John L. Harris

A Short History of American Diplomacy

HARPER'S HISTORICAL SERIES

Under the Editorship of Guy Stanton Ford

A Short History of
American Diplomacy

by

L. ETHAN ELLIS
RUTGERS UNIVERSITY

HARPER & BROTHERS, NEW YORK

**A SHORT HISTORY OF
AMERICAN DIPLOMACY**

Contents

Contents

Maps

Preface

ONE WHO ATTEMPTS TO COMPRESS THE LONG STORY OF American foreign relations within manageable limits faces a formidable task. For essaying such a task, however, the author offers no apologies. It is his belief that a succinct account, such as he has tried to present, has a proper place in the literature of the field. Probably no two readers, professional or amateur, will agree entirely with the omissions he has been forced to make in order to achieve brevity. The guiding principle has been to include such material as would give the reader a working tool for understanding the main forces which shape American foreign policy and the chief avenues which that policy has followed. If the book contributes to such an understanding, he will be content.

Any writer of a general account lays himself under heavy initial obligations. To the usually unsung bibliographers he owes much, as well as to the patient compilers of monographs whose product he must distill into a paragraph or two. Nor can he forget the textbook writers, from Carl Russell Fish and John Bassett Moore, through John Holladay Latané, Randolph G. Adams, and Louis M. Sears, to Samuel Flagg Bemis and Thomas A. Bailey, whose varied approaches to the problem of exposition afford him both precept and example. Likewise the colleagues and coworkers who thoughtfully con his pages and curb his native propensity to error must share whatever success he achieves.

The present writer gratefully acknowledges all these obligations, and particularly those owing to his wife, Elizabeth Breckenridge Ellis, who patiently presided over typewriter, galley sheets, and in-

ix

dexing paraphernalia. His colleagues in the Department of History and Political Science, Ardath W. Burks, Charles C. Cumberland, Irving S. Kull, and Henry R. Winkler, have succumbed to the perils of propinquity and read critically the chapters covering their fields of competence. Others, more distant but equally willing, have rendered similar service, among them Philip C. Brooks, A. L. Burt, Albert B. Corey, E. Wilson Lyon, Alice Morrissey McDiarmid, Dwight C. Miner, Ludwell Lee Montague, Julius W. Pratt, Durward V. Sandifer, Joe Patterson Smith, and Charles M. Thomas. With all of these the author gladly shares such commendation as his work may merit; he cheerfully absolves all of them from the errors which their industry has not prevented him from perpetrating.

L. ETHAN ELLIS

Rutgers University
February, 1951

A Short History of American Diplomacy

1 The Problem of Diplomacy

THE WORLD WAR OF 1939–1945 PROFOUNDLY DISTURBED
not only world politics but individual thinking. It grew out of the inequities and pressures generated by the War of 1914–1918 and its
settlement in the Treaty of Versailles (1919). These pressures of the
interwar years contributed to the appearance in Europe of dictatorships of the Left and of the Right, equally subversive of those individual and social liberties which the western world had learned to
cherish. Hostilities broke out when the international machinery established at Versailles proved inadequate to check aggressive German ambitions. American talent had contributed largely to the creation of this international machinery, but the American verdict was
against participating in its operation. Recoiling against the rising
international rivalry, American thinking became ever more provincial and the isolationism of the later 1920's was sharpened by the
events of the 1930's. The serious domestic crisis of this decade occupied much of American energy and contributed to economic isolationism through the prohibitively protective Hawley-Smoot Tariff of
1930. When the European crisis began to loom large in middecade,
political isolationism was added through the misnamed neutrality
legislation of 1935–1937. Thus the approach of war found many
Americans uneasily hopeful that the Atlantic barrier, added to the
economic and political ones already established, might avert involvement.

Despite these attempts to remain aloof, the very urgency of events
made Americans more than ever aware of international problems.

1

In fact, the generation which attained middle age between 1939 and 1945, having lived through two world-wide struggles, was probably more consciously interested in such problems than any of its predecessors. The war, demolishing distance and intensifying the methods of destruction, ended false dreams of isolationism. American participation in the struggle transformed mere interest in world problems into a decision to assume the nation's long-deferred role of leadership in international coöperation, and again as in 1919 American thinking contributed largely to the formulation of the war-born United Nations. This time the United States joined the group and its citizens found themselves immediately concerned on a global scale with that conduct of international affairs which generally goes under the name of "diplomacy." The average citizen, however, discovered that he knew little of the history of his country's foreign relations and of the jargon which diplomats and historians use in discussing them. Since the ultimate objective of this book is to examine the history of those relations, some definitions and introductory comment on the origins and machinery of diplomacy may well serve as a background for particular American developments.

Diplomacy—Terms and Machinery

An initial and sharp distinction should be made between the formulation of policy and the machinery by which it is carried out. The citizenry of democratic countries has recently, and rightly, demanded more information about policy and a larger voice in its formulation. Most definitions with which the individual citizen or student is concerned deal, however, with machinery—the agencies through which determined policy is negotiated and enforced. The word diplomacy itself is from the Greek "diploun," to fold, and derives from the fact that Roman passports and other official papers were inscribed on folded metal plates. The manipulation of these documents became a skilled profession, and the first "diplomats" were really archivists and students of past relations. Over the centuries the diplomat came out of the library and became a skilled practitioner in his field. It is perhaps significant that modern definitions of diplomacy stress the fact that it is the art, rather than the science, of conducting the relations between states.[1]

A state may be defined as a particular group of people, so united as to form a political entity. The existence of such independent units makes diplomacy a necessary instrument of intercourse. States have ever claimed the attribute of sovereignty which, by asserting total freedom from external control, complicates matters for the diplomat, since each, jealous of its rights and ignoring practical realities, claims legal equality regardless of size. The diplomat's task has been to mitigate these jealousies and to compromise conflicting assertions as to these rights. In performing this task he wears the traditional velvet glove to clothe the iron hand of force which, until very recently, has furnished the only imaginable alternative as well as the ultimate authority for his work.

The speculatively inclined have pushed the origins of diplomacy back into the early dawn of history. Sixteenth-century theorists held that the earliest diplomats were angels, acting as messengers between Heaven and earth. Another theory traces the origin of diplomacy to the feminine curiosity of Pandora, whose opening of the forbidden box loosed a flood of evils upon the world—evils presumably susceptible of diplomatic solution. The Greeks evidently had a well-developed diplomatic service by the fifth century B.C., beginning with the herald, under the tutelage of the tricky god Hermes, and progressing through the orator, whose value in pleading his city's cause was in direct proportion to the volume of his voice, to the trained professional observer. As used in the modern sense, diplomacy dates from thirteenth-century Italy, where the combination of the Papacy and the atomized city-state system of the northern peninsula made relations intimate and violent, and where machinery was required to minimize the inevitable frictions. In this atmosphere diplomacy was ill-omened, ill-paid, and dangerous, but gradually prestige and rewards increased and important men of

[1] Sir E. M. Satow, the dean of writers in this field, in his *A Guide to Diplomatic Practice*, Longmans, Green, 3rd ed., 1932, p. 1, calls it "the application of intelligence and tact to the conduct of official relations between the governments of states. . . ." See also Harold Nicolson, *Diplomacy*, Harcourt, Brace, 1939, for a spirited account.

letters (Dante, Petrarch, Boccaccio, Chaucer, Sir Philip Sidney) added negotiation to their other accomplishments. Francesco Sforza, Duke of Milan, established the first permanent diplomatic mission of modern record at Genoa in 1455, and by the end of this century the permanent embassy had taken its place alongside the standing army—twin agents of international relations.

Diplomatic machinery develops independently in each nation; however, custom and inertia unite to produce a fairly uniform pattern which differentiates domestic from external instruments. Since the early days when expanding problems first forced the sovereign to rely upon assistance, his foreign minister (known as the Secretary of State in the United States) has occupied an important place in the official family. Normally chosen today for political reasons rather than for technical proficiency, this minister assists in formulating policy as well as carrying it out. His role in formulating policy varies widely with the constitution of the particular country, his own personality and that of the chief of state. As an administrator of policy already determined he is the go-between in the relations of his government with others, serving as the normal channel of communication in both directions—only rarely does one chief of state address another directly. The minister instructs his government's foreign agents and through their reports watches and analyzes the movement of world events. Special negotiations come under his general supervision and, if sufficiently important, his personal direction. From his office issue the voluminous documents which record the story of foreign relations; copies of these documents, and those received in reply, remain in his custody for a considerable period of time. When such documents outlive their current usefulness and any possible incendiary influence on international relations, they go into archives, to gather dust until disturbed by some industrious student. As diplomacy operates under today's complex conditions, the foreign minister stands at the apex of an ever-growing pyramid of expert assistants in the legal, political, and economic aspects of his duties.

The external machinery of diplomacy consists of a mission at each capital with which a nation maintains relations, operating under the close supervision of the Foreign Office and the Executive. This mission is in charge of an ambassador, minister, or charge d'affaires, depending upon the degree of importance attached to the relations with a particular nation. Heads of important embassies top smaller pyramids of secretaries, attachés, and clerks, and stand high among government servants. This has not always been the case, as in earlier days ambassadors were often agents for royal skullduggery. This phase of their activity was pointed up by a witty if ill-chosen remark of Sir Henry Wotton, sent to Venice as James I's ambassador. In a guest book in 1604 he wrote what was intended as a pun: "Legatus est vir bonus peregre missus ad mentiendum reipublicae causa." The sentiment, "An ambassador is an honest man, sent to lie [reside] abroad for the good of his country," did not appeal to his Stuart majesty, and Sir Henry joined the unemployed. Three centuries have hardly sufficed to erase from the popular mind all traces of this connotation.

Until recently diplomacy has been a function of the elect rather than the skilled. Royalty naturally enlisted the services of nobility as its agents in the early days, as more capable of dealing with contemporary royalty and better able to keep up the necessary style. This was true save in impecunious pre-Columbian Spain, which relied on the better-educated and more frugal-living friars, who presumably were less subject than their secular fellows to local pressures, especially of the petticoat variety. As foreign relations passed increasingly under popular control the practice of diplomacy gradually became a profession, save in the United States, where its richest plums were long reserved to reward the party faithful. Here since 1924 a persistent effort, not yet entirely successful, has been made under the Foreign Service Act of that year and subsequent legislation to foster the creation of a professional class.

As in any field, a successful practitioner of diplomacy needs special qualities, some of which change with the times, but most of which remain basic to the task in hand. Few ambassadors are now expected to lie in order to gain their objectives; less attention need be paid today to the personal foibles of those in power. Fundamental, however, are such characteristics as patience, courtesy, good temper, firmness, quick insight, and calm deliberation balanced when necessary by decisive action. Loyalty, truthfulness, and modesty are likewise essential; vanity is a failing a diplomat cannot afford. The ability to subordinate his own convictions is also necessary; William E. Dodd's outspoken criticisms of Hitlerism in its German stronghold seriously embarrassed his superiors in Washington in the mid-1930's. Wealth, particularly for an American, is no handicap, though the anecdote attributed to Joseph H. Choate will probably not be repeated. At a time when his government owned few embassies and forced its representatives to find quarters at their own expense, a London bobby stopped him on a late evening stroll and inquired why he was not at home, where he belonged. "I have no home," replied Mr. Choate, "I am the American ambassador."

Once established in his post, an ambassador promptly assumes obligations to his own government and to that of his host nation. Among his highest functions is that of supplying his foreign office with the raw material from which the foreign minister may fashion a picture of the contemporary world; this the ambassador does by distilling for home consumption the climate of opinion by which he is surrounded and whose changing manifestations his position and contacts give him unique opportunities to sample. More humdrum but vastly important are the handling of routine and emergency trade questions, assisting in the extradition of fugitives from justice, and the custody of embassy records. Should life threaten to become a dull social round, there are the inevitable tourists who overstay their passports, who wish to meet celebrities or be presented at court, and who, when in trouble, shout loudly that no one can solve their unique and urgent problems except the ambassador himself.

Like any guest, the ambassador strives to make himself agreeable in his personal as well as his official capacity. Much of diplomacy never appears in the documents, and the significance of culture, social aplomb, a gracious wife, a well-spread table, must be guessed at rather than measured; they must not, however, be forgotten. The amenities disposed of, the diplomat gets down to more serious things. Important among these is serving as a reverse channel of in-

formation, enlightening the local government and public on affairs
at home. This may take the form of appearing at numerous public
functions, where the duty of presenting a few well-chosen remarks
affords the opportunity to insert propaganda favorable to his own
government. In more official contacts, often under the tutelage of
his foreign office but sometimes at his own discretion, he interprets
the despatches, toning them up or down as occasion demands, and
sometimes communicating orally sentiments which if written might
lead to friction. He conducts special negotiations on occasion. If his
host nation goes to war he finds himself beset by his own nationals
wanting to get home out of harm's way, and he is possibly charged
as well with looking after the interests of his host's enemy nationals,
left stranded on hostile soil. He must, finally, scrupulously refrain
from expressing himself on local social or political issues. The indiscretion of Sir Lionel Sackville-West in advising a pseudo-Democrat
of English extraction to vote for Grover Cleveland in 1888 because
of the latter's low-tariff sentiments received sufficient airing to serve
as an example to generations of his successors.

In conclusion, there is still much truth in the advice given by the
Earl of Malmesbury in 1813 to a neophyte in diplomacy:

> The first and best advice I can give a young man on entering this career,
> is *to listen, not to talk*—at least, not more than is necessary to induce
> others to talk. I have in the course of my life, by endeavouring to follow
> this method, drawn from my opponents much information, and concealed
> from them my own views, much more than by the employment of spies
> or money.
>
> To be very cautious in *any* country, or at *any* court, of such as, on your
> first arrival, appear the most eager to make your acquaintance. . . . I have
> ever found their professions insincere, and their intelligence false. . . .
>
> Never attempt to export English habits and manners, but to conform as
> far as possible to those of the country where you reside—to do this even
> in the most trivial things—to learn to speak their language, and never to
> sneer at what may strike you as singular and absurd. . . .
>
> Not to be carried away by any real or supposed distinctions from the
> sovereign at whose Court you reside, or to imagine, because he may say
> a few more commonplace sentences to you than to your colleagues, that
> he entertains a special personal predilection for you. . . . This is a species

of royal stage-trick, often practiced, and for which it is right to be prepared. . . .

It is scarcely necessary to say that no occasion, no provocation, no anxiety to rebut an unjust accusation, no idea, however tempting, of promoting the object you have in view, can *need*, much less justify, a *falsehood*. Success obtained by one, is a precarious and baseless success. . . .[2]

---

[2] Quoted by Satow, *op. cit.*, pp. 92–94.

2 Europe and America Before the Revolution

BEGINNING STUDENTS OF OUR HISTORY ARE TOO PRONE TO forget their country's youth and its relatively recent emergence as a world power. The two hundredth anniversary of independence is over 25 years away as this is written. By contrast, America had been known to Europe 271 years when the Treaty of Paris (1763) brought down the curtain on French pretensions on this continent. During most of these centuries American territories had figured in European calculations not as ends in themselves, but as counters in the interminable game of colonial rivalry played among Europe's crowned heads. These rivalries, in turn, were but part of the larger dynastic and imperial competition by which the new nation-states of western Europe sought to dominate not only their own continental corner but the whole world. The student does well, therefore, to set present greatness in proper perspective alongside the long and often galling years of subordination which it is the purpose of this chapter to examine. It is well also, however, to note that while (until 1754) American factors were always subordinate, the seeds of importance were being sown, seeds which would bear fruit in the mighty duel between France and England which culminated in British victory in 1763 and eventually in the birth of the United States as a nation itself capable of playing the same game in which it had so long been a pawn.

In Europe, the years from 1492 to the American Revolution are marked by vastly important internal and international develop-

9

ments. The aftermath of early discovery elevated Spain to a position of temporary predominance which was soon challenged in politics and on the sea by Elizabethan England, resulting in the defeat of the Spanish Armada in 1588. Simultaneously the Netherlands and France launched attacks on Spanish continental hegemony, which was well on the decline by 1600. The seventeenth century witnessed the consolidation of absolute monarchy in France and its imperialistic expansion on the continent under Louis XIV. In England political affairs took a different turn when the would-be absolutism of the Stuart dynasty faded before the rise of a parliamentary party which triumphed in the Glorious Revolution of 1688. This was based upon a type of natural-rights philosophy which was to be of profound importance in the development of the United States. Protestant and relatively democratic Britain became a natural European rival of the French Catholic absolutism; the competition produced a series of wars spanning with intermissions nearly a century after the accession of William of Orange to the English throne in 1689. This duel had its colonial counterpart in the French and Indian Wars, the defeat of France and the emergence of a victorious Britain in possession of France's continental American holdings. No sooner had French possessions been acquired, however, than a family quarrel developed that eventuated in the American Revolution which disrupted the British Empire in America.

Exploration and Discovery

Before this Anglo-French duel brought America forward as a subject of diplomacy the area had long been an object of colonial ambitions and territorial rivalry. These years of subordination to Europe's concerns may be divided into three periods, toward the end of which an important issue (the French and Indian War) first takes its rise in affairs on the American side of the Atlantic. The first period, one of exploration and discovery, dates from Christopher Columbus' landfall in 1492 to the establishment of British sea power by the defeat of the Armada in 1588. During this time America was less an objective than an obstacle, lying across the road to the Orient, and Europe's energies were only gradually diverted from seeking routes through or around it into channels of immediate interest. Columbus confided to his journal a week after sighting land: "It is certain that this is the main-land. . . ." and John Cabot sailed from England four years later in an effort to reach "the island of Cipango [Japan] and the lands from which Oriental caravans brought their goods from Alexandria." Both were to be disappointed. The reasons for their search and for their disappointment take us, via the profit motive, to the eastern Mediterranean.

The Crusades and other contacts with the Levant stimulated European appetite for Far Eastern wares of many sorts. In a day devoid of refrigeration, spices helped to cover less desirable tastes in meat and added piquancy to wines of ordinary vintage. Crusaders, and crusaders' wives, enjoyed the silks and jewels which from time immemorial had come from the East. All these, however, cost money, and during the fifteenth century western Europeans began to think they cost too much money; therefore, after the manner of consumers, they sought relief from high prices by establishing more direct contact with the sources of supply. The reason for these high prices, and consequent search for direct routes to the source of supply, was believed for many years to be found in the capture of Constantinople by the Ottoman Turks (1453) and subsequent Turkish restrictions upon the flow of goods from east to west. Later research has shown, however, that its real origin lay in the Italian monopoly of trade between Europe and the Levant.[1]

Asiatic wares had for generations made their slow way eastward via one of three routes. The southern, after edging down the China Sea, through the Straits of Malacca and around India, entered the Red Sea, from the shores of which goods moved by caravan to the Nile and down its waters to Cairo and Alexandria. The central route, originating in the same way, turned north from the Indian Ocean to the Persian Gulf and proceeded up the Tigris-Euphrates Valley and

---

[1] A. H. Lybyer, "The Ottoman Turks and the Routes of Oriental Trade," *English Historical Review*, vol. 30 (1915), pp. 577–588, and "Influence of the Rise of the Ottoman Turks upon the Routes of Oriental Trade," *Report of the American Historical Association, 1914*, Government Printing Office, 1916, vol. 1, pp. 125–133. Professor Lybyer showed quite conclusively that the Turks interfered but little with the Italian trade prior to 1516, and that the European price level had risen less than it would inevitably have done had Turkish restrictions been severe.

then across country to Black Sea or eastern Mediterranean ports such as Aleppo and Antioch. The northern land route traversed the high plateau of Central Asia and, after passing Samarkand and Bokhara, forked north of the Caspian Sea to the Don and the Volga, and south to the Black Sea and Mediterranean ports. At all of these termini Italian middlemen had established mutually profitable relationships with the local politicos, resulting in Italian monopoly of the transit to Italy. Fanning out from the peninsular city-states a complex network of routes brought the treasures of Cathay to eager European buyers—at a good Italian profit. During the fifteenth century Portuguese and Spaniards wearied of paying these extortionate prices. As a result hardy Portuguese expeditions, under an impetus initially furnished by the great Prince Henry the Navigator (1394–1460), began edging down the African coast seeking direct routes to the East. In 1445 Denis Diaz reached Cape Verde on the bulge of Africa; 1488 saw Bartholomew Diaz at the Cape of Good Hope; and in 1498 Vasco da Gama reached Calicut on India's west coast. Columbus' urging put Spain tardily in the race, and in the course of his first voyage, quite accidentally, America was discovered. It was thus Italian exactions rather than Turkish impositions which caused the Iberian nations to reach out for direct eastern contacts.

The Portuguese resented the appearance of a competitor, particularly a trespasser. As was not unusual in those days, they complained of Spanish poaching to the Pope who, in his capacity as an arbiter of temporal affairs, had conferred on them jurisdiction over an undetermined area beyond that actually discovered. But they took their case to the wrong court, since the current pontiff was Alexander VI, a Spaniard, and not averse to doing his countrymen a favor. Considerable negotiation produced a series of papal bulls or edicts which divided between the two nations all land not already ruled over by a Christian prince, whether discovered or yet to be found; Portugal was to have all east of the line and Spain all west. This Papal Line of Demarcation (1493) ran from pole to pole, 100 leagues west of the Azores and Cape Verde Islands. Portugal was thus forced to share her area of exploitation and joined Spain in the Treaty of Tordesillas (1494), which preserved the papal principle of share-and-share-alike but moved the line 370 leagues west of the Cape Verde Islands to a point intended to be midway between them and Columbus' landfall. The expedition under Ferdinand Magellan which completed the first circumnavigation of the globe (1519–1522) created further problems by opening a vast new area to exploration. The nations were equal to the occasion, however, and the Treaty of Saragossa (1529) extended the circuit of division from pole to pole through the eastern hemisphere, giving the Philippine Islands to Spain, with later consequences of considerable magnitude for the United States.

There followed a period of Spanish and Portuguese monopoly in colonization, not because of papal priorities but because other nations were too busy with other concerns to develop active interest in overseas adventures. The papal line failed to prevent other Catholic states from staking out claims, mostly in the nearer reaches, perhaps on the theory that a bird in the hand was worth two in the East Indies, but because of preoccupation with matters closer home they made relatively few actual settlements. Thus the voyages of John and Sebastian Cabot established British claims to the North American mainland and the venturesome journeys of Giovanni da Verrazano, Jacques Cartier, Louis Joliet, and Louis Hennepin took the French flag across the ocean and into the American interior basin via the St. Lawrence Valley. Meantime Spain's claims to all of North America were reinforced by the active enterprise of Hernando Cortez, Juan Ponce de Leon, Francisco Vasquez Verrazano, and others whose activities, however, extended only into the lower reaches of the present United States. The defeat of the Armada therefore found the continent blanketed by overlapping claims which contained the seeds of conflict but which had not so far produced active hostilities because they did not involve friction between actual settlers.

Colonization

These frictions became apparent in the second period, one of colonization running from 1588–1688, a century which found Spain's European power declining before the onslaughts of Britain, France, and the Netherlands. Her imperial position was correspondingly weakened, while French and British colonial enterprises flourished.

The former penetrated the interior basin and consolidated their position in the St. Lawrence Valley. The British settlement at Jamestown (1607) was followed by Plymouth (1620), Massachusetts Bay (1630), and others until colonies fringed the coast. The Dutch appeared briefly in the picture at New Amsterdam, but were elbowed out by the British in 1664. Against a background of European wars the lines of colonial empire were drawn on North American soil, while contrasting colonial policies were being developed. The Anglo-French invasion of the Spanish monopoly was foreshadowing another kind of demarcation line. French and British expansion brought outposts into proximity and policies into conflict. French interest in the fur trade was not conducive to the founding of permanent settlements. Neither was the high degree of political centralization which characterized French domestic administration favorable to local liberty in French America. New France was organized, therefore, along the lines of a continental French province. The need for furs, coupled with French adaptability to the life of the forest, counseled a policy of good relations with the Indians. British settlements, on the other hand, were predicated upon a stable population, fundamentally agricultural, which advanced slowly but steadily into the interior, and were characterized by considerable local political liberty. Such policies necessarily involved dispossessing the Indians, which in turn engendered ill-feeling, since the aborigines had the curious notion that the land belonged to them. Thus the period, brought to a close by the Glorious Revolution of 1688, saw rough boundaries drawn, while rivalry between France and England increased, and while Spain's star was on the wane.

The Anglo-French Duel for North America

The last period (1688–1763) witnessed the culmination of Anglo-French rivalry in complete British victory. The overthrow of the Stuarts in 1688 brought William of Orange to the British throne. In British politics this change of rulers resulted in a deeper involvement in continental affairs, since one of William's main objectives in accepting the crown was to annex British sea power as a weapon in his long struggle to thwart Louis XIV of France. This clash of policies helped to launch Europe on four wars which entangled the colonies of both nations and resulted in final overthrow of France on the North American mainland. The story of these wars should dispel once and for all the myth of American isolationism, for each involved American men, money, and interest, even though until the final struggle colonial issues were distinctly secondary.[2] The first struggle, promptly initiated, properly bore King William's name and lasted from 1689–1697. (This was the War of the League of Augsburg in its European manifestation.) Urged on by the exiled Stuarts and eager to extend his frontiers to the Rhine, Louis XIV entered the conflict willingly, and soon the colonies of the two powers followed. French forays into New England struck isolated towns in New Hampshire and Maine and in 1690 Schenectady was burned. A retaliatory expedition moved northward and captured Port Royal in Acadia but failed to take Quebec. The colonists were rewarded for their activity in the Treaty of Ryswick (1697), which as part of the settlement of the European conflict returned Port Royal to the French.

European dynastic and religious considerations produced Queen Anne's War (War of the Austrian Succession, 1702–1713). Again Port Royal fell before a colonial expedition and again Quebec was an unattained objective. In the Treaty of Utrecht (1713) French failures in Europe initiated the concessions which were to lead to her final downfall. Acadia and the Hudson's Bay country went to Britain, though in neither case were boundaries defined. A British protectorate was established over the Iroquois Indians. The French replaced Port Royal, forfeited at Utrecht, with another fortress at Louisbourg, but the third war, named after King George II (War of the Austrian Succession, 1744–1748), saw it fall before colonial arms in its turn. The Treaty of Aix-la-Chapelle (1748) returned Louisbourg to France like Port Royal before it, and kindled in colonial minds a keen distaste for this disregard of American interests. In each war to date Americans had come in as a tail to the European

---

[2] H. L. Osgood, *The American Colonies in the Seventeenth Century*, Macmillan, 1904–1907, 3 vols., and *The American Colonies in the Eighteenth Century*, Columbia University Press, 1924, 4 vols., tell the story of these wars in great detail.

kite, and in each, American desires had been considered last, if at all. All were forerunners for the final showdown which, unlike the others, took its rise west of the Atlantic.

The slow but steady advance of British settlement toward the Alleghenies induced French fears for their tenuous hold on the great interior basin. When the British topped the mountains and spilled into the Ohio Valley the fear became a menace. Both powers adopted a now-or-never attitude toward this area and in it was produced the friction which lighted the match of the French and Indian War, 1754–1763 (Seven Years' War, 1756–1763). Here was launched a decisive conflict which highlighted the divergent motives and methods developed by the protagonists. France held lightly, by a chain of forts and trading posts, a vast semicircle of territory; years of regimentation had schooled and disciplined her comparative handful of colonists to take orders. The slow British advance into the interior, made against the steady resistance of hostile Indians, re-sulted in contiguous settlements and consolidated gains. A vast numerical superiority was almost canceled, however, by a spirit of local independence. This spirit, fostered by generations of salutary neglect on the part of British administrators, made the colonies un-willing to coöperate fully with each other or to respond wholeheart-edly to British requests for assistance in a war whose successful out-come would undoubtedly be of advantage to colonies as well as to Britain. The slow British penetration, with its threat to the French connection between Canada and the Gulf of Mexico, made the Ohio Valley the focal point of claim and counterclaim.

Each party claimed the valley; to each its possession was essential. French claims rested upon exploration, upon control of the mouth of the Mississippi which drained it, and more immediately upon the expedition of Céloron de Bienville who in 1749 traversed it and left leaden plates bearing formal claims of ownership. The French need was obvious: A link forged firmly between the St. Lawrence and the Lakes to the north and Louisiana to the south would confine the English to the coastal area and the nearer hinterland and would guarantee the benefits of the fur trade, most lucrative of French economic contacts with her continental colonies. Pursuant of these motives they followed up Bienville's journey by beginning the erection of a chain of forts running to the Gulf of Mexico. British legal claims had their strongest basis in the somewhat vague terms of colonial sea-to-sea charters; even less valid as bases were their protectorate over the Iroquois, who claimed the Northwest, and their trade relations with the Valley Indians. Their need to cut the territorial link matched French urgency to forge it; moreover, no very long view was required to envision trans-Appalachia as a legitimate and necessary area for expansion. So it was inevitable that when the French appeared near the junction of the Monongahela and the Allegheny and started erecting forts, one on ground seized from a British outpost, Governor Robert Dinwiddie of Virginia should take counsel. The result was an expedition under the youthful George Washington, sent to oust the French from their Fort Duquesne, newly built at the Forks of the Ohio. His expedition was a failure, but a sufficiently respectable one to permit him to retire with the honors of war. This backwoods operation presently spread to Europe and the far places of the earth; for once an American issue had forced a larger one which was shortly fought in the West Indies, in Europe, and in the Far East, where Anglo-French rivalry in India was fought out to eventual British victory.

Political as well as military considerations played their part in British victory. William Pitt, who entered the Cabinet in 1757, completed a diplomatic revolution whose results redounded to British credit. A prewar realignment took Austria out of an earlier alliance with England and into one with France, intended to isolate Frederick the Great. Pitt combined diplomacy with strategy by allying with the lonely Prussian and furnishing him with the sinews for continental warfare. This permitted concentration of British efforts on sea power and overseas combat. The young and vigorous Jeffrey Amherst and James Wolfe replaced their elders and waged successful war in America, culminating in Wolfe's victory in his epic duel with Louis-Joseph Montcalm for possession of Quebec. British interests presently triumphed in all theaters of warfare and in 1763 a nexus of agreements, commonly referred to jointly as the Treaty of Paris, created a new North American situation which was to be pro-

PACIFIC

OCEAN

ATLANTIC

OCEAN

MIQUELON
ST. PIERRE
(French 1763)

Mississippi

Rio

Grande

ISLAND OF
NEW ORLEANS
(Spanish, 1763)

**BRITAIN TRIUMPHS
IN THE NEW WORLD
1754-1763**

Scale of Miles
0   200   400   600   800

Russian, 1754, 1763

Spanish, 1754,

Spanish gains from
France, 1763

British, 1754

French, 1754

British gains from
France, 1763

British gains from
Spain, 1763

foundly significant for the history of the United States. France surrendered to Britain all her continental territories in Canada and in
Louisiana east of the Mississippi except for an area of approximately
2800 square miles, called the Island of New Orleans, east of and
close to the mouth of the river and including the city of New Orleans. Britain expressly reserved the right to navigate the river's

lower reaches. Thus Canada and the eastern portion of French Louisiana became British. France retained portions of her island empire in the West Indies, including Guadeloupe and Martinique, as well as St. Pierre and Miquelon in the Gulf of St. Lawrence. A contemporaneous Franco-Spanish agreement gave to Spain Louisiana west of the river, plus the Island of New Orleans, thus insuring Spanish control of the river's mouth. This was supposedly in return for surrender of the Floridas, but actually it was a maneuver on the part of the French foreign minister, the Duc de Choiseul, to induce Spain to conclude peace before British demands expanded, possibly so much as to include the French West Indies and all of Louisiana. An Anglo-Spanish arrangement gave Britain the Floridas and all Spanish territory east of the Mississippi except the Island of New Orleans. Cuba, recently under British occupation, was returned to Spain, but Britain retained sufficient hold on the area around the Bay of Honduras to involve her later in the question of an isthmian canal. By a proclamation (also of 1763) Britain divided her Florida acquisition into two portions, East and West Florida, with the Apalachicola River as the dividing line and the 31st parallel as the northern boundary of West Florida. She also set up the Province of Quebec in Canada, leaving the intervening territory unorganized, but closing it to further colonial occupation west of the Appalachians for the time being, until a policy could be determined for its settlement and government. These arrangements had far-reaching results: Spain's position in North America, despite the loss of the Floridas, was temporarily improved by the extinction of French claims to western Louisiana and the mouth of the Mississippi; France, defeated, was disgruntled and would anxiously await an opportunity to take revenge on Britain; victorious Britain's restrictions on western settlement aggravated her colonists and were of no small importance in the development of Anglo-American tensions. But more important than this was the removal of the French menace in loosing centrifugal forces in the British Empire, forces long developing and to be noted just below, which would within the next two decades contribute largely to the American Revolution.

3 Revolution and Peace

A Revolutionary Half-Century

THE SECOND HALF OF THE EIGHTEENTH CENTURY WAS ONE of the great periods of change in historic times. In Europe it saw the outbreak of a spirit of innovation which uprooted the social and political mores of generations, and in America its passage saw the rupture of the British Empire and the launching of the American experiment in self-government under forms more democratic than had ever been tried on such a large scale. In the stirring years of the French Revolution the stability of long-established social relationships was disturbed by the upsurge of the underprivileged demanding equality. Any approximation of equality meant of course that those who for ages had had preëminence must descend at least part way to the level of those whom they had considered beneath them in the scale; by the same token those who had been nobodies upgraded themselves toward their former betters. Though distinctions were by no means wiped out, their sharpest edges were softened. The same ones who demanded equality in the social sphere clamored for political liberty. This again involved a revolt against a royal authority long recognized as paramount and the adjustment was a violent one. The seizure of political power by those inexperienced in its exercise is always a dangerous experiment and the urge to democracy which the Revolution engendered soon worked itself into a stage of excess which opened the way for the inevitable man on horseback who bides his time and rides to power through the ranks of bewildered patriots betrayed by demagogic leaders. When the smoke of the

22

Napoleonic Era had cleared away it was seen that the full realization of political democracy was yet to come. Socially and politically, however, the Europe of 1800 differed vastly from that of 1750.

In America too a spirit of domestic unrest was at work. Here too were found distinctions which laid a galling burden on many shoulders—mute evidence that equality and democracy were not self-generating on American soil. They were the common distinctions between the haves and the have-nots, centering largely around the relations between the propertied and the poor, the low country and the back country, the well-churched and the Dissenter. The back-country man who paid taxes and saw all the roads built along the coast, who was unable to vote because his property holding was insufficient, who had to travel weary miles to the low-country seats of justice to settle his legal squabbles, and who contributed perforce to help pay the clergy of the established church, Anglican or Congregational, that paid him no heed, and then dug further into his scanty funds to support the Baptist or Presbyterian itinerant who actually ministered to him, was ripe for change. To him the nature of the forces bringing change need not be too clearly defined; an excuse for action against immediate abuses was what he mainly craved. He could be persuaded, perhaps, to harness his energies to a cause somewhat distant from his immediate needs, in the hope that success for the larger cause might remedy the present inequities. Historians can probably never measure the precise influence of these cumulative unrests, but they furnished a fertile soil for the germination of Anglo-American differences.

These differences, in which the American Revolution took its start, had been long preparing, but were brought into sharp focus by the British decision to take Canada and the Mississippi Valley at the close of the last Intercolonial War. While the war was being fought, colonial support of the war effort had never been more than lukewarm and the colonies had persisted in carrying on their accustomed trade with the enemy French in the West Indies, even in time of peace a violation of the Molasses Act of 1733. Acquisition of the new territory, peopled by alien French and hostile Indians, saddled the British with large expenses of administration and defense—expenditures which would operate in part to colonial advantage. Under these circumstances Britain adopted a policy as logical as it was unsuccessful: She would at once discipline the colonies for their wartime trade with the enemy by enforcing the Acts of Trade, and tax them to support the new imperial establishment. The Sugar Act (1764) was designed to tax as well as regulate trade with the French sugar islands, a trade which had helped New England to make enough to pay her adverse trade balance with the mother country. The Stamp Act (1765), by taxing newspapers and legal documents, levied direct burdens on the most vocal elements of the population. Together the intent of these acts was to raise funds by parliamentary enactment. The right of Parliament to tax the colonies has been the subject of impassioned argument; whatever the legalities, this was the first practical attempt to exercise the right. Thus discipline and fiscal exactions—never popular with immature minds—were invoked at the very moment when those minds were first freed of the French menace, the only real tie binding them to the mother country.

The British taxing policy introduced the more fundamental problem of the relation of colonies to metropolis, with Britain asserting and reasserting a degree of control which Americans were unwilling to admit, thus posing an issue which Britain was not up to solving. There followed a decade of trial and error, of advance and retreat, of passing laws and revoking them in the light of colonial petulance, and then of repeating the whole exasperating cycle. Ten years of this against the background of three thousand miles of water and the consequent irritating lag in communications produced tensions adroitly fostered by demagogues and patriots, mounting to a point where a Declaration of Independence broke the imperial tie. The succession of allegedly oppressive British actions, culminating in the Intolerable Acts (1774), had meantime drawn the colonies together in tentative union for organized protest through the Continental Congress (September, 1774) and its successor, scheduled to meet in May, 1775. Before the Second Continental Congress assembled, armed hostilities had broken out at Lexington and Concord in April, 1775. This body, now faced with the waging of a war, was a prey to divided internal councils and the same spirit of independence in intercolonial relations which had long characterized Anglo-American affairs.

The Deane Mission to France

Thus, under fire, Congress started building domestic institutions and simultaneously began the development of a foreign policy. This was guided first by the Committee of Secret Correspondence, constituted in November, 1775, and in charge until April, 1777, when it gave way to the Committee on Foreign Affairs. The principle of the union of powers exemplified in Congress operated poorly through the committee system and in October, 1781, a Secretary of Foreign Affairs was appointed; he continued to function until the new constitution went into operation in 1789. Congress still adhered to the union of powers, however, and committees and secretary were closely checked at all times. The first committee guided the initial tentative, and abortive, moves toward diplomatic negotiations, carried on through the mission of Silas Deane which grew directly out of Indian policy. January 27, 1776, Congress authorized the committee to contract for the exportation of colonial goods to the amount of £40,000 sterling, to be exchanged for imports, "in order to preserve the friendship and confidence of the Indians, and to prevent their suffering for want of the necessaries of life. . . ." Deane and other merchants contracted with the committee and he departed under instructions of March 2, 1776, for France, "there to transact such Business, commercial and political, as we have committed to his care. . . ." Though the political aspects of his mission never materialized, he may properly be called our first diplomatic agent.

Leaving Deane for the moment on the high seas, attention should turn at this point to the evolving policy of France, whose aid he was to invoke.[1] The motivation of this policy, which resulted in the Alliance of 1778 and was of high importance in the American vic-

---

[1] Edward S. Corwin, *French Policy and the American Alliance of 1778*, Princeton University Press, 1916. Any subsequent account must lean heavily, as does the following, upon Samuel Flagg Bemis, *The Diplomacy of the American Revolution*, Appleton-Century, 1935. Useful also is James Brown Scott's "Historical Introduction" to Volume I of Samuel Flagg Bemis (ed.), *The American Secretaries of State and Their Diplomacy*, Knopf, 1927–1929, 10 vols. The student will find that he, like the author of this text, must draw extensively upon this excellent series.

tory, derives from France's humiliation in 1763 and her desire to redress in her own favor the European balance thus created. At least three sets of influences focused from divergent directions upon King Louis XVI. The leading opponent of American aid was Anne Robert Jacques Turgot, Minister of Finance, whose thankless and impossible task it was to try to write French finances, even now heading for the debacle of 1789, in black ink. He believed that France's true interest lay in "measures of caution" and economy. On the other side stood a group of young intellectuals, readers of books, who took seriously the new social gospel of the French *philosophes* with its emphasis on democratic institutions, overlooking the obvious fact that in any such regime their personal position and privileges would be the first to suffer. Foremost among these was the dashing Marie Joseph Paul Roch Yves Gilbert Motier, Marquis de Lafayette. On the same side, and of decisive influence, stood two influential figures: Charles Gravier, Comte de Vergennes, Louis XVI's Foreign Minister, was a diplomat of the old school, trained in the wiles of his trade at half a dozen courts, a mercantilist economist and a politician of the balance of power. Ably abetting, and possibly instigating, Vergennes, was the remarkable Caron de Beaumarchais, jack-of-all-trades and royal errand-boy. In the latter capacity he found himself in London in the summer of 1775, where he seems to have come under the influence of the American Arthur Lee.

Vergennes and Beaumarchais began early in 1776 to concert measures looking toward assisting the Americans. By March, long before Deane set foot on French soil, Vergennes was memorializing the King with arguments along this line. The first, a weighty proposition in which he himself did not believe, urged that whatever the immediate result of the Anglo-American war, France would eventually have to fight in the Caribbean. A victorious Britain would have to keep her troops occupied. A victorious America forced to fight for markets would find the West Indies a likely place. A peace of attrition would result in continued union and the inevitable next war would see England and America combined against France. The most telling argument favored aggressive assistance in order to strike at England politically by breaching her economic empire. British sea power precluded a direct attack, but the same result might be approached, and English influence on the continent lessened, by aiding the Americans and so weakening Britain: Thus money spent on an American war might accrue to French advantage vis-à-vis Britain. These points were so cogently presented that King Louis ordered a million livres ($200,000) placed at American disposal. His brother monarch, Charles III of Spain, matched the amount. The channel of disbursement, doubtless chosen with one eye on Great Britain, was a dummy corporation, Roderique Hortalez et Cie., for whose mythical head Beaumarchais furnished a cheerful and ever-present substitute. This was essentially the picture of affairs into which Deane stepped on his arrival at Paris, May 7, 1776.

His appearance touched off a hectic chapter lasting more than a generation. His contracts with Beaumarchais eventually began to move goods westward in such volume and of such character that they were probably decisive in the American victory at Saratoga. This was accomplished under conditions of considerable difficulty due to slow communications and perhaps to Congressional occupation with a multiplicity of affairs. At any rate, Deane was increasingly unable to maintain good relations with superiors at home and colleagues in Paris. These frictions eventually undermined Congressional confidence to such an extent that Deane was ordered home in November, 1777, purportedly to give information on the condition of European affairs, actually to stand trial on charges of falsifying his accounts. After a difficult experience with Congress he left the country and took service with the British. Meantime he had failed completely to implement the political aspect of his instructions, as Vergennes was not yet ready to submit his government to the wager of battle with the British which would follow well-nigh automatically upon a French diplomatic commitment.

Deane's troubles multiplied against a growing domestic concern with foreign policy which developed three points of view in Congress. John Adams, perhaps the original isolationist, opposed all European entanglements at this stage of American development; Benjamin Franklin favored diplomatic approaches to France alone, on the theory that a friendly France would draw other nations after her; still others suggested overtures to several countries at once, a policy which was eventually followed without attaining conspicuous success.[2] The whole matter of foreign contacts came into sharp focus with the introduction (June 7, 1776) of Richard Henry Lee's resolutions favoring independence, foreign alliances, and confederation among the States, which set in train many significant developments. After independence was declared, Congress appointed (September 26, 1776) a mission more avowedly diplomatic than Deane's, composed of Franklin, Arthur Lee, and Deane himself. Of these the greatest was without doubt the good Doctor from Philadelphia. Long the best-known of Americans, Franklin accepted at the age of seventy the heavy responsibility of inducing bankrupt France to honor the usual petitions of revolutionaries, material aid (already under way through Deane's agency), recognition of independence, and treaties of commerce and of alliance. Adopting the guise of a disarming and deceptive simplicity, he captured the French popular imagination to a point where John Adams, not distinguished as one of his great admirers, could write: "His reputation was more universal than that of Leibnitz or Newton, Frederick or Voltaire, and his character more beloved and esteemed than any or all of them. . . . His name was familiar . . . to such a degree that there was scarcely a peasant or a citizen, a valet de chambre, coachman or

---

[2] In the interests of brevity this account can make but the merest mention of other diplomatic aspects of the period. Spain, like France, had been injured by Britain's recent successes. It was part of Vergennes' plan, therefore, to involve Spain in the war—not too difficult when the prospect of regaining Gibraltar and the Floridas became apparent. By the Franco-Spanish Convention of Aranjuez (April 12, 1779) the two powers covenanted to fight until Gibraltar was secured, but Vergennes failed to bind Spain on the matter of American independence, to which he himself was by that time pledged. John Jay spent many months in unsuccessful efforts to secure effective Spanish aid in the American war, during which he acquired a highly developed suspicion of that nation's policy which bore fruit during the peace negotiations to be noted presently. The Dutch committed a series of offenses against the British sense of propriety, most flagrant of which was to make a great deal of money by allowing their barren West Indian island of St. Eustatius to serve as the point of exchange in transactions between the revolutionaries and continental nations. Even while they themselves derived advantages from St. Eustatius' position as a free port, the British made demands which the Dutch refused to honor, and on December 20, 1780, Britain declared war. In 1782 John Adams signed with the Dutch a treaty of amity and commerce similar to that with France, making the Netherlands the only other nation to recognize American independence prior to 1783. Agents sent to Prussia, Russia, and Tuscany made no particular headway.

footman, a lady's chambermaid or a scullion in a kitchen, who was not familiar with it, and who did not consider him a friend to humankind. . . ."[3]

This first full-fledged diplomatic mission paid its collective respects and presented its collective petitions to Vergennes in late December, 1776. He deftly turned aside the request for open assistance and a treaty, since the latter would involve recognition, and he was not yet ready for the certain consequences in war with Britain. This is readily understandable, since the only possible immediate gain from recognition was free trade. This was a dubious reward, since France, like the rest of Europe, was a mercantilist state which believed in a minimum of economic contacts with competing areas. Furthermore, three thousand miles of water and England's possession of the world's strongest navy threatened the success of trade relations, and the Americans had yet to prove themselves in the field. The British had captured New York and were eyeing Philadelphia; Gentleman Johnny Burgoyne was about to move south from Canada to cut off New England; and Britain was chiding France on her obvious violations of the Treaty of Utrecht which bound her not to let privateers fit or bring prizes into French ports. To soften the sting of refusal Vergennes promised to continue the secret aid and credit already being given, and with this, for some months, the Americans were forced to be content.

By July of 1777, however, Vergennes had decided to take the plunge, due partly to Franklin's continued exertions and partly to Britain's continued pressure; on the 23rd he sent a memoir to his master advising an offensive and defensive alliance. The date of this memoir should effectively dispose of one misconception long embedded in the textbooks, to the effect that it was the defeat of Burgoyne at Saratoga (October 17, 1777; news received in Paris December 3) which determined the issue of French recognition. The American victory, of course, strengthened Vergennes' convictions. It also brought a British peace offer on the basis of home rule, which the Americans refused. After some months of futile effort to

---

[3] F. Wharton (ed.), *The Revolutionary Diplomatic Correspondence of the United States,* Government Printing Office, 1889, vol. 1, p. 488.

induce Spain to become a fellow belligerent, he finally announced on
January 8, 1778, his willingness to proceed to negotiate treaties with
the United States. Matters then moved rapidly and on February 6
a treaty of amity and commerce and one of alliance were signed.

The First Alliance

The first was based largely on a draft which Franklin had brought
to Europe with him, called the Plan of 1776. This document, drawn
up by a Congressional Committee of which he was a member, had
its origin in existing treaties among the small-navy nations of Europe,
and naturally contained principles that were anathema to the mistress of the seas. Prominent among these was the doctrine that free
ships make free goods, intended to prevent a belligerent from capturing enemy goods (save contraband, always subject to capture on
the high seas) on a neutral ship. Another provision likely to irk the
British defined contraband in such narrow terms as to exclude many
items which under British definition and the usage of the day were
subject to capture. Two articles touched on questions of neutrality
destined to cause trouble later. One stated that if either country
were at war, with the other neutral, belligerent warships and privateers might enter the neutral's ports with prizes and depart freely,
while the other party to the war was denied such sanctuary except
under stress of wind and weather. It should be noted carefully, in
view of later complications, that nothing was proposed here concerning the disposal of such prizes in neutral ports. Another, applying also to a period when one party was at war and the other neutral, forbade the belligerent's enemy to fit ships or sell goods in the
neutral's ports, beyond the minimum necessary to carry to the near-
est home port. Again, in view of the future, it should be noted that
there is no permission here given to the allied belligerent to fit ships
or to sell goods.

One provision hitherto unique in commercial treaties introduced a
new interpretation of the already common most-favored-nation
clause. As long used in European diplomacy, this clause simply
meant that when two nations adopted the principle each gave the
other automatically any further concessions that either granted to

third (or most favored) nations. By Article 2 the two parties engaged "mutually not to grant any particular Favour to other Nations in respect of Commerce and Navigation, which shall not immediately become common to the other Party, *who shall enjoy the same Favour, freely, if the Concession was freely made, or on allowing the same Compensation, if the Concession was Conditional.*" (Author's italics.)[4]

This introduces the so-called "conditional most-favored-nation" idea, long to be part of American diplomatic paraphernalia. In this interpretation the United States has held that the making of bilateral reciprocity treaties, in which concession was traded for concession, did not bind her to extend such concessions to third parties except in return for similar concessions on their part; to make the matter specific, the United States need not give France for nothing what she gave another nation for a consideration. It appears likely that this peculiar interpretation was suggested by the French, seemingly as a means of convincing the Americans of their unselfishness, and was inserted in the treaty without full realization of its implications.

The treaty of alliance provided that if an Anglo-French war should eventuate during the course of the Anglo-American hostilities, a consequence of course inevitable, the parties should "make it a common cause, and aid each other mutually with their good Offices, their Counsels, and their forces, according to the exigence of Conjunctures as becomes good & faithful Allies." The end of the treaty was asserted to be "the liberty, Sovereignty, and independence" of the United States, and each promised not to make peace or truce without previously obtaining the consent of the other. Each guaranteed the American possessions of the other as these might stand at the conclusion of the war, with the United States permitted to capture, up to the limits of its ability, British continental possessions, plus the Bermudas, while France might exercise her talents upon any British West Indian holdings except the Bermudas. A separate and secret article provided hopefully for Spanish adherence

---

[4] Hunter Miller (ed.), *Treaties and Other International Acts of the United States of America*, Government Printing Office, 1931 ff., vol. 2, pp. 3–47. This monumental and definitive edition of United States treaties will be used hereafter, wherever available, for treaty excerpts.

to both agreements. Vergennes allowed the British to learn the contents of the commercial agreement, but tried to keep the alliance a secret. Deane's secretary, Dr. Edward Bancroft, was a British spy, however, and boasted that his real employers were informed of both treaties within forty-eight hours.[5] Anglo-French hostilities began June 17, 1778.

Open alliance produced open aid, and French ships and men soon entered the American lists. The wholeheartedness of this assistance has been a matter of dispute: Some assert that naval aid was seasonal, the French fleet appearing in American waters only with the warm breezes of spring; others allege that French interests were concentrated in the West Indies, where French conquests might most likely occur and that, had the full French potential been brought to bear, the war's end might have been hastened considerably. Be this as it may, the fact remains that a French fleet did appear at a crucial moment while Lord Charles Cornwallis was penned in the peninsula between the York and the James Rivers, and played an important role in aiding combined Franco-American forces to compel his surrender at Yorktown, October 19, 1781. This resulted in a British peace offer, refused until French aspirations in the West Indies were ended by a shattering defeat in the Battle of the Saints, April 12, 1782. All in all, it seems fair to conclude that France provided the foreign assistance without which independence could not have been won, and Americans probably should not quibble over the obvious fact that the aid was not entirely selfless in its motivation.

Peace Negotiated

With typical American optimism, stimulated by a proposed Spanish mediation, Congress began to consider peace negotiations as early as August, 1779, and sent John Adams to Europe armed with instructions in the premises. These insisted that independence must be recognized prior to a treaty of peace and be confirmed in any

---

[5] American naïveté, or British adroitness, may be inferred from the fact that Bancroft served various American agencies in Europe throughout the war and the peace without being suspected.

such document (later modified so that recognition of independence might accompany a truce). An attempt was made to delimit boundaries, in such fashion as would have given much of Canada north of Lakes Erie and Ontario to the United States. Congress also considered other matters, but left them out of Adams' final instructions. Some of these are worth present mention because of their recurrence in American thinking and their divisive character in domestic affairs. One was the proposal to annex Canada, destined to become a hardy perennial in some American quarters. Access to the northern fisheries and to the use of the Mississippi River aroused sectional differences, since New England fishermen were not interested in the river and southern frontiersmen not conspicuously concerned with codfish.

Adams' role as peacemaker was destined to postponement. He soon saw that Vergennes' interests were primarily European; his own great talents did not include forbearance, and he was presently writing the Foreign Minister lectures as able as they were tactless, an exercise which resulted in Vergennes' decision to deal only with Franklin, and in Adams' departure for the Netherlands. Vergennes also worked through his own agent in the States to have Adams surrounded by a commission, so that when the final group for peace negotiations was constituted, June 15, 1781, it consisted of Franklin, Adams, John Jay (who had spent an agonizing period following the impecunious Spanish court about the country), Henry Laurens (who was a prisoner in the Tower of London, released only in time to participate in the late stages), and Thomas Jefferson, who reached Europe too late to play any part whatever. Less stringent instructions insisted only upon independence and strict adherence to the French treaties; beyond this the plenipotentiaries were told to secure "the interest of the United States in such manner as circumstances may direct. . . ." However, in a remarkable display of confidence, Congress instructed its agents in making peace "to make the most candid and confidential communications upon all subjects, to the ministers of our generous ally the King of France; to undertake nothing in the negotiations for peace or truce without their knowledge and concurrence; and ultimately to govern yourself by their advice and opinion. . . ."[6]

Meantime the European atmosphere was favorable to peace overtures. Rising dissatisfaction with the war played a considerable part in the fall of the North ministry, followed by one under Rockingham who in turn gave way to Charles Shelburne, under whose aegis peace negotiations were finally completed. For his part, Vergennes was not averse to seeing things begin to move, but he was glad to have the initiative arise elsewhere. His two allies, Spain and the United States, were not on good terms, and he had made promises to each which might be difficult to fulfill. The former demanded Gibraltar and the Floridas, which had proved difficult of attainment, and Vergennes had promised not to make peace without the latter. Under these circumstances a British move would afford him opportunity to maneuver; he believed that he could still control the negotiations and time the Anglo-American settlement to coincide with the general European peace. Franklin made it possible for the British to make this move. Over the teacups he met Lord Cholmondeley, passing through Paris (enemy country, incidentally) on his way home from wintering at Nice. Cholmondeley offered to carry a note to Shelburne, long Franklin's personal friend. In this the venerable Franklin (he was now seventy-six) expressed the pious hope that peace might follow the recent Cabinet upheavals. Unbeknown to Franklin, these upheavals had just elevated Shelburne to be Secretary for Home Affairs, from which post he hoped to manage any peace negotiations. Thus encouraged, he sent Richard Oswald, a retired Scottish slave-trader whose American business had contributed to his fortune and whose years matched Franklin's with one to spare, to talk informally of peace.

These worthies, old friends, conferred at some length and on July 9, 1782, Franklin submitted tentative peace suggestions. Three conditions were necessary: Complete independence and withdrawal of British troops; a boundary settlement likely to restrict Canada to the St. Lawrence Valley; and the right to fish on the Newfoundland

---

[6] *Journals of the Continental Congress, 1774–1789*, Government Printing Office, 1904–1937, vol. 20, p. 651.

Banks "and elsewhere." To these "musts" were added other desirable proposals. British forces had accomplished considerable devastation of American towns; Franklin admitted that his request for an indemnity of £500,000 to £600,000 was large, but argued that "it would not be ill bestowed, as it would conciliate the resentment of a multitude of poor sufferers, who could have no other remedy, and who, without some relief, would keep up a spirit of secret revenge and animosity for a long time to come against Great Britain; whereas a voluntary offer of such reparation would diffuse a universal calm and conciliation over the whole country." The British, further, should acknowledge their error in "distressing those countries" as they had done. American ships should be admitted into British and Irish ports on terms of equality with British vessels. Franklin's final touch of optimism counseled giving up "every part of Canada."[7] Oswald seemed agreeable to these proposals and Franklin suggested to Shelburne (recently elevated to the prime ministership) that their discussions should be formalized by granting Oswald a commission. Shelburne, however, showed signs of unwillingness to recognize American independence prior to a treaty, and Franklin forthwith repudiated his original terms and told Oswald that he must confer with Jay, who was then ill. The foregoing account should make it clear that Franklin deliberately took the road to separate negotiations with the British, a dubious honor usually reserved for Jay.

His suspicions of Shelburne confirmed by subsequent events, Franklin took Jay to Vergennes for advice. The latter suggested going ahead, even though the form of Oswald's commission might not meet completely the Americans' desires. The more experienced Franklin felt justified in accepting Vergennes' advice and Oswald's proposed commission, but not Jay. At this point Jay became even more suspicious of Vergennes than Franklin had been of Shelburne, and was convinced, correctly as we now know, that Vergennes was deliberately delaying the American negotiations, and consequently recognition of American independence, pending realization of his

---

[7] Jared Sparks (ed.), *The Works of Benjamin Franklin*, Hilliard, Gray, 1840, vol. 9, pp. 354–355, n.

own European objectives. Events now focused Jay's suspicions upon
Anglo-French motives to a point where he became willing to make
separate Anglo-American negotiations not strictly in accord with
Congressional instructions to be guided in all things by France.
Three particular factors produced this decision. The British intercepted, translated, and thoughtfully handed Jay a copy of a letter
written by Francois Barbé-Marbois, French Secretary of Legation in
Philadelphia, to Vergennes. This contained arguments against American postwar use of the inshore fisheries, perfectly permissible since
France was not bound to support American claims, and perfectly
logical since the realization of those claims would have subjected
French fishermen to New England competition. Again, Jay had had
discouraging conversations with Pedro de Aranda, Spanish Minister
in Paris. In these the Spaniard had claimed for his country a large
part of the area east of the Mississippi which Jay thought should
pass to the United States. Joseph de Rayneval, Vergennes' private
secretary, presented to Jay proposals jeopardizing American claims
in the valley to the advantage of the British. Finally, Rayneval visited
Vergennes at a most undiplomatic hour in the morning and then
departed posthaste for London. Jay jumped to the conclusion that
France was conniving with Britain to the detriment of his country's
cause.

Action followed rapidly upon conclusion. Without consulting
Franklin who, he wrote, "did not concur with me in sentiment . . ."
he sent one Benjamin Vaughan to urge Shelburne to complete
Oswald's commission on terms satisfactory to himself. This involved
changing the original form, in which the British had proposed to
treat with representatives of the "colonies or plantations." Jay felt
that this was an inadequate guarantee of independence. After
Vaughan's appearance, but more in response to Oswald's urging, the
Cabinet voted on September 19 "that a Commission be made
out . . . for enabling Mr. Oswald to treat with the Colonys under
the title 'of Thirteen United States, inasmuch as the Commissioners
have offered under that condition to accept the Independence of
America as the First Article of the Treaty." Thus Jay had been
stampeded by his suspicions into abandoning the American demand

for prior recognition of independence and into a position where he was willing to accept independence as the first article of a peace treaty in return for prompt and separate negotiations. Franklin concurred in the parleys which Oswald's new commission inaugurated, though illness kept him from active participation in them. Jay and Oswald were thus the chief architects of the draft which was completed on October 5. It should be emphasized that Jay at no point envisaged a separate peace; he merely abandoned that close coöperation with the French which his instructions had enjoined, a departure which Franklin's earlier actions had foreshadowed. It seems fair to note, furthermore, that Vergennes, by no means ignorant of what went on, was not sufficiently perturbed to object, which he assuredly would have done had it been to his advantage to do so.

News of British victory at Gibraltar, received in London September 30, stiffened the British to a point where several provisions of the preliminary draft were rejected and a watchdog (Henry Strachey) set to keep an eye on Oswald in the renewed negotiations opening on October 28. The newly arrived Adams played a part in these and Franklin gave acquiescence and coöperation. The signing of preliminary peace terms on November 30 brought the separate negotiations to a conclusion and posed a problem which has furnished writers with much food for reflection on the ethics and honesty of American conduct. The consensus of such reflection stands at this writing about as follows: The American legalist can maintain successfully that the letter of the law was complied with; the agreement of November 30 was tentative and preliminary, and the definitive settlement was made later with French knowledge and consent. His politically-minded brother can successfully defend the proposition that the technique adopted was more likely to succeed than one involving simultaneous Anglo-French and Anglo-Spanish discussions in which American interests would doubtless have bulked fairly small. If the family contained a moralist, however, he might point a critical finger at what undoubtedly was, and was intended to be, an evasion of the spirit of the French alliance.

To Franklin was delegated the somewhat delicate task of informing Vergennes of recent events. On November 29 he despatched a

note, followed the next day by a copy of the Anglo-American draft.
Vergennes indicated that the Americans had "managed well." On
December 14 the whole delegation signed a note of explanation,
which was intended to reënforce another in the long list of requests
for loans. When the petition for money was not honored immediately, so that part of the cash could be shipped on an early-depart-
ing vessel, Franklin was sufficiently sharp with Vergennes to nettle
the latter into an even sharper reply. Thus warned, Franklin composed an oft-quoted model of diplomatic soothing syrup containing,
perhaps, more sound elements than many such concoctions: "Nothing has been agreed to in the preliminaries contrary to the interests
of France; and no peace is to take place between us and England,
till you have concluded yours. Your observation is, however, apparently just, that, in not consulting you before they were signed,
we have been guilty of neglecting a point of *bienséance* [propriety].
But, as this was not from want of respect for the King, whom we all
love and honor, we hope it will be excused, and that the great work,
which has hitherto been so happily conducted, is so nearly brought
to perfection, and is so glorious to his reign, will not be ruined by a
single indiscretion of ours."[8] Having thus disarmed Vergennes he returned to the matter of the money, announcing that the ship had not
yet sailed and that he would wait hopefully (as he did successfully)
for the loan.

Peace Confirmed—The Treaty of Paris, 1783

Between these maneuverings 'and the signature of the definitive
treaties (September 3,1783) came the termination of European hostilities, the negotiation of European agreements, and another British
cabinet upheaval. The ultimate arrangements confirmed American
independence and vindicated the ability of American amateurs to
operate in competition with their more experienced European counterparts. Little more than this can be said of the Treaty of Paris as
a settlement of Anglo-American difficulties; in fact, aside from assuring independence, every important clause was honeycombed with
such loopholes, ambiguities, and omissions as would furnish prob-

---

[8] Sparks, *op. cit.*, vol. 9, p. 451.

lems for diplomats to solve and students to ponder for generations to come. In Article 1 the King acknowledged that the United States were "free sovereign & Independent States; that he treats with them as such, and for himself his Heirs & Successors, relinquishes all Claims to the Government Propriety & Territorial Rights of the same & every Part thereof." Thus was achieved the aim of patriot and demagogue, of soldier and diplomat. Succeeding articles, however, went far to nullify, for years at least, the promise of the first.[9]

Prominent among the troublemakers was Article 2, on boundaries. In this area matters of principle were to be agitated until the 1840's; details of settlement persisted through succeeding decades. So many controversies have hinged upon its interpretation as to warrant extensive quotation:

And that all Disputes which might arise in future on the Subject of the Boundaries of the said United States, may be prevented, it is hereby agreed and declared, that the following are and shall be their Boundaries, Viz. From the North West Angle of Nova Scotia, viz. That Angle which is formed by a Line drawn due North from the Source of St. Croix River to the Highlands along the said Highlands which divide those Rivers that empty themselves into the River St. Lawrence, from those which fall into the Atlantic Ocean, to the Northwestern-most Head of Connecticut River: Thence down along the middle of that River to the forty fifth Degree of North Latitude; From thence by a Line due West on said Latitude until it strikes the River Iroquois or Cataraquy; Thence along the middle of said River into Lake Ontario; through the Middle of said Lake until it strikes the Communication by Water between that Lake & Lake Erie; Thence along the middle of said Communication into Lake Erie; through the middle of said Lake, until it arrives at the Water Communication between that Lake & Lake Huron; Thence along the middle of said Water-Communication into the Lake Huron, thence through the middle of said Lake to the Water Communication between that Lake and Lake Superior, thence through Lake Superior Northward of the Isles Royal & Phelipeaux to the Long Lake; Thence through the Middle of said Long-Lake, and the Water Communication between it & the Lake of the Woods, to the said Lake of the Woods; Thence through the said Lake to the most Northwestern Point thereof, and from thence on a due West Course to the River Mississippi, Thence by a Line to be drawn along the

---

[9] Miller, *Treaties*, vol. 2, pp. 96–107, 151–157.

Middle of the said River Mississippi until it shall intersect the Northern-most Part of the thirty first Degree of North Latitude. . . .[10]

Despite this deceptively simple language, practically every step aroused controversy. Determination of the starting point at the St. Croix River would appear relatively easy, but rival territorial ambitions produced rivals for the name, and a decade was not long enough to decide the issues thus raised. Exact determination of the source of a river is no task for a summer afternoon. Again, the northeastern forests are replete with "highlands," but to decide just which ones constituted the Atlantic-St. Lawrence watershed could be done only by painstaking surveys. Even the 45th parallel, which had been surveyed in 1774, was found to be in error at a crucial point. Daniel Webster, who, with Lord Ashburton, was to draw much of the final line in 1842, was less than two years old when the treaty was signed.

Article 3 was to give birth to another series of controversies over the fisheries which recurred in one serious form or another until 1909, when a comprehensive arbitration removed its fundamental issues from the realm of diplomatic dispute. The wording of the article involved a contest in the use of terms, a contest won by the British at the expense of John Adams and the New England fishing interest. The Americans wished to retain unimpaired the use of all those northern fisheries which they had frequented as colonists. These included two main areas, the Grand Banks of Newfoundland and the inshore fisheries in territorial waters along the Canadian coast. The British operated upon the principle that they had no control over the Banks fisheries, which were outside territorial waters and thus subject to international rather than municipal control; on the other hand, they claimed the right to determine whether the coastal area should be opened to outsiders or not. Pursuant of this principle they persuaded Adams to accept the following language: "It is agreed that the People of the United States shall continue to

---

[10] Preliminary alternatives suggested (1) a line extending the 45th parallel, as it formed the northern boundary of New York, through to the Mississippi River; or (2) from the intersection of this parallel with the St. Lawrence, northwesterly to Lake Nipissing, thence westerly to the river. Such boundaries would have surrendered considerable areas north and west of Lake Michigan and might have resulted in the loss of fabulously rich mineral deposits.

enjoy unmolested the *Right* to take Fish of every kind on the Grand
Bank. . . . And also that the Inhabitants of the United States shall
have *Liberty* to take Fish of every Kind . . . on the Coasts Bays &
Creeks of all other of his Britannic Majesty's Dominions in America.
. . ." (Author's italics.) They persuaded Adams, as he later wrote,
that right was liberty and liberty was right, and the New England
lawyer, who should have known better, justified himself by saying
that he did not think it worth while to contend for a word. New England's interest would have been better served had he done so, as the
British privately held that "liberty" meant a grant, revocable at pleasure, and proceeded to act upon this theory during the War of 1812.
Judgment on Adams should not be too severe, however, as securing
use of the inshore fisheries even upon sufferance was no small accomplishment.

At the time the treaty was made it was thought that the Mississippi River took its rise in Canada. Article 8 guaranteed free use of
its waters to both parties. Since Spain controlled the lower reaches
and mouth of the river it was important to secure rights in that area.
The British took good care to do this in their own negotiations with
Spain, and the American delegates thought they had secured the
same rights, only to have their claims rudely denied by Spain. The
controversy thus engendered was not to be settled until 1795.

Articles 4 and 5 covered American debts owed to Englishmen and
Loyalist claims to compensation for lost estates. These settlements
reflect the loose character of the American confederation and the
consequent inability of its agents to make Congressional commitments which would be binding upon the States. The best that could
be done in the case of private creditors was a promise that they
should "meet with no lawful Impediment to the Recovery of the
full Value in Sterling Money, of all bona fide Debts heretofore contracted." Here, be it noted, was no guarantee of hospitable treatment
by local courts and juries, an omission which was fully apparent
when cases came to trial. As to confiscations, it was "agreed that the
Congress shall earnestly recommend it to the Legislatures of the respective States to provide for the Restitution of all Estates, Rights
and Properties which have been confiscated belonging to real Brit-

ish Subjects. . . ." Both sides recognized quite clearly that such a recommendation would be honored only to the extent of State respect for Congress, even then slight and destined to decline. A British promise to evacuate a chain of frontier posts "with all convenient speed" was later to emerge into intimate connection with the debt question.

The weaknesses of the treaty, to be disclosed in future years, should not obscure the fact that the American negotiators accomplished a real success in their first attempt. Their territorial achievements were more than commensurate with the success of American arms and the validity of American claims, if actual settlement be used as a criterion. Use of the inshore fisheries was more than they had a right to expect. Their standing among the nations was still problematical, and the fact that they had done so well in dealing with their former masters is a tribute to their own ability. The student should not, however, lose sight of the fact that the way was smoothed by British desire to make peace as well as by American adroitness.

4 Machinery of Diplomacy Under the Constitution

Confederation and Constitution

INDEPENDENCE CREATED MORE PROBLEMS THAN IT SOLVED, whether domestic or foreign. The so-called Confederation Period, 1781–1789, was one of frustration in practically every field, frustration which finally reached a point that threatened extinction of the new experiment and drove a group of leaders to the creation of a new form of government in the Philadelphia Convention of 1787. Constitutionally the period marked a transition stage between subordinate membership in the British Empire and independent nationhood. During it the country faced, and failed to solve, the same problem of political relationships which had split the British Empire in the Revolution. The British failed to create a workable relationship between central authority and local liberty by emphasizing the former at a time when the latter had received a great impetus in America from removal of the French threat in 1763. Fresh from this experience the framers of the Articles of Confederation set up a form of government minimizing central authority to a point where local liberty (state rights) was so unlimited that it threatened to run away with itself and wind up in chaos. Inability of the central government to secure, under the Articles, any element of State compliance with fiscal or other obligations to central authority was a major factor in the movement for the Convention. At Philadelphia the Founding Fathers approached this weakness by establishing

Dual Federalism, a working compromise which has to date withstood all tests, including that of civil war.

Social and economic conditions in the country paralleled political instability. The liquidation of wartime prosperity found debtors facing creditors across an age-old barrier of hostility. Debtors sought the usual remedies in currency inflation and postponement of debt payments, and met the usual obstacles from the creditors, entrenched in political power in the State legislatures. The pre-Revolutionary frictions between the haves and the have-nots reappeared, with the propertied elements usually retaining control and their less fortunate brethren becoming increasingly disgruntled. Prewar channels of American trade were thoroughly disrupted. War and independence did not destroy the American appetite for British manufactures, and Britain promptly reopened the channels of direct trade with the United States. There remained, however, the old matter of the adverse trade balance. The colonies had made this up by various types of trade involving the British and Foreign West Indies. Under mercantilism both Britain and France closed their West Indies to American traders, throwing long-established trade channels into confusion and necessitating development of new avenues of commerce. American ingenuity was equal to the task, and the foundation of the China trade was the result. This materialized, however, only after a period of considerable confusion which contributed to the general unsettlement. A final sample of confusion is to be found in interstate trade relations, where suspicion resulted in crippling tariff barriers.

Foreign humiliations matched domestic complications. The weaknesses of the peace settlement produced controversies with Great Britain and Spain.[1] John Adams and John Jay struggled valiantly but unsuccessfully to solve the difficulties, but these nations saw slight need to make concessions to a government so new and so obviously weak. As a result Adams' pleas for a trade treaty gained no hearing in England, which in turn began to ask embarrassing questions about prewar debts and Loyalist claims. Jay's agreement

---

[1] Relations with these nations, chief foreign problems of the Confederation Period, will be noted in their appropriate connections below.

with Don Diego de Gardoqui, the only important arrangement made during the period, was defeated by a split in Congress which made its ratification impossible. Finally, no attempts had been made to meet the debts incurred from France and the Netherlands during the Revolution. Foreign difficulties therefore contributed their part to the complex of troubles which produced the movement for the Constitution, and the Convention faced along with its other tasks the problem of evolving foreign policy machinery which might improve the national standing in the world of nations.

The Revolutionary and Confederation Periods taught the framers of the Constitution many lessons through unfortunate experience, and the machinery for conducting foreign relations which was created at Philadelphia differed widely from earlier models. This machinery, as it emerged and as it has been modified under usage, should be surveyed briefly before proceeding with the narrative of events. Such a survey should aid the student to understand something of the principles which the framers wrote into the Constitution; it should also indicate how these principles have been applied, and how the experience of the Republic has brought their alteration at several important points.

An Executive Power Emerges

It will be remembered that Congressional control of foreign policy characterized affairs down to 1787. This had proved unwieldly in practice, and considerable discussion at Philadelphia resulted in shifting control to the executive. The framers operated on the principle of the separation of powers among executive, legislative, and judicial branches of government. Fearful of possible tyranny at the hands of any one arm of the government, they also applied the principle of checks and balances, a complicated design whereby each branch acted as a watchdog on the other two. Under this arrangement, though both the Senate and the House form part of the machinery of diplomacy, and though the courts interpret judically the finished product, the President is clothed with principal responsibility and authority in this field. His position rests in part upon specific constitutional provisions and even more on the intangibles of initiative and discretionary power inherent in the executive office.[2] The constitutional clauses pertinent to the conduct of foreign affairs would include the following collection:

The executive Power shall be vested in a President of the United States of America. . . . The President shall be Commander in Chief of the Army and Navy of the United States, and of the Militia of the several States, when called into the service of the United States. . . . He shall have Power, by and with the Advice and Consent of the Senate, to make Treaties, provided two thirds of the Senators present concur; and he shall nominate, and by and with the Advice and Consent of the Senate, shall appoint Ambassadors, other public Ministers and Consuls. . . . The President shall have Power to fill up all Vacancies that may happen during the Recess of the Senate, by granting Commissions which shall expire at the End of their next Session . . . he shall receive Ambassadors and other public Ministers; he shall take Care that the Laws be faithfully executed, and shall Commission all the Officers of the United States.

These specific grants plus the tradition of executive power inherent in his office make him, *par excellence,* the prime mover in diplomatic affairs. The possession of initiative and discretion in the conduct of foreign relations further strengthens his position and places him a step ahead of other branches of government, by that much tending to remove him from their control. John Marshall in his famous opinion in Marbury *vs.* Madison (1803) alludes to this point:

By the Constitution of the United States, the President is invested with important political powers, in the exercise of which he is to use his own discretion, and is accountable only to his country in his political character and to his own conscience. To aid him in the performance of these duties, he is authorized to appoint certain officers, who act by his authority, and in conformity with his orders. In such cases their acts are his acts; and whatever discretion may be used, still there exists, and can exist, no power to control that discretion.

Despite later specific grants and broad discretionary implications, there are nonetheless considerable legal and practical limitations

---

[2] Edward S. Corwin, *The President's Control of Foreign Relations,* Princeton University Press, 1917; T. C. Lay, *The Foreign Service of the United States,* Prentice-Hall, 1928; J. M. Mathews, *American Foreign Relations: Conduct and Policies,* Century, 1928.

upon the executive's freedom of action. His nominations to diplomatic positions must receive Senatorial confirmation; many of his executive commitments remain unfulfilled until implemented by appropriations which, under our system, must originate in the House of Representatives. The two Houses may singly or together petition him by resolution to pursue a given course of action, which it is of course within his discretion to adopt or to reject. When such Congressional petitions reflect a well-developed public opinion, a wise chief executive trims his sails to the obvious breeze. It should be noted, however, that present-day facilities furnish an aggressive President with the means of influencing public opinion in the direction he may wish it to take. The annual and the special message to Congress, the letter to a friend, released "by authority" to the press, the occasional address, the fireside chat over the air, project presidential personality and policies to a world-wide audience. Alongside these tremendous initial advantages the checks imposed by domestic pressures, by the loose framework of international law, and by the tentative limitations of international organization tend to shrink into relative insignificance.

Partly by constitution and partly by usage, certain additional functions have come within the reach of the executive. Prominent among these is the recognition of new governments, a problem which may arise at any time due to revolution or the fortunes of war.[3] In the absence of express constitutional provision, and following the common usage that recognition is the prerogative of that branch of the government conducting foreign relations, the President performs the act of recognition, normally through official reception of a diplomatic agent. Constitutionalists differ as to whether the power of recognition is exclusively his, and examples will be cited later of Congressional attempts to influence action in this field. Practice, however, is in favor of executive recognition. Some opinion in the early days of the Republic held that the power to instruct diplomatic agents and to declare neutrality rested with Congress, but in both instances executive control was soon estab-

---

[3] H. Lauterpacht, *Recognition in International Law*, Cambridge University Press, 1947, presents considerable material on American policy in this area.

lished. Finally, the Constitution confers upon the President, "by and with the Advice and Consent of the Senate," the power to make treaties, an important function which should receive more extended consideration.

Techniques of International Agreement

The framers undoubtedly intended that the international policies of the United States should be carried out through the treaty-making power. This procedure was followed in the majority of instances during the first hundred years of national history. The third half-century witnessed a shift in procedure in which two-thirds of American international compacts followed one of two alternative patterns. The first of these patterns is the independent executive agreement, which goes into operation without the action of either House of Congress. The other is the so-called joint resolution procedure whereby an international agreement is either previously authorized or subsequently sanctioned by a majority of both Houses, actual completion being handled by the executive within the framework thus established. This is aptly illustrated by the reciprocal trade agreements program inaugurated by Cordell Hull in the 1930's, under which the President negotiates specific agreements within broad rules previously laid down by legislation.[4] Since the treaty procedure has been historically the favored technique, and since it seems likely to remain the method used for reaching important political agreements, it will receive major consideration here.[5]

The scheme whereby the executive, checked by one House of

------

[4] Wallace McClure, *International Executive Agreements, Democratic Procedure under the Constitution of the United States,* Columbia University Press, 1941, is the standard treatise on this subject. See also John Sloan Dickey, "Our Treaty Procedure Versus Our Foreign Policies," *Foreign Affairs,* vol. 25 (1947), pp. 357–377.

[5] The already voluminous literature on the treaty-making process was expanded after 1920 by the adverse termination of the Senate debate on the Versailles Treaty. In addition to the works already cited, valuable contributions have been made by George H. Haynes, *The Senate of the United States: Its History and Practice,* Houghton Mifflin, 1938, 2 vols.; Denna Frank Fleming, *The Treaty Veto of the American Senate,* Putnam, 1930, an account critical of the status quo; Royden J. Dangerfield, *In Defense of the Senate,* University of Oklahoma Press, 1933, a statistical study attacking the misconception that the Senate has been the great obstacle in the effectuation of treaties; and W. Stull Holt, *Treaties Defeated by the Senate,* Johns Hopkins Press, 1933, which studies the practical workings of the two-thirds rule.

Congress, conducts treaty procedure was an evolution in the Convention of 1787 away from the Confederation plan which gave the treaty-making power to Congress. As it has developed, the procedure includes four steps: negotiation, ratification, exchange of ratifications, and proclamation, the last three of which are essentially executive functions. Negotiation includes everything up to the point of ratification, which is an executive act, though journalists and many scholars refer to Senate "ratification" of treaties. The framers obviously intended that the Senate, then a small as well as highly selected body, should serve the President as an advisory council in the actual drafting of treaties, thus combining the "advice and consent" functions of the constitutional clause. President George Washington evidently took the provision in good faith and approached the Senate concerning a treaty with the Indians. An unpleasant experience with the doughty William Maclay of Pennsylvania, resulting in long discussion, delay, and submission of his proposals to a committee, disillusioned Washington concerning the usefulness of Senatorial advice. Maclay's desire to be heard was not unique among the members of his House; in addition he represented the spirit which was to bring into being the Anti-Federalist party. This combination of volubility and partisanship made it expedient for Washington and succeeding Presidents to forego formal Senatorial "advice" of the sort envisioned by the framers, while remaining bound to secure Senatorial "consent."[6] Increasing size and the rise of political parties completed the doom of what was doubtless from the first an unworkable partnership.

It should not be inferred, however, that the President pays no attention to the Senate while a treaty is being drafted. The obvious necessity of securing consent to his proposals forces him to negotiate in terms of what the Senate is likely to accept. He may gauge his chances by contacts with individual Senators or with his party's leader in the Committee on Foreign Relations. He not infrequently chooses Senators as negotiators, as did William McKinley after the Spanish-American War and Warren G. Harding in picking his dele-

---

[6] Charles A. Beard (ed.), *The Journal of William Maclay*, Boni, 1927, pp. 125–129.

gation to the Washington Conference of 1921–1922. Franklin D. Roosevelt and Harry S. Truman in a later day assured themselves of a measure of bipartisan support by allowing Senators Tom Connally and Arthur H. Vandenberg at least to skirt the fringes of world-shaping events. The outstanding exception was Woodrow Wilson's failure to take a Senator to Paris in 1918.

Once drafted, the treaty begins its course through the Senate. Here pitfalls await it, so numerous that John Hay once pessimistically likened it to a "bull going into the arena; no one can say just how or when the final blow will fall—but one thing is certain—it will never leave the arena alive."[7] Routine reference to the Committee on Foreign Relations is normally followed by a report calling for one of three dispositions: Unconditional acceptance, unconditional refusal, or conditional consent. The last involves the addition of amendments or reservations, which can be done by a bare majority, thus on occasion forcing the friends of the treaty to accept unwanted changes as an alternative to the defeat of a generally desirable arrangement. Experience with approximately nine hundred treaties down to 1928 seems to indicate that amendments kill relatively few treaties. The Senate altered 146 by amendment or reservation; of these the President or the other party dropped 48, making it apparent that amendment caused the defeat of not more than one out of three treaties. The essential factor, of course, is the number of crucially important treaties so defeated, and here the Versailles debacle has caused some of those who would reform treaty procedure to advocate limiting Senatorial action to acceptance or rejection, eliminating the possibility of amendment.

Once approved by the Senate, Presidential discretion may be invoked to refuse ratification, should amendments prove unduly objectionable. Alterations compel the executive to seek their acceptance by the other party, and if this is secured he normally proceeds to ratification, exchanges ratifications, and proclaims the treaty to be in effect. It will be seen that the door to success may be closed at a number of points. The President may not submit the treaty to

---

[7] William Roscoe Thayer, *The Life and Letters of John Hay*, Houghton Mifflin, 1908, vol. 2, p. 393.

the Senate (as in the case of the Monroe-Pinkney Treaty of 1806). An adverse committee report may be damning; reservations and amendments may emasculate the treaty to the point where the President refuses to ratify; outright rejection may be secured by one-third of a quorum, plus one. If amended, and ratified by the President, the other party may refuse to accept the amendments; indeed, the other party may nullify all these domestic steps by itself refusing ratification of its negotiator's work. Of all these pitfalls the most publicized and maligned, however, has been the rule whereby "two thirds of the Senators present" must judge it affirmatively prior to Presidential ratification.

The charges leveled against the Senate here are that it defeats and delays treaties. Pure statistics fail to convict the Senate on either count. Less than a dozen first-rate treaties popular enough to secure a majority vote failed to receive a two-thirds majority. Dangerfield's figures absolve the Senate of undue delay; 621 treaties which he considered were acted upon after an average delay of 107.7 days, not excessive in view of the parliamentary complications involved and in comparison with the time required to pass ordinary legislation. Eighty percent of all treaties were agreed to within the average delay period, and the Senate held only 6 percent over one year. The greatest average lapse of time occurred between Senate action and proclamation, a period in which responsibility must be divided between the President and the other party to the agreement.

On other than statistical grounds, however, the two-thirds rule is more vulnerable. Although few first-rate treaties have been defeated, several of these, such as the Versailles Treaty (1920) and the World Court Protocol (1935), have been of transcendent importance. Quantitatively, the two-thirds rule gives each opposing vote twice as much weight as each supporting ballot. When this is added to the fact that partisanship on occasion outweighs statesmanship, the handicap becomes even greater. A further burden is the imposition of undesirable amendments and reservations which may be done by a simple majority, whereas the final consent must be given by a two-thirds majority. Shifting blocs of votes may attach amendments which may make the total product unacceptable. In addition to these specific drawbacks, and perhaps more important than any, is the handicap under which the procedure places American policy-makers in the international field. Forced to negotiate in the face of certain partisan opposition, the executive may well hesitate to advocate measures of far-reaching national and international importance. He may try, alternatively, to by-pass the Senate by taking refuge in the executive agreement or joint resolution procedures. The first of these is hardly an adequate vehicle for the conduct of large-scale international operations; its frequent use can only aggravate already touchy interdepartmental relationships and cause alarm as to democratic control over foreign policy. The latter, flexible and less vulnerable, enhances the degree of popular supervision, but threatens always to offend Senatorial self-esteem.

The foregoing brief critique points a way to improved procedure, but does not indicate the chief obstacle to its realization. The obvious remedy for a bad rule is to change it, and suggestions to this end are numerous: Among them are the transfer of the Senate's power to a majority of both Houses (most frequently proposed); giving the power to the House of Representatives alone; reducing the "consent" figure to a bare Senatorial majority; or limiting Senatorial action to mere acceptance or rejection. Unfortunately the only way to effectuate any of these is by a constitutional amendment, requiring a two-thirds vote of the Senate for adoption, and that body has shown no great desire to commit this particular sort of hari-kari. Until such a spirit of Senatorial self-abnegation develops, the best that can be hoped for is continued use of alternative techniques within their limitations, and reduction of the frictions inherent in the situation by mutual understanding between departments. Only a congenital optimist can hope for removal of the frictions, regardless of the techniques, as long as the system of checks and balances remains rooted in American thinking.

Once proclaimed, the treaty is subject to interpretation and enforcement. All three branches of the government are involved here, and the ramifications are too varied to fit into a brief treatment. Certain distinctions and criteria may be mentioned as useful guideposts. It is obvious that any enforcement agency must act according to its lights; hence whatever branch of the government is involved in enforcement must interpret the provisions in question. If, however, the executive has indicated its own interpretation, the courts will pay great attention to this expression. Furthermore, if executive or Congress has terminated a treaty as an international agreement, a political decision, it can have no force as domestic law and so is nonenforceable in the courts. This brings up an important distinction between the international and municipal aspects of treaties. Upon proclamation by both parties a treaty becomes an international agreement, binding upon each. Its self-executing provisions become, by Senatorial consent and Presidential ratification, part of municipal law and so enforceable by the courts without further ado. Other provisions, however, may require legislative implementation, usually involving appropriations, before they can become effective. This raises a nice constitutional question: Is Congress obligated to take action to effectuate a duly negotiated and ratified treaty? This arose first in connection with bills appropriating money to meet the expenses of arbitration boards proposed by the Jay Treaty of 1794. Some members of the lower House, jealous of their rights, felt that the circumstances offered an opportunity for the House to judge the merits of the treaty itself, and to grant or withhold the appropriations accordingly. As has usually been the case in similar disputes since that time, long debate was followed by passage of the bill, though not until the amenities had been observed by passage of a resolution to the effect that "it is the constitutional right and duty of the House of Representatives, in all such cases, to deliberate on the expediency or inexpediency of carrying such Treaty into effect, and to determine and act thereon, as, in their judgment, may be most conducive to the public good." It is thus apparent that a treaty may be both a valid international agreement and the law of the land, but inexecutable until Congress has acted affirmatively; furthermore, there seems to be no way in which such action can be compelled—in fact, on at least one occasion a treaty has been brought to naught by failure of Congress to pass supplementary legislation.

The dual nature of treaties also complicates the question of their termination. As international contracts they may be terminated in a number of ways. If a new agreement specifically supersedes an older one the latter automatically passes into limbo, as was the case when the Hay-Pauncefote Treaty (1902) replaced the Clayton-Bulwer Treaty (1850) in regulating Anglo-American policy relative to an isthmian canal. The same result obtains when the provisions of a new treaty are inconsistent with a former one, without specific abrogation. The dissolution of one party or its absorption into another state raises questions of treaty obligations which are frequently settled when the absorbing state assumes by treaty the obligations of the deceased state. Full execution of its provisions acts as an automatic termination. Other treaties expire at the end of an agreed period. A variant of this is found in the establishment of a specified period, with a proviso that the agreement shall run on indefinitely subject to termination by either party after giving due notice, the terms of which are clearly indicated.

As in the case of negotiation, the executive is usually the agent in terminating treaties. He may act independently; frequently such action is underwritten by one or both Houses, but such approval is evidently not necessary. Only once has Congress acted independently, in 1798 terminating the French treaties of 1778, which by that time had become undesirable obligations. Congress frequently tries to induce the executive to act, though it is doubtful whether he can legally be forced to terminate an international agreement. Congress may, however, legislate in the municipal sphere in such fashion as practically to compel him to follow its wishes regarding a treaty. Professor J. M. Mathews cites in this connection the Seamen's Act of 1915, wherein Congress "requested and directed" the President to give notice of termination of certain treaty provisions then in conflict with the newly enacted municipal law. Had he failed to comply he would have found himself in the ludicrous position of enforcing, as municipal law, provisions in conflict with binding international agreements.

This power of municipal legislation actually gives Congress considerable control over treaties. Termination of the French treaties in 1798 is again a case in point, as Congress intended its action in the premises to extend to both their international and municipal aspects. In the ordinary course of legislation a treaty may be adversely affected whenever Congress, in exercising its municipal functions, enacts a law conflicting with a treaty but otherwise constitutional, pursuant of the legal principle *leges posteriores priores contrarias abrogant.* As stated by Attorney-General J. J. Crittenden in 1851, "The last expression of the law-giving power must prevail and have effect, though inconsistent with a prior treaty." This rose to plague the government in 1888 when Congress passed restrictive legislation violative of the Sino-American treaty of 1880 regulating Chinese immigration. The Supreme Court on hearing the evidence agreed that the law violated the treaty, but asserted that the law was "not on that account invalid or to be restricted in its enforcement. . . . A treaty is in its nature a contract between nations, and is often merely promissory in its character, requiring legislation to carry its stipulations into effect. If the treaty operates by its own force, and relates to a subject within the power of Congress, it can be deemed in that particular only the equivalent of a legislative act, to be repealed or modified at the pleasure of Congress. In either case the last expression of the sovereign will must prevail." Municipal legislation derogatory of treaty rights may give the injured party ample grounds for grievance, but such grievance constitutes a political question, which must be threshed out with the executive branch of the government.

The Department of State

A brief word should be said in conclusion concerning the Department of State, established by Congress to aid the President in conducting his functions in the field of foreign relations.[8] The Constitution does not specifically authorize creation of executive depart-

---

[8] In addition to the authorities already cited, the following give useful information or criticism on the organization and functioning of the Department: Blair Bolles, "Reorganization of the State Department," *Foreign Policy Reports*, August 15, 1947; Bertram D. Hulen, *Inside the Department of State*, McGraw-Hill, 1939; Gaillard Hunt, *The Department of State of the United States: Its History and Functions*, Department of State, 1893; James L. McCamy, *The Administration of American Foreign Affairs*, Knopf, 1950; Graham H. Stuart, *American Diplomatic and Consular Practice*, Appleton-Century, 1936, and *The Department of State: A History of Its Organization, Procedure, and Personnel*, Macmillan, 1949.

ments, but by permitting the President to require the opinions, in writing, of the heads of such departments, it clearly postulates their establishment. Congress acted promptly, creating the Department of Foreign Affairs by Act of July 27, 1789; when it was found that some domestic functions were unassigned they were allotted to the Department, necessitating a change of name, by Act of September 15, 1789, to the Department of State. First established on a very modest scale, with a staff of six including Secretary Jefferson, and an annual budget of $5950, its complement of personnel lagged far behind its expanding duties. It was not until the nation began to face up to its international obligations in the 1940's that the Department began to draw anything approximating its due share of government funds, with consequent staff increases. As of March, 1947, authorized personnel totalled 7290; the Foreign Service, State's field arm, had a similar quota of 12,373.

No general account can cover more than a broad outline of organization, which follows herewith. The functions of the Secretary of State are those of his counterparts in Foreign Offices the world over (covered in Chapter 1), except that his degree of responsibility for the policy which he helps to formulate and carry out is less than in a parliamentary government, where the Cabinet stands or falls on its ability to range a legislative majority behind its measures. The American system not infrequently develops a situation in which President and Cabinet are on opposite sides of the political fence from the majority in one or both Houses of Congress. The Secretary is a political officer whose possession of technical skill is a fortunate accident of unhappy rarity. Congress tardily recognized this fact in 1919 by providing an Undersecretary to relieve his chief of routine, to act for him in his absence, and to assist him in his policy-making function. The intent was to follow a European pattern in which the Undersecretary is a permanent, nonpolitical career official who acts as a coördinating element regardless of party changes and thus serves to perpetuate the traditions of the Department. This aim was not immediately realized; appointments have normally been political choices of the Secretary and incumbents have changed frequently. Fortunately this has been offset somewhat by the high level of ability available for the position. The Solicitor and the Legal Adviser afford counsel on the multifarious questions of international law and relations which the Department faces in its day-to-day routine.

On the next level and above the numerous and frequently shifting bureaus and divisions, which can receive no attention here, are the Assistant Secretaries, whose duties are divided according to changing concepts of successive Secretaries. These are regarded as political appointments, but conspicuous exceptions have kept unusually able men in this grade for many years, particularly Alvey A. Adee, who was Second Assistant Secretary from 1886 until 1924. William Roscoe Thayer thus apostrophized him in his biography of John Hay: "Presidents ignorant of diplomacy and international law felt reasonably safe in appointing as their chief secretaries gentlemen as ignorant as themselves, because they knew that Adee was there to guard against blunders." The most common division of duties among the Assistant Secretaries has been on some geographical basis, under which particular parts of the world are assigned, not always with entire logic, to a particular Assistant, with departmental administration allocated to one of the number. This leads to a somewhat compartmentalized approach to foreign policy, since the incumbents of the various "desks" over which pass the routine matters relating to individual countries tend to lack the overall view so essential in formulating a rounded policy. This limitation was aggravated, beginning in the later 1930's, by the development of a functional approach to foreign policy, involving such aspects as economics, information, and intelligence, carrying supranational or world-wide connotations.

Inevitable conflicts of objective and of jurisdiction resulted from this combination of geographical and functional approach; to these were added postwar growing pains due to absorption into the Department of wartime organizations whose usefulness appeared likely to survive and whose personnel emphasized the functional approach. The combination of conflict and of growing pains produced some confusion and friction within the Department with resultant loss of efficiency. In an effort to attack the problem Secretary George C. Marshall made two changes in 1947. One involved another of the periodic reorganizations of the geographic desks, grouping them into four offices covering well-defined areas and placing all under the coördinating direction of a single Assistant Secretary. The other was the creation of a Policy Planning Board whose members had no administrative duties, previously the bane of policy-makers. This group was given access to all information in the Department's possession, at whatever level, in the hope that it might enable the Secretary to formulate policy more efficiently. As this account is written it is too early to evaluate the results of these changes, but they seem as logical as their need was apparent.

5 America in the World

GEORGE WASHINGTON TOOK THE PRESIDENTIAL OATH IN New York on April 30, 1789. Within a few short weeks the assembling of the Estates General set in train the French Revolution which in a matter of months embroiled France with most of the rest of Europe. This war, opening in 1793, perched the United States uneasily at the apex of a triangle completed by the belligerents. A weak nation, largely dependent upon overseas commerce for existence, was bound for trouble in following its natural desire to trade with vigorous antagonists, one of them the great maritime power of the day. To this economic dilemma was added an ideological one which threatened to become political: The followers of Alexander Hamilton were men who felt that the English side was better as well as more profitable, while Thomas Jefferson's disciples believed that the watchwords of the Revolution held out hope for mankind even when its excesses filled the baskets with severed heads. Thus foreign relations found a counterpart in domestic issues.

As a haven from these conflicting pressures the government resorted to an assertion of neutrality, then a relatively new device. Around the policy thus launched were to be written several troublesome chapters of American history, chapters troublesome whether they concerned a weak nation struggling for existence among strong rivals or, as in 1914–1917, a powerful nation seeking to avoid involvement in a battle among its peers. They would prove, over a span of a century and a half, that the device was inadequate to the recurring stresses which it faced, and that interest, or principle, or fear, in varying proportions, would involve the nation in each suc-

ceeding full-dress international conflict. Thus neutrality became a
hardy perennial in the thorny crop of international complications
and furnished material for a bitter lesson in the inability of the
United States, or any first-line nation, to hold itself successfully and
permanently aloof from hostilities involving any large proportion of
its fellow nations. Fortunately, perhaps, not all of this was clear to
Washington and his advisers in 1793.

The idea that a nation can remain at peace among warring neighbors is a relatively modern concept, contrary to the political and
religious theories of the Middle Ages, when both church and state
were organized on the basis of suzerainty, in which each individual
owed allegiance to someone on a higher level.[1] In such a situation a
quarrel among any was likely to involve all. With the development
of the national state came slowly the idea that a nation's attitude
toward an unjust war might differ from that toward a just one, even
to the point of abstaining from the former. The geographical discov-
eries of the sixteenth and seventeenth centuries induced wars as well
as increased commerce. The one interfered with the other; hence
the politically powerful merchants sought from government rules of
war whereby they might ply their trade in spite of surrounding hostilities. By the time the United States appeared upon the scene ideas
of neutrality were current; they were still sufficiently novel that
American practice added considerably to their content. As advanced
by this country and developed down to 1914, neutrality has come
to involve (1) an automatic declaration of abstention from European
wars; (2) insistence upon certain rights upon the high seas, usually
reflecting a relatively weak maritime position; and (3) the recognition of corresponding obligations to act in such a way that neither
belligerent can benefit by the partisan action of the neutral government.

The years 1793–1815 produced many practical tests of these matters in a period when the United States was a military nonentity and
a naval cipher. American efforts to establish neutral rights, cutting

---

[1] Philip C. Jessup and Francis Deak, *Neutrality, Its History, Economics, and Law,*
Columbia University Press, 1935, vol. 1; Edwin M. Borchard and Wm. P. Lage,
Neutrality for the United States, Yale University Press, 1937.

athwart British sea power, were not destined to easy success and contributed to the War of 1812. Neutrality next rose to importance between 1861–1865, when the United States was a belligerent, with its interests largely reversed. The War of 1914–1918 again found America first an uneasy neutral and then a belligerent, but this time with a power potential that made it important in determining the final issue. Within the earliest period noted above, the years 1793–1801 (to which this chapter will be devoted) witnessed the emergence, elaboration, and first trials of neutrality. During these years the United States, always desiring peaceful trade, swings as it were at the extremities of a giant pendulum, first into difficulties with France, then with Great Britain, and finally to the verge of war with France. It should be noted, however, that these gymnastics succeeded in keeping the peace and in loosing the bonds of the French treaties of 1778. To the narration of these events, bearing the names respectively of the Genêt Affair, the Jay Treaty, and the X Y Z Affair, we now turn.

Genêt Generates a Policy

The first swing of the pendulum began with the French declaration of war on Great Britain, February 1, 1793.[2] This war, spasmodically continued until 1815, afforded a great opportunity and posed a great problem for the young nation. The opportunity lay in the accelerated economic development which came from purveying sup-

---

[2] The abortive Nootka Sound Affair of 1790 foreshadowed the neutrality policy. Anglo-Spanish rivalry on the west coast of North America focused on Vancouver Island where British traders poaching on the Spanish preserve erected a trading post at Nootka Sound in 1789. Spanish capture of the traders threatened a European crisis which failed to materialize because Revolutionary disorders precluded French support of Spain. British pressure soon forced Spain to permit the English to trade and settle in unoccupied parts of the coast. This prospective war stirred fears in American quarters. Anglo-Spanish conflict might aggravate efforts which both were making to alienate American frontiersmen. Further, suppose the British should request the right of transit across American territory to attack the Spanish in the Mississippi Valley? This might involve friction around the western posts, in British hands since the treaty of Paris. Washington received the usual conflicting advice from his official family, but the note which Jefferson finally wrote to Gouverneur Morris, Minister to England, said, "We wish to be neutral . . ." and clearly predicted the American attitude. The standard account of this episode is William R. Manning, "The Nootka Sound Affair," in *Report of the American Historical Association, 1904*, Government Printing Office, 1905, pp. 279–478.

plies to belligerent Europe. The prosperity thus secured strengthened the United States against domestic discord and the growth of the nation relieved the ever-present threat of British and Spanish encroachment on the borders—threats virtually at an end by the end of the period. More pressing, however, was this problem: What were American obligations to France under the treaties of 1778, now for the first time likely to become a liability rather than an asset?[3] The news of war which reached Philadelphia in April did not catch the administration completely napping. Jefferson had been writing to David Humphreys, Minister to Portugal (March 22, 1793), that in the event of war he was to "be particularly attentive to preserve for our vessels all the rights of neutrality. . . ." Washington, cutting short a holiday at Mount Vernon, wrote Jefferson that "it behoves the Government of this Country to use every means in its power to prevent the citizens thereof from embroiling us with either of those powers, by endeavouring to maintain a strict neutrality," and hastened to Philadelphia to develop a policy. This policy, contained in the Proclamation of April 22, 1793, was based on the solid agreement of Washington's advisers that noninvolvement in war was desirable; it was hammered out by vigorous blows of Hamilton's pro-British hammer on the anvil of Jefferson's Francophilism, and expressed Washington's true neutrality in the language of Attorney General Edmund Randolph.

The day after his arrival at Philadelphia the President submitted to his advisers (April 18) thirteen questions, most of which were probably drafted by Hamilton. Three of these epitomize the principal issues facing American policy makers:

1. Shall a proclamation issue for the purpose of preventing interferences of the citizens of the United States in the war between France and Great Britain, &c.? Shall it contain a declaration of neutrality or not? What shall it contain?

2. Shall a minister from the Republic of France be received? . . .

4. Are the United States obliged by good faith to consider the treaties

---

[3] W. K. Woolery, *The Relation of Thomas Jefferson to American Foreign Policy, 1783–1793*, Johns Hopkins Press, 1927, and C. M. Thomas, *American Neutrality in 1793*, Columbia University Press, 1931, portray the interplay of personalities and events which produced the neutrality policy.

heretofore made with France as applying to the present situation of the parties?

Of these the first and last were momentarily most pressing. The first produced divergences of detail rather than principle. Jefferson believed in neutrality, but not in proclamation, which he thought unwise and beyond the province of the executive; perhaps his shrewd political mind saw some gain in leaving the matter to the decision of the new Congress, which would probably be controlled by his followers. He yielded gracefully to Hamilton's arguments in favor of an executive proclamation on condition that the word "neutrality" be omitted. Washington proclaimed Randolph's draft of April 22, directing it, since official notice of the war had not yet been received, to the government's own citizens, who were warned "carefully to avoid all acts and proceedings whatsoever, which may in any manner tend to contravene . . . a conduct friendly and impartial toward the belligerent powers. . . ."

The fourth query was the most crucial—how far were the treaties of 1778 binding in a new framework? Suppose, for example, that the French should ask implementation of Article 11 of the Alliance, guaranteeing France's West Indian possessions? Hamilton and his Anglophiles hoped temporarily to avoid performance of whatever commitments the treaties contained. He therefore argued that they were "temporarily and provisionally suspended" until a qualified French government was established. He argued that the treaties had been made with Louis XVI, whose death had removed their obligation, and that they were "defensive," whereas the present war was an "offensive" one. Jefferson replied that treaties were interstate rather than intergovernmental obligations, pointing out drily that the United States, as well as France, had changed its form of government since 1778 without thereby attempting to evade its legal commitments. Hamilton's second argument, developed to make possible the evasion of the guarantee provisions, was more difficult to answer, since France had declared war; he had, however, conveniently ignored the bellicose attitude of Austria and Prussia and their machinations in assisting Louis XVI to overthrow the constitutional regime which the Revolution had forced upon him. Jefferson demonstrated that since it would not be immediately necessary to fulfill these guarantees, Hamilton's fears of a war with England were premature. These arguments well illustrate Jefferson's technique, which was to preserve the binding obligation of the French treaties, but to avoid performing such of them as might offend England to the point of war.

Washington's query about the reception of a French minister was given point by the triumphal progress from Charleston to Philadelphia of Edmond Charles, Citizen Genêt. This vigorous and loquacious revolutionary had made himself *persona non grata* at the Russian court; the Girondists in control of the French government sent him to the United States, where sentiments were, it was to be hoped, more in line with French Republicanism. Contrary winds, he asserted, blew his ship south from its intended berth in Philadelphia; they certainly wafted him to a warmer political climate, as Governor William Moultrie received him cordially. Sending his ship ahead, Genêt proceeded overland to the capital through an almost uninterrupted ovation, arriving on May 16 to find neutrality an accomplished fact. His prospective arrival raised the constitutional question of the power of recognition. Hamilton had proposed to qualify Genêt's reception with such reservations as would postpone implementation of the French treaties, but discussion modified this to the point where the reception was unqualified; since it was tendered by the President, a precedent of executive recognition was established which has obtained ever since.

Popular enthusiasm and official recognition did not insure personal success. Genêt won Jefferson's initial approbation by not invoking the guarantee provisions of the treaty of alliance. The French felt that neutrality, enforced rigorously toward Great Britain and benevolently toward France, was more valuable than any hypothetical naval support in the West Indies. The commercial treaty provided that free ships made free goods and excluded naval stores and foodstuffs from the contraband list; it also prohibited France's enemies from outfitting privateers or bringing prizes into neutral American ports. If the United States could successfully insist upon British recognition of the provisions on foodstuffs and contraband, she might constitute herself the French lifeline. Likewise, a tolerant attitude toward privateers and prizes (such, say, as France had exhibited toward John Paul Jones during the American Revolution) could be most advantageous to France.

Genêt's program, geared to these objectives, was not unlike what Franklin and his colleagues had sought from France not long before. It aimed at political sympathy, money for France, and the use of American soil as a base of propaganda and military operations against France's enemies. Political sympathy was ready to hand in the predilections of the Jeffersonian group for French ideals as against the conservative monarchism of the enemy coalition. A good case could also be made for Genêt's financial requests. The American revolutionary debt to France was being paid by instalments designed to liquidate it early in 1807. Genêt suggested the prepayment of the remainder (two and one-half million dollars in round numbers), promising to spend it locally for supplies. A precedent had been created by an advance of 1792 to succor French refugees from a slave insurrection in Santo Domingo, and he felt justly abused when his plea was rejected. Most important, however, were his plans for American-based operations against the enemy. The propaganda aspects, lesser of his two objectives in this regard, included dissemination of material designed to induce revolt in British Canada and Spanish Florida, thus building a backfire to the European struggle. Military and naval operations occupied a larger place in Genêt's schemes, and raised sharply the issue of American obligations under the treaty of amity. He hoped that a liberal interpretation of this treaty (see above, p. 30) would enable him to outfit privateers and dispose of prizes on American soil. He knew that as the treaty stood it contained no such permission. Optimistically he proposed to translate hope into reality by a new treaty amplifying the earlier one in favor of French claims; meantime he sought government complaisance toward actions which would have been permissible only under the terms of the proposed new agreement.

Pursuant of this design he fitted armed privateers in American ports, established prize courts on American soil, and prepared to launch military expeditions against the Spanish. He brought with him 250 blank privateering commissions, of which 14 were issued, resulting in the capture of over eighty prizes. It should be noted that his government never officially claimed the right to fit privateers, though Genêt personally asserted it to Jefferson. The American government was quite clear that it was not obligated to accommodate him; the question of its obligation to Genêt's enemies raised the problem of neutral duty, and discussion produced the unanimous opinion that it was bound to prohibit such actions as those of Genêt in American ports. This was conveyed to Genêt, whose impudent reply was to outfit the *Little Democrat* in Philadelphia. Privateering is conducted for profit as well as for injuring hostile commerce; and its success depends upon access to courts where prizes may be condemned prior to sale. Genêt assumed a treaty right and authorized French consuls to act as prize court judges. This practice was halted only after the government revoked the *exequatur* of a particularly obnoxious consul at Boston. Finally, Genêt recruited Americans for service afloat and ashore. Informed that he had no right to recruit privateering crews, he refused to desist on the ground that he could find no law or treaty prohibiting it. The government's efforts to prevent the practice were hindered temporarily when a jury released one Gideon Henfield, arrested for enlistment on a French privateer, despite the fact that Randolph and Hamilton prompted the prosecutor. Genêt presently made contact with George Rogers Clark, whose grandiose advertisement in the *Centinel of the North-Western Territory* (Cincinnati, January 25, 1794) proclaimed him a "Major General in the Armies of France, and Commander in Chief of the French Revolutionary Legions on the Mississippi River," and contained his proposals "For raising the volunteers for the reduction of the Spanish posts on the Mississippi, for opening the trade of the said river, & giving freedom to its inhabitants. . . ."[4] At one time the French consul at Charleston had several hundred men under arms for an attack upon Spanish Florida. These antics jeopardized American efforts to solve the problems of the Florida frontier and Missis-

---

[4] Archibald Henderson, "Isaac Shelby and the Genêt Mission," *Mississippi Valley Historical Review,* vol. 6 (1920), pp. 451–469.

sippi navigation, then at an acute stage, and steps were taken to prevent either expedition from materializing.

Genêt's disregard of the proprieties measured his rising unpopularity with the government, which in turn was reflected in the increasing asperity of his communications to it. His letter of June 22 was so insolent that no reply was made; shortly afterward he threatened to appeal to the people over the President's head, and in August copies of his correspondence were transmitted to his government with the request that he be recalled. Meantime, since several months must elapse, he was told what had been done, which sobered his actions but not his tongue. The French government had moved to the left and the Jacobins were almost as anxious to lay hands on Genêt as Hamilton was to get rid of him. Washington declined to consign him to their tender mercies and allowed him to remain in the country and exercise whatever talents he possessed in domestic pursuits as the son-in-law of Governor George Clinton of New York.

Genêt's major significance is that he contributed to the establishment of the principles of neutral obligation later known as the doctrines of impartiality and abstention, under which the United States undertook to refrain from all unneutral acts and to make all belligerents behave alike. Hamilton directed a circular containing these principles to the collectors of customs, August 4, 1793, and they were enacted into the first Neutrality Act of 1794. They denied the right of belligerents to add original arms or military equipment to ships in American ports; permitted belligerent merchant ships to equip; sanctioned the acquisition of equipment which could be adapted to either peaceful or warlike uses; and prohibited recruiting. The problems of neutral duties, to which this episode gave rise, carried the country far along the way to trouble with France under the interpretation of the treaties of 1778, trouble which was to come to a focus in the X Y Z Affair after a sharp skirmish with Britain over neutral rights, culminating in the Jay Treaty.

John Jay and the Rights of Neutrals
The second swing of the pendulum takes the United States over into a sharp controversy with Great Britain in which long-developing

problems growing out of the peace settlement of 1783 are mingled with questions of neutral rights produced by the Revolutionary wars. It will be recalled that the Treaty of Paris provided for the evacuation of Britain's western posts (now on American soil) "with all convenient speed" and also attempted to smooth the way for recovery of debts by Loyalists and British merchants. As events moved, these two matters became connected in British policy and Anglo-American relations.[5] The British had originally intended to retain the posts at least temporarily in the interest of fur traders who stood to lose by their surrender.[6] Before news of the definitive treaty of peace reached American shores, Governor Frederick Haldimand reminded Lord North of another important factor. In the Treaty of Fort Stanwix (1768) the British had made certain territorial promises to the Ohio Valley Indians. The Paris negotiators had ignored these, and had surrendered much of the land to the United States without consulting the Indians. The latter, highly incensed, denied that such arrangements could be binding without their consent. In the fortunate position of those whose principles and interests coincide, the British postponed surrender of the posts in order to prevent the bloody repetition of Pontiac's Revolt, forecast by Haldimand if the posts were given up. Meantime Haldimand had been approached by an agent who demanded surrender of the New York posts, and in conversation suggested as his personal opinion that evacuation should be preceded by execution of the debt provisions of the Treaty of Paris favorable to the Loyalists. This idea appealed to the agent so much that he suggested it to his home government, which seized upon it as justification for retaining the posts. As the Confederation Period went its weary way the posts became increasingly desirable as bases from which Britain might recover parts of her lost territory which seemed likely to disintegrate from centrifugal force. Thus the twin problems of debts and posts continued to exercise their mis-

---

[5] S. F. Bemis, *Jay's Treaty*, Macmillan, 1923, and A. L. Burt, *The United States, Great Britain and British North America*, Yale University Press, 1940, provide the most thorough studies of this period.

[6] The principal posts, British retention of which jeopardized American frontier and expansionist interests, were Oswegatchie (Ogdensburg), Oswego, Niagara, Presque Isle (Erie, Pennsylvania), Sandusky, Detroit, and Michilimackinac.

chievous force in Anglo-American relations until the French Revolutionary wars brought questions of neutral rights to the fore.

The problem was easily stated: How could a weak maritime nation achieve its desire to trade with two parties to a war, one of whom was mistress of the seas and accustomed to dictating the rules of maritime conduct? Trade with one side was no problem—indeed, relaxed British mercantile regulations permitted American trade with British West Indian ports and opened to American shipping the "long haul" from the Indies to Britain, closed since the separation.[7] It was when Americans tried to apply the principles of the treaty of 1778 (free ships, free goods, the right of a neutral to trade from port to port of a belligerent in innocent goods, a short contraband list) that trouble ensued. Direct trade with France developed rapidly but was neatly detoured by the "Provision Order" of June 8, 1793, directing that ships carrying the principal grain products to France be brought to British ports, where the cargoes were purchased at British prices; the ships were freed, perhaps in the hope that the trip might be repeated. Five ports in the French West Indies had been opened to American trade prior to the outbreak of war; hostilities opened others to neutral commerce, after the custom which France had developed during earlier wars with Britain when she needed neutral carriers for her island products.[8] As had happened before, a British Order in Council (November 6, 1793) forbade neutrals to engage in this carrying trade, although the five ports opened before the war were later excepted from its operation. American ingenuity surmounted this crisis by bringing French West Indian products into the United States, entering them at the customs, and reëxporting them to France. When the ships were overhauled by British cruisers, the ships' papers indicated that the goods were American—had they not paid duty? This "broken voyage trade" became very lucrative until outlawed by the *Essex* decision in 1806.

---

[7] Robert G. Albion and Jennie B. Pope, *Sea Lanes in Wartime: The American Experience, 1775–1942*, Norton, 1942, p. 67; G. S. Graham, *Sea Power and British North America, 1783–1820: A Study in British Colonial Policy*, Harvard University Press, 1941, pp. 56–73.

[8] During the French and Indian War France had opened her carrying trade to the neutral Dutch. The British countered with the "rule of War of 1756," which stated that a trade closed in time of peace could not be opened during a war.

Trade was still subject to galling restrictions, however. The long and purposely vague British contraband list adapted itself aggravatingly to the character of neutral cargoes. Annoying also was British reliance on blockade by proclamation rather than by patrol. Most objectionable of all, since it involved danger to American lives, was the British practice of "impressing" seamen. This custom, a reflection of British dependence upon the fleet, permitted the transfer of sailors (above a bare minimum) from merchantmen to warships. The war called for new American sailors at higher wages than were paid in the Royal Navy; mercantile service was also less hazardous. Desertions were frequent, recruiting easy. Many deserters availed themselves of the easy American naturalization law and the still easier practices developed in course of time. This ran foul of the British doctrine of indefeasible allegiance, which proclaimed "Once an Englishman, always an Englishman." This doctrine enabled British warships to seize naturalized citizens of British extraction in violation of American law; very occasionally, too, a bona fide American was included in the press gang's haul, and it was easy to charge that this resulted more from design than from accident.

The preceding factual recital measures but poorly the emotional tensions of the middle 1790's. The aftermath of the peace settlement of 1783 created bitterness on the frontier; the British flouted American neutral "rights" in ways which might at any moment precipitate hostilities; Hamilton's influence in the councils of the administration was growing and his contacts with the British agent in the United States becoming closer. Small wonder that the end of 1793 saw Jefferson leaving the post in which he had labored so diligently and in many directions so successfully. Small wonder, either, that the Federalist leadership, freed of the Jeffersonian incubus, resolved to try to settle once and for all the problems endangering peace with Britain. The agent chosen for this well-nigh impossible task was John Jay, now recalled to his former practice of diplomacy just as he was becoming well-settled in the Chief Justiceship. His long career in the foreign service had developed experience and training in high-level negotiations; it had also contributed to an anti-French and pro-English bias which, together with certain personal traits, rendered

him somewhat vulnerable to a talented antagonist. He was described
by a contemporary as one who "argues closely, but is long-winded
and self-opinioned. He can bear opposition to what he advocates
provided regard is shown to his ability. He may be attached by good
treatment but will be unforgiving if he thinks himself neglected . . .
almost every man has a weak and assailable quarter, and Mr. Jay's
weak spot is *Mr. Jay*."[9] Much more damaging, however, was the
essential vulnerability of his position. Representing a nation virtually
without a navy, he was a petitioner charged with securing maritime
favors from the mistress of the seas; needing the utmost in the way of
unified support from the administration, he was subjected to simultaneous and often conflicting advice from Washington, Hamilton,
and Randolph, the last of whom did not enjoy the full confidence of
his superiors. His own biases reflected a sharp national division between the Republicans who were strongly pro-French and the Federalists who were as strongly pro-British and antiwar. Small wonder,
then, that his three months' negotiation failed to produce all the
desired results; that he secured any results at all should be remembered to his credit.

Jay's instructions gave him discretion except in two respects: He
was to sign nothing contrary to American engagements to France
and to make no commercial agreement which did not include access
to the British West Indies. Beyond this he was charged with recti-
fying the mistakes of the Revolutionary settlement and clarifying
his country's position as a neutral among warring nations. It may be
doubted whether he accomplished any of these objectives successfully or completely. This was due partly to his own susceptibilities
and maladroitness, partly to the iron necessity which drove the British to stick to their maritime policy, partly to cabinet squabbles at
home which left him prey to conflicting instructions, and partly to
the fact that Hamilton nullified what might have been a cogent
argument for concessions. Efforts, which proved abortive, were in
the making to launch an Armed Neutrality among European neutrals
to resist British exactions; had this materialized, and had the United
States joined it, Jay would have been in a much stronger position;

---

[9] Quoted in Bemis, *Jay's Treaty*, p. 205.

any trepidation which Britain might have felt was relieved in advance, however, by learning from Hamilton via George Hammond, the British Minister to the United States, of America's decision not to enter. Hamilton has indeed been depicted as a gambler's accomplice, holding a mirror in which Jay's cards could be read.[10]

The net result was a none too satisfactory treaty, signed November 14, 1794, after over three months of negotiation. The major success was the British promise to evacuate the western posts by June 1, 1796, a promise not actually implemented until several weeks after this date despite American impatience, because American troops were not ready to take the posts over. By Article 12 American ships of not over seventy tons' burden (too small to continue across the Atlantic) could enter the West Indian trade provided (1) that they carried goods only to the United States; and (2) that the United States would "prohibit and restrain the carrying any Melasses, Sugar, Coffee, Cocoa or Cotton in American vessels, either from His Majesty's Islands or from the United States, to any part of the World, except the United States. . . ." This provision, deleted in the first Senate reservation to a treaty, would have prevented the reëxport of goods from either the British or French West Indies, the latter recently recognized as legal by British courts under the "broken voyage" technique; it would also have prevented the export of the listed items, products of the American states themselves—only a year after Whitney's cotton gin had opened the door to a great growth of cotton production.

The treaty's provisions on the position of neutrals gave France ground for claiming violation of the treaties of 1778. Article 24 prohibited France from outfitting privateers or disposing of booty in American ports. Article 25 allowed the British to bring prizes into American ports and depart freely; this privilege was denied the French. A definition of contraband (Article 18) subjected naval stores to confiscation and permitted seizure of foodstuffs if compensation were made. Article 17 abandoned the principle of free ships,

---

[10] Frank Monaghan, *John Jay*, Bobbs-Merrill, 1935, p. 380. The position taken by Bemis, *Jay's Treaty*, pp. 246–268, that adherence to the Armed Neutrality might have influenced the British is countered by Burt, *op. cit.*, p. 155, n. 34.

free goods by allowing the British to take enemy goods from neutral ships. By omission, Jay consented to the Rule of 1756 and opened the way for continuance of the British device of the paper blockade. It would be difficult to justify these articles as keeping faith with the agreements of 1778 with the French.

Jay made no headway in the matter of impressments, despite frequent discussions with his opposite number, Foreign Secretary William W. Grenville. The best that he could elicit was a sarcastic note suggesting that the impressment of Americans was "contrary to the King's desire," but sometimes happened because "there so often exists an interest and intention to deceive" on the part of the Americans.

The score should not be added up, however, without noting one considerable accomplishment in providing for arbitration of a number of the long-standing points of friction. Four arbitration commissions resulted, and although only one succeeded without further negotiation, Jay's contribution to the use of arbitration as a technique of diplomacy was important. Two had to do with boundaries and two with fiscal matters. Article 4, stemming from the likelihood that the line of the Treaty of Paris, due west from the northwest corner of the Lake of the Woods to the Mississippi, could not be drawn because the river rose some distance to the south, called for a joint survey of the gap, to be followed, if the facts were as suspected, by negotiation of a line. The survey was never carried out.[11] Eleven years after peace, the identity of the St. Croix River, upon which the entire northeast boundary hinged, had not been established. Article 5 called for the only commission which recorded an initial success; this commission was charged with determining the mouth and source of this river. Working from 1796 to 1798 a three-man board picked a stream previously called the Schoodic, a blow to American contentions. Article 6 proposed the establishment of a board to determine the amount owed by Americans to British subjects at the end of the Revolution. It broke up in disagreement after sessions running from 1797 into 1799, and the question was finally

---

[11] S. F. Bemis, "Jay's Treaty and the Northwest Boundary Gap," *American Historical Review,* vol. 27 (1922), pp. 465–486.

settled by a treaty of 1802 which gave Britain £600,000. Under
Article 7 five men attempted to adjudicate the losses suffered by
Americans through British seizures under the Order in Council of
November 6, 1793, and by Englishmen through damages inflicted by
American-outfitted French privateers. It too broke up, but was re-
constituted under the treaty of 1802 and completed its work in 1804
by awarding the United States $10,345,200 and Great Britain
$143,428.

Although contemporary Republicans and many later scholars have
judged Jay's failures harshly, it should be remembered that war was
the probable alternative to his mission. His concessions to England
and his myopia toward the Treaties of 1778 undoubtedly purchased
his country a period of sorely needed peace which contributed to the
growth of nationality and of the prosperity provided by overseas
trade and Hamilton's financial measures. These long-run benefits
were not apparent to Jay's contemporaries, and the treaty (submitted to a special session of the Senate on June 8, 1795) ran a
gamut of partisan opposition which saw Hamilton stoned for trying
to support it in New York, and saw Jay burned in effigy throughout
the country before the Senate consented to ratification by a party
vote of 20 to 10. Neither did his treaty appeal to the critical eyes of
the French Republic, and publication of its terms pushed the pendulum into another swing which carried Franco-American relations to
the verge of war.

X Y Z and Naval War

This French crisis, culminating in the Naval War of 1798 and the
Convention of 1800, began coincidentally with the Jay Mission and
was part of Federalist efforts to keep the peace with Britain. As Jay
went to England the Republican and much less discreet James Monroe was sent to replace pro-Bourbon Gouverneur Morris in a deliberate attempt to keep France quiet while Jay was negotiating in
England.[12] Monroe's youthful enthusiasm was ill-suited to cope with
the French temper, disappointed in its hope of benevolent neutral-

---

[12] The standard account of Monroe's tribulations is Beverly W. Bond, Jr., *The Monroe Mission to France, 1794–1796*, Johns Hopkins Press, 1907.

ity, angry at Morris' intrigues with the monarchists, fearful of the possible effect of Jay's negotiations on Franco-American relations, and unsettled by the domestic confusion attendant upon the fall of Robespierre. Approaching his official duties after a heart-warming reception which led him to promise more than his principals would have approved (though what he said was justified by his instructions), Monroe found that the French were, somewhat less noisily, infringing on American rights under the Treaty of 1778 just as vigorously as the British had done. His first task, successfully achieved, was to persuade them to abandon their violations and return to strict recognition of American rights under the treaty; furthermore, they promised payment for damages incurred by their violations of it.

This honeymoon period lasted only until France learned (in January, 1795) the content of the Jay Treaty. It was then obvious that both Monroe and the French had been deceived; Monroe had slight stomach to argue that Jay's agreement was compatible with Franco-American obligations. The Directory, which presently assumed control of French affairs with the remarkable Charles Maurice de Talleyrand as its guiding genius, proclaimed (July 2, 1796) prospective resumption of depredations on American commerce, and attempted to dragoon the United States back into line by recalling its Minister to that country. A growing lack of sympathy between Monroe and his superiors at home, combined with his lack of success abroad, led to his recall in November, 1796, and to the appointment of Charles C. Pinckney as his successor. A parting ceremony almost as touching as his original reception emphasized his personal popularity nearly as much as his country's shortcomings. His mission, although an ultimate failure, accomplished the administration's objective of keeping France quiet until the English problem could be settled.

With Monroe's departure the clouds thickened rapidly. After lingering in Paris for some weeks Pinckney was informed that he was a stranger, present without permission; taking this hint, he secured a passport to Holland. In dismissing Pinckney the Directory underlined the breach by stating that it would "no longer recognize nor receive a minister plenipotentiary from the United States, until after a reparation of the grievances demanded of the American government, and which the French republic has a right to expect." The breach became a gulf with the promised renewal of depredations on American commerce through a series of Decrees (1797–1798) which far outpaced earlier British exactions on American shipping in grounds of seizure and approached the British total in extent of authenticated claims.[13] Against this background of worsening relations the campaign of 1796 had witnessed an unsuccessful French attempt to defeat the Federalist John Adams—an interference with domestic affairs which called forth Washington's Farewell Address.[14] Spoliations and interference bred a war spirit which Adams suppressed for the moment in favor of another diplomatic sally. Attempting to make Pinckney more palatable to the French, he added a Republican (Elbridge Gerry) and another Federalist (John Marshall) to the mission. Marshall probably drafted his own instructions for this, his only essay into diplomacy, and they reflected Adams' desire to avoid war. The three foregathered in Paris in October, 1797, a moment almost as inauspicious as that of Monroe's début some months earlier. Napoleon Bonaparte had just defeated the First Coalition and France was surrounding herself with dependent republics. Talleyrand, still at the helm of the Directory, found this situation made to order for one of his peculiarly acquisitive talents for negotiation—talents which he presently directed optimistically but vainly at the American delegation.

Early American efforts to see Talleyrand were effectively parried but on October 18 Pinckney received a gentleman mysteriously calling himself Monsieur "X." This worthy announced that he brought three demands from Talleyrand, as follows: Certain passages in a message of President Adams to Congress, offensive to members of the Directory must be softened before the delegates could be re-

---

[13] In 1915 the United States Court of Claims awarded $7,149,306.10 compensation for the so-called spoliation claims. Actual payments could be made only after congressional appropriations, which have amounted to only $3,910,860.61. G. A. King, *The French Spoliation Claims, Senate Document 451,* 64th Congress, 1st Session, tells the story of these claims before Congress and Court through 1915. Other types of claims arising between 1793 and 1800 increased the total by $5,000,000.

[14] See below, p. 131.

ceived; a "douceur" of $250,000 must be placed at Talleyrand's disposal; finally, France needed a loan. Monsieur X did not know which passages were offensive, nor how large the loan, but the pocket-money was definite. Messieurs "Y" and "Z" presently joined this eighteenth-century alphabetical agency, and gradually the demands were specified. The American government was to handle the loan by furnishing the Directory with the par value of a 32,000,000-florin issue of Dutch bonds, then worth about fifty cents on the dollar—with "Y's" bland assurance that the Dutch would be able to pay out after the war was over. American reluctance was followed by French bullying and further blunt refusal, culminating in Pinckney's famous "no; no; not a sixpence" rejoinder to a demand of "X," later exaggerated into the more magniloquent "Millions for defense but not one cent for tribute."[15]

Numerous conferences and much writing of notes running well into the spring of 1798 produced no concrete results. Talleyrand, indeed, felt himself in such a good position that argument and discussion were superfluous; he was confident that if the American delegation returned without an agreement John Adams would be forced from office. He finally wrote a haughty note on March 18 in which he announced that in view of the uncoöperative spirit of Marshall and Pinckney "the Executive Directory is disposed to treat with that one of the three, whose opinions, presumed to be more impartial, promise in the course of the explanations, more of that reciprocal confidence which is indispensable." Another note of April 3 hinted pointedly that the Federalist members should leave Paris, which they proceeded to do, leaving Gerry to continue equally fruitless negotiations until he received a peremptory recall issued under date of June 25.

President Adams submitted the correspondence retailing the above narrative to Congress in seven instalments published at intervals between May, 1798, and January, 1799. War spirit developed

---

[15] Herman V. Ames (ed.), *The X. Y. Z. Letters; University of Pennsylvania Translations and Reprints* . . . , The University of Pennsylvania, 1899, vol. 6, No. 2, contains the documentary story of the X Y Z Affair in the official reports of the delegates. Albert J. Beveridge, *The Life of John Marshall*, Houghton Mifflin, 1916–1919, vol. 2, pp. 214–334, is the most extended account.

rapidly. Congress created the Navy Department as a separate branch
of the Executive, expanded naval construction considerably, took
steps to raise the army to a strength of ten thousand men, and abrogated the French treaties of 1778. While Adams did not share the
enthusiasm for war he was properly indignant at French tactics and
declared in a ringing statement: "I will never send another minister
to France, without assurances that he will be received, respected,
and honored as the representative of a great, free, powerful, and
independent nation." Actual hostilities reached a scale sufficient to
warrant use of the term "The Naval War with France" for the developments between 1798 and 1801. Nearly 50 warships and over
350 privateers pursued and captured over 100 armed French ships,
including 2 warships, avoiding the attacks on unarmed vessels which
would have characterized an all-out war.[16]

A number of factors prevented the pseudo-war from reaching its
logical conclusion in full-dress hostilities. Adams, who had ill-ad-
visedly retained most of Washington's Cabinet upon entering his
term, had watched the group steadily act under the domination of
Hamilton, who disputed with him the leadership of the party. Hamilton was now happy at the prospect of adding military glory to his
civilian honors; he had been placed second to Washington in command of the expanded army, doubtless to Adams' chagrin. A war
would render Hamilton not only insufferable but even more powerful. A war with France would thus have gratified Adams' enemies in
his own party; by the same token any steps to soft-pedal hostilities
would encounter Federalist wrath. Events across the water made
Talleyrand think twice before precipitating war. British sea power
effectively bottled up the main French fleet; the American navy
had developed a sting out of proportion to its size; Franco-American
war would produce Anglo-American *rapprochement*. Finally, Talleyrand's dream of regaining Louisiana was approaching fruition; it
would never materialize if war intervened. Under all these circumstances he reversed his recalcitrant attitude and told William Vans
Murray, American agent at the Hague, that an American diplomat
appearing in France would "undoubtedly be received with the re-

---

[16] Gardner W. Allen, *Our Naval War with France*, Houghton Mifflin, 1909.

spect due to the representative of a free, independent and powerful nation"—a reiteration of Adams' own stout statement.

This offer presented Adams with an opportunity and a dilemma. The opportunity lay in preserving the nation from the danger of war with France; his dilemma was that any move to ameliorate the French problem would create political disturbances at home, at a time when the breezes were already freshening for the election of 1800. The Hamiltonian branch of the Federalists, still dominant in the Cabinet, would hardly countenance a peaceful gesture toward France. Mindful of the dilemma, Adams seized the opportunity; disregarding the Cabinet, which would have overruled him, he accepted Talleyrand's gesture by nominating Murray as Minister to France. Public opinion forced acceptance of the French proposal to negotiate; factional suspicion forced Adams to accept a mission (Chief Justice Oliver Ellsworth, W. R. Davie, formerly Governor of North Carolina, and Murray) instead of an individual agent. The consequences of this personal choice were momentous: By it Adams completed the intraparty breach which resulted in Republican victory in 1800, thus assisting effectively in digging his own political grave. That he considered this sacrifice of person and party worthwhile is indicated by his later statement that a sufficient epitaph would be "Here lies John Adams, who took upon himself the responsibility for peace with France in the year 1800."

Bonaparte had assumed control of French affairs by the time the American mission assembled in Paris, but Talleyrand, whose talent for survival was well-nigh unique in the shifting tides of French politics between 1789 and 1815, was retained as foreign minister. Napoleon curbed Talleyrand's acquisitive tendencies while making full use of his talents as a negotiator. The result was that the discussions eventuating in the Convention of 1800 were geared to Talleyrand's plans for regaining possession of Louisiana from Spain (a scheme which fitted nicely with Napoleon's dream of a revived western empire). Since the Spanish plan materialized slowly, it became Talleyrand's task to avoid closing the American deal while preventing a further Anglo-American *rapprochement*. This delayed signature of the Franco-American agreement until September 30, 1800.

The discussions reflected the shrewdness of Talleyrand and an essential weakness in the American position. The Americans had been instructed to demand nearly $20,000,000 in damages for spoliations going back to 1793, plus French acceptance of Congressional action in abrogating the treaties of 1778. The French argument, extremely difficult to combat, was to the effect that the treaties were operative, or they were not. If, thanks to the Congressional repeal of 1798, they were not operative, their termination was an act of war; hence the spoliations were acts of war and certainly no grounds for claims upon France. If on the other hand they were still operative, the two countries were still allies and under them France could claim American support against her enemies. Talleyrand magnanimously offered a compromise which recognized suspension of the treaties and left all claims pending under them to subsequent negotiations, which never materialized. Thus France traded American spoliation claims for suspension of the treaties of 1778, leaving to the United States the problem of quieting the complaints of her citizens.

This was probably a good bargain, except for those whose descendants had to wait over a century for the satisfaction of their claims at the hands of their own government. The acceptance of the French proposals of 1800 was in considerable measure a recognition that the Jay Treaty was out of harmony with the spirit, if not the letter, of the 1778 agreements. This concession was made (as indeed had been Jay's concessions of 1794) in the interest of keeping the peace. It would seem that this prevention of hostilities was the most important accomplishment of Federalist diplomacy, and in the light of history Federalist leaders should not be condemned too severely for resorting to some rather adroit diplomatic moves in achieving this vastly important goal. Peace, indeed, was highly important in affording time for the consolidation of national resources and the development of that national unity without which the stresses of the succeeding years could not have been weathered. In passing the torch to the Republicans the Federalists had charted a course and followed it successfully—more successfully in fact than the Republicans in 1801–1812, or Woodrow Wilson in 1914–1917, were able to do. So far, however, neutrality had stood the test.

6 Neutrality Loses

THE TURN OF THE CENTURY FURNISHED BOTH NEUTRAL AND belligerent with a breathing space. At Lunéville (1801) and Amiens (1802) Napoleon made peace with Continental and British enemies, which gave him time to consolidate gains, carry out domestic reforms, crown himself Emperor (1804), and prepare for further hostilities. These were precipitated in May, 1803, when fear of Napoleonic designs caused Britain to break the truce of Amiens and declare war. Europe remained in turmoil until the liquidation of the French hegemony at Vienna (1815). The principal protagonists, fighting each other to a recognized death struggle, scrupled little about neutral rights or welfare; moreover, both belligerents were beginning to recognize in the United States a potentially dangerous commercial rival. The policy of each was therefore compounded of desire to hurt the other and crush the upstart. Under these circumstances it is not strange that Jefferson and Madison after him faced a succession of crises which kept them walking a diplomatic tightrope from which Madison finally slipped or was pushed into war in 1812. The events leading up to this climax bring to culmination the first great trial, and the first failure, of the neutrality policy born of expediency and necessity in 1793.

The historiography of the causes of the War of 1812 reflects interpretations which have changed with the years and are still in process of clarification.[1] Through the nineteenth century the vindication of

---

[1] W. H. Goodman, "The Origins of the War of 1812: A Survey of Changing Interpretations," *Mississippi Valley Historical Review*, vol. 28 (1941), pp. 171–186, ably surveys these changes. Julius W. Pratt's *Expansionists of 1812*, Macmillan, 1925, is a major study which, while according due prominence to maritime grievances,

national honor against attacks on neutral shipping furnished writers with their principal approach. When it presently became apparent that New England, hurt most by strictures on neutral rights, was but lukewarm toward the war, a school of thought developed which sought causes on the American continent. These were found in western suspicions that the English were conniving at Indian efforts to block settlements in the Indiana country, and in expansionist urges to acquire the Canadian and Florida borderlands which could only be satisfied in a war of conquest. Still later attempts were made to rehabilitate maritime grievances as the prime cause. Tracing the narrative of events will perhaps suggest that there is truth in all these approaches and that no one of them is all-sufficient.

Europe's War Troubles Yankee Trade

Renewed hostilities posed for President Jefferson problems similar to those which he had faced earlier as Secretary of State. As Napoleon's grip tightened on Europe's mainland and as the Battle of Trafalgar Bay (October 21, 1805) confirmed Britain's maritime supremacy, the necessities of war multiplied neutral commercial opportunities; multiplied also were the dangers to which neutral trade was exposed and the difficulties of avoiding involvement. The problems of the 1790's reappeared, sometimes modified or aggravated, and to them were added others which inhibited the urge to profit which has always characterized the American makeup. Renewed hostilities found American commerce in a relatively favorable position. Lenient British interpretation of the broken voyage trade had permitted American ships to carry goods to both belligerents and the new ships of the merchant marine had found profitable cargoes during the 1790's, a situation which the new war renewed briefly. For example, combined American imports and exports amounted to $52,000,000 in 1792; this figure was up to $205,000,000 in 1801, but slumped to $110,000,000 with peace in 1803. Anglo-French hostilities

---

stresses frontier and expansionist factors as causes. A. L. Burt, *op. cit.*, reëmphasizes, and according to most students somewhat overemphasizes, the traditional maritime approach.

provided a stimulant which raised the total to \$162,000,000 in 1804, to \$215,000,000 in 1805, to \$221,000,000 in 1806 (despite restrictions to be mentioned shortly), and to \$246,000,000 in 1807.[2] This expansion, most of which was in the carrying trade, was so profitable as to encourage attempted evasions of whatever restrictions the belligerents might apply. No volume of profit, however, could still the howls of anguish which went up at the capture of an ill-fated cargo. The new shipping also called for between four and five thousand new sailors each year, at wages triple the normal figure. The combination of new ships, high wages, and the fact that under the American flag one was not so likely to be shot at, induced many British tars to desert merchantmen and the Royal Navy for the American merchant marine. They often added American citizenship to their escapades through the easy naturalization law and still easier practice of the day. Thus when the exigencies of the war forced the British to resort once more to visit and search and impressment, the stage was well set for complications reminiscent of the 1790's, with variations.

British assertion of the right to visit and search American merchantmen on the high seas, accompanied by the practice of impressment, opened and gouged deeper an old sore which Jay's Treaty had failed to heal.[3] The British claimed the right to visit and search for deserters on the high seas; the United States advanced the then novel doctrine that a ship was a "detached portion" of American soil and so immune from search. British concern may be appreciated from the estimate that 2500 desertions occurred each year. Immediate difficulties ensued. Search parties did not always draw a sharp line between British deserters and bona fide Americans; the latter often found themselves shanghaied aboard British men-o'-war. Moreover, the British balked at the other novel American doctrine of expatriation, which would have protected naturalized citizens from impressment. The result was a mounting tension not measurable in

---

[2] Albion and Pope, *op. cit.*, pp. 93–96.

[3] Burt, *op. cit.*, pp. 212–214; J. F. Zimmerman, *Impressment of American Seamen*, Columbia University Press, 1925, is the standard treatise on this subject.

statistics, which at best are uncertain. The usual estimate is that at least 10,000 Americans were impressed; on the other hand the British Admiralty guessed that 20,000 Englishmen had deserted to the Americans. Furthermore, probably only one in ten of those impressed (i.e., 1000) turned out to be British subjects, so that it is likely that British tactics regained only one deserter out of twenty. Setting this ratio of success over against the aggravation of Anglo-American relations caused by this interference with American life and liberty raises doubts as to the usefulness of impressment as a device. These considerations, of course, did not enter British calculations at the moment.

Impressment was not the only limitation on American trade. Mention has already been made of American ingenuity in evading the British Rule of 1756 by the device of the broken voyage. This evasion had made possible the continuance of lucrative trade during the 1790's; a British admiralty court had sanctioned it in the case of the *Polly* (1802). This involved a cargo of sugar and cocoa, laden at Havana and brought to Marblehead, Massachusetts. Duty was paid and the cargo discharged while the ship was under repair. Repairs completed, the cargo was reloaded, along with some New England fish, the duty for the most part refunded, and the *Polly* proceeded to Bilbao, a belligerent Spanish port. The presiding judge did not consider the matter of the tariff refund. The British acquiesced, with minor modifications, when this trade was resumed in 1803. Under pressure of domestic economic interests, injured by American competition, the British courts reversed themselves in the case of the *Essex* (1805). The facts resembled the earlier decision but the court this time held that the tariff rebate destroyed the neutrality conferred on the goods by importation and payment of duties. Thus the cargo was really on a *continuous voyage* between belligerent country and colony; the device of entry at a neutral port did not alter its character. Since such trade was closed in time of peace, under the Rule of 1756 it could not be opened in time of war. By thus extending the Rule of 1756 through the doctrine of continuous voyage the British exerted an adverse effect on much lucrative trade, undertaken in good faith and sanctioned by the *Polly* decision. A further

British restriction denied neutrals access to the coasting trade of France or her allies.[4]

The *Essex* decision prompted legislative retaliation in the non-importation act of April 18, 1806, which set November 1 of that year as a deadline after which, unless other issues had been previously compromised, a list of British manufactures would be excluded from the States. During the interval Jefferson launched what was to prove a fruitless negotiation through the agency of an older and more experienced James Monroe and William Pinkney. Among the important issues at stake were trade questions raised by the *Essex* case, British blockade practices, and impressments, which last was in such an aggravating state that the envoys were told to sign no treaty which did not improve British practice. The British were adamant as to the right of impressment, though seemingly willing to modify their *practice* by undertaking to see to it, according to a note of November 9, 1806, collateral to the treaty, "that the strictest care shall be taken to preserve the citizens of the United States from any molestation or injury; and that immediate and prompt redress shall be afforded upon any representation of injury sustained by them." Deeming this better than nothing, the Americans went on to further negotiations resulting in a treaty (signed December 31, 1806) in which they gave up the principle of free ships, free goods and the British almost (but not quite) gave up the Rule of 1756. This provision allowed neutrals to carry the produce of foreign colonies to unblockaded European ports on payment of a 1 percent ad valorem duty, which was not to be refunded. The word "blockaded" was the joker, since under British practice a stroke of the pen accomplished a blockade. Failure on impressments and equivocal success on trade questions was capped by inability to secure any promise relative to the extensive British spoliations, and when the treaty arrived Jefferson felt constrained not to submit it to the Senate, a decision for which commentators have generally criticized him.[5]

---

[4] C. B. Elliott, "The Doctrine of Continuous Voyages," *American Journal of International Law*, vol. 1 (1907), pp. 65–95.

[5] For a good discussion of this episode, more than usually favorable to Monroe and Pinkney, see Burt, *op. cit.*, pp. 235–239.

Soon after the Monroe-Pinkney fiasco the *Leopard-Chesapeake* incident (June 22, 1807) capped the climax of the impressment issue. The *Chesapeake,* a United States warship (it should be noted that the British had not previously extended their impressment pretensions to naval units), had left Hampton Roads bound for the Mediterranean. Her decks were so cumbered with gear that normal naval maneuvers were impracticable. She was presently overhauled by the British frigate *Leopard,* under orders from Vice-Admiral G. C. Berkeley, commandant at Halifax, and ordered to surrender four alleged deserters. Commodore James Barron refused a request for permission to search his ship and was answered by an attack which resulted in three killed and eighteen wounded among his crew. The ship's honor, if not her safety, was vindicated by firing one gun touched off by a live coal carried from the galley in the fingers of an officer, after which the colors were struck and four men taken off. One turned out to be a British deserter, who was shortly hanged. The others were American citizens whose previous records had been somewhat confused. Not until 1812 did Britain surrender the two survivors and make amends for the *Chesapeake's* casualties.

According to Henry Adams this startling episode produced for the first time a "feeling of true national emotion." Jefferson closed American territorial waters to the British fleet, which had been using them under a provision of the Jay Treaty (it might be noted in passing that the *Leopard* sallied from an American port to launch her attack). He called a special session of Congress and ordered militia quotas held in readiness, but made no further warlike moves. Indeed, he attempted to use this warlike episode to promote peace; having the British on the run (for the boarding of a warship was unprecedented), he tried to force them to abandon impressment as a recompense for their error. This they could not do, of course, and the martial ardor of 1807 was dissipated in extended negotiation.

Elephant Fights Whale

These Anglo-American frictions developed against a background of European events. Anglo-French hostilities reached a point of threatened stalemate which caused the protagonists to adopt measures seriously affecting the neutral. Trafalgar established British naval dominance. To offset this Napoleon fashioned a remarkable series of land victories over his continental enemies—Prussia, Austria, and Russia—at Jena, Ulm, Austerlitz, and Friedland, which by July, 1807, had inflicted the ultimate humiliation of Tilsit upon the Third Coalition. Napoleonic supremacy on land and British impregnability afloat suggest the analogy of the elephant and the whale, each relatively invulnerable in its own element, but under severe handicaps when adventuring into the other's realm. Under these circumstances both adopted economic devices intended to exact from the enemy a maximum economic toll, in the hope that economic weakness might bring military and political defeat. The British desired also to curb rising American competition and to channel neutral trade with the continent through British ports, with consequent profits to the royal exchequer.[6] Such a rivalry brought obvious dangers to neutral shipping.

The Berlin Decree (November 21, 1806) inaugurated Napoleon's Continental System. This was in effect a closure of the ports under Napoleon's control whereby, ostensibly under the guise of retaliation for British strictures on neutral trade with France, Napoleon declared a blockade of the British Isles. This was obviously a mere gesture, since Napoleon had no effective means of enforcement. More threatening were provisions interdicting trade in goods produced by Britain and her colonies, and denying access to French-controlled ports to ships coming from or calling at British or British colonial ports. Had Napoleon had a fleet on the high seas this would have placed him on a par with Britain as a violator of neutral rights. Since he did not, the Berlin Decree was preëminently an attempt to close Continental ports to neutral bottoms carrying English goods.

---

[6] British policy was to a considerable extent implemented by theories put forward by James Stephen in 1805 in *War in Disguise, or the Frauds of the Neutral Flags,* a very influential philippic against neutral rights. Pertinent at this point is the following statement: "neither the Continental system nor the Orders in Council were aimed at actually cutting off supplies from the foe. They were instead primarily financial measures. Napoleon sold Continental produce to England in order to drain away its gold more rapidly. England, in its turn, supplied the Continent with sugar, coffee, and tobacco, for its policy of 'no trade except through England' was not to deprive the Continent of such articles, but to see that Britain alone reaped the entrepôt profits." Albion and Pope, *op. cit.,* p. 97.

He hoped thus to bring the British to their knees through inroads on their commerce and industry. British counterobjectives were equally clear. Far from wishing to destroy trade with France (except in contraband), Britain wished to encourage neutral bottoms to carry both British and colonial goods through the French self-blockade to continental ports, but only after the goods had passed through British hands and contributed various fees and taxes. Britain hoped thereby to defeat Napoleon's self-blockade and at the same time make money to support military action against him.[7]

Lord Howick's Order (January 7, 1807) inaugurated a series ostensibly retaliatory to the Berlin Decree but actually designed to strengthen British trade against neutral competition.[8] It extended the Rule of 1756 by forbidding neutrals to engage in port-to-port coastal trade of countries dominated by Napoleon. This was followed by a cluster of three Orders (November 11, 1807) which registered the heart of British policy. These applied a strict blockade to all enemy territory and made confiscable any property, ships, or cargo, wherever found, destined to such territory. A saving clause permitted neutral ships to travel to enemy ports by first entering a British port, paying fees, and securing a license. This made it possible to compel all trade with Napoleonic areas to pass through Britain, who could supervise its character and at the same time derive considerable income. For example, 1600 such licenses were issued in 1807, 15,000 in 1809, and 18,000 in 1810. Napoleon's reply was not long delayed; the Milan Decree (December 17, 1807) declared that any ship which permitted search by British naval units, which altered its course to

---

[7] E. F. Heckscher, *The Continental System: An Economic Interpretation*, Clarendon, 1922; A. C. Clauder, *American Commerce as Affected by the Wars of the French Revolution and Napoleon, 1793–1812*, University of Pennsylvania Press, 1932; and W. Alison Phillips and Arthur H. Reede, *Neutrality: Its History, Economics and Law, Volume II, the Napoleonic Period*, Columbia University Press, 1936, are standard treatises on maritime restrictions.

[8] Fox's Order (May 16, 1806) was an ineffective effort to forestall passage of an American nonimportation act. It proposed to ease the burden of the *Essex* decision by blockading the continental coast from Brest to the Elbe River, making the blockade effective, however, only between Ostend and the Seine. At the extremities of the zone British naval officers were instructed to pass inbound neutrals not laden at an enemy port and outbound neutrals not destined for such port. This tacitly reopened the broken-voyage trade with such ports as Rotterdam, Bremen, and Bordeaux, but subsequent frictions rendered the device ineffective.

enter a British port, or paid tribute to the British tax-collectors became legally British and as such was fair prize at sea or in port.

The Neutral is Caught

With later embroidery in detail, these constituted the opposing policies. Strictly enforced, they left the neutral in a hopeless position. If he tried to trade with Napoleon without obeying British regulations the latter could seize him; if he subjected himself to British rules Napoleon was waiting to pounce. His only salvation lay in the exigencies which moderated the letter of the law. On the British side the profit motive inspired the system of licenses; Napoleon was unable to enforce his system completely and presently took to granting exceptions. Furthermore, the defection of Spain, Russia, and the Scandinavian lands from his orbit opened these areas to trade via Britain. These mitigations did not eliminate severe burdens on neutral trade; although losses probably never caught up with profits, principles were violated right and left. Devotion to principle led Thomas Jefferson and his successor to a series of expedients which grew more desperate as they became less successful and which played no small role in the outbreak of hostilities in 1812. These expedients, three in number, were resorted to in the hope of achieving an accommodation with one or both belligerents which would make it possible to continue trade and avoid war. As each move failed to secure the desired accommodation, the next became more liberal and hence, in the temper of the times, less likely to succeed.

The first and most vigorous move was the Embargo, the embodiment of Jefferson's matured philosophy that peace was the best state for a nation to be in, as well as his practical realization that his country was ill-prepared for war.[9] It was launched by news of Napoleon's Berlin Decree, which preceded reports of the British Orders of November 11. First, however, came the enforcement of the Non-Importation Act of 1806, keeping out a considerable list of British manufactures, effective December 14, 1807, under pressure resulting from the *Chesapeake* affair. The law was enacted quickly, modeled on a Federalist policy of 1793–1794, and went into opera-

---

[9] Louis M. Sears, *Jefferson and the Embargo*, Duke University Press, 1927.

tion December 22. Like the Continental System, it was a self-blockade, forbidding departure to "all ships and vessels in the ports and
places within the limits or jurisdiction of the United States, cleared
or not cleared, bound to any foreign port or place." It came as an
unannounced and unwelcome Christmas present to the port of New
York, where it caused a wild flurry of unscheduled departures. It
met with complete hostility and wholesale evasion from the mercantile interests; legitimate shipping remained paralyzed for its duration and the government revenues suffered accordingly. The planter
South was hurt badly but remained loyal to Jefferson on ideological
grounds; restricted areas along the border profited greatly by smuggling; New Englanders could engage in profitable violation or begin
to move their capital into manufacturing, meanwhile cursing Jefferson, the architect of Federalist defeat in 1800. Various semirespect-
able loopholes were presently discovered. Coasting vessels gave bond
for delivery of their cargoes in the United States, "dangers of the sea
Excepted." A remarkable number of leaking hulls and broken spars
developed in proximity to Canadian and Caribbean ports; the cargoes, of course, had to be sold to pay for the repairs. Whalers were
permitted to carry on as usual; one varied from the norm by bringing one cask of whaleoil from Halifax along with hundreds of bales
of British woolens. Nearly six hundred clearances in ballast were
granted for the purpose of fetching home property "stranded
abroad." John Jacob Astor was allowed to send a ship to China to
return a Chinese Mandarin, "stranded by the embargo." His $200,-
000 profit from the voyage doubtless assuaged the injury inflicted on
his feelings by invidious contemporary comment that high-ranking
Chinese never left home.[10]

Despite evasions the embargo affected British economy adversely.
Food prices went up, cotton manufacturing was seriously incon-
venienced, and the Caribbean colonies went on short rations. Discomfort, however, was insufficient to induce concessions, particularly
since Britain considered American action a bid to France. So did
Napoleon. The embargo concerned him but slightly anyway since
he had trouble getting goods through the British blockade; on the

---

[10] Illustrations of evasive tactics from Albion and Pope, *op. cit.*, pp. 99–102.

assumption that the United States was adopting his own policy of boycotting Great Britain, he told his American agent to propose an alliance. Moreover, many American ships, abroad when the embargo was adopted, were still at large. Napoleon shrewdly declared that since no American ships could legally leave port, these were English ships and so subject to seizure under his Bayonne Decree (April 17, 1808). By this adroit strategem he enriched his coffers by $10,000,000 within a few months. Thus the embargo failed alike as an instrument of foreign policy and as an experiment in domestic politics; it brought neither belligerent to time, and Jefferson lost the support of the middle states which was necessary to its continuance; he was unable to muster strength to prevent its repeal, except as to England and France, to take effect on March 15, 1809. The embargo's merits as a substitute for war should be remembered, however, to Jefferson's credit; by postponing hostilities it contributed much-needed time to apply to the consolidation of national wealth and feeling.

Nonintercourse, the second American strategem, succeeded the embargo and remained in effect until May, 1810. This variation on the theme of economic coercion forbade American ships to enter the ports of either belligerent, closed American ports to both after May 20, 1809, and permitted the President, should either relax its restrictions, to reopen trade with that one, while continuing adamant against the other.[11] While continuing pressure against the belligerents, this law invited concessions and permitted trade with the few neutrals, thus affording American ingenuity a back-door access to belligerent markets. Though like the embargo ostensibly impartial, nonintercourse favored the British, who would gain more by concessions than would the well-blockaded French. George Canning, British Foreign Secretary, commissioned David M. Erskine to try to take advantage of this opportunity. Erskine was pro-American, due perhaps to predisposition or to an American wife. His efforts were more earnest than effective. Specifically instructed to offer re-

---

[11] The nonintercourse with France gave Napoleon another excuse to seize American ships appearing in his ports. Vienna Decree, August 4, 1809; Rambouillet Decree, March 23, 1810.

peal of the 1807 Orders upon acceptance of three conditions, he soft-pedaled their less favorable aspects in his conferences with Secretary of State Robert Smith. The United States was to repeal nonintercourse, accept the Rule of 1756, and permit the British navy to enforce the continued nonintercourse with France. Smith suggested that a specific statement on the Rule of 1756 was unnecessary; the Erskine Agreement (April, 1809) did not mention the explosive question of British enforcement of American law.[12] Madison naïvely accepted Erskine's signature as equivalent to Canning's approval and his announcement that intercourse with Britain would reopen on June 10, 1809, launched domestic shipowners on feverish preparations. The stated day saw six hundred cargoes on their way. Rejoicing was short-lived, however, for Canning promptly repudiated Erskine's arrangement, cannily accepting the cargoes as they arrived. This brief spurt of trade complemented British profits from recently acquired access to the ports of Spain and Portugal and their colonies, now in revolt against Napoleon's power, and vitiated any further coercive efforts which Madison might adopt. This episode vastly increased the strains on Anglo-American relations and did much to render the administration attentive to the possibilities of *rapprochement* with Napoleon.[13]

Canning's next appointment of Francis James Jackson seemed deliberately calculated to irritate. Jackson's instructions charged that the "American government cannot have believed that such an arrangement as Mr. Erskine consented to accept was conformable to his instructions." This approach hardly made Jackson popular; his own attitude worsened matters and after some oral discussion Smith insisted that all communications be written. Shortly even this medium became too explosive and Jackson was told that "no further communications will be received from you." Neither he nor his successor, Augustus J. Foster, made any headway in easing Anglo-American relations.

The last maneuver, Macon's Bill No. 2, reflected American despera-

---

[12] Professor Burt supports Erskine's disregard of the letter of his instructions in favor of their spirit, and suggests that if Canning had adopted a like conciliatory attitude the War of 1812 might have been averted: *op. cit.*, pp. 270–275.

[13] Smith's somewhat bumbling conduct of the Department of State is described by C. C. Tansill in vol. 3 of Bemis' *American Secretaries of State*, pp. 149–197.

tion. In effect May 1, 1810, a few days before nonintercourse was due to expire with the adjournment of Congress, it opened commerce to all the world; should either belligerent agree to respect American rights before March 3, 1811, the President should, after a three-month interval to allow the other belligerent to follow suit, reinstitute nonintercourse against the recusant nation. This made Napoleon uneasy, as it permitted revival of American trade with Britain; Macon's Bill signified little to him since the rush was to Britain. He promptly countered with an adroit half-promise contained in a letter addressed by his Foreign Minister, J. B. N. Champagny, the Duc de Cadore (August 5, 1810), to the American minister in Paris. The Emperor seems to have been willing to let Madison *think* (incorrectly) that he was planning to revoke his Decrees; it was hoped that on the strength of this misapprehension Madison would restore nonintercourse with Britain, thus provoking an Anglo-American war. This masterpiece of circumlocution can be appreciated only in quotation: "I am authorized to declare to you, sir, that the decrees of Berlin and Milan are revoked, and that after the 1st of November they will cease to have effect; it being understood that, in consequence of his declaration, the English shall revoke their orders in council, and renounce the new principles of blockade, which they have wished to establish; or that the United States, conformably to the act you have just communicated, shall cause their rights to be respected by the English." Madison cooperated with Napoleon by accepting this conditional repeal as an actual one (as of November 2, 1810). Under the Macon Bill this would apply nonintercourse to Great Britain as of February 2, 1811, unless the Orders in Council were repealed. The British, who read documents more carefully than the harried Madison, informed him quite properly that they failed to find repeal in the Cadore Letter. Congress implemented renewal of nonintercourse by an Act of March 2, 1811, which caused considerable hardship in the cotton mill towns and precipitated a flood of petitions for repeal of the Orders. Pressure of public opinion over a number of months induced the government to take advantage of a technicality to repeal the Orders, June 18, 1812 (published in the Gazette of June 23), the very day that Madison signed the declaration of war. Unfortunately,

America was inadequately represented in Britain after February, 1811, and Foster, who arrived in Washington late in June, 1811, was unaware of the changing situation at home. Minus the services of an Atlantic cable and lacking adequate diplomatic representation which might have alerted both governments to changing sentiments, the long-festering sore of bad commercial relations thus affected Anglo-American affairs adversely to the very end of the chapter.[14]

The West Wants War—and Gets It

Meantime events on the far frontier increased the chance of friction —events which for a time received such attention from historians as to overshadow the maritime factors just described. These may be considered under the not unrelated topics of British relations with the frontier Indians and the rise of the War Hawk expansionists. Land-hungry Americans had long been whittling away at Indian holdings in the interior basin; successful military operations compelled successive treaties surrendering rights of settlement. The Treaty of Fort Wayne (1809) pushed the frontier westward by about three million acres to the Wabash River. This surrender, to which not all of the interested chieftains had acceded, stimulated a move already underway to unite the tribes against the whites. A one-eyed Shawnee fanatic appropriately named The Prophet stirred his people to hate the white man and all his works; his half-brother Tecumseh channeled this hatred into a growing political confederacy. Their headquarters since 1808 had been a village at Tippecanoe Creek on the banks of the Wabash. After repeated threats to the western settlements Tecumseh left toward the end of 1811 to visit the southern tribes. Western fears during the summer and autumn of this year stemmed in part from Indian activities and still more from the alleged fact that the braves were being backed by British supplies furnished from settlements near Detroit.

Governor William Henry Harrison caught the fever in September and wrote the War Department:

A trader of this country was lately in the King's store at Malden, and was told that the quantity of goods for the Indian department, which had

---

[14] Phillips, *op. cit.*, pp. 189–205.

been sent out this year, exceeded that of common years by £20,000 sterling. It is impossible to ascribe this profusion to any other motive than that of instigating the Indians to take up the tomahawk; it cannot be to secure their trade, for all the peltries collected on the waters of the Wabash, in one year, if sold in the London market, would not pay the freight of the goods which have been given to the Indians.

Thus land-hunger linked with fears of British-supported Indian depredations led the westerners to demand at once the destruction of the Tippecanoe settlement and the expulsion of the British from Canada. British officials were actually not eager for Indian hostilities at the moment, preferring to maintain friendly relations until a more auspicious occasion presented itself—such, for example, as an Anglo-American war.[15] Harrison, acting on what the westerners thought rather than on what the British wanted, mounted an expedition and approached Tippecanoe, probably with the idea of bluffing rather than fighting. Lacking Tecumseh's restraining influence, the Indians attacked on November 7, 1811, and considerable blood was shed. The issue was not decisive; it has indeed been suggested that Harrison's conviction of victory was in direct ratio to his distance from the scene of the battle. However, the episode stirred the west to fever heat and contributed to the events about to take place in Washington.

The new Congress meeting in special session but three days before Tippecanoe provided the arena where the final decision for war was taken. The driving force in this direction was furnished by a group of young (most of the leaders were under thirty-five) frontiersmen who, while not unaware of maritime factors, were mainly interested in driving the British from Canada and the Spanish from Florida, thus adding territory, ridding the borders of dangerous neighbors, and at the same time preserving the balance between slavery and freedom which was even then an important consideration.[16] These

---

[15] C. B. Coleman, "The Ohio Valley in the Preliminaries of the War of 1812," *Mississippi Valley Historical Review*, vol. 7 (1920), pp. 39–50; Bernard Mayo, *Henry Clay: Spokesman of the New West*, Houghton Mifflin, 1937, p. 397, n. 4.

[16] This is a brief statement of the Pratt thesis which has been much to the fore since the publication of *Expansionists of 1812* in 1925. It has been challenged by Professor Burt and subjected to detailed scrutiny and some modification by Dr. Goodman but its basic importance cannot be dismissed.

youngsters, soon dubbed War Hawks, were spearheaded by Henry
Clay (who exchanged his Senate seat for one in the Lower House
in order to foment war with Britain and was promptly chosen
Speaker), John C. Calhoun, Peter Porter, and others. They found
the President not averse to military preparations and under increasing pressure of events he sent a message (June 1, 1812) publicly
urging the war which he had privately held for years was the only
honorable course for his country to pursue.[17] The House passed the
necessary legislation promptly (June 4) but two weeks passed before the war party mustered enough recruits to carry the Senate,
nineteen to thirteen (June 17). War was officially declared on June
18, the very day the Orders in Council were revoked. This coincidence in dates, plus the fact that a change of four votes would have
altered the Senate majority, has induced the speculatively inclined
to conjecture that an Atlantic cable would have averted war by furnishing news of the impending reversal of British policy.[18] Granting
that much work remains to be done before a balance can be struck
as to the cause of the war, it seems fair at this point to suggest the
continuing importance of frontier factors and the likelihood that
these would in time have overborne the results of both British concessions and the lack of warlike ardor in mercantile circles.

A good case can be made against the wisdom of going to war in
1812. Whereas the Revolution engendered French coöperation, in
1812 Napoleon was preparing his punitive expedition against Russia
and so was in no position to extend aid; furthermore, within his
limitations he had been as disregardful of American rights as the
British, the chief difference being that his depredations cost American dollars whereas the British took lives. Again, the United States
went to war when the cycle of British exactions was on the down-
swing, as evidenced by the repeal of the Orders in Council; had the
War Hawks been willing to play for time instead of territory the
story might have been different. Finally, the poor state of prepara-

---

[17] Mayo, *op. cit.*, pp. 511–513; Abbot Smith, "Mr. Madison's War: An Unsuccessful Experiment in the Conduct of National Policy," *Political Science Quarterly*, vol.
57 (1942), pp. 229–246.
[18] Phillips, *op. cit.*, pp. 206–207.

tion for war and only moderate success in its prosecution augured ill
for diplomatic success at its conclusion. Military measures failed to
prevent invasion and the burning of the nation's government build-
ings in Washington. Brilliant individual actions on the high seas
failed to hide the fact of overall inferiority; only on fresh water, on
Lakes Erie and Champlain, was signal success achieved. Add to this
New England's lack of sympathy for the war's aims, her willingness
to profit by supplying enemy expeditions, and the separatist threat
of the Hartford Convention, and Madison's disposition to discuss
peace can be understood.

Madison Seeks Peace—and Secures It

The President sought to end the war when it was barely a week old.
Instructions to Jonathan Russell, left in London to look after American interests, authorized an armistice if the British would (1) revoke the Orders in Council (already done); and (2) stop impressments. The last the British refused to do and the war went on. It
soon proved so irksome, however, to Czar Alexander I of Russia,
now out of the Napoleonic orbit and back in the war as an ally of
Great Britain, that he offered mediation. This may have been due
to that mercurial monarch's momentary leanings toward republicanism.[19] At any rate the Anglo-American war was a fire in the rear of
his British ally, and had ended American exports to Russia, which in
1811 had totalled over six million dollars; he therefore sought peace
between his political ally and his commercial friend, despite the advice of his Chancellor that the British would not appreciate a third
party's meddling in their affairs. John Quincy Adams eagerly transmitted the proposal to President Madison, who sent his Secretary
of the Treasury, Albert Gallatin, and James A. Bayard (a Federalist)
to join Adams in St. Petersburg. By the time they arrived the British
had declined the Russian offer, ostensibly because "their differences
with the United States were of a nature *involving principles of the
internal government of the British nation*" (i.e., impressment), actually because they had no stomach to see questions of neutral rights

---

[19] F. A. Golder, "The Russian Offer of Mediation in the War of 1812," *Political
Science Quarterly*, vol. 31 (1916), pp. 380–391.

thrown into open international discussion where their own position might be challenged by one as powerful as Alexander.

In the autumn of 1813 the British proposed direct negotiations, the offer was accepted, and Henry Clay and Jonathan Russell joined the original three to constitute an extremely able but somewhat ill-assorted group of negotiators. As their opposite numbers the British delegated Lord James Gambier, a former admiral, Henry Goulburn, a junior governmental functionary, and William Adams, a lawyer; their unimpressive background and personalities doubtless reflected the fact that Britain's first-rate negotiators were then engaged in unscrambling the Napoleonic omelette at Vienna and wanted to keep firm hold on the subordinates who conducted the less important conversations which opened at Ghent on August 8, 1814.[20] The American delegation more than matched the British, despite the handicaps of impossible instructions and sharp domestic cleavages. They were helped no little, furthermore, when the British presented extreme demands which were supported neither by the facts nor the deteriorating European situation. The final settlement, in comparison with the original British demands, represents a triumph in pleasing contrast with the modest success of American arms.

European conditions underlined American difficulties. Napoleon was exiled to Elba; two war-hardened British armies were seeking American objectives; the "Iron Duke" of Wellington was at liberty should need arise. In the face of these discouraging circumstances American instructions demanded abolition of impressments as an essential condition of peace, an impracticable proposal which was withdrawn by later orders of June 27, 1814. The orders reiterated practically all the traditional neutral programs which had been pushed so unsuccessfully, omitting only free ships, free goods; blockade, the long contraband list, the Rule of 1756, all came in for censure. Captured Negroes must be returned or paid for; American right to arm on the Great Lakes must be retained; British access to the Mississippi denied; compensation made for destroyed property

---

[20] F. A. Updyke, *The Diplomacy of the War of 1812*, Johns Hopkins Press, 1915, is the most thorough account. C. E. Hill, *Leading American Treaties*, Macmillan, 1924, pp. 103–135, gives a good working account of this as of other important treaty negotiations. Burt, *op. cit.*, pp. 346–372, is the best brief treatment.

and towns; and captured territory should be mutually restored (the *status quo ante bellum* principle).

Submission of the British demands indicated the distance between the parties. There was to be no concession on impressments or on the infringements of neutral rights which had long been so troublesome; a huge Indian buffer state must be established south of the Great Lakes; the boundary must be altered to furnish real British access to the upper reaches of the Mississippi, to afford a right of way from Quebec to Halifax and St. John, and control of strategic border points; British control of the Lakes must be assured; use of the inshore fisheries, abrogated with the war, must not be restored without a *quid pro quo;* and territorial arrangements were to be made on the basis of *uti possidetis,* or what each held at the conclusion of hostilities. Only on neutral rights and impressment were the British instructions ironclad; elsewhere concessions might be made.

The extreme disparity of the instructions and the powerful position of the British suggested the only possible American tactic: To keep the negotiations open and to minimize their opponents' extreme demands wherever possible. The British amiably coöperated at this game. Goulburn, evidently at Colonial Office instigation, early advanced the Indian buffer state as a *sine qua non,* only to have the Americans reject it and the Foreign Office abandon it for a proposal that each side approach its Indian enemies with peace terms. This the Americans accepted, thus keeping the pot boiling and the negotiations alive. Next came the unwise British assertion of *uti possidetis* and a flat American refusal. At this point the British adopted dilatory tactics in the hope that news of military victories would strengthen the diplomats' hands; the news from America was otherwise. Furthermore, British diplomacy was experiencing its usual difficulties in keeping wartime allies together at the peace table; Alexander's desire to be King of Poland endangered the peace not yet made. British merchants yearned to pour their piled-up wares on the American market, and Parliament was skittish about sinking more money in the American war. Finally, Wellington wrote Lord Liverpool, the Prime Minister, November 9, 1814, that though he was willing to head a military expedition to America, "I don't

promise myself much success there. . . . That which appears to me
to be wanting in America is not a General, or General officers and
troops, but a naval superiority on the Lakes. . . . In regard to your
present negotiations, I confess that I think you have no right from
the state of the war to demand any concession of territory from
America." He thought the *status quo ante bellum* a good basis for
peace.

Wellington's advice persuaded the Ministry to use an American
proposal of November 10 as a real basis of discussion instead of
grounds for delaying debate, and it became the foundation of the
treaty, which was signed on December 24, 1814. Peace was restored.
Captured slaves were to be returned or paid for and each side
pledged efforts to suppress the slave trade (this long-time British objective will receive attention later as a factor in the Webster-Ashburton discussions). Boundaries were to be based on the *status quo*,
but some sectors were still in doubt. Four commissions were established to delimit these. One drew most of the line through the islands
of Passamaquoddy Bay in 1817, though final details were not ironed
out until 1910. One charged with the line between the source of the
St. Croix and the St. Lawrence disagreed and its functions were
passed on to arbitration by the King of the Netherlands in 1827 (see
below, p. 206). A third finished most of the river-and-lake boundary
from the St. Lawrence to Lake Huron, leaving the remainder to
Webster and Ashburton to work out. The last one likewise failed in
its task of completing the Lake Huron–Lake Superior–Lake of the
Woods link, which also fell to Webster and Ashburton.

The treaty's omissions were almost as remarkable as its provisions.
Maritime rights were ignored; technically impressment might have
accompanied any succeeding war, but fortunately peace obtained
generally until the United States had outgrown her position of semi-
tutelage. If the Americans secured no renunciation of British interference with neutral rights, the British did not continue that
interference; both saved face. The twin questions of fisheries and
Mississippi navigation evoked a similar solution. Adams was actively
concerned to restore use of the inshore fisheries which his father had
failed to secure finally in 1783; Clay was not interested in codfish,

but heartily opposed any concession on the Mississippi question; Adams cared little how many Englishmen used the river. Gallatin, after joking his hot-headed and antagonistic colleagues into a semblance of unity, proposed that both questions be omitted from the treaty, subject to later discussion without prejudice to the claims of either party. This the British accepted with the proviso that they would make a bargain when the fisheries question came up.

The treaty, like the war, was indecisive. The War Hawks got no territory, the merchants no damages, but no concessions of principle had been made. The British stopped short of possible territorial successes which could have been won only by a long and costly struggle. On the other hand, as Professor Burt has suggested, the settlement "did nothing that had to be undone, which is more than can be said for many treaties of peace. . . ." This contributed to two consequences of vast importance in American history: In the first place, future Anglo-American controversies could be settled over a table instead of across a rampart; and secondly, the struggle played no small part in the growth of that American nationality which blossomed vigorously under the guidance of those who so recently had been the War Hawks of 1811–1812.

7 The Infant Nation Starts to Grow

Imperialism—American Style

THE PREPONDERANCE OF COLLEGE SOPHOMORES, SOME-what startlingly, give a negative answer when asked whether it had previously been suggested to them that the United States might be classed as an imperialistic nation. This characteristic myopia seems to stem partly from the fact that the word "imperialism" carries a connotation which one dislikes to apply to oneself; "manifest destiny" is a more palatable term.[1] Another extenuating factor makes the term applicable only to territory far away and overseas. The chief element appears to be simple ignorance, which in fairness should not be laid entirely to earlier instruction. Seldom, indeed, have public men or state documents avowed the expansionist urge suggested by a map showing the territorial growth of the United States between 1800 and 1855.

Representatives of nations at whose expense this growth was accomplished return a vociferous and unanimous verdict to the effect that the United States is no better, and perhaps worse, than others. Listen, for example, to the Spaniard, Don Luis de Onís, writing in 1821:

---

[1] The late Professor James W. Garner quoted the English publicist Philip Guedalla in an illuminating remark in this connection: "I have a feeling that imperialism is very much like an open window. If you open it, it is fresh air. If the other fellow opens it, it is called a draught." See the penetrating essay, "Imperialism and 'Dollar Diplomacy,'" in *American Foreign Policies*, New York University Press, 1928, pp. 69–93.

The United States had scarcely seen their independence acknowledged, tranquillity and good order established in their republic, and the place settled which they were to hold among independent powers, when they formed the ostentatious project of driving from the continent of America the nations that held possession of it, and of uniting under their dominion by federation or conquest the whole of the [Spanish] colonies. . . . The Americans . . . believe that their dominion is destined to extend, now to the Isthmus of Panama, and hereafter over all the regions of the New World. . . . They consider themselves superior to the rest of mankind, and look upon their republic as the only establishment upon earth founded upon a grand and solid basis, embellished by wisdom, and destined one day to become the most sublime colossus of human power, and the wonder of the universe. . . .[2]

And to Señor Lucas Alamán, Mexican Secretary of State in 1830:

The United States of the North have been going on successfully acquiring, without awakening public attention, all the territories adjoining theirs. Thus we find that, in less than fifty years, they have succeeded in making themselves masters of extensive colonies belonging to various European Powers, and of districts, still more extensive, formerly in possession of Indian tribes, which have disappeared from the face of the earth; proceeding in these transactions, not with the noisy pomp of conquest, but with such silence, such constancy, and such uniformity, that they have always succeeded in accomplishing their views.[3]

The literature, of course, contains expressions of confidence in the large future of the country. Jedidiah Morse commented as early as 1789 on the westward course of empire, and announced that "Probably her last and broadest seat will be America. Here the sciences and arts of civilized life are to receive their highest improvement. . . . Here Genius . . . is to be exerted . . . planning and executing a form of government . . . which shall be calculated to protect and unite, in a manner consistent with the natural rights of mankind, the largest empire that ever existed." John Quincy Adams, then the stoutest of imperialists, told a cabinet meeting in 1819 that the world must be "familiarized with the idea of considering our proper dominion to be the continent of North America." And in 1823 he instructed a new Minister to Spain that "In looking forward to the

[2] E. C. Barker, *Mexico and Texas, 1821–1835*, P. L. Turner, 1928, pp. 6–7.
[3] Quoted by Carl Russell Fish, *American Diplomacy*, Henry Holt, 1915, p. 243.

probable course of events for the short period of half a century, it seems scarcely possible to resist the conviction that the annexation of Cuba to our Federal Republic will be indispensable to the continuance and integrity of the Union itself." The high-water mark of imperialism in the public documents is doubtless found in the Ostend Manifesto (October 18, 1854), which reflected the desire of the Pierce administration to secure Cuba. James Buchanan, Pierre Soulé, and J. M. Mason signed this remarkable statement which recommended offering up to $120,000,000 for the island and then

if Spain, dead to the voice of her own interest, and actuated by stubborn pride and a false sense of honor, should refuse to sell Cuba to the United States . . . the question will arise, What ought to be the course of the American government under such circumstances? . . . After we shall have offered Spain a price for Cuba far beyond its present value, and this shall have been refused, it will then be time to consider the question, does Cuba, in the possession of Spain, seriously endanger our internal peace and the existence of our cherished Union?

Should this question be answered in the affirmative, then, by every law, human and divine, we shall be justified in wresting it from Spain if we possess the power. . . .

Academicians have outspokenly assessed their country's methods and objectives. As early as 1915 William Milligan Sloane wrote in *Current History* that "Our own history since independence is an unbroken record of expansion and imperialism. . . . This is the light in which European nations see us; our identity in this policy from the dawn of our national existence onward they consider a proof of our national character." J. Fred Rippy points out that "It is in vain that we plead our innocence of imperialism. Our whole history gives the lie to such a plea, unless one wishes to quibble over the term 'imperialism!' " And P. T. Moon suggests that "For a non-aggressive nation, the United States has done remarkably well, as compared with rivals candidly intent on imperial expansion. Only Great Britain has done better." Thus in spite of the mild disclaimer of S. F. Bemis that "In the achievement of the Manifest Destiny of continental expansion, the European powers were loosened of their titles by the peaceful process of diplomacy unaccompanied by any threats of force—

there was no force with which to threaten . . ." the academic con-
census rates the United States at least on a par with others in territorial self-seeking.

Supporting this thesis of an expanding and expansionist nation the
present chapter will consider three continental episodes of that expansion, the Louisiana Purchase, the acquisition of Spanish Florida,
and the penetration and annexation of Texas. It should be noted that
here, as so often in our history, American success exceeded the
American power potential and resulted largely from Europe's preoccupation with its own affairs. From the Louisiana deal through the
British boundary controversies American transcontinental progress
has been closely intertwined with the facts and complications of
Europe's wars and national and international politics.[4]

First Steps Westward—Louisiana

Ever since the Treaty of Paris (1783) gave the United States a foothold on the east bank of the Mississippi and the navigation of the
river, the control of its mouth and the ownership of its western valley have bulked large in American economic and political thinking.
The pioneers, pouring in mounting thousands across the Appala-
chian passes, saw in the river a broad highway for the trade on
which their prosperity depended and which could not profitably
move eastward via the tortuous overland route. The goal of the policy, after one false start, was to secure first the use and then the ownership of the river from source to mouth. The end of the Revolution
left Spain in possession of the mouth, the western valley, and to the
east the Floridas, with an undetermined northern boundary. Spain's
control of the river's mouth, her attempts to push the Florida boundary northward, her relations with the valley Indians, and the uncertain status of Spanish-American trade made it incumbent upon the
government of the Confederation to attempt an overall settlement.
The ensuing negotiations between John Jay and Don Diego de Gardoqui (1785) were characterized by a cavalier treatment of valley

---

[4] The story of American success through European preoccupation has received
extended treatment in many writings of S. F. Bemis and in J. Fred Rippy, *America
and the Strife of Europe,* University of Chicago Press, 1938.

interests which no succeeding American negotiator dared repeat.[5]
His anxiety to secure trade concessions led Jay (an easterner) to
propose that Congress should for thirty years forbear to *use* the
river, though not yielding claim to the *right* of navigation. This immediately roused the five southern states to opposition, and though
the seven northern and eastern states united in support (Delaware
was unrepresented at the moment), Jay could not secure the required two-thirds vote and Spain kept the lower river closed until
the Treaty of San Lorenzo (1795).

Meantime Spain had courted the favor of the frontiersmen in an
effort to wean them from allegiance to their faraway government.
This move had not succeeded as she had hoped. Several factors,
compounded of European political considerations and the failure of
the colonial policy envisioned for Louisiana, determined the Spanish
to make concessions amounting to a surrender in the Mississippi valley. A treaty signed by Don Manuel de Godoy and Thomas Pinckney
at San Lorenzo (October 27, 1795) conceded the substance of the
Spanish-American dispute but left annoying strings attached to the
Spanish capitulation. The Florida boundary, which Spain had long
argued lay on the line of 32° 28′ N. Lat. was dropped to 31°, claimed
by the United States. Americans obtained free navigation of the river
and the right to deposit and transship goods at New Orleans for
three years. Spain might thereafter close the deposit at New Orleans
on condition of opening another port. This treaty tacitly acknowledged that Spanish power in the neighborhood of the Mississippi
was past its zenith; it was a direct forerunner of the retrocession of
Louisiana to France and so the first key to American expansionism.[6]

The rights of navigation and deposit conferred by the treaty did
little to ease Spanish-American frictions. In fact legal access to river
and port gave new opportunities for unpleasantness which few
Americans neglected to cultivate. The Spanish hosts were no angels,

---

[5] S. F. Bemis, *Pinckney's Treaty: A Study of America's Advantage from Europe's
Distress,* Johns Hopkins Press, 1926, and A. P. Whitaker, *The Spanish-American
Frontier: 1783–1795,* Houghton Mifflin, 1927, and "New Light on the Treaty of San
Lorenzo," *Mississippi Valley Historical Review,* vol. 15 (1929), pp. 435–454, cover
the story of the Jay-Gardoqui negotiations and of the Treaty of San Lorenzo.

[6] A. P. Whitaker, "The Retrocession of Louisiana in Spanish Policy," *American
Historical Review,* vol. 39 (1934), pp. 454–476.

either, but on balance were more sinned against than sinning.[7] Their failure to attract the American frontiersmen, plus cumulated grievances over the deposit, made Spain receptive to ceding Louisiana back to France. This idea had cropped up frequently in French official thinking during the late 1790's, resulting in ineffective overtures from the Directory in 1795, 1796, and 1797. The scheme was revived in 1800 while Napoleon and Talleyrand were discussing continental affairs with Spain. That nation, pursuant of her age-long desire to play a role in Italy, was exploring the prospects of an Italian throne for a Spanish prince. Seeking to use Louisiana as a make-weight in this affair, Spain made the first move, the motives of which are clearly indicated in a letter written (June 22, 1800) by Don Luis de Urquijo, Spanish Foreign Minister, to his Minister to France:

Between ourselves, this [province] *costs us more than it is worth . . .* and it would be a great advantage to us to interpose between the latter and ourselves a barrier against their [the Americans'] ambitious plans of conquest, especially if that barrier were raised by such a nation as France, which has neither an active colonizing spirit nor, in view of its absorption in European affairs, the resources for colonization. *Above all, I repeat, this would be an advantage to us because of the recent treaty* [of San Lorenzo] *by which we granted the free navigation of the Mississippi and the principal points that served us as a barrier to the Gulf of Mexico—a concession the ultimate consequences of which you can foresee.*[8]

From this it becomes clear enough that Spain was willing to be rid of Louisiana; no compulsion was exercised by Napoleon, as was formerly believed. The only question was agreement on a proper price.

The proposal fitted admirably into Napoleon's thinking. It offered a territory vastly valuable in intrinsic resources and of great possibilities for colonization. It might furnish a base of operations for an up-river move on his long-time British enemy. Restoring territory which the royal Bourbons had lost would be a feather in the upstart Corsican's cap. Probably most important of all, it might become the

---

[7] A. P. Whitaker, *The Mississippi Question, 1795–1803: A Study in Trade, Politics, and Diplomacy,* Appleton-Century, 1934, and E. W. Lyon, *Louisiana in French Diplomacy,* University of Oklahoma Press, 1934, cover developing French and Spanish policy in detail.

[8] Whitaker, in *American Historical Review,* vol. 39, pp. 469–470.

continental aspect of a grandiose scheme even then taking shape for restoring French commercial and territorial empire in the New World. By the Treaty of Basle (1795) Spain had ceded to France a portion of Santo Domingo; he viewed this as the keystone of his imperial arch but realized that a source of foodstuffs must be found. Louisiana would be the commissary. With Spain eager to sell, with Napoleon eager to buy and able to offer inducements, the business moved ahead.

The resultant Treaty of San Ildefonso was signed most secretly on October 1, 1800, the day after the Franco-American arrangement already noted. Napoleon would create an Italian Kingdom of Etruria for the son-in-law of Queen Maria Louisa; a good bargain, had it been fulfilled, for by it Spain would exchange fifty thousand outlanders for over a million nearby subjects and a place in the European sun. Six months after the new monarchy had been properly recognized, Louisiana was to pass back to French control, "with the same extent that it now has in the hands of Spain, and that it had while France possessed it, and such as it ought to be according to the treaties subsequently concluded between Spain and other states." Napoleon would simultaneously receive six battleships and share with the still sticky-fingered Talleyrand a three-million-dollar bribe. Continental factors prevented the early recognition of Etruria, but when the Peace of Amiens (1802) temporarily relieved Napoleon of British pressure he reverted to his idea of empire and took steps to secure Louisiana, even though he had not paid for it. He lulled the Spanish by promising that he would never alienate Louisiana to a third power, and bullied them into completing the transfer in October, 1802.

Against this continental backdrop Napoleon prepared the second act of his imperial drama: Santo Domingo had been ceded, now it must be conquered, as a preliminary to the occupation of Louisiana. The heroic Touissaint L'Ouverture now rallied his black legions to the defense of his native soil against French invasion. The expeditionary force, entrusted to General Victor E. Leclerc, Napoleon's brother-in-law, defeated the natives but bowed in surrender to disease. L'Ouverture was speedily captured, his armies beaten, and he himself packed off to Europe to die. The desperate resistance of the blacks, however, delayed complete conquest until yellow fever added its ravages to raise the toll of Santo Domingo to fifty thousand Frenchmen, including Leclerc (in the autumn of 1802), disheartened French armies, and eventually aided in discouraging Napoleon himself. The weather rather than the Dominican mosquito furnished the ultimate obstacle. Disregarding bad reports from the Indies, Napoleon was readying a fleet for a late sailing to occupy Louisiana when an unseasonably early cold snap closed the Dutch port of embarkation. Before spring thaws freed the fleet, Bonaparte had given up the Dominican adventure as a bad job and turned his attention to renewed hostilities in Europe. Abandoning Santo Domingo destroyed the *raison d'être* for retaining Louisiana; moreover, the province would fall an easy prey to British sea power in case of war. The United States might have it—for a proper price. Such a maneuver would strengthen the United States territorially and commercially and by that much weaken Britain; finally, the purchase price would be a useful item. These developments came to a focus on April 11, 1803, when Napoleon suddenly directed his Finance Minister, François Barbé-Marbois, to offer Louisiana to the United States. Let us leave the American Minister, Robert R. Livingston, while his astonishment merges into delight, and bring the advancement of American policy into step with Napoleon.

Jefferson, friend of France, came to the presidency under favorable omens. The Convention of 1800 had eliminated points of friction; the peace of Amiens, by ending Anglo-French hostilities, reopened prospects of profitable trade; the West, whence came some of Jefferson's main support, was filling with settlers who might shortly be expected to challenge Spanish control of the Mississippi Valley. To disturb this pleasant picture came rumors that France was about to regain control of Louisiana; the secret of San Ildefonso was leaking out. At first Jefferson could get no confirmation, but eventually (early in 1802) he found his fears justified and proceeded to take steps in a remarkable letter of April 18 to Livingston, illustrating aptly the agility of statesmen in the face of political emergency. This document, delivered by Pierre S. du Pont de Nemours, pointed out the dangers to France should her possession of New Orleans result in an Anglo-American *rapprochement* which aggressive French policy in America would render necessary. Jefferson the Anglophobe, the friend of France, the destroyer of the American navy, whose "entangling alliances with none" had confirmed the Washington doctrine of noninvolvement, now wrote:

> The cession of Louisiana and the Floridas [it was thought, but not known, that Napoleon was in control here] by Spain to France, works most sorely on the United States. . . . It completely reverses all the political relations of the United States, and will form a new epoch in our political course. . . . There is on the globe one single spot, the possessor of which is our natural and habitual enemy. It is New Orleans. . . . France, placing herself in that door, assumes to us the attitude of defiance. Spain might have retained it quietly for years. . . . The day that France takes possession of New Orleans, fixes the sentence which is to restrain her forever within her low-water mark. It seals the union of two nations, who, in conjunction, can maintain exclusive possession of the ocean. From that moment, we must marry ourselves to the British fleet and nation. We must turn all our attention to a maritime force . . . and having formed and connected together a power which may render reinforcement of her settlements here impossible to France, make the first cannon which shall be fired in Europe the signal for the tearing up any settlement she may have made, and for holding the two continents of America in sequestration for the common purposes of the United British and American nations.[9]

Livingston was to use this sharp warning as a sales talk to persuade Napoleon to part with the Floridas and the Island of New Orleans, which last would give control of the river. He worked faithfully but unsuccessfully during the summer, since Napoleon's Dominican adventure had not yet met disaster.

Things came to a sharp focus when, on October 18, Juan Ventura Morales, Spanish Intendant of Louisiana, apparently acting under direct orders of the Crown and without French complicity, withdrew the right of deposit granted by the San Lorenzo Treaty without opening an alternate port, as the treaty stipulated. This action resulted from complaints that Americans had been using the deposit

---

[9] H. A. Washington (ed.), *The Writings of Thomas Jefferson*, Taylor and Maury, 1853–1854, vol. 4, pp. 431–434.

to cover smuggling and evade paying duties.[10] Although the right of navigation was not withdrawn, the West was immediately up in arms and a first-rate political threat developed. Jefferson, like most incumbent Presidents, had one eye on the next election, in which his success would be jeopardized should the current crisis align the West with the vocal Federalist minority. Forcing the issue, however, might bring France to Spain's support. Jefferson's message of December 15, 1802, to Congress therefore merely mentioned casually that Spain seemed to be ceding Louisiana to France, with probable repercussions on American foreign relations "which will doubtless have just weight in any deliberations of the Legislature connected with that subject." Pressing Spain to renew the deposit (which was done April 19, 1803), he wooed the west by sending James Monroe, a prominent land speculator, to aid Livingston in his assigned mission, authorizing the two to pay up to 50,000,000 *livres* for New Orleans and the Floridas. In case of failure they might seek an English alliance.

Livingston's efforts meantime had been unfruitful, even though he offered of his own motion to buy Louisiana north of the Arkansas River. Hearing of Monroe's appointment (Monroe left the States March 8, 1803) and anxious to secure his own prestige, he redoubled his efforts without visible success until April 11, when in the middle of a conference Talleyrand asked if he would like to buy the whole of Louisiana. This astonishing proposal resulted from the train of events already chronicled, but the act was not played exactly as Napoleon had intended. On April 10 the First Consul, respecting Talleyrand's ability more than he trusted his honesty, had consulted Barbé-Marbois relative to the sale of Louisiana *in toto*. Receiving affirmative advice, he had instructed Barbé-Marbois, early in the morning of the eleventh, to see Livingston. Talleyrand in some way knew of the plan and he substituted himself for Barbé-Marbois in the crucial interview. Without instructions, Livingston kept the matter open for the time being; Monroe arrived meantime, and was anxious to share in the proceedings. The night of April 12–13 Living-

---

[10] E. W. Lyon, "The Closing of the Port of New Orleans," *American Historical Review*, vol. 37 (1932), pp. 280–286.

JEFFERSON'S PRIZE PACKAGE
- Definitely located portion of boundary
- Western Florida, claimed by Jefferson under Louisiana Treaty
- So-called "Natural Boundary"
- Texas, claimed by both United States and Spain

Scale of Miles
0   100   200   300   400

ston and Marbois, who had again insinuated himself into the picture, settled on the principle of purchase, prior to Monroe's formal accreditation. Monroe agreed to bidding for all of Louisiana, and a month of negotiations followed, during which both Americans piled up claims to major responsibility which have never been unraveled.

The net result was registered in three agreements dated April 30, 1803, by which the United States paid to France 60,000,000 francs and to her own citizens, in satisfaction of their claims against France, another 20,000,000 francs. In order to effect an orderly transfer, France formally took over Louisiana, held it twenty days, and yielded control December 20, 1803. This deal was remarkable in many respects. By it Napoleon sold something which he had not paid for, which he had never actually possessed, and which he had solemnly stipulated never to alienate to a third party. Livingston and Monroe, authorized to spend ten millions for New Orleans and the Floridas, had spent about fifteen millions for Louisiana, the extent of which no man knew. The treaty said that it was the same territory which France had just bought from Spain, in the indefinite language of San Ildefonso. This doubled, by the most modest estimate, the area of the United States; the more optimistic might ask whether Texas and the Floridas were not included as well. The astute Talleyrand, like every other party to the negotiations, knew that Florida was not included, but was not above planting a disruptive idea. When Livingston asked him how far eastward the Purchase extended, he replied that "he did not know; we must take it as they had received it. I asked him how Spain meant to give them possession? He said . . . I do not know. Then you mean that we shall construe it our own way? I can give you no direction; you have made a noble bargain for yourselves, and I suppose you will make the most of it." The next section will describe the mental gymnastics which this uncertain boundary inspired in American minds.

The consequences of this adventure in expansion were most significant. The Spanish were puzzled to decide whether to be more irked with Napoleon or with the Americans; the former had sold a fair portion of Spain's birthright without paying for it; the latter had profited by the unholy deed. Jefferson parried their complaints by referring them to Napoleon, from whom he said his own title derived. British feelings, which must have been mixed at seeing the United States strengthened, were more immediately concerned with the rising European storm. At home the New England Federalists suffered anguish to see such an addition of territory in the exploitation of which they were unlikely to share. Furthermore, they had hitherto been starved for valid grounds on which to criticize the administration. John Marshall had perpetuated Federalist judicial interpreta-

tion; Albert Gallatin was bringing money into the treasury and paying the debts which the Federalists themselves had incurred; here
for the first time was something they could get their teeth into. The
Purchase, they shouted, was an unconstitutional exercise of executive authority and an immoral compact with the robber Napoleon.
It was, indeed, broad construction with a vengeance and as such
worried Jefferson so greatly that he proposed a constitutional
amendment to legalize what his own strict-construction doctrines
told him exceeded his authority, only to abandon the scheme on the
urging of his advisers; the emergency was so pressing that scruples
were discarded. A most interesting aspect of the story is the easy
evasion practiced by politicians of both parties—the earliest of many
examples of tailoring constitutional principles to fit political patterns. Finally, the territory added by thus taking advantage of Europe's embroilments set the face of the new nation toward a West
which continued to beckon until the flag dipped in the far Pacific.

Spain Yields the Floridas

The Transcontinental Treaty of 1819 (so named by Professor Bemis)
added the Floridas and strengthened claims westward of the Mississippi; it opened the first real avenue to the further ocean, though
Britain and Russia were claimants still to be dislodged. A cartographic problem of considerable complexity, the story becomes in-
telligible only by close scrutiny of a map.[11] Spanish Florida, surrendered to Britain in 1763, had extended to the Perdido River, west of
which French Louisiana lay athwart the Mississippi. France in 1763
ceded to Britain her holdings east of the river save for the Island of
New Orleans, which went to Spain. The British split their gains into
East and West Florida at the line of the Chattahoochee-Apalachi-
cola River, leaving the northern boundary of East Florida indeterminate and fixing that of the western province successively by royal

---

[11] I. J. Cox, *The West Florida Controversy, 1798–1813,* Johns Hopkins Press, 1918,
H. B. Fuller, *The Purchase of Florida,* Burrows, 1906; H. E. Chambers, *West Florida
and Its Relation to the Historical Cartography of the United States,* Johns Hopkins
Press, 1898; P. C. Brooks, *Diplomacy and the Borderlands: The Adams-Onís Treaty
of 1819,* University of California Press, 1939; and C. C. Griffin, *The United States
and the Disruption of the Spanish Empire, 1810–1822,* Columbia University Press,
1937, cover the Florida story in detail.

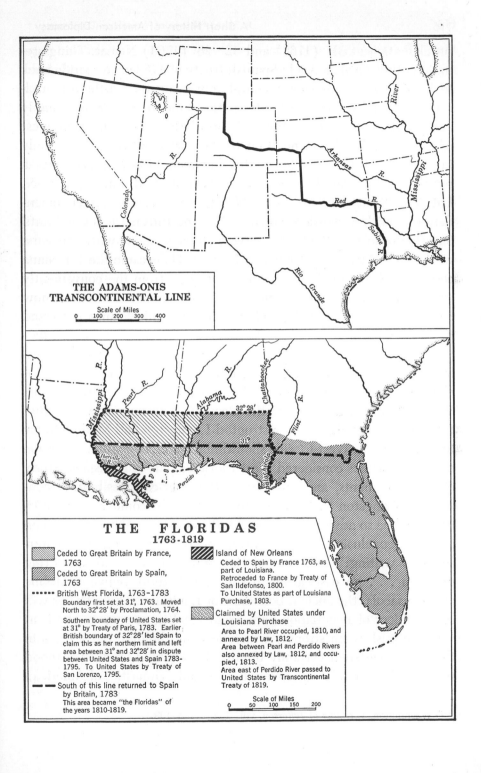

THE ADAMS-ONIS
TRANSCONTINENTAL LINE

Scale of Miles
0   100   200   300   400

THE FLORIDAS
1763-1819

Ceded to Great Britain by France, 1763

Ceded to Great Britain by Spain, 1763

••••• British West Florida, 1763-1783
Boundary first set at 31°, 1763. Moved North to 32°28' by Proclamation, 1764.

Southern boundary of United States set at 31° by Treaty of Paris, 1783. Earlier British boundary of 32°28' led Spain to claim this as her northern limit and left area between 31° and 32°28' in dispute between United States and Spain 1783-1795. To United States by Treaty of San Lorenzo, 1795.

━ ━ South of this line returned to Spain by Britain, 1783
This area became "the Floridas" of the years 1810-1819.

Island of New Orleans
Ceded to Spain by France 1763, as part of Louisiana.
Retroceded to France by Treaty of San Ildefonso, 1800.
To United States as part of Louisiana Purchase, 1803.

Claimed by United States under Louisiana Purchase
Area to Pearl River occupied, 1810, and annexed by Law, 1812.
Area between Pearl and Perdido Rivers also annexed by Law, 1812, and occupied, 1813.
Area east of Perdido River passed to United States by Transcontinental Treaty of 1819.

Scale of Miles
0   50   100   150   200

proclamation at 31° (1763) and 32° 28′ (1764) N. Lat. Things remained thus until an Anglo-Spanish treaty of 1783 gave Florida back to Spain, without, however, completely fixing the northern boundary. The Anglo-American treaty of the same year drew reasonably acceptable northern limits for East Florida. Spanish pretensions west of the Apalachicola extended far to the north, but the area actually in dispute with the United States between 1783 and 1795 was a rough parallelogram bounded by the two rivers, 31° and 32° 28′ N. Lat. The Treaty of San Lorenzo (Pinckney's Treaty, 1795) surrendered Spanish pretensions north of 31°, and thus matters stood until San Ildefonso gave the Island of New Orleans (along with Louisiana west of the Mississippi) back to France. Then came the Louisiana cession with its ambiguous wording, copied from the conveniently vague language of San Ildefonso: "with the same extent that it now has in the hands of Spain, and that it had while France possessed it. . . ."

This language presented interesting possibilities to several statesmen. If purchased as France had once held it, Louisiana surely included land east of the Mississippi, perhaps so much of Spanish West Florida as lay west of the Perdido. The fact, however, that Jefferson and Madison had instructed Livingston and Monroe to try to buy East and West Florida should make it clear enough that none of these worthies considered West Florida a part of Louisiana. Study of the documents, and possibly of the political possibilities, convinced Livingston that a claim to the Perdido could be substantiated, and he so advised Jefferson. Madison seems to have reached an identical conclusion independently, and by August 12, 1803 Jefferson was writing:[12] "The boundaries, which I deem not admitting question . . . go eastwardly to the Rio Perdido, between Mobile and Pensacola, the ancient boundary of Louisiana. These claims will be a subject of negotiation with Spain, and if, as soon as she is at war, we push them strongly with one hand, holding out a price in the other, we shall certainly obtain the Floridas, and all in good time." This statement epitomizes the mental gymnastics of American

---

[12] Washington, *Writings of Jefferson*, vol. 4, pp. 498–499.

statesmen, foreshadows Jeffersonian policy, and shows American expansionism, hardly launched in the Louisiana Purchase, again on the march.

Jefferson's moves to implement his remarkable discovery did not show effect during his presidency. Congress in the Mobile Act (February 24, 1804) extended jurisdiction over the territory east of the Mississippi, acquired from France in 1803 and allegedly extending to the Perdido, and authorized establishment of a customs district. This Jefferson instituted in May, seeking to soften the inevitable Spanish anger by locating the port of entry well inside American territory, north of 31°. Further complicated Jeffersonian maneuvers to secure all or part of the Floridas failed, largely because he received no coöperation from Napoleon, who was himself becoming increasingly interested in controlling Spain, which he seized in 1808. This provoked a revolution which tortured the Iberian peninsula until 1814. Meantime the United States broke relations with the Bourbon monarchy and did not resume them with Napoleon's puppet brother who succeeded it.

So disturbed at home, Spain lacked energy to control her colonies, where violence and revolution became the rule. This weakness brought numerous restless Americans to West Florida, attracted by weakening Spanish authority and the natural advantages of the area. The combination was too tempting to resist; when they were ready for action in 1810 they found Madison eager to assist. On June 14 we find Governor William C. C. Claiborne of the Orleans Territory writing to William Wykoff of his Executive Council that the example of revolution in Spain's South American colonies was likely to prove contagious. Revolution in West Florida might necessitate intervention, which would look much better if undertaken at the request of the local populace. Claiborne therefore sent Wykoff in, on a government expense account, to foment revolution or guide such movement as he might find already under way. Curiously, an uprising occurred no later than September at Baton Rouge, up river from New Orleans.

This disturbed General L. M. Turreau, Napoleon's Ambassador, whose embarrassing questions drove Secretary of State Smith to the following reasonably equivocal statement:[13] "As for the Floridas, I swear, General, on my honor as a gentleman, not only that we are strangers to everything that has happened, but even that the Americans who have appeared there either as agents or leaders are enemies of the Executive, and act in this sense against the Federal government as well as against Spain." His prevarication was matched by the suspicious ease with which Madison transposed public documents in government files in the hope of keeping future searchers from knowing of his complicity in later events. On the strength of the September revolution the President (October 27, 1810) extended American jurisdiction to the Perdido River, prudently limiting actual occupation to the area west of the Pearl, because of the possible obstacles offered by active Spanish garrisons at Mobile and Pensacola. The Pearl-Perdido gap was closed in April, 1813, its occupation (doubly justifiable because of Spain's alliance with the British enemy) affording the sole territorial consolation of the War of 1812.

On January 15, 1811 Congress authorized the President to extend national control beyond the Perdido into East Florida if occupation by a foreign power seemed imminent, or if the local authorities could be persuaded to such an arrangement. An experiment modeled after the West Florida *coup* placed the aged General George Mathews in charge of federal forces charged with invasion and establishment of a local regime favorable to annexation; the administration adroitly arranged matters so that its ties to Mathews could be easily severed. He occupied Amelia Island but failed to capture St. Augustine, the Spanish capital. His previous activities had so embarrassed his superiors that he was repudiated and relieved of command but they continued to hold the territory he had seized until after the outbreak of the War of 1812. Thus the postwar period found the United States in full possession of West Florida and Spain still precariously holding the eastern portion.

The resolution of this unstable equilibrium fell to John Quincy Adams, Secretary of State under James Monroe and one of the great

---

[13] Henry Adams, *History of the United States of America,* Scribner, 1889–1891, vol. 5, p. 313.

American apostles of expansionism, and Don Luis de Onís, who had since 1809 been in the States as the agent of that Bourbon who after the Restoration became Ferdinand VII of Spain. With Ferdinand's government formally recognized, Onís and Adams opened conversations toward the end of 1817. The American occupation of West Florida and the obvious ability to treat East Florida similarly at will made surrender of the Floridas all but an accomplished fact.

Meantime, however, larger implications had arisen. The western limits of the Louisiana Purchase had never been satisfactorily drawn and Adams, seeing in the present circumstances an opportunity to remove Spanish claims on a line extending to the Pacific Ocean, directed the major portion of his efforts to this end. Spain rather promptly promised to yield the Floridas in return for American assumption of claims arising under suspension of the deposit in 1802 and others stemming from Spanish captures during the Napoleonic wars.[14] The western boundary was less easily arrived at. Instructed to drop back by stages from his extreme demand that the line be drawn at the Mississippi, Onís was not prepared to yield as much as Adams demanded. Spanish policy was evidently geared to the hope of securing British assistance, but Britain, tired of embroilments, had just agreed in the Rush-Bagot Agreement (April, 1817) to mutual disarmament of the Great Lakes and would in 1818 settle the northern boundary along the 49th parallel to the summit of the Rockies; Spain derived no support in British quarters. Finally convinced of this, the Spanish government modified Onís's instructions (April 25, 1818) to permit him to make a more elastic western settlement. All this give and take had been so time-consuming as to postpone final agreement until negotiations were rudely interrupted by that fractious frontiersman, Andrew Jackson.

Violence had long characterized the Georgia-Florida frontier. Spain had been unable to prevent Indian raids, as she had bound herself to do under the Treaty of San Lorenzo. Fugitive slaves, renegades, and cattle rustlers added to the confusion. Jackson went south

---

[14] The United States had ratified a convention of August 11, 1802, providing for adjudication of the latter, but Spain rejected it on learning of the Louisiana Purchase; she ratified it during the Adams-Onís negotiations.

late in 1817 under instructions to "concentrate your forces, and to adopt the necessary measures to terminate a conflict which it has been the desire of the President, from considerations of humanity, to avoid, but which is now made necessary by their [the Indians'] settled hostilities." Jackson suggested to Monroe that his expedition afforded a golden opportunity to acquire territory. Acting, he always insisted, with governmental approval, he crossed the border into Florida and campaigned vigorously against the Seminoles.[15] Rushing rapidly from place to place, he made things unpleasant for the Indians, seized the royal archives at Pensacola, and captured, court-martialed, and executed a Scot, Alexander Arbuthnot, and a Britisher, Lt. Robert C. Ambrister of the Royal Colonial Marines, for inciting the Indians. These actions interrupted the diplomatic conversations and upset the British until they were persuaded by Adams that the charges were well-founded; they brought Jackson's speedy recall, earned him the noisy plaudits of the masses, and an all but unanimous Cabinet judgment that he had exceeded his authority, a judgment particularly vigorous on the part of Secretary of War John C. Calhoun, his immediate superior. Only Adams considered Jackson's strong tactics justifiable pressure to make Spain admit her obvious inability to deal with Florida affairs.

Shortly after the conversations were resumed Adams proposed what was to become the outstanding achievement of the negotiation —the establishment of a Spanish-American frontier extending to the Pacific. Developing circumstances assisted him toward his goal: The Jackson Raid made Florida's complete vulnerability apparent; speed was desirable lest border troubles further expose Spanish impotence and lead to reprisals; a drive to recognize the independence of Spain's Latin American colonies, adroitly fostered by Henry Clay for

---

[15] The so-called "Rhea Letter controversy" has occasioned much speculation. Jackson, on the strength of an alleged reply to his letter of January 6, 1818, to Monroe, insisted that he had been authorized to invade Florida. Monroe denied this. A fair statement of present opinion would be that Monroe probably did not give specific permission but, by failing to issue restraining orders, should share responsibility. Brooks, *op. cit.*, pp. 93, 140–141. Marquis James, *Andrew Jackson: The Border Captain*, Bobbs-Merrill, 1933, pp. 308–309, 408–411, surveys the question, adding his critique of the analysis in John Spencer Bassett, *The Life of Andrew Jackson*, Doubleday, 1911, vol. 1, pp. 247–249.

partisan reasons, was increasingly difficult to control. Possibly a sensible settlement of the Florida question would stave off such recognition. After arduous weeks during which the good offices of the French Minister, Hyde de Neuville, were offered and accepted, a solution was reached and agreement signed, February 22, 1819. The United States secured the Floridas and surrendered claim to much Texan territory which might have been obtained had Adams been more insistent, since Onís had been instructed to yield territory as far as the (Texas) Colorado River. The line as established followed the Sabine River to 32° N. Lat., running thence north to the Red River, along it to 100° W. Long., north along that meridian to the Arkansas, up it to its source, which the negotiators believed to lie at 42° N. Lat., but which was actually 183 miles south of that parallel. When the facts became known it was, of course, necessary to run the line northerly from the river's actual source to 42° N. Lat., along which the boundary was then extended to the pacific. Spain thus surrendered claim to the Oregon country and American pretensions to the Southwest were shelved for the time being. Each party agreed not to press claims for damages against the other; the United States promised to assume its citizens' claims on Spain up to $5,000,000. The adjudicated claims amounted to slightly over five and one-half millions, which were prorated. Provisions of earlier treaties permitting Spain to navigate the Mississippi were omitted.

The treaty called for ratification within six months. The United States Senate gave its approval two days after the signing, an action which almost proved precipitate. Article 8 had validated all land grants made by the King of Spain prior to January 24, 1817; it presently appeared that that monarch had surrendered most of the remaining public lands to royal favorites in three huge grants, two of them dated December 17, 1817. Adams, however, insisted successfully on the revocation of these gifts. Spain delayed action beyond the stipulated period, partly because of domestic complications and partly in an effort to dissuade the United States from recognizing the independence of Latin America. She finally yielded to the suggestion of forcible occupation and ratified, with express nullification of the land grants, October 24, 1820; the Senate again agreed, February 19,

1821, and ratifications were exchanged three days later. Thus a second successful chapter in American expansionism was made possible by Spain's weakness and her inability to muster friends in Europe; again American pretensions had succeeded beyond the dreams of all but the most far-sighted, largely because of Spain's distresses which made possible Adams' undoubtedly predatory tactics. There were those, however, who felt that he had not been predatory enough, and the West soon began clamoring because he had surrendered Texas—a clamor never entirely stilled until annexation was finally achieved in 1845.

Texas Enters the Fold

Texas opened the way for conquest in the Mexican War, shifting momentarily the target of expansionism from Europe to an American rival, and rectified Adams' "error" in the Florida negotiations. Chronologically the problem divides itself neatly into two parts, Texas-Mexican relations prior to the revolution of 1835, and the subsequent three-cornered involvement of Texas, Mexico, and the United States ending in annexation a decade later.[16] The sequence of events involves the recognition of Mexican independence in 1822 and the almost immediate beginning of American emigration to the Texas borderland. These emigrants were typical frontiersmen, self-reliant, individualistic, impatient of near neighbors, and many of them in economic straits after the Panic of 1819 and disgusted with a Federal policy which would exact a cash price of $1.25 an acre for land which the settler was even then beginning to think should be free in return for his pioneering efforts. Contrasted with this was the liberal policy of Coahuila (a Mexican state of which Texas was politically a part) which offered heads of families land at about four and one-half cents an acre. Local politicos not only permitted but encouraged this immigration, to their ultimate discomfiture, and the estimated Anglo-American population of Texas in 1835 was 30,000.

---

[16] Professor E. C. Barker has devoted most of his scholarly career to the study of Texan affairs. Particularly notable are *The Life of Stephen F. Austin, Founder of Texas, 1793–1836,* Dallas, Cokesbury, 1926, and *Mexico and Texas, 1821–1835,* Turner, 1928. Also useful are Marquis James, *The Raven: A Biography of Sam Houston,* Bobbs-Merrill, 1929, and Samuel Flagg Bemis, *The Latin American Policy of the United States, An Historical Interpretation,* Harcourt, Brace, 1943, pp. 75–81.

Texan realities failed to match the colonists' expectations. Political affairs were handled in such fashion that the Americans had small voice in state government. Judicial procedure was Latin, mysterious, and often unintelligible—baffling to a litigious people. Periodic upheavals in the central government and that government's touchy problems affected the Americans adversely. Four specific factors aggravated this unstable situation. Long juggling with the slavery question brought a national decree of emancipation in Mexico in 1829. Professor E. C. Barker has effectively disposed of the charge that the penetration of Texas was a slaveholders' conspiracy to add new territory, and has indicated that anxiety over slavery does not appear to have played an important part in the actual outbreak of revolution.[17] Nevertheless, there were many slaves in Texas and Southern migrants would wish to bring in more; emancipation created a serious crisis. The Governor of Coahuila secured exemption from the decree for his Texan constituents, relieving momentary tension but leaving an uncomfortable feeling that the situation might recur. Again, immigrants had feared the alleged lack of liberality of the Roman Catholic Church, though this was rather a conditioning than a causative factor.

More important were immigration restrictions and the administration of justice. The year 1830 saw the introduction of regulations forbidding foreigners to cross the frontier without passports, and prohibiting "the citizens of foreign countries lying adjacent to the Mexican territory . . ." (the United States was the only adjacent country) from "settling as colonists in the states or territories of the republic adjoining such countries." Under pressure, the authorities suspended these restrictions, effective in 1834, but possible repetition hung like a Damoclean sword thereafter. Delays and confusions in court procedure constituted the "most exasperating and persistent" grievance. Important civil and criminal cases could be appealed to the supreme court of the state, located at Saltillo, about seven hundred miles from that part of Texas where the Americans had mostly congregated. The Anglo-Saxon tradition of jury trial had not taken

---

[17] E. C. Barker, "The Influence of Slavery in the Colonization of Texas," *Mississippi Valley Historical Review*, vol. 11 (1924), pp. 3–36.

hold of Mexican jurisprudence, the local Alcaldes were ignorant and often prejudiced, and frequent references to Saltillo might extend the process of appeal for years. All in all, the future did not look too bright under continued Mexican domination.

Despite these mounting pressures, Stephen F. Austin, long the dominant figure in the American colony, had tried to hold his people aloof from the recurrent revolutions which shook the Republic. A newer element, represented by Sam Houston, was increasingly convinced that separate statehood, divorced from Coahuila, would solve Texan problems. A convention in the Spring of 1832 drafted a constitution and instructed Austin to present it to Mexico. He secured some concessions but was returning with a denial of statehood when (in January, 1834) he was arrested and jailed for several months. While he was in jail a spirit of independence developed rapidly in Texas; confinement generated like sentiments in Austin, who returned north in time to assume the lead in events culminating in revolution (October 2, 1835) and a declaration of independence in March, 1836. Texan victory at San Jacinto, April 21, 1836, implemented the declaration and further military operations made Texan independence practically assured.

Revolution inaugurated the second phase of the Texas problem, involving as it soon did the attitude of the United States toward Mexico and its Texas territory. Sympathy for the Texans permeated large sections and all levels of the American populace. Recruiting was blatantly carried on under the guise of organizing "emigrant" groups; when Mexico protested, Jackson asked for specific evidence that the neutrality laws had been violated. Since the "proof" was long since engaged on the Texas-Mexican front, it was somewhat difficult to produce. It is probably fair to say that Jackson steered a reasonably cautious course in view of his own desire to secure Texas for the United States. Belligerency was not recognized, and though both sides used the term neutrality in public documents, the United States undoubtedly failed to observe the spirit of the inadequate neutrality laws then in effect. In extenuation of the government's lukewarm attitude toward its obligations it should be noted that partisan and sectional feeling over the slavery aspects of the Texas question was near the boiling point and that any vigorous stand would have endangered the nation's peace.[18]

Close-coupled with neutrality were questions of recognition and annexation.[19] Request for recognition of independence, a natural consequence of victory in the field, met with extended delay due to domestic factors. Texas had stirred the fires of antislavery propaganda to white heat. Benjamin Lundy, perhaps the first professional abolitionist, had returned from a trip to Texas filled with the idea that the whole Texan movement was a conspiracy to add new slave territory to the Union.[20] John Quincy Adams, seen earlier in this chapter as an ardent expansionist and now representing his Massachusetts district in Congress, had reached a point (aided by Lundy's propaganda) where abolition was more important than territory. He preached the Lundy doctrine with true Adams vociferousness and influenced northern opinion so deeply as to threaten Democratic solidarity and the election of Martin Van Buren as Jackson's successor in 1836. Thus Jackson dared not take action until after the election was won. Urged by congressional opinion and driven by fear that failure to act would induce commercial favors to Britain, Jackson recognized the independence of Texas (March 3, 1837) by nominating a diplomatic representative whose expenses the House had already underwritten pending the exercise of executive discretion.

Van Buren, bedeviled by the still existent Jacksonianism, was promptly (August, 1837) pressed to annex the Lone Star Republic. He too feared the disruptive influence of Texas on domestic politics, knowing that both parties were divided on the question. He parried the request by expressing doubts as to his constitutional authority to annex independent territory, particularly in view of the American treaty of amity with Mexico, with which Texas was still technically

---

[18] E. C. Barker, "The United States and Mexico, 1835–1837," *Mississippi Valley Historical Review*, vol. 1 (1914), pp. 3–30.

[19] Justin H. Smith, *The Annexation of Texas*, Baker and Taylor, 1911, is the standard work. Also useful are G. L. Rives, *The United States and Mexico, 1821–1848*, Scribner, 1913, 2 vols., and J. S. Reeves, *American Diplomacy under Tyler and Polk*, Johns Hopkins Press, 1907.

[20] In addition to Barker's work in refutation of this theory may be cited C. S. Boucher, "In Re That Aggressive Slavocracy," *Mississippi Valley Historical Review*, vol. 8 (1921), pp. 13–77.

at war. Thus rebuffed, Texas embarked on a career which, it was confidently predicted, would enable her to "embrace the shores of the Pacific as well as those of the Gulf" and become "an immense cotton and sugar growing nation in intimate connection with *England,* and other commercial and manufacturing countries of Europe." This was a culmination ardently desired by Britain and France, alike happy at the prospect of an area into which they could push their industrial products over a low tariff wall, whence raw cotton might be derived to relieve them of their galling dependence on supplies from the United States. The only barrier was slavery; British activities were now being directed against the peculiar institution which conflicted with British humanitarianism and the profits derivable from free black labor in the British West Indies. Texas would go only so far as a treaty (1842) denying the legality of the slave trade and permitting mutual visit and search in its suppression. British policy was for years directed toward maintaining an independent Texas which would not join the United States.[21]

Texan dreams of expansion and flirtations with Britain pushed annexation off-stage during Van Buren's administration but circumstances revived the question under John Tyler, a hardly-reformed Virginia Democrat who became President on the death of Harrison, his Whig superior, in 1841. Not unwilling to be reëlected in his own right, Tyler had had his troubles with the Whig congressional leadership and seemingly hoped to make personal capital out of the Texas question which was by this time beginning to intrude itself on the national consciousness once more. Tyler's Secretary of State, the South Carolinian Abel P. Upshur, inaugurated conversations with a Texas agent in 1843 and pursued matters to the point of promising that once Texas had accepted annexation, she would receive protection (by force if necessary) until the Senate acted upon the treaty. At this crucial point a gun blew up aboard the U.S.S. *Princeton,* exploding at once Mr. Upshur and, temporarily, his treaty. Tyler invited Calhoun to be Upshur's successor as he had previously been his adviser, and the treaty went to the Senate April 22, 1844, with

---

[21] These British manuevers are detailed in E. D. Adams, *British Interests and Activities in Texas, 1838–1846,* Johns Hopkins Press, 1910.

the Upshur protective clause intact. John Quincy Adams entered this lachrymose remark in his diary: "The treaty for the annexation of Texas to this Union was this day sent into the Senate; and with it went the freedom of the human race."

More immediately involved, however, was the presidential race, since the party conventions met within a month. Clay and Van Buren, the leading preconvention candidates, sensitive to the explosive character of the Texas question, had concocted pussyfooting statements opposing immediate annexation, but leaving the usual exit in case the political breeze should shift. Clay received the Whig nomination by acclamation and the platform deferred to his wish and said nothing about Texas. The Democratic convention kicked over the traces and made James K. Polk the first dark-horse candidate. His Texas position was as vigorous as his nomination was startling, and it went into the party platform to balance a demand for Oregon: "*Resolved,* that our title to the whole of the territory of Oregon is clear and unquestionable; that no portion of the same ought to be ceded to England or any other power; and that the re-occupation of Oregon and the re-annexation of Texas at the earliest practicable period are great American measures, which this convention recommends to the cordial support of the Democracy of the Union." Polk campaigned forthrightly on this platform while Clay continued his written efforts in two letters "explaining" his original statement, one of which cost him votes in the North, the other in the South. Polk stood squarely on his expansionist platform and was elected by a narrow margin. Meantime the Upshur-Calhoun treaty had been defeated, June 8, 1844, by a vote of 16 to 35.

Polk took his modest margin of victory as a mandate on expansionism, though the facts do not bear out his contention. The figures indicate that Clay would have won had not some hundreds of New York Free-Soilers, who after all preferred Clay's Texas stand to Polk's, cast enough protest votes for James G. Birney, candidate of the Liberty Party, to give Polk that decisive state. Though Polk was prepared to implement his victory, he reckoned without John Tyler, who resolved to salvage some remnants of prestige for his badly battered administration. With Calhoun at his elbow, Tyler suggested

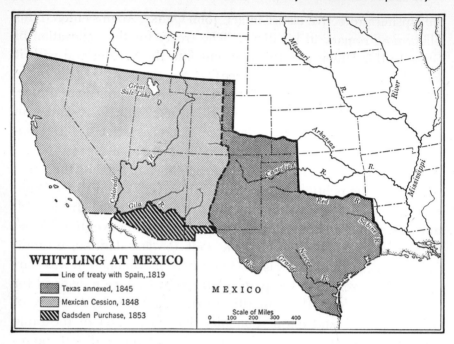

WHITTLING AT MEXICO
— Line of treaty with Spain, 1819
▦ Texas annexed, 1845
▨ Mexican Cession, 1848
▧ Gadsden Purchase, 1853

MEXICO

Scale of Miles
0   100   200   300   400

annexation by joint resolution, an artful proposal to short circuit the
Senatorial opposition which had killed the earlier treaty. The success of this method matched its novelty, but only after long and bitter debate. The joint resolution was signed March 1, 1845, accomplishing annexation so far as American action could do. Polk came
in three days later with only the Oregon half of his expansionist program of 1844 still to be achieved. By a vote of July 4, 1845, a Texas
convention agreed to annexation and on December 29, 1845, Polk
signed a resolution which formally transformed the Lone Star Republic into the Lone Star State.

The incidents related above reveal a young republic on the march.
They illustrate vividly the elements out of which American expansion was fabricated—a brash aggressiveness, an opportunism which
took instant advantage of Europe's necessities and allowed no constitutional or political consistency to place obstacles in the way of
success, a ruthlessness ready to take full advantage of a neighbor's
internal turmoil. Small wonder that this adolescent self-assertiveness,
combined with a democratic political ideology out of harmony with

prevailing European doctrine, made the United States an unpleasant junior member of international society. Indeed, aside from the fact that its power potential was vastly inferior by comparison, the United States was hardly less popular by the middle of the nineteenth century than was that other Johnny-come-lately, Russia, in the middle of the twentieth.

8 Retreat to the West

ISOLATION
NONINTERVENTION
THE MONROE DOCTRINE

CUTTING ACROSS DECADES OF TIME AND EPOCHS OF NA-
tional growth, three policies have mirrored prevailing concepts of
national self-interest. These, isolation, nonintervention, and the
Monroe Doctrine, have mainly reflected the desire of the young nation, still largely dependent upon Europe, to avoid involvement in
that continent's difficulties and to keep those difficulties from involving the American hemisphere and so endangering the national welfare. During much of our history these policies were fairly consonant
with the facts of geography, with leisurely communications, and
with the status of a minor power. They gathered prestige from repeated pronouncements by the nation's great and so became deeply
embedded in popular thinking. When, fairly recently, the nation became powerful and the speed of communication increased, the older
ideas remained fixed in the popular mind. Thus it happened that occasional efforts to align national policy with changing national status
met domestic resistance as well as foreign hostility, and that American opinion adjusted only tardily to the concept of an international
community.

We Should Stay out of Entanglements
Though developing in series chronologically and sharply differenti-
ated as to content, the three policies together formed a framework
within which the nation might seek its own destiny unfettered by
outside political forces. Isolationism is the oldest and hardiest of the

three. Though its origins are often erroneously traced to Washington's Farewell Address, it antedates the birth of the Republic.[1] When separated from numerous glosses and reduced to the language of its earliest advocates isolationism becomes the negation of political alliances with European nations. In this definition its first practitioner was John Adams who urged Congress (in the session of 1775–1776) that relations with France be limited to a commercial basis, since alliance "would entangle us in any future wars in Europe. . . ." This warning was not heeded and the French agreements of 1778 resulted. In reporting to Congress on the peace negotiations (November 11, 1783) Adams reverted to the idea of limiting American relations with France and England to the commercial sphere. The writings of the period between the peace and ratification of the Constitution show Jay, Hamilton, Madison, and Jefferson joining Adams in similar expressions of isolationism. The story has already indicated how the conflicts of the 1790's pushed the government into neutrality, the wartime counterpart of isolationism.

French complications of the mid-decade drew from Washington the most influential of all statements, weighty with the prestige of the elder statesman, but withal couched in phrases so elastic as to enable advocates of widely variant ideas to stretch the Farewell Address to meet their momentary needs. Washington's "Great Rule" developed immediately from an overt attempt of Pierre A. Adet, French Minister to the United States, to influence American voters to elect Thomas Jefferson President in 1796. This interference with domestic affairs so incensed Washington (who had himself decided not to seek a third term) that he determined to read the foreigner a lesson in minding his own business. Written (as were many of Washington's state papers) in collaboration with Hamilton, the Address

---

[1] J. F. Rippy and Angie Debo, *The Historical Background of the American Policy of Isolationism*, Department of History, Smith College, 1924, traces the pre-Farewell Address story. S. F. Bemis, "Washington's Farewell Address: A Foreign Policy of Independence," *American Historical Review*, vol. 39 (1934), pp. 250–268, analyzes the Address. Valuable interpretative material is found in A. K. Weinberg, "The Historical Meaning of the American Doctrine of Isolation," *American Political Science Review*, vol. 34 (1940) pp. 539–547, and "Washington's 'Great Rule' In Its Historical Evolution," in E. F. Goldman (ed.), *Historiography and Urbanization: Essays in American History in Honor of W. Stull Holt*, Johns Hopkins Press, 1941, pp. 109–138. J. W. Garner, *op. cit.*, pp. 47–68, surveys the problem briefly.

appeared in a Philadelphia paper September 9, 1796, and warned the French sharply that American domestic affairs were of concern only to Americans. Almost as a corollary of this assertion of autonomy Washington warned his people to avoid foreign political ties which would jeopardize that independence upon which alone could be built solid the foundations of national security. He said:

The great rule of conduct for us in regard to foreign nations is, in extending our commercial relations to have with them as little *political* connection as possible. So far as we have already formed engagements let them be fulfilled with perfect good faith. Here let us stop.

Europe has a set of primary interests which to us have none or a very remote relation. Hence she must be engaged in frequent controversies, the causes of which are essentially foreign to our concerns. Hence, therefore, it must be unwise in us to implicate ourselves by artificial ties in the ordinary vicissitudes of her politics or the ordinary combinations and collisions of her friendships or enmities.

Our detached and distant situation invites and enables us to pursue a different course. If we remain one people, under an efficient government, the period is not far off when we may defy material injury from external annoyance; when we may take such an attitude as will cause the neutrality we may at any time resolve upon to be scrupulously respected; when belligerent nations, under the impossibility of making acquisitions upon us, will not lightly hazard the giving us provocation; when we may choose peace or war, as our interest, guided by justice, shall counsel.

Why forego the advantages of so peculiar a situation? Why quit our own to stand upon foreign ground? Why, by interweaving our destiny with that of any part of Europe, entangle our peace and prosperity in the toils of European ambition, rivalship, interest, humor or caprice?

It is our true policy to steer clear of permanent alliances with any portion of the foreign world, so far, I mean, as we are now at liberty to do it. . . .

Taking care always to keep ourselves by suitable establishments on a respectable defensive posture, we may safely trust to temporary alliances for extraordinary emergencies. . . .[2]

Thus was launched, in language lucid and completely applicable to an immediate set of circumstances, yet susceptible of endless reinterpretation under developing conditions, a doctrine which has

---

[2] J. D. Richardson (comp.), *A Compilation of the Messages and Papers of the Presidents, 1789–1897*, Government Printing Office, 1896–1899, vol. 1, pp. 222–223.

since served statesmen and propagandists on both sides of every important question concerning American involvement with the outside world. As a mirror comfortingly affirms each successive user's conception of his own good points, so the Address, like many another secular and religious document, has underwritten the conflicting convictions of passing generations. This mass of interpretation and of pure inference makes any attempt to cut through to Washington's real meaning somewhat presumptuous; however, the consensus of academic interpretation leans to the conclusion that his warning was first a temporary one, to be heeded until the nation had attained the essentials of time, space, and unity which he so coveted for it, and second, that it pointed to the danger of additional permanent political alliances with particular portions of the world.[3] Whatever Washington's intent may have been, it was given bipartisan support and the cloak of language when Jefferson's first inaugural announced that "peace, commerce, and honest friendship with all nations, entangling alliances with none . . ." would be an essential principle of Republican government.

These generalizations have been embodied in practical action by (1) the policy of automatic neutrality already discussed above; and (2) maintaining freedom of action, mainly by avoiding permanent political alliances. However, like many policies, isolationism has been honored in the breach as well as in the observance. Numerous agreements, covering wide geographical areas, attest the nation's willingness to depart from a political principle to safeguard a supposed national interest. Concern with an isthmian canal, for example, produced two definitely entangling agreements in the mid-nineteenth century; one of 1846 guaranteeing to New Granada the permanent neutrality of the Isthmus of Panama, and the Clayton-Bulwer Treaty of 1850 establishing joint Anglo-American control of any future transisthmian project. Budding overseas imperialism produced the Anglo-German-American agreement of 1889 setting up a condominium over the Samoan Islands, definitely an international "en-

---

[3] Dr. Weinberg's comment in Goldman, *op. cit.*, p. 112, is a pertinent one: "Thus ideological testaments are not stable in content but pass from generation to generation with the same diminution or expansion, the same deterioration or improvement, that mark the career of a legacy of material wealth."

tanglement." Concern with Caribbean stability led to guarantee treaties relative to Panama (1903) and Haiti (1915) which were equally foreign to the spirit of the Address.

Despite such occasional departures, governmental policy generally reflected popular sentiment in maintaining freedom of action down to the outbreak of the War of 1914–1918. At the end of this struggle a combination of the concept of community interest among nations, Wilsonian idealism, and fear of a reviving Germany produced two treaties which would have sounded the death knell of isolationism. French demands for security in the face of a possibly renascent Germany produced a treaty (signed June 28, 1919) in which the United States and Britain guaranteed France against unprovoked German aggression. The same day witnessed the signature of the Versailles Treaty, carrying in the Covenant of the League of Nations Article 10 which guaranteed "the territorial integrity and political independence" of League members. This is not the proper place to chronicle the upsurge of real isolationism which combined with postwar disillusionment and partisan maneuver to defeat both guarantees and membership in the League of Nations; the story demonstrated clearly the vigor of the sentiment.

The sentiment fed upon itself and upon the increasing international tensions of the 1920's and 1930's to produce an era of increased withdrawal from the relatively narrow area of international coöperation created by the League. This withdrawal was pointed up by the pseudo-neutrality developed in answer to totalitarian threats prior to the outbreak of war in 1939. Meantime, however, the leaven of coöperation had been at work and the national influence was thrown wholeheartedly into the effort which produced the United Nations, successor to Wilson's League. Thus was tardy recognition given to the fact that no first-rate power can remain isolated under conditions of instantaneous communication and well-nigh instantaneous transportation; the nation did not repeat the mistake of 1919–1920.

We Should Let Others Alone

It was only reasonable that a nation wishing, as did the United States, to hold aloof from foreign entanglements should itself forgo interference with the domestic affairs of other states. Thus was born the policy of nonintervention, followed during most of the national period with respect to most nations.[4] This policy has been defined as avoiding "any trespass upon the external or internal sovereignty of others that is not warranted by defense of serious national rights."[5] Occasions for intervention frequently accompany revolutionary changes which endanger the lives or property of foreign nationals; domestic legislation prejudicial to such interests also affords occasion for outside interference. A policy of nonintervention is therefore apt to focus largely on questions of recognition of revolutionary governments, since failure to accord recognition to a successful revolution may easily become an act of intervention. The fact that the United States was the fruit of a successful revolution bred sympathy for similar movements and an accordingly generous recognition policy.

This doctrine of de facto recognition was roughed out by Thomas Jefferson when he said in 1792 that "It accords with our principles to acknowledge any government to be rightful which is formed by the will of the nation, substantially declared." Its full content, after over a century of operation, was stated by Alvey A. Adee in 1913 to be "dependent upon the existence of three conditions of fact: the control of the administrative machinery of the state; the general acquiescence of its people; and the ability and willingness of their government to discharge international and conventional obligations." These requirements were temporarily tightened in the post-Civil War period by William H. Seward's pronouncement in 1868 to the effect that "revolutions in republican states ought not to be accepted until the people have adopted them by organic law, with the solemnities which would seem sufficient to guarantee their stability and permanency. . . ." This added requirement was in effect but a short time and the country returned to a de facto policy until the days of Woodrow Wilson. He announced in 1913, principally in relation to Latin America, what has come to be known as the doctrine of "constitutional legitimacy" according to which no governmental change

---

[4] A more positive form of nonintervention commits a nation to try to prevent other states from interfering in the affairs of third parties; this active aspect of nonintervention as exemplified in the Monroe Doctrine will be examined below.

[5] Weinberg, in *American Political Science Review*, vol. 34, p. 543.

not based upon constitutional processes could merit recognition. This remained in effect until renounced in 1930 as to South, but not Central, America, to be followed by a return to the de facto policy. In 1933 at Montevideo the United States made full and final renunciation of the right of intervention in Latin America.

It will thus be seen that since de factoism has dominated the recognition policy of the United States, nonintervention has also been a keynote. It should be noted, however, that the Wilsonian exceptions (particularly concerning the Huerta regime in Mexico) were important negative applications of the power of recognition as an interventionary instrument. Moreover, several instances illustrate the use of recognition as a positive factor to aid in procuring stability or respectability for regimes which the United States was interested in establishing on a de facto foundation. Thus Cuban (after the Spanish-American War), Panamanian (1903), and Czechoslovak (during the War of 1914–1918) governments were recognized when their de factoism was largely fictitious. On the whole, however, the record is a creditable one.

Europe Should Leave Us Alone

Background and Enunciation

The Monroe Doctrine, third of the American triad of defense-mechanisms designed to achieve a self-contained existence was originally, like so many other American policies, a by-product of European developments; its successful maintenance long depended upon continuing European divergencies and an Anglo-American community of interest in its main objectives—this last despite the fact that Anglo-American rivalry in Latin America had much to do with its beginnings.[6] Its origins may be traced at least as far back as

---

[6] No aspect of American foreign policy has been subjected to more extensive scholarly investigation than this; no lengthy discussion of its bibliography can here be attempted. From the authors whose works are noted below may be obtained the results of the most recent scholarship. Other titles will be cited in support of particular phases of the story. The most prolific writer on the Doctrine in English is Professor Dexter Perkins. His *The Monroe Doctrine, 1823–1826,* Harvard University Press, 1927, details the European background and origins of the Doctrine. *The Monroe Doctrine, 1826–1867,* Johns Hopkins Press, 1933, and *The Monroe Doctrine, 1867–1907,* Johns Hopkins Press, 1937, carry the story into the twentieth century.

the French incursion into Spain which supplanted (1808) the Bourbon dynasty with a lesser Bonaparte, Joseph. Spain's American colonies presently revolted against this Napoleonic intrusion, continuing their struggle for independence after the Bourbon restoration of 1815 against the futile efforts of Ferdinand VII to reëstablish Spanish control. Realizing his own impotence, the Spanish monarch sought to enlist the assistance of the Holy Alliance.

This organization grew out of a proposal presented to the rulers of Austria and Prussia, and later to the other European sovereigns, by Czar Alexander I of Russia. Alexander, a curious compound of liberalism and conservatism, brought to the Napoleonic peace-table a temper as sanguine, ideas as unacceptable to many, and power almost comparable to those exhibited by Woodrow Wilson a century later at Versailles.[7] All signed it except the Pope, whose power was not hereditary; the Sultan, whose faith was not based upon the same Holy Book which it invoked; and the King of England, whose power was hereditary but limited by Parliament. Its pious platitudes about "reciprocal service" and "unalterable good-will" found the signatories acknowledging that the Christian world had "in reality no other sovereign than Him to Whom alone power rightfully belongs. . . ." After the hard-bitten Prince Clemens Metternich recovered from his irritation at its "religious phraseology" he proceeded to make it the instrument of the Concert of Europe, a most realistic engine of repression.

The Alliance (the terms Concert and Holy Alliance, though not strictly synonymous, are used interchangeably by most textbooks), acting upon the principle of maintaining the *status quo* established at Vienna, constituted itself the sworn enemy of European liberalism. Acting as its agent Austrian troops put down an Italian revolt in

Hands Off: A History of the Monroe Doctrine, Little, Brown, 1941, summarizes the first three volumes and brings the narrative down to date. E. H. Tatum, Jr., *The United States and Europe, 1815–1823*, University of California Press, 1936, counters previous authors in finding the Doctrine's origins in American conditions and its objective in fear of Britain. A. P. Whitaker, *The United States and the Independence of Latin America, 1800–1830*, Johns Hopkins Press, 1941, and S. F. Bemis, *Latin Am. Policy of U.S.*, add detail and modify some conclusions of Perkins' works. J. W. Garner, *op. cit.*, pp. 95–139, is a stimulating essay.

[7] W. P. Cresson, *The Holy Alliance: The European Background of the Monroe Doctrine*, Oxford University Press, 1922.

1821; the Congress of Verona (1822) authorized France (which had been admitted to the fold) to suppress revolt in Spain. The threat of intervention in Spain increased British doubts of the Alliance, with which she had been acting though not strictly a member, and her delegate at Verona served notice that his Government intended to continue relations with Spain regardless of Alliance action. When France invaded Spain in the summer of 1823 Britain announced that she would remain neutral only so long as France did not meddle with Spain's rebellious American colonies. The passing summer increased the likelihood of such meddling and George Canning, British Foreign Minister, by threatening that French interference would bring British recognition of the Spanish colonies' independence, forced Prince Jules de Polignac, French Minister in London, to sign a memorandum (October 9, 1823) disavowing on behalf of his Government any designs of armed intervention in Spanish America. Thus weeks before any public American pronouncement, British pressure and the Polignac Memorandum had effectively removed the threat of European interference in American affairs.

Economic opportunity rather than lofty idealism explains this increasing British coolness toward the Alliance. As early as 1801 Spain had been forced to ease her monopolistic trade practices and open her colonial ports to British and American trade. These new markets had helped take up the slack caused by the Jeffersonian embargo and subsequent American variations on the theme of trade restrictions. If the restored Bourbons regained colonial empire through French agency they might recur to colonial monopoly. These factors turned British policy first toward recognition of Latin American independence (tentatively, in 1822), and then toward negotiations with the United States in the summer of 1823, preceding the pressure on France mentioned just above. Canning also wished to find out whether the United States had any designs on Cuba and, if so, to thwart them. Anglo-American relations were in better state than usual, thanks to the Rush-Bagot Agreement of 1817, providing for disarmament on the Great Lakes, and the Convention of 1818 which restored American access to the Northeast fisheries and established the Canadian-American boundary at 49° between the Lake of the Woods and the Rocky Mountains.

The United States shared one British motive for interest in Latin America. The lifting of Spanish trade restrictions had made it possible to market crockery, textiles, and furniture in return for hides and semitropical foodstuffs. Moreover, Latin American governmental forms had been patterned on a North American model; consequently the United States would look askance at any effort to disturb such institutions. Finally, the United States had in 1822 recognized the independence of the Latin American states, an action which Britain had so far only contemplated. These circumstances constitute the background of the Rush-Canning conversations of August, 1823, which furnish the immediate impetus to the Monroe Doctrine.

These opened on August 16 when, in an interview on other matters, the American Minister, Richard Rush, raised the question of possible French intervention in Latin America, then becoming a matter of comment. Rush intimated that British policy would doubtless not be indifferent to such French action. Canning countered with a point-blank question as to whether Rush thought his own government would join Britain in preventing intervention. Rush, being without instructions, replied by hinting that British recognition should precede common action. Canning followed up the conversation with the famous note of August 20:

Is not the moment come when our governments might understand each other as to the Spanish-American Colonies? And if we can arrive at such an understanding, would it not be expedient for ourselves and beneficial for all the world that the principles of it should be clearly settled and plainly avowed?

1. For ourselves we have no disguise. We conceive the recovery of the Colonies by Spain to be hopeless.

2. We conceive the question of the recognition of them as independent states to be one of time and circumstances.

3. We are, however, by no means disposed to throw any impediment in the way of an arrangement between them and the mother country by amicable negotiation.

4. We aim not at the possession of any portion of them ourselves. [This

was Canning's adroit attempt to feel out American designs on Cuba; endorsement of Canning's note would have estopped action in that quarter.]

5. We could not see any portion of them transferred to any other Power with indifference.

If these opinions and feelings are, as I firmly believe them to be, common to your government with ours, why should we hesitate mutually to confide them to each other, and to declare them in the face of the world? . . .

Do you conceive that under the power which you have recently received you are authorized to enter into negotiation and to sign any convention upon this subject? . . . Nothing could be more gratifying to me than to join with you in such a work, and I am persuaded there has seldom in the history of the world occurred an opportunity when so small an effort of two friendly governments might produce so unequivocal a good and prevent such extensive calamities.[8]

Three days later Canning learned that the Alliance powers would probably meet to discuss the colonial question as soon as Spanish hostilities were ended. Writing from Liverpool, August 23, he again requested joint action. Rush's statements of August 23 and 26 indicated awareness that Canning's concern for British trade outweighed his interest in Latin American liberty; nevertheless he hinted even more strongly at a joint pronouncement, despite lack of instructions from his Government, provided Canning would first recognize Latin American independence. This Canning would not do, and the important phase of the conversations ended at this point.[9] Rush referred matters, as so far developed, back to Washington. After some abortive attempts to secure Cabinet support for recognition of Latin America, Canning felt that the European situation precluded waiting for Monroe's reply and embarked upon the course of action resulting in the Polignac Memorandum.

The story as so far unfolded, minus the Polignac Memorandum

---

[8] Quoted in J. H. Powell, *Richard Rush, Republican Diplomat, 1780–1859*, University of Pennsylvania Press, 1942, pp. 158–159.

[9] Professor Whitaker suggests that had Canning fallen in with Rush's proposal for precedent recognition, Monroe would probably have honored Rush's commitment, the joint pronouncement would have followed, and the consequent Anglo-American *rapprochement* might have obviated a generation of bickering. *U.S. and Indep. of Lat. Am.*, pp. 447–448.

which was not known to Rush until November 24, reached Monroe and Adams early in October. Their deliberations on its possibilities may perhaps be interrupted at this point to introduce another phase of the Doctrine's background. The western coast of North America was the scene of the overlapping territorial claims of Spain, Russia, Great Britain, and the United States. John Quincy Adams' instrumentality in extinguishing Spanish pretensions north of 42° has already been indicated. His term of office had also witnessed, in the Convention of 1818, the partial clarification of Anglo-American relations north of that line (See below, p. 212, n.) Russia, however, presently threatened to become a problem. Russian interests had been confided to the care of the Russian-American Company, primarily concerned with trade and profits. On behalf of this concern Alexander I issued (September 14, 1821) an imperial *ukase* forbidding foreign ships to come within 100 Italian miles (6,085.2 feet) from shore between 51° and Bering Straits. This unjustifiable claim to jurisdiction over the high seas, combined with the prospective extension of Russian activities on land, induced Adams to inform the Russian Minister (July 17, 1823) that "we should contest the right of Russia to *any* territorial establishment on this continent, and that we should assume distinctly the principle that the American continents are no longer subjects for *any* new European colonial establishments." This pronouncement, stemming from Adams' fear that colonization might be followed by commercial monopoly as well as settlement, was to be incorporated almost bodily in Monroe's December message.

Monroe's receipt of the Rush-Canning correspondence introduces the question of the authorship of the Monroe Doctrine, one of the most thoroughly canvassed problems of American historiography.[10]

---

[10] W. C. Ford, "John Quincy Adams and the Monroe Doctrine," *American Historical Review*, vol. 7 (1902), pp. 676–696; 8 (1902), pp. 28–52, plays up Adams' role. W. A. MacCorkle, *The Personal Genesis of the Monroe Doctrine*, Putnam, 1923, stresses Monroe's contribution, which is also emphasized by Perkins in the work already cited and in his sketch of Adams in Bemis (ed.), *Am. Sec. of State*, vol. 4, pp. 56–103. T. R. Schellenberg, "Jeffersonian Origins of the Monroe Doctrine," *Hispanic American Historical Review*, vol. 14 (1934), pp. 1–31, plays up the influence of Jefferson upon Monroe. Whitaker's volume bolsters the position of those (in the majority among recent scholars) who emphasize Monroe.

Adams' influence in shaping the noncolonization phase of the Doctrine is indisputable. His statement of July, 1823, has already been quoted. His suggestions for the December message proposed a repetition of the idea; Monroe accepted the proposal and Adams drafted this part of the message in language almost identical with his July pronouncement. The nonintervention statement is the end result of a much more complicated process of combination and elimination which takes the narrative back to receipt of the Rush-Canning correspondence in October. Monroe submitted copies to the elder statesmen, Jefferson and Madison, accompanying his request for advice with his own initial judgment favorable to the joint pronouncement proposed by Canning. Both agreed that Canning's proposal should be accepted but differed beyond that point. The problem presented, then, is to weigh the contributions of Madison, Jefferson, Adams, and Monroe himself to the evolution of the unilateral pronouncement which finally emerged.[11]

The evidence available indicates that Monroe from the first intended a statement on the colonial question and that Adams was mainly influential in modifying and moderating somewhat his chief's choices among the alternative courses proposed. The first draft of the message (submitted to the Cabinet November 21) followed a Jeffersonian suggestion that the world divided itself into two spheres with interests distinct from each other.[12] It also incorporated, somewhat incongruously, Madison's desire for a statement supporting those who in Greece and Spain were struggling to maintain democracy. Adams pertinently suggested the unwisdom of this last, as equivalent to throwing down the gauntlet to the Holy Alliance, and it was toned down. He supported, from somewhat different motives, the Jeffersonian notion of the two spheres, which was retained. Thus his chief influence lay in aiding Monroe to make a choice between Jefferson's and Madison's conflicting advice. He had also suggested

---

[11] Both Whitaker and Powell, *op. cit.*, stress Rush's suspicion of British motives, sharply put in a despatch of October 10, in Cabinet hands November 16 during the crucial stages of the drafting of the message.

[12] Schellenberg, *loc. cit.*, Whitaker, *U.S. and Indep. of Lat. Am.*, pp. 474–477, and Laura Bornholdt, "The Abbé de Pradt and the Monroe Doctrine," *Hispanic American Historical Review*, vol. 24 (1944), pp. 201–221, contribute material on the two-spheres idea.

earlier (November) his personal opposition to a joint pronouncement, saying that "It would be more candid, as well as more dignified, to avow our principles explicitly to Russia and France, than
to come in as a cock-boat in the wake of the British man-of-war."
The question of joint or unilateral pronouncement, however, was
largely determined by Canning, since Rush's despatch of October 10
(received November 16) made it clear that the British had abandoned the idea of joint representations; a statement would be made
unilaterally or not at all, and it was Monroe who decided to make it.
Thus the idea that the United States "rejected" Canning's proposal
must itself be rejected. These strictures upon Adams' contributions
to the basic ideas of the Doctrine should not obscure his important
part in the actual framing of the principles which were settled upon.
To Monroe's final credit should be placed the first formal affirmation
that his country would fight to protect the freedom of the American
states against a possible French attack, though Monroe evidently did
not expect to have to implement his words by deeds.

As finally worked out the Doctrine appeared in widely separated
paragraphs in the message of December 2, 1823, containing first a
caution against further colonization and second, a warning against
foreign intervention in the political affairs of American nations, together with a reiteration of American intention to abstain from involvement in European wars or politics.[13] The pertinent passages of
the Doctrine are as follows:

At the proposal of the Russian Imperial Government, made through the
minister of the Emperor residing here, a full power and instructions have
been transmitted to the minister of the United States at St. Petersburg to
arrange by amicable negotiation the respective rights and interests of the
two nations on the northwest coast of this continent. A similar proposal
has been made by His Imperial Majesty to the Government of Great
Britain, which has likewise been acceded to. The Government of the
United States has been desirous by this friendly proceeding of manifest-
ing the great value which they have invariably attached to the friendship

---

[13] It has been pointed out that this statement of abstention carries no obligation
which would prevent the protection of legitimate American interests or serve as a
cover for isolationism. Dexter Perkins, "The Monroe Doctrine Up to Date," *Foreign
Affairs*, vol. 20 (1942), pp. 253–265; F. O. Wilcox, "The Monroe Doctrine and
World War II," *American Political Science Review*, vol. 36 (1942), pp. 433–453.

of the Emperor and their solicitude to cultivate the best understanding with his Government. In the discussions to which this interest has given rise and in the arrangements by which they may terminate the occasion has been judged proper for asserting, as a principle in which the rights and interests of the United States are involved, that the American continents, by the free and independent condition which they have assumed and maintain, are henceforth not to be considered as subjects for future colonization by any European powers. . . .

It was stated at the commencement of the last session that a great effort was then making in Spain and Portugal to improve the condition of the people of those countries, and that it appeared to be conducted with extraordinary moderation. It need scarcely be remarked that the result has been so far very different from what was then anticipated. Of events in that quarter of the globe, with which we have so much intercourse and from which we derive our origin, we have always been anxious and interested spectators. The citizens of the United States cherish sentiments the most friendly in favor of the liberty and happiness of their fellow-men on that side of the Atlantic. In the wars of the European powers in matters relating to themselves we have never taken any part, nor does it comport with our policy, so to do. It is only when our rights are invaded or seriously menaced that we resent injuries or make preparation for our defense. With the movements in this hemisphere we are of necessity more immediately connected, and by causes which must be obvious to all enlightened and impartial observers. The political system of the allied powers is essentially different in this respect from that of America. This difference proceeds from that which exists in their respective Governments; and to the defense of our own, which has been achieved by the loss of so much blood and treasure, and matured by the wisdom of their most enlightened citizens, and under which we have enjoyed unexampled felicity, this whole nation is devoted. We owe it, therefore, to candor and to the amicable relations existing between the United States and those powers to declare that we should consider any attempt on their part to extend their system to any portion of this hemisphere as dangerous to our peace and safety. With the existing colonies or dependencies of any European power we have not interfered and shall not interfere. But with the Governments who have declared their independence and maintained it, and whose Independence we have, on great consideration and on just principles, acknowledged, we could not view any interposition for the purpose of oppressing them, or controlling in any other manner their destiny, by any European power in any other light than as the manifestation of an unfriendly disposition toward the United States. In the war between those new governments and Spain we declared our neutrality at the time of their recognition, and to this we have adhered, and shall continue to adhere, provided no change shall occur which, in the judgment of the competent authorities of this Government, shall make a corresponding change on the part of the United States indispensable to their security.

The late events in Spain and Portugal shew that Europe is still unsettled. Of this important fact no stronger proof can be adduced than that the allied powers should have thought it proper, on any principle satisfactory to themselves, to have interposed by force in the internal concerns of Spain. To what extent such interposition may be carried, on the same principle, is a question in which all Independent powers whose governments differ from theirs are interested, even those most remote, and surely none more so than the United States. Our policy in regard to Europe, which was adopted at an early stage of the wars which have so long agitated that quarter of the globe, nevertheless remains the same, which is, not to interfere in the internal concerns of any of its powers; to consider the Government *de facto* as the legitimate government for us; to cultivate friendly relations with it, and to preserve those relations by a frank, firm, and manly policy, meeting in all instances the just claims of every power, submitting to injuries from none. But in regard to those continents circumstances are eminently and conspicuously different. It is impossible that the allied powers should extend their political system to any portion of either continent without endangering our peace and happiness; nor can anyone believe that our Southern brethren, if left to themselves, would adopt it of their own accord. It is equally impossible, therefore, that we should behold such interposition in any form with indifference. If we look to the comparative strength and resources of Spain and those new Governments, and their distance from each other, it must be obvious that she can never subdue them. It is still the true policy of the United States to leave the parties to themselves, in the hope that other powers will pursue the same course.[14]

Monroe's dictum aroused much less contemporary excitement than some of its later ramifications. John Randolph voiced the loudest domestic criticism, but people were used to hearing his condemnatory tirades. Latin American liberals approved mildly, though more interested in the British attitude than their northern neighbor's. Canning was shrewd enough to see that Monroe's threats ran as strongly against Britain as against the Holy Alliance and that the President was keeping the rain off Latin America with a British um-

---

[14] As quoted in Richardson, *op. cit.*, vol. 2, pp. 207–220.

brella, since no adequate American force could have been mustered in the face of a European invasion. He prepared himself for the heightened commercial rivalry which was the most significant immediate result of the episode and, in order that the world might know whence came the real preventive of Alliance action, saw to it that the Polignac Memorandum was promptly published.[15]

The foregoing account has been perhaps unnecessarily explicit in order to underline the limits of the Doctrine as enunciated; the passing years and the country's real or fancied needs have brought its expansion to a point far beyond anything envisioned by its author. This expansion, gradual for a long time and then exceedingly rapid, transformed it from an instrument of well-being for Latin America to an agency of northern intervention which became one of the most mischievous forces in Hemispheric affairs. Only recently has the United States developed sufficient statesmanship to realize that the early twentieth-century policy is not a useful one.

Slow Growth Through the Century

The Doctrine, after one or two tentative and relatively unimportant interpretations, was heard little of until the 1840's; it was violated with impunity when the British in 1833 ousted Argentina from the Falkland Islands, to which the latter had a valid title,[16] and by British encroachments in Central America in the same decade. By the time James K. Polk blustered his way to success in the election of 1844 British rivalry had become sufficiently apparent in Texas and on the west coast to make advisable a revival of Monroeism aimed at Britain. In his message of December 2, 1845 Polk stated that

The nations of America are equally sovereign and independent with those of Europe. They possess the same rights, independent of all foreign interposition, to make war, to conclude peace, and to regulate their internal affairs. The people of the United States can not, therefore, view

---

[15] Perkins' concluding estimate is of interest at this point: "The action taken by the President in 1823 ought, from the standpoint of his own time, to be regarded as a significant episode and as little more than that. . . . From the standpoint of its immediate results, it was close to a futility." *Monroe Doctrine, 1823–1826*, pp. 257–260.

[16] J. L. Goebel, *The Struggle for the Falkland Islands: A Study in Legal and Diplomatic History,* Yale University Press, 1927.

with indifference attempts of European powers to interfere with the independent action of the nations on this continent. . . . We must ever maintain the principle that the people of this continent alone have the right to decide their own destiny. Should any portion of them, constituting an independent state, propose to unite themselves with our Confederacy, this will be a question for them and us to determine without any foreign interposition. We can never consent that European powers shall interfere to prevent such a union because it might disturb the "balance of power" which they may desire to maintain upon this continent . . . it should be distinctly announced to the world as our settled policy that no future European colony or dominion shall with our consent be planted or established on any part of the North American continent. . . ."[17]

In expanding both phases of the Doctrine, Polk's message constituted a major contribution to its growth. Whereas Monroe had inveighed against possible armed intervention in Latin America, Polk warned against even such advisory and diplomatic action as Britain had recently offered to Texas. And whereas to Monroe noncolonization had implied the acquisition of unoccupied territory, Polk's use of the word "dominion" extended the prohibition to include already established settlements; moreover, it was his intention to forbid the transfer of American territory to Europe even by voluntary cession of its inhabitants. Here is to be found, indeed, the earliest step in the metamorphosis of the Doctrine into an instrument of intervention, limiting not only European interference but American freedom as well. It has been suggested that by emphasizing North America Polk intended to restrict his application of the Doctrine to that continent.[18] Although such emphasis is obvious, it is not necessarily exclusive, since he quoted approvingly Monroe's plural statement: "The American continents . . . are henceforth not to be considered as subjects for future colonization . . ." and spoke of the "wisdom and sound policy" of the original Doctrine.

The new doctrine was soon tested. The Mexican War was accompanied by disturbances in Yucatan, where a white minority in revolution against Mexico was endangered by an Indian uprising. In

---

[17] Richardson, *op. cit.*, vol. 4, pp. 398–399.
[18] Bemis, *Lat. Am. Pol. of U.S.*, p. 101, for example, asserts that in line with his continental policy Polk "had to desert the Monroe Doctrine in South America in order to defend it in North America."

view of Mexican impotence an agent of the whites offered to transfer "the dominion and sovereignty of the peninsula" to the United
States, Great Britain, or Spain in return for aid. The acquisition of
about half of Mexico had recently satisfied Polk's own appetite for
territory; his message of April 29, 1848, sought to warn Europe
against action by reiterating that his Government "could not consent
to a transfer of this 'dominion and sovereignty' either to Spain,
Great Britain, or any other European power." He was saved from
further concern by Europe's lack of interest.

The period of the American Civil War marked the Doctrine's
victory, after repeated violations, over the most vigorous and temporarily successful challenges ever directed against it.[19] The Doctrine's vigor in these years matches that of the United States itself.
During the period of domestic turmoil violations were frequent, but
military success assisted appreciably in ending the outstanding violation and discouraging subsequent ones. Affairs in Santo Domingo
early posed a difficult problem for Abraham Lincoln and William H.
Seward. Shortly after Fort Sumter was fired upon Spain reannexed
(May 19, 1861) that island republic.[20] Despite the complexities of
domestic affairs Seward advised Lincoln (April 1, 1861) to demand
"categorical explanations" from Spain as to her Dominican policy
and, wanting a satisfactory reply, counseled a declaration of war.
The following day Seward invoked the Monroe Doctrine in a sharp
note of inquiry to Spain. He began to hedge, however, in the face of
a belligerent reply that the annexation was an accomplished fact,
and Spanish withdrawal in 1865 was chiefly dictated by forces other
than the Doctrine.[21]

The Doctrine came of age with the French challenge in Mexico.[22]

---

[19] The Monrovian implications of the Clayton-Bulwer Treaty of 1850 and its aftermath in the early 1880's will be discussed below in connection with isthmian diplomacy.

[20] C. C. Tansill, *The United States and Santo Domingo, 1798–1873,* Johns Hopkins
Press, 1938, pp. 213–286. It may be noted that in 1854 joint Anglo-French interven-
tion forced the current dictator to declare his intention not to sell, lease, or alienate
Dominican territory—a distinct violation of the Doctrine.

[21] Seward's successful invocation of the Doctrine in Spain's invasion of the Chincha
guano islands off the coast of Peru may have had some influence. Bemis, *Lat. Am.
Pol. of U.S.,* p. 113.

[22] The French adventure in Mexico will receive further consideration in the next
chapter; the effort here is to confine the narrative as closely as possible to the Monroe
Doctrine.

Here a succession of misadventures caused France, Spain, and Britain to intervene in order to collect debts long overdue. Seward declined an invitation to participate but acquiesced in forcible action by the powers (only in the twentieth century has the Doctrine been used to oppose armed hostilities against American states) and issued a mild warning hoping that there would be no territorial exactions and no attempt to deprive the Mexicans of self-government. When allied action seemed likely to move from the economic to the political realm in 1862 he protested, on Monrovian principles, what seemed likely to occur, though the Dominican experience taught him the wisdom of not mentioning the Doctrine by name. The offering of a Mexican throne to the French puppet, Maximilian of Habsburg, in 1863, brought another protest, mild, as had been that of 1862, in view of domestic uncertainties.

As Northern arms grew stronger, so did Seward's voice; by the end of 1865 he was applying vigorous pressure for French withdrawal and President Andrew Johnson's message of December 4 informed Congress (and Napoleon III) that the United States would "regard it as a great calamity to ourselves, to the cause of good government, and to the peace of the world should any European power challenge the American people, as it were, to the defense of republicanism against foreign interference." The French withdrew fairly promptly, due to a variety of circumstances prominent among which was American pressure under the Monroe Doctrine, now for the first time stoutly supported by an aroused public opinion. Henceforth the Doctrine must be counted as an essential element of American ideological paraphernalia.

The early postwar period also marks the formal emergence of the no-transfer corollary, indicating opposition to the transfer of American territory from one European power to another. This position, taken independently of the Monroe Doctrine as early as 1811 with respect to the possible transfer of part of Florida from Spanish possession, had been frequently reiterated and was not fully connected with the Monroe Doctrine until the 1860's. Seward protested when in 1864 it seemed likely that the Danish West Indies might change hands because of European diplomatic moves; U. S. Grant's message of 1869 asserted, apropos of a Cuban revolution, that "These dependencies are no longer regarded as subject to transfer from one European power to another." American business interests presently presumed upon Grant's gullibility to secure his coöperation in a remarkable scheme to annex Santo Domingo. A treaty to this effect went to the Senate early in 1870 and when it encountered opposition Grant sent a naïve message, May 31, supporting the proposal on the ground that it would be "an adherence to the 'Monroe Doctrine.'" He went on to make the first broad and rigorous statement of the no-transfer idea: "and I now deem it proper to assert the equally important principle that hereafter no territory on this continent shall be regarded as subject of transfer to a European power," and continued that he had "information which I believe reliable that a European power stands ready now to offer $2,000,000 for the possession of Samaná Bay alone. If refused by us, with what grace can we prevent a foreign power from attempting to secure the prize?" The treaty was defeated, but on July 14 Secretary of State Hamilton Fish submitted a memorandum which confirmed the no-transfer corollary as part of the Monroe Doctrine.[23] Lest, however, the government be credited with too great a reputation for consistency, Fish's successor blandly ignored an early violation in the transfer (in 1877) of Swedish St. Bartholomew to France.

The Doctrine's Voice Changes

The next great chapter in the Doctrine's history, written under the goad of turn-of-the-century imperialists, marks the first real threat of aggressive action in its support. Grover Cleveland's demands of Britain in settlement of the British Guiana-Venezuela boundary must have given some comfort to the young jingoes, so pained by his inaction in the face of the opportunity to annex Hawaii. But it was a completely unjustifiable extension of the Doctrine to assert the right of Cleveland's Government to demand the settlement by arbitration of any dispute between an American power and a non-American power having American possessions, which the two had been unable to settle by diplomatic means. The setting of this

---

[23] Tansill's account, *U.S. and Santo Domingo*, p. 338 ff., throws much new light on the Dominican intrigue.

episode is typical of Anglo-American relations; a combination of surface aggravations obscured temporarily a solid body of common interests. As at other periods, the volatile character of the surface elements endangered the basic substructure; as at other periods, too, the fundamental common sense of both parties, plus the usual European diversion, intervened to prevent a catastrophe.

British acquisition of Dutch territory in 1814 touched off a long-standing boundary controversy which at its peak saw Venezuela claiming over half of British Guiana and Britain demanding a lesser but expanding share of Venezuela.[24] Sir Robert Schomburgk drew a tentative boundary in 1840 which as time passed came to be looked upon by the British as final. Decades of unsuccessful Venezuelan efforts at adjustment resulted in a breach of relations in 1887. Venezuela repeatedly appealed to the United States for assistance, with a liberal misrepresentation of the facts, and in 1887 the Department of State unsuccessfully suggested arbitration. Despite much note-writing no great change had occurred when Cleveland took office in 1893. He was promptly put under fire for his lukewarmness toward the pending Hawaiian annexation treaty; Henry Cabot Lodge, Theodore Roosevelt, and Alfred Thayer Mahan, prophets of a more vigorous foreign policy, were full of demands and threats; Cleveland's only mild affection for the British was not increased by British occupation of the customs house at Corinto, Nicaragua, in the spring of 1895. Lodge's article in the June *North American Review* asserted that "the American people are not ready to abandon the Monroe Doctrine, or give up their rightful supremacy in the Western Hemisphere. On the contrary, they are as ready now to fight to maintain

---

[24] The following titles are useful additions to those already cited: C. C. Tansill, *The Foreign Policy of Thomas F. Bayard*, Fordham University Press, 1940; Grover Cleveland, *Presidential Problems*, Century, 1904, pp. 173–381, is a presidential apologia; P. R. Fossum, "The Anglo-Venezuela Boundary Controversy," *Hispanic American Historical Review*, vol. 8 (1928), pp. 299–329; Allan Nevins, *Grover Cleveland: A Study in Courage*, Dodd, Mead, 1932, pp. 629–649; T. C. Smith, "Secretary Olney's Real Credit in the Venezuela Affair," *Proceedings of the Massachusetts Historical Society*, vol. 65, pp. 112–147, defends Olney's conduct of the affair, especially in its later stages; N. M. Blake, "Background of Cleveland's Venezuela Policy," *American Historical Review*, vol. 47 (1942), pp. 259–277, demonstrates the contemporary pressures which made Cleveland pursue a policy seemingly contradictory to his policy toward Hawaii; and A. L. P. Dennis, *Adventures in American Diplomacy, 1896–1906*, Dutton, 1928, pp. 17–62.

both as they were when they forced the French out of Mexico. . . .
The supremacy of the Monroe Doctrine should be established and at
once—peaceably if we can, forcibly if we must. It will be the duty
and the privilege of the next Congress to see that this is done."[25]
Altogether, the usually placid Cleveland became irritated and decided to make an issue.

The result was a note of July 20, 1895, drafted by the new Secretary of State, Richard Olney, softened by Cleveland, but still notable
in its disregard of the diplomatic proprieties, in its underestimate of
the British spirit, and in its optimistic concept of the Monroe Doctrine and the power of the United States to implement such a concept. Stating that "the United States is practically sovereign on this
continent, and its fiat is law upon the subjects to which it confines its
interposition," he announced that there was "a doctrine of American
public law . . . which entitles and requires the United States to
treat as an injury to itself the forcible assumption by an European
power of political control over an American state," and concluded
that existing conditions called for "a definite decision upon the point
whether Great Britain will consent or will decline to submit the
Venezuelan boundary question in its entirety to an impartial arbitration."[26] A combination of factors delayed for over four months the
British reply to this peremptory note. The new Salisbury Government was busy learning the ropes and dealing with a touchy Near
Eastern situation, and Ambassador Thomas F. Bayard did not adequately emphasize the urgency of the case. Realizing that an initial
surrender to arbitration would bring added demands, Salisbury desired to build up the strongest possible argument. Then his aides
miscalculated the date when Congress convened; finally, the tardy
reply was sent by mail instead of cable under date of November 26
and was not received until December 7, after Congress had assembled.

It was not reassuring. Salisbury was as well convinced of his own
worth and of his country's position as was Olney. He denied the

---

[25] Vol. 160 (1895), p. 658.
[26] *Papers Relating to the Foreign Relations of the United States, 1895,* Government Printing Office, 1896, pp. 558–562.

applicability of the Monroe Doctrine to the existing circumstances, challenged its validity in international law, and peremptorily rejected the arbitration proposal. This left no diplomatic recourse and gave Cleveland pause. The result was his message to Congress, December 17, in which he reasserted the validity of the Monroe Doctrine and declared that British intransigence made it incumbent upon the United States to run the disputed line; he requested an appropriation for a commission for that purpose. Once the line was drawn it would have to be maintained by the United States. He concluded: "In making these recommendations I am fully alive to the responsibility incurred and keenly realize all the consequences that may follow." Congress promptly voted the money and the rejoicing jingoes scanned the horizon for war clouds, conveniently forgetting their country's total unpreparedness for hostilities.

Fortunately for both nations, soberer counsels prevailed. Clerics and scholars attacked Cleveland's untenable position, particularly the eminent international lawyer John Bassett Moore, who wrote exposing Venezuela's lack of frankness and hoping that the President would "not be willing to launch his country on a career as mad and as fatal as that on which France was started by Louis XIV." Such Englishmen as had ever heard of the boundary question were disposed to minimize its importance. Several prominent leaders were married to American women; the distaff influence was doubtless invoked. The general tendency was to deprecate the quarrel and seek its termination. Each government, however, had placed itself far out on a long limb; Cleveland had threatened an intervention intolerable to Britain; Salisbury had closed the door to negotiation; an impasse was at hand.

Its resolution was aided, as on so many other occasions, by outside forces. On January 2, 1896, while tempers were still warm but beginning to cool, news arrived in London that the Transvaal Boers had beaten off invading English raiders led by Dr. L. S. Jameson. The following day Kaiser Wilhelm II of Germany sent his historic telegram to President Paul Krüger of the Boer Republic:[27] "I express

----

[27] Quoted in W. L. Langer, *The Diplomacy of Imperialism*, Knopf, 1935, vol. 1, p. 237.

to you my sincere congratulations that you and your people, without appealing to the help of friendly powers, have succeeded, by your own energetic action against the armed bands which invaded your country as disturbers of the peace, in restoring peace and in maintaining the independence of the country against attacks from without." This startling pronouncement exposed Britain to a crisis much more crucial than a Venezuelan swamp and found her, without friends, staring Germany in the face. There followed a reorientation of British policy, one element of which involved liquidating the American issue.[28] The day after the publication of the Krüger Telegram Joseph Chamberlain, Colonial Secretary, wrote Salisbury asking whether it might not be wise to make "a serious effort to come to terms with America." The British gave in and the principle of arbitration was embodied, after months of discussion in which the United States coöperated, in an Anglo-Venezuelan treaty. This pretty well protected British interests east of the Schomburgk Line by excepting from the discussions land which either party had held for fifty years. The final award of 1899 mainly followed the Schomburgk Line, with some important concessions to Venezuela which, however, Britain had offered to make as early as 1844.

This episode, in addition to demonstrating American ineptitude in the brash promulgation of the Cleveland-Olney Corollary, registered also an American desire to play a role in world affairs, a desire at the moment out of proportion to American ability, but an earnest of America's coming of age as a world force. No longer would Europe calculate policy without estimating the position of the United States; particularly, British statesmen began currying American favor as part of the British turn-of-the-century campaign to win friends. By the same token, continental opinion turned correspondingly hostile. A significant aftermath was the signing (January 11, 1897) of a general Anglo-American arbitration treaty which a jealous Senate first amended and then rejected. Domestically, the Monroe Doctrine

---

[28] This reorientation, which impinges on American foreign relations at a number of points, is ably detailed in Professor Langer's study. It is likely that the Anglo-American crisis would have been resolved without the Krüger Telegram; recent writers such as Professor Allan Nevins have pointed out that the crisis was beginning to wear itself out when the telegram was published. *Grover Cleveland,* p. 646.

grew in popular knowledge and esteem; prompt congressional acceptance of its obligations enhanced its prestige. Latin America viewed the episode with mixed emotions, the less powerful nations seeing the United States as a benefactor, the more vigorous ones (including Venezuela) as a potential dictator.

Several significant signs and portents preceded the Doctrine's next and greatest enlargement under Theodore Roosevelt. The jingoes finally had their way in the Spanish-American War, which made the nation responsible for far-flung territories unfamiliar to its people. Fast on the heels of this came the end of British attempts to share the control of the Caribbean; the United States must now maintain a new alertness to all that happened in that area as related to transisthmian transportation. With an isthmian canal in prospect, any European interest in adjacent areas was bound to cause concern; the numerous if often ill-conceived schemes of Wilhelm II were supposed (whether rightly or wrongly is immaterial at the moment) to include an attempt to see how far the United States would go in support of the Monroe Doctrine. Last but by no means least among the new phenomena was Theodore Roosevelt, sidetracked into the vice-presidency by political maneuver and thence elevated to the presidency by the assassin's bullet. Seldom in the history of nations have man and circumstances been better met. Unlike his domestically minded predecessor he liked the international stage; his equipment for dealing with world affairs exceeded that of most Presidents, as did his opportunities for influencing them. That his methods were sometimes less circumspect than the cautious might have wished was a product of the Rooseveltian personality, well expressed by his oft-quoted statement: "I have always been fond of the West African proverb: 'Speak softly and carry a big stick, you will go far.'"

Later dramatic developments have tended to obscure the first Rooseveltian pronouncement upon the Doctrine, which was itself of a routine character.[29] The current Venezuelan dictator was Cipriano Castro, whom Roosevelt pungently characterized as an "unspeakably

---

[29] Authorities of special value in addition to the general accounts already cited are Dennis, *op. cit.*, pp. 282–308; H. C. Hill, *Roosevelt and the Caribbean*, University of Chicago Press, 1927, pp. 106–147; and A. Vagts, *Deutschland und die Vereinigten Staaten in der Weltpolitik*, Macmillan, 1935, 2 vols.

villainous little monkey." His willingness to incur debts was exceeded only by his reluctance to repay them; the list of his creditors was long and distinguished—distinguished too, as time went on, by increasing impatience with his dilatory tactics and by increasing conviction that he must be forced into a realization of his obligations. The fact that American consent was sought before giving Castro his richly deserved chastisement is a tribute both to the adult status of the United States and to increasing world recognition of its dogma. As early as December, 1901, a German memorial to the Department of State indicated the possibility of forcible measures against Venezuela, disclaiming any intention of permanent occupation. John Hay's memorandum of December 16 quoted Roosevelt's first annual message to the effect that the United States did "not guarantee any State against punishment if it misconducts itself, provided that punishment does not take the form of the acquisition of territory by any non-American power." This, it should be noted, is the only actual connection of the Monroe Doctrine with the Venezuela episode; the subsequent story deserves brief recital because of its implications for Roosevelt's other, and greater, contribution to the Doctrine.

A year passed between the first German representations and actual action against Castro; meantime Britain and Italy joined the protesting nations. In December, 1902, a blockade was followed by bombardment of ports and seizure of ships. Castro quickly gave up and asked Roosevelt to propose arbitration by the American Minister to Venezuela. The President forwarded the request to London and Berlin (December 12, 1902) without comment. The suggestion appealed to the British and within a week both powers had accepted the principle of arbitration, which was eventually effected through the Hague Tribunal.[30] Since the Roosevelt Corollary is the logical con-

---

[30] Years later during the War of 1914–1918, W. R. Thayer asked Roosevelt to describe the events of 1902 for a biography of Hay, then in preparation. Thayer's suggestion that any evidence of "German duplicity and evil plotting . . . could not fail to help the American patriotic cause," plus the anti-German feeling of the day, stimulated Roosevelt into a highly colored account in which it appeared that he had personally bulldozed a reluctant Germany into arbitration by threats of naval reprisals in the Caribbean. The fact that his account gave no dates, and was not supported by evidence in *Die Grosse Politik*, the great collection of German archives published after the war, led historians to scorn it as a typical bit of Theodorian bombast. While no categorical statement is possible, gradually cumulating evidence seems to indicate

sequence of this reference to the Hague Court, it is not too much to say that it was the most significant aspect of the episode. Forcible Anglo-American intervention to collect debts had thus been given legal sanction. The Caribbean being what it was, repeated interventions might be expected, to the ultimate danger of the prospective isthmian canal. What more logical then, than that the United States, fearful of the effects of intervention on its Panama preserves, should assume responsibility for Caribbean stability, even to the point of itself intervening to forestall the necessity of European intervention? Of the logic of the above argument there can be no doubt; of its logical connection with the Doctrine as originally conceived there is no evidence. Logic and evidence, however, were not to stand in Roosevelt's way.[31]

Events of 1904, long preparing in the unhappy history of Santo Domingo, called forth the Roosevelt Corollary, one of the most vigorous and certainly the least creditable glosses upon Monroe's dictum, and a reflection of advancing American pretensions in the Caribbean.[32] The Dominican Republic, eastward portion of Columbus' Isle of Hispaniola, suffered a fiscal malady similar to Venezuela's of some months earlier. Her debt of over $32,000,000 was serviced

---

the possibility of a Rooseveltian threat. Such evidence will be found in Dennis, *op. cit.*; H. F. Pringle, *Theodore Roosevelt, a Biography*, Harcourt, Brace, 1931; T. A. Bailey, *A Diplomatic History of the American People*, Crofts, 1946, 3rd ed.; and S. A. Livermore, "Theodore Roosevelt, the American Navy, and the Venezuelan Crisis of 1902–1903," *American Historical Review*, vol. 51 (1946), pp. 452–471. Livermore points out that on December 18 John Hay warned the German chargé that "unless Germany quickly reached on agreement on arbitration, Congress might adopt a resolution directing the President to look to the preservation of the Monroe Doctrine." While having no direct bearing on Roosevelt's veracity, the comment throws interesting light on the story, since the contemporary situation was such that no such resolution would have been likely unless inspired from the White House.

[31] Perkins notes how willing the British were to have things go as they did. In a conversation some time later Roosevelt pointed out to the British Ambassador that the American people opposed the forcible collection of debts. The Ambassador replied: "I supposed in that case he would be ready to police the whole American Continent and prevent the general repudiation which would most likely follow any declaration by the United States of such a policy." Roosevelt took the bait beautifully by asserting: "That is just why I took the lines I did in my two messages." Here is the background of the Police Power Corollary. See also Bemis, *Lat. Am. Pol. of U.S.*, pp. 151–152.

[32] It should be noted that between Roosevelt's two pronouncements on the Doctrine events of 1903 had committed his Administration to the construction of a Panama Canal, thus making the United States sensitive to any untoward Caribbean developments.

mainly by customs receipts which were pledged, customs house by customs house, to various creditors; default permitted creditors to demand control of customs houses. Increasing political instability in 1904 increased the likelihood of default which in turn might lead to what would amount to intervention, with consequent violation of the Monroe Doctrine. Matters came to a focus in the autumn when the debts payable to an American firm, the San Domingo Improvement Company, were given a preferred position as compared with the other creditors. The vigorous protests of these other creditors foreshadowed intervention and forced Roosevelt to seek a solution, which he found in stretching the Monroe Doctrine to cover the facts. His message of December 6, 1904 contained the Roosevelt or Police Power Corollary which established the United States as the policeman of the Caribbean:[33]

If a nation shows that it knows how to act with reasonable efficiency and decency in social and political matters, if it keeps order and pays its obligations, it need fear no interference from the United States. Chronic wrongdoing, or an impotence which results in a general loosening of the ties of civilized society, may in America, as elsewhere, ultimately require intervention by some civilized nation, and in the Western Hemisphere the adherence of the United States to the Monroe Doctrine may force the United States, however reluctantly, in flagrant cases of such wrongdoing or impotence, to the exercise of an international police power.

As things had been developing, some such situation was probably the inevitable alternative to repeated interventions, intolerable in the light of the Panama Policy. To support it by the Monroe Doctrine, however, was taking liberties; as Perkins points out, Roosevelt transformed the Doctrine from one of nonintervention by Europe to one of intervention by the United States. This idea had been partially outlined by Polk in the 1840's and approached repeatedly in succeeding years;[34] its full emergence stemmed from the exuberant na-

---

[33] The message repeated the substance of a letter of May 20, 1904, to Elihu Root, designed for publication. Text is found in *Congressional Record*, 58th Cong., 3d Sess., p. 19. J. F. Rippy, "The Initiation of the Customs Receivership in the Dominican Republic," *Hispanic American Historical Review*, vol. 17 (1937), pp. 419–457, describes how Santo Domingo's customs passed under American control. Detailed discussion of this will be reserved for the section on the Caribbean.

[34] J. F. Rippy, *The Caribbean Danger Zone*, Putnam, 1940, pp. 42–53.

tionalist attitude of the early twentieth century. European creditors
received it as a comforting assurance of fiscal security. Latin America
tardily but all too surely learned that it merely substituted one kind
of intervention for another; as financial protectorates followed in
procession, the Colossus of the North, the United States, came to be
regarded as the nearer, and so the worse, of possible evils. The passing years saw the Corollary and its results become the great obstacle
to that inter-American solidarity which many were trying so hard to
cultivate. Gradually the advantages of solidarity outgrew the necessities of security and the Corollary was abandoned. Immediately,
however, Roosevelt had gone far, carrying a big stick, but not walking softly.

The Doctrine was collaterally connected with the Magdalena Bay
Episode of 1912, also an outgrowth of isthmian policy.[35] This lonely
harbor and its hinterland, lying not far from the lower tip of Southern California and within striking distance of the Canal, had been
the scene of successive and increasingly unsuccessful attempts at exploitation by American interests. Its current owners entered negotiations for disposing of their rights to a Japanese syndicate. Inquiry at
the Department of State elicited an opinion sufficiently discouraging
to end the incident, had not Senator Lodge got wind of it. He asserted (February 29, 1912) that a foreign power had been indirectly
seeking control of an American harbor. This stimulated the hair-
trigger Japanophobia of William Randolph Hearst and a furore resulted, despite proper denials of improper intent by all parties concerned.

Eventually a Senate resolution proposed that the Government
view with "grave concern" the possession of strategically important
areas "by any corporation or association which has such a relation to
another Government, not American, as to give that Government
practical power of control for national purposes." In the debate
Lodge said that the resolution was "merely a statement of policy,
allied to the Monroe Doctrine, of course, but not necessarily dependent upon it or growing out of it," and could be based independ-

---

[35] T. A. Bailey, "The Lodge Corollary to the Monroe Doctrine," *Political Science
Quarterly*, vol. 48 (1933), pp. 220–239.

ently on the principle of national self-preservation. He had earlier stated, however, that he desired to extend the Monrovian definition of "colonization" to cover foreign companies as well as foreign nations, and this extension, as well as the application to Asia, together called the Lodge Corollary, was acted upon by the Department of State on several occasions. Thus since 1912 the prohibition on colonization has included acquisition by seizure, by voluntary cession (Yucatan), and control through corporations.

The Doctrine played some role in Woodrow Wilson's valiant but vain efforts to establish a society of nations. His address to the Senate on essential peace terms (January 22, 1917) adopted the broad support of self-determination which Madison had suggested to Monroe in 1823:[36] "I am proposing, as it were, that the nations should with one accord adopt the doctrine of President Monroe as the doctrine of the world: that no nation should seek to extend its polity over any other nation or people, but that every people should be left free to determine its own polity, its own way of development, unhindered, unthreatened, unafraid, the little along with the great and powerful." This support of self-determination everywhere was continued in the last of his Fourteen Points, wherein he proposed an association of nations "for the purpose of affording mutual guarantees of political independence and territorial integrity to great and small states alike," and in Article 10 of the Covenant of the League of Nations, in which the members undertook "to respect and preserve as against external aggression the territorial integrity and existing political independence of all Members of the League." Its position was, presumably, both recognized and further safeguarded by Article 21: "Nothing in this Covenant shall be deemed to affect the validity of international engagements such as Treaties of Arbitration, or regional understandings like the Monroe Doctrine for securing the maintenance of peace."

Senator Lodge and the isolationist majority, however, interpreted membership in the League as an abandonment and repudiation of the Doctrine. Lodge stated on February 28, 1919, that "If we put aside forever the Washington policy [he had been discussing the

---

[36] *Record,* 64th Cong., 2d Sess., p. 1743.

Farewell Address] in regard to our foreign relations we must always remember that it carries with it the corollary known as the Monroe Doctrine. Under the terms of this league draft reported by the committee of the peace conference the Monroe Doctrine disappears." And the fourth of the proposed Senate reservations refused to "submit for arbitration or inquiry by the assembly or the council of the League of Nations provided for in said treaty of peace any questions which in the judgment of the United States Senate depend upon or relate to its long-established policy, commonly known as the Monroe Doctrine; said doctrine is to be interpreted by the United States alone, and is hereby declared to be wholly outside the jurisdiction of said League of Nations and entirely unaffected by any provision contained in the said treaty of peace with Germany." By adopting this reservation and defeating the League-burdened treaty the isolationists preserved to their own satisfaction the integrity of the Doctrine.

Latin America Grows Restive

From the early 1920's until the world picture began to darken under the clouds of dictatorship in the 1930's the Monroe Doctrine was a family problem among the American nations, since the likelihood of a dangerous outside challenge to American security seemed remote. Like many family problems it turned on the desire of the younger members to share in something previously the exclusive possession of the senior member. As Latin America approached maturity its nations came to resent the increasingly interventionist aspects of the Monroe Doctrine and to demand a share in its interpretation and enforcement. The United States, like many elder brothers, for long insisted on a monopoly, but presently the pressure reached such a point as to endanger another cherished family project, Pan-Americanism, upon which the United States had lavished much time and attention. It finally became apparent that insistence upon the Monroe Doctrine was making successful Pan-Americanism impossible of achievement, and adjustments were made accordingly.

The fifth Pan-American Congress at Santiago (1923) saw an attempt to put the Doctrine on an international basis sharply rebuffed by the American delegation. Secretary of State Charles Evans

Hughes soon attempted (in speeches at Philadelphia, August 30, and at Minneapolis, November 30) the difficult task of reassuring his southern neighbors and of emphasizing the Doctrine's unilateral character. While denying that it was aggressive or that it looked to a protectorate over Latin America, he insisted that it was "distinctively the policy of the United States," which nation "reserves to itself its definition, interpretation, and application." Such a policy "implies neither suspicion nor estrangement. It simply means that the United States is asserting a separate national right of self-defense, and that in the exercise of this right it must have an unhampered discretion." This attempt at mollification did not obscure continued insistence upon the right of intervention, chief source of Latin American hostility. The only mitigating circumstance was that both pronouncements narrowed the scope of intervention to the Caribbean area so crucial to the control of the canal.

Landing of marines in Nicaragua late in 1926 alarmed Latin America anew, though the executive did not invoke the Doctrine in support of the action. Thus when the sixth Pan-American Conference assembled at Havana in 1928 nothing reassuring had been added to the record. Here, although the Doctrine was studiously kept out of the debates, much was said about the abstract legal question of the right of intervention in international law, and Mr. Hughes, chairman of the American delegation (Frank B. Kellogg was now Secretary of State), was made amply aware of Latin American hostility to the practice. This strong feeling impelled Hughes to make an extraconference statement justifying but deprecating the existing interventions in Haiti and Nicaragua: "We have no desire to stay. . . . We entered to meet an imperative but temporary exigency; and we shall retire as soon as it is possible." Within a few weeks he himself was calling the Doctrine a "cover for extravagant utterances and pretensions," and in January, 1929, the Senate condemned the Roosevelt Corollary.

The United States Retreats

Meantime Secretary Kellogg had requested and Undersecretary J. Reuben Clark had prepared a historic Memorandum on the Doctrine, submitted December 17, 1928, and published in 1930. It repudiated the Roosevelt Corollary and thus cut out one of the sorest spots in inter-American relations, the claim to a right of intervention under the Doctrine; this while still maintaining the Doctrine's effectiveness against European intervention and not abandoning the inherent right of intervention for national security or self-preservation:

> The Doctrine states a case of United States *vs.* Europe, not of United States *vs.* Latin America. . . . The so-called "Roosevelt corollary" was to the effect, as generally understood, that in case of financial or other difficulties in weak Latin American countries, the United States should attempt an adjustment thereof lest European Governments should intervene, and intervening should occupy territory—an act which would be contrary to the principles of the Monroe Doctrine . . . it is not believed that this corollary is justified by the terms of the Monroe Doctrine, however much it may be justified by the application of the doctrine of self-preservation.[37]

Since 1930 there has been no right of intervention under the Doctrine.

Latin American skeptics doubted northern good intentions in spite of Franklin D. Roosevelt's inaugural statement of good neighborliness.[38] Action taken at the seventh Pan-American Conference at Montevideo late in 1933 helped to silence these by embodying in Article 8 of a Convention on the Rights and Duties of States a formula denying to any State the right "to intervene in the internal or external affairs of another." Together with the Clark Memorandum this helped to quiet Latin American fears of intervention; there remained vestiges of suspicion, however, since Secretary of State Cordell Hull had insisted upon attaching some reservations to the Montevideo agreement. Roosevelt shortly (December 28, 1933) forecast his government's acquiescence in what Latin America had long been

---

[37] J. Reuben Clark, *Memorandum on the Monroe Doctrine*, Government Printing Office, 1938.

[38] Subsequent developments may be traced through the following: Dexter Perkins, "The Monroe Doctrine Up to Date," *loc. cit.*, vol. 20 (1942), pp. 253–265; "The Monroe Doctrine To-Day," *Yale Review*, vol. 30 (1941), pp. 686–702; Bemis, *Lat. Am. Pol. of U.S.*, pp. 269–294; F. O. Wilcox, "The Monroe Doctrine and World War II," *loc. cit.*, vol. 36 (1942), pp. 433–453; and Joseph L. Kunz, "The Inter-American Treaty of Reciprocal Assistance," *American Journal of International Law*, vol. 42 (1948), pp. 111–120.

urging—the continentalization of the Doctrine. Speaking to the Woodrow Wilson Foundation he announced that "The maintenance of constitutional government in other Nations is not a sacred obligation devolving upon the United States alone," and that the breakdown of orderly governmental processes in any country "becomes the joint concern of a whole continent in which we are all neighbors."

Another step was taken at the Inter-American Conference for the Maintenance of Peace, assembled at Roosevelt's suggestion in December, 1936, at Buenos Aires. This completed the adoption of non-intervention in a Protocol (December 23, 1936) which declared "inadmissible the intervention of *any one* of them, directly or indirectly, and for whatever reason, in the internal or external affairs of any other of the Parties." (Italics added.) This protocol, be it noted, abandoned the Hull reservations to the Montevideo agreement. A Convention for the Maintenance, Preservation and Re-Establishment of Peace (of the same date) called (without providing any machinery) for "consultation" between the American states in case the peace of the Americas was threatened. Implementation was provided in the Declaration of Lima (December 24, 1938), adopted after Hitler's moves in Austria had alarmed the world. The Declaration called for consultation, by invitation of any of them, among the Prime Ministers of the American nations. With the coming of the War two such meetings were held, at Panama (September 23–October 3, 1939) and at Havana (July 21–30, 1940), which last declared that "any attempt on the part of a non-American State against the integrity or inviolability of the territory, the sovereignty, or the political independence of an American State shall be considered as an act of aggression against the States which sign this declaration." Such an emergency might be met with proper defensive action by any American State. From the war also emerged the Act of Chapultepec (March, 1945) which specified the "use of armed force to prevent or repel aggression." This Act, binding for the duration of the war, also called for the negotiation of a permanent treaty of a similar character after the war's conclusion.

Actual drafting of this agreement was postponed until after the

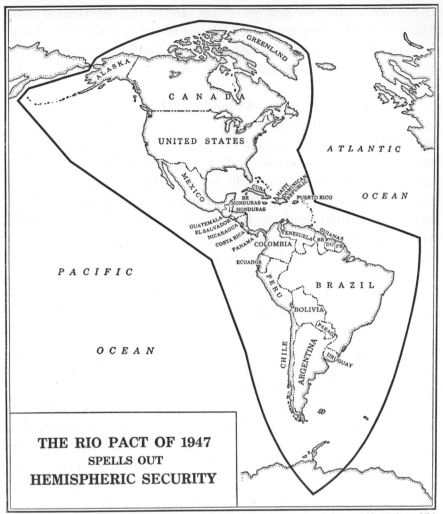

THE RIO PACT OF 1947
SPELLS OUT
HEMISPHERIC SECURITY

(*Adapted from* Major Problems of the United States Foreign Policy, 1948–1949, p. 87.)

establishment of the United Nations, and the Inter-American Defense Treaty signed at Rio de Janeiro, September 2, 1947, was a prototype of regional agreements under Article 51 of the United Nations Covenant. It established, on a solidly founded treaty basis, the obligation of mutual defense against aggression from outside the hemisphere, or by one American State against another. When it was ratified by the requisite number of nations and became effective on

December 3, 1948, the process of continentalizing the Monroe Doctrine was finally completed; the Colossus of the North was bound as firmly, but much more willingly, than any Gulliver, and the hovering fear of intervention from within or without was exorcised by agreement.

It remains only to chronicle sundry unilateral expansions of the Doctrine brought about by the developing world crisis. Even before Munich Roosevelt had brought Canada under the Doctrine's protection when at Kingston, Ontario, he declared (August 18, 1938) that his country "would not stand idly by" were the Dominion attacked. The circumstances of the destroyers-for-bases deal announced on September 3, 1940, made it clear that Bermuda and Newfoundland were also included within its shelter and when in April, 1941, protection of Greenland was assumed under an agreement with Denmark's Minister in Washington, the Doctrine was specifically invoked. Thus while its enforcement was being continentalized, its application was being broadened.

This chronicle of the Doctrine ends as it began, in an effort to maintain American independence of outside aggression. Its development has mirrored in some measure that of the nation which has sponsored it. It was born of the young nation's insecurity and fear lest disturbances in neighboring areas endanger its own safety; initially it succeeded less because of the nation's own strength than because its interests partly coincided with those of a stronger power. Once the immediate emergency was past, the Doctrine was conveniently unused for years. Then followed a long and slow development followed by a sudden and rapid expansion in which the nation, now vigorous and powerful but still wary of its own security, used the Doctrine as a bludgeon to keep its less thrifty neighbors from laying themselves open to outside attack. Aware, presently, of the ill will thus created, the nation, even more vigorous and powerful, first denied itself the use of the bludgeon and then merged the Doctrine's security functions into a partnership of enforcement against aggression from within or without.

9 Mexico and Her Northern Neighbor

ELATIONS BETWEEN THE UNITED STATES AND MEXICO
have followed an intimate but changing pattern. Mexican independence (recognized in 1823) found the republics not too far apart in population and territory; their cultural heritage was widely disparate. In Mexico a white minority governed a huge majority of Indians and mixed-blood *mestizos* in the Spanish tradition of overlordship and subservience; to the north an Anglo-Saxon tradition of self-government had provided the base for a stable polity advancing by evolutionary change. This was foreign to the Latin background of Mexican life—where, indeed, experience in self-government long bred disorder instead of improvement. This meant that, once territorial relationships had been stabilized, Mexico receded into the position of a supplier of raw materials and staples and thus fell a prey to exploiters from above the border. There ensued a period in which United States capital was protected by a Mexican regime of iron repression. Revolution loosed the pent-up Mexican energies in 1910 and sent investors scurrying to Washington seeking protection for their interests against the encroachments of a Mexican government increasingly sensitive to its own rights and the social welfare of its people. External pressure to protect foreign interests not only antagonized Mexico but jeopardized inter-American relations; hence for years United States policy walked an uneasy tightrope with the balance being gradually shifted southward by advancing Mexican nationalism. Finally the need to maintain wartime hemispheric solidar-

ity brought Mexican emancipation from foreign domination underway since 1920.[1]

The War with Mexico

James K. Polk must have heard the echo of John Tyler's amused
chuckles when he entered the White House on March 4, 1845; three
days earlier Tyler's signature to the joint resolution annexing Texas
had accomplished half of Polk's annexationist program. Less amus-
ing was the Mexican threat that annexation would constitute valid
grounds for war. Polk's campaign slogan, "Fifty-four Forty or Fight,"
had already committed him to the possibility of one war; another
might be one too many. He therefore despatched John Slidell on
what was to be an honest but futile attempt to settle the Texas question short of war.[2] Brief comment should be made here on changing
interpretations of the Mexican War. For many years Whig historians
of a Democratic war pictured the United States as a huge power
bullying a helpless Mexico. Latterly, however, a revisionist school
has found a vigorous spokesman in Justin H. Smith.[3] Without attempting to be dogmatic on the ethical justification of war, the facts
warrant the conclusion that Mexican incompetence contributed to
grievances which would have tried a man even more honestly patient than Polk, and that, however peacefully inclined the United
States might have been, Mexico was definitely bent on war.

Mexican treatment of American citizens heads the list of grievances. Many Americans found themselves in trouble with Mexican
authorities; not infrequently the proceedings were terminated by
firing squads without benefit of trial. Most Americans so treated
richly merited their fate, but such precipitate Mexican action violated the established rules. Again, Mexico dealt arbitrarily and capri-
ciously with treaty-based trade rights. Last but longest-lived was

---

[1] Justin H. Smith, *The War with Mexico*, Macmillan, 1919, vol. 1, pp. 1–28, ably
describes differing popular backgrounds. Ernest Gruening, *Mexico and Its Heritage*,
Century, 1928, is an excellent popular account, while J. Fred Rippy, *The United
States and Mexico*, Knopf, rev. ed., 1931, and James Morton Callahan, *American
Foreign Policy in Mexican Relations*, Macmillan, 1932, are the standard narratives of
diplomatic relations.

[2] Louis M. Sears, *John Slidell*, University of North Carolina Press, 1925.

[3] Smith, *War with Mexico*, pp. 58–116.

Mexico's cavalier treatment of American claims. Trade with a politically unstable area incurred large risks and brought high rewards. When the risks interfered with the rewards, injured Americans sought ample recompense. Since the harried Mexicans could rarely make amends, the Americans sought governmental assistance in collecting their private claims. Steady pressure, increased from time to time, had failed to secure payment of claims which had been arbitrated and accepted as valid.

Available evidence also indicates that Mexican leaders viewed the possibility of war with equanimity if not with enthusiasm. Perhaps on the basis of performance in the War of 1812, American military prowess was viewed with some disdain; whereas Mexican training and experience in repeated domestic hostilities reënforced the normal human belief of the Mexicans in their own military valor. The likelihood that Texas would be the scene of battle seemed an advantage, since Mexico would there be fighting nearer home and on the defensive. Sectional and partisan differences over slavery seemed likely to prevent the United States from achieving unity in prosecution of a war. Finally, European desire for cotton and Anglo-American antagonism over Oregon might gain for Mexico an offer of mediation after some degree of military success. It is thus not too hard to agree with General Antonio López de Santa Anna's remark of 1847 that Mexico wanted a war.

Slidell's mission was hopeless from the start. He represented a nation whose desire for territory was unsatisfied and a President who, though he probably did not want war, did want Texas to extend to the Rio Grande River—a boundary some distance beyond the limits of effective Texan control and including a strip, between the Nueces and the Rio Grande, which had never been part of Texas. Slidell was accredited to a government whose hold on power was so precarious that any territorial concession was likely to cause a revolution that would bring its downfall. He was under instruction to agree to assume the unpaid claims, for which Mexico had already accepted responsibility, in return for a Rio Grande boundary for Texas; he was authorized to offer as much as $25,000,000 additional for varying portions of Mexican territory up to and including California. For some time after arrival he cooled his heels while the Government canvassed the probable consequences of receiving him and decided that the risks were too great. On December 21, 1845, he was told that he could not be received, since Mexico had only agreed to accept an agent to discuss outstanding problems, whereas his credentials were those of a minister plenipotentiary resuming full diplomatic relations. News of this perfectly legal but unwise decision caused Polk to order troops into the disputed area of Texas, greatly increasing the likelihood of trouble.

General Zachary Taylor began his advance on March 8, 1846, under orders to treat as a warlike act a Mexican crossing of the Rio Grande in force. He reached the river twenty days later. Slidell began his homeward journey while Taylor was on the march, and arrived in Washington May 8. Satisfactory adjustment of the Oregon boundary had removed the likelihood of hostilities with Britain; Slidell's report confirmed Polk's growing disposition toward war, and on May 9 a Cabinet meeting debated a war message but deferred action after two members had suggested that a declaration could be better supported following an act of Mexican aggression. That very day news arrived that Mexican forces had crossed the Rio Grande, attacked Taylor's troops, and shed American blood on American soil. The Cabinet met in evening session and decided upon war, and Polk and Secretary of the Navy George Bancroft spent the Sabbath drafting the war message which went to Congress on Monday the 11th and was promptly implemented by both Houses.

Taylor, without further formalities, crossed the river and began hostilities on Mexican soil, fighting the battle of Palo Alto the very day of Slidell's homecoming. This launched a thrust into northern Mexico which lasted until the winter of 1847, helped to make its leader into presidential timber, and was one of the war's principal if not decisive campaigns. The spring of 1847 saw another expedition landed at Vera Cruz under the command of General Winfield Scott. Its successful push inland brought it almost to the capital city by autumn and it too kindled presidential ambitions in its commander. It brought Mexico to the verge of defeat and induced peace negotiations.

The politics of the election of 1848 made the choice of a negotiator a delicate matter. Slidell, perhaps the logical choice, was unacceptable to Senator Thomas Hart Benton; no other prominent man (save possibly Secretary of State James Buchanan) could be chosen without offending Slidell's powerful faction. To minimize political reverberations, Polk chose an executive agent (not a fully accredited diplomatic representative, but qualified to act[4]) of relatively minor status, Nicholas P. Trist.[5] This remarkable man, after a career including West Point, legal study under Thomas Jefferson, and consular service at Havana, had become Chief Clerk in the Department of State. This position, while one of considerable responsibility (Trist acted as Secretary in Buchanan's absence), carried no political weight; Trist could be sent, as Polk proposed, as a civilian accompanying the army, and could thus await a favorable opportunity for negotiation without offending any powerful faction. Moreover, if Trist were not received, Buchanan could always head a full-fledged diplomatic mission. Trist's varied experience had not brought him a large share of humility; furthermore, his superiors placed him in a difficult position vis-à-vis General Scott, whose army he joined, bearing instructions and a sealed State Department despatch for the eyes of the Mexican Government. He was authorized to show both to Scott, but did not do so, only asking Scott to forward the despatch. The General, fighting a difficult campaign, in trouble with his service of supply, and suspicious of Polk, took umbrage at instructions from his immediate superior, Secretary of War William L. Marcy, authorizing Trist to order the suspension of hostilities when he considered the time was ripe for negotiation. To Scott this appeared to be placing a civilian superior to himself; he refused to forward the despatch. This initiated a vigorous correspondence which gave free rein to Trist's penchant for letter-writing. His masterpiece attained a length of thirty pages; Scott cooled his temper for a week before venturing to reply: "The Jacobin convention of France never sent to one of its armies in the field a more amiable and accomplished instrument. If you were armed with an ambulatory guillotine, you would be the personification of Danton, Marat, and St. Just, all in one."

---

[4] H. M. Wriston, *Executive Agents in American Foreign Relations*, Johns Hopkins Press, 1929, is the standard work on this subject.

[5] L. M. Sears, "Nicholas P. Trist, A Diplomat with Ideals," *Mississippi Valley Historical Review*, vol. 11 (1924), pp. 85–99.

The reconciliation between Scott and Trist which presently followed was as complete as the quarrel had been stormy. With failing military fortune, Santa Anna asked for an armistice and Trist presented the draft treaty which he had brought with him—his minimum territorial demand equaled Slidell's maximum: Surrender of territory included in New Mexico and Upper California. For this he might pay $15,000,000 in cash and the United States would assume claims up to $3,000,000. The cash payment could be doubled in return for the addition of Lower California and a right of way across the Mexican narrows at Tehuantepec. Santa Anna used the armistice to consolidate his position and submitted a counterproposition at variance with Trist's original proposal. The latter agreed to transmit this to Washington. While this was being done hostilities were renewed and Scott occupied Mexico City (September 14, 1847). Trist's lack of progress and his willingness to ignore his instructions caused Polk to order him home (October 6, 1847) in terms precluding any further negotiation after receipt of the notice. Trist took the recall in good faith but circumstances prevented immediate departure; presently a renewed opportunity for negotiation presented itself and Trist boldly decided to ignore his recall in the interest of a prompt settlement.

On February 2, 1848 (gold was discovered in California on January 24), he signed a treaty at Guadalupe Hidalgo, site of a famed shrine to the Virgin near Mexico City. The treaty tallied closely with his original instructions: Mexico surrendered about half her territory, including Texas to the Rio Grande and all or part of the present States of California, Nevada, Arizona, Utah, New Mexico, Colorado, and Wyoming. The cash payment was $15,000,000 and the amount to be assumed for claims was raised to $3,250,000. It seems likely that one reason for agreeing to this relatively modest acquisition of land was Trist's belief that Polk wanted all of Mexico; Trist would forestall such a complete conquest. Polk did not want all of Mexico, though many Americans of his day did, and the relatively prompt passage of Trist's treaty doubtless helped to thwart their plans. Curiously enough, the chief opponents of the all-of-Mexico drive were southern slaveholders who felt that the area would not prove hospitable to the institution of slavery, while its supporters were New

Yorkers who hoped for Mexican markets and eastern devotees of Manifest Destiny.[6] Trist's conduct angered Polk but his treaty was generally acceptable, since it conformed to his original instructions and was in line with Polk's own wishes; refusing it would invite Whig reprisals. Moreover, new negotiations would take time which would play into the hands of the all-of-Mexico group. Polk sent the treaty to the Senate, which approved it with slight changes (March 10, 1848), thus confirming Mexican dismemberment and completing, with the Oregon treaty of 1846, the nation's advance to the Pacific.

It soon became apparent, however, that not enough territory had been secured. The 1850's witnessed feverish agitation over the choice of a route for a railway to the Pacific empire, since ideas and institutions would travel over the rails as well as goods and gold. Furthermore, embarrassing questions had arisen over Article 11 of the Treaty of Guadalupe Hidalgo which obliged the United States to restrain or punish Indian invasions of Mexican territory. Surveys indicated that the best southern railway route lay through the Mesilla Valley, in territory whose ownership had not been settled, and south of the Gila River, an area unquestionably Mexican.[7] James Gadsden, a railroad expansionist, went as Minister to Mexico to make a deal. Here Santa Anna, impecunious as ever, was back in power for the time being and willing to sign (December 30, 1853) a treaty selling 19,000,000 desert acres in southern New Mexico and Arizona essential for the railway route and adjusting the problems arising out of Indian depredations. The Senate cut $5,000,000 from the agreed $15,000,000. This completed major boundary adjustments and stabilized the territorial relationships between the two republics.

Seward and Napoleon

The Civil War provides the backdrop for the next important episode of Mexican-American relations. Seward's suspicion of European motives relative to Mexico developed before hostilities broke out, and he declined the invitation to join France, Britain, and Spain in de-

---

[6] J. D. P. Fuller, *The Movement for the Acquisition of All Mexico, 1846–1848,* Johns Hopkins Press, 1936.

[7] P. N. Garber, *The Gadsden Treaty,* University of Pennsylvania Press, 1923.

manding payment of Mexican debts (December 4, 1861). Since the
Monroe Doctrine had not as yet been invoked to prevent coercion of
American states, the powers exacted promises, after which Britain
and Spain withdrew. Napoleon III, an upstart whose promises were
not equaled by his performance, sought to distract his people's attention by foreign adventure; he kept troops in Mexico and presently
(October, 1863) offered a Mexican throne to Prince Maximilian of
Habsburg. The year 1863 was no time to say much about this violation of the Monroe Doctrine, so Seward replied softly to Napoleon's
request for recognition of his puppet, saying that since there was
still opposition to Maximilian Seward's government preferred to err
on the side of caution. An aroused public opinion began, after the
conclusion of hostilities, to connect Napoleon with the Monroe Doctrine. Military leaders were also urging action, and General Philip
Sheridan was sent to Texas with 50,000 seasoned troops; by the autumn of 1865 Seward applied such pressure that Napoleon informed
the American Minister on Christmas Eve that he expected his forces
out of Mexico by the following autumn. On February 12, 1866, Seward delivered a virtual ultimatum: "we shall be gratified when the
Emperor shall give to us . . . definitive information of the time
when French military operations may be expected to cease in Mexico," and announcement of prospective French withdrawal followed
on April 5, 1866. It seems likely that this would have happened without Seward's pressure, since French taxpayers were beginning to
resent the heavy military expenditures involved in keeping Maximilian's throne secure. Seward had meantime resumed diplomatic relations with the fugitive government of Benito Juárez as a tactic in his
pressure on Napoleon. Maximilian's death before a Juárista firing
squad (June 19, 1867) completed the tale except for meeting the
ensuing Austrian resentment. Mexican-American relations were free
to seek their own level once more.

Wilson and Mexico

From a decade of confusion compounded of border quarrels, Indian
raids, smugglers, and bandits emerged the figure of Porfirio Diaz,
whose power and sense of international responsibility increased until

his government was recognized in 1876.[8] His regime, one of iron dictatorship and economic realism, placed Mexico accurately in the scheme of things: As a land rich in staple and raw materials but poor in capital, she must for a long time depend upon outside capital to finance the extractive industries which were her chief birthright; only assurance of political stability, for which Mexico had not previously been noted, would bring such capital in adequate volume. Diaz made Mexico safe, and the money rolled in. There followed what Professor J. Fred Rippy has called the era of Pacific Penetration during which, under favorable legislative and administrative measures, two billion foreign dollars, half of them from north of the border, went into Mexican land, cattle, railways, mines, and oil, until the land hummed with activity.

The land presently hummed also with discontent, as Diaz' policy conferred few economic, social, or cultural benefits on the common man. This common man was generally too downtrodden and inarticulate to speak for himself, but during the first decade of the twentieth century he began to find spokesmen whose voices inveighed against Diaz and the foreigner whose interest he had served so long. When political security was threatened, Diaz' experience suggested only repressive measures which in turn bred violent revolution. Such a revolution flared up in November, 1910, and culminated in Diaz' resignation, May 25, 1911. The spearhead of this revolt was Francisco I. Madero, who became President late in 1911. Most writers to date have dismissed Madero as a visionary political reformer whose concept of the revolution did not encompass the social and economic dynamics which later characterized it.[9] Whatever his vision, Madero's days as President were short and full of trouble: Revolution was brewing before he was firmly in the saddle; his foreign relations were always precarious; and his career was cut short early in 1913

---

[8] Pauline S. Relyea, *Relations between the United States and Mexico under Porfirio Diaz, 1876–1910*, Smith College, 1924. Rippy's is the best account of the infiltration of American capital into Mexico.

[9] A reinterpretation of Madero, pointing out that he was not unaware of these larger aspects, but believed that political reform must pave the way for them, is contained in Charles C. Cumberland, *Francisco I. Madero, Revolutionary* (unpublished dissertation, the University of Texas, 1949). The distance between peasant realities and even the first step toward political democracy is aptly if perhaps apocryphally

by assassination at the hands of agents of General Victoriano Huerta, who seized power and held it until July 15, 1914.

The alarm of United States investors at these events requires no elaboration. Their fears, and interests, were well served by the American Ambassador, Henry Lane Wilson, who opposed Madero from the beginning and greatly encouraged his enemies; he was in close touch with Huerta at the time of Madero's overthrow. The Taft administration had meantime followed the normal policy of de facto recognition of Madero; as his power waned it took to scolding him, on Wilson's recommendation. Since Huerta at first seemed likely to favor foreign capital, Wilson promptly recommended that he be recognized. Taft, now a "lame duck," hesitated to commit his successor to a Mexican policy; Wilson was sternly admonished to take no steps without specific instructions. Thus at Woodrow Wilson's inauguration Mexican relations needed clarification. American business, and the American Ambassador, favored Huerta; what would Wilson do?

He decided that the Mexican problem was larger than his countrymen's dollar investment.[10] It was intimately connected with the larger problem of Latin American relations, on which Wilson had formulated his ideas by March 11, 1913, evidently without consulting Secretary of State William Jennings Bryan or holding the exploratory conversations with the larger southern powers usually preliminary to such important pronouncements. His policy would be one of coöperating only with such governments as rested upon the undoubted consent of the governed: "We hold . . . that just government rests always upon the consent of the governed. . . . We can have no sympathy with those who seek to seize the power of government to advance their own personal interests or ambition." Such a lofty ideal of responsible government accorded thoroughly with

---

illustrated by an anecdote retailed by Gruening, *op. cit.*, pp. 96–97. Two peons watching a *Maderista* demonstration were intrigued by the oft-repeated "Viva Madero! Viva la Democracia!" One queried the other "And what, *amigo*, is this *democracia* for which all are shouting?"

"Why, it must be the lady who accompanies him," replied the other, pointing to Madero's wife.

[10] From the voluminous Wilson bibliography the following titles add to those already cited: Ray Stannard Baker, *Woodrow Wilson: Life and Letters*, Doubleday, Page, 1927–1939, 8 vols.; S. A. MacCorkle, *The American Policy of Recognition Towards Mexico*, Johns Hopkins Press, 1933; Harley Notter, *The Origins of the Foreign Policy of Woodrow Wilson*, Johns Hopkins Press, 1937.

Wilson's philosophy; it departed sharply, however, from the de facto recognition policy which his country had pursued for over a century; by tacitly disapproving of Huerta it contributed immediately to the very disorders which Wilson so deplored. It pleased neither foreign investors nor Huerta. British investors, and Huerta, took some comfort when Britain recognized him; American investors vainly pushed Wilson in the same direction; and a long-simmering revolution under Venustiano Carranza was presently in full swing. Wilson posed, too, an ominous hint to Latin America that the "orderly processes of just government based upon law" would be subject to the unilateral interpretation of the United States.

Wilson's hands-off policy having produced no results by midsummer, Wilson, who had meantime recalled Ambassador Henry Lane Wilson, despatched as his personal representative ex-Governor John Lind of Minnesota, a faithful party member ignorant of Spanish and innocent of diplomatic experience, to tender friendly offices.[11] Bearing a remarkable letter of accreditation addressed "To Whom It May Concern," he modestly suggested (August 14, 1913) an immediate armistice, to be followed by an early and free election in which Huerta should not be a candidate; universal acceptance of its results would bring Wilsonian approval of a bankers' loan to Mexico. Huerta's sarcastic refusal (August 16) evoked from President Wilson a series of pronouncements eventually designed to force Huerta's resignation. Starting off on a moderate note Wilson told Congress (August 27) that "everything that we do must be rooted in patience and done with calm and disinterested deliberation. . . . While we wait, the contest of the rival forces will undoubtedly for a little while be sharper than ever, just because it will be plain that an end must be made of the existing situation, and that very promptly. . . ."[12] Application of a strict arms embargo accompanied this statement of the policy of "Watchful Waiting."[13] Despite renewed demands for intervention by domestic business interests, he reiterated at Mobile, Alabama (October 27), his belief in responsible government, taking oc-

---

[11] G. M. Stephenson, *John Lind of Minnesota,* University of Minnesota Press, 1935.
[12] *Foreign Relations of the U.S., 1913,* pp. 822–823.
[13] Elton Atwater, *American Regulation of Arms Exports,* Carnegie Endowment, 1941, p. 65 ff., covers the embargo aspects of American policy.

casion to assert that his country would never again seek to conquer territory. This was delivered in the face of Huerta's recent dissolution of Congress (October 10) and his triumphant, if farcical, election as President (October 26).

Wilson applied still sharper pressure on November 7 in a note proclaiming his "immediate duty to require Huerta's retirement from the Mexican Government. . . ." His hand was strengthened by a bargain made in mid-November whereby the British agreed to withdraw their recognition in return for repeal of domestic legislation exempting American coastwise shipping from paying tolls in the Panama Canal (see below, p. 254). On the 24th Secretary of State Bryan notified Huerta directly, through Nelson O'Shaughnessy, American Chargé d'Affaires, that "The present policy of the Government of the United States is to isolate General Huerta entirely; to cut him off from foreign sympathy and aid and from domestic credit, whether moral or material, and to force him out. . . ." Congress was informed (December 2) that "There can be no certain prospect of peace in America until Gen. Huerta has surrendered his usurped authority. . . ."

These representations left Huerta's armor undented; they brought American investors, who were losing huge sums, buzzing around Wilson's ears insisting that order was better for even the Mexican peon than the self-government which, thanks to Wilson's policy, was degenerating into anarchy. Humanitarians, also, deplored the scores of American lives being sacrificed on the altar of nonintervention. Early in 1914 Wilson lifted the arms embargo to permit munitions to reach Carranza, upon whom he was by this time beginning to pin his hopes, and stationed American naval units off Vera Cruz to hinder the entry of European shipments. However, it took two specific episodes and a complete severance of diplomatic relations to accomplish Huerta's final removal. On April 9, 1914, an unarmed boat's crew from the U.S.S. *Dolphin* approached Tampico (in the heart of the Mexican oil district) to secure supplies. Innocently entering a restricted area, they were arrested by Huerta's troops despite the cover of the United States flag. They were released promptly, with verbal apologies from a superior officer, but Admiral H. T. Mayo peremptorily demanded that the port commander apologize formally, promise to punish the responsible officer, and hoist the American flag ashore, giving it a twenty-one-gun salute. Mayo acted without consulting Washington, though communication was open, and opinion was divided as to his wisdom, some feeling that sufficient amends had been made; nevertheless it was felt that he must be supported, lest Huerta make capital of the incident.[14] That worthy succeeded in evading the salute, despite a warning that a refusal would probably result in intervention.

Congress granted (April 22) Wilson's request for permission to use force to secure redress of grievances, but meantime the Vera Cruz Incident (the night of April 20–21) resulted in an armed landing on Mexican soil. Informed that a German ship, the *Ypirango*, was approaching with munitions, Bryan advised Wilson to use the navy to prevent a landing. Secretary of the Navy Josephus Daniels consented, and on April 21 the customs house was occupied peaceably; resistance by naval cadets precipitated a skirmish, and bloodshed accompanied the subsequent occupation of the city.[15] Huerta promptly handed O'Shaughnessy his passports, completing a breach which he hoped would rally both friends and enemies to his cause. When this failed, his stock declined rapidly and Wilson gratefully accepted the proffered mediation of the A B C Powers, since the landing at Vera Cruz might well commit him to further intervention for which he had no desire. Huerta eventually (July 15, 1914) acted on a mediatory suggestion that he resign in favor of a government with which the United States could negotiate.

After months of struggle Carranza emerged in the forefront of the Mexican confusion. His de facto recognition (October 9, 1915) mended the breach existing since Henry Lane Wilson's departure early in 1913. Opposition continued, however, particularly by Pancho Villa in the north. Villa participated in the death of Americans on both sides of the border, shooting a number of mining engineers entering on invitation, with Carranza passports, at Santa Ysabel, and

---

[14] Josephus Daniels, *The Wilson Era: Years of Peace, 1910–1917*, University of North Carolina Press, 1944, pp. 186–191, gives the Secretary of the Navy's version of this episode; he believed that Mayo should have consulted Wilson.

[15] *Ibid.*, p. 192 ff.

being credited with repeated raids into Texas and New Mexico in the spring of 1916. The combination of territorial invasion and a presidential election threatened to create support for the interventionists and made Wilson's policy of abstention an extremely difficult one to follow. After the Santa Ysabel murders William E. Borah proclaimed in the Senate that he would "protect the American passport when issued at whatever cost. I would make even the fiends of Mexico know its worth," and many another Republican took up the cudgels to belabor Wilson's inactivity.

When a raid on Columbus, New Mexico (March 9, 1916), resulted in seventeen deaths, General John J. Pershing was ordered, with Carranza's reluctant consent, to pursue Villa into Mexico. The farther Pershing went the less hospitable was his reception, and he was finally told that if he moved south, or east, or west, he would be attacked. A skirmish at Carrizal cost several lives on both sides and rendered impossible further coöperation in chasing Villa. Despite numerous conferences no agreement could be reached, and Wilson finally withdrew the expeditionary force early in 1917 as war with Germany loomed large. Although at times driven to forcible measures, he had by and large held to his policy of nonintervention, even under severe pressure from domestic economic interests; his patient maneuverings averted war, however narrowly, and earned for him the grudging admiration of Latin America, as well as Carranza's defiance. American entry into the World War in April, 1917, pushed Mexican-American relations into the background, the while internal developments of a fundamental character were taking place to the south.

Carranza's Constitution

Under Carranza the pendulum of the Mexican revolution took a wide sweep. Madero's political liberalism had not had time to prove itself; Huerta's swing backward toward Diaz conservatism had been thwarted; underlying both was a ferment of hostility toward the three bulwarks of conservative control—the great landlord (foreigner and native *hacendado*), the Roman Church (also a great landlord), and the foreign capitalist. The Constitution of 1917 spelled out the urge to limit these elements, and to advance the

Mexican people, however haltingly, toward the realization of social, economic, and political goals. The great task of those who have guided Mexican-American relations since 1920 has been to balance the developing Mexican political and economic nationalism shown in this document against the threatened security of American business interests.

The document was formulated by a convention which assembled December 2, 1916, and was proclaimed on February 5, 1917. Though drafted under the aegis of a dictator, it contained many advanced ideas of social readjustment directed toward improvement of the hitherto submerged classes; it protected labor, guaranteed minimum wages, and provided social insurance. Most important to foreign investors was Article 27, designed to restore national control of the land and its subsoil minerals. It provided in part:[16]

The ownership of the lands and waters . . . is vested originally in the Nation, which has   . . the right to transmit title thereof to private persons, thereby constituting private property. . . .

In the Nation is vested the direct ownership of all minerals or substances [in the subsoil] . . . solid mineral fuel; petroleum, and all solid, liquid or gaseous hydro-carbons . . . the ownership of the Nation shall be inalienable and imprescriptible. . . .

Only Mexicans by birth or naturalization and Mexican corporations have the right to acquire ownership of lands, waters and their appurtenances, or to obtain concessions for working mines or for the utilization of waters or mineral fuel in the Republic of Mexico. The Nation may grant the same right to aliens, provided they agree before the Ministry of Foreign Relations to consider themselves as Mexicans in respect to such property, and bind themselves not to invoke the protection of their Governments in matters relating thereto; under penalty, in case of noncompliance, of forfeiture to the Nation of property so acquired.

Under no circumstances may foreigners acquire direct ownership of lands and waters within a zone of 100 kilometres along the frontiers and of 50 kilometres inland from the seacoast. . . .

Centres of population which have no ejidos or are unable to have same restored to them due to lack of title, impossibility of identifying such lands, or because they have been legally alienated, shall be granted sufficient lands, forests, and waters to constitute same, in accordance with their requirements . . . and for that purpose land shall be expropriated

---

[16] Quoted in N. L. Whetten, *Rural Mexico,* University of Chicago Press, 1948, pp. 616–622.

by the Federal Government and be taken from that adjacent to the villages in question. . . .

Landowners affected by resolutions already handed down granting or restoring ejido lands or waters to villages, or who may be affected by future resolutions shall enjoy no ordinary legal rights or recourse, and they cannot institute injunction proceedings. . . .

Provisions in Articles 3, 5, 27, and 130 looked to curtailing the economic position of the Church, subjecting it to state control, and sharply limiting foreign (Spanish) influence among its clergy.

Although most of these provisions became effective only after legislative implementation, their threat to cattle, mining, and petroleum interests was immediately apparent. Particularly disturbed were the owners of land purchased for its actual or potential subsoil content; they saw their prospective wealth being thus siphoned out of their pockets, and they were not consoled by the fact that this was largely a reversion to previous practice. Spanish colonial land grants had customarily and thriftily reserved subsoil gold and silver rights to the Crown. Mexico continued after independence to permit exploitation of subsoil products only on special grant and under careful regulation. In 1883, however, a constitutional amendment permitted Congress to pass mining codes, pursuant of which laws of 1884, 1892, and 1909 specified that ownership of the surface conferred control of subsoil *petroleum* and allied products. Armed with this favorable exception, huge amounts of foreign capital moved into Mexican oil; considerable development had already taken place, but much land remained unexploited. Unfavorably interpreted, the new Constitution would be a rude threat to holdings thus confidently secured during the Diaz regime. Article 27 contained still another threat: It proposed means of regaining state control over agricultural land in order to reëstablish the *ejidos* or communal holdings which had been the basis of rural life before the peasants sank into peonage. This endangered the holders, native or foreign, of any land suitable for agriculture, regardless of its subterranean treasures.

Mexico Comes of Age—Slowly

The World War over, the threatened vested interests began a campaign to stimulate American public and governmental opinion against Carranza who, in addition to his strange ideas about property, had been more than suspected of sympathy for the German cause. The pressure presently worked its way up to Congress, which became a sounding board for numerous anti-Carranza speeches. The most effective propaganda device, however, was the "Preliminary Report and Hearings" of a Senate committee headed by Albert B. Fall of New Mexico, soon to gain ill-repute as a tool of oil magnate Edward L. Doheny in the Teapot Dome Scandal of the 1920's. Thousands of pages paraded Carranza's sins of omission and commission in an effort to arouse support for a "strong" Mexican policy. With President Wilson still largely out of touch with affairs the interventionist group gained dangerous strength in the autumn of 1919, aided by the detention of W. O. Jenkins, an American consular agent, in a Mexican jail. A resolution for severance of diplomatic relations had been introduced into Congress before Wilson was informed of developments and called a halt. Carranza soon succumbed to his own deficiencies in carrying out his own constitution, and was overthrown and killed in 1920.

Following Taft's example, Wilson left to Warren G. Harding's administration the problem of dealing with Carranza's successor, General Alvaro Obregón, who rose to the top of a confused situation and was inaugurated President on December 1, 1920. It seems apparent that the early Hughes-Harding policy toward Obregón was dictated by deference to American economic interests; Obregón stoutly resisted this pressure for many months, and presently both sides saw political profit in a compromise, which was worked out in the Bucareli Agreements of August, 1923, whereby Obregón gained recognition and the oil companies temporary satisfaction.[17] As part of what the *Nation* called a policy of "Bumptious Bullying" the United States

---

[17] The following add pertinent information on the oil question, which becomes increasingly important during the subsequent story: R. B. Gaither, *Expropriation in Mexico: The Facts and the Law*, William Morrow, 1940, an attack on the policy; W. C. Gordon, *The Expropriation of Foreign-Owned Property in Mexico,* American Council on Public Affairs, 1941, particularly useful on the agrarian side; H. S. Person, *Mexican Oil: Symbol of Recent Trends in International Relations*, Harper, 1942; H. W. Briggs, "The Settlement of Mexican Claims Act of 1942," *American Journal of International Law*, vol. 37 (1943), pp. 222–232; and A. W. MacMahon and W. R. Dittmar, "The Mexican Oil Industry Since Expropriation," *Political Science Quarterly*, vol. 57 (1942), pp. 28–50, 161–189.

offered Obregón (May 27, 1921) a draft treaty of amity and commerce which he was supposed to accept as a condition precedent to recognition. Its crucial provisions sought to guarantee American property owners against loss through application of the land provisions of the Constitution of 1917, so far being implemented mainly through executive decrees rather than legislation. When Obregón delayed, Hughes announced that "when it appears that there is a Government in Mexico willing to bind itself to the discharge of primary international obligations, concurrently with that act its recognition will take place." Obregón replied via a message to his own Congress (September 20) refusing to purchase recognition at the risk of abandoning the Constitution, and later (November 19) listed the concessions which he was prepared to make. Months of controversy followed before the parties reached an agreement.

Meantime the Mexican courts, sensitive to executive wishes, rendered five decisions (the first on August 30, 1921) favorable to the oil companies. These held under Article 14 of the Constitution ("no law shall be given retroactive effect to the prejudice of any person. . . .") that Article 27 could not apply retroactively, and that the companies thus retained whatever rights of exploitation they had received from Diaz under the laws of 1884 and 1909. Obregón's practice followed the decisions, but the United States held off for some months. Continued refusal, however, subjected the Administration to attack, even from such staunch Republicans as Senator Borah, then Chairman of the Foreign Relations Committee. By the spring of 1923 both American and Mexican administrations were beginning to think about the next election, and each was willing to make some concession to stabilize relations. The result was a conference (May 14–August 15, 1923) between a Mexican delegation and John Barton Payne and Charles Beecher Warren, resulting in the Bucareli Agreement and the subequent recognition of the Obregón government (August 31, 1923). This was an executive agreement, not binding on succeeding chief executives, and represented a fairly successful Mexican effort to withstand the weakening northern pressure.

Obregón agreed that, subsequent to recognition, he would negotiate claims conventions covering (1) those arising since the last general arbitration of 1868; and (2) revolutionary claims accruing from 1910–1920. The American delegates also made some concessions regarding payment for land expropriated for the *ejido* system. The question of subsoil rights was the most important aspect of the negotiation. Here the Americans admitted the Mexican right to control resources, but insisted that such control could not be made retroactive, i.e., projected backward prior to May 1, 1917. Mexico agreed that the performance of a "positive act" prior to the 1917 date would confirm concessionaires in their rights. The agreed definition of a positive act was extremely liberal, conferring subsoil rights for "drilling, leasing, entering into any contract relative to the subsoil, making investments of capital in lands for the purpose of obtaining the oil in the subsoil, carrying out works of exploitation and exploration of the subsoil and in cases where from the contract relative to the subsoil it appears that the grantors fixed and received a price higher than would have been paid for the surface of the land because it was purchased for the purpose of looking for oil and exploiting the same if found. . . ."[18] Owners of land who had failed to perform such positive acts received a preferred position as against third parties.

It is important to remember that this was not a treaty engagement, but an executive agreement; its duration depended upon the good will of succeeding Presidents. Moreover, experience was to demonstrate that application of the positive acts doctrine made it possible for Mexico to recapture a very substantial portion of her unexploited oil regions. The Agreement, in fact, was followed by a tendency on the part of the oil companies to shift their explorations and investment toward South America.

Obregón was succeeded in 1924 by Plutarco Elias Calles, the strong man of the group which had overthrown Carranza and the man who was to control Mexican destinies from either front- or backstage until 1936. His administration, and that of Calvin Coolidge in the States, saw the last sharp conflict between the American Government, backing American vested interests, and the rising tide of Mexican nationalism. A combination of bad taste to the north and

[18] *Proceedings of the United States–Mexican Commission Convened at Mexico City, May 14, 1923*, Government Printing Office, 1925, p. 47.

aggressive action to the south stimulated the clash; it was softened
by a reversal of northern tactics and a modification of southern motives. It was followed by a long and sometimes painfully slow process of accommodation, with Mexican nationalism gradually realizing
many of its objectives under the influence of the Good Neighbor policy and the need for hemispheric solidarity in the face of totalitarian
aggression. The likelihood that Mexico would legislate on oil and
land in the spring of 1925 evidently alarmed the American Ambassador, James R. Sheffield, to a point where he sent disturbing reports
to Frank B. Kellogg, who had become Secretary of State in March.[19]
Kellogg loosed a public blast (June 12) designed to warn Mexico to
tread warily in relation to foreign capital and the maintenance of
internal peace:

it should be made clear that this Government will continue to support
the Government in Mexico only so long as it protects American lives and
American rights and complies with its international engagements and
obligations.

The Government of Mexico is now on trial before the world. We have
the greatest interest in the stability, prosperity and independence of
Mexico. We have been patient and realize, of course, that it takes time to
bring about a stable Government, but we cannot countenance violation of
her obligations and failure to protect American citizens.[20]

Calles' counterblast, equally and pardonably vigorous, evoked general domestic enthusiasm.

The Mexican Congress passed two laws in the autumn (to become
effective January 1, 1927) designed to implement Article 27 of the
Constitution, which had hitherto been enforced mainly by presidential decree. These reflect Calles' belief that he was not bound by the
Bucareli Agreements, and represent a fundamental departure from
the policy of those agreements toward foreign-owned property. The
Petroleum Law required foreign operators to exchange their supposedly permanent concessions before January 1, 1927, for others
limited to fifty years' duration; its definition of a positive act was less
liberal; and it contained a so-called "Calvo Clause" requiring alien

---

[19] D. Bryn-Jones, *Frank B. Kellogg: A Biography*, Putnam, 1937, pp. 171–185.
[20] New York *Times*, June 13, 1925.

corporations to waive their right of appeal to the home government in case of controversy with the Mexican authorities. When the larger oil companies failed to apply for the new concessions they found it increasingly difficult to secure drilling permits. The Land Law, designed to aid in breaking up the huge estates, implemented the constitutional prohibition on alien ownership of land within 100 kilometers of the frontier and 50 kilometers of the coast; it also applied a Calvo Clause to alien landowners. These laws, plus drastic anticlerical legislation, agitated property owners and Catholics north of the border as well as the government. The resultant barrage of correspondence ran through most of 1926, with the United States maintaining a consistently stiff attitude toward the Mexican legislation. The only concession made by Mexico, however, was a promise of reasonable enforcement, and the laws went into operation on January 1, 1927. Simultaneously Secretary Kellogg sent a memorandum on "bolshevik Aims and Policies in Mexico and Latin America" to the Senate Committee on Foreign Relations. It is perhaps significant to note that despite executive pressure a Senate resolution (January 27) unanimously recommended arbitration of the Mexican dispute.

The year 1927 witnessed important developments. The Mexican revolution was in a lull during which many of its leaders (Calles included) reaped the pecuniary rewards of their earlier military prowess, with consequent relaxation of their reforming zeal. To the north President Calvin Coolidge, after yielding for a time to the combined humanitarian, business, and religious pressures which sought stronger measures, shifted to a policy of "vigilant patience" (the phrase is Professor Rippy's). This resulted in the resignation of Sheffield and the appointment as Ambassador of Dwight W. Morrow, Coolidge's Amherst classmate and a highly successful partner in J. P. Morgan and Co., who began a three-year tour of duty in October.[21] His personal qualities soon placed him on excellent terms with President and people alike; he confirmed an initial good impression by stage-managing the Mexican appearance of Charles A. Lindbergh, fresh from his solo crossing of the Atlantic, and of that homespun philosopher Will Rogers, whose diverse talents had wide ap-

---

[21] Harold Nicolson, *Dwight Morrow*, Harcourt, Brace, 1935.

peal. In the intervals of these amenities he devoted himself to study-ing the Mexican situation in the light of the new and softer policy of his Government.

Morrow concluded that the day of threats was over and that the best prospect of success lay in persuading Mexican leadership to seek solutions within a purely Mexican framework. Working first on the oil problem, which he rightly regarded as the most pressing, he achieved considerable success. It will be remembered that the laws of 1925 had directed foreigners holding oil lands to apply for limited confirmatory concessions before January 1, 1927, on pain of forfei-ture. Few applications were made, but the government had not acted to void the remaining concessions. Following conversations between Morrow and Calles the Mexican Supreme Court mirrored an executive change of heart by declaring (November 17, 1927) that insistence upon limited concessions was confiscatory and that therefore sections 14 and 15 of the Petroleum Law were unconsti-tutional. The Mexican Congress was equally agreeable and on De-cember 26 adopted at Calles' suggestion a law (effective January 10, 1928) granting unlimited confirmatory concessions to lands on which the necessary positive acts had been performed prior to May 1, 1917. Thus by Morrow's efforts the status of oil had been secured against any attack except the ultimate step of expropriation.

Morrow also sought, less successfully, to compose the church-state differences which had become acute by 1927.[22] Here he achieved only a temporary amelioration. Calles' anticlerical measures had re-sulted in the clergy's repudiation of the Constitution, in refusal to register priests as demanded by the civil authorities, and in the sus-pension (in midsummer, 1926) of all public religious activities re-quiring the services of a priest. Since the church had been identified with the great landlords and the foreign interests which the Revolu-tion sought to curb, Morrow's task was a delicate one. After consid-erable progress his initial efforts were interrupted when a Catholic fanatic assassinated President-elect Obregón and he had to begin

---

[22] Walter Lippmann, "Church and State in Mexico: The American Mediation," *Foreign Affairs*, vol. 8 (1930), pp. 186–208, gives a sympathetic account of Morrow's efforts. C. L. Jones, "Roots of the Mexican Church Conflict," *Ibid.*, vol. 14 (1935), pp. 135–146, is less optimistic of Morrow's accomplishment.

anew. Ultimately (June, 1929), resumption of public worship was permitted under a considerable degree of state control. Morrow was unable to restrain permanently the anticlericalism of the Revolution, but his efforts here and in the oil situation stabilized Mexican-American relations for some time to come.

The Mexican swing to the right, mentioned above, continued through a succession of chief executives subservient to Calles, who registered his increasing conservatism by announcing (early in 1930) the failure and abandonment of the program of peasant communal landholdings. Toward the end of the term of Abelardo Rodríguez land distribution was revived, however, and in December, 1933, Calles proclaimed a Six-Year Plan as a goal for the next presidential term, which had been obligingly lengthened at his behest. Its leftward swing was rapidly accelerated after the inauguration (November 11, 1934) of Lázaro Cárdenas. This aggressive leader took the Six-Year Plan so seriously as to rouse the opposition of his sponsor, Calles, whom he promptly (1936) exiled.[23] His administration resembled that of Franklin D. Roosevelt in more than the accident of contemporaneity. Both moved leftward from their immediate predecessors; each was attentive to the interests of domestic labor; each in his own way was interested in the inter-American system, Roosevelt through the Good Neighbor Policy and Cárdenas through the nonintervention formula which his agent sponsored vigorously at Buenos Aires in 1936; both faced anxiously the world threat of totalitarianism. Circumstances developed from these factors which under the threat of war went far to remove the problems of the Revolution.

In his first three years Cárdenas outpaced the accomplishments of his combined predecessors since 1920. This was first apparent in the speed-up of land expropriations for ejidal holdings. A million acres

[23] The following, in addition to authorities already cited, throw light on Mexican-American relations in the late 'thirties and early 'forties: *Foreign Policy Reports*, August 1, 1937, August 15, 1937, August 15, 1938; W. H. Shepardson and W. O. Scroggs, *The United States in World Affairs: An Account of American Foreign Relations, 1937*, Harper, 1938, pp. 115–134; Hudson Strode, *Timeless Mexico*, Harcourt, Brace, 1944; Betty Kirk, *Covering the Mexican Front: The Battle of Europe versus America*, University of Oklahoma Press, 1943; W. O. Scroggs, "Mexican Anxieties," *Foreign Affairs*, vol. 18 (1940), pp. 266–279.

were seized at once in October, 1936, and before Cárdenas delivered his valedictory to Congress in September, 1940, he had distributed over 45,000,000 acres as against less than 17,500,000 acres previously given out. Since neither Cárdenas nor his predecessors had troubled much about compensation for these agricultural lands, a first-rate international problem was soon in the making. His Government's policy toward foreign-owned oil properties soon gave further cause for alarm. Late in 1936 the highly unionized industry engaged in a complicated dispute with its foreign owners involving demands for better wages and working conditions, union demands for a share in management, and insistence upon sharply increased social welfare benefits which the employers contended they were unable to meet. The dispute progressed wearily through conference and strike until it reached the Supreme Court. This body, rendered more than usually amenable to executive pressure by a law ending life tenure and making the judges' terms coincide with that of the President appointing them, awarded the workers wage and benefit increments amounting to 26,329,393 pesos annually. The Government's attitude had been obviously sympathetic toward the workers' interests, whether or not, as has been suggested, it was deliberately taking cover under the Buenos Aires nonintervention formula to launch an attack on foreign capital. Further efforts at compromise ended suddenly and evidently unexpectedly when Cárdenas acted under an extremely broad act passed in 1936 to expropriate most of the foreign-owned oil properties (March 18, 1938).[24]

The American Government thus found itself in the middle of a tug of war between American investors and the Good Neighbor policy which lasted until the threat of war settled the issue in 1941. All Latin America watched closely, particularly those areas with confiscable foreign-owned resources, to see whether Washington would stick to the Good Neighbor policy to the disadvantage of American capital. The oil companies promptly launched a campaign to edu-

---

[24] Properties belonging to seventeen companies, four British and thirteen American, were involved, with the estimated potential values fairly evenly divided. British values were tremendously increased by the recently granted concession to the Poza Rica field, not yet under development.

cate government and country to the merits of a strong policy. Hull's first statement (March 30) frankly admitted the right of expropriation, but insisted that the companies receive fair compensation. Roosevelt elaborated this two days later by setting up a yardstick of the amount actually invested and still unamortized and excluding profits from oil still underground. This displeased the companies, which based their claim to $450,000,000 compensation on the estimated total potential value of the fields, far above the Mexican valuation. The same day Washington applied the first hint of pressure. The United States Treasury had for some time kept the Mexican peso stable by buying the major portion of Mexico's silver exports (the mines were mostly owned in the United States) at a price above the world level. These purchases were discontinued, thus forcing Mexican silver into the world market at a much lower price and greatly endangering national financial stability.

The sharp divergence between Mexican and company valuations led to months of negotiation, during which Hull's voice was often sharp but never peremptory while the companies stood valiantly by their refusal to accept a valuation lower than their own. The agrarian claims, whose owners were less vociferous than the oil companies, were also under discussion, and as time passed it seemed to many that Hull was seeking to settle them first as a lever to open the oil question. Mexico, despite extremely difficult circumstances, refused to increase her valuation of the oil lands. Mere possession of the fields had not resulted in the hoped-for benefits for Mexico, as the companies denied machinery and transportation facilities, thus cutting off markets as effectively as would a blockade. This drove Mexico into barter deals with Germany, Italy, and Japan which doubtless increased Axis influence in Mexico and underscored the imperative need to settle the problem. Lengthy conversations brought substantial agreement on all outstanding points of difference except oil-land valuation by September, 1941. By this time, too, the world picture had darkened to a point where hemispheric solidarity outweighed oil; the American government sacrificed the companies to the larger interest and on November 19, 1941 (shortly before the Pearl Harbor disaster) signed with the government of President Ávila Camacho an agreement settling other aspects, and opening the way to an oil settlement.

Mexico settled the agrarian claims by promising to pay $40,000,-000, of which $3,000,000 had already been paid under a 1938 agreement, and a like amount was turned over upon exchange of ratifications (completed April 2, 1942). The balance of $34,000,000 would be paid in annual installments of not less than $2,500,000. The United States promised to establish a $40,000,000 fund to underwrite the peso, to issue through the Export-Import Bank a $30,000,-000 credit for the benefit of Mexican highway construction, to resume the purchase of Mexican silver at a price considerably above its market value, and to proceed to the negotiation of a reciprocal trade agreement. These terms make it abundantly clear that both parties negotiated in the light of the world emergency; generous northern contributions to common defense matched Mexico's recognition and payment of her long-standing obligations. As to oil, each party agreed to appoint an expert to arrive at an equitable joint valuation of the American-owned properties. Both governments would accept this valuation; if the oil companies were not satisfied, they might have recourse to the Mexican courts—not a particularly pleasant prospect in light of recent experience. Mexico deposited $9,000,-000 on account, recognizing thus the principle of responsibility, while the United States, by tacitly abandoning the companies, recognized Mexican control of subsoil rights. The figure of $23,995,991 was announced on April 18, 1942.[25] Since this figure is considerably above earlier Mexican estimates, it seems reasonable to assume at least a slightly more favorable Mexican attitude toward the companies.

This chapter of Mexican-American relations opened with an account of one war and closes with another under way. In the first war Mexico fought the United States more or less as an equal; the second found her largely dependent upon northern aid against a common

---

[25] To this should be added $8,500,000 accepted by the Sinclair oil interests in an individual settlement arrived at in May, 1940, and $1,100,000 awarded Cities Service by a separate agreement announced simultaneously with the general appraisal.

enemy. Meantime, however, she had achieved, after passing through a period of economic tutelage, a national stature which it once seemed she might never attain. The fact that she was able to achieve it bears witness alike to her own progress, to the growth in stature of her northern neighbor, and to the expanding community of nations in the western hemisphere.

10 The United States and Britain, 1815-1903

T HOUGH THE WAR OF 1812 WAS THE LAST ANGLO-AMERI-can dispute to be settled by the sword, the decades which followed were by no means devoid of controversy. The developing pattern of relationships resembles, if one resists the usual temptation to push analogies too far, that between a parent and an adolescent child. Earlier frictions over fisheries and boundaries were family problems not unlike the tensions accompanying adolescent efforts to snap finally the bonds of parental authority. The serious issues arising out of the Civil War commanded respectful attention on both sides, with the United States still fearful of British intervention and Britain wary of giving offense. By the turn of the twentieth century the former parent, seeking friends in the world community, recognized the former offspring as an equal and frankly offered concessions to obtain good will in the areas of isthmian and Alaskan diplomacy. Thus the wheel turned full circle from somewhat angry incompatibility in 1815 to a comfortable coöperation which was to bring mutual advantage between 1914 and 1918.

Piscatorial Complexities

The Northeast Fisheries question, hardy perennial among Anglo-American problems, stemmed from John Adams' failure to persuade British negotiators in 1782 to apply the word "right" to both inshore and offshore areas, and from John Quincy Adams' inability to insert a fisheries clause in the Treaty of Ghent.[1] The deep-sea fisheries thus remained, as always, open to New England exploitation, but the inshore areas continued under the prohibition established during the War of 1812. British seizures along the coast sharpened New England's desire for legal access to the inshore fishing grounds, and John Quincy Adams succeeded as Secretary of State in retrieving his failure of 1814. Acting under his direction Richard Rush and Albert Gallatin negotiated in 1818 a Convention (signed October 20) which secured temporary relief and laid a solid foundation for fisheries relations in the future—a settlement which fashioned a permanent victory out of a strategic retreat.[2] The American technique, embodied in the Convention, traded an earlier claim of access to the whole inshore area for the right to permanent access to restricted and carefully stipulated portions of the northern coasts. Both parties derived advantage: Britain narrowed American pretensions quantitatively and the United States attached the word "forever" to the area of accessibility.[3]

The Convention created a fair basis for relationships; its interpretation, however, created difficulties. Moreover, changing British policy and changing patterns of fishing produced developments unfore-

---

[1] The following titles cover the important aspects of the fisheries question: Burt, *U.S., Gt. Brit. and British N. Am.*, pp. 399–420; J. M. Callahan, *American Foreign Policy in Canadian Relations*, Macmillan, 1937, pp. 241–269, 326–386, 438–465; Hugh Keenleyside, *Canada and the United States*, Knopf, 1929, pp. 242–294; Robert Lansing, "The North Atlantic Coast Fisheries Arbitration," *American Journal of International Law*, vol. 5 (1911), pp. 1–31; D. C. Masters, *The Reciprocity Treaty of 1854*, Longmans, Green, 1937, pp. 15–211; Allan Nevins, *Hamilton Fish: The Inner History of the Grant Administration*, Dodd, Mead, 1936, pp. 413–485; J. H. Powell, *op. cit.*, pp. 104–178; L. B. Shippee, *Canadian-American Relations, 1849–1874*, Yale University Press, 1939, pp. 262–401, 426–448; Goldwin Smith, *The Treaty of Washington*, Cornell University Press, 1941; C. C. Tansill, *Canadian-American Relations, 1874–1911*, Yale University Press, 1944, pp. 1–120, 267–295; *For. Pol. of Thomas F. Bayard*, pp. 185–323.

[2] Text in Miller, *Treaties*, vol. 2, pp. 658–662.

[3] Americans might catch, dry, and cure fish along southern Newfoundland from Cape Ray to the Rameau Islands, and northward indefinitely from Mt. Joly along Labrador, subject to the rights of the Hudson's Bay Company and to securing prior consent of the inhabitants to dry and cure (but not to fish) in settled areas; they might fish, but not dry or cure, along western Newfoundland from Cape Ray to Quirpon Island and around the Magdalen Islands; they might seek shelter or supplies of wood and water anywhere in British North America. Burt, *op. cit.*, pp. 418–419. These provisions were more generous than the proposals contained in Adams' instructions.

seen in 1818. The resulting serious friction threatened hostilities in
the 1850's and contributed to the Elgin-Marcy agreement of 1854.
Two questions of interpretation arose. The Convention allowed
Americans to use the fisheries "in common with the subjects of His
Britannic Majesty"; how did this apply to the actual policing of the
area? Americans objected instantly and vociferously to the contention that the nationals of both powers should be subject to British
local regulations, loudly demanded autonomy, and were not too
scrupulous in observing the limits laid down in the Convention. In
response Nova Scotia passed a Hovering Act (1836) allowing local
authorities to board vessels operating illegally within the three-mile
limit outside the treaty area, and authorizing seizure and confiscation on failure to depart within twenty-four hours of notice. Prince
Edward Island followed suit, and between 1839 and 1854 numerous
seizures occurred. Again, the United States had relinquished access
to territorial waters outside the treaty area; the method of fixing this
three-mile limit produced controversy. British lawyers presently announced the headland-to-headland theory, which would locate the
limit three miles seaward from a line drawn between the headlands.
This potential closure of all large bays promptly evoked the contrary
doctrine that the line should follow the sinuosities of the coast. These
two matters remained at issue for decades.

Passing time and changing policies engendered further frictions.
British colonial ports were opened to American merchant shipping
in 1830. The provision of the Convention of 1818 permitting fishing
vessels to enter northern ports for shelter and supplies thereafter became a cover for smuggling operations as profitable as they were
aggravating. About 1850 Britain reversed a long-standing policy and
opened Newfoundland to settlement; the island's increasing population did not appreciate the American exercise of treaty rights along
their coasts. Finally, American fishermen began taking mackerel and
herring, which brought them into sharp competition with local rivals
in the large bays. These ominous signs were aggravated in the early
1850's by the appearance in Canadian waters of naval contingents
representing both sides.

General Anglo-American tensions made a broad settlement desirable. The Clayton-Bulwer Treaty of 1850 had not ended Central American rivalry. A noisy and poverty-stricken Canadian minority sought annexation to the United States. The agent chosen to clear the atmosphere was Lord Elgin, Governor General of Canada, ably abetted, according to his secretary's memoirs, by liberal quantities of champagne. Whatever the merits of Elgin's anecdotes and champagne as weighed against his diplomatic talents, his efforts resulted in signature with William L. Marcy (June 5, 1854) of the treaty bearing their joint names. This agreement carried commercial reciprocity as a sop to the disgruntled Canadians. Its fisheries provisions, a considerable liberalization of the 1818 arrangements, restored most of the privileges extended under the Treaty of Paris. To compensate for this generosity Canadians were permitted to fish American coastal waters as far as 36° N. Lat. The undoubted economic advantages of reciprocity faded before disagreements arising from the Civil War and the United States exercised its right to terminate the Elgin-Marcy Treaty in 1866, leaving fisheries matters in an indeterminate status. At first the various British provinces in North America (Canadian Confederation was achieved in 1867) continued to extend the privileges of the Elgin-Marcy agreement upon payment of nominal fees proportioned to ship-tonnage. American reluctance to secure these licenses resulted in increased fees and finally a Dominion Order in Council of January 8, 1870, abolished all privileges and restricted Americans to the area granted by the Convention of 1818.

The following summer found the Americans still trespassing; four hundred ships were boarded and fifteen were condemned, accompanied by considerable violence. As in the 1850's, other issues complicated fisheries questions. Canadian independence still intruded itself into Anglo-American relations; conflicting attitudes on the *Alabama* claims had not been resolved; a remnant of the Northwest Boundary controversy lingered on; and post-Civil War high tariffs still irked the Canadians. On the other hand, New England thrift sought to regain full use of the inshore fisheries without bothersome limitations. Complicated negotiations produced the Treaty of Washington (accepted by the Senate, May 24, 1871), in which fisheries matters occupied an important part. Again, for a ten-year period and thereafter until two years after formal notice of desire to abrogate, the inshore fisheries were opened to Americans virtually without limits; again Canadians were admitted to fish United States shore waters, this time south to 39° N. Lat.; each country might ship fish and fish oil to the other duty-free. It was admitted that the southern neighbor had the better of the bargain; this was the first of a number of occasions when Canada was asked to contribute to Anglo-American good will and her great Prime Minister, Sir John A. Macdonald, was soundly if briefly berated at home for his alleged gift. An arbitral commission meeting in Halifax in 1877 determined that the United States should pay Canada $500,000 a year to even the score. The size of this award pleasantly surprised the Canadians; even their own historians have admitted that it was unjustifiably large. Partly because of it the United States gave notice in 1883 and the treaty ceased to operate as of July 1, 1885.

Matters thus returned to the status of the Convention of 1818, which the Dominion enforced with enthusiasm. Canadian efforts to use the fisheries as a club to compel tariff concessions and American seizures of Canadian sealers in Bering Sea developed dangerous tendencies in the late 1880's. Finally an Act of March, 1887, which was never enforced, authorized retaliation when, in the judgment of the President, American fishermen were badly treated in British North America. An attempted settlement in the abortive Bayard-Chamberlain Treaty was defeated in 1888, but produced a *modus vivendi* of February 15, 1888, which under various Canadian regulations remained the practical basis for use of the fisheries until it was abrogated at the end of 1923 in retaliation against the Fordney-McCumber Tariff. By it American fishing vessels were permitted, on payment of a license fee of $1.50 per ton, to enter ports from which they had recently been excluded to purchase bait and supplies, a practical arrangement which placed matters on a reasonably amicable basis.

Meantime the economic significance of the fisheries declined and the temper of Anglo-American relations improved to a point where a general arbitration treaty (signed April 4, 1908) referred disputes to the Hague Tribunal. This was followed by a convention (signed January 27, 1909) detailing seven questions for arbitration. The Hague Court award, published in December, 1910, was a compromise which on the whole served American economic interests while preserving British sovereign control. Among the important awards was one covering local regulation of fishing in territorial waters. The Tribunal denied the American argument for joint regulation but held that Anglo-Canadian rules must be appropriate and necessary, must bear equally upon both Canadians and Americans, and must not violate the Convention of 1818. Machinery for nipping future disputes in the bud was forecast by provision for their reference to a permanent mixed commission, established under a convention of July 20, 1912. Another dealt with the American practice of hiring local fishermen after working their ships to the fishing grounds with skeleton crews, a custom disapproved by the Newfoundlanders. The Court rendered a somewhat equivocal judgment to the effect that the Americans might ship crews of nonnationals, but that the local authorities might close the fisheries to ships partly manned by British citizens. A third applied to the nature and location of the three-mile limit, least important economically of all the questions considered. Here the American argument reverted to the decades-old contention that the line followed the windings of the coast, making accessible all bays more than six miles wide at the mouth. The Court approved the British headland-to-headland theory, but since this was difficult to apply in practice, recommended an arbitrary settlement in the case of several bays, covering the rest by resurrecting a provision of the never-ratified Bayard-Chamberlain Treaty which called for a line three miles out from the point where the entrance narrowed to ten miles. This friendly settlement, plus the declining importance of the fisheries, put an end to the long disagreement which had more than once endangered Anglo-American peace.

Fur Seals and *Mare Clausum*

The migratory and breeding habits of the genus *Callorhinus alascanus* (fur seal) gave rise to a minor but long-standing Anglo-American complication. These valuable contributors to the satisfaction of feminine vanity travel widely but return annually to the Pribilof Islands in Bering Sea to bear young and to mate.[4] The older males dominate family life at the rookeries, with the young bulls herding by themselves. These habits make it possible to slaughter discriminatingly, leaving the females to their reproductive function and maintaining males to preserve the herd. The sole right to kill males on the islands was leased to a corporation. Since, however, the creatures migrate along fairly definite sea lanes on a fairly definite schedule, pelagic sealing developed where, by rifle, dynamite, and harpoon, seals were killed outside territorial waters. Here it was impossible to distinguish between the sexes, and the death of a female deprived the herd also of an unborn and a nursing pup; moreover, only about half of the seals killed at sea were recovered. The United States fell heir to this problem in biology and conservation with the purchase of Alaska (including the Pribilof Islands) in 1867.

A laudable desire to avoid decimation of the herd through pelagic sealing led to an ill-advised reversal of the traditional American doctrine of freedom of the seas. In 1881 a Treasury official, apparently without consulting the Department of State, claimed jurisdiction over all waters east of the line of the Alaska Purchase Treaty, on the strength of Alexander I's *ukase* of 1821 closing the waters of Bering Sea to a distance of one hundred Italian miles from shore, to which right the United States supposedly succeeded with the Purchase. This application of the *mare clausum* doctrine to Bering Sea was implemented in 1886–1887 by the seizure, over sixty miles from land, of several Canadian pelagic sealers. British and Canadian protests elicited a memorandum from the Department's Solicitor to Secretary of State Thomas F. Bayard (January 17, 1887) stating that "there were no concessions whatever . . . by which we as assignees of Russia, can claim any right to seize British sailing vessels on the high seas outside of the three mile band. . . ." Patriotic fervor was

---

[4] The following supplement the titles already cited: T. A. Bailey, "The North Pacific Sealing Convention of 1911," *Pacific Historical Review*, vol. 4 (1935), pp. 1–14; J. Stanley-Brown, "The Bering Sea Controversy from an Economic Standpoint," *Yale Review*, vol. 2 (1893), pp. 194–210; Tansill, *Can.-Am. Rel.*, pp. 267–371; E. A. Falk, *From Perry to Pearl Harbor: The Struggle for Supremacy in the Pacific*, Doubleday, Doran, 1943, pp. 80–85.

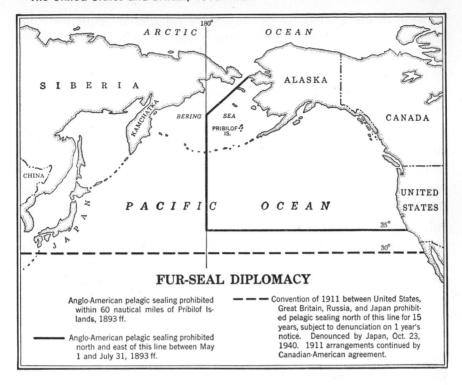

FUR-SEAL DIPLOMACY

Anglo-American pelagic sealing prohibited within 60 nautical miles of Pribilof Islands, 1893 ff.

——— Anglo-American pelagic sealing prohibited north and east of this line between May 1 and July 31, 1893 ff.

— — — Convention of 1911 between United States, Great Britain, Russia, and Japan prohibited pelagic sealing north of this line for 15 years, subject to denunciation on 1 year's notice. Denounced by Japan, Oct. 23, 1940. 1911 arrangements continued by Canadian-American agreement.

stirred as further seizures followed, and Cleveland left office just after signing (March 2, 1889) a law authorizing the President to seize predatory vessels outside territorial waters in Bering Sea. The new Secretary of State, James G. Blaine, thus found an aroused public opinion pushing him toward an untenable legal position.

His initial note of January 22, 1890, avoided asserting a claim to *mare clausum,* but asserted that Canadian seizures were opposed to public interest; moreover, he asserted that since Russia had maintained undisputed and unmolested the right to control the Bering Sea fisheries until 1867, the United States had by prescription acquired a similar right. Blaine presented these tenuous arguments with something of the bluster which was to become synonymous with his diplomatic exchanges. Lord Salisbury replied through Sir Julian Pauncefote, with the conscious righteousness and something of the unctuousness of a British Foreign Secretary standing on unassailable legal ground, that his Government would "hold the Gov-

ernment of the United States responsible for the consequences that
may ensue from acts which are contrary to the established principles
of international law." Further complicated correspondence produced
an agreement (signed February 29, 1892) submitting the whole matter to an arbitration held at Paris between February 23 and August
15, 1893, in which the United States deservedly lost every point. The
problem was ultimately solved only after delicate multilateral negotiations, protracted for some years by tender Canadian sensibilities.
Meantime failure to set up adequate local controls permitted Canada
to continue pelagic sealing. After 1900 the added activities of Japanese sealers again threatened the herd with extinction. Finally, on
July 7, 1911, a four-power agreement (Russia was also involved) put
an end for fifteen years to pelagic sealing north of 30° N. Lat. An
American monopoly of the catch was established, and Canada and
Japan each received 15 percent of the skins in return for abandoning
pelagic activities. The treaty was to continue in force, subject to one
year's notice, which Japan gave, October 23, 1940, on the dubious
ground that the now well-replenished herd was depleting her fish
supply. The Pearl Harbor disaster interrupted an investigation of the
Japanese contention that the catch should be increased in order to
reduce the herd.

Webster and Ashburton Split the Difference

The Canadian-American boundary line first drawn so long ago, and
so unsuccessfully, at Paris in 1782 was virtually completed in the
1840's. This final settlement of sharp differences was achieved, with
reasonable honor to both sides, in the face of a grasping American
appetite for territory which during the same decade swallowed half
of Mexico, and of Anglo-American difficulties which had been piling
up since the War of 1812. Both British superiority and American im-
maturity were factors in these difficulties. Englishmen (and women)
returned from cursory examination of American life and customs and
wrote derogatory volumes.[5] Americans, on the other hand, were still

_____

[5] For a good survey of the matter in this paragraph see R. G. Adams, *A History
of the Foreign Policy of the United States,* Macmillan, 1925, pp. 212–218.

so unsure of their emancipation from Britain that they felt called upon to assert it at the top of their voices. Succeeding Independence Days offered occasion for twisting the British lion's tail; intervening opportunities were not lacking. The resulting tensions were only slowly offset by growing economic bonds such as British dependence upon American cotton and increasing British investments in American industry and transportation. Meantime specific frictions might at any time kindle a real fire.

These frictions were numerous in the later 1830's.[6] They were initiated by the *Caroline* Affair. A waning Canadian revolution against British authority, led by William Lyon Mackenzie and largely manned by anti-British Americans thrown out of work by the Panic of 1837, made a stand on Navy Island, Canadian territory in the Niagara River. The *Caroline*, a Yankee boat, brought provisions from the American side. Aiming to destroy this life line of revolution, a Canadian force embarked for Navy Island on the night of December 29, 1837. Not finding the vessel, the expedition constituted itself an invasion force, continued across the river, fired the *Caroline*, and cut her adrift to sink in the river above the Falls. Amos Durfee, an American citizen, was killed in the melee. This invasion of American sovereignty would better have been preceded by formal complaint through diplomatic channels, and was by no means justified by any contribution the *Caroline* had or could make to the overthrow of British authority. In November, 1840, just as the heat caused by this episode was dying down, the New York State au-

---

[6] The following is a representative selection from the voluminous literature on the Northeast Boundary and its ramifications: Burt, *The U.S., Gt. Brit., etc.*, pp. 185–195; Callahan, *Am. For. Pol. in Canadian Rel.*, pp. 185–214; A. B. Corey, *The Crisis of 1830–1842 in Canadian-American Relations*, Yale University Press, 1941, pp. 34–43, 146–184; R. N. Current, "Webster's Propaganda and the Ashburton Treaty," *Mississippi Valley Historical Review*, vol. 34 (1947), pp. 187–200; C. M. Fuess, *Daniel Webster*, Little, Brown, 1930, vol. 2, pp. 93–130; Hill, *Leading American Treaties*, pp. 175–194; Keenleyside, *Canada & U.S.*, pp. 112–116, 167–187; Thomas LeDuc, "The Maine Frontier and the Northeastern Boundary Controversy," *American Historical Review*, vol. 53 (1947), pp. 30–41; E. W. McInnis, *The Unguarded Frontier: A History of American-Canadian Relations*, Doubleday, Doran, 1942, pp. 158–171; L. F. Martin and S. F. Bemis, "Franklin's Red-Line Map was a Mitchell," *New England Quarterly*, vol. 10 (1937), pp. 105–111; Alastair Watt, "The Case of Alexander McLeod," *Canadian Historical Review*, vol. 12 (1931), pp. 145–167.

thorities arrested, for the third time, one Alexander McLeod, a former deputy sheriff of Upper Canada, charging that he had drunkenly boasted of killing Durfee.

Bail was arranged, but a mob prevented McLeod's release and he was presently under indictment in New York courts for the murder. The British Government, previously not much interested, promptly insisted that if McLeod were guilty as charged, his act had been performed as a member of Her Majesty's armed forces, and so was not subject to American judicial process. Secretary of State Daniel Webster accepted this position in April, 1841, and sent his Attorney General to indicate to the New York authorities that were McLeod under Federal jurisdiction the indictment would be dismissed. The suggestion raised embarrassing questions of Federal and State relations and New York's doughty Governor, William H. Seward, ignored Webster's hint. McLeod, tired of staying in jail, rejected a proposed effort to remove his case to the Federal courts, and was brought to trial at Utica on the fearful charge that

not having the fear of God before his eyes, but moved and seduced by the instigation of the devil . . . with a certain gun of the value of five dollars, then and there loaded and charged with gunpowder and one leaden bullet . . . then and there feloniously and wilfully, and of his malice aforethought and with a premeditated design to effect the death of the said Amos Durfee, did shoot and discharge, and the said Alexander McLeod with the leaden bullet aforesaid, out of the gun aforesaid, then and there by the force of the gunpowder and shot sent forth as aforesaid, the said Amos Durfee in and upon the back of the head of him . . . did strike, penetrate and wound, giving to the said Amos Durfee . . . one mortal wound . . . the said Amos Durfee, then and there . . . did languish, and languishing, did die.[7]

The enormity of the indictment was not justified by the ascertainable facts. The prosecution was not even able to prove McLeod's presence on the *Caroline* expedition; two of its main witnesses disappeared at a crucial moment in the trial, and McLeod was acquitted in October, 1841. Even had he been found guilty, Governor Seward had promised Webster a pardon. The issue raised by his arrest and trial, how-

---

[7] Quoted in M. L. Bonham, "Alexander McLeod, Bone of Contention," *New York History*, vol. 18 (1937), pp. 189–217.

ever, was one which could recur with less happy consequences at any time.

The slave trade furnished a long-standing Anglo-American controversy. British abolition of this traffic in 1807 had been followed (1808) by a fairly ineffective American gesture in the same direction, and by British abolition (1833) of slavery itself. To humanitarian opposition to slavery and the slave trade was added the economic fact that the British colonies would now have to compete with goods produced by slave labor. Americans, and others, stimulated by large profits and continued demand, repeatedly violated the British legislation of 1808 under the cloak of the American flag. The understandable British desire to end the traffic had been implemented by forcible visit and search of ships suspected as slavers during the Napoleonic Era, on the theory that the trade was piratical. When a court decision denied this contention in 1817 the British sought to continue the practice by establishing treaty-based mutual agreements—an arrangement favorable to a powerful maritime nation. By 1841 the United States was the only dangerous rival not covered by such a treaty. The latter fought shy of British blandishments with the result that most of the remaining slave-traders took refuge under the American flag. This issue was to come to a dramatic focus during the forthcoming negotiations.

Against these mounting tensions the Northeast Boundary question increasingly demanded attention.[8] The negotiators chosen to compose these differences were singularly well-suited to their complex task. Daniel Webster was the last member of Harrison's Cabinet remaining in John Tyler's service. His career as the nation's greatest orator and expositor of the Constitution had included a recent visit to Britain, where he had met, and liked, many leaders and had drawn from Thomas Carlyle the comment: "This is our Yankee Englishman; such limbs we make in Yankee land!" Whether a Yankee Englishman or not, Webster was well-disposed toward England. His opposite number, Alexander Baring, Lord Ashburton, entertained similar sentiments toward the United States. The American interests

---

[8] Texas, already discussed, and Oregon, to be noted directly below, important as they were, received only slight consideration.

of his banking house, Baring Brothers, dated back to the financing of
the Louisiana Purchase and had grown more intimate with the passing years; his wife was the daughter of an American Senator; his
own chief aim during thirty years in Parliament had been, in his own
words to Webster, "to impress on others the necessity of, and to promote myself, peace and harmony between our countries. . . ." Seldom have better-intentioned agents dealt with thorny questions. A
brief review will indicate some of the thorns which had sprouted
along the boundary.

It will be recalled that an arbitration (1798) under the Jay Treaty
had determined the first section of the line, running to the source of
the St. Croix River. The passage of forty-odd years found the intervening distance to the St. Lawrence still largely undetermined. It
was to run, according to the Treaty of Paris, north from the source
of the St. Croix to the highlands separating the Atlantic from the St.
Lawrence watersheds, along them to the northwesternmost head of
the Connecticut River, down the middle of the stream to the forty-
fifth parallel, and along it to the St. Lawrence. Geographic facts
failed to provide the systematic highlands laid down by the treaty,
and ownership of a roughly triangular area of about 12,000 square
miles northward of Maine fell into dispute; claim to its disposition
was shared by Massachusetts when Maine achieved statehood in
1820. Differences over the source of the Connecticut created controversy over another 200 square miles. Finally, one of the arbitration commissions under the Treaty of Ghent discovered a surveyor's
error of the 1770's which raised the forty-fifth parallel a half-mile
northward across the head of Lake Champlain, surrendering 61
square miles of British territory to New York and Vermont. This
gained importance after American construction, on land technically
British, of extensive fortifications at Rouse's Point. Thus, though the
arbitrations provided under the Treaty of Ghent failed to settle the
crucial aspects of the St. Croix–St. Lawrence boundary, they established some facts and laid the foundation of further claims. The facts
were submitted, under a treaty of 1827, to arbitration by the King
of the Netherlands. That monarch decided that the facts as given
him were "inexplicable and impractical," and that instead of trying

to apply them, he would try to draw a reasonable line. His efforts failed, for after both the British and President Jackson agreed to his working compromise Maine refused to accept the loss of land entailed in the proposal. The Senate then advised Jackson to reject the arbitral award on the ground that the King had acted beyond his commission. It is interesting to note that Maine would have received more territory under this award of 1831 than she gained by the Webster-Ashburton agreement. Here matters rested legally until the negotiations of 1841–1842.

Meantime a strategic factor came to bulk large in British thinking. With ice closing the St. Lawrence for several months each year, the only route open between Montreal and Quebec, the open sea, and the great military base at Halifax was the valley of the St. John, flowing through the upper portion of the disputed triangle. The abortive Canadian revolution of 1837 aptly pointed up the need of an overland road. Economically the spruce forest north of the river promised little to either party to the controversy. West of the St. John, however, the valley of its confluent, the Aroostook, formed an island of rich limestone soil in an otherwise unproductive area. Settlers from both Maine and New Brunswick flocked thither in the 1830's, and in 1838–1839 the appearance of numerous Canadians brought conflict dangerously near. Names were called and fists waved on both sides in this "Restook War" until the Federal authorities despatched a military peacemaker in the person of General Scott, who arranged a precarious truce under which each party continued to hold territory to which the other claimed it had no right. Thus was established an unstable balance which might at any moment be displaced, with violent results.

Such were the difficulties which Webster and Ashburton had to resolve in their negotiation which opened at Washington in April, 1842. Presenting their solutions in the same order as their problems are listed above, a series of notes disposed of the *Caroline* affair. A year earlier (April 24, 1841) Webster had warned the British Government that action such as that taken by the expeditionary force could be justified only by showing "a necessity of self-defence, instant, overwhelming, leaving no choice of means, and no moment for

deliberation. It will be for it to show, also, that the local authorities
of Canada, even supposing the necessity of the moment authorized
them to enter the territories of the United States at all, did nothing
unreasonable or excessive; since the act, justified by the necessity of
self-defence, must be limited by that necessity, and kept clearly
within it."[9] In opening the matter at Washington Webster chided
Ashburton's Government for permitting five years to pass without
any conciliatory gesture. Ashburton in replying used the word "apology" which Webster later said was the result of two days' work on
his part, and stated that "what is, perhaps, most to be regretted is,
that some explanation and apology for this occurrence was not immediately made; this, with a frank explanation of the necessity of
the case, might, and probably would, have prevented much of the
exasperation, and of the subsequent complaints and recriminations
to which it gave rise." Webster accepted the explanation and promised, on behalf of the President, to "make this subject, as a complaint
of violation of territory, the topic of no further discussion between
the two governments." The issues raised by the McLeod case were
reduced in intensity by an act (passed August 29, 1842, twenty days
after the Treaty was signed) allowing removal to Federal jurisdiction of those charged before State courts with offenses committed
under orders of a foreign authority. Never again would an Alexander
McLeod muddy the waters of international affairs.

The *Creole* case brought the slave trade sharply to the negotiators'
attention and contributed indirectly to the content of their treaty.
A coastal slave-trader, bound from Virginia to New Orleans, her
slave cargo mutinied, killed one of their owners, and took refuge in a
British West Indian port. Here those guilty of the murder were
hanged, and the rest set free. Existing machinery afforded no means
of securing their return since the extradition provisions of the Jay
Treaty had expired in 1807. Webster attempted unsuccessfully to
include "mutiny on board ship" in a list of categories to be contained
in the treaty clause on that subject, the list reading "murder, or
assault with intent to commit murder, or Piracy, or arson, or robbery,
or Forgery, or the utterance of forged paper. . . ." As to the trade

---

[9] *The Works of Daniel Webster*, Little, Brown, 1851, vol. 6, p. 261.

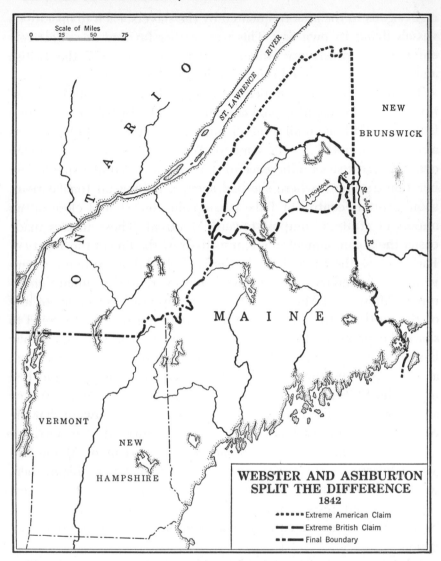

Scale of Miles
0   25   50   75

ST. LAWRENCE RIVER

O N T A R I O

NEW
BRUNSWICK

Aroostook R.

St. John R.

M A I N E

VERMONT

NEW
HAMPSHIRE

**WEBSTER AND ASHBURTON
SPLIT THE DIFFERENCE
1842**

•••••• Extreme American Claim
▬ ▬ Extreme British Claim
▬•▬• Final Boundary

itself, the British of course were unable to secure the right of mutual
visit to establish identity because of vivid memories of impressment
(on which, incidentally, Ashburton's Government would allow no
negotiation), plus perhaps the realization that any really effective
curb on the trade might raise domestic political complications. A
compromise provided that each nation should maintain a fleet of

eighty guns in the area frequented by the slavers, each to operate on vessels flying its own flag. This was neither favored nor effectively enforced by proslavery Administrations, and in 1857 the British again boarded suspected slavers under the American flag.

The actual boundary settlement resulted from a curious combination of strategy, cupidity, and cartography. The British concern for a frontier providing an all-weather route to Montreal and Quebec has already been noted. By the same token, the United States was much concerned lest strict adherence to the forty-fifth parallel should lose her Rouse's Point, where she had spent a million on fortifications, should forfeit control of Lake Champlain, and should close off an important strategic outpost toward Montreal. These factors made easier the abandonment of attempts to draw the line of the Treaty of Paris and, as the King of the Netherlands had done, propose a conventional boundary. This involved, however, the pecuniary interests of Maine and Massachusetts, which opposed surrender of any of the northern triangle, since upon separation they had agreed to share the proceeds from the exploitation of their common public lands. Pursuant of this attitude, the Maine legislature had declared, as early as 1838, the inexpediency of a conventional line and had urged the State's Congressional delegation to press for the survey and adoption of the line of 1783. Webster was well aware that the constitutional proprieties attendant upon surrendering territory claimed by a State involved obtaining the consent of Maine and Massachusetts to any prospective arrangement. His problem, then, was to reconcile the States to surrendering a portion of their birthright in the interests of national strategical objectives. He did this by a judicious use of cartographic legerdemain, cash, and propaganda.

A brief account of the "Red-Line Map Controversy" must suffice. Seeking a means of persuading Maine and Massachusetts to be reasonable, Webster resorted to a recent discovery of the historian Jared Sparks in the French Archives. Back in 1782 Vergennes had asked Franklin for a map showing the boundaries as drawn in the preliminary peace negotiations. Under date of December 6 Franklin obliged, writing that he had drawn the boundary "with a strong red line." All maps accompanying the negotiations had disappeared, but Sparks found a d'Anville map of 1746 which had a boundary, marked in red, which more than supported the British contentions of 1842. Webster had in his possession also a Mitchell map (the negotiators at Paris were known to have used a Mitchell map) formerly the property of General Frederick William von Steuben, with the boundary drawn by an unknown hand in support of the British claim. Webster promptly despatched Sparks to Augusta, armed with the foregoing information and a drawn-from-memory copy of the d'Anville map, in a successful effort to persuade Maine to agree to a conventional line. This conversion was undoubtedly hastened by a promise that the Federal authorities would pay each State $150,000 in lieu of the lost lands, by the inclusion in the treaty of a provision allowing Maine's citizens use of the St. John River (vastly important in their economy) for movement of their agricultural and forest products, and by the insertion in the local press of inspired articles supporting the treaty. Subsequent investigation has shown that there is no evidence indicating that Sparks' d'Anville map was the one Franklin sent to Vergennes; on the contrary, excellent evidence supports the view that Franklin sent Vergennes a Mitchell, bearing a line supporting the American contention. Thus it may be argued that Webster gave away some five thousand square miles of land to which the United States was entitled.[10] At the moment, however, strategy was more important than territory, and the deal progressed.

Under the final boundary provisions the northern triangle was divided with the United States receiving 7,015 square miles and the British 5,012. In return for this concession Webster secured navigation rights on the St. John, some concession in the area of the Connecticut, and the "rectified" boundary along the forty-fifth parallel. Finally, in innocent ignorance and evidently without any reciprocal concession, Ashburton agreed to a line between Lake Superior and the Lake of the Woods which gave the United States the fabulously rich Mesabi iron deposits. As matters stood at the time, however, the

---

[10] Curiously enough, the British had a Mitchell map marked to support the American claim. It might be noted, too, that Ashburton was under instructions to offer compensation to Maine and Massachusetts, but generously deferred to Webster in this respect.

arrangement was an eminently fair one. It gave each nation an important strategic location, it compensated Maine and Massachusetts, it settled long-standing controversies freighted with immense possibilities of trouble. The fact that the Opposition press howled for months about "Ashburton's Capitulation" and that Webster was also vilified for surrendering as much as he did should also help to indicate the essential fairness of this complicated settlement made by men of good will.

Aberdeen Surrenders

The last leg of the international boundary, from the Rockies to the Pacific, was also drawn during the 1840's.[11] It marked the culmination of a long historic process which eliminated two of the four nations which claimed the west coast of North America (exclusive of Alaska, which will be treated below) from the picture and divided the territory between the remaining pair.[12] Of the four claimants Spain's withdrawal south of the forty-second parallel by the Transcontinental Treaty of 1819 has already been detailed. By a treaty of 1824 Russia agreed to accept N. Lat. 54°40' as her southern, and the United States as her northern, limit of settlement. Britain and Russia made an almost identical delimitation in 1825.

---

[11] The Rush-Gallatin (fisheries) Convention of 1818 had drawn the line from the northwest corner of the Lake of the Woods to the forty-ninth parallel, thence along it to the summit of the Rocky Mountains. The link from Lake Superior to the Lake of the Woods was completed in 1842, as indicated above. It should be noted, perhaps somewhat repetitiously, that Webster and Ashburton also completed the work of two of the arbitration commissions established under the Treaty of Ghent, one relating to the line between the St. Lawrence and Lake Huron, and the other to that between Lakes Huron and Superior.

[12] The Oregon story is covered in the following: Callahan, *Am. For. Pol. in Canadian Rel.*, pp. 215–240; McInnis, *Unguarded Frontier*, pp. 171–179; T. P. Martin, "Free Trade and the Oregon Question, 1842–1846," in *Facts and Factors in Economic History: Articles by Former Students of Edwin Francis Gay*, Harvard University Press, 1932, pp. 470–491; Frederick Merk, "British Government Propaganda and the Oregon Treaty," *American Historical Review*, vol. 40 (1934), pp. 38–63; "British Party Politics and the Oregon Treaty," *Ibid.*, vol. 37 (1932), pp. 653–678; "The Oregon Pioneers and the Boundary," *Ibid.*, vol. 29 (1924), pp. 681–699; "The British Corn Crisis of 1846," *Agricultural History*, vol. 8 (1934), pp. 95–123; J. W. Pratt, "James K. Polk and John Bull," *Canadian Historical Review*, vol. 24 (1943), pp. 341–349; Reeves, *op. cit.*, pp. 190–265; Walter N. Sage, "The Oregon Treaty of 1846," *Canadian Historical Review*, vol. 27 (1946), pp. 349–367.

Thus by the mid-1820's "Oregon" extended northwardly from 42° to 54°40′ and westwardly from the Rockies to the Pacific, and was subject only to the conflicting claims of Britain and the United States.

These claims, of long standing and multiple foundation, were, as far as the crucial area was concerned, somewhat weighted in favor of Britain. Britain's were based first on Drake's circumnavigating voyage of 1578, which paused on the west coast. Two hundred years later Captain James Cook followed in Drake's footsteps, and in 1792 Captain George Vancouver took the English flag a hundred miles up the Columbia River. The search for furs brought the first overland passage when Alexander Mackenzie reached the Pacific in 1793, to be followed by many more who soon laid the valley of the Columbia under the light but strong bonds of the trader. Captain Robert Gray visited the coast in 1788–1789 and again in 1791–1792, giving the name of his ship to the Columbia River, but so far as is known making no claim of ownership for the United States. Jefferson's famous pathfinders, Meriwether Lewis and William Clark, extended their exploration of the newly purchased Louisiana to include a winter at the mouth of the Columbia in 1805–1806. The first bona fide settlement at Astoria (1811), perpetuating the name of John Jacob Astor, was prudently sold to British fur traders upon news of the War of 1812, and presently (1821) Britain conferred jurisdiction over the Oregon country upon the Hudson's Bay Company. Few Americans felt the urge toward Oregon for some time; not until the mid-1830's did Methodist missionaries pit the persuasiveness of their brand of belief, without conspicuous success, against that of the Catholic missionaries also on the ground. The few Americans who arrived were hospitably received, because the Hudson's Bay Company encouraged agricultural settlements near their posts in the interest of food production. The Bay Company factors, under orders, kept Americans from settling north of the Columbia River, possession of which was long deemed essential to British west-coast policy. Indeed, it was only the Panic of 1837 that started the trek into Oregon so dramatically portrayed in Francis Parkman's *Oregon Trail*. The few hundred American settlers already on the

ground were joined in 1843 by about eight hundred more; the turbulent activities of their numerous successors pushed Oregon into the
full current of the diplomatic stream.

That stream was full of rocks, sharpest of which was the undefined boundary, most unsatisfactory to the migrants of the 1840's
who came to found homes and had no wish to improve land to which
they could not prove title. The *status quo* was ultimately based upon
the Rush-Gallatin Convention of 1818, which had established the
forty-ninth parallel as the boundary to the Rockies. John Quincy
Adams tried to continue the line to the coast, as he was doing at the
same time with the Spanish, but was unsuccessful. The convention
opened the transmountain area claimed by Britain or the United
States for ten years to settlement by nationals of both powers without prejudicing the claims of either. After considerable discussion
had failed to produce a permanent agreement, the 1818 terms were
continued indefinitely (1827) subject to termination on either side
after one year's notice. At one time or another, however, each party
had advanced its own idea of a proper boundary, thus implicitly
abandoning claim to further territory. For the United States, this
was the forty-ninth parallel; for Britain, the Columbia River; thus
the area really in dispute was narrowed to the roughly triangular
tract south of the parallel and north of the river. Such was the state
of affairs when Oregon became a political football.

As early as March, 1844, Lord Aberdeen, Foreign Minister in the
Tory Government, was willing to surrender the disputed triangle
and draw the boundary along the forty-ninth parallel to the Straits
of Juan de Fuca, thus yielding the whole substance of the Oregon
dispute. This decision was based on the conclusion that the Columbia was not such an essential link to a valuable hinterland as had previously been held—a conclusion to be reënforced from a number of
angles during the coming months. Aberdeen hesitated to act on his
conviction, however, for fear of jeopardizing his Government's domestic program and of antagonizing Lord Palmerston in the Opposition, hardly yet recovered from his wrath over Ashburton's "capitulation" of 1842. At this point the American Democratic National
Convention took the bit in its teeth, nominated James K. Polk as a

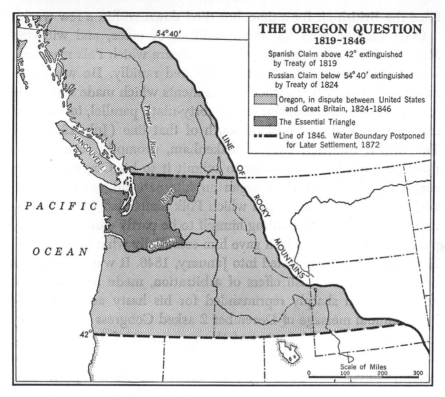

dark-horse candidate for President, and adopted a platform demanding the acquisition of both Texas and Oregon, insisting "That our title
to the whole of the Territory of Oregon is clear and unquestionable
. . . and that the re-occupation of Oregon and the re-annexation of
Texas at the earliest practicable period are great American measures. . . ." During the campaign, which Polk won by a narrow
margin, the slogan "Fifty-four Forty or Fight," coined by some
bumptious disciple of expansionism among Polk's followers, reiterated his party's expansionist program. He himself returned to the
charge, though somewhat less vigorously, in his inaugural address,
asserting that "Our title to the country [note omission of the adjective used in the platform] of the Oregon is 'clear and unquestionable,' and already are our people preparing to perfect that title by
occupying it with their wives and children." Both Aberdeen and Sir
Robert Peel, his Prime Minister, replied vigorously and war talk

filled the British air for a time, but died down within a few weeks.

Once saddled with the responsibilities of office, and with the Mexican situation threatening war, any desire which Polk may have had to fight for fifty-four forty moderated rapidly. He was fortunately able to discover earlier commitments which made it possible for him to offer a settlement on the forty-ninth parallel, including a free port on Vancouver Island south of that line (July 12, 1845). The British Minister, Richard Pakenham, promptly rejected this (July 29), mistakenly refusing to submit it to his Government for consideration. This refusal began an international game of bluff, with Oregon as the stakes, in which Polk demanded more than he really wanted, later permitting himself to be partly eased and partly pushed into a retreat which gave him essentially what he was after. His period of bluffing lasted into January, 1846. It was inaugurated by refusing two British offers of arbitration, made by Pakenham, who had been sharply reprimanded for his hasty action of July. Polk's annual message of December 2 asked Congress for authority to give notice of termination of the agreement of 1827, and contained also his interpretations of the Monroe Doctrine, already discussed, which were obviously directed toward British pretensions on the west coast. Though nothing was said about fifty-four forty, all signs pointed to Polk's renewal of this demand in the face of British recalcitrance. Backstage, however, his Secretary of State, James Buchanan, was shortly writing to Louis McLane, Minister to England, that if the British had an offer to make, Polk "would feel inclined to submit it to the Senate for their previous advice" (December 13, 1845). Ten days later Polk told the Cabinet that he would probably submit a British offer of the forty-ninth parallel to the Senate. Outwardly, however, he continued to bristle, confiding in his diary (January 4, 1846) that he had told a Congressman "that the only way to treat John Bull was to look him straight in the eye . . . that if Congress faultered [sic] or hesitated in their course, John Bull would immediately become arrogant and more grasping in his demands. . . ."

Meantime other developments softened the British demand for the line of the Columbia and heightened British desire for a settlement. Attention has already been called to Aberdeen's reluctance to act on his own willingness to settle on the line of 49°. Events of the summer and early winter of 1845–1846 pushed him in the direction of his convictions. Bad weather during the summer helped to cut the Irish and Scottish potato crops in half and threatened large groups with starvation, plus creating a shortage of seed for the following year. American grain furnished the logical alternative supply, but it could be admitted only by modification of the long-standing system of protection embodied in the Corn Laws. Such legislation endangered the delicate balance of British domestic politics and made it undesirable to risk diplomatic involvement with Britain's potential source of grain.[13] By this time, too, the American cotton crop was essential to the maintenance of British industry. Palmerston, however, stood ready to pounce on any sign of governmental weakness in compromising the American issue, had not certain events of early 1846 served to silence him. On December 28, 1845, Edward Everett, former American Minister to England, wrote Lord John Russell, leader of the Whig Opposition, asking him to quiet Palmerston. This was done, first in Russell's speech at Glasgow, January 12, 1846, in which he indicated his belief that the Oregon question could be settled short of war, and second in his private statement to Aberdeen early in February, 1846, that his Opposition would not hinder Governmental attempts at settlement.[14] This put Aberdeen, who still wanted to settle, in a position to bluff a bit on his own.

Under date of January 3, 1846, McLane reported an interview with Aberdeen in which the latter indicated that certain British naval activities then under way would be "useful and important" in case of an Anglo-American breach. This was promptly reported to Polk, who as promptly (January 29, 1846) authorized informal intimations to Aberdeen that he was willing to ask the Senate's advice

[13] Historians differ as to the influence of this factor. Contrary views are expressed in the articles by Thomas and Merk (*Agricultural History*, vol. 8), cited above.

[14] Russell wrote Palmerston, February 3, 1846: "My opinion upon the whole is that we may well and with due regard to our own interests give up the Columbia river, and I have let Aberdeen know privately that he will have no opposition from me on that ground." Quoted by Merk, "British Party Politics and the Oregon Treaty," *loc. cit.*, p. 658.

(the reader should note this abdication of presidential responsibility) on a settlement along the forty-ninth parallel. By early February (and before Polk's intimations were available to him) Aberdeen was relieved of the Palmerston menace by Russell's statement of abstention. He accordingly increased the force of his bluff. At an interview with McLane (February 3) he sharply criticized the American attitude and suggested that his patience had been tried to the point of considering the abandonment of opposition to preparations "founded upon the contingency of war with the United States." Polk learned on February 21 of this strong language from one who had long wished to settle the Oregon dispute; within a week he assured Aberdeen that he was always willing "to receive and to treat with the utmost respect" any British proposals for compromise, by submitting them to the Senate. Buchanan, who conveyed these assurances, indicated privately his opinion that the Senate would act favorably. These steps of course indicate Polk's abandonment of his demand for fifty-four forty. But one who had so recently boasted of looking John Bull in the eye could hardly admit this openly; hence the device of promising acceptance only after Senatorial consent had been received—a reversal of normal process.

Once this shadow-boxing was completed, events marched rapidly. Congress authorized (April 27, 1846) termination of the agreement of 1827, but in terms indicating a desire for peaceful settlement. On receipt of the notice a draft agreement was sent to Pakenham; Polk objected to a clause giving the Hudson's Bay Company free navigation of the Columbia, but the Cabinet advised submitting the draft to the Senate for advice. The treaty was signed June 15, after the Senate had advised acceptance. The urgency of events may have overcome Polk's scruples over the use of the river; the Mexican War began in May, and there was need to settle British complications. The treaty as ratified gave the Hudson's Bay Company the right to use the Columbia River, protected British property rights, drew the boundary along the forty-ninth parallel to midchannel between the mainland and Vancouver Island, and purported to draw the water boundary thence to the Pacific. Arbitration of property rights resulted (1869) in payment of $650,000. The water boundary, due to imprecise cartographical information, had likewise to be arbitrated, and was not settled until 1872. These, however, were matters of detail; Britain had yielded the substance of the dispute for the sake of peace, although her claims probably had the soundest base. Polk's hands were free to deal with Mexico.

Alaska, Bought and Bounded

The Alaska Purchase was the dreary end-product of the magnificent imagination of Secretary of State William H. Seward, whose fate it was to beat his imperialistic brains against a wall of postwar indifference to expansionism. Thus his dream of a United States encompassing the continent, and including the Danish West Indies, Santo Domingo, and Hawaii, shrank to the acquisition of a remote and presumably worthless area opprobriously labeled "Seward's Folly."[15] This resulted from a deliberate Russian decision to unload the Alaskan white elephant upon the United States. The exploitation of this remote area had been entrusted, unprofitably, to the Russian American Company, whose charter expired in 1862, but which continued to operate on sufferance through the rest of the American Civil War. In the postwar period Russia decided to cultivate an earlier and abortive American interest in Alaska, and a conference at St. Petersburg in December, 1866, instructed Baron Edoard de Stoeckl, Minister to the United States, to part with the territory for not less than $5,000,000. Upon his return to the United States in March, 1867, Stoeckl maneuvered Seward into proposing the sale.

After the matter was cleared with President Andrew Johnson and the Cabinet, negotiations proceeded rapidly. Seward's eagerness to buy enabled Stoeckl to raise the price to $7,000,000; the necessity of extinguishing some claims of the Russian American Company caused a hitch at this point and Seward added $200,000 to the

---

[15] The following titles cover the purchase of Alaska: T. A. Bailey, "Why the United States Purchased Alaska," *Pacific Historical Review*, vol. 3 (1934), pp. 39–49; F. R. Dulles, *America in the Pacific: A Century of Expansion*, Houghton Mifflin, 1932, pp. 80–97; W. A. Dunning, "Paying for Alaska," *Political Science Quarterly*, vol. 27 (1912), pp. 385–399; V. J. Farrar, *The Annexation of Russian America to the United States*, W. F. Roberts, 1937; F. A. Golder, "The Purchase of Alaska," *American Historical Review*, vol. 25 (1920), pp. 411–425; R. H. Luthin, "The Sale of Alaska," *Slavonic Review*, vol. 16 (1937), pp. 168–182; B. P. Thomas, *Russo-American Relations, 1815–1867*, Johns Hopkins Press, 1930, pp. 143–166.

agreed amount in return for a title cleared of this encumbrance, making the total price $7,200,000. Seward, eager for action, asked Stoeckl to cable his Government a summary of the agreement, and after an all-night drafting session the treaty was signed and submitted to the closing hours of a Senate session on March 30, 1867. Announcement of the deal made Seward the immediate butt of criticism, much of it humorously malicious, which he countered in a shrewdly conceived propaganda campaign capped by enlisting the powerful aid of Senator Charles Sumner, Chairman of the Foreign Relations Committee and archenemy of the President. Nineteenth-century "ghost writers" helped Sumner remedy his abysmal ignorance of Alaska, and his three-hour speech aided in pushing the agreement through a special session of the Senate on April 9, 1867, by a practically unanimous vote. Formal transfer was accomplished on October 17, 1867.[16]

Payment for Seward's prize package evoked prolonged debate and the breath of scandal. Postponed until after the impeachment and trial of Johnson, the appropriation bill was passed between May and July, 1868, by a Congress fresh from the bitter antagonisms engendered by the two-and-a-half-year fight between Congress and Executive, with the vocal and voting support of many of Johnson's chief opponents. When, presently, it became apparent that not all of the $7,200,000 turned over to Stoeckl had found its way to Rus-

---

[16] The connection of the Russian fleet episode with the Alaska Purchase should be mentioned briefly. In the autumn of 1863 Russian naval contingents unexpectedly appeared at New York and San Francisco, where they remained for some time. This was generally taken as an earnest of Russian support of the United States in the event of Anglo-French adherence to the Confederate cause. Actually, the ships were seeking sanctuary whence, should war break out in Europe as then appeared likely, they could sally forth and emulate the Confederate cruiser *Alabama*. It has been stated by most recent writers that the contemporary American interpretation of the visit was arrived at incorrectly, without knowledge of the true facts, and that the resultant feeling of gratitude toward Russia was somewhat influential at the time of the purchase. See Professor Bailey's article, cited in Note 15; F. A. Golder, "The Russian Fleet and the Civil War," *American Historical Review*, vol. 20 (1915), pp. 801–813; E. A. Adamov, "Russia and the United States at the Time of the Civil War," *Journal of Modern History*, vol. 2 (1930), pp. 586–603. William E. Nagengast, "The Visit of the Russian Fleet to the United States: Were Americans Deceived?" *Russian Review*, vol. 8 (1949), pp. 46–55, introduces contemporary evidence to support the thesis that Americans believed the Russian visit a gesture of friendship even though they understood "that self-interest was the driving motivation behind Russia's diplomatic maneuvers."

sia, rumors culminated in an article in the Worcester (Massachusetts) *Spy* alleging irregularities in connection with the legislation.
The ensuing Congressional investigation produced much smoke but
little fire; Seward's carefully calculated replies evaded several embarrassing questions. Subsequent research supports the conclusion
that, in addition to legitimate expenditures in the field of what
would now be called "public relations," Stoeckl used some funds to
buy votes. The tenuous evidence available makes it impossible to
state categorically who got how much; that guilty knowledge has
long since passed beyond the grave with its possessors. Probably
more important in the bill's final passage was a desire to compensate
for recent Russian good will and the realization, based largely on
Seward's well-conceived propaganda, that Alaska was not the bad
bargain it had first seemed. Possession of Alaska was presently accepted and for some time taken for granted; only tardily did the
question of what, exactly, Seward had purchased intrude itself on
the public consciousness.

This question, long postponed, is the culmination of the story of
Anglo-American boundary disputes and writes a chapter in the
story of Rooseveltian impetuosity in foreign relations. It impinges,
also, on the story of growing Anglo-American *rapprochement* around
the opening of the twentieth century, and portrays Canada, once
again, paying the price of Anglo-American good will.[17] The background must be traced to the mid-1820's. Reference has already
been made to the Russo-American agreement of 1824 which abandoned American claims north of fifty-four forty. British and Russian
diplomats, working from faulty maps and without first-hand knowledge of the terrain, shortly signed (February 28, 1825) a treaty
purporting to set the boundary between western Canada and Alaska,

---

[17] The delimitation of the boundary is covered in the following: T. A. Bailey,
"Theodore Roosevelt and the Alaska Boundary Settlement," *Canadian Historical Review*, vol. 18 (1937), pp. 123–131; Callahan, *Am. For. Pol. in Canadian Relations*,
pp. 465–493; Tyler Dennett, *John Hay: From Poetry to Politics*, Dodd, Mead, 1934,
pp. 224–239, 350–363; Dennis, *op. cit.*, pp. 134–156; C. E. Hill, *op. cit.*, pp. 250–276;
Keenleyside, *op. cit.*, pp. 210–230; McInnis, *Unguarded Frontier*, pp. 298–320; Allan
Nevins, *Henry White: Thirty Years of American Diplomacy*, Harper, 1930, pp. 186–
203; Tansill, *Can.-Am. Relations*, pp. 121–230; S. R. Tompkins, "Drawing the Alaska
Boundary," *Canadian Historical Review*, vol. 26 (1945), pp. 1–24.

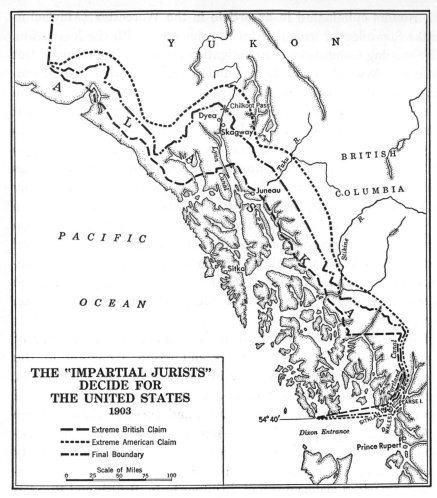

THE "IMPARTIAL JURISTS"
DECIDE FOR
THE UNITED STATES
1903

— — Extreme British Claim
••••••• Extreme American Claim
— •• — Final Boundary

Scale of Miles
0   25   50   75   100

including the long Panhandle stretching southward to the Russo-American frontier. Along the Panhandle the line was supposed to "follow the summit of the mountains situated parallel to the coast," a legal statement of a nonexistent geographical situation, since the mountainous coast was devoid of an orderly system. Indeed, Dr. Tyler Dennett remarks aptly that the supposed treaty line "started from a point which subsequent surveys showed not to exist, and proceeded from crest to crest of a mountain range which never was." Despite this cartographical ambiguity, the intent of the total Anglo-

Russian arrangement was perfectly plain: To deprive the British of access to navigable salt water by establishing an unbroken *lisière* or coastal strip. The subsequent story makes noteworthy the fact that an official Canadian document and map of 1874 recognize the condition of affairs just indicated.

Some practical investigation of the area during the 1880's showed conclusively that the line of the treaty could never be drawn and that a conventional line must be substituted; no agreement as to this could be reached. Increasing Canadian pressure for a settlement in the 1890's complicated the Anglo-American *rapprochement* which was in the making during the same decade. A gold strike in the Klondike (1896), along the upper Yukon River in territory indubitably Canadian, brought matters into sharp focus, since the best means of access lay through the Lynn Canal, a narrow inlet deeply penetrating the coast, along which lay Dyea and Skagway, important points of ingress and egress. In the summer of 1898 Canada advanced claims which would reverse the well-established historical intent of the treaty of 1825, insisting upon a line giving the Dominion control over important harbors. These claims were pressed at the meetings of a Joint High Commission (August 23–October 10, 1898; November 11, 1898–February 20, 1899), called in the hope of settling a number of Anglo-American differences (an earlier section has already noted the fur-seal aspects of its deliberations). Alaska wrecked the Commission and its work was important mainly in bringing out conflicting proposals for settlement. The British proposed arbitration by a board of three, representing the interested parties and a third power, but Secretary of State John Hay, mistrusting impartial umpires, supported the plan finally adopted, namely, a board of six, representing the two parties equally. In such a negotiation, with Britain courting American friendship, as Professor C. C. Tansill remarks, Hay "realized that . . . the United States could not lose. In the fluid condition of existing world politics there was an excellent chance that Canada might be called upon to pay the price of Anglo-American friendship."

Matters remained in suspension for some time under an arrangement of October, 1899, which earned Hay some political oppro-

brium because it conceded temporary British occupation of some
disputed localities. Meantime, however, coöperation on the Open
Door Notes of 1899 and the consummation of the Hay-Pauncefote
Canal Treaty of 1902 strengthened the informal Anglo-American
entente. Meantime, too, the more dynamic Theodore Roosevelt, succeeding William McKinley, had retained the services of John Hay,
sponsor of the six-man board scheme for settling the Alaskan question. The summer of 1902 saw the matter suddenly reopened. In
conversation with Henry White and Joseph H. Choate of the American Embassy in London in late June and early July, Sir Wilfrid
Laurier, the Canadian Prime Minister, raised the question of Alaska
and asked aid in securing a settlement in order to avert the frictions
which might arise were gold discovered in the disputed area. Laurier, clearly anxious for a settlement, even an unfavorable one, indicated his realization that Dominion claims were exorbitant, and
hinted at willingness to accept the six-man board for which Hay had
contended earlier. On February 23, 1903, the Senate agreed to a
convention establishing a "tribunal" (deletion of the word "arbitral"
removed the last vestige of such a connotation from the negotiation)
to draw the boundary.

The plan called for each nation to appoint "three impartial jurists
of repute" for the task in hand. Roosevelt, presuming on Laurier's
desire to settle and supported by a correct but somewhat arrogant
concept of American rights, made selections which belied the terms
of the agreement and raised protests both north and south of the
Canadian border. The ability of Secretary of War Elihu Root was
unquestionable; few would doubt that of Senator Henry Cabot
Lodge of Massachusetts; few knew much about that of former Senator George Turner of Washington. But Root's connection with the
Administration, Lodge's continued and vociferous Anglophobia, and
Turner's geographical identification with Seattle, the commercial
capital of Alaska, thoroughly impeached their impartiality.[18] Laurier

---

[18] Claudius O. Johnson, "George Turner," *Pacific Northwest Quarterly*, vol. 34
(1943), pp. 367–392, gives a more favorable picture of Turner, and indicates that
though convinced of the justice of American claims, he was prepared to vote against
them if they were disproven. Roosevelt evidently approached two or more justices of
the Supreme Court, but met with refusals.

sent a private messenger to Washington to protest the choice of Lodge and Turner. Canadians occupied two of the three British seats: Sir Louis A. Jetté, a Quebec provincial official, and Allen B. Aylesworth, a Toronto attorney, were as thoroughly Canadian as one could ask. The burden of contributing any semblance of impartiality to the tribunal rested upon the shoulders of Lord Chief Justice R. E. W. Alverstone, British chief judicial officer. Having shown his intentions by the agents he had appointed, Roosevelt reëmphasized the rightness of his cause by instructing these agents that certain crucial points were not debatable; he wrote also (July 25, 1903) a letter to Justice Oliver Wendell Holmes, in England for the summer, with the suggestion that it reach the eye of Joseph Chamberlain, Colonial Secretary, and Prime Minister Arthur Balfour, in which he proposed to "take a position . . . which will render it necessary for Congress to give me the authority to run the line as we claim it, by our own people, without any further regard to the attitude of England and Canada. If I paid attention to mere abstract rights, that is the position I ought to take anyhow. I have not taken it because I wish to exhaust every effort to have the affair settled peacefully and with due regard to England's honor."[19]

The tribunal assembled at London on September 3, 1903. The determined position of President Roosevelt and of five of the board's members placed Lord Alverstone in an unenviable position. Beset on the one side by American determination and on the other by Canadian urgency, he was finally, and privately, subjected to pressure by his own Government to prevent a deadlock. This resulted in a settlement favorable to the United States by a vote of four to two, under circumstances which convict Alverstone of (1) departing from his strictly judicial function and slipping over into the role of arbitrator; and (2) going back on his own written opinion. In the first instance, he insisted upon narrowing the width of the *lisière* in the region of the important inlets. Had he adhered strictly to his judicial function, he should have either insisted upon a wider *lisière* (the American contention) or accepted a British line which cut across the mouths of some inlets. By narrowing the *lisière* he be-

---

[19] Quoted in W. R. Thayer, *op. cit.*, vol. 2, p. 210.

came a compromiser rather than a judge. Again, he had in writing
supported his Canadian colleagues' claim to four islands in the
mouth of the Portland Canal. After learning the wishes of his Government he agreed to divide them equally with the United States.
Thus the Americans traded a narow *lisière* for two islands, maintaining, however, effective control of the coast, as the treaty of 1825
had intended. Alverstone, under pressure, traded Canadian interest
for Anglo-American good will; again, Canada paid the fee for a
larger bargain. Her anger was leveled almost equally at her near
neighbor's choice of jurists and at the mother land's political betrayal of Dominion interests. The main effect of the anger was a
determined Canadian drive for autonomy in foreign policy. The
episode just described brings to a happy and, on the whole, reasonable, solution a long and tangled series of Anglo-American border
disputes, whose settlement, while at times turbulent, in the long run
advanced the cause of international comity.

11 The United States and Britain, 1815-1903

CIVIL WAR

ISTHMIAN DIPLOMACY

AMERICAN HOSTILITIES, 1861–1865, WERE A FOREIGN-policy laboratory as well as a Brothers' War. Here were tried out on a considerable and crucial scale numerous questions of recognition, of the rights and duties of neutrals, and of the Monroe Doctrine (already discussed above), in many of which the belligerent North was embarrassed by its previous policies as a neutral. This was particularly true since Britain, the most interested neutral, would watch and cherish carefully any actions which could be turned to her own advantage when positions might again be reversed.[1]

The persons most important in the Northern scheme of things were President Abraham Lincoln, Seward, his Secretary of State, and Charles Francis Adams, his Minister to Britain.[2] Lincoln, to out-

---

[1] The present account will concentrate, in the interests of brevity, on Anglo-American relations, since neither France nor Russia, the other most interested nations, exercised more than a peripheral influence.

[2] The following highly selected titles embody a fair sampling of the literature: C. F. Adams, *Charles Francis Adams,* Houghton Mifflin, 1900, pp. 117–398; E. D. Adams, *Great Britain and the American Civil War,* Longmans, Green, 1925, 2 vols.; Albion and Pope, *op. cit.,* pp. 148–173; F. Bancroft, *The Life of William H. Seward,* Harper, 1900, vol. 2, pp. 123–442; M. P. Claussen, "Peace Factors in Anglo-American Relations, 1861–1865," *Mississippi Valley Historical Review,* vol. 26 (1940), pp. 511–522; C. B. Elliott, "The Doctrine of Continuous Voyages," *loc. cit.,* pp. 61–104; C. E. Hill, *op. cit.,* pp. 276–314; H. D. Jordan and E. J. Pratt, *Europe and the American Civil War,* Houghton Mifflin, 1931; A. M. McDiarmid, "American Civil War Precedents: Their Nature, Application, and Extension," *American Journal of International Law,* vol. 34 (1940), pp. 220–237; Jay Monaghan, *Diplomat in Carpet Slippers: Abraham Lincoln Deals with Foreign Affairs,* Bobbs-Merrill, 1945; Nevins, *Hamilton Fish,* pp. 142–175, 201–230, 372–399, 449–493, 518–566; F. L. Owsley,

ward appearances and to the casual observer, was at the war's outset
an uncouth Midwestern politician, new to the presidency, beset by
office seekers, inexperienced in national administration, and abys-
mally ignorant of the serious military and diplomatic problems with
which he would obviously have to cope. Not yet had his innate genius and his martyr's death at a peak of success begun that apotheosis
which turned him into a world figure. In his own eyes, Seward was
all that Lincoln was not. His influence in the party and his long experience in affairs destined him inevitably to stand at Lincoln's right
hand; persuaded as to his own capabilities, he was convinced that
his hand would guide the ship of state. One of Lincoln's achievements would be to convert Seward's ignorance and impulsiveness
into useful channels.[3] Adams, son and grandson of Presidents, had
followed the family pattern of careful education and broad public
service; his talents included the combination of superlative tact (a
rarity among his kin) and vigorous perseverance essential in dealing with the delicate problems arising during his tour of duty. Appointed at Seward's behest, he saw Lincoln but once before leaving
for his assignment. Lincoln's preoccupation with domestic matters
may be inferred when he turned to Seward, at the close of Adams'
well-chosen remarks, with "Well, governor, I've this morning decided that Chicago post-office appointment."

Britain's attitude concerned both North and South: If it was unfavorable to the North the Union stood in jeopardy; if favorable to
the South, Southern victory was likely. As secession slipped into
what looked increasingly like a long war to preserve the Union
rather than to emancipate the slaves, important groups in England

---

King Cotton Diplomacy, University of Chicago Press, 1931; J. G. Randall, *Lincoln
the President: Springfield to Gettysburg,* Dodd, Mead, 1945, vol. 2, pp. 29–54; Sears,
Slidell, pp. 186–228; E. C. Stowell and H. F. Munro, *International Cases: Arbitrations and Incidents Illustrative of International Law as Practised by Independent
States,* Houghton Mifflin, 1916, vol. 2, pp. 381–405.

[3] Stoeckl testified to his ignorance in a despatch of May 25, 1861: "he labors
under a complete ignorance on international questions; at the same time his self-
conceit is such that he refuses to listen to anyone. His arrogance does more harm
to the Administration than the ineptitude of his colleagues." Quoted in Tansill,
U.S. and Santo Domingo, p. 213. His hare-brained scheme to restore the Union by
the desperate expedient of risking war with France and Spain was embodied in a
remarkable document, "Some Thoughts for the President's Consideration," dated,
appropriately, April 1, 1861. Quoted in Bancroft, *op. cit.,* vol. 2, pp. 132–133.

abandoned an initial pro-Northern sentiment for a feeling that separation of North and South would be to Britain's advantage. Long-continued hostilities would deprive British mills of the uninterrupted supply of raw cotton essential to their operation. The South had of course counted heavily on this to secure British recognition and assistance; the "King Cotton" philosophy had been set forth arrogantly by Senator J. H. Hammond of South Carolina when in 1858 he remarked to the North: "you dare not make war on cotton. No power on earth dares to make war upon it. Cotton is King." An independent South would not only insure this uninterrupted supply but would probably support low tariff or free trade, an attitude important to a British mercantile economy rebuffed by the high-level Morrill Tariff of March 2, 1861. It was also argued that independence would improve Southern economy to the point where heavy British loans would be more secure.

Other items were less tangible but nonetheless significant. British aristocrats had much more in common with their Southern opposite numbers than with any Northern social product. An independent South oriented toward Britain would doubtless lessen the perennial American urge to annex Canada. Moreover, the United States was the object of active and probably well-merited dislike in Britain. What had first been an ingrate child, wantonly breaching the British Empire, had all too rapidly become a swaggering, grasping, and powerful commercial and imperial rival. The check which division would give such a rival was obvious. The London *Economist*, indeed, preferred three or four republics, which it believed would be

more conducive to the peace of Europe. We can feel little doubt that it will also be more conducive to the civilization of America. Limitation will produce modesty and caution. . . . There may be jealousies and quarrels—as there are among contiguous European countries; but we are much inclined to think that these, even if they occasionally proceed to bloodshed, will have a far less demoralizing influence on all concerned than the conviction of boundless power and unmatched grandeur which now inflates the bosom, disturbs the brain and damages the principles and sense of justice of nearly every American citizen. The several commonwealths will keep each other in order.[4]

---

[4] March 9, 1861. Quoted in Owsley, *op. cit.*, p. 200.

Offsetting these factors and to some extent conditioning in favor of the North the diplomatic negotiations which will be the chief concern of the present account were the persistent efforts of certain English liberals such as John Bright and Richard Cobden, who believed that both freedom and democracy were intimately involved in the issues of the war. British labor, not yet enfranchised but awakening politically and sufficiently numerous to influence the formulation of any government policy, had read Harriet Beecher Stowe's powerful tract, *Uncle Tom's Cabin,* and identified itself with the antislavery cause as a means of improving the position of free labor everywhere. A North minus slavery, where the common man had a voice in affairs, offered a refuge even more enticing than that which had already attracted myriads of their friends and relatives.

Recognition—The South Wins and Loses

Recognition of Confederate belligerency was the first important specific question of Civil War diplomacy. Here Seward put himself in the position of the small boy who would both have his cake and eat it too—and both impulses were foredoomed to frustration. Two executive proclamations of April 19 and 27, 1861, blockaded Southern coasts, an action in itself tantamount to Union recognition of Southern belligerency. When, however, reports from England indicated that the British might receive Confederate agents, Seward resolved on drastic action. He instructed Adams, under date of May 21, 1861, that he should "desist from all intercourse whatever, unofficial as well as official, with the British Government, so long as it shall continue intercourse of either kind with the domestic enemies of this country." This was a serious threat, and might well have been followed by dangerous consequences, had it been necessary to carry out the threat. However, by the time Adams arrived events had moved to a point which made this unnecessary. Lincoln's blockade was reported informally in London on May 4. Moving with considerable speed, the Government formally authorized a proclamation of neutrality (which of course recognized Southern belligerency, as well as accepting the fact of the Northern blockade) on May 13, and it was officially published the following day. Meantime Adams, who had delayed his departure for some weeks in order to attend his son's wedding, arrived in Liverpool on May 12, with the formalities of his reception still unsettled. He was thus faced with a *fait accompli* on the first recognition question.

He was given some discretion in applying the orders of May 21, and told Lord John Russell that even an unofficial continuation of relations with the South "could scarcely fail to be viewed by us as hostile in spirit, and to require some corresponding action accordingly." Russell replied that his Government had no intention of seeing the Confederate agents further. This was unsatisfactory but immediately reassuring; with recognition of belligerency accomplished prior to his official arrival, and with further British action postponed for the moment, Adams could assume his post without formally invoking the instructions of May 21. British action, unexceptionable except perhaps for its promptness, increased Confederate respectability and by the same token disappointed the North; it was, of course, the only possible action under all the circumstances.

The question of British recognition of Confederate independence, which came to a head toward the end of 1862, was much more serious.[5] This crisis was postponed largely because the King Cotton theory failed to materialize. Britain entered the war with a huge surplus because of bumper crops in 1859 and 1860, glutting British warehouses with three hundred million excess pounds of raw cotton and large supplies of manufactured textiles, and preventing the practical embargo established in the South from becoming immediately effective. However, by September, 1862, the feast of 1861 had become a veritable famine, with stock on hand down to 100,000 bales. The historian of the cotton famine estimates that when unemployment reached its peak in December, 1862, approximately two million people were receiving government assistance. Confederate military successes accompanied the mounting cotton shortages. The annual Union move on Richmond, this time under General George B. McClellan via the Peninsula, had met with its annual check, and the late summer saw Robert E. Lee and Thomas J.

---

[5] The *Trent* Affair, which drew much more public attention, preceded this in point of time, but will be treated later in connection with another topic.

("Stonewall") Jackson undertaking a powerful sortie into the North which threatened the safety of Washington itself. In light of the developing economic and military situation John Slidell and J. M. Mason presented formal demands for recognition of independence to France and Britain, respectively, late in July. While rejecting these demands, the British Cabinet felt compelled to discuss the possibility of intervention as an alternative to domestic revolution.

News of Jackson's spectacular move at Harper's Ferry (August 29–30, 1862) prompted the Prime Minister, Lord Palmerston, to write his Foreign Secretary, Lord John Russell, on September 14 a note which may be regarded as the inception of the so-called Russell Mediation Plan. In it he proposed, should Lee capture Baltimore or Washington as then appeared likely, that France and England should jointly suggest settlement of American difficulties "on the basis of separation." Russell replied three days later, agreeing to mediation, which he thought might be proposed without the military conditions, since he felt that the South had already proven itself. He added, moreover, that should the North refuse mediation, Southern independence should be recognized, and proposed a meeting of the Cabinet in October to take the necessary action. Lincoln was of course fully alive to the possible consequences of recognition, though not aware of the details of the Russell scheme. His own political and military stock was at low ebb in the summer of 1862; recognition could only be followed by friction, inevitable incidents, and possibly war with Britain. The facts entitle the speculatively inclined to wonder whether recognition might not have insured a Confederate victory before the superior Northern potential could have been brought fully to bear. Here, indeed, was Lincoln's great diplomatic crisis.

The Russell Plan was never implemented. Lee's inability to continue his military success in the Battle of Antietam Creek in mid-September contributed largely to this result. News of this check reached Britain before the date set for Cabinet discussion of mediation, and Palmerston grew increasingly lukewarm to any action not supported by Southern military success. Probably on a par with this was Seward's threat of war in case Britain recognized the South, conveyed in a note of August 2, 1862, to Adams. The entire story has not been unraveled, but it appears that W. E. Forster, a friend of Adams and a confidant of the Ministry, brought the substance of this note to Cabinet attention in October. Of underlying importance, from this point on, was Palmerston's widely shared unwillingness to risk a war which would endanger vulnerable Canada, expose the British merchant marine to attack, and threaten the huge profits accruing to many interests.[6] Considerable Cabinet discussion of mediation came to naught and, though Napoleon's Mexican troubles led him to repeated pressure on the British and to an independent offer of mediation (January, 1863), he received no British support. Lincoln had surmounted his great obstacle.[7]

Roles Reversed—The Shoe Pinches

Questions of neutral rights and obligations were of much greater contemporary and long-run importance. As a long-time champion of neutral rights the United States was uncomfortable as a belligerent, being compelled to adopt and elaborate policies previously considered reprehensible. The *Trent* Affair involved belligerent removal of persons from a neutral vessel and called forth more contemporary and subsequent comment than any other Anglo-American episode of the period. When his original agents proved misfits, Jefferson Davis despatched John Slidell and J. M. Mason to France and England. While traveling from Havana to St. Thomas via the British mail steamer *Trent* they were overhauled on November 8, 1861, by the American sloop *San Jacinto*, Captain Charles Wilkes commanding. Wilkes, acting without orders, removed the

---

[6] Professor Owsley emphasizes the role of war profits in lessening British desire to intervene, showing that the cotton shortages enabled the large operators to make two hundred millions while their mill-hands were going hungry. Linen and woolen interests, munitions manufacturers, and shipbuilders profited directly, while the blockade-runners were earning huge sums and the British-built Confederate raiders were destroying the Northern merchant marine. *Op. cit.*, pp. 569–577.

[7] He could not, of course, know this in 1862 and resorted to emancipation in a desperate effort to stave off British recognition. First suggested to the Cabinet in July, the proclamation was deferred until after Antietam, and issued under date of September 22. Professor E. D. Adams has amply demonstrated that it had no immediate effect in determining the Cabinet against mediation. In the long run, of course, working-class sympathy with its objectives operated as a deterrent to any pro-Southern moves by the Cabinet.

envoys and their secretaries and brought them to the States. His
achievement, although not unlike previous British searches and seizures of American ships, brought public and official acclaim pro-
portionate to the lack of Northern accomplishment in the war to
date.

It brought, also, sharp protest from Great Britain. A Cabinet
meeting held after receipt of the news decided to deliver a virtual
ultimatum, refusal of which might well have led to war. Albert, the
Prince Consort, though well advanced in the illness that caused his
death in mid-December, presented a memorandum, the substance
of which Queen Victoria adopted, counseling a less threatening procedure; in this the Cabinet acquiesced. Russell suggested to Lord
Lyons in Washington (November 30) that, if Seward did not voluntarily propose to release the prisoners, he should be asked to do so,
and to apologize for their capture. Privately Lyons was told to leave
Washington if, after seven days, the envoys were still held. He was
cautioned, however, to handle Seward gently, and evidently did so.
Nevertheless, naval and military measures (several thousand troops
were sent to Canada, some of which entered, ironically enough, by
the overland passage through Maine, due to ice in the St. Lawrence) pointed up Britain's earnestness in the matter. Moreover,
sober opinion in the States realized the similarity of Wilkes' action
to earlier high-handed British acts, and the likelihood that retaining
Mason and Slidell might contribute to war with Britain and consequent Confederate independence.

After a Christmas-day debate the Cabinet decided to release the
captives, but the inevitable public indignation made a face-saving
argument necessary. In it Seward dubbed Mason and Slidell "personal contraband," subject to capture even though traveling not to
a belligerent, but to a neutral state, at the top of the *Trent's* speed.
Wilkes had erred, therefore, only in not bringing the ship as well as
the passengers to port for adjudication. Seward attempted to gloss
over the poverty of his legal argument by praising the British for
at last accepting the American principles of neutral rights at sea.
With this placating gesture, Seward ordered the envoys' release; a
British ship deposited them late in January, 1862, on British soil,

where they were much less useful to the Confederate cause than had they remained in prison in Boston.

A second, and minor, question of neutral rights involved the practice of privateering. After the Crimean War the principal maritime powers had drafted the Declaration of Paris (1856) which, among other provisions, outlawed privateering. This the United States had never accepted because dissatisfied with one of its remaining provisions. In 1861, however, hostilities quickly brought home the danger of privateering, particularly if engaged in, or connived at, by neutrals. Seward promptly ordered the Declaration accepted, only to be rebuffed by British insistence that ratification take effect only after the close of existing American hostilities. This left privateering still legal, but it was quite innocuous, for Britain on June 1, 1861, denied both belligerents the right to bring prizes into British ports. The blockade soon made brnging prizes into Southern ports so difficult that only about forty ships were taken and privateering was virtually abandoncd by the summer of 1861.

British desire to emulate an earlier American example by engaging in broken-voyage trade with the Confederacy raised the most serious question of neutral rights. Such trade became necessary because of the increasingly tight Union blockade, in which the British acquiesced despite the limitations imposed on their trade, because of the possibility that British and American positions might again be reversed in the future; any American easing of the definition of blockade would constitute precedent for later use by a belligerent Britain against a neutral United States.[8] With the blockade a recognized fact, the broken voyage became the recognized evasive technique. Goods shipped in neutral bottoms to West Indian ports were transshipped to blockade-runners for the hazardous, and very profitable, journey to Gulf or Atlantic ports.[9] Complications soon developed, since the efficiency of the blockade-runners compelled the

[8] J. P. Baxter, 3rd, "The British Government and Neutral Rights, 1861–1865," *American Historical Review*, vol. 34 (1928), pp. 9–29, 77–91; "Some British Opinions as to Neutral Rights, 1861 to 1865," *American Journal of International Law*, vol. 23 (1929), pp. 517–537.

[9] Professor Owsley, *op. cit.*, pp. 250–291, makes a persuasive, but not completely documented, case against the blockade's effectiveness. Whatever the statistics, the blockade was tight enough to cause resort to the broken voyage.

Union Navy to capture cargoes on the first leg of the journey. The British repeatedly contended that bona fide intention to land goods at neutral ports immunized such goods from capture until leaving such ports—even though obviously contraband, and bearing the telltale initials "C.S.A." Contrariwise, the United States argued that the *ultimate destination* was the significant thing, and claimed the right to interfere with any trade between neutral ports which appeared to be a subterfuge to break blockade; in effect asserting that since the British intent was to violate blockade by transshipment, such cargoes were subject to capture.

Three outstanding cases may be mentioned briefly. In the *Dolphin* case the Federal District Court applied the doctrine of continuous voyage to blockade. The vessel, ostensibly on a voyage from Liverpool to Nassau with a cargo composed partly of arms, was captured before reaching the latter port. A letter found aboard indicated that the cargo was really destined for Charleston, South Carolina, or Wilmington, North Carolina. In condemning ship and cargo, the court said: "the act of sailing for a blockaded port, with the knowledge of the existence of the blockade, and with an intent to enter, is itself an attempt to break it. . . . The cutting up of a continuous voyage into several parts by the intervention or proposed intervention of several intermediate ports . . . cannot make a voyage which in its nature is one to become two or more voyages, nor make any of the parts of one entire voyage become legal which would be illegal if not so divided."[10] In the *Springbok* case the Supreme Court upheld the confiscation of goods whose *ultimate destination* was the Confederacy, regardless of transshipment at intermediate ports. In the *Peterhoff* case the Supreme Court justified capture on the high seas of *contraband* destined for land transport to the Confederacy.[11] Thus the urgencies of war drove the United States to adopt a large-naval-

---

[10] Stowell and Munro, *op. cit.*, vol. 2, p. 385.

[11] Blockade was not involved in the *Peterhoff* case, since it involved goods ostensibly destined to Matamoros, Mexico, which was not blockaded; neither did their further transport to Brownsville, Texas, violate blockade.

A. M. McDiarmid, *loc. cit.*, minimizes the role of the United States as an innovator, showing that English prize courts had already passed on cases involving contraband, blockade, and ultimate destination long before the Civil War. The fact remains, however, that these received slight publicity in comparison with the Civil War cases.

power attitude toward neutral sea-borne commerce. The British, be it noted, avoided political pressure on behalf of their injured nationals, and stored up the Civil War precedents for refurbishing after 1914.

Britain Minds Her Manners—Tardily

The United States had set a relatively high standard in the observation of neutral obligations during the Revolutionary and Napoleonic wars and was thus justified in expecting a like performance from the British. Some of Adams' most trying experiences, however, were in store before this standard was finally established in 1863. Meantime, Confederate adroitness and British complaisance enabled the South to derive considerable British assistance. Northern naval superiority dictated, perforce, Confederate naval policy, the keynote of which was to achieve a maximum harassment of Northern commerce. Lacking shipbuilding facilities, the Confederate Government commissioned Captain James D. Bulloch to negotiate for the construction of ships which might become commerce-destroyers. Arrived in Britain, Bulloch encountered the Foreign Enlistment Act of 1819 which denied British nationals the right to "be concerned in the equipping, furnishing, fitting out, or arming, of any ship or vessel, with intent or in order that such ship or vessel shall be employed in the service" of a belligerent. Violations entailed severe punishments which, however, were applicable only after due proof of guilt.

British legal counsel furnished Bulloch with a loophole in the law: Violations occurred only when a ship was both built and equipped in British territory; any construction could be carried on, and any equipment purchased, so long as union of ship and equipment was accomplished elsewhere. The *Florida,* the *Alabama,* and the *Shenandoah,* constructed under this subterfuge, wreaked terrific havoc on the Northern merchant marine through actual destruction, increase in marine insurance rates, and a veritable panic which resulted in transfer of about 774,000 tons of shipping to foreign registry, whence it was by law forbidden from returning. Estimates of actual damage run to about 100,000 tons, valued, with cargoes, at between twenty and twenty-five million dollars, of which the *Alabama* bagged about one-third. This raider was hustled out of port in late July, 1862, to avoid detention as a result of Adams' pressure, picked up armament, and sailed 75,000 miles around the Horn, through the China Sea, the Straits of Malacca, and back via the Cape of Good Hope to the English Channel. She was sunk by the *Kearsarge* in July, 1864. She and her sister ships hastened a decline in the American merchant marine already under way for almost a decade. Overproduction of clipper ships and the Panic of 1857 had begun a process which the replacement of wood by steel and of sail by steam would have completed as surely but more slowly.

Bulloch's activities gave Adams plenty of ammunition to pepper the British with demands for seizure of "No. 290," as the *Alabama* was known in the yards, basing his case on British legal advice. Alarmed, the authorities determined upon detention, but illness of a key official delayed matters until the ship was offshore and away. Bulloch promptly started the construction of the *Alexandra* and two ironclads armed with underwater "piercers" designed to poke holes in the wooden blockading ships and, hence, in the blockade itself. Adams' increased protests, plus the raiders' exploits, presently demonstrated to British policy-makers what a subsequent war might mean to them in terms of neutral-built *Alabamas;* they seized the *Alexandra,* April 5, 1863, an earnest of future policy. The courts, however, freed her and she put to sea. Adams' continued pressure culminated in his famous declaration of September 5, apropos Russell's statement that the Government had no legal grounds to retain the Laird Rams: "It would be superfluous to point out to your Lordship that this is war." Adams had meantime been aided by two other factors. Smashing Northern victories at Gettysburg and Vicksburg in early July, 1862, confirmed the growing British belief that the South could not win the war. Worrisome also was the passage (March 3, 1863) of a bill authorizing Lincoln to issue privateering commissions. Inquiry elicited the reply that its purpose was to provide ships to chase the *Alabama,* a somewhat ludicrous explanation in the light of her proven prowess. Reflection caused Russell to fear that the United States might contemplate establishment of a "cruising squadron blockade" in British waters, a device not unfamiliar to Britain, which would inevitably be irritating, and might be dangerous. All in all, the Government decided to detain the Rams, and orders were issued on September 3, two days before Adams' dramatic statement. Henceforth, although an occasional cruiser escaped to sea (including the *Shenandoah,* in the autumn of 1864), British intentions were of the best. Good intentions, however, failed to solve the aggravating problem of American claims for damages, which for years remained a sore spot in Anglo-American relations.

Settlement of these claims merged with several other Anglo-American controversies and was complicated by the fierce domestic discord growing out of a policy for the reconstruction of the conquered South.[12] Finally the Johnson-Clarendon Convention was signed (January 14, 1869) and defeated (April 13, 1869), after a debate made notable by Senator Sumner's speech, aptly called by Professor Allan Nevins "one of the most unfortunate . . . ever made by an American leader upon foreign affairs." In it Sumner asserted that but for three factors, all British, the Civil War would soon have been over: The neutrality proclamation without which it could not have started, and British cruisers and pro-Southern sympathy, without which it could not have persisted. He demanded, in satisfaction for these derelictions, $15,000,000 in payment for the actual shipping destroyed, plus "indirect" claims for (1) collateral damage at sea—higher insurance rates and the like—$110,000,000; (2) damage due to the prolongation of the war which, but for British actions, would have been over by July 4, 1863—$2,000,000,000; a grand total of $2,125,000,000 which even the sanguine Senator had no expectation of collecting. He modestly suggested, however, that ceding Canada would satisfy all claims. Needless to say, the negotiation lapsed.

Various events of 1870 facilitated an overall Anglo-American settlement. The Franco-Prussian War gave Britain concern; the fisheries question urgently demanded solution; Sumner was deposed

---

[12] Among the problems may be mentioned the final determination of the San Juan water boundary, the aftermath of the denunciation of the Elgin-Marcy Treaty in 1866, and the repercussions of the Fenian movement.

from the chairmanship of the Foreign Relations Committee after a stormy experience with President Ulysses S. Grant over Santo Domingo; Lord Clarendon's death removed a somewhat stiff-necked Britisher from the picture; Canada finally made clear her preference for the British connection; and Sumner's exorbitant demands gradually faded from public memory. Complicated negotiations produced a formula: Britain would propose a Joint High Commission to settle the water boundary, the fisheries, and other minor issues; the United States (which had previously refused to arbitrate) would suggest including the *Alabama* Claims in the discussion; Britain would agree. The Joint High Commission, laboring from February 27 to May 8, 1871, drafted the Treaty of Washington. This called for submission of the Claims to an arbitration commission, a concession agreed to only after Hamilton Fish had successfully demanded that the High Commission (and the Treaty) define neutral duties respecting outfitting ships for belligerents, and that this definition should be retroactively applied to the Claims arbitration. The result was the elaboration of the famous "Three Rules of Neutral Duty," in which, after expressing regret for the escape of the *Alabama* and her sister-raiders, it was agreed that a neutral was bound to use "due diligence" to prevent the actions which had permitted the raiders to escape. By ratifying this Britain admitted guilt; the only real task of the arbitration was to determine the amount of damages.

The Commission, composed of representatives of Italy, Switzerland, and Brazil, in addition to the interested parties, met at Geneva, December 15, 1871, and completed its work on September 14, 1872. The American case unwarrantedly revived the indirect claims, thus endangering the whole proceeding. A demand that the British not only pay the cost of the war after July 4, 1863, but also pay 7 percent interest on the amount due, added insult to injury. This curious and unjustified renewal of exorbitant demands is possibly explainable by hasty drafting of the American case. Fish perhaps allowed the inclusion of the demands in order to persuade the Senate to act favorably on legislation implementing the Treaty of Washington; he intimated in a private memorandum that he did not consider them well-founded, but told William M. Evarts, of the American counsel, that he might use them in closing his speech "as bars upon which the spread eagle might perch." After great excitement and a near-breakup of the Commission, a compromise stated that the Commission was incompetent to pass upon the indirect claims, but would, had it had jurisdiction, have regarded them unfavorably, since they had no basis in international law. Applying the Three Rules to the direct claims, Britain was convicted of failing to use "due diligence" with regard to the raiders, and was ordered to pay $15,500,000 in gold, which she did cheerfully. As Professor Robert G. Albion points out, this was a cheap price for a competitor to pay for the long-run damage to the American merchant marine. For the moment, a most aggravating Civil War issue had been liquidated.

Isthmian Dreams Become Reality

The dream of a man-made water-passage linking the Atlantic and Pacific Oceans appealed to those with venturesome imaginations not long after the hazards of the Northwest Passage and the unbroken character of the American continents were established. This became a matter of general interest to the United States as early as 1826, when Secretary of State Henry Clay counseled his delegates to Simon Bolívar's Pan-American Conference that the benefits of any canal "ought not to be exclusively appropriated to any one nation."[13] Special interest appeared around the midcentury when acquisition of land and gold on the West coast and sharp Anglo-American rivalry in the Caribbean threatened peace and the safety of transisthmian land routes. Interest became focused in the 1880's when, emerging as a world power, the United States became alarmed at possible encroachments on what were coming to be considered her preserves. It became paramount around the turn of the twentieth century when expanding Caribbean and Far Eastern interests counseled a policy of Caribbean hegemony. Anglo-American interests

---

[13] As geographical knowledge increased, several potential routes received more or less serious consideration. From north to south they were: (1) across the narrowed waist of Mexico's Isthmus of Tehuantepec; (2) through Honduras; (3) a joint Nicaragua–Costa Rica route, utilizing the boundary San Juan River and Lake Nicaragua; (4) across the narrow neck of Panama; (5) across the Isthmus of Darien; (6) the Atrato River route, in Colombia. Of these, the Nicaragua—Costa Rica and Panama routes were most popular and practicable.

impinged closely at several points of this long route; toward its end larger interests dictated British withdrawal from the scene; the last chapter is written as a strictly inter-American one.

Two midnineteenth-century treaties involved the United States thoroughly in isthmian affairs and insured her at least a share in any future venture.[14] On December 12, 1846, Benjamin A. Bidlack signed a commercial treaty with New Granada which contained, at New Granada's solicitation, an article (35) conveying to the United States "the right of way or transit across the *Isthmus of Panamá* upon any modes of communication that now exist, or that may be, hereafter, constructed." In return the United States guaranteed "positively and efficaciously to New Granada, by the present stipulation, the perfect neutrality of the before mentioned Isthmus, with the view that the free transit from the one to the other sea, may not be interrupted or embarrassed in any future time while this Treaty exists. . . ." The Granadan offer was motivated by fear of British encroachments and of an expedition being readied in London under Ecuadorian auspices for an attack on New Granada, and followed similar, and unsuccessful, overtures to Britain and France. Subsequent developments make it important to note that contemporary opinion agreed that the guarantee provision ran against outside invasion rather than domestic revolution. Polk submitted the agreement, with its guarantee commitment, to the Senate, which accepted it June 8, 1848, to run for twenty years, terminable thereafter upon twelve months' notice. Contemporary evidence makes it clear that Polk did not wish exclusive possession; he was willing to have other

---

[14] Earlier phases of the isthmian story are covered in the following titles, some of which also deal with its later stages: Eleanor E. Dennison, *The Senate Foreign Relations Committee*, Stanford University Press, 1942, pp. 54–72; C. C. Hyde, "The Isthmian Canal Treaty," *Harvard Law Review*, vol. 14 (1900), pp. 52–58; J. B. Lockey, "A Neglected Aspect of Isthmian Diplomacy," *American Historical Review*, vol. 41 (1936), pp. 295–306; Gerstle Mack, *The Land Divided*, Knopf, 1944; D. C. Miner, *The Fight for the Panama Route: The Story of the Spooner Act and the Hay-Herrán Treaty*, Columbia University Press, 1940; E. T. Parks, *Colombia and the United States, 1765–1934*, Duke University Press, 1935, pp. 151–481; Perkins, *Monroe Doct., 1826–1867*, pp. 198–243; R. W. Van Alstyne, "British Diplomacy and the Clayton-Bulwer Treaty, 1850–60," *Journal of Modern History*, vol. 11 (1939), pp. 149–183; "The Central American Policy of Lord Palmerston, 1846–48," *Hispanic American Historical Review*, vol. 16 (1936), pp. 352–357; M. W. Williams, *Anglo-American Isthmian Diplomacy, 1815–1915*, Lord Baltimore Press, 1916.

nations, specifically France and Britain, share in guaranteeing neutrality. By the same token, neither did the United States wish any other nation to enjoy exclusive possession. This sentiment contributed to the formulation of the Clayton-Bulwer Treaty of April 19, 1850.

Ratification of Bidlack's Treaty followed closely on the Mexican cession in the Treaty of Guadalupe Hidalgo. American diplomats busily sought to improve communications with the new Pacific empire by negotiating treaties with Nicaragua and Honduras dealing with canal rights and strategic sites. Ratification of these agreements would have infringed British claims being established by simultaneous negotiations, and would have inevitably brought sharp Anglo-American friction. Furthermore, long-standing British establishments in Central America had recently been expanded by seizure, in the name of the Mosquito Indians (over whom the British had a protectorate), of Greytown, at the mouth of the San Juan River, part of the potential Nicaragua canal route. This was followed by seizure of Tigre Island in the Bay of Fonseca, commanding its Pacific terminus. In order to stave off the rivalry thus developing into a dangerous threat of war, the two nations negotiated, through Secretary of State J. M. Clayton and Sir Henry Lytton Bulwer, the treaty bearing their names (signed April 19, 1850).

In addition to his efforts to soften existing antagonisms and set bounds to American expansionism, Bulwer sought to insinuate British influence into the canal situation. A negotiation of considerable complexity, in which verbal maneuvering played an important part, produced an agreement that neither power would "ever obtain or maintain for itself any exclusive control . . ." over the proposed Nicaragua Canal; neither would erect fortifications commanding it. The principle of joint control was also extended to any other trans-isthmian route; this constituted a block to later American efforts at unilateral action until it was removed by the Hay-Pauncefote Treaty. Both nations derived considerable advantages from the treaty. Each promised to abstain from further territorial acquisitions, but Clayton tacitly (he dared not do so publicly for fear of domestic political repercussions) recognized British pretensions in the Mosquito protectorate, Belize, and the Bay Islands. Britain remained a Central American power, with equal rights in any future canal project. The United States secured a British promise to forego the expansionism which had caused so much recent alarm. She also secured canal rights which she had not previously possessed, though they were held in partnership instead of in exclusive right; this was an advantage, however, as she was in no position at the time to maintain the latter. Finally, a threatening rivalry had been halted.[15]

The idea of an exclusively American canal emerged soon after the Civil War, stimulated by the organization of a privately financed French company in 1878–1880 designed to exploit the name and talents of Ferdinand de Lesseps, fresh from triumphant completion of the Suez Canal, in the construction of a canal at Panama.[16] Fear that the French Government might eventually become involved in de Lesseps' scheme exercised American public opinion to a degree which caused President Rutherford B. Hayes and his Secretary of State, William M. Evarts, to issue warning pronouncements. Recognizing but conveniently glossing over the continuing obligation of the Clayton-Bulwer Treaty, Hayes told Congress (March 8, 1880) that "The policy of this country is a canal under American control. The United States cannot consent to the surrender of this control to any European power or to any combination of European powers." This was reënforced by a report (March 9) in which Evarts asserted that "The paramount interest of the United States in these projects of interoceanic communication across the American isthmus has

---

[15] Much has been written about the relationship of the Clayton-Bulwer Treaty to the Monroe Doctrine, and a categorical statement is difficult. Bulwer himself thought he was implicitly setting it aside by securing American recognition of new British colonial holdings. Professor Perkins, on the other hand, holds that the treaty "seems rather to have been an important affirmation of the Monroe declaration, rather than a denial of its validity. Indeed . . . it represents the only occasion upon which a European nation bound itself by solemn agreement to abstain from doing those things which Monroe's message forbade." *Monroe Doctrine, 1826–1867*, p. 211. It might be fair to suggest that the arrangement countenanced an existing violation for the sake supposedly of preventing subsequent violations. It might further be noted that contemporaries did not regard the joint agreement as violating the Doctrine, however much scholars of a later time may have insisted that it was such.

[16] Miner points out, *op. cit.*, p. 17, that Seward forecast the idea of an American canal before leaving the Department of State, and that Grant had espoused it as early as September, 1869.

seemed quite as indisputable to the European powers as to the States of this continent." Within a few months the House of Representatives advised Hayes to secure release from the joint obligations of the Clayton-Bulwer Treaty.

This effort fell to the lot of President James A. Garfield's somewhat bellicose Secretary of State, James G. Blaine. The latter's note of June 24, 1881, to James Russell Lowell, American Minister to Britain, asserted that the guarantee of the 1846 treaty with New Granada was all-sufficient, and needed no "re-enforcement, or accession, or assent from any other power." This remarkable stand proposed to circumvent the Clayton-Bulwer Treaty by the simple expedient of ignoring it. Becoming restive at Britain's failure to reply, Blaine, in a note of November 19, 1881, instructed Lowell to seek modification of that treaty, alleging that it had been "made more than thirty years ago, under exceptional and extraordinary circumstances which have long since ceased to exist . . ." and that the joint guarantee which it contemplated was contrary to the Monroe Doctrine. Lord Granville's reply to Blaine's June note, delayed until November 10, succinctly reflected the current British position, calling the impatient Blaine's attention to the obvious fact that the isthmian relations of the two nations were still governed by the Clayton-Bulwer Treaty, "and Her Majesty's Government rely with confidence upon the observance of all the engagements of that treaty." Blaine's successor, Frederick Frelinghuysen, returned to the charge, urging complete abrogation of the 1850 agreement by arguments essentially similar to Blaine's. This abandonment of neutralization and joint guarantees of course reflects the increasing power, financial stature, and Caribbean interests of the United States; Britain's reaction likewise reflects her unwillingness, as yet, to accept these facts in relation to her own position in the Caribbean and in the world at large.

While British and Americans discussed, the French prepared to dig; the French Company's excavations, begun in 1883, continued until 1889. These labors moved 72,000,000 cubic yards of Panama's soil, but tropical diseases, coupled with extravagance and inefficiency in management, bankrupted the company. The original concession expired, but renewals postponed until 1904, and later (on payment of 5,000,000 francs) until October 31, 1910, the day when the canal must be in operation. The New Panama Canal Company was organized in October, 1894, to conserve French isthmian interests, more likely by selling the franchise rights than by actually completing construction. American interest and opinion on the canal question developed against this background. The interest increased with the expansion of the American economy and the nation's increasingly outward look. Opinion at this time generally favored a Nicaraguan canal, particularly after an American corporation, the Maritime Canal Company of Nicaragua, was chartered (1889) and began operations halted only by its bankruptcy in 1894. Early in 1896 the French Company employed William Nelson Cromwell, an exceedingly capable New York attorney, to look after its interests. His principal early work consisted of propagandizing against a Nicaraguan canal until the time when positive pressure in favor of Panama might become effective.

American victory in the Spanish-American War served to focus attention sharply upon isthmian policy.[17] The U.S.S. *Oregon* rushed 13,000 miles around Cape Horn to join the Atlantic Fleet in defending the East Coast against a Spanish attack which proved to be purely imaginary. A canal would have made the distance scarcely a third as great; the next enemy might be more formidable. The war launched the United States formally upon a career of overseas imperialism long in the making, with new interests in the Caribbean (Puerto Rico a possession and Cuba virtually a protectorate) and the Pacific (Hawaii, the Philippines, Guam, and part of the Samoan Islands), coupled with the new commercial opportunities thus afforded. Strategy and economics alike brought an isthmian short cut to the fore.

The Clayton-Bulwer obstacle remained. Since the days of Blaine

---

[17] The following supplement the titles already listed: Baker, *Woodrow Wilson*, vol. 4, pp. 394–422, 426–430; Philippe Bunau-Varilla, *Panama, the Creation, Destruction and Resurrection*, McBride, Nast, 1914; W. H. Callcott, *The Caribbean Policy of the United States, 1890–1920*, Johns Hopkins Press, 1942, pp. 140–165; Dennett, *John Hay*, pp. 248–263, 364–383; Dennis, *op. cit.*, pp. 156–170, 309–346; C. E. Hill, *op. cit.*, pp. 347–389; C. L. Jones, *The Caribbean Since 1900*, Prentice-Hall, 1936, pp. 278–339; J. F. Rippy, *The Capitalists and Colombia*, Vanguard, 1931, pp. 91–102.

and Frelinghuysen, however, events (some of which have already been chronicled) had tended to moderate British insistence upon its continued force. Britain's policy of abstention from the European alliance system was wearing thin in the face of an aggressive Germany which was challenging British naval superiority. The Boer War had proved a troublesome, if minor, nuisance; upstart nations were challenging British hegemony in China to a point where some counterweight must be developed; even though the United States had resisted repeated British overtures for alliance, her postwar position made her worth cultivating as a friend to whom might safely be entrusted the military domination of the Caribbean, long considered essential to British interests. Here lies the key to the Hay-Pauncefote Treaty of 1900–1901.

The British were evidently willing to revise the Clayton-Bulwer Treaty favorably to United States interests as early as February, 1899, as part of the Joint High Commission negotiations, but, as already noted, this body broke up over the question of the Alaska Boundary. After the ensuing hard feelings had cooled, Hay reached agreement (February 5, 1900) with the British Ambassador, Sir Julian Pauncefote. The treaty granted the United States sole canal-construction rights, subject to the neutralization provisions governing the Suez Canal, which would have limited rather severely American control of the finished waterway; it denied the right of fortification, left the Clayton-Bulwer Treaty in effect except where specifically superseded, and proposed to invite the adherence of other powers to its arrangements. Publication of these terms evoked criticisms well-founded in terms of the national interest, since the nonfortification provisions would permit the use or seizure of the canal by the nation's enemies in time of war, and European participation in an American enterprise under the joint-guarantee clause might constitute a precedent prejudicial to the Monroe Doctrine. Senate amendments remedied these defects by specific supersession of the Clayton-Bulwer Treaty, affirmative permission of fortification, and elimination of the joint-guarantee article, but the British objected to this gazing into the mouth of the gift-horse and rejected the amended agreement (March, 1901).

Hay resigned in pique at Senate treatment of his agreement, but was persuaded to reconsider. The continued worsening of Britain's position vis-à-vis the Boers and Germany afforded opportunity for renewed negotiation and a Second Hay-Pauncefote Treaty emerged (signed November 18, 1901; accepted by the Senate, December 16, 1901). This formally repealed the Clayton-Bulwer Treaty and omitted the joint-guarantee provisions. Nothing was said about fortifications, but in a memorandum (August 3, 1901) Lord Lansdowne conceded the right to fortify, which was specifically included in the Hay–Bunau-Varilla Treaty with Panama. This earnest of withdrawal from any attempt to dominate the Caribbean, implemented within a few years by reduction of British forces in the area, marked another step in the advancing British respect for the United States shown in several episodes already noted. It concludes this long chronicle of Anglo-American relations on a much more harmonious note than that sounded when the story began.

Optimistically discounting the Clayton-Bulwer obstacle, Americans had long argued the merits of alternative canal routes. Panama and Nicaragua, the most likely, found adherents who developed powerful lobbies; railroad interests, wary of water-borne competition, opposed whichever lobby seemed ahead at the moment. Final choice of the Panama route resulted from these pressures and counterpressures upon Congressional policy. Public and technical opinion, reënforced by both Houses of Congress, generally favored the Nicaraguan route, which was evidently the one taken for granted by the negotiators of the Hay-Pauncefote Treaty. The ultimate choice of Panama was a triumph of lobbying activity, credit for which must be shared by Cromwell, Senator Marcus Alonzo Hanna of Ohio, and a remarkable and ebullient Frenchman, Philippe Bunau-Varilla. The real battle opened with the report (November 16, 1901) of the Walker Commission, established in 1899 to survey possible routes, in favor of a Nicaragua canal.

This body preferred the Panama route from the physical standpoint, but recommended a Nicaragua canal because the French company set a value of $109,141,500 on its properties and franchise. The Hepburn Bill, embodying the Commission's recommendation,

passed the House promptly (January 9, 1902) by a vote of 308 to
2. Meantime the French company, seeing the prize about to slip
from its grasp, cabled (January 4) an offer to settle for the $40,000,-
000 figure which the Walker Commission had estimated its rights
and properties to be worth. The Commission thereupon reversed itself (January 18) and recommended in favor of Panama. Before the
Hepburn Bill reached the Senate floor acceptance of the second
Hay-Pauncefote agreement had cleared the way for action. The
June, 1902, debate was marked by Mark Hanna's vigorous defense
(June 5–6) of the Spooner Amendment substituting a Panama route.
Whatever contributions Cromwell and Bunau-Varilla may have
made to the ultimate success of Panama, the immediate impetus
came from Hanna's conversion to its cause.[18] The Hepburn Bill
became the Spooner Act (June 28, 1902) in a triumph of the lobby-
ist's art. It authorized acquisition of a right of way from Colombia
or, if such should prove impossible, of a Nicaraguan right of way.

The Panama Revolution emerged from the ensuing period of complicated maneuvering. The immediate problem was to reach agreement with Colombia. Here affairs rested under the uneasy control
of José Marroquin, a professor turned Vice-President, who had
assumed control late in July, 1900, by the simple expedient of im-
prisoning the aged chief executive. Power did not bring peace, however, and revolution made Marroquin's position so precarious that
any yielding to the United States would endanger his hold on office.
This never became clear to Roosevelt, who to the end believed him
a trickster trying his hand at extortion. By the same token, Marroquin seems to have been poorly informed as to Roosevelt's attitude; moreover, Hay, evidently under Cromwell's influence, adopted
a policy well calculated to antagonize Colombia. Negotiations,
therefore, began, and remained, on a plane of misunderstanding
and mutual suspicion.

---

[18] This statement is made with due regard to Bunau-Varilla's heroic work with
stamps. The New York *Times* of May 29, 1902, reported an eruption of Mt. Momo-
tombo, a Nicaraguan volcano a hundred miles or so from the proposed canal route.
Bunau-Varilla, calling to mind a recent Nicaraguan stamp depicting an active volcano,
secured a supply and laid one on each Senator's desk with the suggestive legend: "An
official witness of the volcanic activity of Nicaragua." Bunau-Varilla would have been
the last one to deny the influence of this episode on the final decision.

Long discussions produced the Hay-Herrán Treaty (signed January 22, 1903; accepted by the Senate, March 17), forced on the reluctant Colombian diplomat by Hay's implied threat to turn to Nicaragua, offering $10,000,000, plus an annual stipend of $250,000, for a one-hundred-year lease, renewable repeatedly at the sole option of the United States, for a right of way, and the right to buy out the French company. Marroquin, lacking constitutional power to act alone, and unable to exert effective personal pressure because of his precarious position, presented the treaty to his Congress, where debate was postponed until mid-July. Matters were complicated by a Colombian attempt to milk the French company of ten of the forty million dollars anticipated from the United States, and to increase the ten-million-dollar payment of the Hay-Herrán Treaty to fifteen; the American Minister's threat that his Government might turn to Nicaragua was neither well-received nor taken seriously. The Senate rejected the treaty on August 12, amid Colombian charges of coercion, echoed by Rooseveltian snorts of "international blackmail." These events reanimated the Nicaragua lobby; the ensuing stalemate stimulated moves already under way to sever Panama's rather tenuous ties with Colombia.

A local *junta* received word from Cromwell, shortly before the treaty was defeated, that he would coöperate enthusiastically in a revolution, and plans were made accordingly. Dr. Manuel Amador-Guerrero, a politically ambitious physician, arrived in New York early in September; his meetings with Cromwell were terminated abruptly when the latter received a warning that aid to revolution would result in forfeiture of the French concession. Amador's laconic telegram *"desanimado"* (discouraged) well described his depression, which ended only with the appearance in New York (September 22) of Bunau-Varilla with a head full of plans and a purse containing, he thought, enough money to finance a small-scale revolution in Panama. He revived Amador's spirits and busied himself in interviewing various American dignitaries (he saw Roosevelt on October 9 and Hay a week later), eliciting from the latter enough information to justify a shrewd guess that they would not grieve at a Panamanian uprising. He eventually promised Amador $100,000, payable after revolution had succeeded, and packed him off to Panama, armed with a declaration of independence, a proposed constitution, a code for communication, a hastily stitched flag designed by Mme. Bunau-Varilla, and a message to be sent, once the revolution was accomplished, inviting Bunau-Varilla to become the first Panamanian Minister to the United States. Observing the development of thought and action in American government circles will indicate that his confidence in Amador's prospects was not ill-founded.

About mid-August Roosevelt received Professor John Bassett Moore's memorandum arguing that Colombia should not be allowed to obstruct the completion of the canal. Early in October he drafted a tentative statement for submission to Congress in December, asking authority to extinguish French rights and proceed with construction in spite of Colombia's attitude. Should Congress oppose this policy, he proposed, under the Spooner Act, to revert to the Nicaraguan route. A revolution would, of course, make such action unnecessary. His attitude toward Bunau-Varilla at the interview of October 9 was quite correct, but that worthy left with the distinct impression that revolution would not displease him.[19] Hay so encouraged Bunau-Varilla that the latter promised Amador the protection of American forces within forty-eight hours after the revolution took place. About the same time, learning from two army officers just returned from Panama that a revolution was likely during the first three weeks of November, Roosevelt ordered several naval units to Colombian waters. It is thus quite fair to conclude that Hay and Roosevelt were pleased at the likelihood of revolution and had so disposed the fleet as to hinder Colombian repressive measures. This is amply confirmed by the text of the so-called "Fifty Mile Order," issued on November 2 to naval commanders in the area: "Maintain free and uninterrupted transit. . . . Prevent landing of any armed force, either Government or insurgent, with hostile intent at any point within 50 miles of Panama." The consul

---

[19] Roosevelt's letter to Albert Shaw, October 10, 1903, confirms this impression: "Privately, I can freely say to you that I should be delighted if Panama were an independent State, or if it made itself so at this moment. . . ." Bemis, *Am. Secs. of St.*, vol. 9, p. 164.

at Colón was further instructed: "Government force reported approaching the Isthmus in vessels. Prevent their landing if, in your judgment this would precipitate a conflict." Since on this day there was no revolution, and since the insurgents had no ships, this could only mean that Washington was determined to prevent Colombia from suppressing revolt against her own authority; Roosevelt thus handed Panama over to the revolution.

It occurred on schedule, engineered on November 3 by the Panama City fire department. The only human casualty was a Chinaman; the same bombardment from a Colombian gunboat ended the life of a donkey in a local abbatoir. Meantime Colombian troops, landed at Colón on the opposite side of the Isthmus on November 2, were at first unable to proceed to Panama City because the railroad officials, acting in concert with the revolutionaries, had thoughtfully removed most of the rolling stock; later the Fifty Mile Order functioned to the same end. By November 6 both Panama City and Colón were in revolutionary hands; the same day saw the new government officially recognized as de facto; and on November 18 the Hay–Bunau-Varilla Treaty (ratified by the President, February 25, 1904) made the new Republic a protectorate of the United States. It also granted, in return for $10,000,000 in cash and an annual gold rental of $250,000 (the latter to begin nine years after ratification), the right to build the canal in a ten-mile-wide zone, and to construct the necessary fortifications.

Roosevelt's high-handed action evoked a storm of protest both in Colombia and the United States. Sober second thought compels the conclusion that this criticism was valid. It cannot be held that the use of force to prevent Colombia from suppressing revolution accorded with either the letter or the spirit of Bidlack's Treaty. Moreover, the precipitate recognition of Panama's independence subjects the Government to the charge of intervention in order to secure that very "sovereignty and independence" which it had prematurely recognized. Almost as serious, from the standpoint of statesmanship, is Dr. Tyler Dennett's cogent assertion that patience and forbearance would in all probability have overcome Colombian opposition and secured a workable agreement. Roosevelt, constrained to justify his action, set up an ingenious but legally untenable doctrine of the international right of eminent domain which gave the United States " a mandate from civilization" to clear the way for a great and necessary public work. Years later (March 23, 1911) he revealed his real objectives in an exuberant speech to some California college students which Henry F. Pringle has said was to cost the United States twenty-five million dollars:

if I had followed the traditional . . . method I should have submitted an admirable state paper . . . detailing all the facts to Congress. . . . In that case there would have been a number of excellent speeches . . . in Congress; the debate would be proceeding at this moment with great spirit and the beginning of the work on the canal would be fifty years in the future. Fortunately the crisis came at a period when I could act unhampered. Accordingly *I took the isthmus,* started the canal and then left Congress not to debate the canal, but to debate me . . . while the debate goes on the canal does too, and they are welcome to debate me as long as they wish, provided that we can go on with the canal.[20]

The evil influence of Roosevelt's action on inter-American relations soon inspired efforts to soothe Colombia's injured feelings. A treaty negotiated in 1914 expressed "sincere regret" at the interruption of Colombian-American friendship and proposed to repair the breach by payment of $25,000,000. Colombia promptly accepted, but the negotiators had reckoned without Mr. Roosevelt, who fulminated in the *Outlook* that it would be "an act of infamy to pay even a dollar to a nation which, in crooked greed, tried by blackmail to smirch the good fame of America." The matter remained in abeyance until 1921, by which time Colombia's oil prospects were a matter of international moment; moreover, American reputation in Latin America was none too good. It was suggested rather pointedly in the Senate that a favorable attitude toward Colombia might beget concessions on oil in return, and on April 20, 1921, the Senate agreed to pay $25,000,000, without apology. Colombia in return recognized American canal rights. This move, both just and expedient, soothed Colombian feelings and was of some slight help in improving inter-American relations.

---

[20] Quoted in Mack, *op. cit.,* p. 477; italics supplied.

A final word remains to be said concerning the tolls-exemption issue. With the canal about to open, Congress began discussing a law exempting domestic coastwise shipping from payment of tolls, on the basis of a rather peculiar interpretation of Article 3 of the Hay-Pauncefote Treaty which stated that "The canal shall be free and open to the vessels of commerce and of war of all nations observing these Rules, on terms of entire equality. . . ." The British protested during the debate on the ground that "all nations" should include, rather than exclude, the United States, but Congress proceeded to enact the law early in 1912. Plenty of evidence was offered to indicate that the American interpretation contradicted opinion contemporary to the treaty, and before Woodrow Wilson had been long in office he concluded that the law must be repealed. Somewhat scanty evidence points to the conclusion that Wilson bargained with the British to work for repeal in return for their withdrawal of recognition of the Huerta Government in Mexico. It seems likely, also, that the bargain resulted in British pressure on Weetman Pearson (Lord Cowdray) to contract his extensive plans for the exploitation of areas bordering the Caribbean and the Gulf.

12 Expansionism: World Phase

THE FINAL DECADE OF THE NINETEENTH CENTURY BROUGHT into focus a reviving imperialism whose fruits were territorial, economic, and strategic. It was linked in spirit with that earlier burst of expansionism which after the Gadsden Purchase of 1853 had been forced into the background by the issues of slavery, war, and reconstruction. That it never died out completely is witnessed by the Ostend Manifesto, by W. L. Marcy's effort to annex Hawaii in 1854, by the grandiose but abortive schemes of William H. Seward, by continued interest in Canadian annexation, and by some tentative moves of Andrew Johnson and U. S. Grant. By and large, however, domestic concerns dominated the 1870's and 1880's. These decades produced, among other things, a huge industrial machine, attracting millions of rural Americans and of immigrant Europeans into urban centers where they created a mounting volume of goods and capital. The owners of these surpluses were led, like their European counterparts in earlier decades, to seek markets to absorb their goods and gold; they found, however, that most of the pleasant places of the earth were already under the flags of nations which had felt the same urges earlier. As a result the New Imperialism, heir of Manifest Destiny, contented itself with relatively modest but favorably located territorial acquisitions, the subject of the present chapter, and became likewise an imperialism of invested dollars whose promotion and defense became a function of the government. The rank and file of Americans observed but casually this change from rural to urban, from importer to exporter, from poor to rich. Some shrewd prophets of a new day, however, saw the possible implications and urged fulfillment of the new destiny. Among these were such writers and public figures as Captain Alfred Thayer Mahan, the youthful Theodore Roosevelt and his friend Henry Cabot Lodge, and Professor John W. Burgess. Playing upon the varied strings of sea power and empire, the widely circulated writings of these and others laid the groundwork for the burst of enthusiasm which bore fruit in the 1890's; it should carefully be borne in mind, however, that the spirit of the 1840's never died completely, and that this spirit had begun in somewhat guarded fashion to move overseas, to Hawaii and Samoa, in the 1870's.

Wedge into the Pacific

The acquisition of the Hawaiian (Sandwich) Islands, completed incidental to the Spanish-American War in 1898, well illustrates the combination of economic and strategic factors characterizing the New Imperialism. It was a consummation long-delayed but often foreshadowed from that far-off day in 1789 when the first American expedition made its landfall.[1] Lying so close to the continent's western shores, it was at once a natural next step to expansionist-minded Americans and a potential danger in the hands of any other power. This became increasingly apparent as the advent of the Clipper Ship and the steam engine quickened the tempo of transportation and enhanced the value of coaling stations. It soon became apparent, too, that Hawaiian sugar could help fill the yawning cavity that was America's sweet tooth. This last discovery appealed particularly to

---

[1] T. A. Bailey, "Hawaii and the United States during the Spanish-American War," *American Historical Review,* vol. 36 (1931), pp. 552–560; Jean I. Brookes, *International Rivalry in the Pacific Islands, 1800–1875,* University of California Press, 1941, pp. 344–365; Dennis, *op. cit.,* pp. 101–117; D. M. Dozer, "The Opposition to Hawaiian Reciprocity, 1876–1888," *Pacific Historical Review,* vol. 14 (1945), pp. 157–183; Dulles, *Am. in the Pacific,* pp. 138–199; Nevins, *Cleveland,* pp. 549–562; J. W. Pratt, *Expansionists of 1898,* Johns Hopkins Press, 1936; "The Hawaiian Revolution, a New Interpretation," *Pacific Historical Review,* vol. 1 (1932), pp. 273–294; W. A. Russ, "The Role of Sugar in Hawaiian Annexation," *Pacific Historical Review,* vol. 12 (1943), pp. 339–350; Tansill, *Foreign Policy of Bayard,* pp. 359–409; A. F. Tyler, *The Foreign Policy of James G. Blaine,* University of Minnesota Press, 1927, pp. 191–217.

descendants of the missionaries who had begun their highly successful work among the impressionable natives in 1820. Succeeding generations abandoned the vineyard of the Lord for the more profitable plantations until they shared largely in American economic control of the islands. A brief chronicle will indicate the developments which convinced the dominant American group that its only safety lay in annexation to the United States.

Missionaries, visiting whalers, and other commercial venturers advertised the islands and in 1842 a Hawaiian mission to the West requested an international guarantee of the monarchy which was even then in danger of passing under foreign domination. President John Tyler and his Secretary of State, Daniel Webster, were not eager to assume such an obligation, as the nation had not yet acquired the Pacific foothold which would make feasible the policy of joint control applied to an isthmian canal in the Clayton-Bulwer Treaty of 1850. Webster was, however, sufficiently concerned to suggest pointedly that while his Government had no desire for annexation, it would deprecate such action by any other power. Temporary occupation by the British (1843) and French (1849) indicated continuing European interest; by the latter year the Mexican War had advanced American boundaries to the shores of the Pacific, and consequently increased concern with Hawaii. The result was a treaty of amity and commerce signed December 20, 1849, just as French influence was mounting. The Hawaiian monarch was evidently willing to cede his kingdom in 1851, but the Polk regime had given way to the more cautious Millard Fillmore with Webster once more Secretary of State, and the matter rested. Franklin Pierce's Democratic administration had no such inhibitions; the possibilities of Hawaiian sugar had begun to dawn on California; finally, continued exposure to the blessings of civilization rendered the native population increasingly incapable of self-government. Secretary of State William L. Marcy therefore initiated negotiations looking to annexation and a draft treaty emerged in August, 1854. Two unsatisfactory provisions caused delay: One called for annuities of $300,000 to numerous members of Hawaiian royalty whom annexation would place in the ranks of the unemployed; Marcy's top figure had been $100,000. Again, a promise of statehood boded ill to the trembling balance of sectional hostility which characterized the 1850's. While Pierce delayed, illness carried off the king who signed the agreement; his successor fell under anti-American influence and the opportunity disappeared in the gathering storm of domestic conflict.

Postwar annexationism remained for some time secondary to a growing movement for reciprocity. Continental sugar interests opposed this for obvious reasons; annexationists feared that it might postpone or defeat their goal. Their fears were somewhat assuaged, however, by the agreement signed January 30, 1875, allowing Hawaiian sugar into the States duty-free and carrying a promise that the kingdom would never alienate ports or territory to any other power. The feeling that this was a convenient stepping stone to annexation, plus fear of possible British ascendancy, smoothed the way to acceptance of this arrangement. Continued British gestures drew from James G. Blaine a statement (December 1, 1881) which, while rendering lip service to the notion of Hawaiian neutrality as against other nations, stressed the necessity "of drawing the ties of intimate relationship between us and the Hawaiian Islands so as to make them practically a part of the American system without derogation of their absolute independence . . ." and pointedly asserted that should neutrality prove impracticable, Blaine's government "would then unhesitatingly meet the altered situation by seeking an avowedly American solution for the grave issues presented." The Arthur administration signed (December 6, 1884) a treaty extending the life of the reciprocity agreement, but its passage was delayed for months. Finally, in the spring of 1886, the Committee on Foreign Relations accepted an amendment offered by Senator John T. Morgan of Alabama, but unknown to Secretary of State Thomas F. Bayard until he read it in the newspapers, giving the United States a naval station at Pearl Harbor, near Honolulu. Senate acceptance of amendment and treaty (January 20, 1887) emphasized the growing strategic importance of the islands and secured a port whose name would blaze into world-wide prominence in the flames of Japanese destruction in 1941. Meantime island sugar had so prospered under reciprocity as to gear Hawaiian economy so thoroughly into that of the United States that any disturbance of the economic relationship would be bound to have profound political repercussions.

This economic prosperity depended increasingly upon Chinese and Japanese workers whom the sugar planters had brought in to augment the inadequate native labor supply; by 1890 the pure-blood native population had decreased to around 34,000 (from 132,000 in 1832). The white minority which had long dominated Hawaiian affairs looked fearfully to a future in which a preponderantly oriental population might lead to Eastern political domination. These uncertainties were magnified when the McKinley Tariff of 1890 threatened the Hawaiian economy by allowing Cuban sugar free entry to the American market, giving continental producers a countervailing bounty of two cents per pound, and levying import duties on many Hawaiian products which had entered freely under the reciprocity agreement. The cup of danger overflowed with the accession to the throne (1891) of Lilioukalani, sister of the deceased Kalakaua, an avowed opponent of the Constitution of 1887 which had entrenched white control. Under these circumstances annexation appealed to many as the only solution of a complex problem: Those who feared Japanese aggression foresaw security under American protection; some planters supported the move because it would make them eligible to receive the sugar bounty (it should be noted that others opposed annexation, fearing that application of exclusion legislation would cut off the supply of cheap oriental labor essential to the plantation system); advocates of white supremacy could thus avoid the perpetuation of the corruption and inefficiency which characterized the native government.

Matters came to a head when the Queen, influenced by anti-American advisers, proposed (January 14, 1893) to promulgate a constitution based on the theory of Hawaii for the Hawaiians and real power for Lilioukalani. Two days later the American Minister, John L. Stevens, providentially returned from a vacation cruise aboard the U.S.S. *Boston,* and in response to the insistence of a local Committee of Public Safety that it was unable to protect

American interests, landed marines who, curiously enough, deployed so as to intimidate the Queen rather than protect Americans. While the monarch was still in her palace Stevens recognized (January 17) a provisional government which thirty hours earlier had been unable to preserve order; within two weeks he was writing to Washington: "The Hawaiian pear is now fully ripe, and this is the golden hour for the United States to pluck it." Events then moved with commendable speed. Within five days a mission was en route to the United States; it arrived in San Francisco January 28, was in Washington February 3, and twelve days later a treaty of annexation was before the United States Senate.

Here progress halted abruptly. The lame-duck Republican Administration failed to act on the treaty; the House rebuked Stevens by adopting a resolution (February 1) opposing the annexation which he had advocated and the protectorate which he had proclaimed. Grover Cleveland, a convinced anti-imperialist, investigated island affairs through James H. Blount, who reported that the minority of annexationists would not dare risk a plebiscite on their favorite proposal. Cleveland's new Minister, A. S. Willis, exploring the possibility of restoring the Queen, was discouraged by her stout reply to his query as to her likely disposition of the revolutionary leaders: "My decision would be, as the law directs, that such persons should be beheaded and their property confiscated to the Government." Equally disturbing were Willis' efforts to oust Judge Sanford B. Dole, head of the revolutionary government; the judge began preparations for defense. Faced with this dilemma, Cleveland passed the matter on to Congress in a message of December 18 in which he paid his respects to the methods by which American armed forces had contributed to the establishment of the Dole regime. Congress kept hands off through the Cleveland Administration and no further action was taken beyond a recognition of the Dole government which occurred in 1894 after Lilioukalani had bowed to the inevitable.

Continuing Hawaiian pressure for annexation contributed to the signature of a new treaty (June 16, 1897) early in the McKinley Administration. Three days later the Japanese vigorously protested this menace to the future of 25,000 of their nationals domiciled in Hawaii. Republican annexationists exploited this thinly veiled threat of a nation only recently become, by its victory in the Sino-Japanese War, a world power and a potential destroyer of the Pacific balance. There were, however, too many Democratic anti-imperialists in the Senate and progress halted until after Commodore George Dewey's startling victory at Manila Bay, May 1, 1898. Here was an opportunity not to be neglected; a joint resolution (following the Texas pattern of half a century earlier) replaced the languishing treaty. It was speciously argued that the islands must be annexed to protect Dewey's rear; more cogent realities of naval strategy converted other doubters; and still others succumbed to the "jingo bacillus" at the time ravaging the land. July 7, 1898, McKinley signed the joint resolution annexing Hawaii and erecting it into a United States Territory. Thus was finally consummated an arrangement long since true in all but name, the product of complex forces of Church, of dollars, and of strategy—a consummation which, but for the impetus of war, might nevertheless have been indefinitely postponed.[2]

Samoan Strategies

American interest in Samoa presents a combination of economic and strategic factors similar, although in somewhat different proportions, to that which has appeared in the Hawaiian story. It demonstrates again that the imperialist urge which characterized the 1830's and

---

[2] John W. Foster who was Secretary of State during a portion of the period covered above, has left a statement typical of the moderately imperialist point of view: "It would have been the excess of political unwisdom to allow this group of islands to fall into the hands of Great Britain or Japan, either of which powers stood ready to occupy them.

"The native inhabitants had proved themselves incapable of maintaining a respectable and responsible government, and lacked the energy or the will to improve the advantages which Providence had given them in a fertile soil. They were fast dying out as a race, and their places were being occupied by sturdy laborers from China and Japan. There was presented to the American residents the same problem which confronted their forefathers two centuries before in their contact with the aborigines of the Atlantic coast.

"A government was established in Hawaii which had all the elements of a *de jure* and *de facto* sovereignty, and had vigorously maintained itself for four years. It sought for incorporation into the American Union. Under all the circumstances the President and Congress of the United States would have been recreant to their trust if they had failed to take advantage of the opportunity." *American Diplomacy in the Orient*, Houghton Mifflin, 1903, pp. 384–385.

1840's was dormant rather than in complete eclipse after the Civil War. The Samoan group consists of fourteen islands, located strategically about midway between Honolulu and Sydney, New South Wales, and possessing at Pago Pago on the Island of Tutuila a rival to Pearl Harbor in adaptability as a naval base and coaling station.[3] The islands produce copra, dried cocoanut meat which yields an oil useful in various culinary and cosmetic products. American economic concern in Samoa was always secondary and lagged far behind that of Great Britain and Germany, the other powers actively involved. Strategic concepts, ably pushed by private shipping interests with profits in prospect, gradually led the government to develop such an interest in an area five thousand miles from San Francisco as to depart from two cardinal principles of its foreign policy, nonintervention and the avoidance of entangling alliances.

Long-standing but minor commercial contacts merged suddenly into political concern in the early 1870's. A group of California speculators worked out an abortive if time-honored scheme for fleecing the natives of their land with "gifts" of firearms and firewater. More ambitious was the proposal of William H. Webb, a New York shipbuilder, who hoped to launch, under government subsidy, a line of steamships from San Francisco to New Zealand and Australia. He sent an agent, Captain E. Wakeman, to Samoa in 1871 to secure information likely to loosen Congressional pursestrings. Returning, Wakeman paused at Honolulu and sang the praises of Samoa so loudly to the American Minister and Commander R. W. Meade of the Pacific Squadron that the latter, without authority from Washington, signed a treaty (February 17, 1872) with Chief Mauga of Samoa, giving the United States the sole right to establish a naval station at Pago Pago and promising Mauga and his successors "the friendship and protection of the

---

[3] Brookes, op. cit., pp. 288–343; Dennis, op. cit., pp. 103–117; Dulles, Am. in the Pacific, pp. 98–138; J. W. Ellison, "The Partition of Samoa: A Study in Imperialism and Diplomacy," Pacific Historical Review, vol. 8 (1939), pp. 259–288; Opening and Penetration of Foreign Influence in Samoa to 1880, Oregon State University, 1938; Sylvia Masterman, The Origins of International Rivalry in Samoa, 1845 to 1884, Stanford University Press, 1934; G. H. Ryden, The Foreign Policy of the United States in Relation to Samoa, Yale University Press, 1933, the standard work; Tansill, Foreign Policy of Bayard, pp. 3–119; Tyler, op. cit., pp. 218–253.

great Government of the United States of America." Webb placed copies of Wakeman's report of September, 1871, on the desks of officials high in the State and Navy Departments, and Secretary of State Hamilton Fish received Meade's treaty in April, 1872. His study of the documents led him to urge its adoption and Grant sent it to the Senate with a favorable recommendation, May 22.[4] The Senate proving indifferent, Webb applied pressure to Grant through Col. A. B. Steinberger, a former army officer of German birth who was Webb's friend and agent and a personal friend of the President.

This colorful character met Grant in August, 1872, and proposed his own despatch to Samoa as a representative of the United States to investigate conditions in the islands and report to the government. The wheels turned but slowly and it was not until June 29, 1873, that he sailed from San Francisco on a privately chartered ship, as an unsalaried special agent, receiving only $12 per diem for his expenses. His two-month stay in the islands encouraged the natives to hope for at least a protectorate. He brought back a petition for annexation, one argument for which was the chief's knowledge of American "paternal care of the Indians." Grant, however, failed to present this petition to Congress and Fish forwarded Steinberger's glowing report to the Senate in April, 1874, without comment. Though quite without authority, Steinberger continued to work for annexation, and to act as if he expected in that event to become his government's agent in the islands.

On the strength of his prospects Steinberger, unknown to Fish, made a remarkable deal (September 16, 1874) with J. C. Godeffroy & Co., the Hamburg firm which for decades had been the leading mercantile concern at Apia, promising to accord the company governmental favors in return for substantial commissions payable to himself. He next persuaded Fish to authorize a second trip to Samoa, this time at Steinberger's own expense, though he was given passage on a government vessel. Fish's instructions of December 11, 1874, were explicit on annexation: It was "more than doubtful

---

[4] While the treaty was before the Senate the Secretary of the Navy wrote Webb of the Department's "strong interest" in his line of procedure and promised "all the support we can properly give you."

whether . . . these considerations would be sufficient to satisfy our people that the annexation of those islands to the United States is essential to our safety and prosperity." Such being the case, Steinberger's functions were strictly limited "to observing and reporting upon Samoan affairs, and to impressing those in authority there with the lively interest which we take in their happiness and welfare." His actions belied his instructions, for within little more than three months after his arrival (April 1, 1875) he had eased out one of the two kings who were in control, had written a new constitution making all actions of the remaining monarch dependent upon the countersignature of the prime minister, and had modestly assumed that office for himself. His assumption of authority soon merged into delusions of grandeur which involved him in such trouble that he was presently deported aboard a British warship. Professor G. H. Ryden, the leading authority on Samoan-American relations, concluded that had the Grant administration's domestic difficulties been less engrossing, Steinberger's grandiose ideas might have had some chance of success.

Their original hopes dashed, the Samoans tried again in 1877–1878 when through their agent, La Mamea, they offered themselves to the United States either by annexation or protectorate. Congressional leaders were still hostile, however, and the best that could be secured was a treaty of amity and commerce (in effect February 13, 1878) by which the United States secured naval station rights (not exclusive, as in the Meade agreement) at Pago Pago, and in turn promised to use its good offices in case of future Samoan disputes with other powers. Thus by the close of the 1870's the United States stood committed to the extent of opposing the acquisition of the islands by any other power, though congressional lethargy had defeated any possible executive desire for annexation.

An ensuing period of confusion witnessed a sharpening rivalry among the three interested powers, with the Germans insisting that their political position be made commensurate with their economic preponderance. This was unsatisfactory to both Samoa and the United States, and in 1887 American initiative produced a three-power Washington Conference on Samoan affairs. The American proposal for tripartite control foundered on the rocks of an Anglo-German community of interest. Prince Otto von Bismarck was just launching the new German Empire upon a colonial program, and by making concessions elsewhere secured British support for his demand for a sole mandate over Samoa. The conference dissolved and Samoan confusion mounted as German commercial interests gained the upper hand. International tension increased and at its height Germany had three warships, the United States a like number, and Britain one, in the harbor of Apia. Cleveland had meantime turned the Samoan situation over to Congress, which appropriated $500,000 to protect American lives and property and a fifth as much to improve the works at Pago Pago, neglected during a parsimonious decade. These appropriations marked not only an attempt to meet a particular situation but a growing interest in the Pacific which neither Webb nor Steinberger had been able to arouse. The elements intervened just when it seemed that hostilities were inevitable, and a great storm sank or beached all except the British vessel (March 16, 1889).

This manifestation of Nature coincided with a Bismarckian change of heart, and in January, 1889, negotiations were resumed at Berlin. Blaine instructed his agents to insist upon the integrity of the native government and equality of trade rights in Samoa. Under German pressure they abandoned the first of these in the establishment of the Tripartite Agreement or Condominium (signed June 14, 1889) which placed large segments of Samoan affairs under joint foreign control. Ratification of this agreement also violated the American principle of no entangling alliances; the fact that the Government would sign such an arrangement indicates the lengths to which it was willing to go to avert the only possible alternative—complete German control.[5]

So artificial an arrangement could hardly succeed; moreover, its

---

[5] Professor Ryden quotes John Bassett Moore aptly in this connection: "The significance of the Samoan incident lies, however, not in the mere division of territory, but in the disposition shown by the United States, long before the acquisition of the Philippines, to go to any length in asserting a claim to take part in the determination of the fate of a group of islands, thousands of miles away, in which American commercial interests were so slight as to be scarcely appreciable." *Op. cit.*, p. 520.

principle offended the anti-imperialist Cleveland, whose Annual Message of December 3, 1894, referred to the Condominium as "signally illustrating the impolicy of entangling alliances with foreign powers," and forthrightly requested Congress to consider abandoning it. He was ignored, however, and matters rested until after the Spanish-American War had officially registered the United States among the imperialistic nations. Difficulties incident to the Samoan royal succession afforded an opportunity to reopen the whole question; at another three-power conference in 1899 Germany suggested that the United States take Tutuila and some small islands commanding the approaches to Pago Pago and let Britain and Germany divide the rest. Agreement to this effect was signed December 2, 1899, and Tutuila passed under American control. Germany received all the rest, Britain taking in lieu of her share German rights in the Tonga Islands, part of the Solomons, some territory in West Africa, and relinquishment of German extraterritorial rights in Zanzibar. The islands thus acquired were placed under the supervision of the Secretary of the Navy, but long remained in an anomalous position since the Government failed to recognize Samoan cessions of territory made in 1900 and 1904 until 1929, in which year they were formally incorporated in American territory. Thus was concluded the second rehearsal for the New Imperialism.

Leap to the Far East

The preceding story should have suggested the conclusion that the Spanish-American War expressed rather than originated the New Imperialism.[6] Its causes lie deeply imbedded in the intangibles of a

---

[6] The changing American spirit is well described in J. W. Pratt, "The 'Large Policy' of 1898," *Mississippi Valley Historical Review*, vol. 19 (1932), pp. 219–242, and pp. 1–33 of his *Expansionists of 1898*. The following titles cover the war itself: T. A. Bailey, "Dewey and the Germans at Manila Bay," *American Historical Review*, vol. 45 (1939), pp. 59–81; F. E. Chadwick, *The Relations of the United States and Spain: Diplomacy*, Scribner, 1909, pp. 411–589; Dennis, *op. cit.*, pp. 63–101; Dulles, *Am. in the Pacific*, pp. 199–292; H. E. Flack, *Spanish-American Diplomatic Relations Preceding the War of 1898*, Johns Hopkins Press, 1906; C. E. Hill, *op. cit.*, pp. 314–346; Holt, *op. cit.*, pp. 165–177; Walter Millis, *The Martial Spirit: A Study of Our War with Spain*, Houghton Mifflin, 1931; J. W. Pratt, "American Business and the Spanish-American War," *Hispanic American Historical Review*, vol. 14 (1934), pp. 163–201;

long Spanish-American antagonism, but more immediately in developments of the 1880's and 1890's. During these years Spain's increasing inability to maintain order in an area so close to a potential isthmian canal impinged sharply on the consciousness of those who were beginning to think seriously of such an interoceanic link. Too, American investments in Cuba were extensive (about fifty million dollars in tobacco and sugar as of 1898) and subject to both embarrassment and danger from local disturbances that piled up claims which proved uncollectable.[7] On the other hand, rebellious Cubans, often possessors of *ad hoc* citizenship, launched repeated filibustering expeditions against Spanish authority in their native island; Spanish claims for damages were irritating, even when the American Government had not been overly zealous in suppressing the filibusters. Imponderable but important was the fact that the United States was a strong power, with a newly constructed navy, and had had no recent test of the strength which many of its citizens were so eager to see used.

American tariff policy acted as a catalyst in both Spanish-Cuban and Spanish-American relations. The McKinley Tariff of 1890 put raw sugar on the free list and reduced to one-half cent per pound the duty on the refined product. The Wilson-Gorman Act of 1894 levied duty of 40 percent ad valorem on raw sugar and one-eighth of a cent per pound on the refined article, which meant disaster for the Cuban producers. Spain could well subscribe to the old adage that Satan finds work for idle hands, for insurrection soon developed (February 24, 1895). Filibustering was renewed with gusto and questions of neutrality rose apace, with Spain more angry at the one expedition out of three which got through to Cuba than grateful to the American Government for stopping the other two. The

---

L. B. Shippee, "Germany and the Spanish-American War," *American Historical Review*, vol. 30 (1925), pp. 754–777; M. M. Wilkerson, *Public Opinion and the Spanish-American War*, Louisiana State University Press, 1932; J. E. Wisan, *The Cuban Crisis as Reflected in the New York Press (1895–1898)*, Columbia University Press, 1934.

[7] It should be emphasized that American business as a whole, aside from interests actually endangered, was opposed to war in 1897 and early 1898, but adjusted with remarkable ease to the concept of imperialism after Dewey's victory at Manila Bay. On this subject see Pratt's article, "American Business . . ." cited above.

rebels paid no more attention to the niceties of warfare than their
Spanish enemies, a fact which was conveniently played down in the
American press. Spanish repressive measures were entrusted, in
February, 1896, to the none too tender mercies of General Valeriano
("Butcher") Weyler. He promptly inaugurated the *reconcentrado*
policy in order to prevent the populace from aiding the *insurrectos*.
Under this scheme all civilians in disaffected areas were ordered into
camps and all persons taken in opposition to government troops
were to receive "summary" treatment. By thus concentrating the
population, Weyler thought to starve the rebels into submission.
Contrary to his calculations, the women and children crowded the
camps, while the able-bodied men joined the insurrection and lived
off the country. Weyler was neither able nor willing to look after the
crowds of unfortunates, and they died by the thousands.

Their unfortunate plight excited the pity and anger of honest
humanitarians in the States. It excited also the cupidity of two
towering figures of American journalism, Joseph Pulitzer and William Randolph Hearst, whose activities did much to create a public
opinion which swayed Congress and ultimately pushed an insuffi-
ciently resistant McKinley over the brink of war. Immigrant Joseph
Pulitzer, after a varied apprenticeship, had bought Jay Gould's
moribund New York *World* in 1883, promptly changing it into the
first of all "yellow" journals. By using all the devices of sensational-
ism then known, inventing others, and combining all with a crusad-
ing zeal which often attached itself to burning social issues, he cured
the *World's* financial ills to his own considerable profit. Such success
could only breed imitation. In September, 1895, according to Mr.
Walter Millis, "a tall, horse-faced, rather unprepossessing youth
. . . arrived in New York equipped with an idea and $7,500,000."
The possessor of these interesting perquisites was the son of a
wealthy mining Senator, George Hearst of California, who in 1887
had given his son a San Francisco newspaper as a plaything. Successful with his toy, young Hearst (he was thirty at his New York
début) followed Pulitzer into the New York field by purchasing the
Journal, which was, like the pre-Pulitzer *World,* in dire financial
straits. Imitating all of Pulitzer's tricks, Hearst added others, and a

merry race ensued. Cuban difficulties afforded a heaven-sent opportunity to match wits and circulation; Weyler's activities, real or invented, were chronicled in enormous and misleading headines and equally deceptive news columns. Widely copied by the back-country press, the rivals built up a public indignation which soon made trouble for the policy makers.

This thankless role first fell to Grover Cleveland, already painted as an anti-imperialist normally unwilling (except for his temporary lapse in the Venezuela affair) to embark his Government upon uncertain paths. His was an unenviable position as he faced the rising tide of public opinion generated by Hearst and Pulitzer and the only slightly less provocative outpourings of Lodge and Mahan. He stood valiantly to his guns, however, refusing to recognize Cuban belligerency in the face of tremendous pressure, and, moreover, refusing to pay attention to Congressional pronouncements, insisting to the end of his term that the Executive must determine the foreign policy of his Government. His sole concessions to the state of Cuban affairs were a proclamation (June 12, 1895) recognizing that Cuba was "the seat of serious civil disturbances, accompanied by armed resistance to the authority of the established Government of Spain," and an offer of friendly mediation (April, 1896) which Spain ignored. He stood firm, too, despite the adoption of a concurrent resolution (April 6, 1896) favoring recognition of belligerency and reqesting the President to use his good offices to obtain for Cuba a peace of independence. His final word, after his party's defeat, was a hope, in his message of December 7, 1896, that Spain would offer Cuba autonomy, with a gentle warning that American patience might not last forever. As on other occasions, Cleveland had to await the historian's favorable verdict on his actions; for his contemporaries he was all too cautious.

William McKinley profited briefly from Cleveland's sagacity and the assassination of a reactionary Spanish Prime Minister who was succeeded in October, 1897, by the more conciliatory P. M. Sagasta. His Government replied unfavorably to McKinley's tender of good offices (made September 23, 1897), but gave earnest of good intentions by recalling Weyler in October and announcing (November 25) a scheme of Cuban autonomy dependent only upon prior cessation of hostilities. These developments encouraged McKinley, after hinting at the possibility of intervention, to adopt a wait-and-see policy in his first annual message. If Sagasta's reforms could bring peace to Cuba, McKinley would be happy; his main interests had been domestic, his program was domestic, and the business interests which had elected him were generally uninterested in foreign adventure. Domestic jingoes, spurred on by Hearst and Pulitzer, found the message too mild for their mounting desires. Cuban interests, too, found Sagasta's proposed reforms uninviting. Sagasta's offer of autonomy, if accepted, boded ill for the Spanish element of Havana, destined to short shrift under Cuban home rule. Neither did Sagasta's plan appeal to the *insurrectos*, now hopeful of American intervention on their behalf. Matters remained in unstable equilibrium during the autumn and early winter of 1897–1898 until the balance was tilted against peace by two events of February, 1898—the unfortunate letter of Señor Dupuy de Lôme, the Spanish Ambassador, and the destruction of the U.S.S. *Maine.*

De Lôme's official reaction to McKinley's message, as conveyed to his Government, had been correct enough; privately he wrote José Canalejas, a friend in Cuba: "I consider it bad. Besides the natural and inevitable coarseness with which he repeats all that the press and public opinion of Spain have said of Weyler, it shows once more what McKinley is: weak and catering to the rabble and, besides, a low politician who desires to leave the door open to himself and to stand well with the jingoes of his party."[8] This letter by devious paths came into Hearst's hands, and was printed in facsimile (other papers had to be content with the text) on February 9. Days of headlines preceded and accompanied the Minister's resignation before his Government could reply affirmatively to an American request for his recall, but the fat was already in the fire. Spain's letter apologizing for de Lôme's monumental *faux pas* was overshadowed by the *Maine* disaster of February 15, 1898.

Anti-autonomy (pro-Spanish) elements had rioted in Havana on January 12, endangering American lives. Since mid-December,

---

[8] Quoted in Wisan, *op. cit.*, p. 380.

1897, the *Maine* had been at Key West, subject to the request of Consul General Fitzhugh Lee for her presence in Havana. On January 24, under circumstances which have never been completely clarified, and despite Lee's request for delay, she was ordered to Havana, arriving on January 25, the first American naval unit to enter the harbor in three years. She remained at anchor until February 15, when an explosion destroyed the ship and took the lives of two officers and 258 men. The yellow journals promptly shrieked for vengeance; soberer opinion urged suspension of judgment pending investigation, which was undertaken simultaneously but independently by each government. The American Court of Inquiry reported, March 28, that the disaster had been caused by an external explosion which in turn detonated one or more forward magazines, but the Court refused to fix responsibility for the event. A more thorough investigation in 1911 confirmed the verdict, but again declined to fix responsibility, after which the ill-fated vessel was sunk in water too deep for prying eyes. Much hard work and many conjectures have failed to solve the riddle of "Who blew up the *Maine?*" but it may be pointed out that Spain had everything to lose by such an overt act, though it might have appealed to venturesome underlings; the insurgents had much to gain but hardly the necessary resources or technicians; one may reasonably doubt whether Spanish underlings or successful insurgents had the necessary self-restraint to avoid eventual boasting over so great an achievement. There remains, too, the possibility of accidental explosion of an external mine, or an equally accidental internal explosion.[9]

Developments followed rapidly in the *Maine* disaster. Though McKinley clung to peace, some of his big business supporters began by mid-March to feel that war was inevitable. On March 9 Congress responded to mounting public pressure by appropriating, without a dissenting vote, $50,000,000 "for national defense and each and every purpose connected therewith. . . ." This killed any slim remaining chance for the success of Spanish autonomy proposals and raised the interventionist hopes of the 1898 version of the American War Hawks. On March 17 Redfield Proctor of Ver-

---

[9] See Millis' analysis of the situation, *Martial Spirit,* pp. 128–129.

mont reported to the Senate on his one-man investigation of Cuban conditions. Proctor was no jingo; his account documented, in soberer language, the tales of Hearst and Pulitzer and convinced thousands who had refused to believe the "yellows." It was against the mounting pressure of these events that McKinley's policy must be recounted and evaluated. The day before the *Maine* Court of Inquiry reported, Minister Stewart L. Woodford was instructed to sound out the Spanish Government on three proposals, the last less urgent than the others, and together embodying McKinley's idea of essential peace conditions: (1) An immediate armistice, to continue until October 1, to give the President time to mediate between Spain and the insurgents; (2) prompt abandonment of the *reconcentrado* policy, permitting native farmers to return to work and allowing American relief agencies access to the Cuban needy; (3) if possible, a Spanish promise that in case peace efforts had not succeeded by October 1, McKinley should be final arbiter of Spanish and insurgent differences.

Though not in the accepted form of an ultimatum, the urgency of the American request was apparent to the Spanish Government, which was torn between the danger of losing power because of capitulation to the American demands and possible war for not capitulating. Attempting to avoid either alternative, the Ministry offered to submit the issues raised by the *Maine* episode to arbitration, agreed to a Cuban armistice if requested by the insurgents—hardly likely under the circumstances—and on March 30 revoked the *reconcentrado* order, thus accepting one of McKinley's conditions. On April 9 a long step was taken toward meeting the armistice proposal by an order directing the commanding general in Cuba "to grant immediately a suspension of hostilities for such length of time as he may think prudent to prepare and facilitate the peace earnestly desired by all." Though substituting the general's discretion for McKinley's October 1 date, this was probably as far as any Spanish Government could go without prospect of immediate domestic revolution. The following day (Sunday, April 10) Woodford cabled McKinley: "I hope that nothing will now be done to humiliate Spain, as I am satisfied that the present government is going, and is loyally ready to go, as fast and as far as it can. With your power of action sufficiently free you will win the fight on your own lines."

Before these developments had been completed McKinley had already given way to the public clamor and prepared for delivery on April 5 a message submitting the Cuban question to Congress; in the state of popular frenzy, this was equivalent to a declaration of war. Action was postponed over the succeeding week end in order to permit evacuation of Americans from Havana. Receipt of the armistice order (in McKinley's hands on Sunday, April 10) failed to halt the President's program; the message as originally prepared went to Congress on Monday, April 11, with a brief appended statement indicating the developments of the 9th. In it McKinley requested authority to intervene forcibly in Cuban affairs, urging such action on grounds convincing to an inflamed public but generally agreed to have been legally inadequate. He concluded the message with a futile gesture toward the Spanish move of April 9:

Yesterday, and since the preparation of the foregoing message, official information was received by me that the latest decree of the Queen Regent of Spain directs General Blanco, in order to prepare and facilitate peace, to proclaim a suspension of hostilities, the duration and details of which have not yet been communicated to me.

This fact, with every other pertinent consideration, will, I am sure, have your just and careful attention in the solemn deliberations upon which you are about to enter. If this measure attains a successful result, then our aspirations as a Christian, peace-loving people will be realized. If it fails, it will be only another justification for our action.

As Millis aptly puts it, "The fact that Spain had surrendered was imparted in two brief paragraphs, inserted at the end of nine closely printed pages written on the assumption that she had not." Thus did McKinley abdicate the position maintained by Cleveland and allow free play to the warlike forces which had long been building in the country.

These forces had their way promptly. A joint resolution of April 19 declared that Cuba was independent, demanded that Spain relinquish authority over the island, directed the President to use force to attain these ends, and, in the "Teller Amendment," disavowed "any disposition or intention to exercise sovereignty, jurisdiction, or control over said island except for the pacification thereof, and asserts its determination when that is accomplished to leave the government and control of the island to its people." McKinley signed this the following day and on the 25th Congress declared that war had been in effect since April 21, matching the date of Spain's declaration.

As too often before and since, American military preparation was inadequate. Naval affairs, particularly in the Far East, were in better condition, due in part to the extracurricular activities of Assistant Secretary of the Navy Theodore Roosevelt. This youthful statesman, along with Lodge, Mahan, and others had for years been urging the advantages of sea power and colonies in the advancement of the American economy. He combined action with thought. When the command of the Asiatic Squadron fell vacant, Roosevelt, who wanted Manila, set about finding a man whom he believed would, given the opportunity, fight for it. His choice fell on George F. Dewey, ineligible for the post, but elevated to it through Roosevelt's insistence and Senator Proctor's connivance. Once Dewey was installed, Roosevelt saw to it that he was ready for any emergency. On February 25, during the height of the *Maine* excitement, Secretary of the Navy John D. Long left the office in his assistant's charge while he stole a few hours' rest. Gleefully abetted by his friend Lodge, Roosevelt issued numerous orders which caused his superior to confide plaintively to his diary that "the very devil seemed to possess him yesterday afternoon." Among the orders was one to Dewey to concentrate his squadron on Hong Kong, to fill his bunkers, and to stand ready for an attack on Spanish holdings in the Philippines. Though he chided Roosevelt for his presumption, the Secretary did not rescind Dewey's instructions.

Thus it happened that on the night of April 30 Dewey's squadron ran the batteries at the entrance of the deep and narrow Bay of Manila and early the next morning was in position to attack the Spanish defending squadron, ordered by the timorous governor general to stand out in the Bay from the fortress guns which might have afforded some protection. Smoke forced a recess after three

American volleys at the Spanish fleet; firing was resumed at 11:16 A.M. and scarcely forty-five minutes later the Spanish admiral ceased firing, unable to continue the action further. This startling victory cost nine casualties, the most serious of which was a broken leg. Making many Americans for the first time aware of the existence of the Philippines, it set the stage for immediate complications and momentous long-run developments.

Though Manila was vulnerable, Dewey had to wait for ground troops before attempting occupation. Meantime he encountered difficulties with a squadron instructed to look after German interests in case the United States should decide against annexing the archipelago. Blockade regulations gave rise to sharp differences between Dewey, harassed by heavy responsibilities and outgunned by the superior German fleet, and the German Admiral; Dewey sent an angry message offering the German a fight if he wanted one. Calmer counsels prevailed and the crisis blew over, though later writers were to extend it in time and magnify its proportions by alleging that the Germans were preparing to attack Dewey's flank during the bombardment of August 13 and were only deterred when British warships took up an intervening position. Professor Bailey has demonstrated that the Germans were innocent of evil intent and that the British change of station was designed only to improve their view of impending hostilities. Dewey's other embarrassment was Emilio Aguinaldo, a former Filipino insurrectionary, in Singapore when the war scare was in the making. Urged by an American consul, he visited Dewey at Hong Kong and later, after the Manila battle, Dewey invited him to the Islands and assisted him in starting another insurrection against Spanish control as an auxiliary to the American expeditionary force. On the strength of promises allegedly given him by the two Americans, Aguinaldo claimed United States recognition of his Philippine Republic. Dewey vigorously denied any commitment to Aguinaldo, but the latter honestly believed that such had been made; when his demands for recognition were not honored he went into the opposition and forced the United States to spend two years and engage 70,000 troops before catching up with the dusky patriot.

The Caribbean issue was decided quickly but without particular credit to American arms. The barnacle-covered Spanish fleet took uneasy shelter in Santiago Bay, where it was soon blockaded. A young naval officer, Richmond Pearson Hobson, made a dramatic but unsuccessful attempt (June 3, 1898) to close the entrance to the Bay by ramming the antiquated collier *Merrimac* into the bank in such a way that the shifting tide would swing her stern across the narrow channel. An almost ludicrous chapter of accidents dogged the expedition: All but two of the torpedoes fastened alongside to sink the ship at the proper moment were rendered ineffective by Spanish shots which shattered the wiring of the wet-cell batteries then in use; opening the sea-cocks failed to sink the vessel; an unusually accurate Spanish shell shattered the rudder, and the anchor dragged; finally the ship grounded by the stern, but was lifted by the tide and drifted into such a position that when she finally sank the channel was only closed to such an extent as to make night navigation impracticable. Nevertheless, Hobson, who was picked up by the Spanish and returned unharmed, became a minor hero of the war.[10] Its major hero, perhaps, was Theodore Roosevelt who, deserting his recent naval affiliation, became lieutenant colonel of a volunteer regiment of "Rough Riders." These, along with other American troops, reached Cuba tardily after a period of mismanagement and inefficiency characterized by the issue of winter clothing for a subtropical expedition. Early in July a combined land-sea engagement defeated Spain completely; her fleet surrendered after a token resistance, and she admitted the end of her power in the New World by asking French assistance in making peace.

The French ambassador signed a protocol on Spain's behalf on August 12, 1898, agreeing that Spain would relinquish Cuba and evacuate it promptly, cede Puerto Rico (occupied by the United States during the war) in lieu of an indemnity, along with one of the Ladrones, to be chosen later by the United States; the latter, finally, was to "hold and occupy the city, bay, and harbor of Manila, pending the conclusion of a treaty of peace which shall determine the control, disposition and government of the Philippines." Negotia-

[10] See the account of his exploit in the New York *Times,* June 10, 1934.

tions proper opened at Paris on October 1. McKinley chose as his delegation three members of the Senate, C. K. Davis, chairman of its Committee on Foreign Relations, W. P. Frye, its President Pro Tem, and George Gray of Delaware, the sole Democrat and the only convinced anti-imperialist. Secretary of State W. R. Day[11] and Whitelaw Reid, publisher of the New York *Tribune,* completed the group.

Cuba and the Philippines received major attention in the delegation's deliberations. Resigned to losing Cuba, Spain spent almost a month trying unsuccessfully to shift the island, and more particularly her own debt of $400,000,000 incurred in administering and attempting to pacify it, to the United States. Disposition of the Philippines made it impossible for the United States to evade any longer the question of overseas imperialism. Public and executive opinion through the summer and autumn grew increasingly complacent at the thought of accepting a share of that White Man's Burden which other nations had borne so long and so profitably. The business community, which had been largely apathetic to overseas expansion despite the praises of imperialism sung for a decade by the youthful jingoes, developed a sudden alertness after Dewey's victory at Manila. The impending partition of China into spheres of foreign influence might offer a great actual and potential market; a combined stepping stone and naval base in the Philippines would complete the bridge to Asia begun by acquisition of Hawaii during the war. Moreover, Far Eastern markets were becoming more desirable than ever because of retaliatory restrictions leveled against the high rates of American protection in the McKinley (1890) and Dingley (1897) tariffs. Naval interests, intent on the strategic implications of the Philippines, quickly seconded this business interest in the Far East. Finally, the fact that millions of Filipinos were heathen and other millions Roman Catholic offered American Prot-

---

[11] Day had been Assistant Secretary. He succeeded his aging chief, John Sherman, on April 28, 1898, after months of anxiously shepherding his superannuated superior, who had been kicked upstairs to make room in the Senate for Mark Hanna, kingmaker to McKinley. Archie Butt, the shrewd gossip of the Taft Administration, retails an illustrative if perhaps apocryphal anecdote to the effect that Sherman once decided, while crossing the street from the Department to the White House, that the United States should declare war upon Austria. A. W. Butt, *Taft and Roosevelt: The Intimate Letters of Archie Butt,* Doubleday, Doran, 1930, vol. 2, pp. 565–566.

estantism an outlet for its perennial proselyting zeal. All in all, contemporary Americans found much to be said for overseas imperialism.[12]

Under these circumstances it is not strange that McKinley, essentially a follower rather than a leader of public opinion, moved toward annexation. As early as June 3, Day was writing to John Hay that McKinley's thinking on peace terms envisioned a Philippine port to be selected by the United States. The Manila provision of the peace protocol kept the door open. The instructions of September 16 to the peace delegation insisted upon no less "than the cession in full right and sovereignty of the island of Luzon." A period of uncertainty as to whether to make further demands came to a focus in late October. During this month the President listened attentively, on a Midwestern tour, to the volume of applause following his references to colonial empire. Shortly after his return the Commissioners at Paris reported to Hay (October 25). Three of them argued for retaining all the islands. This confirmed McKinley in a decision he had probably reached already. Results were prompt: On the 26th Hay cabled Paris that the cession "must be of the whole archipelago or none."[13] Spain protested vigorously but vainly: The demand violated the protocol, which called only for the provisional occupation of Manila, and in no way impaired Spanish sovereignty over the islands. Embarrassed by this demonstration that claims

---

[12] These sentiments did not motivate all Americans; a vocal anti-imperialist movement developed for a time a considerable organization, but its elements were too diffuse and its sentiments too negative, in the face of the exuberant nationalism of the day, to exert a controlling effect. On this movement, see F. H. Harrington, "The Anti-Imperialist Movement in the United States, 1898–1900," *Mississippi Valley Historical Review*, vol. 22 (1935), pp. 211–230.

[13] McKinley's famous attribution of his decision to the Almighty, made over a year later to a visiting delegation of Methodist divines, describes how he walked the floor and prayed for guidance: "And one night late it came to me this way—I don't know how it was, but it came: (1) That we could not give them back to Spain—that would be cowardly and dishonorable; (2) that we could not turn them over to France or Germany—our commercial rivals in the Orient—that would be bad business and discreditable; (3) that we could not leave them to themselves—they were unfit for self-government—and they would soon have anarchy and misrule over there worse than Spain's was; and (4) that there was nothing left for us to do but to take them all, and to educate the Filipinos, and uplift and civilize and Christianize them, and by God's grace do the very best we could by them, as our fellow men for whom Christ also died. And then I went to bed and went to sleep and slept soundly." Quoted by Millis, *Martial Spirit*, pp. 383–384.

could not be based upon conquest, McKinley (November 21) offered to pay $20,000,000, ostensibly to reimburse Spain for expenses in erecting public works, and Spain accepted under duress.

The Treaty of Paris, signed December 10, 1898, and accepted by the Senate February 6, 1899, closely followed the protocol: Cuba was independent; Puerto Rico went to the United States, as did the Philippines (for $20,000,000); Guam was chosen from the Ladrones; citizens' claims were mutually waived. The Senate had not approved an important treaty for twenty-five years; this one proposed to embark the nation on a new and untried course; more than a third of the Senate was opposed to McKinley, but the treaty went through. This remarkable result is universally and correctly attributed to William Jennings Bryan, who came to Washington early in the fight and remained through most of its course, persuading a sufficient number of Democrats to assure consent to ratification. Bryan's motivation has been the subject of much controversy, the most usual explanation being a political one, that he was seeking to commit the Republicans to imperialism as an issue on which to defeat them in the 1900 election. Whatever his motivation, war, treaty, and surrounding circumstances point sharply to a new national orientation, achieved with seeming suddenness but long preparing, which brought the United States out into the open as a rival of other less self-righteous nations for the spoils of world commerce and empire.

13 Advance and Retreat in the Caribbean

O THE SOUTH AND EAST OF MEXICO THE UNITED STATES has watched carefully and often fearfully developments in eleven Central American, South American, and Island Republics ringing the American Mediterranean. Here live close to thirty million people of the most diverse racial background ranging from Black Haiti to predominantly Indian and mixed-Indian Guatemala, Salvador, and Colombia, with only Costa Rica exhibiting a dominantly Caucasian population. While no generalizations can accurately reflect such diversity, cultural and economic conditions are generally unfavorable. Illiteracy varies from 20–25 percent (Costa Rica) to upwards of 90 percent (Haiti); the cultural level of the great popular masses is inevitably low. An area distinguished chiefly for its staple and raw materials faces the likelihood of low-level economy or foreign exploitation, or both. Such a combination of cultural and economic backwardness boded ill for the political structure. Statesmen attempting to graft republican institutions upon such a shaky stem found the task impossible; those who cavil at the resultant decades of revolution, dictatorship, and intervention would do well to remember the precarious early years of the United States, which was bred in the British tradition of self-government and blessed with repeated European wars to absorb its surplus staples.[1]

---

[1] The following titles culled from the voluminous literature of the Caribbean contribute to a general understanding of the area; all of them, moreover, should be consulted for their specific contributions to the story of the four states chosen for discussion. Selig Adler, "Bryan and Wilsonian Caribbean Penetration," *Hispanic*

The Caribbean loomed larger than ever in northern perspective as the nineteenth century merged into the twentieth. The Spanish-American War conferred ownership of Puerto Rico and tutelage over Cuba to the north. Isthmian developments already related made the American government sensitive to political disturbances in any locality lying athwart canal approaches. Mounting debts, often owed to European creditors, brought the possibility of intervention, increased in the prewar years by particular fears of German imperialism. These factors convinced the Department of State that the influence of the United States in the area must be sufficient to discourage any other power from attempting domination of the Canal or its approaches. This feeling produced such policies as the Roosevelt Corollary to the Monroe Doctrine and some of the less palatable phases of so-called "Dollar Diplomacy" in which the Government urged American bankers to substitute dollars for francs and pounds in Caribbean debt-balances lest the latter encourage political interference; it led finally to actual American intervention and domination of a number of Caribbean nations. Caribbean usefulness as a market, a source of raw materials, and an investment field must not be overlooked; with the possible exception of Cuba, however, American interest has been much more than commensurate with the amount of capital invested.

This mounting concern was thoroughly bipartisan, shared fully by the bumptious Theodore Roosevelt, the traditional Dollar Diplomats, William Howard Taft and Philander C. Knox, and the ostentatiously anti-imperialistic Woodrow Wilson. Roosevelt inherited the Platt Amendment relative to Cuba, established a lien on the Canal Zone, and first proclaimed and then applied to Santo Domingo the police-power corollary bearing his name. Taft maintained the ascendancy established by Roosevelt and extended control over Nicaragua while alert to the usefulness of the American dollar as an

---

American Historical Review, vol. 20 (1940), pp. 198–226; Bemis, *Lat. Am. Pol. of the U.S.*; W. H. Callcott, *op. cit.*; C. L. Jones, *Caribbean Since 1900*; D. G. Munro, *The United States and the Caribbean Area*, World Peace Foundation, 1934; Dexter Perkins, *The United States and the Caribbean*, Harvard University Press, 1947; J. F. Rippy, *Caribbean Danger Zone*; Sumner Welles, *The Time for Decision*, Harper, 1944.

instrument of policy. Wilson, surrendering none of his predecessors'
gains, implemented the Nicaraguan ascendancy and, while popular
attention was focused on European affairs, forcibly expanded Dominican controls and compelled Haiti to abject submission. Thus at
various periods beginning with 1912 United States Marines policed
three ostensibly sovereign American states (Nicaragua, Santo Domingo, and Haiti); less immediate though no less effective controls
were continued over two more—Cuba through the Platt Amendment
and Panama through the Hay–Bunau-Varilla Treaty. This period of
tutelage witnessed great, though somewhat arbitrary, improvements.
Debts were stabilized and, amazingly, paid off. The sanitary and
prophylactic zeal of the Anglo-Saxon worked many small wonders,
improving and sometimes bewildering natives who did not always
approve of wonders. Public works, often too extensive for native
economy to support, were constructed lavishly. The Pax Americana
supplanted revolution or the uneasy peace of dictatorship. What
Professor Rippy calls the "sense of a civilizing mission" found wide
scope.

The 1920's, however, witnessed considerable restlessness at this
assumption of Caribbean leadership and before the last marines
were withdrawn (from Haiti in 1934) an equally bipartisan retreat
from the early-century imperialism had taken place. The cynical-
minded may suggest that this withdrawal could be both easy and
graceful because the War of 1914–1918 and the supposed security measures of the Washington Conference of 1921–1922 had
demonstrated American might and rendered European interference
with the safety of the Canal unthinkable and Asiatic meddling unlikely. Even such stark realism as this should not be permitted to
exclude entirely the belief in equality and spirit of fair play which
made many Americans ashamed of the coercive tactics of the preceding two decades. As Republicans had inaugurated the advance,
so they initiated the retreat. Warren G. Harding sounded the first
note, perhaps a false one, when in the campaign of 1920 he attacked
the Democrats for their high-handed tactics. Discussion of withdrawal from Nicaragua was initiated in 1923 and implemented in
1925; it proved premature and another intervention occurred; the

Dominican intervention was ended in 1924. Mounting domestic dissatisfaction persuaded Calvin Coolidge to send that exceedingly useful citizen, Henry L. Stimson, to iron out Nicaraguan difficulties in 1927. Under Coolidge's auspices, the Clark Memorandum, displacing the Roosevelt Corollary, was elaborated. No sooner had Herbert Hoover won the 1928 election than he set out on a tour designed to woo Latin American good will. Although his signature on the Hawley-Smoot Tariff of 1930 did much to nullify his more gracious gestures, Hoover nevertheless made solid progress toward departure from the Caribbean. His withdrawal from Nicaragua (1933) and his acceptance of the principle of withdrawal from Haiti (1932–1933) paved the way for his successor. Finally he abandoned, as applying to South America, the Wilsonian doctrine of refusal to recognize governmental changes brought about by revolutionary means; this return to de factoism on the Southern Continent cleared the path for the broader noninterventionism which ensued.

The second decade saw Woodrow Wilson reluctantly following Republican patterns of advancing imperialism; in the fourth, Franklin D. Roosevelt embraced, first casually and then enthusiastically, the Republican pattern of retreat. His off-hand inaugural remarks about the "good neighbor" were given no particular orientation. Little more than a month later he took time from the pressing domestic matters which were the primary concern of his first administration to address the Pan-American Union (April 14, 1933) in terms which beamed the good neighbor idea on a southward bent which soon gave it capital initials and capital importance in Rooseveltian diplomacy. Though the Clark Memorandum had renounced the right of intervention as a consequence of the Monroe Doctrine, the general right of intervention was specifically retained; moreover, Wilsonian nonrecognition of revolutionary change was still effective outside South America. The story of Roosevelt's gradual abandonment of all pretensions to interventionist powers, from Montevideo to Buenos Aires and beyond, has already been told in connection with the Monroe Doctrine and need not be repeated here. Further concrete examples of Democratic good neighborliness included the abrogation of the Platt Amendment (1934), the untying of Panamanian

apron strings (1936–1939), and completion of withdrawal from
Haiti and Santo Domingo. Thus, ere totalitarianism cast its shadow
over the Caribbean in the late 1930's, the control of decades had
been ended and a new and sounder unity could be created to meet
the new menace. The wheel had turned full circle, impelled in both
the up- and down-sweep by both Republican and Democratic leadership.

Four brief case-histories will serve to make explicit the pattern of
this bipartisan policy. In Cuba the Platt Amendment gave legal
sanction to an intervention which was used infrequently and usually
reluctantly. Nicaragua, Haiti, and Santo Domingo eventually presented such pictures of domestic instability, financial indigence, or
vulnerablity to outside influence as to bring about intervention without previous consent; these nations endured, in varying degrees and
for long-continued periods, military occupation, political domination, and financial subordination. Together wth Cuba, they fill in
the outline presented in the pages immediately preceding.

Cuban Protégé

Cuban-American relationships from 1900 to the middle 'thirties
stemmed largely from two documents. In one of these, the so-called
Teller Amendment of April 20, 1898, Congress renounced territorial
designs and affirmed its determination to evacuate the island following the establishment of peace. As if dismayed at its own temerity, the dying session of the same Congress took back part of the
gift of freedom, tying fiscal, political, and military strings to the new
Republic through the Platt Amendment.[2] This resulted from the

---

[2] The following titles build up the information given in those already cited as
general references: Carleton Beals, *The Crime of Cuba,* Lippincott, 1934; R. L. Buell
et. al., *Problems of the New Cuba,* Foreign Policy Association, 1935; C. E. Chapman,
A History of the Cuban Republic: A Study in Hispanic American Politics, Macmillan,
1927; R. H. Fitzgibbon, *Cuba and the United States,* Banta, 1935; H. F. Guggen-
heim, *The United States and Cuba,* Macmillan, 1934; L. H. Jenks, *Our Cuban Colony,*
Vanguard, 1928; Jessup, *Root,* vol. 1, pp. 304–326, 532–540; David A. Lockmiller,
Magoon in Cuba, University of North Carolina Press, 1938; C. A. Thomson, "The
Cuban Revolution: Fall of Machado," *Foreign Policy Reports,* Dec. 18, 1935; "The
Cuban Revolution: Reform and Reaction," *Ibid.,* Jan. 1, 1936; C. de la Torriente,
"The Platt Amendment," *Foreign Affairs,* vol. 8 (1930), pp. 364–379; P. G. Wright,
The Cuban Situation and Our Treaty Relations, Brookings Institution, 1931.

failure of the Cuban Constitutional Convention (in session during late 1900 and early 1901) to provide what was considered a proper basis for the future relations of the two republics. Early in January, 1901, Secretary of War Elihu Root began putting on paper the ideas which eventually bore the name of Senator O. H. Platt of Connecticut. After waiting vainly for the Cubans to take the initiative, and with the war Congress about to end, Platt embodied most of Root's proposals in an amendment to the Army Appropriation Bill (February 25, 1901; passed March 2).[3] Its importance in subsequent Cuban-American relations justifies quotation at length:

I. That the government of Cuba shall never enter into any treaty or other compact with any foreign power or powers which will impair or tend to impair the independence of Cuba, nor in any manner authorize or permit any foreign power or powers to obtain by colonization or for military or naval purposes or otherwise, lodgment in or control over any portion of said island.

II. That said government shall not assume or contract any public debt, to pay the interest upon which, and to make reasonable sinking fund provision for the ultimate discharge of which, the ordinary revenues of the island, after defraying the current expenses of government shall be inadequate.

III. That the government of Cuba consents that the United States may exercise the right to intervene for the preservation of Cuban independence, the maintenance of a government adequate for the protection of life, property, and individual liberty, and for discharging the obligations with respect to Cuba imposed by the treaty of Paris on the United States, now to be assumed and undertaken by the government of Cuba.

IV. That all Acts of the United States in Cuba during its military occupancy thereof are ratified and validated, and all lawful rights acquired thereunder shall be maintained and protected.

V. That the government of Cuba will execute, and as far as necessary extend, the plans already devised or other plans to be mutually agreed upon, for the sanitation of the cities of the island, to the end that a recurrence of epidemic and infectious diseases may be prevented, thereby assuring protection to the people and commerce of Cuba, as well as to

---

[3] Root had proposed that the United States "reserve and retain the right of intervention" in Cuba; as adopted, the United States was "to exercise the right to intervene. . . ." Root felt that deriving the right from a Spanish grant in the Treaty of Paris afforded sounder legal ground than a Cuban grant. Point 5 was suggested by General Leonard Wood; Points 6 and 8 were not of Root's devising.

the commerce of the southern ports of the United States and the people residing therein.

VI. That the Isle of Pines shall be omitted from the proposed constitutional boundaries of Cuba, the title thereto being left to future adjustment by treaty.

VII. That to enable the United States to maintain the independence of Cuba, and to protect the people thereof, as well as for its own defense, the government of Cuba will sell or lease to the United States lands necessary for coaling or naval stations at certain specified points, to be agreed upon with the President of the United States.

VIII. That by way of further assurance the government of Cuba will embody the foregoing provisions in a permanent treaty with the United States.

The Cuban Convention incorporated the Amendment in the Constitution (June 12, 1901); to prevent Cuba from amending it out of the Constitution it was embodied in a treaty (signed May 12, 1903). Meantime, to allay Cuban fears of the possible consequences of Article 3, Root instructed General Leonard Wood to state that the intervention therein authorized was "not synonymous with the intermeddling or interference with the affairs of the Cuban Government, but the formal action of the Government of the United States, based upon just and substantial grounds, for the preservation of Cuban independence and the maintenance of a government adequate for the protection of life, property and individual liberty and for discharging the obligations with respect to Cuba imposed by the Treaty of Paris upon the United States." Root seems to have been honestly concerned lest Cuban weakness or inefficiency invite future territorial acquisition or political interference by either the United States or some European nation.[4] This self-denying interpretation becomes of considerable importance in view of subsequent actions by the United States Government; it makes perfectly clear that to responsible contemporaries intervention was permissible only for the protection of Cuban independence against outside aggression. It is equally clear, too, that Articles 1, 3, and 7 established an American quasi-protectorate over Cuba.

---

[4] Years later he wrote Professor Philip C. Jessup: "You cannot understand the Platt Amendment unless you know something about the character of Kaiser Wilhelm the Second." Dec. 20, 1934. Jessup, *Root*, vol. 1, p. 314.

The next three decades of Cuban-American relations hinged largely on (1) Cuba's well-nigh complete dependence upon sugar, financed largely by United States capital highly sensitive to political instability; (2) domestic and international troubles inevitably incident to a self-administered course in the principles and practices of self-government; and (3) the interpretation of the Platt Amendment developed by successive Presidents and Secretaries of State. The net result was a succession of incidents in which the Third Article of the Amendment was used either actually or potentially to preserve order in Cuba, frequently at the expense of the Latin urge to revolution, often in violation of Root's formally expressed interpretation. The first bona fide intervention followed an insurrection against President Estrada Palma in 1906. As it proceeded, Palma repeatedly embarrassed the Roosevelt Administration by requesting warships; Root, then Secretary of State, was barnstorming Latin America as a messenger of good will and intervention would make a mockery of his protestations. Finally, however, when Cuban refusal to coöperate in an honest effort at settlement made anarchy imminent, Roosevelt's proconsul, Man Friday, and Secretary of War William Howard Taft proclaimed himself provisional governor (September 29) just as Root's warship steamed up the Potomac. Intervention was formalized under Governor Charles E. Magoon, whose uneasy control, lasting until January 28, 1909, suffered from the evils confronting those administrators who seek to maintain quiet by distributing patronage.

Intervention hereafter becomes a matter of definition. Most scholars point to 1906–1909 as the sole instance; many Cubans would disagree. At any rate, beginning in 1909 Taft and Knox interpreted the Platt Amendment to permit them to urge Cuba to keep out of trouble. Their joint desire for stability and their concern for American vested interests were aptly pointed up by a Cuban publicist's comment that "If there was so much as word that a mosquito was on its way from Havana to the 'White House,' Taft shook loose the thunderbolts of Jove; and if there was the slightest irregularity discovered in the customs, his rumblings were as those of Mars." Woodrow Wilson, pressed by European circumstances, scolded

Cuba vigorously and landed several hundred marines during 1917; the troops remained for some months. The war sent sugar prices to the fantastic level of 22½ cents per pound, delivered in New York; the ensuing crash reduced the island economy to a state of collapse and its politics to the verge of chaos. In the emergency General Enoch H. Crowder went to Cuba in January, 1921, as Wilson's personal representative; President Harding continued his assignment and Secretary of State Hughes pursued the Taft-Wilson pattern of "advice" in a note of April 21, in which he expressed confidence that the Cuban President would "readily agree that his administration will not be able to maintain the high standards of efficiency and integrity which this Government realizes it is his earnest desire to have it maintain, unless his appointees to Cabinet positions are men of the highest ability and unquestioned integrity." Crowder's advice carried the weight of law for a time, but with the temporary easing of the economic situation his influence waned.

There followed a period of depression in the sugar industry, accompanied by an increasingly dictatorial political regime under Gerardo Machado (inaugurated in May, 1925), whom Professor Perkins has called "the most sinister figure in Cuban history." Elected on promises of no second term and no new foreign borrowing, the superficial prosperity of his first term lessened political agitation. His reëlection in 1928 under a constitutional amendment tailored to his wishes and providing for one six-year presidential term, and his pyramiding of foreign debts, aroused political troubles culminating in actual fighting which the Coolidge and Hoover Administrations regarded with a benign indifference in startling contrast with the almost spinsterish concern of Taft, Wilson, and Harding. Indeed, in October, 1930, Secretary of State Stimson stated that the Department was following the Root interpretation of the Platt Amendment. A year later (October 26, 1932) he announced that the Amendment, while conferring a right of intervention, involved no corresponding obligation. In addition to this laissez faire attitude in the face of deteriorating Cuban conditions, the Hoover Administration witnessed the enactment of the Hawley-Smoot Tariff of 1930, levying unusually high rates on Cuban sugar in a time of shrinking markets due to the Depression of 1929, and of increased productive capacity.[5]

The Machado dictatorship presently closed all secondary and higher educational institutions (December 30, 1930), suppressed a revolt of August, 1931, with considerable bloodshed, pursued the "ABC," secret society of his opponents, with ferocity, and encouraged such of his enemies as he was unable to eliminate forcibly to seek safety in exile; the spring of 1933 found a thousand of these refugees in Miami anxiously scanning the horizon. This situation put Franklin D. Roosevelt to one of the severest tests of his early presidency. Realizing that the economic problem was fundamental, he sought to balance the interventionist aspects of the Platt Amendment against his developing Good Neighbor policy. As an earnest of his good intentions he delegated the task of conciliation to Sumner Welles, an old Caribbean hand whom he sent as Ambassador charged with tendering good offices in Cuba's political difficulties. The Welles mediation stirred winds of controversy which are still blowing, but the facts may be stated briefly.

Welles' arrival in Havana, June 1, 1933, inaugurated weeks of delicate negotiation during which it became increasingly clear that the Ambassador desired the elimination of Machado; the latter resisted mounting pressure until a general strike and decreasing military support, combined with Welles' threat of armed intervention, forced his resignation and departure (August 11–12, 1933). There is no doubt that the Welles diplomacy and the threat of force contributed to Machado's overthrow; this was accomplished, however, with relatively little disturbance, was achieved without formal intervention, and was desired by the great majority of Cubans; thus the Good Neighbor formula remained intact. Three rapidly succeeding Administrations (of Dr. Carlos Manuel de Céspedes, Dr. Ramón Grau San Martín, and Colonel Carlos Mendieta) depended largely for success or failure upon the attitude of American diplomats

---

[5] In a memorandum of January 20, 1933, Ambassador H. F. Guggenheim, representing the lame-duck Republican Administration in Cuba, suggested that "the difficulty in our relations with Cuba was not to be found in the policy that we were then pursuing . . . under the Permanent Treaty. The difficulty was with the Treaty itself." *Op. cit.*, p. 236. He recommended negotiation of a new political agreement.

(Jefferson Caffery presently succeeded Welles). Céspedes, who stood well in Washington, was ousted early in September by the "Revolt of the Sergeants," prominent among whom was Fulgencio Batista, destined to become Cuba's "strong man." Their candidate, the leftist Grau, failed to win Welles' good will, never received recognition from Washington, was unable to hold the support of the army, and resigned in mid-January, 1934. The Mendieta coalition had the nod from Washington, the blessing of Batista, now a Colonel, and the support of Cuban conservatives; these favorable auspices, particularly the second, enabled it to survive. The military influence remained strong and favorable to the United States until the exigencies of hemispheric solidarity in the later 1930's came to outweigh all other considerations on both sides.

It seems reasonable to conclude that the Roosevelt Administration, while exerting diplomatic pressure to secure desired changes, resisted domestic influences which might well have led to forcible intervention in other days. Moreover, it took several steps designed to aid Cuba in building an economic foundation for future political stability, in a period when the tides of economic nationalism were running strong at home. Realizing Cuban dependence upon sugar, Roosevelt used powers given him under the flexible provisions of the Hawley-Smoot Act to reduce the duty (June 8, 1934); the first of Cordell Hull's reciprocal trade agreements (in effect August 24, 1934) made a further cut. The resulting reduction of the rates from 2.5 cents to .9 cent per pound contributed to increased producers' profits. The contemporary Jones-Costigan Sugar Control Act (in effect June 8) helped to stabilize production by assigning Cuba a quota of 1,902,000 short tons in the American market for 1934. This, while 300,000 short tons above the 1933 sales, was over a million tons below the average sales for 1927–1930. However, succeeding years saw the quotas increased, and wartime demands for sugar marked their abandonment. Although this economic policy was obviously one of enlightened selfishness on the part of the United States, seeking frankly to improve the Cuban market for its own manufactures, its undoubted benefits to Cuba should not be overlooked.

Roosevelt's most important act relating to Cuba, one having profound repercussions in the realm of inter-American good neighborhood was the signing (May 29, 1934) of a treaty abrogating the Platt Amendment, thus terminating a relationship which since 1901 had like a Damoclean sword menaced Cuban independence. Sumner Welles' role in this significant event, the full story of which remains to be told, did much to erase the memory of his less popular Cuban activities and to lay firm a cornerstone of lasting good will. The story just recounted has been one often undistinguished for broad statesmanship and dominated by a concept of temporary economic or political advantage; the abrogation treaty should live long in the annals of the Good Neighbor.

Canal Vestibule

Nicaragua, itself a potential canal site and distant from the Panama artery by only the span of Costa Rica, early attracted United States interest. The Clayton-Bulwer Treaty of 1850 was but a step removed from the activities of that fabulous filibuster William Walker, who in the mid-'fifties dreamed of a Central American empire with Cuba as a sort of annex and a canal as an end product, a vision rudely shattered by Commodore Cornelius Vanderbilt's successful opposition to his schemes.[6] After this flurry the country passed largely beyond the American ken until the present century.

Sharply split from the west by a north-south mountain system, the eastern section of Nicaragua became a political stepchild mainly valuable for its minerals, lumber, and fruits; the high western plateau containing seven-eighths of the population became the center of political life. This last developed a party system more clearly divided than in most Caribbean states between the Liberals—mainly professionals, smaller merchants, and artisans and based on the town of Leon—and the Conservatives—landholders and larger merchants centering around Granada and well-disposed toward the

---

[6] On the Walker-Vanderbilt rivalry see Laurence Green, *The Filibuster: The Career of William Walker*, Bobbs-Merrill, 1937; W. O. Scroggs, *Filibusters and Financiers*, Macmillan, 1916; "William Walker and the Steamship Corporation in Nicaragua," *American Historical Review*, vol. 10 (1905), pp. 792–811; Arthur D. Howden Smith, *Commodore Vanderbilt*, McBride, 1927, pp. 152–201.

United States, which might some day build a canal and which every day desired stability in the neighborhood of Panama, a stability which was good for business. A revolution in 1893 ended a thirty-year period of Conservative control and placed in power José Santos Zelaya, a Liberal by label but in practice a ruthless dictator whose activities furnished the immediate background of United States intervention.[7]

Excluding Cuba, where interference, however defined, was an impermanent affair, the Nicaraguan intervention began earliest, continued longest (counting a period of withdrawal in the mid-'twenties), was the least active, and produced less local hostility than any to be studied here. It stemmed originally from Zelaya's hostility to American capital. By 1909 he was moving to cancel a mining concession controlled largely by Pittsburgh capitalists for whom Philander C. Knox had been legal counsel before becoming Taft's Secretary of State. Worse, he had refunded the national debt through the Ethelburga Syndicate, a British concern drawing investors from many nations; this indicated his preference for European capital and, to the dollar-conscious Taft-Knox regime represented a loss of potential profits as well as a possible source of outside intervention. A revolution launched at Bluefields, on the east coast, in 1909, and probably fomented by American-connected interests, presently eliminated Zelaya from the scene (he resigned December 6, 1909) and ushered in a confused period from which emerged the figure of Adolfo Diaz, recently a minor employee of the American interests whose scalp Zelaya had sought.

Diaz, who became President early in 1911, was a Conservative, confident that canal policy demanded close relations with the United States, and distrustful of his people's ability to manage their

---

[7] The following supplement the references given in note 1: *A Brief History of the Relations between the United States and Nicaragua, 1909–1928*, Government Printing Office, 1928; Bryn-Jones, *op. cit.*, pp. 185–203; R. L. Buell, "Union or Disunion in Central America," *Foreign Affairs*, vol. 11 (1933) pp. 478–490; I. J. Cox, *Nicaragua and the United States, 1909–1927*, World Peace Foundation, 1929; Lawrence Dennis, "Nicaragua: In Again, Out Again," *Foreign Affairs*, vol. 9 (1931), pp. 496–500; "Revolution, Recognition, and Intervention," *Ibid.*, pp. 204–221; Harold Denny, *Dollars for Bullets*, Dial, 1929; Anna A. Powell, "Relations between the United States and Nicaragua, 1898–1916," *Hispanic American Historical Review*, vol. 8 (1928), pp. 43–64; H. L. Stimson, *American Policy in Nicaragua*, Scribner, 1927.

own finances successfully. These factors dovetailed nicely with the desire of Taft and Knox to bring Nicaragua under northern fiscal control. The Knox-Castrillo Convention, signed June 6, 1911, provided for refunding the Nicaraguan debt, payment to be secured by a customs receivership; it gave the United States the right of intervention. An executive agreement called for arbitration of American claims. Less than a month later (July 1) the government defaulted on the Ethelburga bonds. Without waiting for the Senate to act, Knox confidently persuaded Brown Brothers and J. and W. Seligman & Co., New York bankers, to implement the treaty's provisions before its formal ratification. Nicaragua had asked the bankers for $15,500,000, on condition of ratification of the Knox-Castrillo agreement by September 1, 1911. The Senate adjourned without action and the Nicaraguan government, desperate for funds, secured a loan of $1,500,000, in return for which the bankers received control of the newly founded National Bank of Nicaragua (incorporated in Connecticut) and the government-owned railway. The contract, similar in terms to the unratified Convention, pledged the customs in payment, collection to be in the hands of an American citizen. A Claims Commission, established upon a similarly extracurricular basis, squeezed American claims of $7,500,000 down to $538,750.

The Department of State, still hoping for ratification of the Knox-Castrillo agreement, encouraged and blessed these bankers' measures. In spite of three presidential suggestions, the Senate did not accept the treaty; by the spring of 1912, when its doom was obvious, the bankers had become so involved that the Department felt in duty bound to protect their interests. Thus when domestic dissatisfaction with the treaty brought Nicaraguan revolution, intervention seemed the only possible reply and the marines occupied Managua, August 14, 1912. Their force was soon reduced to a Legation Guard of one hundred whose main function was to prevent the political Opposition from becoming too obstreperous and to see that the financial arrangements continued to work smoothly. Diaz' need for funds and Knox' fear of Germany and anxiety for the canal route produced another treaty in February, 1913, but Taft's term ended before action could be secured.

Bryan, given a free hand in Latin American policy, early attacked the Nicaraguan question. His problem was to balance his own strictures on dollar diplomacy against the obvious necessity of enabling Nicaragua to meet the demands of her European creditors—funds for which could be secured only from the bankers who demanded renewed pledges of security. All this was complicated by Nicaragua's increased strategic importance by reason of the coming opening of the Panama Canal. The result was the Bryan-Chamorro Treaty, signed August 5, 1914 (approved in 1916), in which Bryan, despite his earlier protestations, essentially perpetuated Republican dollar diplomacy. Nicaragua received $3,000,000 in return for a canal route and a naval base; an attempt to insert Platt Amendment provisions failed, but the naval-base provisions made Nicaraguan dependence upon the United States quite apparent. Interim arrangements had continued the bankers' control over the finances through a customs receivership which was consolidated in the Financial Plans of October 20, 1917 and October 5, 1920; eventually actual financial management passed from the bankers to a Joint High Financial Commission. By 1924, however, arrangements had been concluded between Nicaragua and the bankers whereby the Government regained control of the bank and the railroad. Contemporary charges that the bankers had been allowed to make excessive profits through the policy of the Department of State were exaggerated; profits they did make, with the Department's blessing, but the investment was never large and was on the way to liquidation by 1924. Strategic considerations, it is fair to conclude, always outweighed economic ones in policy toward Nicaragua.

The Legation Guard had currently kept Nicaraguan domestic politics on a reasonably even keel. The Constitution prohibited a President from immediately succeeding himself, and Diaz had given way to Emiliano Chamorro, another Conservative, who in turn had ensconced his uncle as President, Chamorro himself keeping an eye on developments as Ambassador to Washington. Meantime the Central American states signed a treaty (February 7, 1923) binding themselves not to recognize any executive securing his position by revolutionary means, or any relative of such; the United States had underwritten its principles in June. Anticipating the stability which ratification of this agreement should provide, the United States notified Nicaragua (November 14, 1923) of its intention to withdraw the Legation Guard after the inauguration of the next President in 1925. In the free-for-all which followed a Conservative-Liberal coalition composed of Carlos Solorzano and Dr. Juan Sacasa defeated the Conservative Emiliano Chamorro, who thereupon raised loud cries of fraud, doubtless with good reason. The coalition, conscious of its inherent weakness, urged retention of the marines, but they departed on August 4, 1925. Previous Conservative regimes, not discontented with the Occupation which sustained their power, had made inadequate provisions for self-government upon withdrawal; the coalition reaped the whirlwind promptly prepared by Chamorro.

Within a month that worthy had started a remarkable series of military and constitutional maneuvers. Intimidating Solorzano and driving Vice-President Sacasa into exile in Guatemala, he instituted a series of steps, each constitutional in itself, which by January 16, 1926, made him President. The military obbligato to these developments was equivalent to forcible revolution, making Chamorro a violator of the 1923 agreements which he himself had signed and precluding United States recognition of his government. This bothered him little as long as funds were available; when these ran low he turned affairs over to a successor equally unacceptable to the United States. Diaz eventually came to the top of a confused situation and was recognized as President on November 17, 1926; his elevation was as illegal as Chamorro's, since he was uncle to one of the latter's lieutenants, but his docility was already proven. His tenure soon became uneasy, however, as Sacasa bobbed up on the Caribbean coast and proclaimed himself constitutional President of the Republic. This embarrassed both the United States and Diaz. The United States was uncomfortable because Sacasa's movement was supported by Mexico, with which Washington was then on bad terms, because his activities wafted the odor of Bolshevism to Secretary of State Frank B. Kellogg's oversensitive nostrils, and because European nations soon became concerned for the safety of their nationals in the disturbed condition of Nicaraguan affairs—a dangerous threat to American prestige. Diaz was embarrassed because Sacasa's Minister of War and commander-in-the-field, José Moncada, was approaching dangerously close to Managua, despite government reports of repeated victories; a few more "victories" might bring disaster.

Faced with these unpleasant facts the Coolidge Administration again landed marines at Managua (January 6, 1927); already on the defensive in Latin America, Coolidge soon commissioned Henry L. Stimson to attempt a settlement. The Tipitapa Agreement was reached in May, 1927, through conversations between Stimson and Moncada. This provided, after some pressure on Stimson's part, for the retention of President Diaz until after an election in 1928, to be supervised by the United States; it decreed general amnesty and immediate peace; Diaz promised to include some Liberals in his Cabinet; a constabulary, officered by Americans, was to be established; the marines would remain to see that all was done in order. In due course Moncada became President after an unprecedentedly decorous campaign; no liquor was sold during registration or election and each voter dipped a finger in mercurochrome before casting his ballot—a technique which might be useful in more advanced political societies.

Although most of the troops were withdrawn in 1929, it was soon necessary to send large expeditionary forces to deal with Augusto C. Sandino, one of Moncada's lieutenants who, refusing to abide by the Tipitapa Agreement, withdrew to the northern fastnesses and began playing tag with the marines. Thus, despite the relatively peaceful political picture, intervention remained a fact and force was being used on Nicaraguan soil between 1929 and 1931. These were trying years in inter-American relations; domestic criticism of continuance of the Haitian and Nicaraguan interventions also contributed to the Hoover Administration's moves for withdrawal from the former in 1929–1930. Responding to a Senate Resolution calling for full information on the course and conduct of the Nicaraguan intervention, Mr. Stimson, now Hoover's Secretary of State, announced (February 13, 1931) his Government's intention to withdraw from Nicaragua following the presidential election of 1932, a promise fulfilled by the departure of the last marine from Managua on January 2, 1933. Thus a lame-duck Republican Administration ended an intervention inaugurated by Republicans and continued by both parties—an intervention undertaken for primarily strategic motives but carrying economic overtones. Both factors continued to be important after the withdrawal, since the Bryan-Chamorro Treaty remained effective and the Joint High Commission continued to collect the customs pledged to the service of Nicaragua's debt.

Occupied Haiti

Economically the most backward and population-wise the most crowded (265 per square mile), Haiti presents the most uniform racial picture of any Caribbean area here discussed. Her wholly Negro and French-mulatto population has always been sharply divided between an illiterate and disease-ridden peasantry and an elite minority. This group, sometimes estimated at not over 3 percent of the total, highly educated, with French culture-contacts, and endowed with only a rudimentary sense of social responsibility, has dominated the nation's turbulent political history. Of the twenty-five men who headed the Haitian government between 1804 and American intervention in 1915 seventeen were deposed by revolution; of these thirteen went into exile. One remained in power twenty-five years, two others over eleven each, eleven less than a single year apiece. During the period under review, indeed, only one Haitian chief executive voluntarily retired from office. Such turbulence hardly conduced to economic progress. Sugar production, important in the colonial period, declined before lack of domestic capital and foreign reluctance to face the political risks involved in Haitian investments; moreover, since the Dessalines Constitution of 1804 no foreigner had been able to acquire title to land on the island. Low economic potential and political instability resulted in repeated borrowing, mostly from French sources; Haiti's foreign debt had reached the staggering total of almost $24,000,000 at the time of occupation.[8]

---

[8] Additional references on Haiti: R. L. Buell, "The American Occupation of Haiti," *Foreign Policy Association, Information Service,* 5 (Nov.–Dec., 1929); P. H. Douglas, "The American Occupation of Haiti," *Political Science Quarterly,* vol. 42 (1927), pp. 228–258, 368–396; C. Kelsey, "The American Intervention in Haiti and

Though actual intervention in Haiti was postponed until Wilson's day, events of the Taft-Knox period prepared the way. In 1910 an American promoter named James P. MacDonald secured a fifty-year concession, on terms most favorable to himself, for constructing railways in Haiti, on the strength of which the National City Bank granted a half-million dollar loan. The same year witnessed the virtual failure of the French-capitalized Haitian National Bank. Both Germany and Mr. Knox demanded a share in the proposed reorganization. Knox succeeded in holding German investors down to 6 percent, and induced the National City Bank and three other New York bankers with German connections (Speyer & Co., Hallgarten & Co., and Ladenburg, Thalman & Co.) to share equally in 20 percent, leaving 74 percent for French interests. Both bank and railroad charters contained Calvo Clauses forbidding appeal to outside governments in case of disputes between Haiti and foreign investors. Both were soon in trouble with the government and both appealed to Washington despite the Calvo Clauses.

Haitian political disturbances and European maneuverings presently led the strongly anti-imperialist team of Wilson and Bryan to consider drastic measures—the years 1911–1915 witnessed a succession of six Presidents of Haiti. With French, British, and German warships hovering in Haitian waters, a Franco-German proposal of March, 1914, for joint customs control stirred Bryan's fears. Brushing this aside, he laid his own plans. Two days after a Cabinet discussion of June 23 Bryan was instructed to draft an agreement modeled on the Dominican customs-control arrangements of 1905–1907, with the addition of a "financial adviser" not part of that agreement. Somewhat later (December 17, 1914), at the bank's request, unarmed marines from the U.S.S. *Machias* removed a half-million dollars in gold from the bank's vaults and transported it to New York, where the National City Bank retained custody—and use—of it until 1919. Almost as soon as Vibrun Guillaume Sam, last of the sorry parade of Presidents, had been inaugurated (March 5,

the Dominican Republic," *Annals of the American Academy of Political and Social Science*, vol. 100 (1922), pp. 113–165; A. C. Millspaugh, *Haiti under American Control*. World Peace Foundation, 1931; L. L. Montague, *Haiti and the United States, 1714–1938*, Duke University Press, 1940, pp. 163–292.

1915), he was approached by two Wilsonian emissaries who proposed a customs receivership. Sam's natural reluctance postponed action until death ended his interest in mundane affairs on July 28. Acting on Sam's instructions, the commandant of the Port-au-Prince prison had executed 167 aristocrats in custody as enemies of the Administration. A mass uprising ensued and Sam was presently dragged from his refuge in the French Legation and murdered with a brutality rare even in Haitian annals. That night the marines occupied the city and another intervention was under way, its foundations largely laid by Bryan although he resigned shortly before it actually took place.

Diverse factors had contributed to this result. The European crisis and evident European interest in Haiti emphasized the island's obvious strategic importance in the neighborhood of the Canal. Wilson's ardent concern for political stability and constitutional government was undoubtedly a factor. Economic interests, though not decisive, exercised some influence; investors in bank and railway were vocal at the Department of State. Internal conditions had reached such an intolerable pass as to justify forcible action. As conditions were worse than in Nicaragua, so the intervention became more drastic. During its course native control of Haiti's affairs was made ineffective by imposing a new Constitution and dissolving the legislature; the executive sank into a position of complete subservience, and an American-officered constabulary assumed military control.

The process of subordination was inaugurated by virtual dictation of Sudre Dartiguenave's election as President, August 15, 1915. At first well-disposed, Dartiguenave became exasperated at what he considered excessive treaty demands and overextension of the military occupation, this last largely due to the zeal of Admiral W. B. Caperton. He finally signed the proffered agreement (September 16) and it received legislative sanction in November after Secretary of the Navy Josephus Daniels had instructed Caperton (November 10) to inform Haiti of his (Caperton's) gratification "that public sentiment continues favorable to the treaty, that there is a strong demand from all classes for immediate ratification, and that treaty will be ratified Thurday." Failing ratification, he was to indicate that his government "has the intention to retain control in Haiti until the desired end is accomplished, and that it will forthwith proceed to the complete pacification of Haiti. . . ." The arrangement thus forced on Haiti was a severe one. It made Haiti into a protectorate by embodying Platt Amendment provisions such as the Administration had been unable to fasten upon Nicaragua; its fiscal provisions included a customs receivership similar to that in Santo Domingo and a financial advisership which that republic was at the moment trying successfully to avoid; a native gendarmerie, officered by Americans, was to be established forthwith; the Haitian public debt might not be increased, nor its tariff diminished, without American consent. The customs receiver and the financial adviser would supervise collection of revenues and their disbursement in four directions: (1) to the expenses of the receivership and advisership; (2) to the liquidation of the Haitian public debt, foreign and domestic; (3) to the maintenance of the constabulary; and (4) to current governmental expenses.

Haiti was brought further under the yoke by the adoption (June 12, 1918) of a constitution largely drafted by Americans, which allowed foreigners to own land, broadened the base of popular education, suspended the legislature, and abolished the parliamentary form of government, which gave the legislature a degree of control over the executive; such control might prevent the United States from dominating even a submissive President.[9] The legislature might be reinstated only when the President called for an election to be held on January 10 of any even-numbered year. Meantime, authority was divided between the President and a Council of State of twenty-one members, chosen by the President, and in turn empowered to choose the chief executive. The legal method of constitutional ratification (by the National Assembly, a joint meeting of both legislative chambers) being impracticable, resort

---

[9] Considerable mystery attaches to the drafting of this document. Vice-Presidential candidate Franklin D. Roosevelt boasted in a campaign speech, August 18, 1920, that he, as Assistant Secretary of the Navy, had been largely instrumental: "The facts are that I wrote Haiti's Constitution myself, and, if I do say it, I think it is a pretty good Constitution." Others assess his contribution less generously.

was had to a marine-controlled "plebiscite" which rolled up a total of 69,377 votes to 335 in opposition. One writer remarks, however, that the really remarkable feature, in view of known United States wishes, was the size of the opposition. Haitians, curiously ungrateful for these blessings, rose in arms and early in 1920 insurgents penetrated the outskirts of Port-au-Prince. Combined marine-gendarmerie action suppressed such foolishness with promptitude and considerable violence, after which local opposition was for some years confined to the realm of thought. Dartiguenave presently gave way to Louis Borno, more amenable to American control.

Haiti's subjection was completed by the elaboration of administrative machinery whose thoroughness was exceeded only by its complexity. The President and Council of State nominally exercised political authority, but both actually answered to the senior American naval officer who, after Caperton's withdrawal, was domiciled at Santo Domingo City where he was acting as President of Santo Domingo. The link between Haiti and the absent overlord was the commandant of the marine contingent in Haiti, who actually ruled the Republic through his control over the constabulary. The civil treaty officials acted independently of Haitian control; the financial adviser, who spent most of his time in Washington, reported to the Chief of the Latin American Division of the Department of State, the customs receiver to the Bureau of Insular Affairs of the War Department, and nonfinancial officials to the Navy Department.

Practical operations modified these arrangements somewhat in succeeding years. Haitian need for an additional loan extended the original ten-year treaty (March 28, 1917) so that it expired May 3, 1936. In 1916–1917 the National City Bank bought out the other American bankers and two years later eliminated the French interests; a protocol of 1919 authorized a new loan and extended the receivership through its lifetime, presumably to 1952. Domestic agitation against imperialism in the early 1920's produced no less than four investigations of Haitian affairs. The most publicized of these was one by a senatorial committee headed by Medill McCormick which, while criticizing the details of Wilsonian intervention, sustained its principles and proposed to strengthen its application by coördinating civilian and military authority under the direction of a High Commissioner with diplomatic status; he was to be responsible to the Department of State except in matters of military administration. Military considerations dictated the designation of Brigadier General John H. Russell, commandant of the marine detachment, to this post. Honest and able, but a Georgian, a marine, and ignorant of civilian administration, his appointment was not popular with the native ruling classes. In 1924 the positions of financial adviser and customs receiver were consolidated. For some years after these developments were completed there was no evidence of a disposition to withdraw from Haiti, though the Dominican intervention was ended in 1924.

The Occupation, thus thoroughly entrenched, accomplished much. The marine-led gendarmerie, having suppressed local opposition with somewhat excessive vigor, was converted rather effectively to the duties of local administration; the usual roads and public works were constructed, though amid some Haitian grumbling at the expense of their maintenance, should the intervention ever be concluded; sound work was initiated in the realm of public health. Realizing that there was no ultimate substitute for popular education, a new treaty service was elaborated in 1924 with the establishment of the *Service Technique de l'Agriculture et de l'Enseignement Professionel,* based on the made-in-the-United-States theory that vocational and agricultural education, suited to the peasant masses, should supplement and eventually largely supersede Haiti's previous classical system, geared to the needs of the elite. A tug of war for funds ensued, with the weight unequally lodged on the *Service Technique* end of the rope, since treaty officials controlled the allocations. The net result was that by 1928–1929 some eighty agricultural and industrial schools, enrolling more than one-eighth of the total school population, received funds amounting to $556,519.26 as against $410,742.85 allotted to approximately a thousand native schools serving nearly seven-eighths of the pupils. Finally, the financial and economic reorganization undertaken by the treaty officials increased Haiti's liquid resources while refunding and substantially reducing the national debt.

Both Haiti and the United States experienced revulsion in the later 1920's at continuance of the Occupation. Haitian dissatisfaction increased when it became apparent that President Borno was not planning to call an election in January, 1930. This indicated his intention to perpetuate his own power until 1936, when the 1916 treaty was due to expire; he would thus be the one to arrange the details of American withdrawal, if such were indeed to take place, a contingency which many Haitians doubted, and which they likewise feared, since the Occupation had done little to train natives for the duties of administration. Haitian unhappiness became violent when a strike, originating at the Central School of Agriculture, October 31, 1929, ultimately resulted in bloodshed and marine intervention. The United States had long been under fire for its occupation of Haiti and Nicaragua (witness Hughes' defensive statement of 1928 at Havana, cited earlier in this volume); in two messages to Congress President Hoover deprecated the occupation and requested funds for a commission to investigate and recommend methods for withdrawal. A five-man commission was promptly chosen; its report of March 26, 1930, severely criticized Occupation methods, made recommendations for immediate improvement, and drew a partial blueprint for retirement. Implementing its proposals, a new President was chosen by extraconstitutional means suggested by the Commission (Eugene Roy, inaugurated May 15, 1930; presently succeeded by Sténio Vincent, regularly elected by the National Assembly to serve until 1936), a National Assembly was elected, and the High Commissioner gave way to normal diplomatic representation, Dr. Dana G. Munro being the first Minister. By October 1, 1931, Haiti had regained control of most of her local governmental functions. Dr. Munro, charged with liquidating the financial protectorate, signed a treaty on September 3, 1932, on the eve of the presidential election in the States. It provided for continuance of American customs collection pending retirement of a 1922 loan authorized under the Protocol of 1919; Haitian public opinion, forgetting that the United States was by now almost as eager as Haiti for complete withdrawal, objected vigorously to this alleged attempt to perpetuate economic control while relinquishing political control.

President Vincent, a vigorous nationalist, hinted strongly that he had accepted this humiliating agreement in order to stabilize Haitian-American relations before Franklin D. Roosevelt, supposed author of the obnoxious Constitution of 1918, could accede to the presidency of the United States. The National Assembly promptly and unanimously rejected it, September 15, and there matters rested during the remainder of Hoover's term; here a Republican administration initiated the liquidation of a Democratic intervention.

Roosevelt at first insisted upon retaining most of the Munro-Blanchet treaty; minus some of its most obnoxious terms but including the fiscal representative feature, it was embodied in an executive agreement of August 7, 1933. Within six months, however, after Secretary of State Hull had turned his personal attention to the problem, Roosevelt reversed himself and announced that in line with the larger policies of the Administration he would welcome any arrangements that Haiti might make with the bondholders. Accordingly, as of July 9, 1935, the Haitian Government purchased control of the Bank which then became its agent in servicing the debt, then amounting to about $11,000,000. The Foreign Bondholders' Protective Council (an organization representing the interests of creditors of many small nations) refused to coöperate with this scheme, alleging that it hurt their interests; as a result the fiscal representative remained in the picture until 1941. The last marines had departed on August 15, 1934, leaving the Haitianized gendarmerie in control; the Treaty of 1916 lapsed quietly on May 3, 1936, carrying with it the right of intervention. Thus a Democrat completed what Democrats had begun in 1915, but on a pattern set by Republicans in 1929–1930.

Dominican Satrapy

East of Haiti lies Santo Domingo. Occupying the remaining two-thirds of the Island of Hispaniola, it has approximately half the population of overcrowded Haiti and much more than its share of the island's arable land. Though a majority of its people have a touch or more of Negro blood, its government likes it to be considered a white country. Its fertile soil produces cacao, raw sugar, coffee, and some tobacco. It originally loomed large on the American horizon during and shortly after the Civil War, first when Spain's temporary reannexation in 1861 elicited one of William H. Seward's less successful invocations of the Monroe Doctrine, and later in the early postwar period when would-be empire-builders eyeing financial profits secured U. S. Grant's ready assistance in a scheme of annexation which foundered in 1870 on the rocks of Charles Sumner's stubborn opposition and the generally anti-imperialistic temper of the period.[10]

Santo Domingo then embarked on the Caribbean path of dictatorship and debt which ultimately contributed heavily to the establishment of the most thoroughgoing of American interventions—one so drastic as to surpass both the Nicaraguan, in which the native government was subjected to a minimum of control, and the Haitian, in which, while the legislature was abolished a puppet executive was retained—in that it included the entire supersession of the native government and substitution of one controlled by the United States Navy. The last and most complete of Caribbean interventions, it was also the first to be liquidated. Two important steps along the path of indebtedness, taken in 1869 and 1888, will illustrate the character of Dominican finance and help in understanding the republic's plight after 1900 when it became enmeshed in the expansions of the Monroe Doctrine. In 1869 Edward H. Hartmont, a great rascal, contracted to raise for Santo Domingo £420,000 by the sale of bonds, of which he was to retain £120,000 as his commission. He never fulfilled his part of the contract, but put the Dominican Government deeply in his debt and obligated it heavily by the sale of bonds in England. In 1888 Ulises Heureaux, dictator from 1882–1899, and something of a rascal in his own right, secured a loan from the European firm of Westendorp in which the Hartmont bonds were exchanged for Westendorp obligations at the ratio of five to one. Together with another loan of 1890, this issue went into default in 1892. A year later the Westendorp interests were turned over to the San Domingo Improvement Company, from which point

[10] See above, pp. 148–150. Nevins, *Hamilton Fish,* p. 257 ff., and Tansill, *U.S. and Santo Domingo,* p. 338 ff., cover the annexation scheme in detail.

United States interest develops rapidly after the turn of the new century.[11]

The Improvement Company, representing mainly British interests, although incorporated in New Jersey, pursued a checkered career in its relations with the Dominican Government. Arrangements concluded between January 31, 1903 and July 14, 1904, resulted in scaling down its claims of approximately $11,000,000 against Santo Domingo to $4,500,000, payable in monthly instalments guaranteed by the customs receipts which formed practically the sole income of the Republic. If payment were defaulted, the agreement entitled the creditor's agent to take over collection of customs at Puerta Plata, Sanchez, Samaná, and Montecristi and turn over the receipts, less costs of collection, to the creditors. Other creditors criticized this plan, contending that the duties from these ports had already been hypothecated to them. This preferred position of an American corporation led to a demand that the United States assume full responsibility for Dominican debts or leave the field free for all; demands for intervention appeared in inspired articles in the *Independent* and *Review of Reviews* in March, 1904. This situation presented Monrovian implications to Theodore Roosevelt (explored above, p. 158), and called forth his letter of May 20, 1904, to Elihu Root. Meantime, the Dominican Government promptly defaulted its first payment (October 11, 1904) and the Improvement Company's agent began collecting customs at Puerta Plata. In quick succession came Roosevelt's Message of December 6, 1904, with its official statement of the Corollary, threats by other creditors to occupy other customs houses, and a request from the

---

[11] The following references may be added to those cited in Note 1: H. C. Hill, *op. cit.*, pp. 148–174; a series of articles by Professor Jacob Hollander, as follows: "The Convention of 1907 between the United States and the Dominican Republic," *American Journal of International Law*, vol. 1 (1907), pp. 287–296; "The Financial Difficulties of San Domingo," *Annals of the American Academy of Political and Social Science*," vol. 30 (1907), pp. 93–103; "The Readjustment of San Domingo's Finances," *Quarterly Journal of Economics*, vol. 21 (1907), pp. 405–426; C. Kelsey, "American Intervention in Haiti and the Dominican Republic," *loc. cit.*, pp. 166–203; M. M. Knight, *The Americans in Santo Domingo*, Vanguard, 1928; Sumner Welles, *Naboth's Vineyard: The Dominican Republic, 1844–1924*, Payson & Clarke, 1928, 2 vols.; and the references cited in connection with the Roosevelt Corollary of the Monroe Doctrine.

Dominican President that the United States assume a customs receivership for the Republic.

Following this, John Hay asked the Dominican executive (December 30, 1904) whether his Government "would be disposed to request the United States to take charge of the collection of duties and effect an equitable distribution of the assigned quotas among the Dominican Government and the several claimants." No other "disposition" being possible, a protocol of an agreement was promptly signed (January 21, 1905) providing for American customs collection, the proceeds, after deduction of expenses, to be divided between the Government (45 percent) and the creditors (55 percent). Senatorial refusal to accept the arrangement failed to stop its effectiveness; two years of extraconstitutional collection of Dominican customs ensued, the substantial amounts collected under this arrangement piling up in New York. This export of currency disrupted the economic system but did not satisfy the creditors; numerous warships in Dominican waters made domestic anti-imperialists unhappy; the constitutional aspects afforded such Senatorial Democrats as "Pitchfork Ben" Tillman an opportunity to attack Roosevelt; something had to be done.

At the request of the Department of State Dr. Jacob Hollander of the Johns Hopkins University elaborated a plan which was put forward on Dominican initiative, a desirable maneuver since it involved scaling book debts of about forty million dollars down to seventeen, not likely to appeal to either American or European creditors. It was written into a treaty which the Senate accepted (February 25, 1907). This regularized the procedure in effect during the previous two years and established a pattern which lasted until 1941; an official appointed by the President of the United States was to collect the customs and divide the net proceeds between Santo Domingo and her creditors. Substantially a financial protectorate, this deal temporarily relieved Santo Domingo of internal bickering and foreign pressures.[12] Long-standing domestic disturbances led to a

---

[12] An administrative oversight permitted Dr. Hollander, who received $32,500 from the Department of State for his services, to collect an additional $100,000 from Santo Domingo, a bit of professorial acumen which aroused somewhat envious disapproval when it came to light.

revolution in 1911, followed by a weak government which unduly increased the public debt; by September, 1912, new revolutionaries had seized two customs houses and laid two others under siege, and the American Minister was urging his Government to assume physical control. Further complications brought a new Administration into office just as Wilson and Bryan took charge of affairs in March, 1913.

Considerable thought convinced Bryan of the necessity of increased activity in Dominican affairs. In June of 1914 the Government accepted the temporary appointment of a new American official with a check on expenditures. For several months following Bryan attempted unsuccessfully to impose a financial advisership in addition to the customs receivership, a scheme being successfully urged on Haiti, which underwent occupation during the summer of 1915. Meantime Bryan gave way (June, 1915) to Robert Lansing, even more determined to bring order out of increasing Dominican chaos. In November Minister W. W. Russell again demanded acceptance of a financial adviser, but the Dominican President dared not publish such proposals. Domestic disorder forced his resignation in May, 1916, partial occupation of the country followed, and American officials began collecting internal revenue, putting the financial advisership into practical operation. No presidential aspirant would coöperate in this violation of sovereignty and after some months of fruitless search Lansing recommended (November 22) full military occupation of the Republic. Wilson emerged from his preoccupation with the world crisis long enough to sanction Lansing's proposal, writing four days later, "I am convinced that it is the least of the evils in sight in this very perplexing situation."

A full-dress occupation was proclaimed on November 29, and the intervention in force for some months became official. A pliant chief executive had still not been found, and it became necessary to confide Dominican affairs entirely to naval officers, who remained in charge until 1924, completely controlling internal administration and even on occasion exchanging diplomatic correspondence with the United States—a complete abrogation of Dominican self-government. For some years the Department of State paid little attention to Santo Domingo and the Navy Department exercised little supervision; the naval officers in charge seem to have been left pretty much to their own devices. Their initiative contributed the usual fruits of occupation: Order was insured through the American-officered constabulary; the fiscal situation was put on an even keel; roads and sanitary projects were constructed, and educational advances were inaugurated—all without too much sympathetic understanding of native needs and without giving much opportunity for native participation.

The successful termination of the War of 1914–1918 left America free to look at developments closer home; Latin American hostility to the interventions grew apace; the election of 1920 gave Candidate Warren G. Harding a chance to weep humanitarian (Republican) tears over the plight of the Haitians and Dominicans; the Department of State also manifested renewed interest in Dominican affairs. As a last gesture Wilson reverted to the anti-imperialist attitude of his earlier years and in December, 1920, ordered the surprised occupation officials to proclaim their country's belief that the time had come to "inaugurate the simple processes of its rapid withdrawal from the responsibilities assumed in connection with Dominican affairs." President Harding implemented Candidate Harding's implied promises, instructing the local officials to proclaim (June 14, 1921) evacuation of the Republic as soon as a proper plan could be developed. Some months of negotiation produced an agreement (signed December 27, 1924) continuing the customs receivership during the life of certain outstanding bond issues and putting some restrictions on changes in the customs system. This sole remaining vestige of control was removed on April 2, 1941, under an agreement signed September 24, 1940. A regularly elected President was installed in office in July, 1924, and the last marines departed in mid-September, concluding the last and most complete of Occupation chapters.

The foregoing appraisal of Caribbean policy has documented the initial suggestion of bipartisan participation in both aggression and withdrawal. The story closes leaving the Caribbean states largely free of the supervisory management of their northern neighbor. The rising Fascist threat of the later 1930's created new problems, demonstrated anew the need for harmonious relations among the states bordering the American Mediterranean, and showed again that the Caribbean nations can never be entirely their own masters as long as foreign threats can endanger the Canal. Meantime, however, a new atmosphere has surrounded inter-American relations, due to Rooseveltian policies of the 1930's, which made the wartime dependence of the 1940's much less galling than that enforced so vigorously by Wilson earlier.

14 The Far East: China

A CONCEPT OF NATIONAL SELF-INTEREST HAS DICTATED American policy in the Far East, as elsewhere. This has from time to time found implementation through a succession and combination of more particular policies: Most-favored nation treatment (beginning in the 1840's), the Open Door (1899 and the years following), and the territorial integrity of China (1900 and subsequently), have been among these policies. Through much of the period under consideration Anglo-American interests have run parallel and the United States has been well content to reap the benefits of concessions forcibly exacted by Britain from the Chinese or to take the lead in pursuing mutually advantageous policies. At no time prior to 1941 has America had a sufficient economic stake in the Far East to enable policy-makers to command public support of measures passing beyond the realm of moral pressure. The end result has been a century of spasmodic efforts, of successive coöperation and go-it-alone, during which neither Chinese welfare nor American self-interest have been entirely subserved.[1]

Americans Ride on British Coattails

The early days of American independence found American merchants, excluded from the West Indies by British mercantilism,

---

[1] Paul H. Clyde, *The Far East: A History of the Impact of the West on Eastern Asia*, Prentice-Hall, 1948, and Harold M. Vinacke, *A History of the Far East in Modern Times*, Appleton-Century-Crofts, 5th ed., 1950, are standard texts. Valuable accounts of Sino-American relations will be found in Tyler Dennett, *Americans in Eastern Asia*, Macmillan, 1922; F. R. Dulles, *China and America: The Story of Their Relations since 1784*, Princeton University Press, 1946; J. K. Fairbank, *The United States and China*, Harvard University Press, 1948; A. W. Griswold, *The Far Eastern Policy of the United States*, Harcourt, Brace, 1938; and H. B. Morse and H. F. McNair, *Far Eastern International Relations*, Houghton Mifflin, 1931.

seeking to recoup their fortunes in the China trade.[2] The inhabitants of the Celestial Empire eagerly exchanged native tea, silks, and porcelains for their cargoes of ginseng root, of furs obtained unscrupulously from the Northwestern Indians, and later of sandalwood from the Sandwich (Hawaiian) Islands. By careful restrictions, however, China kept American and other merchants at arms length. Foreign traders dealt, under strict regulations, with a monopolistic group of Chinese merchants at factories outside the walls of Canton. Access to the interior, whence came the fabulous commodities of trade, and to the court, whence came the policy of exclusion, were alike forbidden by the Chinese, who transmuted their insularity into superiority, replying through an imperial proclamation to George III's overtures for contact with the court as follows (1793): "our Celestial Empire possesses all things in prolific abundance and lacks no product within its own borders. There was therefore no need to import the manufactures of outside barbarians in exchange for our own produce. . . . I do not forget the lonely remoteness of your island, cut off from the world by intervening wastes of the sea, nor do I overlook your excusable ignorance of the usages of our Celestial Empire. . . . Tremblingly obey and show no negligence!"[3]

History does not record the choleric Hanoverian's reaction to this sally, but early in Queen Victoria's reign Chinese efforts to restrict the use of opium (profitably imported into China by British traders) combined with other trade questions to produce the Opium War (1839). Victory in this one-sided struggle enabled Britain to impose the Treaty of Nanking (August 29, 1842) upon the Chinese. By it they agreed to permit the importation of opium, opened several ports to British trade, and ceded to the victors the city and island of Hongkong. More important, Chinese self-interest had dictated a decision, arrived at independently, that such trading privileges as were accorded the British should not be exclusive, but should be granted to all foreigners alike. Thus the principle of the Open

---

[2] Hallett Abend, *Treaty Ports,* Doubleday, Doran, 1944, and F. R. Dulles, *The Old China Trade,* Houghton Mifflin, 1930, deal with this early commerce.

[3] E. T. Backhouse and J. O. P. Bland, *Annals and Memoirs of the Court of Peking,* Heinemann, 1914, pp. 326–331.

Door appears to be of Chinese invention and of venerable origin.

The United States had an anxious observer of the Nanking negotiations in the person of Commodore Lawrence Kearny, whose request of October 8, 1842, that Americans be placed on a most-favored-nation basis was shortly answered by Kiying, the Chinese viceroy: "Decidedly it shall not be permitted that the American merchants shall come to have merely a dry stick."⁴ The Washington authorities desired more definite assurances, however, than Anglo-Chinese treaties and flowery Chinese verbiage; an official mission was shortly sent to obtain for American goods and ships treaty-based access to Chinese ports. Secretary of State Daniel Webster, fancying himself as Minister to England, tried first to ease Edward Everett from London to the East; this maneuver failing, the appointment fell to Caleb Cushing, an able New Englander. The American merchants, at the moment more popular than their British confreres, and receiving everything they wanted from the Chinese, were dismayed lest Cushing's arrival alter their happy situation. Before Cushing's negotiations commenced, a letter from Everett announced that China had placed other foreigners on the same basis as the British, thus accomplishing the main object of his mission. He persisted, however, and on July 3, 1844, signed the Treaty of Wanghia, writing the principal terms of Nanking into a specific Sino-American agreement opening the treaty ports to American trade and conferring extraterritorial rights on American nationals, exempting them from the operation of Chinese law while on Chinese soil. In view of later Chinese pressure to abolish extraterritoriality, it should perhaps be noted that originally the arrangement was mutually agreeable, since one Chinese authority remarked that "The barbarians are like beasts, and not to be ruled on the same principles as Chinese. Were one to attempt controlling them by the great maxims of reason, it would tend to nothing but the greatest confusion."⁵

---

⁴ Quoted in Dennett, *Ams. in E. Asia,* p. 108. See also T. F. Tsiang, "The Extension of Equal Commercial Privileges to Other Nations than the British after the Treaty of Nanking," *Chinese Social and Political Science Review,* vol. 15 (1931), pp. 422–444; vol. 16 (1932), pp. 105–109.

⁵ P. C. Kuo, "Caleb Cushing and the Treaty of Wanghia, 1844," *Journal of Modern History,* vol. 5 (1933), pp. 34–54.

Cushing thus formally secured trade privileges won by a British war, freely offered by the Chinese, and originally bespoken by Kearny.

This policy of riding on British coattails was repeated in the 1850's when the Treaty of Tientsin (signed June 18, 1858) confirmed to the United States further concessions wrung from China by the Anglo-French "Arrow War," after which William H. Seward, coming to the Secretaryship of State in 1861, inaugurated a policy of coöperating with the British, French, and Russian Ministers to China. His collaborator in this new departure was Anson Burlingame, first American Minister to reside at the Imperial court, who reached his post in July, 1862. Together they established most of the principles which were to be so prominently associated with the names of John Hay around the turn of the twentieth century and Charles Evans Hughes in the early 1920's.[6] Arriving during the Taiping Rebellion (1850–1864), Burlingame soon realized that China's domestic weakness would inevitably encourage Westerners, whose commercial desires were about satiated, to demand territorial satisfactions. Such lay beyond American objectives and would endanger American interests. He therefore worked out with the representatives of the powers the following self-denying formula (as reported in a despatch to Seward, June 20, 1863): "while we claim our treaty right to buy and sell, and hire, in the treaty ports, subject, in respect to our rights of property and person, to the jurisdiction of our own governments, we will not ask for, nor take concessions of, territory in the treaty ports, or in any way interfere with the jurisdiction of the Chinese government over its own people, nor ever menace the territorial integrity of the Chinese empire. . . ."[7]

Burlingame Sows Seeds of Trouble

Such a policy depended for success on the continued forbearance of the powers; this wore thin with the passing years and had practically disappeared by 1867 when Burlingame decided to retire from his

---

[6] Tyler Dennett, "Seward's Far Eastern Policy," *American Historical Review,* vol. 28 (1922), pp. 45–62.

[7] *House Executive Document 1,* 38th Congress, 1st Session, Government Printing Office, 1864, p. 937.

Chinese post. The ceremonies attendant upon his departure produced the half-jocular suggestion that he might become China's
spokesman to the outside world. The Chinese seized upon the idea,
with the result that he was made official envoy to the Powers.[8] Well
endowed with Chinese funds and American showmanship, the Burlingame mission left Shanghai in February, 1868, and proceeded to
Washington via San Francisco and the Isthmus of Panama. Before
continuing to Europe, where he died of pneumonia at St. Petersburg
(February 23, 1870), he signed (July 28, 1868) an agreement sup-
plementing the Treaty of Tientsin, bearing his name but drafted by
Seward and representing the latter's wishes. The first two articles
attempted to underline the American idea of international coöperation relative to China and to affirm China's political sovereignty and
territorial integrity, except where these were already compromised
by existing commitments. More immediately important to Sino-
American relations was Article 5, which allowed unrestricted voluntary migration between China and the United States. This reflected
the desire of Seward and, for the moment, of western Americans, for
a supply of cheap labor useful in the railroad construction then
under way. The Seward-Burlingame coöperative policy presently
fell into disuse and the United States reverted to its earlier technique of using its most-favored-nation position to gain the same concessions secured by other nations, until the threatened dismemberment of China in the 1890's led John Hay to turn again to the
coöperative approach.

Meantime Chinese coolies had done yeoman service in building
western railroads. When employment slackened in this quarter they
found temporary refuge in the bonanza mining operations of the
1870's, but when the Panic of 1873 struck the West Coast in 1876
native workers found themselves competing unfavorably with the
frugal Orientals who began to take over the diminishing number of

---

[8] See Knight Biggerstaff, "The Official Chinese Attitude toward the Burlingame
Mission," *American Historical Review,* vol. 41 (1936), pp. 682–701; W. A. P. Martin,
A Cycle of Cathay; or China, South and North, Revell, 1896; Warren B. Walsh, "The
Beginnings of the Burlingame Mission," *Far Eastern Quarterly,* vol. 4 (1945), pp.
274–277; and F. W. Williams, *Anson Burlingame and the First Chinese Mission to
Foreign Powers,* Scribner, 1912.

jobs. Hostility flared into violence in the so-called "Sandlot Riots" of July, 1877, in San Francisco, led by Denis Kearney, a volatile Irishman whose slogan, "The Chinese must go!" roused his followers to a pitch of frenzy. Congress presently succumbed to the anti-Chinese pressure, and in 1879 passed a bill allowing no more than fifteen Chinese to enter the country on any one ship. President Rutherford B. Hayes vetoed this as a violation of the Burlingame Treaty, but in 1880 secured a new agreement permitting the United States by law to "regulate, limit or suspend" but not to prohibit the entry of Chinese laborers. Several legislative enactments of the 1880's and 1890's were followed by a new treaty in 1894 recognizing a ten-year period of exclusion. When China terminated this agreement in 1904 an exclusion act of 1902 was reënacted without terminal date. Thus after long and acrimonious discussion the West Coast had its way and the United States abandoned another Seward-Burlingame principle, joining the "white" nations that wished to trade with China but had no desire to be contaminated by entry of Chinese laborers. This attitude persisted until wartime camaraderie impelled Franklin D. Roosevelt to recommend, and Congress to adopt, a measure (signed December 17, 1943) gearing China into the prevailing immigration system with an annual quota of 105 and granting naturalization privileges to many Chinese already in the country.[9]

A Door is Opened

The turn of the century witnessed a new coöperative phase reminiscent of the days of Anson Burlingame when John Hay, under British urging, proclaimed the Open Door policy as a means of curbing the further partition of China into spheres of influence.[10] The background of this new adventure lies in the phenomenal rise of Japan, which had emerged from almost complete insularity in the 1850's to a point where she could wage a surprisingly successful war with

---

[9] M. R. Coolidge, *Chinese Immigration*, Holt, 1909; R. D. McKenzie, *Oriental Exclusion*, University of Chicago Press, 1928; E. P. Oberholtzer, *A History of the United States since the Civil War*, Macmillan, 1917–1937, vol. 4, pp. 213–308; R. W. Paul, "The Origin of the Chinese Issue in California," *Mississippi Valley Historical Review*, vol. 25 (1938), pp. 181–196.

[10] Dennis, *Adv. in Am. Dipl.*, pp. 170–258; Dennett, *John Hay*, pp. 284–323; and Nevins, *Henry White*, pp. 161–186, give added details on events of 1899–1900.

China (1894–1895) over Korea. Just as Japan reached for the territorial rewards of victory, a combination of mismated European nations, France, Germany, and Russia, "advised" her to surrender the recently seized Liaotung Peninsula. She agreed, perforce, only to watch with chagrin while the three powers proceeded to obtain from China spheres where their own influence would be preponderant.

The year 1898 saw the impotent Chinese Government yield ascendancy over Shantung Province to Germany by a ninety-nine-year lease of Kiaochow, over Kwantung Province to France by a lease on Kwangchowwan, and over the Liaotung Peninsula and Manchuria to Russia from an entry at Port Arthur. The likely consequence of such ascendancy was commercial monopoly in the respective spheres of influence. This prospect alarmed the British, who had long possessed the major economic stake in China, a superiority which had enabled them to maintain a more or less tolerant attitude toward commercial competition. Any multiplication of spheres of influence therefore threatened the British economic position; moreover, the political menace of Russia in Manchuria and in India began to loom large in British calculations. In addition, the British power position grew increasingly vulnerable during the 1890's. The South African Boers had proven to be annoying foemen; their resistance had called forth the admiration of Wilhelm II of Germany. Anglo-French interests clashed at Fashoda, on the upper reaches of the Nile, in 1898. Britain's efforts to mend these matters were at first twofold. First, and somewhat hypocritically, she joined in the scramble for concessions, securing a lease on Wei-hei-wei in northern Shantung, facing the Russians at Port Arthur, and by strengthening her position at Kowloon, opposite Hongkong, strengthening her hold on the Yangtze valley. Her second technique was frantic search for allies to redress the balance now beginning to tilt adversely.[11] Among these moves was one of March 8, 1898, formally requesting American coöperation in maintaining free trade in China for all nations. This date, it will be noted, was about midway between the destruction of the *Maine* (February 15) and the report of the American Commission

[11] Langer, *Dipl. of Imperialism*, vol. 2, details this search.

of Inquiry (March 28). These excitements were sufficient in themselves to account for Secretary of State Sherman's cool response, and a second overture in January, 1899, was likewise rebuffed. Another move, less official, was to be more successful.

Meantime general and particular developments induced a more favorable temper in the United States. It will be recalled that whatever success Americans had achieved in China had been as a beneficiary of the most-favored-nation idea of equal commercial opportunity. The United States would therefore object on traditional grounds to the transformation of the spheres of influence into monopolistic holdings, just as Britain feared the spheres' encroachment on her general trade position and Japan resented their establishment behind a "Hands Off!" sign pointed in her direction (her sphere in Fukien, opposite Formosa, was a poor one compared to those of her competitors). Moreover, since the original British overture in March, 1898, the Spanish-American War had made the United States a full-fledged Pacific power, with hostages to fortune in Hawaii, Guam, and the Philippines. These areas, it should be noted, far outmatched in immediate territorial and strategic value any recent European acquisitions on the Asiatic mainland. Projecting American Pacific imperialism to the continent by joining the scramble for spheres of influence was beyond the scope of American policy, but the hardening of the spheres into protectorates or colonies would be doubly dangerous both strategically and economically, now that American possessions lay so close to Asia. Only one feasible method of preventing further European encroachments presented itself to the Anglophile John Hay (he had assumed the Department of State portfolio in September, 1898), namely, coöperation with Great Britain. Willing prompters in this direction were not lacking in 1899, and out of this complex of circumstances emerged the Notes of September 6.

The Open Door in China was becoming the subject of consideration and exhortation by a wide variety of interests. Cabinet members urged it in Britain and Anglo-American Leagues fostered it in London and New York. Lord Charles Beresford arrived in Washington in February, 1899, after a tour of the Far East and a speech-making junket from the West Coast, and was entertained at luncheon by John Hay. His reiterated pleas for American aid in preserving free commercial opportunity in China were distilled into a widely circulated book, *The Break-up of China.* These British elements gathered American adherents among business interests eager for wider markets, manufacturers (particularly of textiles) seeking outlets for their surpluses, and religious groups concerned by missionary reports of the moral implications of the scramble for concessions. These forces came to Hay's attention in the summer through W. W. Rockhill, his adviser on Far Eastern affairs, and Alfred E. Hippisley, an English employee of the Chinese Imperial Maritime Customs Service who through long years in the Far East had developed a concern for China's welfare as well as a desire to forward British interests in China; with his wife he stopped in the United States on a furlough trip to England and visited the Rockhills. Through Rockhill's agency he was able to influence Hay to favor the Open Door idea, after which circumstances conspired to win President McKinley's somewhat reluctant consent.[12] Jacob Gould Schurman, returning from a Philippine mission, reported that China, rather than the Islands, constituted the core of the Eastern problem. Moreover, Russia, one of the chief potential door-closers, exhibited momentary complaisance by opening Talienwan to all comers for a twenty-three-year period.

Aroused by this last, Hippisley drafted (August 17) a "Memorandum on the 'Open Door' in China," which he submitted to Rockhill four days later. On August 24 Hay instructed Rockhill to draft a memorandum on the same subject; Rockhill's memorandum of the 28th, incorporating Hippisley's ideas of the 17th, converted McKinley and became the basis of the notes which Hay sent to American diplomats in London, Berlin, and St. Petersburg on September 6, 1899 (extended later to France, Italy, and Japan). It will thus be seen that the initiative and phraseology of the notes were of British

---

[12] It is the belief of Hippisley's family, shared by Dr. Hu Shih, Chinese Ambassador to the United States, that Hippisley's action was undertaken out of a sincere desire to aid China. The author is indebted for this information to his colleague, Dr. Ardath W. Burks, who made available to him copies of the relevant documents, secured from the Chinese Embassy at Washington.

derivation; Hay's only contribution lay in his willingness to assume the international initiative (most welcome, of course, to the British) in such a fashion as to achieve coöperation without the locally undesirable complication of a foreign alliance. The notes instructed the ambassadors to secure foreign acquiescence in applying to their respective spheres of influence the following propositions which added up to a plea for equal commercial opportunity:

1. No power would interfere with treaty ports or vested interests in its own sphere.

2. All would continue to allow the Chinese treaty tariff, collected by China, to apply to the spheres.

3. None would levy higher harbor dues or freight charges on nonnationals than on its own people.

Thus did Hay, under British urging, revert in part to the coöperative policy of Cushing and of Burlingame in launching what Professor John K. Fairbank has aptly termed "an Anglo-American defensive measure in power politics." The notes were almost as remarkable for their omissions as for their content. Gone was the Burlingame idea of China's territorial integrity—the spheres of influence were fully recognized as part of the China scene. Here was no plea for equal treatment in the vastly important mining and railroad concessions even then beginning to receive serious attention. Nor was any attempt made to equalize the position of investment capital.

Hay's technique of achieving his proposals was, to put it mildly, a bold one. Each recipient of the notes had been requested to adhere to their principles and to urge the rest to do likewise. The only government consenting unequivocally was the Italian, likewise the only one which had failed in the race for spheres of influence. Each remaining power's acceptance was made contingent on like action by all the rest; Britain, the chief instigator of the policy, refused to apply it to Hongkong, and Russia, the chief target, replied with a thinly disguised rejection of its limitations. Hay braved these depressing circumstances by calmly announcing (March 20, 1900) that since all the Powers had accepted, the United States would consider that the door stood open. Silence in the face of this bland declaration constituted a moral commitment to support, but bound no one, including the United States, by more than moral obligations.

"Fits and Starts"

The Boxer Uprising, the first test of the new policy, was marked by a tentative expansion of the policy followed by a hurried retreat in the face of possible consequences—the beginning of a long succession of advances and withdrawals reflecting at once an earnest American desire to prevent unilateral exploitation of China and an unwillingness to implement this desire effectively because of the slight American economic and public concern with China. Trouble brewed in North China boiled over into a combined anti-Manchu (the Manchu dynasty had long exercised an alien sway over China) and anti-Western uprising in June, 1900, led by secret associations opposed to both types of outlanders and calling themselves the "Fists of Righteous Harmony." The accompanying violence resulted in an international expedition to relieve the Legation District of Peking where several hundred whites and some thousands of Chinese Christians were under siege—an enterprise shared by the United States in defiance of traditional isolationism. China was forced to pay heavy indemnities for the damage to foreign life and property. The American share of these more than compensated for actual losses, and in 1907 the Government refunded over $10,000,-000 to China; the use of part of this amount to provide American education for Chinese students did much to promote Sino-American good will.

The British suspicions which had helped to prompt the Open Door notes of 1899, and which had been heightened by Russian refusal to accept their implications, were borne out by Russian military encroachments in Manchuria during the Boxer troubles. Hay, likewise alarmed, sought to preserve Manchuria for China. His circular note of July 3, 1900, added significantly to the doctrine of 1899: The United States, he said, was determined "to seek a solution which may bring about permanent safety and peace to China, *preserve Chinese territorial and administrative entity*, protect all rights guaranteed to friendly powers by treaty and international law, and safeguard for the world the principle of equal and impartial trade with all parts of the Chinese Empire." [Italics added.] This not only brought Hay back into line with Burlingame, but carried him beyond, for he hinted at a "collective guarantee" of China's territorial integrity, which Burlingame had not envisioned. This note, merely stating the American position, did not require replies from the Powers; only England bothered to answer it. By November, however, Hay had repudiated his forward step and was himself asking, under Navy pressure, for territorial satisfactions at Samsah Bay. And when, some weeks later, Japan asked about his intentions in the event of Russian territorial acquisitions in Manchuria, Hay's reply of February 1, 1901, indicated full retreat from his July position. The United States, he said, "were not at present prepared to attempt singly, or in concert with other Powers, to enforce those views [our well-known views as to the integrity of China] in the east by any demonstration which could present a character of hostility to any other Power." Any contemporary moderation of foreign aggressions on China was achieved by mutual fear of taking the first step, rather than by American pressure; the Open Door had suffered its first setback.

The slight respect paid the dogma prior to the outbreak of the War of 1914–1918 reflects American unwillingness to implement such an essentially interventionist policy; reflects, too, the fact that other nations were unwilling to pay it more than lip service. The Anglo-Japanese Alliance of 1902 struck the first sharp blow at its principles.[13] This first British step out of the lonely grandeur of the 1890's contained in its preamble pious platitudes relative to China's independence and territorial integrity, and the Open Door, but later articles reaffirmed the Chinese spheres of both nations. Russo-Japanese territorial and economic rivalries in the Manchuria-Korea area brought these nations in February, 1904, into a war which jeopardized the Open Door. The Roosevelt Administration approached the

[13] After 1900 the problem of dissociating American relations with the two great Asiatic Powers, China and Japan, becomes increasingly difficult. The present chapter seeks to hew as closely as possible to the line of Sino-American relations, leaving larger Far Eastern and world-wide implications to the next chapter.

matter hopefully and in a circular note of February 20 asked the belligerents to respect "the neutrality of China and in all practicable ways her administrative entity." Each made its acceptance conditional upon the other's, and Russia rejected the proposed neutralization of Manchuria, so this initial effort was not particularly successful. During the negotiations which brought the two parties to the peace table Roosevelt committed Japan to "the position of maintaining Open Door in Manchuria and of restoring that province to China." However, even while the Japanese peace delegation was en route to the United States his Secretary of War was signing (July 29, 1905) the Taft-Katsura Memorandum which traded a Japanese promise to keep away from the Philippines for American acceptance of complete Japanese ascendancy over Korea—hardly a Rooseveltian "victory" for the Open Door.

Japanese designs on Manchuria, developing steadily after the Russo-Japanese War, brought about a *rapprochement* between the recent antagonists concerning their respective Manchurian spheres which boded ill for the Open Door. This was strengthened by agreements with other European Powers and sanctioned at least tacitly by the Root-Takahira Agreement of November 30, 1908, which carried a step further the concession granted in the Taft-Katsura Memorandum. This document, while containing the usual platitudes about the Open Door, committed the parties to the support of the *status quo* in the Pacific region, which could easily be construed as confirming Japan's already-established violations of the Open Door in Manchuria. The parties agreed, moreover, on "supporting by all pacific means at their disposal the independence and integrity of China and the principle of equal opportunity for commerce and industry of all nations in that Empire." It will be noted that only "pacific" means of implementation are stipulated, and that the word "territorial," now a common modifier of "integrity," does not appear. While these refinements of phraseology do not necessarily carry sinister connotations, the tenor of the Agreement indicates Roosevelt's realization that the Open Door could be no more than an ideal unless the United States was prepared to support its policy by force, which was then unthinkable. Rooseveltian maneuvers thus assisted considerably in underwriting Japanese imperialism in Korea and Manchuria.[14]

William Howard Taft and Philander C. Knox reversed the Rooseveltian policy of accommodation toward Japan and attempted to reassert the validity of the Open Door. They seem to have been motivated by an honest desire to help make China strong enough to be independent and so a land of really equal commercial opportunity. Their method was to insinuate American capital into all possible financial operations in China and Manchuria in an effort to help China help herself. Their efforts were almost completely unsuccessful and produced multiple antagonisms. The bankers first had to be persuaded to enter the game and then dragooned into remaining in it. The other Powers resented American intrusion and sought to forestall it. Japan and Russia, jointly alarmed at the Manchurian aspects, were driven into an alliance (completed, aptly enough, on July 4, 1910) which delimited more sharply than ever the spheres of influence staked out by an earlier agreement of 1907; the terms "Open Door" and "integrity of China" did not appear in this document. All in all, neither China, the Open Door, nor United States prestige profited by the Taft-Knox policy.[15]

Three principal episodes may be cited briefly to document the foregoing conclusions. Soon after Taft's inauguration in 1909 an international consortium composed of France, Britain, and Germany

---

[14] Roosevelt wrote Taft in 1910 that "as has been proved by the whole history of Manchuria, alike under Russia and Japan, the 'Open Door' policy, as a matter of fact, completely disappears as soon as a powerful nation determines to disregard it, and is willing to run the risk of war rather than forego its intention." Elihu Root seems to have felt that the Open Door aspects, rather than the *status quo,* would be emphasized in Manchuria, and that thus the Agreement might act as a brake on Japanese imperialism. It is at least arguable, however, that Japan would look at the Agreement as part of the larger pattern of arrangements sanctioning her special position in Manchuria. See T. A. Bailey, "The Root-Takahira Agreement of 1908," *Pacific Historical Review,* vol. 9 (1940), pp. 19–35.

[15] The reader's attention should perhaps be called again to Griswold's study, on which all textbook writers rely heavily for the period after 1900. Additional titles which bear on the Taft-Knox story are Herbert Croly, *Willard Straight,* Macmillan, 1924; C. F. Remer, *Foreign Investments in China,* Macmillan, 1933; W. W. Willoughby, *Foreign Rights and Interests in China,* Johns Hopkins Press, 1927; F. M. Huntington-Wilson, *Memoirs of an Ex-diplomat,* Humphries, 1945; and E. H. Zabriskie, *American-Russian Rivalry in the Far East,* University of Pennsylvania Press, 1946.

was preparing to float a loan for the construction of the so-called Hukuang Railways, to link Hankow and Canton with the interior province of Szechwan. An American banking group, formed at the instance of the Department of State, to finance railroad concessions which might be secured from the Chinese Government, sought to participate. Their agent, Willard Straight,[16] formally petitioned the European bankers for admission to the consortium (July 7), but met with refusal. Taft broke the deadlock by the unprecedented step of personally urging Chinese coöperation upon Prince Chun, the Chinese regent, on July 15. American participation was finally permitted, though only after long negotiations carried on by Straight in China, and the final four-power consortium agreement was not signed until May 20, 1911.

A second episode centered in Manchuria, where Edward H. Harriman had for some time sought to forge a railroad link in his grandiose scheme of world-girdling transportation facilities. His untimely death (September 10, 1909) left matters temporarily in Straight's hands, and on October 2 the latter took the initiative and signed a preliminary agreement, on behalf of the American bankers and a British firm, to build a 750-mile stretch of a proposed line between Chinchow and Aigun, far in northern Manchuria. When the bankers refused to be bound by Straight's action, the Secretary of State offered (December 14) alternative proposals. One suggested joint Anglo-American action looking to the neutralization of all the Manchurian lines under an international board; its alternative was joint participation of all "interested powers," which in Knox's calculations did not include Japan, in the Chinchow-Aigun scheme, with China as nominal owner of the completed line. The neutralization scheme threw Russia and Japan together; only collaboration could have produced their almost identical notes of refusal of January 21, 1910. Their treaty of July 4, mentioned above, deliberately defying the Open Door, was the logical result. February 24 Russia indicated that the Chinchow-Aigun proposal was "exceedingly injuri-

---

[16] Much of the impetus of the Taft-Knox policy seems to have derived from the activities of William Phillips of the Department and of Straight who, first as American Consul at Mukden, later as Chief of the Department's Far Eastern Division, and finally as an employee of the bankers, was incessantly active.

ous" to her position in Manchuria. Opposed by the two Manchurian door-closers and lacking effective support elsewhere, Knox was compelled to witness the defeat of his schemes and the weakening of American prestige in the Far East.

Optimistic despite these rebuffs, he encouraged the Chinese Government to request (September 22, 1910) a large loan to underwrite currency reform and industrial development. The bankers, alarmed at his previous lack of success, announced that they would not be bound to participate in contracts which were objectionable to other powers. Other nations presently entered the picture and there followed a tangled story complicated by the outbreak of the Chinese Revolution (October 10, 1911). Eventually a six-power consortium was developed in 1912, but the final agreement was signed without American participation (April 26, 1913). The bankers were now thoroughly disillusioned and informed Woodrow Wilson the very day after his inauguration that they wanted no more of China and would remain active only under executive pressure. This Wilson refused to exert, and on March 18 withdrew his support of the consortium on the ground that its terms endangered China's "administrative independence." Thus ended Knox's efforts to open the door with dollars.[17]

The War of 1914–1918 took Europe's full attention; it found the United States first deeply concerned with problems of neutrality and continental international complications and then immersed in actual hostilities to a point where the Far East was very "far" indeed. At the same time its distractions permitted Japan to forward a maturing policy of aggression at China's expense. From the standpoint of the Open Door and the accompanying principles of China's administrative and territorial integrity it was a discouraging period. American support of traditional principles, however tentative, served only to mitigate, not to halt, Japanese encroachments, and

---

[17] It may be noted in passing that as early as July, 1916, the Department of State was again asking the bankers to enter the Chinese picture. Again in June, 1918, Wilson set in motion the machinery which induced American bankers to enter a four-power consortium, completed late in 1920, to loan to China, thus reverting to the policy repudiated in 1913.

contributed to a rapid worsening of Japanese-American relations.[18] These developments occurred against the background of Japan's Twenty-One Demands upon China and the Lansing-Ishii Agreement of November 2, 1917.

Japan first occupied German holdings in Shantung Province, effecting the capture in part by an unauthorized military expedition through Chinese territory. A statement of her ultimate intention to return the seized territory to Chinese jurisdiction accompanied the seizure; her next move, indicative of her purpose to reduce all China to subservience, rendered this pious promise somewhat academic. This took the form of twenty-one propositions, communicated secretly to President Yuan Shih-kai on January 18, 1915. In Professor Bemis' telling phrase, every word of the Demands was "packed with anaesthesia for Chinese sovereignty," and by the same token boded ill for the Open Door. Group I committed China to prior acceptance of any German-Japanese dispositions relative to Shantung; Group II demanded Chinese recognition of Japan's "special position" in South Manchuria and Eastern Inner Mongolia; Group IV sought the end of "effectively preserving the territorial integrity of China" by exacting her promise "not to cede or lease to any third power any harbor or bay or island along the coast of China"; Group V proposed Chinese employment of "influential Japanese" as advisers in the formulation of domestic governmental policy, the use of "numerous Japanese" in important police positions, and joint Sino-Japanese control of the domestic munitions industry.

Nearer matters such as Mexico overshadowed American interest in the Far East; Secretary Bryan's note of March 3, 1915, protested vigorously that many of the Demands were derogatory of Chinese political independence and administrative entity; as a result Japan withdrew or modified several, particularly those in Group V. As to the Shantung–South Manchuria–East Mongolia area, however, Bryan made the damaging statement that "the United States frankly

---

[18] The present narrative is devoted mainly to the Open Door aspects of the period; see below, pp. 337–377, for a fuller discussion of Japanese-American relations. On China's role during the period, see T. E. LaFargue, *China and the World War*, Stanford University Press, 1937.

recognizes that territorial contiguity creates special relations between Japan and these districts," an admission somewhat encouraging to Japan.

The revised Demands were resubmitted to China on April 26 and embodied in a Sino-Japanese treaty of May 25 (following a Japanese ultimatum of May 7) by which Japan obtained unwilling Chinese recognition of her position in South Manchuria and Shantung. Meantime this position had been challenged but not seriously threatened by an American note drafted by Robert Lansing (then Counsellor of the Department) and despatched May 11, between the ultimatum and signature of the Treaty. This note, which became the basis of the Stimson Doctrine of 1932, was at the moment merely a face-saving gesture designed to insert in the fast-closing door a wedge which might be driven home later, under more propitious circumstances; circumstances were indeed not propitious on that date, which found the *Lusitania* crisis at high tension. The note refused, on behalf of the United States, to recognize "any agreement or undertaking which has been entered into or which may be entered into between the Governments of Japan and China, impairing the treaty rights of the United States and its citizens in China, the political or territorial integrity of the Republic of China, or the international policy relative to China commonly known as the open door policy." However weak, this was the only protest made on China's behalf, and helped to induce the Japanese maneuvering which resulted in the Lansing-Ishii Agreement of November 2, 1917.

This statement at once reaffirmed the Open Door and permitted Japan to twist its interpretation to her own ends. It reflects increasing Japanese predominance in the Far East and American preoccupation with the War of 1914–1918, which that nation entered in April, 1917, following German renewal of unrestricted submarine warfare on February 1. The submarine crisis enabled Japan to force the European powers into a series of agreements underwriting Japanese claims in any postwar settlement. The Lansing-Ishii Agreement was designed to incorporate the United States in this nexus of promises, and was so interpreted by Japan. Formally denying any intention to "infringe in any way the independence or territorial integrity of China," it reaffirmed the Open Door principle; at the same time it admitted that "territorial propinquity creates special relations between countries. . . ." Viscount Kikujiro Ishii, the Japanese negotiator, had sought to use "paramount relations," but deferred to Lansing in the official document; however, the term "paramount" mysteriously reappeared in the translation furnished the Chinese Government. The Agreement represents at once an exercise in semantics and a complete failure to produce a meeting of the minds: Lansing was convinced that he conceded to Japan only an economic hold on China, while Ishii felt that a political concession had been made as well. At best it was a holding operation, designed to prevent full recognition of Japan's position in China; it left the United States at the end of the war, however, the only important nation holding any reservations of this kind.[19]

Washington Conference—Chinese Phase

The relation of the Washington Conference of 1921–1922 to the Open Door must be approached in the light of China's treatment at the Versailles Conference of 1918–1919 and subsequent American pressures of various sorts on Japan (pp. 356, 357). Briefly, China's hope that the Peace Conference would oust Japan from Shantung was deferred; Japan merely promised to surrender political control in the indefinite future. In the succeeding months the United States repeatedly indicated antagonism to Japan's Asiatic ambitions, often with Chinese ramifications. Among such episodes may be listed friction over Japan's Siberian aspirations, over her tightening grip on Manchuria, her continued aversion to the principles of the Open Door, her refusal to accord the United States cable privileges on the Island of Yap, and her apparent willingness to join the fast-emerging naval-armaments race. Viewed as a move to limit Japanese aggressions, the Conference produced the most vigorous statement yet made on the Open Door and elevated the doctrine from a purely American shibboleth into the realm of conventional international law. China, disturbed and disunited from years of revolution,

---

[19] The Agreement will be explored more fully below (pp. 353, 354) in connection with the story of Japanese-American relations.

thwarted at Versailles, and increasingly burdened by the "unequal treaties," saw in the Conference an opportunity to achieve hopes long deferred; Japan scented danger to established positions. Japan's cautious acceptance of the American invitation insisted that any agenda avoid the introduction of "problems such as are of *sole concern* to certain particular powers or such matters that may be regarded *accomplished facts. . . .*" (Italics added.) Thus she sought to forestall discussion of such ticklish questions as the Twenty-One Demands, Manchuria, and Shantung. Despite the discouraging Japanese reservations, China came to Washington optimistically demanding removal of tariff and extraterritorial limitations, the cancellation of the Twenty-One Demands, and the return of Shantung. She was to be only partly successful in fulfilling her desires.[20]

Attention has already been called to the early assumption of extraterritorial privileges by foreign nations, at first not unwelcome to the Chinese. Since 1842 China's sovereignty had been further restricted by treaty limitations precluding customs levies above 5 percent ad valorem. She had abrogated the treaties granting these privileges to Germany, Austria, and Russia as a result of the recent war, but had as yet reaped slight benefit from this action. She came to Washington hopeful of terminating these particular types of control, and was immediately encouraged by the appointment of subcommittees to draft proposals on both matters. The net results were disappointing; instead of setting the desired date, the Conference referred the extraterritorial question to a commission for study and recommendation, which the Powers could accept or reject individually. Tariff provisions were likewise unsatisfactory; the treaty provided for a special conference to deal with tariff revision. Thus the Conference did little more than dangle a carrot under China's nose; the real battle over the unequal treaties was yet to be waged.

The delegates devoted long and earnest attention to naval disarmament, nonfortification in the Pacific, and a substitute for the Anglo-Japanese Alliance before appreciable headway was made to-

---

[20] Dorothy Borg, *American Policy and the Chinese Revolution, 1925–1928,* Macmillan, 1947, surveys the Chinese aspects of the Washington Conference as well as application of its principles to the particular years of her study. For more detailed reference to the bibliography of the Conference, see footnotes of the next chapter.

ward solving mainland problems. The delegates were becoming restive when, early in January, Mr. Arthur Balfour of the British contingent seems to have hinted to the Japanese that failure to reach agreement here would have unfortunate results in the United States. Japan presently promised to withdraw from Siberia (her December concession of cable-landing rights on Yap was implemented by a treaty signed February 11) and before long (February 4) an agreement was reached on Shantung, less favorable than China had hoped, but a step in the right direction.[21] The Japanese doctrine of sole concern precluded direct Conference action on Shantung, but a complicated procedure in which Hughes and Balfour worked with the Oriental delegations produced an extra-Conference arrangement whereby political sovereignty over the Peninsula reverted to China, while Japan retained her economic control. American pressure failed to dislodge Japan from her treaty-based position in Manchuria; her chief concession here was the withdrawal of Group V of the Twenty-One Demands, in abeyance since 1915.

One of the Conference's most important and in later years most disputed actions covered China's future under the Nine-Power Pact, signed February 6, 1922. Here the United States, which had just rejected international coöperation via the League of Nations, returned to its own earlier Far Eastern policy as embodied in the most-favored-nation demands of the 1840's, the Open Door notes of 1899, and Hay's position of July, 1900. This time, however, coöperation was treaty-based and so was as binding as any international agreement could be made. The initiative, as in 1899, was British. Balfour brought with him a memorandum which Hughes elaborated into a multipartite treaty despite Japan's objections and China's weakness (the Canton Government of Sun Yat-sen was contending with an almost equally powerful regime at Peking for domestic supremacy). In Article I the signatories bound themselves "To respect the sovereignty, the independence, and the territorial and administrative integrity of China. . . ." and "To use their influence for the purpose of effectually establishing and maintaining the principle of equal

---

[21] On this phase of the Conference see Harold and Margaret Sprout, *Toward a New Order of Sea Power*, Princeton University Press, 1940, pp. 249–250.

opportunity for the commerce and industry of all nations throughout the territory of China." Only Hughes' heroic efforts induced Japan to sign what was virtually a renunciation of her further territorial aspirations. Later events were to prove that she would not remain obligated by an agreement no more binding than her pledged word. History has not yet proved the suggestion that she pledged her word in bad faith; on the other hand, history presents several years during which her leaders faithfully observed their promises. The fact remains, of course, that her pledge, like that of all the rest, was a pledge only; international coöperation was still many years away from the time when pledges were to receive the sanction of international force. For the moment, China had fared well at the hands of her friends as well as her potential enemies. The rest of the decade was largely filled with her efforts to achieve domestic unity and stability and to continue (without wholly succeeding) the attack upon the unequal treaties.

China Comes of Age

China's history since the Revolution of 1911 had been almost unbelievably troubled and complicated—in fact, it was only by courtesy that a "government" was recognized for the purposes of Chinese membership in the Conference of 1921–1922. The remaining 1920's witnessed the emergence, out of grinding necessity and developing leadership, of an authority which, while never achieving complete domination of the warlords who from time immemorial have laid tribute on China's boundaries, spoke with increasing firmness for a steadily consolidating nation. One faction based on Peking at first had the recognition of most of the Powers; another attempted to rule from Canton under the influence of Sun Yat-sen. Neither commanded adequate financial support and both were held in derision by the local military potentates. Sun, unable to make headway by himself, accepted proffered Russian assistance and in 1923 began reconstituting the Kuomintang or Nationalist Party along Communist lines. The year 1927 saw the rise to commanding leadership of Chiang Kai-shek who, expelling the Communists from the Kuomintang, consolidated the Peking and Canton factions into what increasingly approximated a fascist dictatorship, ruling from Nanking and encompassing more and more of China until his sway extended over most of the ancient Empire except for Manchuria and some portions still under Soviet influence. It was this China, at first disunited but later gaining in both unity and aggressiveness, which faced and partly solved the problems left by the Washington Conference. Its unity aided in breaking the solid front of the Powers against concessions; its aggressiveness ultimately helped to force Japan into the Manchurian adventure of 1931–1932.

The Commissions provided for by the Conference to deal with tariff and extraterritorial questions accomplished little. The treaty relating to a tariff conference did not become effective until August 5, 1925. Meantime Chinese initiative dictated notes of June 24 chiding the Powers for their inaction. The latter replied in identical notes on September 4; two days earlier Secretary of State Frank B. Kellogg announced that a conference would assemble at Peking in October. His instructions to the American delegates were sympathetic toward Chinese aspirations, but wary of concessions until China had stabilized her domestic affairs. The conference labored intermittently until the summer of 1926 with slight positive results because of the still-existing hostilities between the Peking and Canton Governments and the refusal of the latter to honor the conference's decisions. Though the conference was barren of actual accomplishment, its resolution that China assume tariff autonomy on January 1, 1929, became the goal of Chinese aspirations. Failure to ratify the Washington treaty likewise postponed the proposed commission on extraterritoriality until January 12, 1926. The Soviet-dominated Canton Government refused to receive the commission's traveling emissaries, and its nine months' investigation resulted in a report confined to North China and insisting that far-reaching reforms must precede lifting of the extraterritorial burden. Thus after four years the Washington Conference machinery proved ineffective in removing the unequal treaties; more drastic measures seemed indicated.

These, initiated by China herself and reflecting an aggressively nationalistic spirit, secured tariff autonomy and bade fair to restore judicial autonomy as well, being balked in the latter only by the launching of the Japanese maneuvers of September, 1931. China succeeded largely because of the inability of the Washington Conference Powers to maintain the concert there established; this in turn was due largely to the conciliatory attitude of Secretary of State Frank B. Kellogg; finally, the adroit diplomacy of the Canton Government (which presently gained ascendancy in China) played no small role. The Chinese technique, evolved by Eugene Chen, the Nationalist Foreign Minister, was to apply pressure to Britain, whose China trade had been severely curtailed by a Cantonese boycott and stood in even greater danger from a prospective Nationalist occupation of the Yangtze Valley.[22] The Chinese policy-makers reasoned cogently that the British Labor Government was more sympathetic than its predecessors toward the "lesser peoples"; moreover, a boycott on the China trade, affecting only about 2 percent of Britain's total foreign commerce, would be only a minor irritant. The pressure became sufficiently severe to induce the British to propose (December 18, 1926; published on Christmas Day) that the Conference Powers "should abandon the idea that the economic and political development of China can only be secured under foreign tutelage" and "should expressly disclaim any intention of forcing foreign control upon an unwilling China." Here was a conciliatory attitude, but one which still posited joint action by the Conference Powers.

Chinese pressure exploded from diplomacy into force when on January 3–5, 1927, a mob rudely expelled the British from their important concession at Hankow, then the seat of the Nationalist Government; peaceable British acceptance of this untoward treatment was at wide variance with traditional practice. Secretary Kellogg's statement of January 27 overtook and passed the earlier British proposal. He announced his Government's willingness to enter direct Sino-American negotiations on tariff and extraterritoriality regardless of the other Washington Conference Powers, and pro-

---

[22] The following throw additional light on this particular story: H. B. Elliston, "China in the World Family," *Foreign Affairs*, vol. 7 (1929), pp. 616–627; A. N. Holcombe, *The Chinese Revolution: A Phase in the Regeneration of a World Power*, Harvard University Press, 1930; W. H. Mallory, "The Passing of Extraterritoriality in China," *Foreign Affairs*, vol. 9 (1931), pp. 346–349; R. T. Pollard, *China's Foreign Relations, 1917–1931*, Macmillan, 1933.

posed, moreover, to deal with delegates from both contending Chinese factions if these could agree on joint discussions. This presaged a breach in the Powers' united front; unity was almost restored, however, by another Chinese affront to Western prestige in the Nanking Incident of March 24, 1927. Here again elements of the Nationalists (allegedly Communists, alarmed at Chiang's prospective defection from their ideology and trying by violence to provoke a foreign intervention which would restore their own influence) attacked foreigners in Nanking. A movement rapidly gathered headway, evidently under British leadership and supported by the American Ambassador, Mr. J. V. A. MacMurray, for joint application of sanctions to the Nationalist Government. Mr. Kellogg, however, feeling that public opinion at home was opposed to sanctions, refused to join with the others, causing abandonment of the scheme.[23]

This marked the end of concerted action and left the United States free to implement its promises of January, 1927. The tariff problem was approached first and a draft treaty prepared in the Department as early as the autumn of 1927. Expanding Nationalist control brought increasing pressure for treaty revision, and matters moved rapidly to a conclusion in July, 1928. An agreement signed on the 25th embodying "the principle of complete national tariff autonomy" and the most-favored-nation principle became China's first "equal" tariff treaty. By December 27, 1928, China had signed no less than twelve treaties; her tariff law went into operation on February 1, 1929, though Japan's agreement did not become effective until May 16, 1930, and though Japan and Britain secured a ceiling on rates for varying periods of time. One great Chinese objective had thus been attained, with American coöperation, and through making a breach in the concert established at Washington.

It took a war to achieve the other objective, though China had made some progress even before the abortive conference of 1926. In entering the War of 1914–1918 she abrogated treaties conferring extraterritorial privileges upon nationals of Germany, Austria, and

---

[23] On March 30, 1928, just as Chiang was establishing his ascendancy over the Communists and preparing to set up his Nanking Government as a rival of the Peking group, he apologized and assumed responsibility for the incident, although disavowing its instigation.

Hungary; the peace treaties recognized this and new agreements with Germany (1921) and Austria (1925) accepted Chinese judicial authority. Unilateral abolition applied to Russia (1920) became treaty-based in an agreement of May 31, 1924. The tariff flurry of 1928 stimulated interest, and in July China established regulations covering nationals of all powers (mostly the smaller European nations) not then enjoying extraterritorial privileges. Chinese pressure against the major powers, exerted in 1930, elicited sympathetic responses; Chinese legal codes had been modernized and negotiations with Britain and the United States had reached an advanced stage in the autumn of 1931 when "natural disasters and other calamities in various localities," to wit, the Japanese sortie of September 18 in Manchuria, rudely terminated proceedings. Japanese activities likewise ended resumed discussions in 1937. May 31, 1941, Cordell Hull renewed previous offers to war-torn China, to be implemented upon the return of peace. Instead of peace, Pearl Harbor inaugurated a new phase of world-wide war which found the United States and China fighting Japan together; extraterritoriality became bad manners toward an ally and treaties signed at Washington and Chungking on January 11, 1943, released China from her obligations to both the United States and Great Britain. The wheel whose revolution had begun at Nanking and Wanghia in the 1840's swung full circle a century later to place China, however precariously, back on a footing of international equality.

15 The Far East: Japan

I N SHARP CONTRAST WITH THE EARLY CHINA POLICY OF hanging to British coattails, the United States took an early and positive lead, in the 1850's, in conditioning Japan to western contacts. Americans aided greatly, moreover, in Japan's phenomenal westernization during the ensuing decades. These were years of firm friendship lasting until, around the turn of the twentieth century, both nations emerged as world powers and began each to eye the other watchfully. Thus a potential rivalry succeeded the earlier, easier relationship—a rivalry aggravated by a succession of episodes making it increasingly clear that Japanese maturity in position and possessions could be achieved only by endangering supposed American social, economic, and strategic interests. Japanese-American relations in the present century therefore present a recurring series of crises and near-crises interspersed with periods of uneasy good will, constantly diminishing and finally disappearing in the early 1930's as Japan's supposed necessities drove her to increasingly open imperialism on the Asiatic mainland.[1]

---

[1] See Note 1 of the preceding chapter for general references on the Far East. The following are particularly useful from the Japanese standpoint: F. R. Dulles, *America in the Pacific: Forty Years of American-Japanese Relations,* Appleton-Century, 1937; Sir George B. Sansom, *The Western World and Japan,* Knopf, 1950; Payson J. Treat, *Diplomatic Relations between the United States and Japan, 1853–1895,* Stanford University Press, 1932, 2 vols.; *Diplomatic Relations between the United States and Japan, 1895–1905,* Stanford University Press, 1938; *The Early Diplomatic Relations between the United States and Japan, 1853–1865,* Johns Hopkins Press, 1917; *The Far East: A Political and Diplomatic History,* Harper, 1928; *Japan and the United States, 1853–1921,* Houghton Mifflin, 1921; H. E. Wildes, *Aliens in the East: A New History of Japan's Foreign Intercourse,* University of Pennsylvania Press, 1937.

Perry and the Recluse

When Americans began to develop an interest in Japan, toward the middle of the nineteenth century, their eyes turned to an area almost insulated from outside contacts and on the verge of severe domestic turmoil. Japanese receptivity to Western advances in the sixteenth century brought traders (Spanish, Portuguese, Dutch, and English), missionaries (of the Roman Catholic persuasion), and trouble. In 1624 Japan expelled all foreigners save the Dutch and English; the British were eliminated twenty years later, and the Dutch limited to sending eight ships per year to an island near Nagasaki, a privilege gradually restricted until (after 1790) only a single annual voyage was permitted. The Napoleonic Wars afforded the first American opportunity to visit Japan when the Dutch, fearful of losing their annual venture to British cruisers, allowed American ships to make eight of their voyages between 1797 and 1809.

By the 1820's American whalers began to frequent Japanese waters; the Japanese refused to permit these to secure supplies and treated shipwrecked sailors with contempt. Adventurers in the China trade repeatedly sought to extend their operations across the China Sea in the next two decades; not until 1846, however, did an American naval expedition under Commodore James Biddle anchor in Japanese waters and establish contact with Japanese officialdom. Biddle's experience was not particularly encouraging, as its principal fruit was a warning "to depart immediately, and to consult your own safety by not appearing again upon our coast." When the Mexican War and the Oregon Treaty of 1846 gave the United States undisputed possession of a long Pacific shoreline, interest in Japan developed rapidly; the San Francisco–Shanghai trade needed coaling stations for the steam vessels which would presently elbow the proud clipper ships from the China trade. Together these pressures induced the American authorities to despatch an expedition in an attempt to persuade Japan to open a window to the westward. Commodore Matthew Calbraith Perry, brother of the Oliver Hazard Perry who had "met the enemy" on Lake Erie in the War of 1812, and himself an officer of considerable experience, was chosen for the mission.

Unbeknown to Perry, preparing for his voyage by poring over Dutch books and charts, Japan approached a domestic crisis. Supposedly ruled by a divinely ordained dynasty descended in unbroken (if often badly bent) line from a mythical progenitor living centuries before the Christian era, Japan was long actually governed by a group of court nobles; later a military dictatorship, divorced from court and Emperor and often at odds with both, exercised control. Power had for some centuries been concentrated in an individual titled the Shogun. The Shogunate had gradually become hereditary and had since 1603 been in the hands of the Tokugawa family; its power in turn had been weakening and in the years just before Perry's appearance had largely been placed in the hands of a small group of ministers chosen from the higher nobility. The Emperor lived at Kyoto, while the Shogun's capital was at Yedo (Tokyo), some 350 miles distant. Due to domestic factors which form no part of the present story, a showdown was approaching between the Emperor and the Shogunate, a showdown which Perry's appearance in Japanese waters helped to precipitate and which, lasting well into the 1860's, resulted in the downfall of the Shogunate. Thus Western penetration of Japan's isolation was played against a backdrop of domestic upheaval.

After a year of study and preparation Perry led his small squadron of four ships from the China station, arriving at the entrance of Yedo Bay on July 8, 1853.[2] He was armed with numerous presents calculated to intrigue the Japanese interest and palate and with a well-developed sense of his own importance calculated to stand him in good stead in dealing with the "proud and vindictive" natives. His instructions bade him obtain humane treatment for shipwrecked sailors, secure the designation of one or more ports for trade and procurement of supplies, and survey, if possible, Japanese coastal

---

[2] On the Perry expedition see: E. M. Barrows, *The Great Commodore: The Exploits of Matthew Calbraith Perry,* Bobbs-Merrill, 1936, pp. 212–343; Allen B. Cole (ed.), *With Perry in Japan: The Diary of Edward Yorke McCauley,* Princeton University Press, 1943; F. L. Hawks, *Narrative of the Expedition of an American Squadron to the China Seas and Japan,* D. Appleton, 1856; C. O. Paullin, *Diplomatic Negotiations of American Naval Officers, 1778–1883,* Johns Hopkins Press, 1912, pp. 186–214; Arthur Walworth, *Black Ships Off Japan,* Knopf, 1946, the best secondary account; F. W. Williams, *The Life and Letters of Samuel Wells Williams, Missionary, Diplomatist, Sinologue,* Putnam, 1889, a biography of Perry's interpreter.

waters, largely a closed book to westerners. Mindful of Japan's earlier experiences, he was to renounce any religious objectives, and to
make it clear that identity of language made the United States no
party to any English designs. First formal contact was established
by dropping anchor at Uraga, only twenty-seven miles from Yedo.
After considerable palaver, complicated by Perry's refusal to comply with Japanese demands, arrangements were completed for the
delivery, ashore, of a letter from "his high and puissant mightiness
the Caezar of America," addressed to the Emperor. This took place
on July 14, with a minimum of ceremony, after which Perry was
none too politely invited to leave. Instead, he continued to survey
the waters of the Bay, his advance toward Yedo inducing a corresponding increase in Japanese civility. He stayed nine days and departed, promising to return the following spring for a reply to the
President's communication.

The incumbent Shogun soon died; the modest political talents of
his son-successor left matters more than ever in the hands of the
court clique, whose leader took the unprecedented step of submitting the American proposals to the Emperor and the Daimyos (feudal nobles) for advice. Having made this concession, however, the
Shogun's advisers proceeded to ignore Imperial and noble counsel
to have nothing to do with the foreigner, and determined to reply
amicably to the American requests. When Perry, ignorant to the
end of these domestic developments, returned to Japan in February,
1854, in order to forestall Russian maneuvers, he met with a cordial
reception. During the ensuing social amenities the Japanese con-
sumed Perry's delicacies, particularly the liquid ones, with great
gusto. Gifts were exchanged amid ceremonies out of proportion to
the importance of the treaty which followed (signed March 31,
1854).[3] The principal immediate significance of this agreement was
to insure fair treatment for shipwrecked sailors; its trading conces-

---

[3] Japanese ceremonial gifts included a dried fish, four dogs, and several tons of
rice, encased in 125-pound sacks which were carried two at a time aboard Perry's
ship by professional wrestlers who later entertained the guests at their specialty. Perry
had brought numerous specimens of western handiwork in addition to large supplies
of liquor, and enlivened the occasion by setting up and operating a miniature steam
railway for Japanese edification.

sions were very slight, but opened the door for further negotiations; by placing the United States on a most-favored-nation basis the agreement laid the foundation for future demands. Perry returned to the States and (with some expert assistance) produced a three-volume narrative of his expedition. His importance lies more in what he started than in what he actually accomplished, and even here he served as a catalyst of forces already at work within Japan rather than furnishing an initial impetus.

Japan Goes Western

The Japanese door, opened a crack by Perry, was pushed wide by Townsend Harris, first (1856–1859) Consul and later Minister, after months of wearisome and painstaking negotiations which made his name a household word in Japan.[4] A footloose bachelor, he disposed of a prosperous business in New York City in 1849 and indulged a long-standing wanderlust which took him to China. Appointed upon Perry's recommendation, he arrived at Shimoda, a village on a poor harbor sixty miles from Yedo, opened by the Perry treaty for the procurement of supplies, in the summer of 1856. Japanese desire to avoid further concessions to the West induced dilatory and evasive tactics which soon convinced Harris that all members of the race were congenital liars; ill-health and inadequate instructions likewise complicated his task, accomplishment of which was finally facilitated by his discovery that his co-negotiators understood American champagne better than his diplomatic representations. Out of months of mutual misunderstanding he finally evolved two agreements, one signed June 18, 1857, and the other July 29, 1858.[5]

---

[4] M. E. Cosenza (ed.), *The Complete Journal of Townsend Harris*, Doubleday, Doran, 1930; Carl Crow, *He Opened the Door of Japan*, Harper, 1939; H. H. Gowen, *Five Foreigners in Japan*, Revell, 1936, pp. 226–282; R. S. Morris, *Townsend Harris: A Chapter of American Diplomacy*, Japan Society, 1921.

[5] He caused the Japanese no small concern on his own part. Gowen, *op. cit.*, p. 243, quotes a letter from the Governor of Shimoda to the Yedo authorities, December 22, 1857: "he became angry and refused to listen to our words. We did not understand what he was saying but, pointing his fingers at the Japanese officials who were present, he seemed to be rebuking them in a loud and excited manner. Furthermore, when he saw the attendants bring in tea, he waved his hands and with a sweeping motion hurled them away. This, most likely, meant that he did not desire any

The first specifically admitted the United States to the privileges granted by Japan to Britain, Russia, and the Netherlands, and already effective under the most-favored-nation clause. It opened Nagasaki to American commerce, increased the value of American currency in Japan, and granted extraterritorial rights to Americans. The second, and more important, Treaty of Shimoda came some months after Harris' audience with the Shogun, whom he interviewed under the impression that he was seeing the Emperor. It broadened the commercial base by opening several additional ports to American merchants, established a conventional tariff, granted American rights of residence at Yedo and Osaka, and established diplomatic representation at the respective capitals. Its provisions governed Japan's external relations until 1894. Its negotiation by Lord Hotta, liberal Foreign Minister of the Shogun's party, added a chapter to the developing crisis inside Japan. Increasingly unsure of himself, the Shogun submitted the question of policy involved to the Emperor and the Daimyos, who opposed signing the treaty. The issue was determined by news of recent Anglo-French military victories over China, raising the unpleasant prospect that the victorious Europeans might arrive in Japan to exact concessions by force. It was signed, however, without the Emperor's permission; that he was consulted at all was another earnest of changing times in Japan. Harris' tour of duty (which lasted until 1862) saw the establishment of Japanese-American relations upon a sound basis, partly because of his own patience and ability, partly because of the confused conditions in Japan which worked momentarily to his advantage, and partly because the Japanese preferred to acquiesce in his demands, thus establishing by peaceful means a model preferable to one which might be exacted forcibly by less considerate Europeans.[6]

---

tea. Since his conduct resembles that of a lunatic, if we insist upon consulting with him, it would make matters worse. . . ."

[6] A British consular contemporary wrote enthusiastically that the story of Harris' service was "one of marvelous tact and patience, of steady determination and courage, of straightforward uprightness in every respect, that is not exceeded by any in the entire history of the international relations of the world." Quoted by Treat, *Early Relations,* p. 190.

Japan's domestic crisis was resolved in two directions in the 1860's by the ousting of the Shogun, who had favored enlarged western contacts, and the adoption of his policy by the victorious Daimyos, using the Emperor as a tool. The Shogun and his group, seeing the handwriting on the wall, had, as has been indicated above, favored opening Japan to the West. The Daimyos, in the ascendant with the Emperor, opposed the broadening of outside contacts and for a time made life miserable for the westernizers and for foreigners in Japan (the British and American legations were burned in 1863). Presently, however, the relapse into isolationism was halted when one of the Daimyos overreached himself. In the summer of 1863 Choshu, a leader of the antiforeign group whose feudal holdings abutted on the Straits of Shimonoseki, attempted a one-man purge of foreigners. His guns fired from shore upon ships bearing the flags of the United States, France, and the Netherlands, and when the Shogun was unable to comply with united foreign demands that Choshu be disciplined the Powers took matters into their own hands.

After the United States and Britain had taken individual reprisals, a joint naval expedition was organized and the United States hastily abandoned isolationism to join in chastising the unruly Choshu (September, 1864). American participation was strictly by token, as the steam-powered navy was busy in the Civil War. The government therefore chartered a handy merchant vessel, mounted modest armament, and sent her along with nine British, four Dutch, and three French warships to join in the bombardment. One sequel was an assessment of $3,000,000 indemnity upon Japan, the excessive American share of which ($785,000) was refunded in 1883. Another was the decision on the part of the Daimyos that their own isolation policy was a mistaken one; acting promptly, they overthrew the Shogun, restored the Emperor to his former position (1868), and turned their eyes steadfastly westward.

The present story cannot detail the amazing process of Japan's emergence, around the turn of the twentieth century, as a first-rate nation; recent world history offers no counterpart for this remarkable transformation. The metamorphosis was achieved by the deliberate abandonment, at least outwardly, of centuries-old concepts and the adoption and adaptation to Japanese uses, under the guidance of carefully selected foreign advisers, of Western economic, educational, and military practices and institutions. Japan preceded China by some decades in attacking the unequal treaties conferring extraterritorial and tariff privileges upon foreigners. After years of revising domestic penal codes and petitioning the powers for favors had proven ineffective, she approached the problem obliquely by signing (1888) a treaty with Mexico, a nation having little trade and no resident nationals, conferring Japanese jurisdiction over Mexican subjects in Japan. The following year the United States offered Japan a similar arrangement, but negotiations were interrupted when Count Shigenobu Okuma, the Japanese Foreign Minister, was wounded by a bomb thrown by a fanatic incensed at Okuma's concessions to the foreigners. The first reciprocal and terminable treaty with a great power (Great Britain) became effective in 1894, resulting in the elimination of consular jurisdiction and some tariff limitations six years later.[7] This was followed, between 1894 and 1899, by a general revision of the unequal treaties in Japan's favor, although some tariff restrictions remained operative until 1911.

Japan and the United States Grow Up

Throughout this era Japanese-American friendship remained unmarred, though alarming portents had appeared on both sides before 1900. When the McKinley Administration signed (June 16, 1897) a treaty annexing the Hawaiian Islands, Japan protested vigorously against this prospective disturbance of the Pacific *status quo;* fortunately, Senate Democrats helped allay Japanese fears by preventing adoption of the treaty.[8] Much more portentous was the Sino-Japanese War of 1894–1895 which showed that Japan had

---

[7] F. C. Jones, *Extraterritoriality in Japan and the Diplomatic Relations Resulting in Its Abolition, 1853–1899,* Yale University Press, 1931. It should be noted, in order to correct a misapprehension long current, that the Sino-Japanese War was not responsible for the abolition of extraterritoriality, since the Anglo-Japanese treaty was signed prior to the outbreak of the struggle.

[8] T. A. Bailey, "Japan's Protest against the Annexation of Hawaii," *Journal of Modern History,* vol. 3 (1931), pp. 46–61.

acquired imperialism along with other occidental characteristics. This marked the culmination of a long-standing Japanese desire to dominate Korea, which owed nominal allegiance to China; Japan's lightning offensive "liberated" Korea from China and left Korea vulnerable to Japanese aggression when the time was ripe. The Treaty of Shimonoseki (1895), Japan's first bid for membership in the imperialistic fraternity, compelled China to surrender Formosa, the Pescadores Islands, and the Liaotung Peninsula (Manchuria's window to seaward), and to submit to occupation of Wei-hei-wei pending payment of an indemnity of 200,000,000 taels. Before this complete humiliation of China could be achieved, Russia, whose designs on Manchuria made Japanese ascendancy in Korea and the Liaotung area a dangerous threat, joined France and Germany in forcing Japan to relinquish her claim to the Peninsula. As the China story has indicated, Japan then had to stand by and watch the European nations scramble for concessions at China's expense. This frustration was hardly sweetened by the subsequent emergence of the United States as an equally (and more successfully) imperialistic nation whose new possessions, Hawaii, Guam, and the Philippines, advanced her holdings to Japan's own back yard.[9] Indeed, the final half-decade of the century ended the honeymoon relationship between the two nations; each now emerged into a fiercely competitive world in which their interests overlapped sufficiently to render friction inevitable.

As indicated above, the United States soon sought to protect her Far Eastern interests through the Open Door policy which could evoke only mild enthusiasm in Japan, recently prevented from acquiring a sphere to which the Open Door might apply. Isolated by the Triple Intervention of 1895 and increasingly fearful of Russian encroachments in Manchuria, Japan was ripe for an alliance which might counterbalance these dangers. Her needs complemented Britain's, also on the lookout for allies in the late 1890's. Anglo-Russian relations were becoming increasingly strained in Europe, in the Near East, in India and, as was Japan's case, in China; more-

---

[9] This despite the fact that Japan preferred American control of the islands to that of any nation except her own.

over, Britain was as yet aloof from the European alliance-system. The result of these needs, partly identical and partly diverse, was the Anglo-Japanese Alliance (signed January 30, 1902) which removed both nations from the ranks of the isolated, aligned them together against Russian pretensions in Manchuria, and recognized Japan's special political, commercial, and industrial interests in Korea. Russo-Japanese rivalry in Manchuria, reflected in the Alliance, was aggravated by certain Russian elements eager for an aggressive policy, and furthered by Kaiser Wilhelm II, who knew that if Cousin Nicholas II of Russia were occupied in the Far East he would be less likely to disturb the delicate balance of affairs in Western Europe. The clash of interests thus adroitly fostered culminated in the Russo-Japanese War (1904), in whose wake came the first open signs of Japanese-American antagonism.

The outbreak of war found President Theodore Roosevelt in personal charge of American foreign policy, due to the illness of Secretary John Hay. Roosevelt was already perturbed by complaints of American commercial interests that the Russian advance into Manchuria endangered the Open Door; moreover, he shared the feeling of most Americans, then and during most of the war, that a valiant Japanese mite was standing forthrightly in the way of a bullying giant. He claims to have taken prompt action by a virtual ultimatum to Germany and France committing the United States to war on Japan's behalf should those nations in concert with Russia attempt to repeat their maneuvers of 1895. Unfortunately, as in his story of the Venezuela episode, the evidence does not support his contention.[10] Be this as it may, it was not to his interest to see the complete defeat of either antagonist, since this would create an unstable Far Eastern equilibrium potentially dangerous to American interests. The above, plus his innate desire to participate in whatever drama

---

[10] Vagts, op. cit., vol. 2, pp. 1178–1179. The best account of the war is Tyler Dennett, Roosevelt and the Russo-Japanese War, Doubleday, Page, 1925. It should be used in conjunction with Griswold, op. cit., pp. 87–122, and Dennis, Adventures in Am. Dipl., pp. 389–424; Eleanor Tupper and G. E. McReynolds, Japan in American Public Opinion, Macmillan, 1937, is useful for this and subsequent episodes of Japanese-American relations. P. H. Clyde, International Rivalries in Manchuria, Ohio State University Press, 1928, is helpful from the Sino-Japanese War through the Washington Conference.

was being enacted, will help to explain the alacrity with which he accepted the proffered role of peacemaker in the spring and summer of 1905.

By this time both parties were willing to call quits. Japan had won all the battles, but at tremendous cost in men and materiél; moreover, the deeper her troops penetrated Manchuria the harder it was to keep them supplied. Russia's supply problem bade fair to be eased, if the war continued, by completion of the Trans-Siberian Railway around Lake Baikal. On the other hand, continued defeats humiliated the Russians and contributed to domestic disturbances which presently culminated in revolution. The Kaiser, moreover, was becoming alarmed: A complete Japanese victory might destroy Russia's interest in the Far East and permit the Czar to concentrate upon European affairs, which might lead to cousinly strife; further-more, unchecked popular upheavals in Russia might give his own docile subjects ideas. Finally, France was willing to see her European ally extricated from a difficult position. The initiative, how-ever, came from the hard-pressed Japanese. Three days after their stunning defeat of the Russian fleet at the Battle of Tsushima, their Government requested Roosevelt (May 31, 1905) "directly and en-tirely of his own motion and initiative to invite the two belligerents to come together for the purpose of direct negotiations." The Presi-dent shortly (June 6) sounded out Russia, promising to keep secret any Russian consent to negotiate until Japan had also agreed—which, of course, she had already done. The Czar promptly accepted this overture (June 7) and the following day both powers were formally invited to open joint negotiations. Roosevelt tendered his good offices in arranging the preliminaries; after the American capi-tal city had been rejected because of its abominable summer climate and Newport, Rhode Island, because its social dowagers might look down their noses at yellow-skinned diplomats, the facilities of the Navy Yard at Portsmouth, New Hampshire, were finally agreed upon as the scene of the peace parleys.[11]

---

[11] In the light of subsequent developments it is perhaps pertinent to repeat that Roosevelt had exacted a prior promise that "Japan adheres to the position of main-taining Open Door in Manchuria and of restoring that province to China."

Japanese-American antagonisms emerge openly from the Portsmouth period. A combination of circumstances diverted American
public favor from Japan to Russia. The Russians, realizing their unfavorable position, successfully sought American sympathy by em-
ploying an adroit newspaper man as public relations counsel; on
the other hand, Baron Jutaro Komura, chief Japanese delegate,
adopted an apparently deliberately haughty attitude toward the
American reporters; as a result, Japan received a "bad press" and
Russian stock rose accordingly. Publication of Japan's proposed
peace terms accentuated the shift. These included the cession of
the Island of Sakhalin and payment of a huge indemnity. When
Russian refusal of these extreme demands threatened deadlock,
Roosevelt intervened personally to moderate Japan's grasping tactics. As a result, in part at least, of his influence, Japan abandoned
the indemnity entirely and contented herself with the southern half
of the island. Other terms of the agreement (signed September 5,
1905) registered Japan's thoroughgoing victory and a sharp realignment in Far Eastern affairs. Russia agreed to recognize Japan's
dominance in Korea; pious promises to restore Manchuria to China
were rendered somewhat hypocritical by the transfer to Japan of
Russia's Liaotung leasehold, including the South Manchurian Railway and consequent economic dominance of the area.

The shifting balance of forces on the Asiatic mainland was underwritten still further by the Taft-Katsura Memorandum of July 29.
Secretary of War Taft, briefly ashore in Japan on his way to the
Philippines, was approached by the Japanese Foreign Minister and
agreed with him that the United States would not interfere with
Japanese ambitions in Korea in return for a Japanese hands-off attitude toward the Philippines. Though it was apparently an unauthorized and unpremeditated arrangement, and one binding only upon
the two administrations making it, Roosevelt endorsed it enthusiastically; the Treaty and the Memorandum might well lead Japan to
believe that Roosevelt's earlier insistence upon the Open Door was
subject to modification in the face of changing, if unpleasant, facts.[12]

---

[12] The following add light to the account of the Taft-Katsura Memorandum in
Dennett's *Roosevelt and the Russo-Japanese War:* H. P. Howard and Tyler Dennett,

Rooseveltian complaisance over Korea, however, failed to compensate for other factors which appeared during his Administration. Japanese taxpayers had looked to a Russian indemnity to lighten their load; when their statesmen returned without it and with only half of Sakhalin, Roosevelt and the United States shared the consequent opprobrium. A carefully planned series of public demonstrations in Tokyo fanned the fires of antagonism and resulted in damage to American property in the city. American business interests were promptly and adversely affected by the substitution of Japanese for Russian control in South Manchuria; their complaints soon poured in upon the Department of State.

More important than any of these, however, was the immigration question which rose out of a long background to plague both domestic and international politics in Roosevelt's later days.[13] Like China, Japan suffered from too many people on too little poor soil. When the anti-Chinese movement gained headway in the 1880's and 1890's California's need for agricultural labor stimulated the entry of increasing numbers of industrious Japanese. This influx was sanctioned by a treaty of 1894 which permitted all citizens of each country free entry into the other, vesting in both governments the power to protect domestic interests by legislating against excessive immigration of laborers. American protests had reached a point which induced Japan in August, 1900, to inaugurate a policy of voluntary limitation of emigration through refusal to issue passports to emigrant laborers. This so-called First Gentlemen's Agreement, however, failed to solve the problem, as it did not stop the flow to Hawaii, Canada, or Mexico, whence migration could not be effec-

---

"America's Role in Asia," *Pacific Affairs*, vol. 16 (1943), pp. 485–492; Sir John T. Pratt and Tyler Dennett, "Correspondence," *Ibid.*, 18 (1945), pp. 369–374; Jessup, *Root*, vol. 2, p. 5. Roosevelt lived up to Taft's commitments and in the autumn of 1905 his Government withdrew recognition from Korea and began dealing with Japan on Korean affairs.

[13] T. A. Bailey, *Theodore Roosevelt and the Japanese-American Crises,* Stanford University Press, 1934; R. L. Buell, "Japanese Immigration," *World Peace Foundation Pamphlets*, World Peace Foundation, 1924, vol. 7, Nos. 5–6; and "The Development of the Anti-Japanese Agitation in the United States," *Political Science Quarterly*, vol. 37 (1922), pp. 605–638; 38 (1923), pp. 57–81; K. K. Kawakami, *American-Japanese Relations: An Inside View of Japan's Policies and Purposes*, Revell, 1912, emphasizes the role of West Coast labor in the anti-Japanese agitation.

tively controlled; moreover, its administration was at times only half-hearted. The resultant antagonism was increased by Japan's strong showing in the Russian War to a point where William Randolph Hearst's press could magnify it into a Yellow Peril and where West Coast labor felt called upon to organize (May 7, 1905) a Japanese and Korean Exclusion League. These pressures resulted in a movement for statutory exclusion so strong as to constrain the President, in his message of December, 1905, to argue against discriminatory legislation. Congress heeded his request, but western agitation continued unabated and was brought to a focus by the action of the San Francisco School Board late in 1906.

The city's schools, closed by an earthquake and subsequent fire, reopened to 25,000 pupils on July 23, 1906. On October 11 the School Board ordered the segregation, as of October 15, of all Japanese, Chinese, and Korean children in the so-called Oriental Public School in Chinatown. Local protests failing to bring satisfaction, the board's action was given to the Japanese press and a municipal episode involving ninety-three Japanese pupils flared into an international incident. Japan promptly charged that the board's action violated most-favored-nation rights guaranteed by the Treaty of 1894. Faced with this emergency, Roosevelt invited the San Francisco board to Washington for a conference. The group, accompanied by Mayor Eugene Schmitz, then under indictment for corruption and anxious to brighten his tarnished reputation by contact with the President, negotiated an arrangement whereby the segregation order would be rescinded (accomplished March 13, 1907); in return Roosevelt would try to deal with the immigration question.

The problem resolved itself into one of securing exclusion (which both Roosevelt and the Japanese authorities by now believed essential) without the loss of face attaching to a statutory enactment. Roosevelt plunged promptly into a long and delicate negotiation designed to bring national policy into line with west-coast desires. Meantime, in order to impress both Japanese and domestic opinion, it was announced on July 9, 1907, that the American battle fleet would move from Atlantic waters to San Francisco, a maneuver under consideration in naval quarters for some time but which was doubtless hastened by the publicity-wise President for its immediate effect. It was also seized upon by Mr. Hearst and his fellow sensation-mongers to manufacture a war scare of somewhat formidable if short-lived proportions. Treaty settlement of the immigration question proved impossible, and recourse was had to refurbishing the scheme of 1900. A series of notes of 1907–1908, subsequently known as the Gentlemen's Agreement, affirmed Japan's intention to continue stopping emigration of laborers at the source, a policy scrupulously adhered to in succeeding years.[14] Thus California attained its immediate objective and Japan saved face.

The Roosevelt Administration's final sally into Far Eastern affairs came in the Root-Takahira Agreement of 1908, noted above. Suffice it here to repeat that although reiterating traditional Open Door doctrines it was probably a realistic recognition, in return for Japanese denial of designs on the Philippines and Hawaii, that Japan had supplanted Russia in Manchuria. Thus though the torch of Japanese-American relations burned steadily as Roosevelt handed it to Taft in 1909, each nation, fully grown to adulthood, would view with increasing suspicion any action of the other which might cause the flame to flicker. These international drafts blew with increasing frequency in the next three decades; never after 1909 was Japanese-American friendship as solidly based as when, before 1900, neither nation had grown up.

Though the War of 1914–1918 found the two nations opposing a common enemy, developments of these years sharpened old antagonisms and furnished new points of friction.[15] Japan attempted to substitute her own power for that of Europe in China and the islands of the North Pacific; she tried to maneuver the United States into admitting Japanese control over China in the Lansing-Ishii

---

[14] The correspondence was not published for many years though the Annual Report of United States Commissioner-General of Immigration for 1908 indicated its substance. See *Foreign Relations, 1924* (published, 1939), pp. 339–369, for a resumé of the relevant documents. When a new treaty replaced (1911) the agreement of 1894, the Japanese secured elimination of the clause granting the right to restrict immigration by statute by signing an auxiliary note promising to continue the Gentlemen's Agreement; this arrangement continued the 1907–1908 compromise until 1924.

[15] At this point the reader should remind himself of the Taft-Knox economic policies which kept alive Japanese suspicions of American motives in China and Manchuria and contributed to the Russo-Japanese alliance of 1910.

Agreement; she was irritated at Wilson's role in thwarting what she considered her legitimate objectives in the Treaty of Versailles; she was both angered and perturbed at the prospect of American naval supremacy as envisioned in the so-called 1916 Program. On the other hand, Japan's grasping tactics and her evident intention to use the war to her own advantage raised fears for the American future in the Far East. Conditions, however, did not favor vigorous opposition of Japan's program; successive problems of neutrality, belligerency, and world reorganization so monopolized American attention that American relations with Japan became a series of holding operations, designed to avoid final acceptance of Japanese ambitions pending another and, perhaps, more auspicious day when a reckoning might be demanded. Meantime, the wartime accretions on the difficulties appearing since 1900 laid a heavy burden upon Japanese-American friendship.

The war's outbreak, resulting in withdrawal of fleets and practical removal of European influence from China, contributed to a natural Japanese-American rivalry in that area. Both had surplus capital whose investment might have political implications, though Wilson had abandoned the Consortium of 1913. Japan's Twenty-One Demands and the subsequent treaties of 1915 looked in part to subjecting China to Japanese financial control. When American opposition prevented the full realization of this aim Japan was correspondingly disturbed, particularly when American commercial activities in China increased. Wilson's reversion in 1916 and 1918 to a policy of urging American bankers to make China loans further alarmed the Japanese, especially in the light of the aggressive tactics of Mr. Paul S. Reinsch, the American Ambassador to China, who seemed to them to be trying to substitute American for Japanese influence.

Japan promptly pressed the advantage by presenting China the Twenty-One Demands (January 18, 1915). It will be remembered that Secretary Bryan, in objecting to the Demands, had admitted in his note of March 3 that "territorial contiguity creates special relations" between Japan and various mainland areas; the note of May 11, however, had refused to "recognize any agreement or undertaking . . . impairing the treaty rights of the United States and its citizens in China." This relatively mild warning, plus American commercial and diplomatic aggressiveness, remained for months the only foreign obstacle to realization of Japan's continental objectives. To safeguard the future, Japan built during 1916 and 1917 a network of secret treaties with the European powers (including a military alliance with Russia directed against the United States) designed to guarantee her succession to German rights in Shantung and Pacific islands north of the equator. Her efforts to commit the United States similarly led to the Lansing-Ishii Agreement of November 2, 1917. In January, 1917, Lansing, now Secretary of State, told Aimaro Sato, the Japanese Ambassador, that the latter "must be aware that the American Government recognized that Japan had special interests in Manchuria." It became the task of Viscount Kikujiro Ishii to try to expand this admission into an American commitment to the recognition of Japanese *paramount* interest in *all China*. Arriving ostensibly to discuss general problems of the war, he and the Secretary plunged into prolonged discussion of Chinese affairs.[16]

Early in the conversations Ishii attempted to use the word "paramount" to describe Japan's interest in China, inconveniently pointing out that William H. Seward had thus characterized United States interest in Mexico at an earlier date. Lansing's defense insists that he refused further discussion on this basis, and that Ishii "understood fully that any reference that I made . . . to Japan's interest was based on geographical position and pertained to commercial interests and that the idea of paramount interest applying to political affairs was entirely eliminated from the negotiation." There followed an extended sparring match in which each principal seems to have used the word "special," which finally appeared in the Agreement, according to his own preconceptions. Ishii undoubtedly believed that the United States had conceded Japan's political as well as economic interest on the mainland; Lansing has asserted stoutly

---

[16] The claims of the protagonists have been set forth in W. R. Langdon (tr.), *Diplomatic Commentaries by Viscount Kikujiro Ishii*, Johns Hopkins Press, 1936; Robert Lansing, *The War Memoirs of Robert Lansing*, Bobbs-Merrill, 1935.

that his concession was limited to the latter category. The two shades of meaning well reflect the facts of the contemporary Far Eastern situation: Japan, active, energetic, and on imperialism bent, used her interpretation to further her designs; the United States, far distant, immersed in war, and fearful of those designs, sought to safeguard her welfare (and China's) by a more restricted view. Her position, like her words, was momentarily weaker than Japan's. As has been indicated above, Japan promptly transmuted the "special relations" of the Agreement's text into "paramount relations" as the document was translated into Chinese, and proceeded to assume that this was its proper meaning; no amount of subsequent qualification entirely removed the impression thus created.[17]

The Versailles Peace Conference heightened the antagonism arising from Lansing's somewhat tentative opposition to Japanese imperialism on the Asiatic mainland. Flushed with victory, determined to gain equal status as a great power, and fully entrenched behind complex treaties underwriting her territorial demands, Japan arrived demanding a formal recognition of racial equality and full cession

---

[17] Griswold, *op. cit.*, p. 218, is convinced that Lansing understood that he was making a political concession. It should be noted that Lansing sought and secured a secret protocol (signed October 31, 1917) in which it was agreed that the parties would "not take advantage of present conditions to seek special rights or privileges in China which would abridge the rights of the citizens or subjects of other friendly states. . . ." This was hardly compatible with either the Twenty-One Demands or the secret treaties.

The text of this triumph of ambiguity follows:

The Governments of Japan and the United States recognize that territorial propinquity creates special relations between countries, and, consequently, the Government of the United States recognizes that Japan has special interests in China, particularly in the part to which her possessions are contiguous.

The territorial sovereignty of China, nevertheless, remains unimpaired and the Government of the United States has every confidence in the repeated assurances of the Imperial Japanese Government that while geographical position gives Japan such special interests they have no desire to discriminate against the trade of other nations or to disregard the commercial rights heretofore granted by China in treaties with other powers.

The Governments of Japan and the United States deny that they have any purpose to infringe in any way the independence or territorial integrity of China and they declare, furthermore, that they always adhere to the principle of the so-called "open door" or equal opportunity for commerce and industry in China.

Moreover, they mutually declare that they are opposed to the acquisition by any government of any special rights or privileges that would affect the independence or territorial integrity of China or that would deny to the subjects or citizens of any country the full enjoyment of equal opportunity in the commerce and industry of China.

to herself of German rights in Shantung. Her desires had to be rec-
onciled with those of Woodrow Wilson, a statesman committed to
the highest principles of human rights, but at the same time utterly
devoted to the League of Nations, and not unaware of the effect
which his European conduct might have upon American domestic
politics. It proved impossible to reconcile all these variables and
Japan, falling short of her full objectives, emerged from the Peace
Conference blaming the United States for such reverses as she had
sustained.[18]

Fiercely proud of her nationality and angry at widespread discrimination, Japan proposed (on February 7, 1919) to include in
the League Covenant a statement binding members to accord nationals of all member states "equal and just treatment in every
respect, making no distinction, either in law or in fact, on account
of their race or nationality." The suggestion found no favor in Australia, whose Premier, W. M. Hughes, induced Lord Robert Cecil
and Sir Arthur Balfour of the British delegation to join in opposition.
Forewarned, Japan diluted her proposal to an amendment (offered
April 11 in the Commission on the League of Nations) to the principles contained in the Preamble of the Covenant: "by the endorsement of the principle of equality of nations and just treatment of
their nationals." Wilson had approved the original resolution, which
agreed with his general political philosophy. However, when he
heard Cecil refuse the amendment, and learned that Hughes would
force open debate when the Covenant was brought before the Plenary Session of the Conference, he began to hedge, since he knew
that his own westerners would be no happier about it than Hughes'
constituents who wanted a White Australia. His suggestion that it
would be inadvisable to put the amendment directly into the Covenant did not appeal to the Japanese delegates, who demanded a
record vote, which was favorable, by eleven to six. As Chairman of
the Commission, however, Wilson ruled that unanimity was necessary, and the amendment was therefore lost; Japan, adroitly mis-

[18] The present section confines itself to the contribution of the Conference to
Japanese-American relations; the larger implications of Wilson's policy at Versailles
will be explored in the next chapter.

guided by Hughes' propaganda, shifted the blame for her extremely humiliating defeat from Anglo-Australian shoulders, where it really belonged, to those of the United States.

Thus embittered, Japan redoubled her efforts to secure German rights in Shantung, raising this issue late in April, after Wilson had helped to thwart her move for racial equality, and causing him acute embarrassment. Surrendering to Japan here violated his principle of self-determination, now to be guaranteed by the League to all the world; it countered, too, America's traditional Far Eastern policy of maintaining China's territorial integrity. Coming closer home, it would give his political opponents powerful ammunition in their campaign to defeat the League itself. However, when the Council of Three (the Italians had walked out over the Fiume issue) began to discuss Shantung on April 22, Wilson had already been forced into the process of compromise which he felt was necessary in order to save the League. Japan made it clear that she would follow Italy out of the Conference unless her demands were met; where then would be the League? Her legal position was impregnable; all the interested powers except the United States, and including China, had agreed by treaty to the surrender of Shantung. By adhering to his principles, Wilson could only sacrifice his League. His decision was prompt, but not easy. He surrendered to the Japanese demands *in toto,* his only consolation being Japan's promise that political control of Shantung would ultimately revert to China, and his only hope that his League might some day free the whole world as well as Shantung. Thus the war ended with Japanese-American relations in worse case than when it began, and with several unsettled and aggravating minor issues (e.g., cable rights on the Island of Yap, and the status of Eastern Siberia, where both nations had sizable armies eyeing each other watchfully if not amicably) standing in the way of improvement.

Washington Conference—World Phase

These issues were not resolved in the succeeding months, but took unto themselves others. Japanese-American problems presently so wove themselves into the pattern of Anglo-American, Anglo-Japanese, and British imperial relations as to afford opportunity for a multilateral approach to a number of questions. The result was a gathering whose originally limited objectives broadened into direct and collateral settlements which exerted a far-reaching influence upon world affairs. Indeed, the Washington Conference on the Limitation of Armaments may aptly be likened to a snowball gathering substance and momentum on a winter hillside. That some of its arrangements were only slightly less impermanent than a snowball should not obscure the importance of its achievements, not the least of which was buying nearly ten years of peace for the Far East.[19]

Increasing Japanese-American frictions characterized the years after Versailles. Failure of the racial-equality proposal still smoldered, ready to burst into flame under proper stimulus. The Japanese foothold in Shantung, guaranteed at Versailles, became a take-off for active penetration of Manchuria, to the detriment of the Open Door and of American and other business interests, not to mention its lessening of Chinese sovereignty. The United States, then, still desired to eject Japan from Manchuria. National interests also clashed in Siberia, where both had considerable forces, despatched in an attempt to rescue a Czechoslovak army adrift in Bolshevik territory; the great disparity in numbers (9000 Americans to 72,000 Japanese) made it difficult for General W. S. Graves to carry out his tacit assignment of preventing Japanese seizure of strategically

---

[19] In addition to the works of Clyde, Dulles, Fairbank, Griswold, Jessup, the Sprouts, and Tupper and McReynolds, already cited, the following give most aspects of the much-controverted story: T. A. Bisson, *America's Far Eastern Policy*, Macmillan, 1945; R. L. Buell, *The Washington Conference*, D. Appleton, 1922, an unfavorable account written close to the event, the conclusions of which are modified somewhat in his *Isolated America*, Knopf, 1940; E. A. Falk, *op. cit.*; J. S. Galbraith, "The Imperial Conference of 1921 and the Washington Conference," *Canadian Historical Review*, vol. 29 (1948), pp. 143–152; C. L. Hoag, *Preface to Preparedness: The Washington Disarmament Conference and Public Opinion*, American Council on Public Affairs, 1941; Yamato Ichihashi, *The Washington Conference and After: A Historical Survey*, Stanford University Press, 1928; F. L. Paxson, *Postwar Years: Normalcy, 1918–1923*, University of California Press, 1948; Frank H. Simonds, *American Foreign Policy in the Post-War Years*, Johns Hopkins Press, 1935; Mark Sullivan, *The Great Adventure in Washington: The Story of the Conference*, Doubleday, Page, 1922; Pauline Tompkins, *American-Russian Relations in the Far East*, Macmillan, 1949, pp. 87–180; Eugene J. Young, *Powerful America*, Stokes, 1936. A collection of relevant documents is found in *Conference on the Limitation of Armaments, November 12, 1921–February 6, 1922*, Government Printing Office, 1922.

important places. Retention of the Japanese contingent on the continent after American withdrawal in 1920 deepened existing suspicion of Japanese motives.[20] The name "Yap," attached to a microscopic Pacific island, meant much to the jokesters but more to the Department of State. Formerly German, it had passed under Japanese mandate despite Wilson's efforts to have it internationalized. Its only value, a considerable one, was as a cable landing; repeated efforts to obtain its use for such purposes had failed.

Naval rivalry momentarily outweighed all other factors. The United States had in 1916 announced an enormous program of naval construction. Sidetracked during the war in favor of merchant shipping, this was resumed in earnest after the peace. Japan also had an ambitious program; if both continued to build, friction was inevitable, conflict not impossible, since Japan's postwar sphere of naval dominance overlapped the Philippines and Guam, the far fringes of the American empire. Long-range American plans looked in 1921 to a fleet strong enough not only to protect these outposts but to return victorious from a successful invasion of Japanese home waters. Such a program, though still far from realization, would cost a great deal of money; no first-rate nation could ignore such a development in its own budgetary and strategic calculations. Japan and Britain, both first-rate nations intent upon remaining such, were filled with concern.

So was the American taxpayer, whose thoughts tended toward economy.[21] As early as December 20, 1920, Senator William E. Borah had introduced a resolution asking the President to invite Japan and Britain to discuss reducing naval armaments. This passed the Senate

---

[20] W. S. Graves, *America's Siberian Adventure, 1918–1920,* P. Smith, 1931.

[21] The following statement from Jessup's *Root,* vol. 2, p. 449, merits careful consideration in opening discussion of a negotiation in which it has frequently been asserted that the United States made undue concessions: "At one of the first preliminary meetings of the American delegation, Root asked whether there was any likelihood that Congress would vote the necessary appropriations to continue the naval building program and the concomitant program for the fortification of the Philippines which was an essential element in American naval policy as it was then conceived. . . . Senators Lodge and Underwood were emphatic in asserting that there was no possibility that Congress would appropriate the necessary funds. . . ." That body, moreover, had in recent months rejected three construction plans proposed by the Navy Department.

on May 25 and the House on June 29, 1921, despite President Warren G. Harding's opposition. This brought American statecraft to a
choice among three alternatives; continuing the expensive armaments race, for which public opinion had just registered an aversion;
confining naval objectives within the scope of the existing establishment (which would probably mean getting out of Japan's way on
the Asiatic mainland); or leading in an effort to solve some of the
problems by reducing and stabilizing naval armaments. Secretary of
State Hughes adopted the third alternative, throwing himself into
line with the Borah resolution except for his successful insistence
upon including France and Italy in the deliberations. Again, as in
the days of Seward and Hay, the United States sought a collective
solution of Far Eastern questions—an ironical twist for a nation
which had just forsworn collective action in Europe and whose
Monroe Doctrine hardly invited collaboration in managing American affairs.

British economic and political exigencies dovetailed nicely into
the American economizing temper. Facing critical problems of domestic and foreign debt and industrial unemployment, Britain was
anxious to avoid a naval-construction race with the United States.
On the other hand, British prestige would ill bear the stigma of
initiating discussion of limiting naval armaments. British policy
therefore aimed at maneuvering the United States into making the
first move. In February, 1921, Lord Lee of Fareham, husband of an
American wife and long familiar with and friendly toward the
United States, became First Lord of the Admiralty. By mid-March
his speech to the British Institute of Naval Architects sent up a trial
balloon in the assertion that "If America invites Great Britain to a
conference to come to an agreement on the naval question, I am
prepared to put aside all other business in order to help that matter
forward, for there can be no more pressing business in the affairs of
the world." This overture proving unfruitful, the British adopted another approach through informal channels which would not commit
the Foreign Office. On April 22, 1921, Lee asked Mr. Adolph S.
Ochs, publisher of the New York *Times* and an advocate of armament limitation, to inform Washington of Britain's sympathy with

any such project which might be initiated by the United States; Britain was, he told Ochs, willing to abandon her traditional two-power navy standard and accept equality with the United States, which would make it possible, should it become necessary, for the latter to concentrate its naval power in the Pacific.[22] Lee's proposal reached Edwin Denby, Secretary of the Navy, by the hand of Ernest Marshall, London correspondent of Ochs' paper; it was received politely but noncommittally.

Midsummer saw events move toward a conference which would discuss not only naval matters but Far Eastern affairs as well. Canadian opposition to renewal of the Anglo-Japanese Alliance furnished the reason for this enlarging horizon.[23] This Alliance, renewed from time to time since 1902, was about to expire. It technically bound Britain to aid Japan in case of a Japanese-American war, although the British had stated privately to the United States in 1920 that the Alliance was not applicable in such a case. Since this might involve Canada, Mr. Arthur Meighen, Dominion Prime Minister, vigorously and successfully urged the Imperial Conference of June, 1921, to oppose renewal. His victory was won by July 1, after which the objective of British policy came to be the working out of a substitute for the Alliance which would keep the Dominions happy and avoid offending Japan.

The technique adopted was to try to persuade the United States to call a conference. On July 5 the British suggested to George Harvey, the American Ambassador, that he sound out his government on calling a meeting of interested powers to discuss Far Eastern questions. Two days later David Lloyd George, the British Prime Minister, indicated publicly that Far Eastern matters were under discussion with the United States. In order to avoid losing the initiative, thus in danger of slipping from his grasp, Hughes cabled London, Tokyo, Paris, and Rome (July 8) inquiring whether

---

[22] It might be pointed out that although the British overture was couched in naval terms, Lee even this early had Far Eastern affairs in mind, for Ochs' memorandum of the interview states that "He discussed the fear of the United States of a possible war with Japan. . . ." Young, *op. cit.*, p. 49.

[23] J. Bartlet Brebner, "Canada, the Anglo-Japanese Alliance, and the Washington Conference," *Political Science Quarterly*, vol. 50 (1935), pp. 45–58.

those capitals would be interested in discussing *arms limitation.*
This cable crossed one from Harvey relaying the British request
for a *Far Eastern* conference. Within a matter of hours Hughes'
vision broadened to include the Far Eastern aspects suggested by
the British as well as the enlarged agenda and increased membership thus entailed. On July 11 the press announced that President
Harding was inviting the leading naval nations, and China, to a
conference to discuss limitation of armaments and Far Eastern affairs. Thus a common interest in averting an armaments race was
stirring on both sides of the Atlantic; although British imperial considerations were immediately responsible for injecting Far Eastern
political affairs into the picture, these were close to the surface of
American thinking at the time and the combination was both logical
and easy.

Under the circumstances British acceptance was prompt and
cordial; China, likewise, saw hope here where otherwise there was
no hope. Japan's position was not so simple. Although the mounting
cost of naval armaments could easily be spared, she might well
suspect the political implications of Harding's invitation. For one
thing, the Anglo-Japanese Alliance had long been an anchor to
windward; for another, no discussion of Far Eastern affairs could
proceed far without running foul of Japan's tactics since the Twenty-
One Demands. Unable to persuade Hughes to be specific as to the
Conference agenda, Japan's delayed acceptance of the American
invitation was qualified, as already noted, by the doctrines of "sole
concern" and of "accomplished fact," devices designed to obviate
discussion of some of the more ticklish questions which might arise.

After President Harding had exercised his verbal talents in wel-
coming the delegates of nine nations to the first Plenary Session of
the Conference on November 12, Hughes startled the assembled
representatives, settling back in their seats in anticipation of further
platitudes.[24] Instead of confining himself to the expected amenities,
he stated forthrightly the details of a proposed scheme of armament

---

[24] In addition to the six mentioned in the text above, invitations went also to the
Netherlands, Portugal, and Belgium, on the strength of their holdings, respectively,
in the East Indies, Macao, and Tientsin.

limitation. This adroit maneuver retained American initiative, capitalized on the general popular weariness at paying armaments taxes, and, in case the proposals failed to catch on, neatly shifted the onus to the opposition and bespoke Congressional support for any alternative program to which the Administration might then have to resort. His proposals were startling. Advancing the unusual but curiously appealing hypothesis that disarmament should be achieved by disarming, he proceeded to blueprint the reorganization of the world's larger navies on a lower tonnage level, while retaining roughly the relative positions of the powers. Specifically, he suggested a ten-year holiday in capital-ship construction, accompanied by destruction of tonnage built or building (he named ships so there would be no doubt) so that the ultimate strength of the five leading navies would stand, including all sorts of craft, in the ratio of 5–5–3 for the United States, Great Britain, and Japan, and 1.75 each for Italy and France. Hughes thus touched off the greatest naval holocaust in history for, in Professor Thomas A. Bailey's pungent phrase, "In less than fifteen minutes he destroyed sixty-six ships with a total tonnage of 1,878,043. . . ."

This breath-taking performance opened a session of horse-trading on a global scale which lasted until February 6, 1922. From it or from collateral and simultaneous negotiations emerged three major multipartite treaties (the Four-Power Pact between Britain, France, Japan, and the United States; the Five-Power Pact among the five naval powers; and the Nine-Power Pact signed by all nations seated at the Conference), a Sino-Japanese agreement on Shantung, a Japanese-American treaty relative to Yap (February 11, 1922), a Japanese promise to evacuate Siberia, and the later abrogation (April 14, 1923) of the Lansing-Ishii Agreement. Once the delegates recovered from Hughes' drastic proposals, the Conference settled down to consideration of particular problems. The chief of these was to persuade Japan, ambitious to dominate the Pacific and fiercely opposed to any hint of inferiority, to accept a substitute for the Anglo-Japanese Alliance and a secondary naval position.

Signature of the Four-Power Pacific Treaty (December 13, 1921) as a substitute for the Anglo-Japanese Alliance marked the first great step and a triumph for Hughes' diplomacy. Before the Conference formally opened, Sir Arthur Balfour suggested to Hughes (November 11) the substitution of an Anglo-Japanese-American agreement covering both the Pacific islands and the eastern Asiatic mainland. These proposals contained mutual nonaggression pledges on such terms as to preclude further American opposition to Japan's continental activities. Hughes balked at this and at a somewhat similar Japanese proposal, as undue recognition of British and Japanese interests, and succeeded in broadening the arrangement to include France, and narrowing its scope by confining its application to the island possessions. Thus, instead of committing the United States to accept Japanese aggressions on the continent, the nonaggression pledges bound Japan to respect American possession of the Philippines, a matter of great moment since Japan now controlled the Marianas, Marshalls, and the Carolines lying athwart the principal sea-approaches to Manila. As finally signed, the four powers agreed to respect each other's rights in the island possessions, to confer in case of dispute over these rights, and to consult in case of outside aggression against these rights. Such promises of mutual confidence made possible graceful Japanese renunciation of the British alliance (Article 4) without risking political isolation; though they carried no pledges of military implementation, they eased the way to Japanese acceptance of naval inferiority in the 5–5–3 ratio.

This acceptance, however, was only to be secured at a price, and a dear one in the view of American naval experts. The discussions leading to the Four-Power agreement demonstrated that Japan would demand something beyond the consultative arrangements therein proposed in return for abandoning the British alliance and relegating herself to secondary naval status. Early in December she suggested the possibility of yielding on the naval ratio in return for two American concessions: First, she must be permitted to retain the *Mutsu,* which Hughes had consigned to the scrap heap, and instead abandon the older *Settsu;* built largely with the contributions of Japanese school-children, the *Mutsu* had already been commissioned and had joined the fleet. Second, she demanded mutual restriction of naval power in the Pacific. This was to be achieved by agreeing to maintain the *status quo* as to fortifications, preventing all three powers from further construction of bases and fortifications in certain specified areas. As early as December 2 Hughes intimated in a meeting of delegation chiefs that his Government might move in this direction in return for Japanese acceptance of a four-power entente and the naval ratio. Thus the three matters were tied together, and rapid progress ensued. Hughes' fellow delegates, Henry Cabot Lodge, Oscar Underwood, and Elihu Root, promptly accepted the principle of the *status quo,* on the ground that the economizing temper of Congress would prevent securing the vast appropriations necessary for the proposed Pacific program. On December 12, the day before the Four-Power Pact was signed, Hughes promised to abandon further fortification of Guam and the Philippines. Thus he sacrificed the possible retention of strategic supremacy in the western Pacific in favor of an easing of international political tensions and reduction of naval armaments.[25]

Three days later the Big Three agreed on what later became Article 18 of the Five-Power Naval Treaty (signed February 5, 1922), leaving naval fortifications in the western Pacific *in statu quo.* Japan's subsequent acceptance of the 5–5–3 ratio cleared the decks as far as the Big Three were concerned; at this point French anxieties threatened dire complications. The French had received somewhat cavalier treatment during the Conference; Hughes had occasionally been somewhat less than cordial toward their delegates; moreover, at the opening session their seats were less prominent than those of the British and American representatives; finally, the suggestion that they rated only 1.75 tons of shipping as against 5 for the Big Three deeply wounded their pride. They reacted to these diverse factors by demanding a ratio of 3.5, so vigorously that the Conference was almost wrecked. Their exorbitant demands were allowed to leak out, resulting in world-wide condemnation of their position; Hughes appealed to Prime Minister Aristide Briand and France finally accepted the 1.75 ratio on condition that it be applied only to battle-

---

[25] The Sprouts, *op. cit.,* pp. 171–172, point out that this sacrifice was more apparent than real, since Japan's control of the former German islands, plus new war techniques, probably more than offset any possible American expenditures in this area.

ships. This, one of the Conference's most fateful decisions, opened the way to future competition in submarines, cruisers, and destroyers, thus partially vitiating the principle of arms limitation.

As finally signed, the Five-Power Naval Treaty called for the 5–5–3 ratio for the Big Three, with Italy and France standing 1.75 each. The *status quo* principle entailed a British promise not to increase fortifications at Hongkong or in the Pacific islands east of 110° E. Longitude—in effect retracting the naval frontier to Singapore. The United States renounced the right to fortify further the Philippines, Guam, the Aleutians, and Pago-Pago in American Samoa—correspondingly establishing her naval frontier at Pearl Harbor. The Japanese, after considerable maneuvering, agreed to apply the self-denying provisions to the screen of islands extending north and south from the homeland and including the Kuriles, Bonins, Loochoos, Pescadores, Formosa and Amami-Oshima. The agreement was binding until December 21, 1936, after which it was to remain effective unless terminated upon two years' notice.

The hectic days of early December during which Japan abandoned the security of the Anglo-Japanese Alliance for the Four-Power Pact and accepted an inferior naval ratio found the Nipponese bargaining shrewdly to recoup these losses. Basic decisions on most of the side issues were reached before signature of the Four-Power Pact (December 13, 1921), though formal announcement was usually postponed. A brief recapitulation must suffice. The Sino-Japanese treaty of February 4, 1922, maintained Japan's economic primacy in Shantung while conceding political sovereignty to China. Late in January the Japanese agreed to evacuate their Siberian expeditionary force, a promise implemented before the end of the year. The December days, too, saw Japanese-American agreement, resulting in a treaty of February 11, 1922, carrying American recognition of the Japanese mandate over former German islands north of the Equator; in return the United States received commercial rights in those islands and cable-landing rights on Yap. Finally, and long after the Conference ended, Japan agreed (April 14, 1923) to the abrogation of the Lansing-Ishii Agreement of 1917.

Japan's ultimate act of self-denial was the signature of the Nine-

Power Pact (February 6, 1922), mainly designed to reopen that door which she had been so assiduously closing during the recent crisis years. The preceding discussion must have been revealing and possibly bewildering to Japan; revealing in the vigor of Western condemnation of recent Japanese policies in China and Siberia, and bewildering because Japan in pursuing these policies only aped the methods by which some of her fellow conferees had established themselves in that same Far East which Japan had recently sought to dominate. This strongest of Open-Door statements became, by ratification of the treaty, a part of conventional international law, binding upon all signatories, but binding none of them to use force to make it effective. Its utility depended, therefore, and for a number of years depended successfully, upon the continuance in power of those liberal Japanese statesmen who considered a promise as an obligation. It ignored, however, a deeply rooted Japanese conviction, not unique in Japanese political thinking, that the national interest outweighs all promises. Later, during another crisis not unlike the one which fostered the aggressions of 1914–1917, the conviction would rise to overthrow the promise.

The historiography of the Conference presents a welter of claim and counterclaim, complicated by the fact that the ultimate failure of its work contributed to the disaster of December 7, 1941, at Pearl Harbor. A tentative balance, however, warrants the following conclusions: The results of the Conference developed largely from a common Anglo-American desire to reduce naval expenditures, to dissolve the Anglo-Japanese Alliance, and to limit Japanese aggressions on the Asiatic mainland. This obvious community of interest enabled Japan to bargain successfully for compensatory concessions. In terms of individual profit and loss, the United States obtained battleship parity with the former mistress of the seas, increased the "safe" area around either terminus of the Panama life line, and laid a foundation of Anglo-American coöperation which paid large future dividends. On the other hand, she surrendered a likely victory in a continued armaments race (which might have been less decisive than anticipated because of popular and congressional unwillingness to pay the bill), and with it the ability to defend the Philippines

and Guam. Britain, retreating from predominance to parity in battleships, was able, like Japan, to shift expenditures effectively to the
less expensive smaller categories, thus minimizing her surrender;
and she secured effective naval control of European waters and the
route to India. She jeopardized the safety of her possessions beyond
Singapore and formally abdicated her long-time claim to dominate
the seven seas. Japan secured tactical supremacy in the Far East,
retained the consultative features of the Four-Power Pact, and entrenched herself in the former German islands. To offset these advantages she surrendered the Anglo-Japanese Alliance, resigned
herself to a technically inferior naval status, and accepted a multipartite reproof of her mainland aspirations by signing the Nine-
Power agreement.

The net result was a fabric only as durable as Japan's observance
of the plighted word. The fabric presently faced stresses resulting
from Japanese domestic pressures. The protagonists in the long Japanese struggle between constitutional liberals and reactionary mili-
tarists viewed the Washington settlements differently. The former
hoped to use the new situation to reorient Japan while consolidating
their own control. To the latter the self-denying features of the Nine-
Power Treaty represented a weak surrender of essential continental
rights fairly bought and duly paid for; not unjustifiably, they viewed
the United States as the chief obstacle to realization of their legitimate objectives. Their dissatisfactions furnish the seeds of the ultimate overthrow of the balance established at Washington. During
the decade while these seeds were germinating, however, China
gained valuable time for consolidating her domestic political position; this buying of time may, indeed, prove in the long run the most
important accomplishment of the Washington meeting.

Antagonisms Deepen

Statutory exclusion of Japanese immigrants in 1924 helped to poison
the post-Washington atmosphere.[26] This product of west-coast anti-

---

[26] R. W. Paul, *The Abrogation of the Gentlemen's Agreement,* The Phi Beta Kappa
Society, 1936, and Bailey, *Dipl. Hist.,* pp. 705–706, supplement the titles cited in
Note 13, above.

Orientalism rode into the statute book on a wave of self-protection-
ism which, in the Johnson Act, deliberately discriminated in favor
of supposedly more "desirable" immigrants. With the Gentlemen's
Agreement in effective operation after 1908, California's feelings
had found vent in legislation limiting first (1913) the Japanese
right to own, and then (1920) to lease, agricultural lands. The early
1920's saw over a dozen states following California's example, and
in 1923 the Supreme Court upheld the legality of such legislation.
In the preceding year, moreover, that body had ruled that Japanese
were ineligible for citizenship by naturalization. Western laws represented a refinement of the general feeling which produced the
"quota" system of the Act of 1924 whereby the annual immigration
from any country was limited to 2 percent of its foreign-born nationals resident in the United States under the census of 1890 (a
scheme which would have allowed 250 Japanese to enter annually).
While Congress considered this scheme to stack the cards in favor
of presumably more easily assimilable northern and western Europeans, a proposal was offered specifically and completely excluding
"aliens ineligible to citizenship." Since other legislation covered
other Asiatics, it was perfectly obvious that here was a move to reënforce an accomplished fact by a gratuitous insult.

The amendment alarmed both Secretary Hughes and Japanese
Ambassador Masanao Hanihara. The result was a collaborative effort,
the precise details of which have not yet been fully documented, to
focus the joint pressure of Japan and the Department upon Congress. The instrument was a letter from Hanihara to Hughes (April
10, 1924), drafted after considerable preliminary discussion between
the two parties, which set forth for the first time the gist of the
Gentlemen's Agreement. This useful compilation closed with a note
of warning: "I realize, as I believe you do, the grave consequences
which the enactment of the measure retaining that particular provision would inevitably bring upon the otherwise happy and mutually advantageous relations between our two countries." Though
Hughes deprecated the use of the fighting words "grave consequences" he permitted the note to go forward to Congress in an
effort to deflect the rising anti-Japanese current. This maladroit at-

tempt to tell Congress how to run its own business accelerated an action doubtless inevitable from the beginning: The bill became a law with the objectionable provision intact. This unilateral action, in Elihu Root's phrase "one of the most unpardonable sins in the conduct of foreign affairs—acting in a moment of irritation," evoked loud Japanese protests, including the observation of July 1, 1924, as "Humiliation Day" in Tokyo, during which thousands attended mass meetings and signs urged Japanese to "Hate everything American." Granting the indubitable right of the United States to control its domestic policies, the fact remains that the Law of 1924 pulled the first brick from the edifice built at Washington; it was after only seven more years that Japan's Manchurian adventure was launched.[27]

The middle and later 'twenties brought into focus a number of domestic and foreign problems freighted with heavy consequences for the destiny of Japan and Japanese-American relations. Some phases of Japan's long-standing interest in Manchuria have already entered the present narrative; over a twenty-year span Manchuria had become a veritable life line, whose maintenance seemed absolutely essential to Japanese existence. This life line, moreover, had been secured by a nexus of treaties acquired over the years and effective despite the Washington agreements. China's gropings for national solidarity during the post-Washington period, however feeble, threatened the life line; the consolidating genius of Chiang Kai-shek intensified the threat. And when in 1928 the Young Marshal, Chiang Hsüeh-liang, oriented Manchurian policy toward the Kuomintang, the threat became a present danger with the possibility that the unifying forces of nascent Chinese nationalism would become too strong for Japan to control.

These developments pointed up an internal conflict apparent in Japanese affairs ever since Washington, namely, whether China could best be handled by peaceful means, coöperating under the Washington treaties, or by a "strong" policy designed to bring her

---

[27] It might be noted that in September, 1931, a move was well under way to place Japan under a revised quota system which would have admitted 185 immigrants a year; the Mukden Incident of September 18 ended the negotiations.

forcibly to heel. Advocates of the former policy, representing industrial and business groups, constitutional liberals and international-
ists, led by Baron Kijuro Shidehara, were in control roughly from
1924–1927 and 1929–1931; they hoped that China's nationalism
could be geared into Japan's Manchurian necessities. The "strong
policy" group frowned upon such a weak approach; representing
military and naval elements, small landowners and peasants, and
headed by Baron Giichi Tanaka, they advocated application of force
before it was too late. That it would soon be too late seemed likely in
1931, for their conviction that it was Japan's destiny to rule the East
was endangered by the increasing solidarity of China, by the long
continuance of the moderates in power, and by the repeated disregard of their wishes in the naval treaties of Washington and London (1930).

Against this background American relations remained outwardly
unruffled. Japan signed the Kellogg-Briand Pact for outlawry of
war in 1928 and accepted less than she had asked for in the London
Naval Conference of 1930; the treaty registering this compromise
was adopted in the face of unfavorable recommendations by the
naval authorities. An event of pivotal importance in Japanese-American and world relations ruptured the outward calm when the Japanese military took matters into their own hands and precipitated
the Mukden Incident of September 18, 1931. This seizure of the
initiative by advocates of the "strong policy" was most adroitly
timed. The world was in the midst of a profound depression for the
remedying of which, in the United States, the Administration of
Herbert Hoover had found no formula; an economy-minded people
supported Congressional niggardliness which kept the navy below
the 5–5–3 level of the Washington treaties; Britain had reached such
depths that three days after the Mukden Incident she became the
twenty-first nation to abandon the gold standard. Of the two powers
most immediately concerned, China faced civil conflict and Russian
energies were wholly and not too successfully involved in the first
Five-Year Plan. A more auspicious time for sloughing off inconven-
ient obligations could hardly have been chosen.

An explosion causing minor dislocation of the southbound track of the Changchun-Mukden railway line touched off the crisis.[28] Alleged Chinese firing on a Japanese investigating patrol inaugurated a series of moves which placed all Manchuria under Japanese control by the end of 1932 and resulted (in February, 1932) in establishment of the puppet state of Manchukuo, "ruled" by Henry Pu-Yi, the last Manchu emperor of China. Such aggression was in conflict with all the peace-keeping machinery instituted between 1918 and 1928, the League Covenant, the Nine-Power Pact, and the Kellogg-Briand agreement. China promptly (September 21) appealed to the League under Article 11, which made war or a threat of war a "matter of concern," and to the United States under the Kellogg-Briand Pact; she also proposed immediate investigation on the spot by an international committee. The League Council in the next few days apparently made definite overtures for American coöperation, and received tentative encouragement from Washington, for on September 23 Secretary of State Henry L. Stimson expressed his Government's "wholehearted sympathy" with League efforts and on the 24th he sent identical notes to the parties underwriting the League's notes of the 22d urging cessation of hostilities and a peaceful settlement. He warned Japan, moreover, that her action might involve violations of the Nine-Power and Kellogg-Briand Agreements. He was unwilling, however, to support the proposed on-the-spot investigation, preferring that matters be left to direct Sino-Japanese negotiations; he seems to have hoped for some time that the peaceful

---

[28] The disturbance was so slight that a southbound train traversed the break and arrived on time. Recent writing tends to minimize American willingness to coöperate with the League of Nations, in contrast to earlier assertions that the American non-member was in advance of the recognized agency of collective security. For material on both sides of this question, see Paul H. Clyde, "The American Policy of 'Playing No Favorites': Secretary Stimson and Manchuria, 1931," *Mississippi Valley Historical Review,* vol. 35 (1948), pp. 187–202; Griswold, *op. cit.;* Walter Lippmann and W. O. Scroggs, *The United States in World Affairs: An Account of American Foreign Relations, 1931,* Harper, 1932; *Ibid., 1932,* Harper, 1933; W. S. Myers, *The Foreign Policies of Herbert Hoover, 1929–1933,* Scribner, 1940; *Papers Relating to the Foreign Relations of the United States: Japan, 1931–1941,* Government Printing Office, 1943, 2 vols.; Sara R. Smith, *The Manchurian Crisis, 1931–32: A Tragedy in International Relations,* Columbia University Press, 1948; H. L. Stimson, *The Far Eastern Crisis,* Harper, 1936, and, with McGeorge Bundy, *On Active Service in Peace and War,* Harper, 1947; B. J. Wallace, "How the United States 'Led the League' in 1931," *American Political Science Review,* vol. 39 (1945), pp. 101–116; R. L. Wilbur and A. M. Hyde, *The Hoover Policies,* Scribner, 1937.

elements represented by Baron Shidehara would reassert themselves, and feared that any outside intervention would react unfavorably upon this possibility. The United States should therefore pursue an independent course in order to facilitate direct settlement by diplomatic means. With the United States unwilling to assist and Japan opposed to a commission, the Council abandoned the proposed investigation and Japan soon resumed her aggressive program.[29] Whatever influence the United States wielded during the early days of the crisis was thus by no means in advance of League policy and exercised a deterrent effect on coöperative action. The Council adjourned on September 30 after passing a resolution noting Japan's disavowal of territorial designs in Manchuria and placing on that nation responsibility for future developments.

In October, as in September, American performance lagged behind implied American promises. Encouraged by League inaction, Japan resumed the aggressive, bombing Chinchow on the 8th. Three days earlier Stimson had proffered continued American support and suggested that the Council "in no way relax its vigilance and in no way fail to assert all the pressure and authority within its competence toward regulating the action of China and Japan in the premises." The Japanese offensive induced Stimson to stimulate League action. On October 10 he told Sir Eric Drummond, Secretary-General of the League, that should the Council discuss invoking the Kellogg-Briand Pact, Mr. Prentiss Gilbert, American Consul at Geneva, would accept an invitation to sit with that body for such a discussion.[30] While still unwilling to assume the initiative, Stimson on October 12 expressed his willingness to take concurrent action in

---

[29] Stimson's note of September 24 to Nelson T. Johnson, American Minister to China, may shed some light on his personal feeling relative to the employment of sanctions against Japan. Commenting on the possibility that direct negotiations might prove unsuccessful, Stimson suggested that "this Government would be inclined to favor . . . action under Article 11 *and subsequent articles* of the League Covenant signed by both Japan and China." (Italics added.) Article 15 provided for the use of sanctions.

[30] This proposal was made specific on October 13. At about the same time Stimson was coming to believe that, so great was China's weakness, any Sino-Japanese negotiations should be held in the presence of outside observers as in the Shantung negotiations at Washington; this represents a modification of his September insistence upon direct negotiations.

case the Council invoked the Pact. After considerable discussion the
Council decided to remind Japan and China of their obligations
under the Kellogg-Briand Pact (October 17); the United States
took similar action on October 20. Here the policies of the United
States and the League run most closely parallel, though it should be
emphasized that Stimson's action followed only tardily upon a
League initiative which he himself helped to instigate; the promise
of October 10 had not been adequately implemented. Moreover,
Gilbert's presence at the Council meeting so stirred Japanese hostility and threatened to arouse the anti-League press at home that
Stimson presently made his position that of an observer only. The
Council adjourned October 24 after passing a strong resolution demanding complete evacuation of Chinese territory by November 16,
when the Council was to reconvene at Paris. By the end of the
month Stimson had made it clear that he had no new move under
consideration.

This failure to match promise with performance should not be
laid entirely at Stimson's door, for just as Gilbert was being depu-
tized to the Council, President Hoover entered an absolute veto on
American coöperation in any League measures which might at that
time have proven effective to halt Japan's march through Manchuria. The nation's desperate financial plight postponed Cabinet discussion of Manchuria until October 9; the following day President
and Secretary reviewed the matter, and at or about the same time
Hoover embodied his policy, which of course became that of the
Government, in a memorandum the essential parts of which are
reproduced herewith:[31]

---

[31] Wilbur and Hyde, *op. cit.*, pp. 600–601, print the Hoover memorandum. (Italics
added.) This effectively disposed of any disposition which Stimson may have entertained toward imposition of sanctions; the authorities are not in agreement as to
Stimson's position on this matter, but it seems likely to the writer that he was favorably disposed toward economic sanctions at least. See note 29, above, and Stimson
and Bundy, *On Active Service*, p. 244, where, commenting on cabinet discussions of
January, 1932, it is stated: "Since Mr. Hoover was the President, and since he believed that any policy of embargo or sanctions might lead to war, his position effectively blocked any governmental support for economic sanctions. This was a point
which Stimson had argued with Mr. Hoover several times. The President was always
willing to listen, but he was never persuaded."

The problem lies in three parts:

First, this is primarily a controversy between China and Japan. The United States has never set out to preserve peace among other nations by force and so far as this part is concerned *we shall confine ourselves to friendly counsel.* . . .

Second, our whole policy in connection with controversies is to exhaust the processes of peaceful negotiation. But in contemplating these we must make up our minds whether we consider war as the ultimate if these efforts fail. Neither our obligations to China, nor our own interest, nor our dignity require us to go to war over these questions. . . .

Third. . . . As the League of Nations has already taken up the subject, *we should co-operate with them in every field of negotiation or conciliation. But that is the limit. We will not go along on war or any of the sanctions either economic or military for those are the roads to war.*

This *caveat* limited American policy in the immediate future to continued efforts by independent action and diplomatic representations to mobilize world opinion against Japanese aggression; it prevented any effective coöperation with League efforts of November and December to meet the growing crisis. Charles G. Dawes, American Ambassador to Great Britain, was instructed to go to Paris when the Council reconvened in mid-November, but he was told to use his own discretion as to "whether and when" he should attend its sessions. Mindful of Hoover's dictum, Stimson told Dawes: "I do not want us to push or lead in this matter; neither do I want the American Government to be placed in the position of initiating or instigating League action. . . ." (November 10); and again, when it appeared that the League might turn to sanctions under Article 15, "we do not intend to get into war with Japan" (November 19). Since European leadership was no more inclined to drastic measures than Mr. Hoover, the Council soon reverted to the innocuous but face-saving gesture of an on-the-spot commission of inquiry such as Stimson had rejected in September.[32] The United States now subscribed to the scheme and permitted General Frank Ross McCoy to

---

[32] Since the present account deals primarily with Japan and the United States, no extended consideration can be given to European motives; it may be noted in passing, however, that by December no first-rate European power was disposed toward effective action. Whether this situation might have been altered by more forthright American action must remain a question for the speculatively inclined, but the importance of the joint failure is difficult to overemphasize.

serve on the Lytton Commission which was authorized by Council action on December 10.

With Japan's fingers closing on Manchuria, the treaty structure tottering, and international coöperation a polite fiction, the United States took recourse again to the inkpot to keep the record clear against another and perhaps more favorable day. The result was the Nonrecognition Doctrine announced January 7, 1932. The initial suggestion for this seems to have come from the President, for Stimson recorded in his diary for November 9: "He . . . thinks his main weapon is to give an announcement that if the treaty is made under military pressure we will not recognize it or avow it." This idea closely paralleled Bryan's note of May 11, 1915, at the time of the Twenty-One Demands; Stimson and his advisers repeatedly discussed it during the period when he was still hoping against hope that the better Japanese elements might triumph; Hoover seems likewise to have urged it upon the Cabinet. The occupation of Chinchow on January 3 destroyed any lingering vestiges of optimism and Stimson promptly prepared two drafts for Hoover's consideration, one closely patterned after the Bryan note and another broadened in scope to encompass the obligations of the Kellogg-Briand Pact. On January 4 Hoover chose the broader approach and three days later it was stated that the United States Government

deems it to be its duty to notify both the Government of the Chinese Republic and the Imperial Japanese Government that it cannot admit the legality of any situation *de facto* nor does it intend to recognize any treaty or agreement entered into between those governments, or agents thereof, which may impair the treaty rights of the United States or its citizens in China, including those which relate to the sovereignty, the independence, or the territorial and administrative integrity of the Republic of China, or to the international policy relative to China, commonly known as the open-door policy; and that it does not intend to recognize any situation, treaty, or agreement which may be brought about by means contrary to the covenants and obligations of the Pact of Paris of August 27, 1928. . . .

The effect of the doctrine was to leave the United States as the sole potential obstacle to Japanese aggression, as the British accepted at face value facile Japanese assurances that the door would be kept open. The appearance of virtually the entire United States navy in Hawaiian waters for maneuvers in February did not heighten Japanese good will despite the fact that the concentration had been under plan for two years.

Continued Japanese aggression around Shanghai late in January prompted Stimson to consider further protests, resulting in the letter of February 24 to Senator William E. Borah, Chairman of the Senate Committee on Foreign Relations. His action also stemmed partly from Japanese intimations in early February that the Nine-Power Treaty was no longer binding and that China was now liable to permanent dismemberment and exploitation. He originally hoped through joint Anglo-American representations to induce Japan to parley with the signers of that agreement (note that earlier American statements had been based upon the Kellogg-Briand Pact). This proving impracticable, he determined on a unilateral pronouncement.[33] The Borah letter called pointed attention to the interdependence of the Washington treaties and traded upon the presence of the American fleet in Pacific waters by suggesting that

the willingness of the American Government to surrender its then commanding lead in battleship construction and to leave its positions at Guam and in the Philippines without further fortifications was predicated upon, among other things, the self-denying covenants contained in the Nine-Power Treaty, which assured the nations of the world not only of equal opportunity for their Eastern trade but also against the military aggrandizement of any other power at the expense of China. One cannot discuss the possibility of modifying or abrogating those provisions of the Nine-Power Treaty without considering at the same time the other promises upon which they were really dependent.

Japan, however, had already contrived (February 18) a Manchukuoan "declaration of independence," so that the Borah letter merely kept the American record clear by reiterating refusal to recognize territorial changes which violated the treaty structure.

---

[33] Stimson has suggested (*On Active Service*, pp. 247–248) that British reluctance to coöperate forced him to take independent action. It should be pointed out, however, that British efforts were instrumental in securing the insertion of the non-recognition formula and of a warning to Japan under the Nine-Power Treaty in a resolution of February 16 adopted by twelve members of the League Council. Smith, *op. cit.*, pp. 242–247.

Discouraged by the Council's failure to take adequate steps under Article 11, China appealed to the Assembly under Article 15. Here the Borah letter helped to focus small-state opinion back of an Assembly resolution (March 11) supporting the nonrecognition doctrine.

Thus American policy had been effective only in aiding to mobilize world opinion against Japan's aggression and in focusing Japanese hostility upon the United States. The Lytton Commission's investigation thoroughly documented Japan's bad faith but was no more successful in inducing action. The fact was that no one, Britain, France, the League, or the United States, was at the time willing to pay the price of maintaining collective security. The fact that the United States was not formally part of the peace-keeping machinery undoubtedly contributed, and the unfortunate result was reënforced by American isolationism and by Hoover's personal unwillingness, perhaps a heritage of his Quaker upbringing, to skirt the fringes of effective sanctions. The episode as a whole erected a signpost pointing out the road to aggression to Mussolini and Hitler in the later 1930's. Judging Manchuria as a test of collective security, however, suggests the venerable cliché advanced by apologists for Christianity's alleged shortcomings—that it has never failed because it has never been tried.

American relations with Japan between the 1850's and the early 1930's developed against a backdrop of rapidly shifting domestic and world events. During these years each successively suffered the pangs of national adolescence, leading both at times to pursue policies unpleasant to their older contemporaries. The fact that the United States emerged first from this unpleasant transition to a period of relative maturity and stability while Japan still retained the bumptiousness of youth seems to account for much of the friction which increasingly characterized their relations. Whatever the causes, the story has made the facts apparent; the twentieth century was a period of increasing antagonism, interspersed with short intervals of amicability; exercising the historical prerogative of hindsight, it can now be seen that the trend toward the denouement of Pearl Harbor was already under way by 1932.

16 Neutrality Fails Again

Ⅎ HE WAR WHICH BROKE OVER EUROPE IN THE SUMMER OF 1914 found the American people vastly ignorant of the complex issues involved, psychologically unprepared, but generally predisposed toward the Triple Entente (Britain, France, and Russia), to which Italy adhered in 1915 after weighing the consequences of continued allegiance to her recent German and Austrian partners in the Triple Alliance. Both Britain and Germany stimulated this initial predisposition. British cutting of German-American cable connections (August 5, 1914) destroyed direct communication; British propaganda emanated from Wellington House, an insurance office converted to the uses of international persuasion; the skillful labors of Sir Gilbert Parker and the youthful Arnold J. Toynbee plowed both wide and deep the fields of American public opinion. Few escaped the sweet praises of that democratic way of life which most already preferred to the autocracy of Britain's enemies. For her part, Germany lost few opportunities to demonstrate maladroitness. From the invasion of Belgium through the *Lusitania* and other shipsinkings to the all-out submarine campaign of 1917 her actions grievously burdened her diplomats. Britain had to keep Americans thinking the way they did, and then persuade them to act upon their convictions; German propaganda faced the well-nigh impossible task of making Americans change their minds. Any attempted assessment of American leadership between 1914 and 1917 must be made in the light of this initial predisposition.[1]

---

[1] J. D. Squires, *British Propaganda at Home and in the United States from 1914 to 1917*, Harvard University Press, 1935; H. C. Peterson, *Propaganda for War*, Uni-

As always, the personal factor was important in the evolution of American policy.[2] Most conspicuous bulks the figure of Woodrow Wilson. The strong religious convictions of generations of stern Calvinist forebears rested heavily upon him; that confidence in the rightness of his own opinions not uncommon among academicians was strong within him; that sense of mission which developed rapidly during the peace-making period was always present. All these were topped off by a thoroughgoing devotion to principle which would cause him to adhere to a position once assumed even at the risk of dangerous involvement. To these factors was added a personal preference for the Allied cause bred of long study of democracy in general and of British literature and institutions in particular —a preference which Wilson honestly tried to divorce from his conduct of foreign affairs. It can be truly said of him that he desired to maintain the peace; the story will show that loyalty to his honest convictions led the United States into war.

His top-flight advisers were in varying degrees pro-British and inexperienced, which at once complicated Wilson's efforts to maintain the peace and forced him into reliance upon his own judgment. William Jennings Bryan, his first Secretary of State, was innocent of diplomatic training and came from a background which made it impossible for him to disregard political considerations of a less elevated character, measurably handicapping him for the conduct of high policy. His chief asset, a fine sense of moral responsibility,

---

versity of Oklahoma Press, 1939. Dexter Perkins, *America and the Two Wars*, Little, Brown, 1944, analyzes briefly but penetratingly the American frame of mind.

[2] The following titles bear particularly on the personalities involved. Much material is also contained in titles subsequently cited in connection with particular events: Ray Stannard Baker, *Woodrow Wilson*, vols. 5–6; M. E. Curti, *Bryan and World Peace, Smith College Studies in History*, Smith College, 1931, vol. 16, Nos. 3 and 4, pp. 165–222; Burton J. Hendrick, *The Life and Letters of Walter Hines Page*, Doubleday, Page, 1923, 2 vols.; Lansing, *War Memoirs*; Notter, *For. Pol. of Wilson*, pp. 315–654; *Papers Relating to the Foreign Relations of the United States: The Lansing Papers*, Government Printing Office, 1939–1940, 2 vols.; Carlton Savage (comp.), *The Policy of the United States Toward Maritime Commerce in War*, Government Printing Office, 1936, vol. 2; Charles Seymour, *American Neutrality, 1914– 1917: Essays on the Causes of American Intervention in the World War*, Yale University Press, 1935; Charles Seymour, (ed.), *The Intimate Papers of Colonel House*, Houghton Mifflin, 1926–1928, 4 vols.

led him to a position which Wilson could not share and compelled him to resign rather than compromise his own principles. Robert Lansing's appointment as Bryan's successor brought to the fore a legalistic mind of the type which Wilson never entirely trusted. Though both strove honestly to maintain the peace, Lansing's pro-British bias developed more rapidly than did his chief's. As time passed his advice helped to place the United States in a position vis-à-vis Germany whence retreat became impossible, and his feeling that a break with Britain was unthinkable colored his attitude toward the complicated negotiations with that nation. He had become convinced by the summer of 1915, long before Wilson reached this point, that the likelihood of German victory would necessitate American entry into the war. Colonel Edward M. House, *fidus Achates* to Wilson through the period of neutrality and attempted mediation, and well into the peace negotiations, was avowedly and vocally devoted to the Allied cause. The bias of Wilson's Ambassador to Britain, Walter Hines Page, was exceeded only by that worthy's naïveté. Thus temperament and the qualities of his advisers drove Wilson to be his own Foreign Minister.

Wilson Temporizes with the Allies

Aside from the normal declaration of neutrality, promptly issued on August 4, and a simultaneous tender of good offices which were ignored or turned aside, the war's earliest problems dealt with trade. As always, war's preoccupations provided the neutral's opportunity, particularly valuable in the depressed condition of American industry in 1914. As in earlier days, however, opportunity and danger went hand in hand, expanding trade inevitably breeding controversy with the stronger naval power. As usual, the stronger naval power was Britain, the willing object of the American predispositions mentioned above. The handling of these early controversies offers the key to much that happens later: Unwilling to offend the British, American policy-makers made concessions of principle amounting to the abandonment of an excellent legal position without demanding equivalent compensation. This lenient handling of British derelictions contrasted strongly with the vigorous demands presently made upon Germany. Anglo-American controversies were initiated by discussions centering around the Declaration of London.[3]

This document, drafted in 1909, attempted to sharpen the definition of contraband so as to minimize wartime trade difficulties. The British, always wary of clear-cut definitions, had not ratified it; neither had any other nation, although the United States Senate had consented to ratification in April, 1912. Bryan, anxious to stabilize the situation, asked the belligerents (August 6, 1914) to accept it. Its guarantees offered the Central Powers their only chance for large-scale trade with the neutrals; they promptly accepted, conditional upon enemy agreement. Britain, speaking for the Entente, politely admitted the "great importance" of American views and expressed "keen desire" to go as far as possible to comply with neutral objectives. The equivocal nature of these statements soon became apparent; an Order in Council of August 20 (which established the pattern of British trade regulation for the duration of the war) accepted the Declaration "subject to certain modifications and additions which they judge indispensable to the efficient conduct of their naval operations." By expanding the list of conditional contraband beyond the categories specified in the Declaration, notice was served that Britain did not intend to be bound by its limitations; successive Orders in Council further extended the contraband list, enabling the British to seize many goods, previously fair trade for neutrals, which otherwise would have flowed to Germany through Dutch and Scandinavian ports. This obvious negation of neutral

---

[3] R. W. Van Alstyne, "The Policy of the United States Regarding the Declaration of London, at the Outbreak of the Great War," *Journal of Modern History*, vol. 7 (1935), pp. 434–447, deals in detail with this episode. The following titles give a good general coverage of the neutrality period: Albion and Pope, *op. cit.*, pp. 207–252; Borchard and Lage, *op. cit.*, pp. 33–44, 59–240; C. Hartley Grattan, *Why We Fought*, Vanguard, 1929; Walter Millis, *The Road to War*, Houghton Mifflin, 1935; Alice M. Morrissey, *The American Defense of Neutral Rights, 1914–1917*, Harvard University Press, 1939; F. L. Paxson, *American Democracy and the World War: Pre-War Years, 1913–1917*, Houghton Mifflin, 1936, pp. 198–420; Charles Seymour, *American Diplomacy during the World War*, Johns Hopkins Press, 1934, pp. 1–211; C. C. Tansill, *America Goes to War*, Little, Brown, 1938. A penetrating analysis and critique of the literature of the neutrality period is contained in R. W. Leopold, "The Problem of American Intervention, 1917: An Historical Retrospect," *World Politics*, vol. 2 (1950), pp. 405–425.

wishes produced the first Anglo-American crisis and the first evidence that the United States was not prepared to undertake a thoroughgoing defense of neutral rights.

Here was the point for a vigorous protest against British pretensions; such was prepared and sent to London, but never delivered. Drafted by Cone Johnson, Solicitor of the Department of State, under date of September 26, it spelled out British violations of the Declaration of London in the Order in Council of August 20. Wilson showed Colonel House a copy; the Colonel felt that it was too strong. At his own request House conferred with the British Ambassador, Sir Cecil Spring Rice who, curiously enough, agreed with House. Under their combined inspiration the second note sent on September 28 was devoid of teeth; affirming Wilson's desire to avoid formal protest, it stressed the evil effects of British policy upon American public opinion rather than neutral rights. Even this watered-down protest was further diluted by instructing Page to communicate not its text, but its substance, to the British authorities. Lansing, Acting Secretary of State, presently suggested to Spring Rice that the British might tighten their blockade of the Continent by persuading the Dutch to embargo foodstuffs or promise not to reëxport them, a technique which would shift American criticism from British to Dutch shoulders while permitting the British to proceed unchecked. On October 22 the United States abandoned its efforts to make the Declaration of London effective.

This tender consideration was not lost upon the British, who in successive Orders in Council (September 21, October 29, and December 23) vastly extended the contraband list and put Lansing's suggestion into operation by compelling the continental neutrals to "ration" their exports to Germany. Neutral ships going to Germany and to neighboring neutrals were intercepted by British warships and taken into port, on the ground that submarines rendered search on the high seas too hazardous. Once in port it was not too difficult for the British to expand the doctrine of continuous voyage to justify seizure of goods ultimately destined for the Central Powers; here American Civil War practices came home to roost, and British forbearance at that time now brought its reward. On November 3 the

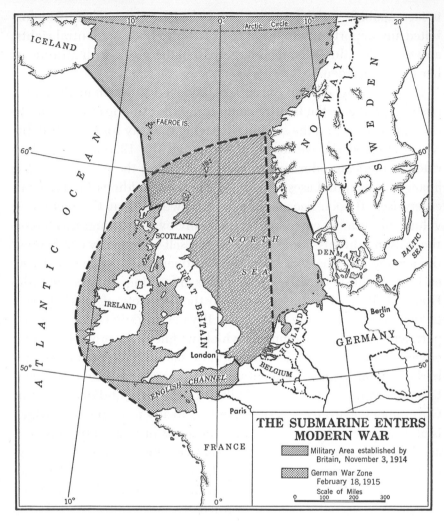

THE SUBMARINE ENTERS
MODERN WAR

Military Area established by
Britain, November 3, 1914

German War Zone
February 18, 1915

Scale of Miles
0   100   200   300

North Sea was declared a military area and was presently mined so
thoroughly as to preclude navigation without British charts, which
were denied ships carrying "dangerous" cargo. These devices, of
course equivalent to a practical blockade of Germany, violated neutral rights as these had been understood prior to 1914; instead, however, of the forthright demands of a nation intent upon maintaining
its rights, the American note of December 26, 1914, protested British
methods instead of challenging British objectives. The conclusion

is inescapable that the United States had by the end of 1914 forfeited any opportunity to bring the British to book on neutral rights,
and that this failure stemmed largely from the pro-British attitude of
her own statesmen.

The financing of war purchases produced a wartime tie and a
postwar problem; the first by committing the American economy to
the Allied cause and the second by paving the way for the war debts
which plagued the western world through the 1920's. Depression-
ridden American industry was anxious to sell to the Allies, who first
financed their purchases by liquidating their holdings in American
enterprises. It soon became apparent, however, that the increasing
volume of business could be financed only by borrowing; this forced
the Wilson Administration, which at first self-righteously condemned
the making of loans, to a tortuous adjustment to economic facts. As
early as August 10, 1914, Bryan was informing Wilson that the
House of Morgan had inquired as to the propriety of making loans
to the French. Lansing, bolstering Bryan's negative advice, asked
pertinently why a government which withheld its protection from
citizens enlisting in belligerent armies should protect dollars embarking upon a similar adventure. Bryan's note of August 15, containing a sentence written by Wilson that "in the judgment of this
Government, loans by American bankers to any foreign nation which
is at war are inconsistent with the true spirit of neutrality," discouraged the bankers temporarily. By mid-October, however, the government was making a distinction, between loans made by private
citizens and government advances, a distinction which favored the
former. A week later bankers warned the Administration that the
belligerents, unless granted temporary credits, would take their business elsewhere; in response to this hint Lansing, who had now
changed his mind about loans, consulted Wilson and dropped a
quiet word to the bankers that there would be no official objection
to credit loans to settle the short-term obligations which were piling
up dangerously. The Morgans and the National City Bank promptly
advanced $10,000,000 to the French Government. This cleared the
way for advances up to the limit of banking resources. By the summer of 1915 this limit was being approached and trade was still

increasing; under Lansing's urging the President surrendered and agreed (early in September) to countenance the floating of general loans by belligerent governments. Thus under economic necessity Wilson shifted from highly moral to merely legal ground. The result was to mesh the American economy thoroughly into the European war effort and to increase the difficulty of ultimate abstention from the war.

Wilson's preventive efforts in a third area produced no positive results and further evidenced American predisposition to the Allied cause. With neutrality becoming increasingly complicated and burdensome, Wilson sought to avoid involvement by mediating peace.[4] The Anglophile Texan, Colonel House, arrived in England in February, 1915, to confer with Sir Edward Grey as "a disinterested friend whose suggestions and offers of service will not be misunderstood and may be made use of to the advantage of the world." Their mutual discourse on "nature, solitude, Wordsworth" brought peace no nearer but impressed Grey's qualities upon House. Succeeding parleys in Paris and Berlin were equally unproductive; neither side had eyed defeat closely enough to really want peace.

In the autumn of 1915 the Colonel began working out a plan whereby, when the British approved, Wilson would threaten the Germans with American intervention unless they agreed to American mediation. This resulted in the House-Grey Memorandum of February 22, 1916, a remarkable document which promised on Wilson's behalf that, on receiving the signal from the Allies, the President would propose a peace conference. If Allied acceptance were followed by German refusal, "the United States would probably enter the war against Germany." If the meeting were held and failed because of German recalcitrance, "the United States would leave the Conference as a belligerent on the side of the Allies." Wilson, more conscious than House of the Congressional function of declaring war, altered the document to read that "the United States would *probably* leave the Conference as a belligerent on the side of the Allies" (italics added). With this single change, Wilson accepted

---

[4] His efforts toward a negotiated peace are detailed in Kent Forster, *The Failures of Peace,* American Council on Public Affairs, 1941.

the implications of the Memorandum to the limit of his ability to speak for the future actions of his Government. This evidence that the United States was morally on their side doubtless gave the British confidence in pursuing their cavalier treatment of American complaints about commerce restrictions, then a matter of sharp controversy. Wilson soon became irked at the British and then involved in his reëlection campaign; these factors postponed further mediation schemes until the autumn.

Germany Is Held Accountable

While timid handling of trade-restriction disputes, increasing complaisance on loans, and a benevolently intentioned mediation policy were tilting the balance toward the Allies by the early months of 1916, developing relations with the Central Powers had produced the issue of submarine warfare. The forthright American attitude on this issue contrasted strongly with its temporizing position on British interference with American rights.[5] This question, bred of German necessity and a somewhat quixotic American insistence upon the right to use wartime seas as if they were peacetime avenues, ultimately took the United States into the war. With blockade measures increasingly effective, British fingers began tightening around the throats of the German civilian population as well as the flow of military materiél. German opportunity to retaliate was practically limited to the submarine, as yet a relatively untried weapon of which Germany had about a score ready for sea duty. Throwing a war zone about the British Isles, she announced that beginning on February 18, 1915, enemy merchant ships would be destroyed in the forbidden area without provision for the safety of passengers and crew. Neutral shipping was warned of the dangers resulting from belligerents' misuse of neutral flags; thus both neutral lives and property were endangered.

This posed an American dilemma. Lacking an adequate merchant fleet, Americans traveled on foreign liners. Submarine sinkings

---

[5] This attitude, it should be noted, appeared before economic ties could have strengthened the original predisposition toward the Allies to the point of final conviction.

would endanger American lives; what position would the Government take? The answer was the "strict accountability" note of February 10:

If the commanders of German vessels of war should act upon the presumption that the flag of the United States was not being used in good faith and should destroy on the high seas an American vessel or the lives of American citizens, it would be difficult for the Government of the United States to view the act in any other light than as an indefensible violation of neutral rights. . . .

If such a deplorable situation should arise, the Imperial German Government can readily appreciate that the Government of the United States would be constrained to hold the Imperial German Government to a strict accountability for such acts of their naval authorities and to take any steps it might be necessary to take to safeguard American lives and property and to secure to American citizens the full enjoyment of their acknowledged rights on the high seas.

This vigorous statement implied not only the right of Americans to travel safely on their own vessels, but by their mere presence to protect the unarmed shipping of enemy belligerents from submarine attack. If such sharp language was intended to frighten Germany into a less drastic policy, it also had another effect, for it placed the American Government, early in the controversy, in a position whence any retreat would be a major diplomatic defeat. It took a stand which, if adhered to, pointed straight to involvement and war —a striking contrast with the tentative policy assumed toward the Allies.

The German Ambassador promptly urged the Department of State to warn Americans against travel on belligerent ships, but his advice was not heeded. With submarines hovering in the converging sea-lanes southwest of the British Isles, incidents were inevitable. On March 28 an American sailor perished in the sinking of the British liner *Falaba* in the Irish Sea. On May 1 the new American oil-tanker *Gulflight* was struck by a torpedo launched in a fight between a submarine and a British naval patrol; she limped into port, but two crew members were killed and the captain died of heart failure. Meantime Bryan, who had signed the February note, was undergoing a change of heart; by April 19 he was asking Wilson: "Why do

Americans take the risk? . . . Why be shocked at the drowning of a few people, if there is no objection to the starving of a nation?" His feeling that an American on a belligerent ship should be asked to take his own chances was strongly opposed by Counselor Lansing, who insisted that the safety of noncombatant nationals on belligerent merchant vessels must be held inviolate. Wilson, initially predisposed toward Lansing's view, delayed decision, but was forced to choose between his conflicting subordinates by the sinking of the *Lusitania* on May 7, 1915; he sided with Lansing, thus making war inevitable unless Wilson or Germany later retreated—and neither retreated.

Despite a warning issued by the German Embassy on May 1 that Americans entered the war zone in British ships at their own risk, well over a hundred lost their lives when the *Lusitania* was sunk, off the southern coast of Ireland, by one of a German submarine's last pair of torpedoes. A verdict of contributory negligence seems justly applicable to the *Lusitania's* skipper, who seemingly did his utmost to invite destruction.[6] Proceeding at slow speed on a straight course close to a headland affording ideal submarine cover, he failed to use her great speed on the usual zigzag course which would have minimized the likelihood of a direct torpedo hit. Americans reacted promptly and violently, more mindful of their dead compatriots' legal right to travel on the British vessel than of their doubtful prudence in thus courting disaster.[7] Indeed, an action better calculated to subserve British interests, defeat German propaganda, and prepare the American mind for war could hardly have been devised. It exercised, also, a fateful influence upon official policy, for it forced Wilson to make up his mind between Bryan and Lansing; supporting the latter, he chose the road which led to war in 1917.

The first *Lusitania* note of May 13, drafted by Wilson and sent

---

[6] T. A. Bailey, "The Sinking of the *Lusitania*," *American Historical Review*, vol. 41 (1935), pp. 54–74, is the most thorough factual study.

[7] The violence of this reaction was not lessened by the publication (May 11) of the report of "The German Outrages Inquiry Committee," headed by the distinguished Lord Bryce and containing circumstantial but poorly authenticated accounts of atrocities committed by German troops in Belgium.

over Bryan's name, insisted upon the right of Americans to sail on
belligerent merchantmen and reiterated the "strict accountability"
position. Five days later, however, the President made a bow toward
Bryan by cabling House that representations would have to be
made, in the interests of consistency, about the unjustifiable British
trade restrictions; the resulting House-Grey conversations were indecisive. Germany's unsatisfactory reply (May 28) to the note of
May 13 precipitated action. Bryan, who had been trying valiantly
to secure equalization of pressure upon both belligerents, felt that
Wilson's draft reply (renewing previous demands and denying German contentions), discussed in the Cabinet on June 1, was a direct
invitation to trouble. On June 4 he told Wilson that he could not
sign the note in its existing state; the following day Wilson indicated
his decision to send the note as drafted, while admitting much of
the substance of Bryan's contention by agreeing that steps should
be taken to warn Americans off ships carrying munitions. After an
agonizing week end Bryan tendered his resignation on June 7; it was
promptly accepted and the Wilson note, carrying Lansing's signature and embodying his point of view, went to Germany on the 9th.
A stand condemning the submarine had been taken, so uncompromising that only German surrender could appease the United States;
should surrender become impossible, the danger of war would become instant.[8]

Germany for some time followed a policy of appeasement. Submarine commanders were privately ordered (June 6) not to sink
liners, even under the enemy flag, without warning. When American
lives were lost in the sinking (August 19) of the British *Arabic* in
violation of these orders, Lansing, now Secretary of State, threatened war unless such actions ceased. Pressure of adverse opinion in
the United States led Count J. H. von Bernstorff, the German Ambassador, to render on behalf of his Government the *Arabic* Pledge
(September 1) containing the substance of the June order. The
submarines transferred their attentions to Atlantic freighters during

---

[8] Considerable further correspondence failing to clarify the *Lusitania* incident, the
matter was still at issue when the United States went to war.

the remainder of 1915; the early months of 1916 found most of them ranging the Mediterranean, and except for the *Sussex* episode they passed off stage for some months.

A German threat of early February, 1916, to treat armed belligerent merchantmen as warships, sinking them without warning, contributed to a domestic political crisis in the United States. The British practice of arming merchantmen had been under way for some months prior to the German announcement; such armament had long been recognized as legitimate defensive technique against cruisers or commerce destroyers, but it became a deadly offensive weapon against a thin-skinned submarine. Since the German threat increased the danger to American citizens, a move was launched to keep those citizens off armed merchantmen, which of course ran contrary to Wilson's contentions as to American rights. Representative Jeff McLemore of Texas introduced a resolution on February 17 requesting the President to warn Americans not to travel on armed vessels. On the 25th Senator Thomas P. Gore of Oklahoma proposed to deny passports to Americans seeking passage on armed belligerent vessels and demanded protection of American trade in non-contraband against illegal Allied restrictions. These were both Democrats; their proposals at once countered Wilson's position that he could not "consent to any abridgement of the rights of American citizens in any respect . . ." and threatened complications with Britain over trade rights. They reflected, undoubtedly, the feeling of many in Wilson's own party that the armed merchantman issue was likely to lead to war if his position was maintained; some thought, indeed, that war was then his intention, though the burden of evidence is against this conclusion. Wilson acted promptly and vigorously to prevent adoption of either resolution and his action, hostile as it was to Germany, mirrored rising American exasperation with that power.

This exasperation was heightened by injury of several Americans in the torpedoing (March 24, 1916) of the unarmed French cross-Channel passenger ship *Sussex* in violation of the *Arabic* Pledge. Lansing's bellicose draft note would have broken relations then and there; Wilson substituted a virtual ultimatum (April 18) according to which relations could be continued only if the submarine were kept under leash. On May 4 Germany agreed, laying down the countercondition that the United States force Britain to respect the rights she was then so flagrantly violating. Wilson, enough of a historian to detect this variant of the Cadore Letter, accepted the pledge but refused to accept the condition. The submarine thereupon ceased to be an issue in German relations until early 1917. Wilson's policy, uneven as it was between the warring powers, still succeeded in keeping the United States on the tightrope of peace.

Meantime British relations worsened rapidly during 1916 to a point where German adherence to her *Sussex* Pledge might well have enabled the United States to remain on the tightrope. Late in October, 1915, Page received a long and detailed protest against British trade practices which he dubbed "an uncourteous monster of 35 heads and 3 appendices." Though vigorous, it hinted nothing stronger than protest, and House wrote Grey that he need not be unduly disturbed at it; within a few weeks House's activities leading up to the Memorandum of February 22, 1916, convinced the British that they had little to fear. They did not bother to reply until late in April, adroitly timing their lengthy rebuttal, an essential denial of the American contentions, to coincide with the peak of the *Sussex* crisis. The interim, moreover, had seen the issuance of new and more obnoxious burdens upon neutral trade. Thus the spring of 1916 found Wilson no more successful in redressing trade grievances than in mediating a peace. British treatment of the Easter Rebellion in Ireland roused the hardly dormant Anglophobia of Irish-Americans which was not lulled by the execution (August 3) of the Irish patriot, Sir Roger Casement. On May 27 Wilson addressed the League to Enforce Peace, hinting at American willingness to abandon isolation and enter an international organization designed to maintain peace. He said, moreover, that his country was not concerned with the causes and objects of the European struggle. The Allies ignored the first statement but pounced upon the second, further irking the President. Another indication of the decline of

Allied stock is to be found in the passage of the largest naval appropriation ever made by a nation not at war; its implications were no more favorable to Britain than to Germany.

The unkindest cut of all, however, was the British announcement on July 18, 1916, of a Blacklist of eighty-five names, covering some thirty American firms which because of suspected dealings with the Central Powers were to be denied the use of British banks, cable services, and ships.[9] This public avowal of a policy to which Britain was undoubtedly entitled to resort stirred American public opinion to the depths when piled upon previous British interference with neutral trade and postal contacts with the continental powers. War-born prosperity was such by this time that the economic effects of the policy were negligible; its psychological impact was tremendous. Five days after its announcement Wilson wrote to House that he was ready to ask Congress to prohibit loans and cut exports to the Allies. Two retaliatory laws passed early in September authorized withholding clearance papers from any ship refusing to accept cargo from blacklisted firms and denying port facilities to the merchant-men of a nation guilty of such discrimination. These discretionary powers were never exercised, partly because the British, realizing their error, eased their policy, and partly because the Secretary of Commerce reported that retaliation would invite counterreprisals while not guaranteeing the desired concessions. (It may be noted that the United States enthusiastically adopted the British policy, blacklisting over 5000 individuals and organizations under wartime legislation.)

The presidential election provided a counterirritant to divert Wilson's attention from British misbehavior, but after his hard-won victory at the polls in November he turned again to thoughts of mediation. Delayed by illness and work on his annual message, he did not until late November complete a draft invitation to a conference of both belligerents and neutrals which would not only make peace but set up an international organization. He found himself faced with a German peace move, directed in part toward defeating

---

[9] T. A. Bailey, "The United States and the Blacklist during the Great War," *Journal of Modern History*, vol. 6 (1934), pp. 14–35.

a domestic drive for the renewal of unrestricted submarine warfare. The German armies had pushed the Allies back at the Somme, they were cutting short British food and military supplies, and they had neutralized a Rumanian offensive and captured Bucharest. Their position was better than it was likely to be again, and on December 12 they published a statement indicating that peace discussions were in order. This took Wilson 'twixt wind and water: Failure to capitalize the German offer, tenuous though it might be, would forfeit the peacemaking initiative which he had long sought; responding to it, on the other hand, would lay him open to the charge of collaboration. After some deliberation he took a middle course, abandoning his proposed call to a general conference for a simple request (December 18) to both parties to state their war aims. This, Wilson's last real move toward peace, was futile. The Germans, still undefeated and preferring direct negotiations to a mediated peace, refused a statement. The Allies replied, but in terms making abundantly clear their insistence upon a victorious peace which would include territorial rearrangements unfavorable to the Central Powers. A few days after receipt of the Allied reply Wilson started formulating his own ideas of a desirable peace settlement. Using the Senate as a sounding board, he chided the Powers (January 22, 1917) for their unwillingness to discuss peace, spoke feelingly of the need for international organization, and insisted upon "peace without victory" under which every people "should be left free to determine its own polity, its own way of development, unhindered, unthreatened, unafraid." By this time, however, decisions had been taken in Germany which, given Wilson's continued insistence upon positions already adopted, would prove fatal to his real desire to keep the United States at peace.

In Germany was culminating a long struggle between military and naval elements believing that unlimited use of the submarine would win the war and civilians fearful that such a policy would bring the United States into the contest. The story has already recounted German retreat from all-out submarine warfare in the face of American threats; events of the summer of 1916 put the politicians on the defensive once more. German arms were stopped on the

Verdun sector, the Allies had launched a trial offensive on the
Somme, in August Rumania entered the Allied camp. The same
month saw the advancement of General Paul von Hindenburg to be
Chief of the German General Staff and of General Erich von Luden-
dorff to be Quartermaster General, with corresponding lessening of
civilian influence upon German policy, since both men were advocates of the submarine. Early in October the Main Committee of
the Reichstag indicated its support of unrestricted submarine warfare whenever the Supreme Command indicated its desirability. In
November leaders of the armed services agreed that unless the forthcoming peace move were successful, the spring of 1917 must see the
submarines turned loose once more. When hope of a negotiated
peace faded in December Chancellor Theobald von Bethmann-
Hollweg, spokesman of the civilian opposition, capitulated and
agreed to slip the submarine leash when it became apparent that
the advantages likely to accrue outweighed the dangers of American
entry into the war. By this time the military had become convinced
that victory must be won by August 1, 1917, or not at all. The Navy
claimed to have 115 efficient submarines ready for duty and many
more building; early in January military and naval leaders agreed
that the submarine was essential, believed that it could force Britain
to capitulate before the American potential could be brought to
bear, and determined to bend Bethmann to their decision. On January 9 he gave in and February 1 was set as the day for renewed
U-boat assaults on all neutral and belligerent shipping.

Count von Bernstorff conveyed this news officially only on January 31; it profoundly shocked Wilson, who only the week before
had addressed the Senate and the world in terms of peace without
victory and who still hoped to mediate a settlement without American involvement. Lansing describes his interview with the President
that evening, at which time Wilson was still hesitant to break relations and resisted his Secretary's advice to that end. By February 3,
however, he had made his decision. That afternoon he addressed
Congress announcing severance of diplomatic relations and Bernstorff received his passports. The logical conclusion of the policy of
"strict accountability" had been reached. Only a miracle could now

prevent an overt act which would precipitate hostilities. Attempting to work this miracle, Wilson asked Congress (February 26) for authority to arm American merchantmen in the hope of frightening the lightly armored U-boats into refraining from attack. The House acted promptly but in the Senate a "little group of wilful men," to use Wilson's irritatedly picturesque phrase, led by Robert M. La-Follette filibustered the bill to the end of the session on March 4. Undeterred by these obstructive tactics, Wilson secured advice allowing him to arm the ships, and before the end of March armed merchantmen were on the seas alert for the submarines which were now enemy in all but name.

Wilson's decision to arm merchantmen reflected in part the revulsion of feeling produced by the Zimmermann Note. This message, directed to Mexico by the German Foreign Minister, was intercepted by the British in mid-January, decoded, and transmitted to Wilson on February 24. Its proposals contained an understandable German attempt to discount the prospective American entry into the war by suggesting a German-Mexican alliance directed to a coöperative war effort which would result in Mexican reconquest of lost territory in southwestern United States. Its promise of "generous financial support" was somewhat fatuous in view of the strains to which the German economy was then subject; its suggestion that Mexico invite Japanese adherence was a red rag to Wilson, who at the moment was keenly sensitive to the mission of his country to preserve "white civilization." Its influence, though not decisive, was part of the cumulative forces driving American opinion rapidly into the Allied camp.

The dreaded overt act was not long delayed. Within six weeks the *Algonquin,* an unarmed American vessel, was sunk (March 12); six days later three more sinkings cost the first American lives of the new campaign. Wilson, now under severe pressure from his advisers and a public opinion moving rapidly toward war, delayed his commitment for some time; as late as March 19 Lansing left a conference still uncertain what his chief would decide. The unanimous advice of his Cabinet on the 20th was influential, and on the 21st Wilson called Congress for April 2. On that day he delivered his

war message, freighted with disappointment of his own highest
hopes for peace and with disaster for thousands of his own people.
The Senate adopted the ensuing war resolution on April 4 by 82
to 6; two days later the House concurred by 373 to 50, and the nation was at war.

In a later decade when the temper of the country was opposed
to foreign entanglements, intensive efforts were made by the Nye
Committee to demonstrate that tender concern for a vested interest
in Allied victory led American Big Business to push the government
into war. No evidence, however, has been offered to prove that such
influence was decisive and none whatever to show that it had any
weight with Wilson. War resulted because the country found itself
in an increasingly intolerable relationship with Germany, one made
intolerable largely by Wilson's position with regard to submarine
warfare assumed in February, 1915, which made loss of American
life practically inevitable. In assessing responsibility, however, attention should be called to the possible alternatives; here it would
seem that involvement could have been avoided only by (1) warning Americans off all belligerent ships; (2) denying her own shipping access to the war zones established by the belligerents; and
(3) being willing to swallow any injuries which might result despite
these precautions. Such a course was unthinkable to one as firmly
persuaded of American rights as was Wilson. Finally, the American
attack was launched, as it had been 105 years earlier, not against
that power which interfered most with American property, but
against that one which took American lives.

Wilson Plans a World Order

Once the die was cast the United States contributed unstintingly
but somewhat independently to the winning of the war. The flow
of credit started promptly and continued liberally, reaching a total
of over seven billions before hostilities ceased, and piling up debts
which bred postwar ill feeling. The flow of man power, at first a
trickle and then a stream which carried two million troops to Europe, created more immediate friction over the question of command. European leaders desired to infuse battle-weary British

armies with fresh American troops, under orders of battle-wise British generals; this subordination was stoutly and successfully resisted by Americans and independent command was maintained, except that all the armies ultimately passed in national units under the supreme authority of Marshal Ferdinand Foch as Generalissimo. In another direction, too, independent status was preserved, the United States never becoming an "ally" of the Allies, but remaining to the end of the war an "associate" in a group of "Allied and Associated Powers."

In some contrast with these gestures of independence was Wilson's willingness to fight the war without a clear and common understanding of its objectives. These were pretty completely spelled out among the Allies in a series of so-called "Secret Treaties" worked out during the preceding months and understood in broad outline by American leaders shortly after American entry.[10] They resulted from a series of deals among the nations, intent on remaking the map to their own advantage following the conclusion of hostilities. The adjective "secret" has attached to them an unduly sinister meaning, obscuring the fact that they resulted from perfectly normal maneuvers on the part of the belligerents to secure support and safeguard the future. The fact remains that many of their provisions countered Wilsonian principles and that Wilson took no steps either to harmonize them with those principles or to exact compensatory concessions. His naïveté in not exacting concessions has been criticized; his critics, however, exaggerate both his chances of securing them and the likelihood that the Powers would have adhered faithfully to promises made under such duress. More important is the fact of conflicting objectives, a divergence which emerged increasingly with the evolution of Wilson's war aims and which boded ill for the day when the two sets of objectives had to be compromised in a peace settlement.

Wilson's thinking about peace and world order developed against this background of military and fiscal coöperation. Attention has already been called to his statement of January 22, 1917, setting forth

---

[10] The essential provisions of the treaties are given by Seymour, *Am. Dipl. during the War*, pp. 264–265.

his conception of a proper basis for peace. Beyond his "peace with-out victory" heresy he then advanced such ideas as equality among the nations, recognition of the popular basis of government, assur-ance to all of access to the sea, a guaranteed freedom of the seas, and a reduction of naval armaments. His war address of April 2, 1917, contained the telling phrase, "The world must be made safe for democracy," and insisted upon security for "the rights of man-kind." Most detailed and influential, however, was the Fourteen Points address of January 8, 1918. This originated as a piece of counterpropaganda to offset the peace drive which culminated in the signing (March 3, 1918) of the Russo-German Treaty of Brest-Litovsk taking Russia out of the war. After the Revolution of No-vember, 1917, the Bolsheviks published the secret treaties with their evidence of imperialistic objectives, demanded an Allied exposition of war aims, and inaugurated a campaign designed to destroy the confidence of European labor in the integrity of these aims. When an Interallied Conference in session at Paris was unable to agree upon a formulation, House urged Wilson to make a unilateral state-ment to fill this diplomatic void.

Wilson drafted his address after consultation with House and study of material furnished by a group called The Inquiry already at work in New York gathering data for a future peace conference.[11] The first five points dealt with matters of world-wide import, de-manding an end of secret diplomacy, freedom of the seas, inter-national establishment of free trade, armament reduction, and ad-justment of claims between colonies and colonial powers; the next eight sought to heal particular sore spots in recent international relations, insisting that Russia be evacuated and invited back into the society of nations, that Belgium be restored intact, Alsace-

[11] This group, having only the most tenuous relations with the Department of State, which would normally conduct such activities, had been functioning since September, 1917, under House's aegis, directly supervised by his brother-in-law, Dr. Sidney E. Mezes, President of the College of the City of New York, and staffed by the youthful Walter Lippmann, Dr. Isaiah Bowman of the New York Geographi-cal Society, and Professor James T. Shotwell of Columbia and several other acade-micians. The latter's *At the Paris Peace Conference*, Macmillan, 1937, describes the Inquiry's work, justifies this use of "crisis organizations" in the wartime emergency, and tells how several of its members were added to the peace delegation and ma-neuvered into positions of considerable importance in the Paris negotiations.

Lorraine returned to France, Italian frontiers rectified along lines
of nationality, autonomy accorded the peoples of Austria-Hungary,
that Balkan boundaries be rearranged along national lines and
Serbia given access to the sea, that Turkish minorities be protected and the Dardanelles opened, and that Poland be made independent. These careful interpretations of Wilson's peace ideals
contained at least a tacit warning to the European Allies that modification of their peace designs must precede any settlement of the
war. Wilson reiterated this warning in a speech to Congress (February 11) in which he insisted that "peoples and provinces are not
to be bartered about from sovereignty to sovereignty as if they were
mere chattels and pawns in a game, even the great game, now forever discredited, of the balance of power . . ." and in subsequent
pronouncements on July 4 and September 11.

The President had begun to think also about a world order to
replace the chaos which produced repeated wars.[12] Starting out as
a convinced isolationist who believed that his country could and
must remain aloof from European troubles, he soon began to play
with the idea of international organization which had intrigued the
speculatively minded for generations.[13] On May 27, 1916, he first
publicly came out for a League of Nations in an address before the
League to Enforce Peace (where, incidentally, the same idea was
supported by Henry Cabot Lodge). Thenceforth the League idea
runs through practically all of the landmark addresses surveyed
above, particularly the war-aims address of January 22, 1917, the
final head of the Fourteen Points speech, and the Mount Vernon address of July 4, 1918. British and French publicists were also elabo-
rating plans during 1918, so that all hands were becoming condi-
tioned to the idea.

The military position of the Central Powers deteriorated progres-

[12] Wilsonian thinking on a League of Nations is covered in C. A. Berdahl, *The
Policy of the United States with Respect to the League of Nations,* Librairie Kundig,
1932, and D. F. Fleming, *The United States and the League of Nations, 1918–1920,*
Putnam, 1932.

[13] His brother-in-law, Dr. Stockton Axson, suggests that he was thinking of a
league as early as the autumn of 1914. See New York *Times,* February 4, 1924. Professor Seymour, *Am. Dipl. during the War,* pp. 259–260, 397–398, credits Sir Edward
Grey with helping to shape his thinking in this quarter.

sively in the summer and autumn of 1918; this afforded Wilson an
opportunity to forward his Grand Design and induced the first clash
between Wilsonian idealism and Allied realism. In a surprise move
the German Government, pressed by its military leaders who foresaw imminent collapse and thought Wilson might be easier to deal
with than enemies of longer standing and greater acumen, asked
him (on October 6, followed by Austria on the 7th) for an armistice
preliminary to a conference which would use the Fourteen Points
as the basis of peace. Wilson spent a month in negotiation, refusing
to deal with a German Government unless he was satisfied that it
represented the German people; this gentle hint contributed greatly
to the abdication and flight (November 9) of Kaiser Wilhelm II
and the organization of a republican government. He put off the
Austrians likewise, indicating that since the United States had recognized the Czechoslovak Republic, claiming territory previously
part of Austria-Hungary, that still somewhat hypothetical entity
would have to speak for itself. While he pursued this tactic of delay
the Habsburg Empire collapsed and signed (November 3) an armistice with Italy, putting itself outside the pale of the Fourteen
Points. Eventually Wilson transmitted the German request to the
Allies for consideration of the military authorities as to whether the
time was ripe for an armistice; only when Foch agreed did the Armistice of November 11, 1918, become effective.

The German move, transmuting the Fourteen Points from mere
counterpropaganda to a possible basis of actual negotiation, precipitated the first conflict between Wilson's point of view and that
of the European leaders. This developed behind the scenes in late
October when representatives of the Allied and Associated Powers
met to consider the German proposal.[14] The British pointed out that
approval of the proposed armistice carried tacit acceptance of the
Wilson program; both French and British denied that they had ever
been asked to accept the Fourteen Points, and David Lloyd George,
the British Prime Minister, promptly entered an objection against
accepting Point 2, the freedom of the seas, "under any condi-

---

[14] Seymour, *Am. Dipl. during the War*, pp. 373–393, covers this secret conflict in
detail; it is based on the papers of Colonel House, who represented the United States.

tions. . . ." During the succeeding discussion House apparently threatened to raise the question of further American support in the war unless the British softened their attitude; ultimately a compromise was worked out whereby the Allies accepted the Fourteen Points as the basis of peace, with two exceptions: (1) they "must . . . reserve to themselves complete freedom" to discuss freedom of the seas in the peace conference; and (2) they demanded, under pressure by the French Premier, Georges Clemenceau, that German restoration of evacuated territory include reparation for war damages to the civilian population. Thus in the first clash between the old diplomacy and the new the latter had won a qualified victory, but at some cost; the issue of principle had been exposed and a compromise had resulted—an earnest of further clashes, and other compromises.

Wilson Builds a World Order

Wilson's decision to participate personally in making the peace (taken against the advice of both House and Lansing) removed him from the pedestal on which his winged phrases and the world opinion of the common man had placed him and tended to reduce him to the level of a fellow negotiator. It also relegated his American fellow delegates, whoever they might be, to relatively minor roles and imposed the prime burden of the peace upon his own shoulders.[15] His Secretary of State was the only lawyer on the dele-

---

[15] In addition to volumes 7 and 8 of Baker's *Wilson*, Nevins' *Henry White*, and Perkins' *America and Two Wars*, already cited, the following titles cover the principal personal and scholarly approaches to the history of the Peace Conference: T. A. Bailey, *Woodrow Wilson and the Lost Peace*, Macmillan, 1944; Ray Stannard Baker, *Woodrow Wilson and World Settlement*, Doubleday, Page, 1922, 3 vols.; R. C. Binkley, "New Light on the Paris Peace Conference," *Political Science Quarterly*, vol. 46 (1931), pp. 335–361, 509–547; and "Ten Years of Peace Conference History," *Journal of Modern History*, vol. 1 (1929), pp. 607–629; Paul Birdsall, "The Second Decade of Peace Conference History," *Ibid.*, vol. 11 (1939), pp. 362–378; and *Versailles Twenty Years After*, Reynal and Hitchcock, 1941; C. H. Haskins and R. H. Lord, *Some Problems of the Peace Conference*, Harvard University Press, 1920; E. M. House and Charles Seymour, *What Really Happened at Paris: The Story of the Peace Conference, 1918–1919*, Scribner, 1921; Robert Lansing, *The Peace Negotiations: A Personal Narrative*, Houghton Mifflin, 1921; David Lloyd George, *Memoirs of the Peace Conference*, Yale University Press, 1939, 2 vols.; David Hunter Miller, *The Drafting of the Covenant*, Putnam, 1928; Harold Nicolson, *Peacemaking, 1919*, Houghton Mifflin, 1933; F. L. Paxson, *American Democracy and the World War:*

gation; before the Conference opened Wilson let it be known that
he did not intend that lawyers should draft the peace, a hint which
removed Lansing to the side lines. House's relations with Wilson,
close at the outset, deteriorated after the President's return to Paris
in March due to the Colonel's overwillingness to compromise, and
became even more formal after the Italian crisis in April. General
Tasker H. Bliss, an able and experienced negotiator, never reached
the inner circle. Henry White, the lone Republican, a schooled diplomat, had been out of harness since the Taft Administration. Selected in preference to Republican Senators and elder statesmen,
he had never been a political figure, and only a political figure could
have satisfied the Republicans. His chief role, as he himself conceived and tried to play it, was to be an instrument of enlighten-
ment and possible adjustment of differences between Wilson and
his own long-time Republican friends, particularly Henry Cabot
Lodge. Wilson, carrying to Paris powerful convictions which in his
mind became increasingly identified with abstract principles of
right, relied upon this group and its subordinate experts for information, but not for advice; the Peace Conference story, indeed,
from the American standpoint, is largely a chapter of Wilsonian
biography.

The President carried heavy burdens to the Conference. There
was first the fundamental clash between his own objectives, among
which the League of Nations loomed increasingly large, and those
of his fellow statesmen to whom peace and division of spoils were
more important. The inevitable postwar reaction which Ray Stannard Baker calls "the Slump in Idealism" had set in prior to his
arrival, and while the plain people awaited his appearance with
bated breath, Lloyd George ran for reëlection in December upon
a demagogic platform proposing to hang the Kaiser and exact the
full cost of the war from Germany; and Clemenceau, who with
Lloyd George had accepted most of the Fourteen Points, was affirming to the French Deputies his continued belief in the old sys-

Postwar Years, Normalcy, 1918–1923, University of California Press, 1948, pp. 1–19,
40–68, 105–124; Bernadotte E. Schmitt, "The Peace Conference of 1919," *Journal of
Modern History*, vol. 16 (1944), pp. 49–59; Edith Bolling Wilson, *My Memoir*,
Bobbs-Merrill, 1939.

tem of alliances. Wilson's claim to a full measure of primacy among his Paris colleagues was further weakened by a defection in the domestic ranks which left informed Europeans skeptical as to his political power and so more willing to oppose his aims. Despite a presidential appeal (issued October 25, 1918, in the face of contrary advice), the voters elected a Republican Congress; the Republican margin of two votes in the Senate, although narrow, enabled the party to organize the committees on a Republican base.[16] Though this reversal was probably the normal culmination of a swing back to the Republican column which had been developing as early as 1914, it released forces long repressed. Not only did the party majority shift across the Senatorial aisle, but the wartime truce on politics was ended and a Congress which had long been subjected to the excess of power which war transfers to the Executive branch was free to redress the balance in its own favor. Europeans made more of this change than did Wilson himself; indeed, its influence toward compromise in the peace negotiations was hardly less significant than its repercussions on the treaty fight which followed.

It should be noted at the outset that Wilson failed to realize all his objectives, as does any statesman who sets his sights at a Wilsonian elevation. Coming to the Peace Table with the determination of "making the League of Nations the center of the whole programme and letting everything revolve around that," he immediately became vulnerable to the maneuvers of those whose motives were more worldly and whose objectives were more immediate; he was speedily forced to continue and broaden the process of compromise over the Fourteen Points initiated in October as those with a particular ax to grind demanded concessions under threat of disrupting the Conference. Again and again Wilson gave an inch in order to advance a yard toward his main goal; even in yielding he kept his eye steady on the principles he was forced to compromise. Perhaps he should be judged finally on what he did not yield;

---

[16] On the election see Selig Adler, "The Congressional Election of 1918," *South Atlantic Quarterly,* vol. 36 (1937), pp. 447–465; Fleming, *U.S. and League of Nations,* pp. 26–53; Holt, *Treaties Defeated by Sen.,* pp. 249–254; and C. P. Howland, *Survey of American Foreign Relations, 1928,* Yale University Press, 1928, pp. 239–246.

against this yardstick the Wilson drawn by recent scholarship tends
to gain in stature what he loses in immediate success. Nor should
the failure of his League under stress of resurgent imperialism, refusal of his own country to join it, and its own structural deficiencies,
detract from its importance as a milestone on the slow road to international order.

The Conference, from Wilson's standpoint, divides logically as
well as chronologically into two parts.[17] The first, ending with pres-
entation of the Draft Covenant of the League to the Plenary Session
of February 14, was one of constructive effort to formulate the details of his Grand Design; the second, opened by his return to the
fray in mid-March after a visit to the expiring Congress in Washington, was one of constant friction and repeated compromise over the
detailed peace settlement, in which his colleagues exacted their respective concessions in return for the League and for certain amendments to its Covenant demanded by Wilson's domestic critics. The
problem of agenda brought Wilson immediately face to face with
his adversaries. A French draft of November 29 suggested that the
chief victors meet in secret, dictate preliminary peace terms for
ratification by the full membership, and then, and only then, turn to
the problem of international organization.[18] No sooner had Wilson
arrived on French soil than he announced, as indicated above, that

---

[17] F. S. Marston, *The Peace Conference of 1919: Organization and Procedure*, Oxford University Press, 1944, is an excellent descriptive critique of the Conference.
The Conference organization presents a pattern of highly concentrated power. The
chief delegates (Prime Minister and Foreign Secretary in each case except the
United States) of the five Great Powers (Britain, France, Italy, Japan, and the United
States) constituted themselves the Council of Ten and possessed the real control
of affairs. Even this concentration proved insufficient during the later and more
controversial stages and power finally gravitated into the hands of Lloyd George,
Clemenceau, and Wilson. For window dressing a series of six Plenary Sessions
permitted delegates of all the thirty-two governments (twenty-seven states and
five British dominions) aligned against the enemy to take final, formal action ratifying
decisions arrived at elsewhere; at other times the minor powers were forced to present their claims to committees, a situation not productive of the most cordial atmosphere. The raw material of the Conference was prepared and most decisions
made for its leaders by fifty-odd commissions, in turn served by numerous expertly
staffed committees. Scanty information on the multifarious activities of these bodies
seeped out to the public; despite American efforts the tradition of strictly secret
diplomacy remained in effect and the Conference failed to secure a good "press."
[18] It is interesting to note that this document proposed to scrap the secret treaties,
which were of slight value to France. Since it postponed the League of Nations,
Wilson did not dignify it with a reply.

the League must be central; when Clemenceau urged the French proposal Wilson told the world, in a speech at Manchester, that only a League of Nations could buy American coöperation in peace discussions. He gained his way, partly by weight of personality and partly, perhaps, by an ill-considered move whereby he conceded Italy a boundary at the Brenner Pass, giving her 200,000 Germans in violation of his own cardinal principle of self-determination. On January 25 the Second Plenary Session voted to include the League in the peace settlement. A Commission, with Wilson presiding, hammered out (beginning on February 3) a draft Covenant which was presented to the Plenary Session of February 14.

Such rapid action was necessarily based on groundwork long preparing. Wilson's attention, as already indicated, had long been directed toward a league. French and British sources had also announced in 1918 proposals for bodies with limited scope and restricted membership which fell far short of Wilson's design. In the summer, House and David Hunter Miller reworked the Phillimore (British) Report for Wilson, who used their draft in his own preliminary formulation, which strengthened the proposed league in several respects. Two more drafts were framed at Paris, incorporating ideas of the South African statesman General Jan Christiaan Smuts, and a later, official, British draft prepared by Lord Robert Cecil. The document finally presented to the League of Nations Commission on February 3 was the work of Miller and Sir Cecil Hurst. In ten strenuous sessions the Commission advanced the work to a point where Wilson could read a tentative Covenant before the full Conference just prior to embarking for the States. At this moment, that of his greatest power, he could picture himself triumphing over his nationalistic adversaries and bringing home the foundations of a new world order. From the time, however, that his transatlantic ferry, the *George Washington*, docked at Boston, the President was to begin paying the price for his triumph.

He had asked Congress not to discuss the League until he could have a chance to state his case, and had evidently intended to withhold comment until reaching Washington. On the high seas, however, he was persuaded that he should speak at Boston, where the

Washington docked. This was a double insult to the easily wounded
Lodge, who felt himself silenced by the President's admonition and
took as a personal affront Wilson's long-planned and quite innocent
return through Lodge's home town. Others were less scrupulous,
however, and before Wilson landed, William E. Borah of Idaho and
James A. Reed of Missouri had unlimbered the guns of opposition.
The tension was not lessened by a historic dinner meeting between
the President and the members of the House and Senate committees
dealing with foreign relations. Here Wilson subjected himself to a
two-hour grilling which did little to clear the air; friends found his
replies reassuring and enemies unenlightening or positively confus-
ing; Senator Frank B. Brandegee of Connecticut is said to have compared the occasion to Alice's Wonderland meeting with the White
Rabbit and the Mad Hatter.

Definitely threatening, however, was the Senatorial Round Robin
of March 4, 1919. While the lame-duck Democratic Congress was
being filibustered to death (necessitating a special session to pass
appropriation bills before the fiscal year ended on June 30 and thus
speeding the day when the Republicans could organize the Senate
in opposition to the President), Lodge and Brandegee proposed and
Philander C. Knox drafted a resolution ultimately signed by thirty-
seven Republican Senators and two Senators-elect. It rejected the
League in its existing form, and opposed consideration of any league
until after the final peace settlement. Introduced in the hectic closing hours, it failed to secure the unanimous consent necessary to its
consideration, but served its purpose: Wilson, and the world, were
put on notice that a league-embracing treaty would receive short
shrift in the Senate. Whatever the world thought, Wilson was confident. Flanked on the platform by the bulky figure of William
Howard Taft, just in from a pro-League tour of thirty states and
nearly two hundred speeches, Wilson spoke at the Metropolitan
Opera House on the evening of March 4 and breathed defiance at
his foes. Said he, boldly if not too judiciously: "when that treaty
comes back, gentlemen on this side will find the covenant not only
in it, but so many threads of the treaty tied to the covenant that you
cannot dissect the covenant from the treaty without destroying the

whole vital structure. The structure of peace will not be vital without
the League of Nations, and no man is going to bring back a cadaver
with him."

The League Costs Wilson Dear

During Wilson's absence Lloyd George also spent time on domestic
duties and Clemenceau was recuperating from a would-be assassin's
attack. House and Sir Arthur Balfour moved matters rapidly through
the various commissions—too rapidly, thought Wilson, when he
learned in an initial interview with House (immediately upon his
arrival at Brest, March 13) the extent to which progress had been
hastened by what the President considered compromises of principle dangerous to the future of the League. No sooner had he
reached Paris, moreover, than Marshal Foch handed him (March
14) a memorandum drawing a bill of particulars designed to protect
France from another 1914. It included heavy but undefined reparations for German destruction of French property and either an
Allied occupation of Germany to the Rhine or the creation of a
Rhineland buffer state. Its brusque surrender of Germans to foreign
control roused Wilson's immediate ire by violating the principle of
self-determination; it showed him only too clearly that the honey-
moon was well over. The remainder of March and the early part of
April witnessed a titanic struggle between Wilson and the French;
at its height he took ill (April 3) and for some days Clemenceau,
Lloyd George, and Vittorio Orlando of Italy sat in an adjacent room
while House served as messenger, relaying French demands and
Wilson's ringing if somewhat feeble refusals. After four days of this,
Wilson bluffed the French by ordering the *George Washington* to
Europe, presumably to take him home unless a compromise could
be evolved.

The bluff worked, but only at the cost of some of Wilson's principles. Successive compromises emerged during the next week; these
included French military occupation of the Rhine's left bank for as
long as fifteen years, depending upon German faithfulness in fulfilling her treaty pledges; demilitarization of a 50-kilometer zone
east of the Rhine; French occupation of the Saar Valley's rich coal

resources until 1935, when a plebiscite should determine its disposition; and a vast addition to the reparations total by the inclusion of
uncalculated and perhaps incalculable payments of military separation and pension allowances. In return for this terminable occupation of enemy territory Wilson agreed to a treaty binding Britain
and the United States to defend France against a future unprovoked
German attack.[19] The Conference had been held together and the
League idea was therefore kept intact, but the Franco-American
friction had generated much heat and some light—light enabling
Italy and Japan to see their own chances to exploit Wilsonian principles to their own advantage.

Both were active before the French crisis was resolved, with the
Italians, a bit in the van, creating a crisis which endangered the
success of the Conference, and thus of Wilson's program, without
solving the specific problem involved. The Treaty of London (April
26, 1915) had purchased Italian defection from the Triple Alliance
by promising Italy a strategic boundary running to the Brenner Pass
and including some 200,000 Germans, as well as territory on the head
and eastern shore of the Adriatic which Italy considered as rightfully Italian. The treaty had specified that the port of Fiume should
belong to Croatia, then part of Hungary but at the war's end part of
the succession state of Jugoslavia, with which Fiume had close
ethnic ties. Encouraged by the unexpectedly complete collapse of
their Austro-Hungarian enemies and, perhaps, by Wilson's injudi-
cious acceptance of the Brenner Pass line, noted above, the Italians
expanded their demands to include Fiume. Committed to the Brenner line, Wilson resolved to prevent a further injustice and opposed
their claims.[20] On April 19 Wilson told the American delegation that
he would never assent to Italian claims to Fiume and Dalmatia; the
same day he repeated his statement to Orlando and his colleague,

---

[19] The Senate looked with a jaundiced eye at this "entanglement," which found
permanent sanctuary in the pigeonholes of the Foreign Relations Committee.

[20] Wilson's slip on the Brenner Pass line had been made at an early date, before
the experts had clarified this violation of his own principle of self-determination. The
Italian episode was complicated by the fact that House and Mezes tried, contrary
to the opinion of the experts, to resolve the Adriatic question in a manner more
favorable to Italy. It seems apparent that House's course at this juncture weakened
Wilson's confidence in him.

Baron Sidney Sonnino. When they proved adamant in their demands for territorial satisfactions, Wilson appealed directly to the Italian people (April 23) to desert their leaders in favor of a peace of justice. The next day the Italians left for home in ostensibly high, but somewhat synthetic, dudgeon, to be received with great acclaim. This gravely threatened Wilson's hopes, as the German delegation began arriving on April 25th and, with the Italians absent, a final peace would be difficult to achieve; they might, moreover, stay out of the League. Negotiations with the Japanese and the Germans proceeded without the Italians, and they returned on May 6, still without Fiume.[21] Again the Conference had been preserved, and this time Wilson's firm stand had helped to avert what would have been a severe injustice to Jugoslavia.

Japan sought to enhance her prestige by committing the Conference to the principle of racial equality; she desired also international recognition of her succession to German rights in Shantung, which she had occupied during the war. Since Wilson had a hand in her failure to secure the first of these, she was in a good position to force his hand on the second, and did so with a delicate sense of timing which must have added to his anguish in having to desert his principles. The League of Nations Commission in February rejected Japan's move to obtain a strong resolution on race equality. Backstage negotiations in March found Premier William Hughes of Australia, whose constituents had no stomach for racial equality, threatening to air the matter on the floor of a plenary session and, moreover, to appeal to the hardly latent prejudice of western Americans should Japan press her point. Japan returned to the charge at the final meeting of the League of Nations Commission, held on April 11 while the French controversy was still in process of liquidation, with a proposal much milder than the one rejected earlier. Forcing this to a vote, she gained the support of all but the British and American delegates. Wilson, in the chair, ruled that since unanimity had not been achieved, the motion was lost.

Four days after this second defeat Japan was asked to agree that

---

[21] It passed under Italian control in 1924 after four years of nominal independence, under the Italo-Jugoslav Treaty of Rapallo (1920).

German rights in Shantung be assigned to the Allied and Associated Powers rather than to herself or to China, and promptly refused. Her wartime occupation of the Province, of course a gross violation of Wilsonian principles, had been sanctioned by secret agreements of 1917 with the European Allies, by agreements of May 25, 1915, and September 24, 1918, with China, and, at least in a left-handed fashion, by the Lansing-Ishii Agreement with the United States. A vigorous argument over Shantung thenceforth played a strident obbligato to the Italian crisis; on April 24, the day the Italians left the Conference, a Japanese note demanded an early settlement. A plenary session was scheduled for the afternoon of the 28th to accept the League Covenant in final form; before it convened a Japanese delegate suggested delicately but firmly to Balfour that, having been asked to accept the League of Nations without racial equality, his group would be in trouble if it went home without Shantung. He threatened, moreover, to raise the race question on the floor of the plenary session and, ultimately, to withhold Japanese signature from the treaty unless he had his way with Shantung. Wilson was bedeviled by other Japanese problems, such as Yap and Siberia; Italy was out of the Conference and might be out of the League; the Germans were growing restive for a clarification of their position. Even so, it was only after a tug of war with Balfour on the morning of the 28th that he sacrificed his principles and surrendered to the Japanese demands. Two more days of argument gained a promise of eventual return of sovereignty over Shantung to China, with Japan retaining only her economic concessions in the Province. Wilson resignedly told Ray Stannard Baker that "the settlement was the best that could be had out of a dirty past."

Paralleling these increasingly acute conflicts Wilson had been compelled to come, hat in hand, and ask his European colleagues to accept amendments to the draft Covenant designed to facilitate favorable action of his own Senate. Such pro-League Republicans as Taft and A. Lawrence Lowell had suggested several amendments which they hoped might improve the Covenant and tend to neutralize the Round Robin of March 4. He secured their adoption at the cost of considerable effort and some reasonably undignified trading, and the attendant circumstances certainly did not help to maintain his position in the conflicts just recounted with France, Italy, and Japan. Among the changes secured was one allowing the United States to avoid participating in the mandate system established to administer the colonies of former enemies; another was designed to prevent the League from interfering with such matters as tariffs and immigration; a third specified that a nation might withdraw from the League upon two years' notice; the most important and hotly debated, and one of the most ambiguous, excepted "regional understandings like the Monroe Doctrine" from the League's jurisdiction.

By May 7 the Allied and Associated Powers were ready to present their completed terms to the Germans, who, denied the opportunity to negotiate, perforce accepted the victors' peace. The vanquished objected vainly to Article 231 carrying an inference of German responsibility for causing the war; objected vainly too, to the discrepancy between the Fourteen Points, on the basis of which they had surrendered, and what they considered the baldly imperialistic terms they were now ordered to accept. Given no choice, they signed, June 28, at a ceremony staged dramatically in the Hall of Mirrors at Versailles where forty-eight years earlier Bismarck had brought the German Empire to birth. Wilson returned home forthwith, bringing a treaty which in many provisions bore the marks of his failure to achieve his unattainable ideals; it bore, however, the League of Nations for the achievement of which those ideals had been sacrificed. When he presented it to the Senate on July 10 the issue turned on whether that body would accept his handiwork.

Victory Turns to Tragedy

There ensued a drama of considerable complexity in which Wilson was less fortunate than Lincoln, his Republican, and Franklin D. Roosevelt, his Democratic, counterparts, in that he lived to participate in its final act; for him it turned to bitter tragedy instead of legendary martyrdom.[22] Involved in the drama were the President

---

[22] In addition to several of the titles already cited in this chapter, the following contribute to the story of the treaty fight: T. A. Bailey, *Woodrow Wilson and the Great Betrayal*, Macmillan, 1945; H. M. Darling, "Who Kept the United States out of the League of Nations?" *Canadian Historical Review*, vol. 10 (1929), pp. 196–211;

himself, at no time as able physically as at Paris and almost completely off stage at crucial moments, less willing to compromise than earlier and toward the end stubbornly inflexible in his insistence upon an unamended Covenant. There was, too, Henry Cabot Lodge, a man of long-sustained and valiant Republican partisanship and a firm advocate of redressing the intragovernmental balance to exalt the Senate at Presidential expense. He had, too, a weather eye on the election of 1920 and an obligation to keep his party intact against such a split as that of 1912, which might continue Democratic—even Wilsonian—ascendancy. His real attitude toward the treaty and its embodied League has been subject of great speculation; scholars tend to doubt the sincerity of his consistent protestations that he wanted the League, with reservations. Certainly, if the League failed because of Democratic refusal to accept reservations, the political onus in 1920 would not rest upon Republicans. Whatever Lodge's motives, his skill was consummate; in the Senate for nearly a generation, he knew men and methods in and out so that no vestige of parliamentary advantage was ever lost to his side. Wilson was less well served. The minority leader, Thomas S. Martin of Virginia, being ill, active command fell upon Gilbert M. Hitchcock of Nebraska. Of only modest ability, his status in the party was not clarified until Martin died during the course of the debate. Add to uncertain status and modest ability his lack of experience as compared with the case-hardened Lodge, and the difficulty of his lot, and of his party's, can be appreciated.

Very much in the forefront in the drama, too, were political factors. Attention has already been called to the imminence of a contest for power within the government. War always exalts the executive, but no Congress has yet enjoyed its wartime subordination; no postwar period but has witnessed Congressional attempts to cut the President down to size, particularly if the two differ in political faith. It is clear, too, that the year 1920 loomed large over the

---

G. A. Finch, "The Treaty of Peace with Germany in the United States Senate," *American Journal of International Law*, vol. 14 (1920), pp. 155–206; Fleming, *Treaty Veto*, pp. 124–168; Holt, *op. cit.*, pp. 249–308; Karl Schriftgiesser, *The Gentleman from Massachusetts: Henry Cabot Lodge*, Little, Brown, 1944, pp. 331–352.

League of Nations debate. If treaty and League were accepted, Democratic self-confidence would know no bounds; Wilson might even be tempted to defy the third-term tradition, and might succeed. To prevent this, Republican solidarity must be maintained, even at the expense of catering to a group like the senatorial irreconcilables who, if they felt themselves ill-treated, could at any time bolt the party and contribute to another 1912. Enough has now perhaps been said to indicate that the verdict for the failure of the League of Nations in 1919–1920 is not an easy one to render, and that laying the responsibility on any one pair of shoulders smacks of oversimplification.

Democratic overconfidence, time, and propaganda worked for the Republicans. None of his domestic informants, Democratic or Republican, had prepared Wilson for the fight he was to encounter; indeed, his somewhat arrogant reply to a reporter who asked whether the treaty could be ratified after Senate reservations was justified on the evidence at hand: "I do not think hypothetical questions are concerned. *The Senate is going to ratify the treaty.*"[23] Public opinion, so far as it could be gauged, was favorable. (Opponents so exalted as Lodge and Borah agreed in April that the Senate reflected this to such an extent as to make an early vote on the treaty inevitably successful.) No peace treaty had yet been defeated; much less would the Senate dare to destroy one where peace and international security were so intimately meshed as in this one. Refusal, finally, would present the unthinkable alternative of falling behind the international parade and embarking upon separate peace negotiations.

Accepting the favorable temper of public opinion, Lodge and Borah, leader of the irreconcilable group which refused the League under any circumstances, contrived a program which would occupy considerable time until measures could be taken to work upon public opinion. The opposition held a trump card in the organization of the new Senate Committee on Foreign Relations. As constituted by Chairman Lodge when Congress assembled in special session on

---

[23] Quoted in Bailey, *Wilson and the Betrayal,* p. 9; the following pages are chiefly based on this excellent monograph.

May 19, 1919, six of the ten Republican members were irreconcilables, thus able to dominate the majority. By controlling the majority
they were able to hold the treaty in the Committee until September
10. The first step in the delaying process involved spending two
weeks in reading the 264-page document; six more weeks (July 31–
September 5) were devoted to public hearings which piled up 1267
pages of testimony, the bulk of it by opponents, and enough of it
definitely prejudiced to hurt the cause of ratification. Meantime a
war chest was sought, and found, through the efforts of Knox and
George Harvey, who persuaded Henry C. Frick and Andrew Mellon
to grease the wheels of propaganda, which soon began to turn with
rhythmic regularity. Senatorial attacks on the League continued
through the hot summer weeks while the Committee sat on the
treaty.[24] Much invective and some solid argument went into the
record, with the advantage in volume and leadership on the side of
the opposition.

Lodge meantime secured another advantage. At his request Wilson entertained the Committee at a luncheon conference on August
19. The President opened the proceedings by reading a prepared
statement asserting that the only obstacle to the ratification of the
treaty was doubt "with regard to the meaning and implication of
certain articles of the covenant of the league of nations; and I must
frankly say that I am unable to understand why such doubts should
be entertained." Three long hours of give-and-take followed this
somewhat inauspicious opening, during which Wilson asserted that
he would accept purely interpretative reservations, not embedded in
the resolution of consent to ratification, and not requiring consent of
other parties to the treaty. Here he seemed to contradict himself,
because on the 15th he had told Hitchcock to tell Senatorial Democrats to oppose reservations. Moreover, he made an obviously in-
correct statement in reply to queries of Hiram Johnson of California
as to his knowledge of the secret treaties among the Allies, denying
categorically that he knew anything of these agreements until he

---

[24] Though the terms "League" and "treaty" appear in the account, the reader
should note that it was the League which was the object of attack; singularly little
fault was found with the treaty, save as it carried the Covenant.

arrived at Paris. His inaccuracy has been proved abundantly; an adequate explanation is still lacking.

With time and propaganda obviously running against him late in August, the President decided to carry out an idea long revolving in his mind and take his case to the people, particularly the westerners who had elected him in 1916 and who were about to be exposed to opposition arguments. In the face of adverse medical and political advice he undertook a 9500-mile tour, in the course of which he delivered 37 speeches averaging 8000 words each in twenty-nine cities over eighteen days. On the return circle, with only a few more addresses to deliver, he broke down at Pueblo, Colorado, on September 25 and was rushed back to Washington. After a few days of discomfort he suffered a stroke on October 2 which completely incapacitated him for some time and kept him more or less out of touch with public affairs until the end of his term, during a period when his leadership was most needed to shepherd his minority resources.

During Wilson's absence Lodge reported the treaty on September 10 and it became the regular order of business five days later, opening eleven weeks of debate in open executive session. Beginning with September 27 the best part of a month was devoted to debating and voting on a series of forty-eight amendments recommended by the Committee. Most of these proposed to eliminate American participation in various bodies carrying out League functions; all were defeated by a combination of Democratic and mild-reservationist Republican votes. On November 6 Lodge reported a resolution of ratification, accompanied by fourteen reservations, many of them designed to replace defeated amendments and all professedly intended to protect American interests allegedly endangered by the League Covenant.

Indulging the historian's prerogative of being wise after the event, it is apparent that at this point Wilson would have done well to exercise the same inclination toward compromise which had enabled him to bring the League back from Paris. Such a policy would have permitted the Democrats and mild-reservationist Republicans to agree on the Lodge reservations, or some modification of them, continuing the alliance formed in voting down the Committee amendments. This would have recognized the existing temper of the Republican majority to demand some safeguards as the price of abandoning traditional American isolation; it might have saved the League. The Lodge reservations, it now seems apparent, would have destroyed neither League Covenant nor treaty of peace; the League could have functioned efficiently, although American obligations under the Covenant would have been somewhat circumscribed.

It becomes useful at this point, then, to examine Wilson's attitude toward reservations. Two days after returning from Europe he dictated his first statement: "The President is open-minded as to every proposition of reasonable interpretation, but will not consent to any proposition that we scuttle." This certainly indicated willingness to accept interpretative reservations, and encouraged the Democrats and mild-reservationist Republicans, who honestly wanted a treaty, to get together. By mid-August, however, Wilson was telling Hitchcock to tell party members to oppose reservations. That he had not completely hardened against them, however, is indicated by the fact that just before leaving on his ill-fated western journey he gave Hitchcock his own draft of four reservations which he would accept if necessary; they were only slightly less limiting than the corresponding Lodge reservations, and bordered closely on the mild-reservationist position of the time. They were, however, under no circumstances to be attached to the resolution of ratification. The events of the intervening months turned him thoroughly against the idea, and when it came time to vote on the Lodge reservations which, it will be remembered, were part of the resolution of ratification, he told his followers in a letter of November 18 that in his judgment the Lodge resolution "does not provide for ratification but, rather, for the nullification of the treaty. I sincerely hope that the friends and supporters of the treaty will vote against the Lodge resolution of ratification. I understand that the door will probably then be open for a genuine resolution of ratification."

Under the Wilsonian injunction forty-two of his loyal followers broke with their previous mild-reservationist allies and joined (November 19) with thirteen irreconcilable Republicans to defeat the

Lodge reservations. The affirmative votes were thirty-five mild-reservationists and four truant Democrats. Defeat of the reservations carried the treaty to disaster also. Had the Democrats been permitted to support moderate reservations, the League and treaty would have been accepted on this ballot by a margin of 81 to 13. Another vote, on unconditional acceptance, was defeated, 38 (1 Republican and 37 Democrats) to 53 (7 Democrats and 46 Republicans). Thus it was apparent that the treaty could not go through with or without the Lodge reservations. This looked like the deadlock for which Wilson seems to have been working, in the hope that it might be followed by ratification with milder, Democratic, reservations; a prompt adjournment of the special session ended this possibility. It can thus be argued that the President himself, by insisting upon party regularity in opposition to Republican reservations, contributed largely to the defeat of his own most cherished dream.

The hope of compromise died hard, however, and after the new session of Congress had convened renewed attempts were made to secure favorable action. A bipartisan group worked during January, 1920, including Lodge in its membership and apparently approaching an agreement whereby Democrats and mild-reservation Republicans would join to pass the treaty. At this point the irreconcilables threatened Lodge with a bolt from the party unless he stuck to his original reservations, whereupon he gave in and the bipartisan effort was soon abandoned. On February 9 the Senate voted to reconsider the treaty and referred it back to the Committee, which reported it the following day with the Lodge reservations intact. Wilson had meantime (January 8) told his party, through a message to the Jackson Day Dinner, that interpretations must accompany, not be part of, the act of ratification—the treaty must not be rewritten in the Senate. Again on March 8, during the debate, he reiterated his opposition to the Lodge position, and on March 19 the treaty with the Lodge reservations was again defeated, 49 to 35, with 21 Democrats this time deserting Wilsonian leadership to join the Republican reservationists. Had seven of the loyal Democrats voted with the bolters the treaty would have been adopted; again

Democratic loyalty had brought defeat. This threw the treaty back to Wilson and left the United States at war; in May, 1920, Congress attempted to declare the war at an end by joint resolution, only to have its action vetoed by Wilson, who by this time placed his faith in party victory in the election campaign then in the offing. The election of Harding was anything but the "great and solemn referendum" which Wilson had sought, and Harding himself refused to take responsibility; Congress again took action and on July 2, 1921, declared the war at an end by joint resolution (implemented further by treaties with Germany and Austria the following month), reserving to the United States all rights secured by the war or the Armistice, rights which she might have obtained under a ratified Versailles Treaty. Neither Lodge's maneuvering nor Wilson's stubbornness had brought great credit to either party.

17 A Decade of Contradictions, 1922-1933

HAVING REFUSED TO TAKE THE FULL PLUNGE INTO INTERnationalism via the League of Nations, the United States momentarily resorted to coöperation in the Washington Conference; there followed then a decade during which American policy oscillated between concern to coöperate in solving the knotty problems of the day and cavalier refusal to recognize these problems or its own connection with them. The withdrawal phase may be partly explained in terms of the normal postwar revulsion of a people who traditionally considered Europe a world apart. Poverty of presidential leadership in the Harding-Coolidge period put a further damper on international-mindedness. Congress occupied itself zealously in the usual effort to regain the power always lost to a wartime chief executive. The laissez faire era of the 'twenties contributed to big scandals, Big Business, and big profits, and the resulting industrial boom and the accompanying speculative mania bred an interest in domestic concerns which left time for only intermittent concern with things European.[1]

One of the clearest indications of a desire to stand aloof from

---

[1] General accounts covering considerable segments of the period under discussion are: O. T. Barck and N. M. Blake, *Since 1900*, Macmillan, 1947; D. F. Fleming, *The United States and World Organization, 1920–1933*, Columbia University Press, 1938; W. C. Langsam, *The World since 1914*, Macmillan, 6th ed., 1948; Drew Pearson and Constantine Brown, *The American Diplomatic Game*, Doubleday, Doran, 1935; Dexter Perkins, *The Evolution of American Foreign Policy*, Oxford University Press, 1948; B. H. Williams, *Economic Foreign Policy of the United States*, McGraw-Hill, 1929.

Europe's vicissitudes is found in the demand for payment of the war debts which ran as an insistent chorus through the 1920's. At the same time successive laws (the Fordney-McCumber Act of 1922 and the Hawley-Smoot Act of 1930) virtually prohibited payment by raising a tariff wall so high as to exclude the goods by whose sale Europe could alone hope to settle her balances. No slightest assurance could be obtained that the United States would underwrite efforts, no matter how minor, to strengthen League of Nations machinery designed to prevent aggression; indeed, the very existence of the League was ignored for some time. The Locarno Agreement of 1925, a multilateral engagement to preserve the existing Franco-German and Belgo-German frontiers and thus supplement the shaky security established in the League Covenant, found no official American support.

On the other hand, by a curious divorce of cause and effect, Americans participated, though not officially, in trying, through the successive Dawes and Young Plans, to solve the reparations problem whose connection with the war debts their Government persisted in denying. Incipient internationalism developed a considerable popular and some Senatorial support for entry into the World Court, but each new formula bred an adverse majority. Initial coldness toward the League, too, thawed into a mild form of coöperation as the decade wore on. Again, serious coöperative efforts were made to reduce the armaments burden, though with only mild success. Finally, the United States undertook vigorously, if somewhat tardily, to promote an initial French overture which became an international engagement in the Kellogg-Briand Pact of 1928 renouncing war as an instrument of national policy. This movement of the pendulum in both directions indicates, perhaps, that the United States was having trouble making up its mind; the swings toward coöperation would become less numerous, and shorter, as depression and dictatorship had their successive ways with Europe.

The Ostrich and the War Debts

Governmental reluctance to recognize the intimate connection between war debts and reparations affords a curious example of official refusal to face the economic facts. At the same time the names of Charles Gates Dawes and Owen D. Young, attached to successive plans of reparation settlement, indicate a sympathetic American interest in solving this pressing problem. German war damages and Allied war costs constituted the raw materials of the complicated debt-reparation problem. The Versailles Treaty authorized establishment of a commission to determine the amount of German reparations; in April, 1921, the French-dominated body set the figure at $32,000,000,000, plus interest, lower than political exigencies had led France to demand, but considerably higher than peace conference experts had suggested as adequate. Meantime there had arisen the question of war debts, divided practically into inter-Allied obligations and those of the Allies to the United States. Britain had loaned heavily to her continental partners; the United States, without too much forethought, but with the general understanding that repayment would be expected, had advanced liberally to all and sundry. As early as December, 1918, the British had intimated to Wilson their willingness to cancel the amounts due from their Allies if he would do likewise with British debts to the United States.[2] Wilson promptly and repeatedly refused, insisting that the debts were valid obligations, unrelated to what the Allies could collect from Germany, and must be paid; his successors repeated his firm stand against cancellation.

The first problem was to establish the amounts due and the terms according to which each debtor should pay. The agency created for this purpose was the World War Foreign Debt Commission (authorized by an Act of February 9, 1922), which between 1923 and 1930 negotiated specific agreements by which the nations accepted, on terms gauged by their capacity to pay, obligations of over eleven and one-half billion dollars, payable over sixty-two years at an average interest rate of 2.135 percent and totaling, principal and interest, well over twenty-two billions.[3] As time passed it became increasingly

---

[2] This involved giving up virtually uncollectable claims of approximately ten billions against her Allies in return for American cancellation of something over four billions of British debt.

[3] In justice to "Uncle Shylock," as the United States was called in Europe, it should be noted that these very substantial settlements still amounted to forgiveness of about half the original principal, and halving of the original interest rate, of admitted obligations. On the debt question in general see H. G. Moulton and Leo

apparent that collection of reparations constituted the only practicable method of paying war debts. This was pointedly drawn to American attention in the so-called Balfour Note of August 1, 1922, addressed to six of Britain's debtors and expressing willingness to remit, "as part of a satisfactory international settlement," both debts and reparations due herself—a not so gentle dig at American refusal to consider cancellation. The American attitude being what it was, the only recourse was to equate British payments to the United States with receipts from Europe: "In no circumstances do we propose to ask more from our debtors than is necessary to pay to our creditors, and while we do not ask for more, all will admit that we can hardly be content with less."

Germany then faced the task of paying reparations, well-nigh hopeless because the scheduled annual payments failed to cover the interest on the total reparations bill, thus insuring that, short of some fiscal miracle, the burden of debt would outpace the calendar. There were no miracle workers among the German fiscal experts, so resort was had to currency inflation in an effort to balance the budget, thrown out of line by high-priced purchases of foreign exchange to meet successive reparations payments. On its way to a peak of astronomical proportions, this inflation disrupted the reparations arrangements; as a result Germany went into default and French, Italian, and Belgian troops occupied much of the industrial Ruhr; this halted reparations payments completely. Germany obviously could not, or would not, pay according to the established schedule; what could she pay?

Although the United States steadfastly refused to admit the connection between reparations and debts, Charles Evans Hughes was willing to coöperate in stabilizing the reparations situation. At his suggestion experts (with Americans taking a leading if unofficial part in the deliberations) were instructed to determine Germany's capacity to pay and to suggest methods to enable her to arrive at this capacity. The result was the successive adoption of the Dawes Plan (effective August 31, 1924) and the Young Plan. The first established a procedure depending for its effectiveness upon contin-

Pasvolsky, *War Debts and World Prosperity*, Century, 1932, and *World War Debt Settlements*, Macmillan, 1926.

ued world prosperity. Germany could pay, it was suggested, if her economy could be restored to a working basis. In order to do this her annual payment of reparations would begin at one billion gold marks, increasing to two and one-half times that figure over a four-year period and continuing into the indefinite future. Meantime Germany should be accorded a loan of 800,000,000 gold marks, mostly to be secured from American investors. Thus was set in train a vicious circle; Americans loaned money to Germany; Germany paid reparations; European debtors liquidated their obligations to the United States.

Certain weaknesses soon manifested themselves. Germany was troubled by the lack of a terminal date; she insisted, and here the economists agreed with her, that the thirty-two-billion-dollar total fixed by the Reparations Commission was too high; she was irked by the presence of foreign agents administering the complicated machinery of payments. Out of these dissatisfactions grew the Young Plan, named for Owen D. Young, who presided over its negotiation. The committee worked for seventeen weeks from its opening session of February 11, 1929, finally proposing that the principal amount of reparations be reduced to $8,032,500,000.[4] The number of annual instalments necessary to liquidate this principal, curiously enough, exactly equaled the remaining number of inter-Allied war debt instalments. To free subsequent payments of political overtones, a Bank for International Settlements would handle the transformation of German currency into those of creditor powers. This plan was embodied in an agreement effective in the spring of 1930, despite vigorous opposition by Germans who felt that the score was still too high. It remained in operation, primed by foreign loans to Germany, until swallowed in the depression of the 1930's, and kept the stream of reparations moving into the European reservoir, whence came the payment of debts due the United States.[5]

The world-wide depression beginning in 1929 inserted an un-

---

[4] At the proposed 5½ percent interest rate the amount paid during the proposed 58½-year life of the Plan would have totaled $26,350,000,000.

[5] Fleming, *U.S. and World Org.*, p. 339, indicates that American investors supplied 55 percent of $2,272,000,000 loaned to Germany on long-term obligations during the seven years ending June 30, 1931; he estimates the American share of a larger volume of short-term loans at $925,000,000.

calculated variable into this unstable equation. German industry had mushroomed under the stimulus of foreign private loans; its structure was not sufficiently solid to withstand the strain of markets destroyed by the depression. In an effort to meet these strains a prospective customs union with Austria was announced in March of 1931.[6] Though Britain approved of this economic move as a step toward stabilization, France viewed it as the possible forerunner of an Austro-German political *rapprochement* dangerous to herself, and a diplomatic furore ensued. In the ensuing crisis Germans rushed to transfer their holdings into foreign currencies and foreign creditors hastily converted their short-term credits into gold. Both operations drained specie from the German Reichsbank so that by the third week in June it had lost over 40 percent of its reserves. With over a billion American dollars tied up in long-term German investments and with hundreds of millions more in short-term loans, the prospective German insolvency became a present threat to many Americans already in the depths of an unprecedented domestic depression. German insolvency not only threatened these investments but the flow of reparations and consequent debt payments. Thus these private investments in German industry finally forced the Hoover Administration to face the unpleasant fact that reparations and war debts were not isolated phenomena.

With the mounting German crisis threatening complete collapse of the Young Plan machinery, Hoover conferred with Congressional leaders and with American diplomats abroad (making use of the recently available trans-Atlantic telephone), and on June 20 made a proposal which had been maturing in his own mind for some days. This involved a moratorium, or postponement for one year from July 1, 1931, of payments on both intergovernmental debts and reparations. Simultaneously, however, he asserted that Allied debt payments were "settled upon a basis not contingent upon German reparations or related thereto," and assured all and sundry that he opposed debt cancellation. French qualms as to the Hoover proposal

---

[6] Walter Lippmann and W. O. Scroggs, *U.S. in World Affairs, 1931*, pp. 132–183; *1932*, pp. 70–85, 132–191; *1933*, pp. 103–118, cover the background and chief developments of the Hoover Moratorium and Lausanne periods.

delayed acceptance until July 6 and modified the scheme in some particulars; the delay contributed to the closing of all the German banks in mid-July. Congress underwrote Hoover's plan on December 22, 1931, but insisted that moratorium predicated neither reduction nor cancellation of the debts. Obviously, further steps were indicated.

Meantime the depression deepened to a point where nation after nation (including Britain, in September, 1931) abandoned the gold standard. In the autumn the French Premier, Pierre Laval, arrived for conferences with Hoover (October 23–25), resulting in a statement that prior to the end of the moratorium some agreement on intergovernmental debts might be necessary "covering the period of business depression," and not merely the moratorium year. This tacit admission that debts and reparations might continue to be related after June 30, 1932, led the hopeful to envision possible revision of the debt schedules. A gesture in this direction emerged from a three-week conference between Germany and her European creditors, opening at Lausanne June 16, 1932. Here Germany was permitted, in lieu of the remaining reparations instalments, to contribute 5-percent bonds to the value of $714,600,000 to a fund for general European reconstruction; one stroke of the pen thus wiped out over 90 percent of the Young Plan reparations total.

This drying up of the reparations stream concerned Germany's creditors for their obligations to the United States; Britain, France, Italy, and Belgium signed a gentlemen's agreement that the Lausanne reduction of reparations should become effective only when Germany's creditors had reached a satisfactory arrangement with their own creditors. The United States refusing to coöperate, the Lausanne agreement fell through; though the Young Plan schedules remained legally in effect, Germany stopped paying reparations. With the termination of the Hoover moratorium on June 30, 1932, this stoppage applied pressure to America's debtors, who during the election campaign of 1932 began requesting debt reduction. No such dynamic political question could be faced during the campaign, but soon after Roosevelt's election notes began arriving from France, Poland, Belgium, Estonia, and Hungary announcing default on the payment due December 15. Other debtors paid, but spoke pointedly of the need for debt revision. The new Administration refused to enter a general discussion to this end, and banned the subject from the agenda of the London Economic Conference of 1933. In June, 1933, Britain, Czechoslovakia, Italy, Rumania, Lithuania, and Latvia made token payments, their last. Only Finland continued to meet her obligations in full. Roosevelt shunted the matter of debt revision to Congress, which reflected current popular opinion by passing (April 13, 1934) the Johnson Act prohibiting loans to nations in default. Thus American policy ended, as it began, on a note of refusal to recognize the relation between reparations and debts, and a continued insistence that the debts were valid obligations.

In the World Court—Almost

Contrasting somewhat curiously with American disinterest in the League of Nations was public, executive, and Congressional support of American membership in the League's auxiliary, the World Court.[7] This apparently overwhelming support was originally rendered ineffective by Senatorial opposition and crippling amendments; its ultimate failure resulted from effective counterpropaganda and lack of affirmative leadership. Charles Evans Hughes made the first tentative move by persuading President Harding to recommend (February 24, 1923) adherence to the Court statute with reservations designed to protect American interests. Within six months (June 21), however, Harding came to fear that the Court's League connections were too close for comfort.

Calvin Coolidge's request for favorable action on the Hughes proposal (December 3, 1923) went the way of many of his recommendations to Congress. With public opinion vigorously affirmative, Senators Lodge and Borah prevented action in the Foreign Relations Committee for some months. In spite of favorable planks in both major party platforms in 1924, it was not until March 3, 1925, that the House voted adherence under the Hughes formula, 301 to 28.

---

[7] In addition to the authorities cited in Note 1, see D. F. Fleming, *The United States and the World Court,* Doubleday, Doran, 1945; and M. O. Hudson, *The World Court,* World Peace Foundation, 5th ed., 1938.

Eventually public pressure overcame Committee inertia and the Senate took action (January 27, 1926) by 76 to 17, but only after the addition of a reservation forbidding the Court to entertain, without American consent, requests for advisory opinions on questions involving American interests. After study a conference proposed counterreservations which found no favor and Coolidge announced (November 11, 1926) that he would drop the matter.

Frank B. Kellogg returned to the charge, however, in the final weeks of the Coolidge Administration, and the aged Elihu Root sailed for Europe in February, 1929, to join a commission considering revision of the Court's statute. To its deliberations he contributed a formula designed to ease American entry by confirming the Senate's veto power over advisory opinions and providing for American withdrawal without prejudice should the Court by some stretch of probability insist on entertaining a motion for an advisory opinion against American wishes. Hoover followed Coolidge's lead and urged Court membership in his inaugural address (March 4, 1929), and during 1929–1930 fifty-four states, including the United States, signed a protocol of adherence. Hoover presented this to the Senate (December 10, 1930), but Borah's influence was important in inducing the Foreign Relations Committee to postpone consideration for a year.

It was not, indeed, until June 1, 1932, on the eve of another Presidential election, that a resolution of adherence emerged from the Committee. Both party platforms followed suit, but Franklin D. Roosevelt was in no hurry to push the matter. There are, indeed, indications that the Democratic Administration was sufficiently concerned with the fate of domestic legislation to avoid risking the endless debate which was likely to accompany effort to discuss the Court while other business was pressing. Successive postponements delayed consideration until a Presidential message of January 16, 1935, urged action. This maneuver afforded opportunity for an early-in-the-session discussion; indeed, there were those who suggested that it was proposed to cover lack of a prepared legislative program. The opposition rallied promptly with Huey P. Long, the Louisiana demagogue, carrying the banner on the Senate floor, Wil-

liam Randolph Hearst training his batteries of newspaper vitupera-
tion, and the "Radio Priest," Charles E. Coughlin, exhorting his un-
seen but vocal audience. Coughlin's final plea of January 27, two
days before the vote was due, resulted in an avalanche of adverse
telegrams. The final vote of 52 to 36 was 7 votes short of the necessary two-thirds, thus finally defeating this tentative move toward
international coöperation which during the 'twenties and early
'thirties had certainly commanded strong popular support.

Flirting with the League
Toward the League of Nations, that archagency of internationalism,
United States policy evolved by 1931 from complete and aggressive
indifference to fairly close coöperation. This was doubtless facilitated by changing attitudes on both sides: American statesmanship
realized that the League was a world phenomenon sufficiently significant to merit consideration; on the other hand developments indicated that the League depended more upon consultation and conciliation than on force, thus minimizing one of the chief dangers
envisioned by its early opponents.[8]

The Harding Administration quickly confronted the problem of
League relations, avoided according to custom during the Wilson
lame-duck period. With the Ohioan in the White House and the
irreconcilables still preening themselves upon defeating the League
in 1919–1920, the only question was how sharp a snub would be
forthcoming. The first technique was complete disregard of League
communications, which piled up in Department of State files. Finally, on June 30, 1921, the American Consul at Geneva informed
Sir Eric Drummond, Secretary-General of the League, "verbally and
unofficially," that communications had been received but that, since
the United States did not maintain relations with the League, no
replies would be forthcoming. When the League sent its commu-

---

[8] The following references add to the works cited in Note 1: "American Coöperation with the League," *Geneva Special Studies, vol. 11, No. 7,* Geneva Research Information Committee, 1931; C. A. Berdahl, "Relations of the United States to the
Council of the League of Nations," *American Political Science Review,* vol. 26
(1932), pp. 497–526; Raymond Fosdick, "Secretary Hughes and the League of
Nations," New York *Times,* October 19, 1924.

nications by registered mail to insure acknowledgment of delivery, the Consul appeared and reiterated his Government's refusal to reply. Early League efforts to enlist American coöperation in the establishment of a World Health Organization and one to suppress the opium traffic were likewise side-stepped. A request of May 21 for information to include in a League statistical publication was ignored until January, 1922, when the American Consul began appearing monthly at the League Secretariat and dropping the data upon the proper desk. By mid-August, 1921, the Department began to notice League mail and on September 22 the Secretary-General received acknowledgments of fifteen communications, each closing with a formula to the effect that "The Secretary of State has taken note of this information for any purpose of relevancy to the United States as a State not a member of the League of Nations."

This ostrich attitude was short-lived, however, and Americans soon appeared, first as unofficial observers and later as full-fledged delegates, at League-sponsored conferences, always with the reservation that their Government was not bound by any decisions taken. By March, 1926, copies of recently signed American treaties were being deposited in League archives and by March, 1930, former Secretary of State Kellogg reported that the United States had sent unofficial representation to over twenty meetings held under League auspices and a comparable number of official delegates to League conferences. By the end of 1931 American representatives in Switzerland were in daily contact with League machinery.

This tendency toward increasing international coöperation characterized both the Coolidge and Hoover Administrations. By the early 'thirties it had manifested itself in such diverse directions as the liquidation of the war (involving a somewhat left-handed connection with operating the mandate system established at Versailles), the promotion of international coöperation, the attempt, however feeble, to prevent future wars, as in the Manchurian episode of 1931–32, discussed above (see pp. 370–377), and an active interest in disarmament, to be noted later in the present chapter. This rather extracurricular *rapprochement* undoubtedly reflected a cooling-off of the arrant isolationism of the early 'twenties and a realization that the United States must adjust to a world in which the League was a definite factor. It was certainly made easier by the fact that League methods of dealing with international complications were obviously veering away from the use of force contemplated under Article 16 of the Covenant toward the milder, and hence less dangerous, techniques of conciliation, conference, and arbitration. It might be concluded, indeed, that American internationalism waxed as League vigor in supporting its original objectives waned.

Dwindling Disarmament

A retrospect of the approach to disarmament in the later 'twenties and the earlier 'thirties affords a glimpse at optimistic futility; the American attitude toward the problem marks a phase of the occasional willingness to coöperate which characterized American policy during these years. It will be remembered that the Hughes formula of apportioning naval tonnage by mathematical ratios, applied to battleships at Washington in 1921–1922, had proved impossible of application to other categories, particularly cruisers. Five years later developing pressure forced the economy-minded Coolidge Administration to enter the Anglo-Japanese competition in cruiser construction. The party, moreover, could use a foreign-policy accomplishment in the forthcoming election campaign. Accordingly Coolidge requested (February 10, 1927) that the five leading Washington Conference Powers permit their delegates to an approaching session of the League's Preparatory Commission on Disarmament, about to assemble at Geneva, to assume the added chore of discussing extension of the Washington Conference ratios to the remaining categories of ship-construction. France and Italy declined to allow their disarmament energies to be diverted from the League's machinery and refused to attend the resultant Geneva Conference, held from June 20–August 4, 1927.[9]

Naval technicians, generally opposed to any limitation, staffed

---

[9] The following supplement the works already cited: P. J. Noel-Baker, *Disarmament and the Coolidge Conference*, Woolf, 1927; Stimson and Bundy, *op. cit.*, pp. 162–174; Merze Tate, *The United States and Armaments*, Harvard University Press, 1948, pp. 141–184; B. H. Williams, *The United States and Disarmament*, Whittlesey House, 1931, pp. 161–225.

the delegations to such an extent as to outweigh civilian influence; British and American objectives clashed sharply, and the result was a conference barren of constructive achievement and significant mainly in embittering Anglo-American relations. This friction emerged promptly on the heels of American suggestions for overall reduction of cruiser tonnage and extension of the capital-ship ratio to other categories. It took the form of British insistence upon the right to construct unlimited numbers of small (7500-ton) cruisers carrying 6-inch guns, allegedly more useful in protecting Britain's numerous and widely scattered possessions. On the other hand, Britain desired sharp limitation of larger (10,000-ton) cruisers carrying 8-inch guns, better adapted to American strategic and defensive needs. Some critics captiously suggested that British quibbling over tonnage was a smoke screen to disguise the Conservative Government's coolness toward reduction of tonnage in the smaller-than-battleship categories. Whatever the explanation, the result was deadlock, and the Conference adjourned after two months of fruitless wrangling. The American reply, somewhat delayed, was found in authorization (February, 1929) for construction of fifteen cruisers of the 10,000-ton displacement, only a month after the signature of the Kellogg-Briand treaty outlawing war.

This incipient Anglo-American naval rivalry faced Hoover on his inauguration. Shortly, Hugh Gibson, an American disarmament expert, suggested a yardstick for measuring fleets according to combat power rather than total tonnage, which would give Britain her small cruisers and the United States her large ones; Hoover himself spoke favorably of disarmament and delayed construction of three of the already-authorized cruisers in May, 1929. During the same months the political breezes blew the Labor Party into power in Britain and the new Premier, Ramsay MacDonald, conducted long disarmament discussions with Charles G. Dawes, the American Ambassador. When these had achieved a considerable measure of agreement, MacDonald visited the United States (in October, 1929) and, on a log beside the Rapidan and in other, more formal, talks carried matters to the point where a new conference seemed likely to promise success.

Britain's invitation (issued October 7) resulted in the London

Naval Conference (January 21–April 22, 1930), attended by the Washington Conference Powers. Profiting by the Geneva experience, the American delegation was dominated by civilians, headed by Secretary of State Henry L. Stimson, assisted by Charles Francis Adams, Secretary of the Navy, Dwight W. Morrow, whose negotiating ability had been amply demonstrated in Mexico, Hugh Gibson, and Senators David A. Reed and Joseph T. Robinson, who represented both political parties. With Anglo-American rivalry somewhat decreased, other obstacles to real disarmament appeared. France exhibited her traditional reluctance to destroy armaments without adequate guarantees to take the place of lost fire power; the American delegation was not permitted to make the necessary political commitments. Japan, moreover, came to London demanding parity in submarines and a 70 percent ratio in other auxiliaries, while the British were, as for some time past, willing to consider abolishing capital ships entirely. Italy, finally, demanded parity with any continental power, which was unthinkable to France, with coastlines on the Atlantic and the English Channel as well as the Mediterranean; this irreconcilable divergence led the two to refuse signature of the important provisions of the treaty and did much to lessen the affirmative achievements of the Conference.

Under these circumstances the three major powers adopted a program of cruiser limitation, qualified by an "escalator" or escape clause permitting Britain to start building again should French or Italian activity threaten her traditional policy of a navy equaling those of her two most important continental rivals. The final compromise established ceilings in cruiser tonnage as well as in all auxiliary categories; it confined Japan to the 10-6 cruiser ratio established at Washington, but accorded her a somewhat better 10-7 ratio in other auxiliaries except submarines, where parity at an upper limit of 52,700 tons was decreed. The capital-ship ratio remained at 10-10-6, but no new keels (except French and Italian battleships authorized at Washington but not yet started) were to be laid until 1936. This postponed construction of ten British, ten American, six Japanese, three French, and three Italian vessels; moreover, five British, three American, and one Japanese capital ships were consigned to the scrap heap. Thus the London Naval Treaty (signed April 22, 1930) set ceilings, put bounds on cruiser rivalry, and reduced and further limited the capital-ship strength of the major powers.

These relatively modest accomplishments resulted from an honest American effort at accommodation. They were vitiated by the escalator clause under which rivalry might recur the moment France or Italy took fright. They might have been more popular in the United States had the cuts been deeper and the ceilings lower, for the American taxpayer, long parsimonious in naval expenditures, was more critical of the billion dollars it would cost him to build *up* to these lowered ceilings than grateful for the savings made by establishing them. This skepticism reflected itself in Senatorial aversion to the treaty, and Hoover was obliged to call a special session and exert executive pressure to secure favorable action (July 21, 1930). The chief promise of the treaty was the postponement, until the treaty's expiration (December 31, 1936), of a naval armaments race. It was apparent that the real work of disarmament was yet to be accomplished.

Meantime the League's Preparatory Commission on Disarmament had stood in adjournment, hoping that the London Powers might reach overall agreement. In the face of Franco-Italian noncoöperation at London, it resumed its efforts, crowning five years' work with the signature (December, 1930) of a convention calling for a general disarmament conference which assembled at Geneva February 2, 1932. Again the United States coöperated, this time with over 200 delegates from about three-score states, in achieving futility. A deadlock caused by repeated French insistence upon security and German demands for equality brought impasse and adjournment in July. Upon resumption of negotiations in February, 1933, Adolf Hitler had assumed office as German Chancellor. More Franco-German friction, and another adjournment (from June until October 16, 1933), made it abundantly apparent that impasse had followed the clock. Two days before resumption was scheduled, Germany announced her withdrawal from the Conference and from the League itself. The succeeding sessions of the Conference, lasting until the spring of 1934, were devoid of success, and armaments appropriations increased apace. The American contribution to this chapter of disillusionment was a Hoover proposal at the original session for abolition of all offensive armaments; when this failed to find favor he made (June 22, 1932) a popularly acclaimed but officially disliked proposal for a 30 percent overall reduction. Thus the armaments problem remained unsettled as international suspicion mounted and as Hoover passed the torch to Franklin D. Roosevelt in March, 1933.

Peace by Promises

Between the issuance of Coolidge's invitations (February 10, 1927) and the assembling of the ill-fated Geneva Disarmament Conference (June 20) had been laid the foundations of the last American experiment in international coöperation to be chronicled in the present chapter—the Kellogg-Briand Pact for outlawry of war. Originating in conversations between M. Aristide Briand, the French Foreign Minister, and Professor James T. Shotwell of Columbia, the project was launched as a joint Franco-American scheme. After a shaky start and considerable delay in the Department of State, it took on new life under the suddenly enlisted aid of Secretary Kellogg and developed into the multilateral pact named for the two statesmen and signed at Paris, August 27, 1928, by the representatives of fifteen nations. The signers, later joined by practically the whole world, bound themselves, without terminal date and without machinery of enforcement, to renounce war "as an instrument of national policy."[10]

Conversations in March of 1927 between Premier Briand and Professor Shotwell, in Europe as a lecturer at Die Hochschule für

---

[10] On the Pact see Bryn-Jones, *op. cit.*, pp. 222–263; Claudius O. Johnson, *Borah of Idaho*, Longmans, Green, 1936, pp. 386–407; David Hunter Miller, *The Peace Pact of Paris: A Study of the Briand-Kellogg Pact*, Putnam, 1928; Denys P. Myers, *Origin and Conclusion of the Paris Pact: The Renunciation of War as an Instrument of National Policy*, World Peace Foundation Pamphlets, Vol. 12, No. 2, World Peace Foundation, 1929; Pearson and Brown, *op. cit.*, pp. 1–43; James T. Shotwell, *On the Rim of the Abyss*, Macmillan, 1936, pp. 105–136; and his *War as an Instrument of National Policy and Its Renunciation in the Pact of Paris*, Harcourt, Brace, 1929, pp. 41–186; and J. E. Stoner, *S. O. Levinson and the Pact of Paris: A Study in the Techniques of Influence*, University of Chicago Press, 1942, especially pp. 212–343.

Politik in Berlin, evidently initiated the original proposal. This was couched in a public statement, not addressed specifically to the American Government, and released on April 6, 1927, the decennial anniversary of American entry into the War of 1914–1918, proposing a Franco-American agreement for the outlawry of war.[11] The coincidence in dates, while doubtless intentional, hardly substantiates the charge that Briand was trying to trick the United States into an alliance with France. The Briand statement fell on deaf ears until, after Shotwell's return to the States, the president of his university, Dr. Nicholas Murray Butler, revived the issue in a letter to the New York *Times* of April 25, 1927. A month of public discussion followed and early in June Briand tendered Myron T. Herrick, the American Ambassador, a suggestion for a bilateral treaty.

Kellogg's reply to this was formal; his indication on June 11 that the Department was willing to discuss matters concerned with preserving the peace was a thinly veiled invitation to drop the matter. It is not at all impossible that the executive branch of the government was ill-pleased with the informality of the original proposal and not overly impressed with academic diplomacy. Briand was not to be rebuffed, however: On June 20 he presented Herrick with a draft treaty which was transmitted to Kellogg, who buried it in Department files. Six months of delay ensued, the causes of which are variously interpreted by Kellogg's friends and his critics. Whatever the circumstances, it seems apparent that the Secretary did not ardently favor a bilateral pact. Indeed, isolationist trends in the United States had made it very difficult for him to do so: Recent cavalier treatment of League of Nations and World Court internationalism would render somewhat ridiculous an Administration which approached the problem of peace by a bilateral political entanglement such as seemed implicit in the Briand proposal.

---

[11] The phrase "outlawry of war" was coined by Salmon O. Levinson, who, along with Dr. Charles Clayton Morrison of the *Christian Century*, had been active in pushing the idea; soon after his phrase appeared in the Briand statement of April 6 he embarked for France and began exerting pressure upon Briand. Dr. Shotwell, through his connection with the Carnegie Endowment for International Peace, had long been active in other aspects of the peace movement. Their work in laying the groundwork of public opinion deserves more appreciation than it has received in most accounts.

However, during the summer the various peace propaganda agencies were busy, focusing their energies with uncommon unanimity upon the Briand proposal of April 6, the only one then publicly known. When Congress assembled in December resolutions in both Houses called for implementation of the Briand scheme. December saw Mr. Kellogg discussing with Borah and other members of the Senate Committee on Foreign Relations the renewal of an expiring arbitration treaty of 1908. According to his own statement, these led him to conclude that the Committee opposed a bilateral arrangement, but would approve a multilateral agreement for the outlawry of war, an idea which, he states, had already occurred to him, and which he embodied in a note dispatched to France under date of December 28, replying to Briand's June suggestion. Thus the Briand proposal, dignified by months of inattention, eventually furnished the impetus for a very different scheme but one with a better chance of surviving. The note of December 28 asked all nations to bind themselves to the Briand renunciation of war proposed in June. Thus the idea of renunciation persisted, its base broadened, and the initiative in negotiation moved westward across the Atlantic. On January 11, 1928, Kellogg published the draft treaty of June 20.

France boggled somewhat at this change of emphasis, perhaps because of a feeling that the United States was trying to steal the limelight. Several weeks of negotiations followed and finally (April 13) the United States assumed responsibility for bringing the matter to the attention of Britain, Germany, Italy, and Japan; the basic subject of discussion continued, however, to be the Briand proposal of June 20, 1927, modified only by changes in wording. On June 23, 1928, the United States submitted this formally to the fourteen governments which eventually signed it on August 27. Its only sanction was the hope that world opinion would prevent violations of its purely moral obligations, and it was to succumb to the first threat launched against it in the Japanese thrust into Manchuria in 1931. From the standpoint of American policy, however, it deserves remembrance as one of the few times, during the decade just described, when American initiative, tardily evoked though it was, led the way to a positive step in international affairs.

18 Descent into Isolationism

FRANKLIN DELANO ROOSEVELT BECAME CHIEF OF STATE ON March 4, 1933, an heir to the Wilsonian tradition of international coöperation. A staggering series of problems arising from economic chaos on the domestic front promptly demanded his attention and challenged his abilities. Their urgency posed the question, which divided the country and the President's official family, whether setting the American house in order was not more important than indulging in international amenities. The Administration deferred for a time, through several outwardly unrelated and unevenly successful policies, to the ideal of coöperation. The prevailing winds of the 1930's, however, blew inward, and whatever internationalism Roosevelt may have brought to the White House was driven under cover by the strong draft of isolationism blowing in the mid-decade. Roosevelt soon grasped the dangers of this phase and started urging his people back along paths which led at once to military coöperation with the democracies in the greatest of all wars and to simultaneous political coöperation for immediate victory and the greatest of all efforts to establish a permanent organization for peace and international security. Thus in hardly more than a decade the wheel turned full circle.[1]

---

[1] Attention is called again to Dexter Perkins' slim but full-packed volume, *The Evolution of American Foreign Policy*, as a cogent analysis of these years. The Government's official exposition and apologia is contained in *Peace and War: United States Foreign Policy, 1931–1941*, Government Printing Office, 1943; Charles A. and Mary Beard, *America in Midpassage*, Macmillan, 1939, 2 vols., provides a narrative account of most of the 1930's.

London Economic Conference

Early in the Administration several tentative gestures pointed, not always successfully, toward a concern for international coöperation.[2] The first, and one of the least successful, of these was the London Economic Conference (June 12–July 27, 1933).[3] Called by the League at the request of the Lausanne Conference, it assembled representatives of sixty-seven nations to consider monetary and economic problems. The Hoover Administration had pledged American participation. During his election campaign Roosevelt had hinted that governmental debts and tariffs might be discussed. Preliminary postinauguration conversations were held with all nations. These determined the Administration against considering the war debts; the developing domestic situation, resulting in abandonment of the gold standard in the interest of higher prices (March–April, 1933), lessened interest in the currency stabilization schemes desired by the remaining gold-standard nations. Secretary of State Cordell Hull, head of the American delegation and a long-time advocate of tariff reform, left for London hopeful of easing the numerous trade restrictions which had followed in the wake of the Hawley-Smoot Act of 1930. On the high seas, however, he received instructions forbidding general discussion and limiting him to negotiating bilateral tariff treaties; this decision forecast the policy of the National Industrial Recovery Act (signed June 16, 1933) and the Agricultural Adjustment Administration, the philosophy of which tended toward higher tariffs as a means of safeguarding the domestic economy. Since the Senate had never yet consented to a tariff-reducing treaty, prospects in this quarter dimmed accordingly.

In Hull's picturesque phrase, the Conference "moved in vicious circles." He desired tariff reduction but had no worthwhile bargaining position; the gold-standard nations (France, Belgium, Italy,

---

[2] The awareness in the early 1930's of international obligations represented in the London Naval Conference of 1930 and the intermittent meetings of the Geneva Conference of 1932–1934, described in the preceding chapter, should be recalled in this connection.

[3] Cordell Hull, *The Memoirs of Cordell Hull,* Macmillan, 1938, pp. 246–269; Walter Lippmann and W. O. Scroggs, *The United States in World Affairs: An Account of American Foreign Relations, 1933,* Harper, 1934, pp. 119–158; Raymond Moley, *After Seven Years,* Harper, 1939, pp. 196–269.

Switzerland, and the Netherlands) would talk tariffs only after currency stabilization, which he was forbidden to discuss; Britain and others wanted debt reduction and again Hull's lips were sealed. Currency-stabilization discussions proceeded fairly far, but were abruptly ended by a peremptory message from the President (July 2, 1933).[4] This was drafted while Roosevelt was cruising on the *Indianapolis* far from official advisers, and struck the Conference like a bombshell. It laid a course diametrically opposed to international coöperation:

I would regard it as a catastrophe amounting to a world tragedy if the great Conference of Nations, called to bring about a more real and permanent financial stability and a greater prosperity to the masses of all nations, should, in advance of any serious effort to consider these broader problems, allow itself to be diverted by the proposal of a purely artificial and temporary experiment affecting the monetary exchange of a few nations only. Such action, such diversion, shows a singular lack of proportion and a failure to remember the larger purposes for which the Economic Conference originally was called together.

A move for immediate adjournment gathered considerable headway, throwing the onus for failure upon the United States, but this was averted and a three weeks' "paper chase" ensued during which unsuccessful efforts were made to salvage something from the wreckage. American isolationism was clearly shown by the record; the bitter bickering between France, Britain, and the United States, moreover, could hardly have gone unobserved by nations like Germany and Italy, whose aggressive plans were soon to become apparent.

American Good Neighborhood

A more successful essay in coöperation, though confined to the Western Hemisphere, emerged in the Good Neighbor policy.[5] Any

---

[4] These were conducted by the Treasury and Federal Reserve experts and by Raymond Moley, Assistant Secretary of State, none of them members of the official delegation; the sharply variant accounts of Hull and Moley are referred to in Note 1.

[5] C. G. Fenwick, *The Inter-American Regional System*, McMullen, 1949; E. O. Guerrant, *Roosevelt's Good Neighbor Policy*, University of New Mexico Press, 1950, pp. 1–22; Perkins, *Ev. Am. For. Pol.*, pp. 117–133. Some ramifications of this policy have already been explored above, pp. 163–165. The object here is mainly to set the policy against its period.

but the strongest partisan will grant previous Republicans a share in its origin: The Clark Memorandum on the Monroe Doctrine, relinquishing the right of intervention under that Doctrine (though, be it noted, not abandoning the right entirely) was drafted under Coolidge; its formal announcement, a landmark in American foreign policy, was made by Hoover; under Hoover, too, came the beginnings of withdrawal from Haiti, and a more kindly policy toward Nicaragua; he, moreover, retreated from the Wilsonian doctrine of constitutional legitimacy toward the historic position of de facto recognition of revolutionary governments. Good Neighborhood owes its documentary origin, however, to Roosevelt's inaugural, where he states, perhaps without specific areas in mind: "In the field of world policy I would dedicate this Nation to the policy of the good neighbor—the neighbor who resolutely respects himself and, because he does so, respects the rights of others—the neighbor who respects his obligations and respects the sanctity of his agreements in and with a world of neighbors." Shortly afterward (April 14, 1933) an address to the Pan-American Union gave it a particular Latin American slant.

Through subsequent developments already elaborated, at Montevideo, Buenos Aires, and Lima, the United States gradually restricted its right of intervention. The Act of Havana (1940) had stated that a non-American act of aggression toward any American state would be accepted as aggression against all. At Chapultepec (February 21–March 8, 1945) this was broadened into an agreement to regard aggression upon one American state by another in the same light as extrahemispheric interference. Furthermore, steps, up to and including armed force against the aggressor, were agreed upon for the war's duration. Wartime commitments became peacetime obligations in the Rio Pact of 1947 (effective December 3, 1948) which put a final quietus on unilateral determination of the right of aggressive intervention of any American state; here it was stated that a two-thirds vote of the American republics on the nature of aggressive action should bind all of them, except that no state could be committed to the use of armed force without its own consent.

Parts of the same pattern of the good-neighbor policy have also been observed in Roosevelt's Caribbean policy, likewise foreshadowed in previous Republican days. The withdrawal from Haiti (1934; forecast in the actions of the later Hoover Administration), the abrogation of the Platt Amendment in the same year, and the signing (March, 1936) of a new treaty with Panama loosening American apron strings on the Republic, are cases in point. American self-restraint in handling the Mexican oil expropriations of 1938 (above, pp. 190–192) demonstrated that the policy was geared to withstand stresses. It should perhaps be kept in mind that many of the developments here hastily outlined took place against an increasingly gloomy international background. Gearing the chronology of developing inter-American comity into the rising European crisis suggests some interesting conclusions; world conditions doubtless accelerated the process of American accommodation. This should not, however, obscure the fact that the policy, firmly laid on a bipartisan base, was developing before the war clouds gathered.

Russia Recognized

The recognition of Soviet Russia, accomplished by notes exchanged between President Roosevelt and Maxim Litvinov, Minister of Foreign Affairs (November 16, 1933), ended over a decade and a half of American refusal to admit the existence of a regime which according to American standards was fiscally irresponsible and ideologically distasteful.[6] The standard reason for nonrecognition of a revolutionary regime, namely that it does not represent the popular will and that it does not control the state's administrative machinery, wore increasingly thin with the passing years. Another normal basis for nonrecognition, Russian refusal to assume the obligations of the previous Czarist and Kerensky regimes to American government and nationals, remained a valid legal obstacle. It appeared increasingly, however, that the real, as contrasted with the legal, grounds for nonrecognition lay in Russia's antidemocratic politico-economic philos-

---

[6] F. R. Dulles, *The Road to Teheran: The Story of Russia and America, 1781–1943*, Princeton University Press, 1944, pp. 188–203; Hull, *op. cit.*, pp. 292–307; John L. MacMahon, *Recent Changes in the Recognition Policy of the United States*, The Catholic University of America, 1933, pp. 56–115; Tompkins, *op. cit.*, pp. 255–263.

ophy and the missionary zeal which sought by any means, fair or foul, to supplant all other philosophies with its own.

Post-1930 developments presently began to lower the barriers. German nationalism developed an ideology different but hardly less offensive than Russian Communism; Japanese aggression on the Asiatic mainland (1931–1932) threatened Russian political and American economic interests. American exports to Russia declined speedily between 1930 and 1933. By the same token, Russia needed formal diplomatic relations to aid in tapping the reservoir of American credit for financing further purchases of the products of American heavy industry so essential to the industrial revolution which the Soviets were trying to impose on the primitive Russian economy. Moreover, beginning about 1928 the Russian dictator, Joseph Stalin, began publicly to soft-pedal the world-revolution aspects of Communism in favor of a more intensive cultivation of its virtues in the fertile Russian soil. Defeat of the Republicans, long the opponents of recognition, in 1932, removed a psychological block of considerable dimensions.

The ostensible moderation of Russian Communism combined with increasing pressure of American economic and financial interests for an improved trade basis to facilitate recognition. As early as May 16, 1933, Roosevelt addressed communications to fifty-four heads of states urging military and economic disarmament; one of these went to Mikhail Kalinin, President of the All Union Central Executive Committee and titular head of the Russian Government. By autumn Roosevelt and Hull were privately canvassing the desirability of recognition and the Russians were actively if circuitously expressing interest. On October 10 Roosevelt requested Kalinin to send an envoy, and Litvinov appeared within a month (November 7) to begin the conversations which resulted in recognition. Roosevelt apparently disregarded his Secretary's advice to secure written commitments on some of the disputed issues, such as Soviet interference in American domestic affairs, a guarantee of religious freedom for Americans in Russia, and the debt question, prior to issuing the invitation. Whatever commitments were made, therefore, were contained in the November 16 exchanges conferring recognition. In these Russia promised faithfully to abjure interference with American domestic affairs; to prevent organizations under her control (the reference here was obviously to the unnamed Third International) from propagandizing in the United States; and not to countenance the existence in Russia of organizations designed to foment revolution against the United States.

From this point the commitments were less firm. A promise, short of an actual guarantee but reasonably acceptable, conferred on American citizens permanently or temporarily domiciled in Russia the right to freedom of conscience and of religion. A postrecognition consular convention would be negotiated guaranteeing fair trial to Americans accused of crimes in Russia. Finally, negotiations would be undertaken to settle mutual claims; Russia waived her claims due to American intervention, toward the end of the War of 1914–1918, in the Vladivostok area, but not those for a like invasion around Archangel. Protracted negotiations failed to bring agreement on the debts, which are still outstanding at this writing. The commitments on propaganda were soon honored in the breach; as early as 1935 American delegates attended the Communist All-World Congress in Moscow. An American protest against this Russian support of Communist propaganda in the United States elicited this remarkable reply: "it is certainly not new to the Government of the United States that the Government of the Union of Soviet Socialist Republics cannot take upon itself and has not taken upon itself obligations of any kind with regard to the Communist International." Recognition failed to furnish the expected commercial stimulus, due largely to Russian unwillingness to settle the debt question, but at least the hurdle of nonrecognition had been topped.

Whittling Down Tariff Walls

It is not unlikely that the perspective of a generation or two may prove the Reciprocal Trade Agreements Act (originally signed June 12, 1934; renewed at periodic intervals and still in operation) to be one of the outstanding accomplishments of the Roosevelt era.[7] This

---

[7] Grace Beckett, *The Reciprocal Trade Agreements Program*, Columbia University Press, 1941; W. S. Culbertson, *Reciprocity: A National Policy for Foreign Trade,*

Act, an amendment to the Hawley-Smoot Tariff Act of 1930, empowered the President to negotiate executive agreements modifying within specified limits tariff arrangements with particular nations. It was an oblique approach to the tariff-reduction problem, an attempt to avoid the full-dress debate and consequent log-rolling which inevitably accompany a thoroughgoing tariff revision. The Hawley-Smoot Act, moreover, had evoked retaliatory rates and import quotas to a point where unilateral American reduction would have served no useful purpose. The Act therefore embodied a bargaining technique whereby, through mutual concessions generalized through the unconditional most-favored-nation principle, it was hoped the trade position of the United States might gradually be improved.

This policy was at once the result of Cordell Hull's thirty years' opposition to protection and an approach to better international political relations through lowered trade barriers. Hull began early in his incumbency to plot an attack upon the tariff problem. His plans were threatened from within the Administration by the point of view represented by the NRA and the AAA, the latter headed by George N. Peek, which held that these domestic price-raising techniques could operate most effectively behind an unbroken tariff wall. The impact of this point of view upon the President at the time of the London Economic Conference has already been indicated; Hull's program was vigorously challenged even after the enactment of his law, but he eventually triumphed to a point where agreements were in operation with thirty-seven nations when he wrote his memoirs in 1948.

The law as passed permitted the President for a three-year period to increase or decrease the Hawley-Smoot rates as much as 50 percent. No item could by this process be added to or removed from the free list. Concessions thus extended to one nation were automatically extended to others in return for similar treatment on their part—the unconditional most-favored-nation provision—except that

Whittlesey, 1937, pp. 64–118; Hull, *op. cit.*, pp. 352–377; J. D. Larkin, *Trade Agreements: A Study in Democratic Methods*, Columbia University Press, 1940, pp. 3–40; H. J. Tasca, *The Reciprocal Trade Policy of the United States*, University of Pennsylvania Press, 1938, pp. 29–99.

the long-standing preferential relations between the United States and Cuba were exempted from the law's provisions. Agreements so negotiated became effective by presidential proclamation, without further reference to the Congress; their term was three years, but they might continue indefinitely, subject to notice of termination by either party. The program produced less rapid and less startling effects than its ardent proponents had hoped. Domestic manufacturers, alert to protect their interests, fought it at every step. Administration negotiators, moreover, were extremely cautious, on both economic and political grounds, to guard domestic producers; caution is a laudable but time-consuming characteristic. Other countries, made wary by previous tariff policy, did not tumble over each other to negotiate. Despite these limitations, however, considerable accomplishments resulted, both positively and negatively. On the one side, the American share in world trade increased during the prewar period, and trade with agreement countries outpaced that with nonagreement countries. On the other side, although this is less susceptible of accurate measurement, it seems likely that the program operated negatively to stop reductions in trade and to minimize the imposition of further restrictions.

Fascism Breeds Isolationism

One striking characteristic of the economic chaos and political confusion following on the War of 1914–1918 was the rise of leaders generally described as "fascist" and of regimes called "totalitarian" from their deëmphasis on democratic ways of thought and of life. Hustling and aggressive, the leaders of these regimes promised their followers surcease from the grinding poverty of postwar dislocations and later of depression conditions. They appealed, too, to the very human desire for revenge against old conquerors and present oppressors. As time passed and their power increased, they took their peoples along paths of aggression threatening international equilibrium established in the League of Nations. The United States, not a member of the League, faced the crucial question of security in the light of these alarming conditions: Was its best choice in continuing tentative coöperation with existing machinery, now be-

ginning to creak badly under the new strains, or would safety be
better served by creating a new isolation behind the broad Atlantic,
such as Britain had maintained for the best part of a century behind
the English Channel after the disturbances of the Napoleonic Era?
The object of the present section, after briefly surveying the rise of
the dictators, will be to chronicle the story of America's choice of the
second of these courses.

Historically the earliest of the European dictatorships, Italian
Fascism, grew rapidly in the early postwar years as an anti-
Bolshevist, antitrade-union, antidemocratic, and ardently nationalist
political group.[8] Under its bumptious and theatrical leader Benito
Mussolini, Fascism eliminated its opponents, solved the generations-
old riddle of reconciling Church and State, and under the disciplined drive of its black-shirted leaders set out to restore ancient
Roman glories. This program marched apace until the depression
years, when rising population, adverse trade balances, currency dislocations, and decline of the lucrative tourist trade jeopardized the
Italian economy.

Under these circumstances Mussolini resorted to a foreign adventure in the hope of diverting attention from domestic woes. This
experiment launched Italian arms at a vulnerable target, Ethiopia,
easy conquest of which promised to round out an African Empire
in emulation of Roman tradition, in a remote area which might
escape serious European attention. An incident in the autumn of
1934 served as prelude to a full-fledged campaign which in 1935–
1936 brought Ethiopian surrender. These developments flouted all
the peace-keeping machinery developed in and under the League
of Nations, the first such defiance except for the Japanese adventure
in remote Manchuria. Americans watched closely the League response to Ethiopian pleas, and League failure to move in defense
of the peace did much to underwrite the isolationism which resulted
in the neutrality legislation of 1935–1937.

---

[8] No attempt is here made to detail the rise of the dictators or to refer to the
voluminous literature of the 'twenties and 'thirties. Workmanlike accounts of these
years will be found in the chapters on Italy, Germany, and the Far East in Langsam,
op. cit., and in F. P. Chambers, C. P. Grant, and C. C. Bayley, *This Age of Conflict*, Harcourt, Brace, 1943.

National Socialism and its leader Adolf Hitler emerged more slowly in postwar Germany. Hitler, son of a minor Austrian customs official, rendered capable if undistinguished service in the War of 1914–1918, after which he cultivated his oratorical talents and sharpened anti-Semitic prejudices acquired in an unhappy prewar period. He eventually dedicated his energies to the National Socialists, one of the numerous postwar splinter parties which gained strength during the depression years by opposing an uncompromising German nationalism to the alleged injustices of the Versailles Treaty and by vigorously denouncing Communism, the great bogey to the East. These policies attracted the landed and industrial aristocrats who subsidized the successive campaigns which gained Hitler the Chancellorship in January, 1933, a few weeks before Franklin D. Roosevelt entered the White House.

Smarting under past humiliations and still convinced of Germany's glorious destiny as set forth by nationalist writers of an earlier day, the Nazis (as they abbreviated the cumbersome title of *Nationalsozialistische Deutsche Arbeiterpartei*) first beat down domestic political opposition and then devoted their tremendous energies to rearmament. This program, carried on under an economy insulated as far as possible from the outside world, gave work to the unemployed. With rearmament well under way by the middle 'thirties, the Nazis assumed the aggressive internationally in an attempt to redress the balance tilted against Germany at Versailles. The year 1935, which saw American entry into the neutrality storm-cellar, witnessed German inauguration of universal compulsory military service, with the objective of an army of 550,000 men; an Anglo-German naval agreement accepting full equality in submarine strength and 35 percent of parity in surface vessels; and the return to Germany, after a plebiscite, of the Saar Valley. Early in 1936 (March 7) Germany capitalized on earlier preparation by occupying the demilitarized Rhineland. The Nazis were on the march.

Some space has been devoted above (pp. 370–377) to the story of American policy toward Japan's open flaunting of the peace machinery in Manchuria. Attention has been given (pp. 358–367, 430–434) to the part of the United States in efforts to limit naval armaments. Japanese imperialism of the 1930's, though successful, had made Japan vastly unpopular in the community of nations. Furthermore, Japan calculated that improvements in naval and particularly in aerial warfare since 1922 had altered the Pacific balance of 5–5–3 to her disadvantage, in favor of a potential attacker. The result, in 1934–1936, was a new Japanese naval policy which furnished further American justification for a retreat into isolationism.[9] The London Naval Treaty of 1930 had provided for a conference during 1935 to draft a new agreement. Preliminary discussions held in October–December, 1934, showed British and American delegates willing to reduce total battleship strength, while maintaining the mathematical ratios of 1922. Japan, however, wished to end the embarrassing "Rolls-Royce—Rolls-Royce—Ford" arrangement; on October 24 she demanded a "common upper limit," covering total tonnage regardless of the type of the ship, and a tonnage reduction creating parity at the Japanese level.

Americans believed that such parity would create an unfavorable security balance in Philippine and Alaskan waters; like the British they refused the Japanese request, and after several weeks of fruitless discussion Japan gave notice (December 29, 1934) terminating the Washington Conference naval treaty on December 31, 1936, the date on which the London Treaty expired by limitation. At the formal conference a year later (December 9, 1935) Japan renewed her demand for a common upper limit, was refused, and withdrew (January 15, 1936). The agreement finally concluded among Britain, France, and the United States (signed March 25, 1936) was mainly useful in minimizing the likelihood of Anglo-American naval competition. The Japanese termination of the Washington agreements absolved the United States, as of January 1, 1937, from its promises not to fortify Pacific bases; the Vinson Act (March 27, 1934), though carrying no appropriations, indicated American determination to rehabilitate its naval arm; and in May–June, 1935, the largest aggregation of naval strength ever gathered under the American flag carried

---

[9] Hull, *op. cit.*, pp. 445–459; Perkins, *Ev. Am. For. Pol.*, pp. 134–148; Tate, *op. cit.*, pp. 185–196; W. H. Shepardson and W. O. Scroggs, *The United States in World Affairs: An Account of American Foreign Relations, 1934–1935*, Harper, 1935, pp. 179–195; *1936*, Harper, 1937, pp. 29–40.

out extensive Pacific maneuvers. Clearly, the climate of the Pacific was becoming less peaceful. Altogether, these developments reën-forced the demand for self-containment and noninvolvement devel-oping in the middle 'thirties, now to be examined.

Retreat into the Storm Cellar

As the international barometer dropped before dictatorial aggres-sions, the American people and their Government had to develop an attitude. Here complex factors forced abandonment of the tenta-tive coöperation of the early 'thirties. Chief among these were a revulsion against involvement in the War of 1914–1918, a feeling that that involvement had been a put-up job on the part of eco-nomic and financial interests, and a determination to avoid at all costs a similar involvement in the future. As always, historians began exercising their function of being wise after the event to revise wartime accounts of the causes of the war. Several less widely disseminated studies had preceded the publication in May, 1935, of Walter Millis' immensely popular *Road to War: America, 1914–1917*.[10] The burden of Millis' plea was that American involvement stemmed from pro-Allied sympathy, adroit Allied propaganda, and a desire for profits. The American Legion and various peace organi-zations had already begun looking with jaundiced eye at the profit factor in war, the former because it enabled some to grow rich while others died, and the latter presumably because of its inducement to belligerency. However, the most important contribution to this approach came from the information turned up by the Nye Com-mittee.

Acting under various pressures the Senate in May, 1934, estab-

---

[10] Houghton Mifflin. Revisionist literature began appearing as early as 1922 with J. K. Turner's *Shall It Be Again?* (Huebsch), was carried on in H. E. Barnes' *The Genesis of the World War: An Introduction to the Problem of War Guilt*, Knopf, 1926, Frederick Bausman's *Facing Europe*, Century, 1926, and C. Hartley Grattan's *Why We Fought*, Vanguard, 1929, but none created the public impact of Millis' vol-ume. Reference has already been made to R. W. Leopold's article, "The Problem of American Intervention, 1917: An Historical Retrospect," *World Politics*, vol. 2 (1950), pp. 405–425, which deals with this problem. H. C. Engelbrecht and F. C. Hanighen, *Merchants of Death*, Dodd, Mead, 1934, while not specifically oriented toward the War of 1914–1918, contributed to the thinking of the period by pointing up the role of the armament-maker from the Middle Ages down to date.

lished a committee headed by Gerald P. Nye of North Dakota to investigate the munitions industry. Its activities, characterized more by industry than by the judicial quality, stretched over most of three years and formed a background for the spate of isolationist literature which characterized the period. Its findings were explicit as to the profits of American munitions makers and bankers between 1914 and 1918; implied but not proven was the charge that the latter fostered American entry into the war in order to protect their loans to the Allies. To an isolationist-minded public the charge was more important than the proof. Among the committee's assigned tasks was to investigate the adequacy of existing legislative controls over the munitions traffic; the burden of its findings raised doubts of the wisdom of permitting such a large degree of unchecked executive discretion in handling foreign affairs as had obtained between 1914 and 1917. The inquiry helped to convince the public mind, increasingly alarmed by the behavior of the dictators, that techniques must be devised to avoid American involvement in future wars.

The developing Italo-Ethiopian crisis of the summer and autumn of 1935 brought matters to a head and furnished the immediate impetus for a series of so-called "neutrality acts" which completely abandoned the traditional concept of neutral trade rights, reflecting current thinking by returning to the position of the Jeffersonian Embargo and attempting to avert involvement by insulation.[11] By mid-summer European affairs had brought the League to consider economic sanctions in an effort to put a brake on Italian designs in Ethiopia; these could succeed only with American coöperation. Meantime the Nye Committee's activities had made it apparent that legislation would be demanded. The Department of State, after several months' study, submitted to the Congressional committees

---

[11] The following highly selected references sample the literature of the time, both descriptive and polemic: Borchard and Lage, *op. cit.*; A. W. Dulles and H. F. Armstrong, *Can America Stay Neutral?*, Harper, 1939, pp. 53–154; J. A. Fairlie (ed.), *Studies in Government and International Law, by James Wilford Garner,* University of Illinois Press, 1943: "Recent Neutrality Legislation of the United States," pp. 515–523, and "The United States 'Neutrality' Legislation of 1937," pp. 524–544; C. G. Fenwick, *American Neutrality, Trial and Failure,* New York University Press, 1940, pp. 25–48; Hull, *op. cit.,* pp. 397–417, 460–474, 504–517, 641–653; Shepardson and Scroggs, *op. cit., 1934–1935,* pp. 255–270; *1936,* Harper, 1937, pp. 129–152; *1937,* Harper, 1938, pp. 39–60, 235–246.

(July 31) a draft bill proposing to grant the President discretionary power to apply an arms embargo against one or all belligerents in future wars. This would permit him to choose between aggressor and victim, withholding aid from one and conferring it upon the other; the embargo would thus become a potent weapon of diplomacy. With the Italian crisis developing rapidly, the Administration proposal was introduced in the House, August 17, and the following day Roosevelt's personal message to Mussolini deplored the possibility of war.

This measure, carrying possible aid to the country attacked and consequent jeopardy to American aloofness, precipitated action. On August 20 members of the Nye Committee announced that they would filibuster against domestic measures until neutrality legislation was adopted; the next day the Foreign Relations Committee, reflecting isolationism rather than the Administration viewpoint, introduced a resolution whose chief feature instructed the President, after proclaiming the existence of a state of war, to enforce a mandatory embargo on all arms shipments. Its prompt passage (with only a few minutes' debate) indicated that it, rather than the Administration-House proposal, reflected public sentiment, and the only concession to the Administration point of view was an amendment putting a six months' limit on the mandatory arms embargo. In signing the measure (August 31), Roosevelt sharply criticized the embargo's inflexible provisions which, he asserted, "might drag us into war instead of keeping us out." It should be noted that the embargo covered only actual arms, ammunition, and warlike implements; primary materials such as oil, steel, copper, and foodstuffs, easily convertible to warlike uses, were not included. Another provision permitted the President to forbid American citizens to travel on belligerent ships except at their own risk. The law went into operation on October 5, running, of course, against Italy in the current Italo-Ethiopian conflict, though less effectively than a full embargo.

The temporary duration of the embargo necessitated further legislation in which the isolationist elements closed some openings which had appeared in the original scheme. Signed on February 29, 1936, the new measure extended the original enactment to May 1, 1937, and forbade extension of loans or credits to belligerents; whereas the President had been *permitted* under the earlier law to extend the embargo to additional nations entering a war, he was now *required* to do so. American republics warring with non-American powers were exempted from the law's restrictions unless they were leagued with other non-American powers. Prior to May 1, 1937, Italy had completely subjugated Ethiopia, Hitler had occupied the Rhineland, and the Spanish Civil War (to which none of the previous legislation, directed only to international wars, applied) had broken out. Congress responded to an executive suggestion and on January 8, 1937, Roosevelt signed a resolution applying earlier restrictions to civil conflicts; he promptly placed an embargo on shipments to both Spanish parties.

The "permanent" Resolution of May 1, 1937, carried the first extension of administrative discretion. The arms embargo was retained, but the President might add nonmilitary items to the embargo list and so had considerable control over items going to an out-of-favor belligerent. Americans were now expressly prohibited from traveling on belligerent ships except under emergency conditions. The 1936 prohibitions on loans and credits were continued, but these did not apply to renewals or readjustments of loans or to the short-term obligations used in the commercial transactions of peacetime. The President might also close American ports to belligerent submarines and armed merchantmen. The most important innovation was the "cash and carry" clause (expiring by limitation on May 1, 1939), giving the President discretion to establish lists of nonembargoed goods salable to belligerents on condition that they be paid for before leaving American shores, and that they leave in non-American bottoms. Though necessarily applied with an impartial hand, such a provision might (as was evidently intended) favor a wealthy maritime nation fighting an impecunious land power, thus partially offsetting the mandatory embargo so damaging to the former. Thus through 1935–1937 did Americans, intent on avoiding repetition of earlier involvements, write into law the abandonment of their traditional attitudes on neutral rights at sea and thus, unintentionally, abet the totalitarian powers, so soon to unleash chaos on the world.

Dictators on the March

Action soon developed, this time in the Far East. Little more than two months after passage of the latest neutrality legislation, Sino-Japanese hostilities broke out in the Marco Polo Bridge incident at Lukouchiao in northern China (July 7, 1937), soon being repeated at Shanghai (August 13), from which fighting spread widely.[12] Conditions resembled those which had produced the original Japanese assault in 1931: Developing Chinese nationalism and improving Chinese economy threatened Japan's mainland interests and the dominant military element seized the opportunity to press an attack before China grew too strong. The international situation was even more advantageous to Japan than six years earlier. Prestige of the League of Nations had ebbed following repeated failures to solve international crises. And whereas in 1931 the United States was a free agent, in 1937 the neutrality legislation tied the executive's hands. Although the Administration obviously favored China, only mild action was possible. The President refused to "find" a state of war, the necessary preliminary to invoking embargoes; this made possible continued shipments to China. Secretary Hull (July 16) reiterated the principles of American Far Eastern policy in such a way as to invite international pressure against Japan, but his overtures were ignored. On September 14 Roosevelt forbade further transport of munitions to China or Japan on government vessels, and placed private shippers on notice that such action was at their own risk; at the same time he indicated that application of the Neutrality Act was on "a 24 hour basis." This of course reacted to Japan's advantage, since private vessels were chary of risking the Japanese fleet in delivering goods to China.

The President's most definite statement of disapproval was de-

---

[12] T. A. Bisson, *op. cit.*, pp. 63–94; Joseph C. Grew, *Ten Years in Japan*, Simon and Schuster, 1944, pp. 209–284; H. S. Quigley, *Far Eastern War*, World Peace Foundation, 1944, pp. 65–84, Shepardson and Scroggs, *op. cit., 1937*, pp. 184–234.

livered at Chicago (October 5) when, in what appears to have been a carefully calculated gesture, he stated, without mentioning Japan, that in case "an epidemic of physical disease starts to spread, the community approves and joins in a quarantine of the patients in order to protect the health of the community against the spread of the disease." Hull followed the next day with a catalogue of Japanese defiance of the peace machinery. The isolationist point of view still prevailed, however; public reaction was largely unfavorable, and the gesture was not repeated. The United States participated in the abortive Brussels Conference in November, 1937, which failed to achieve constructive results. The bombing (December 12) of the plainly marked gunboat *Panay* in the Yangtze River, with loss of American lives, indicated either the unwillingness or the inability (in justice, probably the latter) of the civilian authorities to control the military, but Japanese apologies and reparations were accepted. Two days after the attack, in fact, and largely due to fear that war might result, the Ludlow Resolution proposing a constitutional amendment requiring a national referendum on a declaration of war, except in cases of invasion, was forced to the floor of the House. It was defeated by 209 to 188 only after Roosevelt, fearful that it would weaken his international position, exerted strong adverse pressure. It was clear that the end of 1937 found Americans still concerned with their own affairs to the exclusion, at least, of Far Eastern matters.

This attitude prevailed through most of 1938 until Munich (September 29–30), shortly after which (October 6) the Administration again pointed in detail to Japanese aggressions. Now for the first time the imminence of war began to impress itself upon the public mind. Japan's response, however, was a point-by-point refutation of American charges and occupation of large areas of China. Roosevelt's annual message (January 4, 1939) took a definite position, backed by a public opinion shifting rapidly since Munich; the President also suggested revising the neutrality legislation. Japan matched Hitler's post-Munich aggressions by occupying the Island of Hainan in February and the Spratly Islands in March, 1939. Subsequent difficulties between the Japanese and foreigners in Tientsin and Shanghai strained relations still further and on July 26 Hull gave the required six months' notice terminating the Japanese-American commercial treaty, prospectively threatening the continued flow of American war materials to Japan. This was the state of tension which had developed when the European war broke out in September, 1939.

More slowly, but just as effectively, the German juggernaut rolled over Europe. Aided by British appeasement and the formation in September, 1936, of the Rome-Berlin Axis, Hitler's preparations for conquest continued during 1937; early in 1938 he assumed personal command of the Reichswehr and laid his plans for the absorption of Austria. On February 12 he gave Kurt von Schuschnigg, Austrian Premier, three days to accept a galling ultimatum or face invasion. Acceptance of the ultimatum won only temporary respite; Nazi troops followed a succession of threats across the Austrian border on March 11, occupying Vienna the following day. *Anschluss* was quickly accomplished and Austria's seven million people, her resources, and her industry became a province of the Reich.

The same pressure was applied against Czechoslovakia to secure the Sudetenland, a border area populated by a German minority consisting of three of the nation's fifteen millions of people. Its loyalty to the Czechoslovak republic undermined by a party secretly affiliated with the Nazis, it was soon subjected to German pressures. A crisis developed in May, but passed over without hostilities. Renewed pressure during the summer culminated in a mid-September demand by Hitler's local minion, Konrad Henlein, for annexation of the Sudetenland to Germany. There followed a series of meetings between Hitler and Neville Chamberlain, British Prime Minister, beginning on September 15, after which Chamberlain persuaded Czechoslovakia to make considerable concessions to German self-determination in the Sudetenland. His hopes of settling the crisis were dashed at a second meeting with Hitler on the 22nd when he discovered that the Führer demanded not self-determination, but evacuation of the area by October 1. A week of frantic negotiations, including personal messages from Roosevelt to both Hitler and Mussolini, failed to stop Hitler's plans for mobilization on the 29th, and

Europe trembled on the verge of war. At the last possible moment
Mussolini persuaded Hitler to postpone the mobilization for twenty-
four hours, and arrange a meeting of Hitler, Chamberlain, Edouard
Daladier of France, and himself at Munich for the 29th. Here Hitler's demands were essentially accepted; the Sudetenland was signed
away in return for a German promise to renounce further aggression.

The surge of relief at avoidance of war soon turned to uneasiness
as to Hitler's next move, which was not long delayed. Within six
weeks (November 10), ostensibly in retaliation for the murder of a
German diplomat by a Jewish refugee in Paris, the Nazis perpetrated
the climax of brutality in a pogrom covering many German cities
and extending to Vienna. Four days later the American Ambassador
was called home for consultation. Loss of the Sudetenland loosed
forces long close to the surface of Czechoslovakian politics; German
intrigues fostered these divisions, and by March 15, 1939, Hitler took
advantage of them to annex most of the Republic. The day of the
upstart dictators was indeed come.

America Slowly Awakens

Against this background of aggression in Europe and the Far East
the framers of American policy were compelled to suit their pace to
the slow development of public opinion in the United States.[13] Unfavorable public reaction to the Quarantine Speech, lack of public
concern at the loss of lives in the *Panay* incident, and the narrow
margin by which the Ludlow Resolution was defeated in January,
1938, all indicated the continued ascendancy of isolationism. Under
these circumstances the Administration repeatedly called attention
to the perilous state of the world and repeatedly warned the disturbers of the peace, thus putting its own people on notice as well
as the aggressors, and continued a program of rearmament against

---

[13] Without detailed studies of developing opinion during 1937–1939, it is dangerous to make categorical statements on this subject. It is, however, the writer's opinion that Roosevelt was well in advance of his people, both in appreciating the dangers
inherent in the world situation and in his conception of the measures necessary to
meet those dangers. The best study so far in print on this subject is Walter Johnson,
The Battle Against Isolation, University of Chicago Press, 1944, an account of the
work of William Allen White and the Committee to Defend America by Aiding the
Allies.

the time when the foreign situation warranted an Administration attack on the neutrality legislation.

Even before the German aggressions against Austria in the spring of 1938, and long before the Sudetenland and Munich events, Roosevelt was calling attention to the dangers to the peace and America's need to be strong. As early as January 3 he was telling Congress, and the people, that "we must keep ourselves adequately strong in self-defense. There is a trend in the world away from the observance both of the letter and the spirit of treaties. . . ." Again, on January 28, in asking for increased defense appropriations, he announced that the United States "as a peaceful nation, cannot and will not abandon active search for an agreement among the nations to limit armaments and end aggression. But it is clear that until such agreement is reached—and I have not given up hope of it—we are compelled to think of our own national safety." Throughout the year Hull echoed the executive line in a series of statements vigorously protesting Japan's violation of the Open Door and refusing to condone that nation's efforts to establish a "New Order" in East Asia. Toward the end of the year this disapproval received concrete expression in a loan to the embattled Nationalist Government of Chiang Kai-shek.

Munich and the Sudetenland showed clearly which way the wind was blowing. Encouraged by Congressional willingness to furnish increased armaments in 1938, Roosevelt's message of January 4, 1939, asked for further increases, suggested the desirability of revising the neutrality legislation, and foreshadowed a more vigorous Far Eastern policy:

There comes a time in the affairs of men when they must prepare to defend not their homes alone but the tenets of faith and humanity on which their churches, their governments, and their very civilization are founded. . . .

We know what might happen to us of the United States if the new philosophies of force were to encompass the other continents and invade our own. We, no more than other nations, can afford to be surrounded by the enemies of our faith and our humanity. . . .

In our foreign relations we have learned from the past what not to do. From new wars we have learned what we must do.

We have learned that effective timing of defense, and the distant points from which attacks may be launched, are completely different from what they were 20 years ago. . . .

We have learned that long before any overt military act, aggression begins with preliminaries of propaganda, subsidized penetration, the loosening of ties of good will, the stirring of prejudice, and the incitement to disunion.

Thus did the Chief Executive persistently hammer away at the now-declining public indifference to what was going on in the world.

His second technique, in which he was more adequately supported by Congress and people, was to inaugurate a program of rearmament, initially on the naval side, designed to clothe his political statements with greater authority. To one of his previous experience in naval affairs this could hardly prove other than a congenial task. Even before the failure of naval disarmament in mid-decade Congress had passed (March, 1934) the Vinson-Trammell Act authorizing (without appropriations) a plan designed to bring the Navy up to the Washington Conference limit by 1942. Not until 1938, however, did rumors of Japanese naval construction combine with Hitlerian aggressions in Europe to urge a really ambitious program.[14] In spite of the rebuff to his Quarantine pronouncement in October, 1937, Roosevelt asked Congress in January, 1938, for appropriations to build up both land and naval forces. Shortly afterward (February 5) he joined the French and British in formally querying Japan whether its construction program exceeded the limits of the 1936 treaty in effect between the three Western powers. Japan promptly (February 12) refused to give an answer, and toward the end of March, just as Hitler was completing the digestion of his Austrian morsel, the three powers took all wraps off naval construction; the only remaining limits were Executive imagination and Congressional generosity.

Roosevelt's original request, based on the Vinson-Trammell plan of 1934 and the Washington Conference limits, was implemented in

---

[14] Shepardson and Scroggs, *op. cit.*, *1938*, Harper, 1939, pp. 118–151, and *1940*, Harper, 1941, pp. 84–119, cover the rearmament story.

a law signed April 25, 1938, carrying appropriations of $546,000,000. Encouraged by the House's prompt action (January 21) on this proposal, Roosevelt asked within a week (January 28) for a 20 percent increase in existing authorizations. These two moves indicated clearly the Administration's determination to abandon the naval-limitation policy which the United States had led in inaugurating in 1922. The second measure was reported to the House on March 8 (it will be remembered that the Germans occupied Vienna on the 12th), and passed on the 21st, though with a considerably larger number of opposing votes than were cast against the treaty-limits bill, indicating that the Administration could not yet count upon complete authorization to enter a naval-construction race. The Senate followed suit, and the bill became law on May 17. Not to be outdistanced, the Army secured an appropriation of $459,000,000, the largest since 1921, and $44,000,000 above the 1937–1938 figure. The end of the year saw undisguised naval competition, with Japan's Western rivals far behind as the result of recent economies.

Appropriations continued during 1939, supplemented by attempts to improve the American position in the Pacific. In December, 1938, a Naval board strongly recommended fortifying Guam, lying only 1350 miles from Tokyo and surrounded by Japanese-mandated islands. Fear of offending the Japanese prevented action on this recommendation until March, 1941, when a token appropriation was made. The year 1939 saw also the beginning of a fortification program at Midway and Wake, in the Alaska-Aleutian Islands sector, and along a line of islands running southwesterly from Hawaii.

The actual outbreak of war in the autumn of 1939 stepped up the tempo of American preparedness in 1940. Total appropriations and contract authorizations connected with military, naval, and industrial preparedness for the fiscal year opening on July 1, 1940, reached the then staggering total of over ten and one-half billion dollars. On June 20, 1940, two days before France signed an armistice with Hitler's triumphant legions, a bipartisan measure (the Burke-Wadsworth Bill) proposed the first peacetime program of compulsory military service ever enacted in the United States (it was signed on September 16). It provided for conscription of males from the ages of twenty-one through thirty-five for a year of military service to be followed by a period in the reserve. Likewise under the impetus of the German blitzkrieg, Congress in July, 1940, authorized a naval tonnage increase of 70 percent (1,325,000), bringing the total combat tonnage built and authorized to 3,500,000, writing the new "Two-ocean Navy" policy on the statute book, and facing the economy with a gargantuan construction problem most of which, as events were to prove, was carried out during wartime. All of this, of course, reflected increasing awareness of the dangers inherent in the world situation, made all too apparent by Hitler's attack on Poland in September, 1939.

Against the mounting pressures of the dictators (Hitler's mid-March occupation of the remainder of Czechoslovakia has been mentioned: A companion piece was Mussolini's attack on Albania on April 7, 1939), and with public opinion vigorously condemning their activities, Roosevelt's mind turned to modifying the neutrality legislation. His annual message (January 4) criticized those of its provisions which in case of war would aid an aggressor by withholding needed assistance from a victim. By late March or early April he was writing Secretary Hull of his conviction that the law should be repealed "*in toto* without any substitute," and the Secretary was authorized to pass this judgment along to the Chairman of the Senate Foreign Relations Committee. Hull suggested (May 27) a revision amounting to repeal of the arms embargo and retention of cash-and-carry (which had expired on May 1); this would give the threatened democracies access to American munitions as long as they could continue to pay for them.

The Administration was unable to secure better than a modified arms embargo from the House, and the Senate Committee on Foreign Relations was sufficiently weighted with isolationists to vote 12–11 to postpone consideration of neutrality legislation until January, 1940. Attempting to by-pass the Committee, the Administration conferred with leaders of both parties (July 18) and pointed out at length the seriousness of European affairs. At this session Senator William E. Borah made the remarkable statement that his private advices from Europe convinced him, contrary to the belief of the

Executive branch, that war would not occur. Congress adjourned (August 4) without further action. Roosevelt promptly warned that this failure to afford the democracies access to American munitions had played into the hands of the dictators, and indicated his intention, should war break out, to summon Congress to revise existing legislation. Thus when hostilities developed the United States was still legally fettered by the isolationist mentality, with the law of 1937 still in effect, minus cash-and-carry.

It remains only to recount briefly the climax of dictatorial aggression. In April, replying indirectly to Roosevelt's request for assurances of a ten-year recess on aggression, Hitler told his people that Germany had sufficient territory; before the month's end, however, he was mobilizing troops to back his demand that Poland cede Danzig. This was followed by an Anglo-French statement that an attack on Poland would mean war. Demands for Danzig and the Polish Corridor were stepped up in August, but Poland, relying on Anglo-French promises and hopeful that Russia would join these powers in opposing Germany, resisted stoutly. All hope died when, on August 23, Germany concluded a nonaggression pact with the Soviets, catching Poland in the jaws of a vise. At this point (August 24) Roosevelt made a last-minute appeal to Hitler, to Poland, and to King Victor Emmanuel of Italy to approach the Polish problem by peaceful means. The prospect was too enticing; on September 1 Hitler loosed his troops on Poland, and the promised Anglo-French declaration of war upon Germany followed two days later. The crisis against which the United States had sought for four years to insulate itself had arrived.

19 Through War to Coöperation

WAR'S OUTBREAK POSED MANY PROBLEMS FOR A NATION which, like the United States, had maintained a stubborn aloofness from world affairs; this was particularly true in view of the obvious fact of American sympathy with one side and of the obvious danger to American liberties should the other side triumph. Problems in turn evoked policies, among which, developing in parallel rather than in series, were measures to insure hemispheric security; precautionary steps to avert immediate involvement through untoward incidents; devices, often somewhat circuitous and ever more dangerous, to give material support and psychological comfort to the beleaguered democracies; and, finally, the conduct of prolonged and ultimately unsuccessful negotiations with Japan which, in failing, brought the United States directly into hostilities.

Hemispheric Defense

Hemispheric security constituted the first American line of defense. This was achieved through a process of international consultation whose principles had been set up at Buenos Aires (1936) and implemented at Lima (1938). The latter conference proposed that in case of an outside threat to the peace of the Americas the Foreign Ministers of the Republics should meet to concert countermeasures. Under the impetus of the German threat the Roosevelt policy began paying dividends in a coöperation rare in inter-American annals —born in part of fright, but also, and largely, of the patient nurture

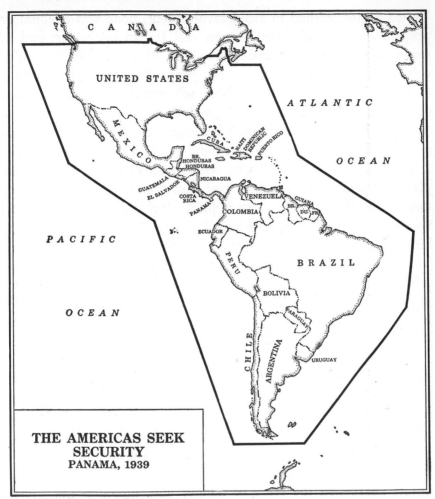

THE AMERICAS SEEK
SECURITY
PANAMA, 1939

(*Based on the text of* Report of the Delegate of the United States of America to the Meeting of the Foreign Ministers of the American Republics, *1940, pp. 63–64.*)

of an Administration which had gradually changed the Colossus of the North into the Good Neighbor of the Continent.[1]

In two conferences, at Panama (September 23–October 3, 1939) and at Havana, the American nations blueprinted security measures for successive stages of a world crisis. The first opened less than a month after Hitler had made Poland the scene of the first full-dress parade of German might. American nations generally, including the

---

[1] Guerrant, *op. cit.*, pp. 135–170; Welles, *Time for Decision*, pp. 211–216.

United States, wished to avoid involvement; none was adequately prepared; some had large German and Italian minorities; and in several the new propaganda technique of the infiltrating "fifth column" had reached embarrassing proportions. The result was a generally harmonious session which achieved its limited objectives of formulating and stating officially the continental desire for neutrality and pointing the way toward improving the continental economic and financial structure for more efficient collective action.

The United States could note with satisfaction that most of the plans adopted followed almost verbatim drafts drawn in Washington. Chief among these were a Joint Declaration of Continental Solidarity underwriting previous Pan-American commitments; a broad declaration of neutrality designed to protect the continent from warlike operations of all sorts, and establishing a maritime safety zone 300 miles or more offshore in which belligerent activities were forbidden;[2] and the establishment of a twenty-one-member Inter-American Financial and Economic Advisory Committee to study both emergency and long-range hemispheric problems.

The Havana Conference met (July 21–30, 1940) in the gloomy shadow of prospective German conquest of Europe.[3] Norway, Denmark, the Netherlands, Luxembourg, Belgium, and France had succumbed and England's air-umbrella, bravely fending off the iron rain from the skies, seemed the sole remaining barrier. Europe conquered, it seemed reasonable to expect German attempts to extend influence across the Atlantic to Dutch or French colonies. This possibility sharpened the sense of danger and, although the United States still attempted to remain correctly neutral, made possible the adoption of more vigorous defense measures than would have been feasible ten months earlier. Among the session's most important accomplishments was a Convention proposing an Inter-American

---

[2] All three belligerents violated this proscription, notably in the episode in which the German pocket-battleship *Graf von Spee*, when about to attack a French merchantman off the coast of South America in December, 1939, was badly injured by Anglo-French naval units and driven into port at Montevideo. Rather than accept the certain annihilation which faced his ship upon leaving port at the end of the 72-hour refuge period allowed him under international law, the skipper ordered his ship's destruction in the Plate River.

[3] Shepardson and Scroggs, *U.S. in World Affairs, 1940*, pp. 140–146, in addition to previous references.

Commission for Territorial Administration, to become effective when ratified by two-thirds of the American republics, which, in case of Nazi threats to the safety of American territory owned by non-American powers, should take jurisdiction over such areas. The Commission would entrust the actual administration to one or more American republics which would manage the areas on a trusteeship basis. Since emergencies might precede procurement of the necessary ratifications, an interim plan called for convening an Emergency Administrative Committee consisting of a representative of each republic. Should even this be too slow, any one or more of the republics might "act in the manner in which its own defense or that of the Continent requires." Several of the Panama Conference agreements were reiterated and new arrangements were made for financial coöperation, underwritten by a half-billion-dollar expansion of the Export-Import Bank's lending facilities, announced during the Conference. Thus, while Europe fought, the Western Hemisphere set its house in order against the day of war which seemed likely to dawn sooner rather than later.

Aid to Democracies

The outbreak of hostilities ushered in a difficult period in the formulation of American policy. Both Administration and public desired an Allied victory; the Administration from the start wished to make American material influence available to the democracies; public opinion was, however, vigorously antiwar. These conflicting forces produced a protracted balancing act in which Administration influence, Nazi victories, the gallant British stand at Dunkirk and in the air, and a gradual public realization of the consequences of Axis victory combined to incline the nation toward participation in the European struggle. These factors, developing in 1940–1941, took the United States away from the strict neutrality of 1939 through a phase of aiding the democracies to a point where active involvement was all but a fact in the summer and autumn of 1941. At this point Far Eastern developments intervened to precipitate actual American entry into the struggle.

American action at the time of war's outbreak reflected the divided feeling indicated above. Roosevelt's fireside chat of September 3, 1939, avoided Wilson's mistake in requesting neutrality of thought as well as of deed by announcing that "Even a neutral has a right to take account of facts." At the same time he asserted that "As long as it remains within my power to prevent, there will be no black-out of peace in the United States," and announced that he was readying a neutrality proclamation, which as announced two days later invoked the existing neutrality legislation by forbidding the export of arms and munitions to the belligerents. On the 8th he proclaimed a state of limited national emergency. Calling Congress in special session on September 21, he asked that the embargo provisions of the Act of 1937 be repealed in order to give the democracies access to American industrial potential. "I regret," he said, "that the Congress passed that Act. I regret equally that I signed that Act." The isolationists, representing honest conviction as well as partisan opposition, made their last stand in the ensuing six weeks of bitter debate which culminated in the enactment (November 4) of a Joint Resolution to Preserve the Neutrality and the Peace of the United States and to Secure the Safety of its Citizens and Their Interests. Congress shared with the President the power to declare the existence of a state of war. The embargo on arms exports was repealed and cash-and-carry was restored. American ships were forbidden to carry goods or persons to any state named by the President, who could also establish so-called combat zones from which American citizens, ships, and airplanes were excluded; an executive proclamation of the same date established such zones, including all belligerent ports, most of the Bay of Biscay, the English Channel, the sea surrounding the British Isles and adjacent islands, and the Baltic and North seas.

Thus equipped, the United States sat back to watch the "phony war" of 1939–1940. British "contraband control" (a euphonious name for blockade) kept American goods from reaching Germany, which power retaliated, as in 1915, with unrestricted submarine warfare. This had little immediate effect on the American economy, since cash-and-carry and the combat zones protected Americans from the consequences of cargo losses and from new *Lusitania* disasters. The

PEACE BY INSULATION
COMBAT ZONES 1939-1941

Presidential proclamations under the Neutrality Act of 1939 forbade American ships or citizens to enter the proscribed zones. Most Canadian ports were also closed, as was the mouth of the Red Sea.

▨ Closed by Proclamation of November 4, 1939
▨ Added by Proclamation of April 10, 1940
▨ Added by Proclamation of June 11, 1940

Scale of Miles
0   200   400   600   800   1000

phony war dissolved into abrupt action in April, 1940, when the Germans struck successfully at Norway and Denmark, followed by the blitzkrieg through the Low Countries and into France, which surrendered via an armistice of June 22. This was paralleled by the British withdrawal from the Continent in the dramatic Dunkirk evacuation (May 29–June 3, 1940) and the development of the German air blitz of the British Isles during the summer. As in the War of 1914–1918, Italy, having calculated the apparent prospects of the two parties, joined the one whose armor seemed heaviest, entering the war on the side of Germany. On June 10, the day when

Italian troops attacked the French rear, Roosevelt recounted to the students of the University of Virginia his efforts to keep Italy out of the war, concluding dramatically that "the hand that held the dagger has struck it into the back of its neighbor."

Allied desperation in the summer of 1940 turned the United States to considering ways and means of assisting in staving off what appeared to be the inevitable doom of Britain. This involved a series of acts which did considerable violence to traditional concepts of neutral obligations. Even before Italy boarded the Nazi band wagon the Administration had evolved and put into operation (June 6) a "trade-in" technique whereby under a law of earlier years the Government could turn over military equipment to armament factories against future delivery of newer and more efficient models. Under this device large quantities of outdated equipment were made available, through the agency of private firms, for European use. Canadian fliers were trained at American fields, British warships were reconditioned in American dry docks, tanks from World War I and merchant vessels of the same vintage were sold to Canada and Britain respectively. Methods were found whereby, through allocation of priorities, the Allies could secure new airplanes ahead of the United States Government and, once in possession, could fly them using their own or American pilots, to the scene of action.[4]

Among the most dramatic episodes, not rendered less dramatic because it was engineered during the heat of a domestic political campaign, was the destroyers-for-bases arrangement. Axis possession of coastal airfields in the Low Countries and in France greatly widened the radius of the war and complicated the British convoy problem. Premier Paul Reynaud on May 14, 1940, four days after the invasion of France, had broached to the United States the sale or loan to his Government of overage destroyers (of which the United States had over one hundred), useful in short-range operations;

---

[4] Forrest Davis and Ernest K. Lindley, *How War Came: An American White Paper; From the Fall of France to Pearl Harbor,* Simon and Schuster, 1942, and Shepardson and Scroggs, *U.S. in World Affairs, 1940,* pp. 242–279, cover the developing program of aid to the democracies in 1940–1941. Hull's story of the destroyers-for-bases deal, to be recounted next, describes that episode from the inside. *Op. cit.,* pp. 831–841.

Winston Churchill had repeated the proposal on behalf of Britain the following day. Roosevelt turned the requests aside at this point on the ground that such action was a Congressional function, but the fall of France changed the complexion of affairs and the question began to attract public attention when General of the Armies John J. Pershing made a radio appeal to turn at least fifty of the ships over to the British, then bearing the brunt of the blitz. Other influential leaders took up the refrain and matters rapidly reached the stage of formal negotiation, which occupied considerable time during August.

Developments were slowed by uncertainties over the exact method of the proposed transaction and over its legality. On August 16 Roosevelt stated publicly that the United States was negotiating for bases on British soil, but said nothing about destroyers; Churchill, on the other hand, had publicly advocated a free gift of leases to bases, without mentioning the destroyers. His continued advocacy of a transaction which must involve mutual free offers ran foul of American constitutional and legal difficulties regarding Presidential gift of government property, particularly in a Presidential year; moreover, it appeared that Churchill was not minded to give as many bases as the United States desired. Eventually a formula was arrived at whereby the British *gave* 99-year leases to bases in Newfoundland and Bermuda and *traded* similar leases to Caribbean bases in the Bahamas, Jamaica, St. Lucia, Trinidad, Antigua, and British Guiana for fifty overage destroyers; thus Churchill was able to make his gift and Roosevelt was able to dispose of Government property by getting something in return.

Further legal obstacles were avoided by an ingenious opinion by Attorney General Robert H. Jackson, who cited two laws and a court decision to support the contention that the President might alienate title to ships and obsolescent material, and that such action would not violate the neutrality laws; finally, and conveniently, he ruled that the act might be performed by executive agreement, thus escaping possible Senatorial delays. In his message announcing the transaction to Congress (September 3) Roosevelt termed the agreement "the most important action in the reinforcement of our na-

tional defense that has been taken since the Louisiana Purchase."
The formal executive agreement was signed on September 6, the
destroyers were turned over as their reconditioning was completed,
between September 9 and November 26, and the whole arrangement
finally confirmed in an exchange of notes on March 27, 1941. That
so little public opposition was aroused by this remarkable arrangement reflects the changing temper of the times. That changing temper was indicated, too, by a Presidential pronouncement of December 29 establishing the United States as the "arsenal of democracy."
By the end of the year the outline of a policy of firm assistance to
Western Europe was apparent.

The European crisis grew more and more ominous during 1941,
while Far Eastern tensions mounted to a point which ultimately
precipitated hostilities. If the American attitude in 1940 had
smacked of pseudo-neutrality, the Lend-Lease Act of March 11,
1941, removed any lingering pretenses of impartiality.[5] The law was
born of the approaching crisis created by the cash-and-carry policy's
drains on Britain's four-and-one-half-billion stockpile of American
dollars. By the end of 1940 the uncommitted balance of this sum was
not much over $500,000,000 and in mid-December the British pur-
chasing agency was placed upon a weekly budget. The idea back of
the legislation had evidently been incubating in Roosevelt's mind
since the late summer, perhaps suggested by the discovery by a
Treasury Department official of an 1892 statute permitting the Secretary of War to lease Army property "not required for public use"
for periods up to five years. It seems to have been fairly well worked
out on Roosevelt's return from a Caribbean cruise on December 16,
1940, just as the British financial plight had become desperate; he
suggested its main outlines in a press interview the following day.

The "arsenal of democracy" speech of December 29 further indicated his intentions, which became explicit in his Message of January 6, 1941, asking Congress for the authority and necessary funds
to manufacture war materiél for shipment to belligerents. A bill was
promptly introduced (January 10) implementing the request. It
would authorize manufacture at government expense, and upon

---

[5] E. R. Stettinius, Jr., *Lend-Lease, Weapon for Victory*, Macmillan, 1944.

government authority, of a long list of "defense articles" for the use of any nation whose defense, in the President's judgment, was vital to that of the United States. The goods so manufactured might be leased, lent, or otherwise disposed of by the government agency at whose order they were manufactured. The sole remnants of caution were found in provisions forbidding convoy of goods manufactured under the law by American naval vessels, and a requirement that the President must report lend-lease activities to Congress at 90-day intervals. The conveniently vague terms of this enactment lodged tremendous powers in Presidential hands; its passage and subsequent operation, moreover, marked the abandonment of that isolationism which had dominated American thinking since the mid-decade and plunged the nation into the middle of a very turbulent stream. Historically it represented an attempt to avoid the unpleasant experience with uncollectable war loans which followed the War of 1914–1918 by frankly recognizing that the advances might never be returned; practically it amounted to an alliance with Great Britain, though the term would still have been abhorrent to many Americans. Alliance it was, however, in all but name.

Episodes of succeeding months evinced an ever wider range of American activity and an ever deeper involvement in the crisis. Over several weeks, between late March and mid-July, Axis merchant ships were seized and turned over to Britain, Axis assets were frozen, German consulates were closed, and Americans were forbidden to have commercial relations with 1800 persons and firms of Axis affiliations. On April 7 an arrangement permitting American defense of Greenland reënforced the lend-lease scheme by making it possible to watch British merchant ships so far on their journey. Three months later, to a day, the defense zone again moved eastward to Iceland, where Americans joined the British who had been there since May of 1940.

Meantime, by late April, Roosevelt had accepted the logical conclusion of lend-lease, namely, protection of the goods on their trans-Atlantic journey. Since the law forbade convoys, a substitute had to be developed, and the President announced a system of "patrols" by which American ships and planes crisscrossed the shipping lanes in search of submarines, whose location they radioed to the British. On May 21 an American ship, the *Robin Moor,* was torpedoed off the coast of Brazil. On May 27 a fireside chat announced a state of unlimited, and undefined, national emergency; the system of patrols was widened to cover the entire Atlantic, with particular emphasis on the vicinity of bases such as Casablanca, Dakar, the Azores, and the Cape Verde Islands which might prove tempting bait for Nazi sallies.

Early in September a German torpedo missed the U.S. destroyer *Greer,* voyaging to Iceland with mail. A week later another fireside chat disclosed that ships and planes had been ordered to shoot on sight. This incident stimulated the President to seek partial repeal of the Neutrality Act of 1939, the spirit of which had long been honored in the breach, and on October 9 he asked Congress to permit the arming of merchantmen and suggested the desirability of allowing them to enter combat zones for the purpose of reaching belligerent ports. The bitter debate which preceded the enactment of a law embodying these ideas marked the swan song of the isolationists whose thinking had ruled the nation while a war was hatching. They died hard, but the facts were against them; two ships were sunk during the debate, the destroyer *Kearny* (October 18) and the *Reuben James* (October 30), and the submarine bag had reached eleven by November 1. By this time the nation was at war in all but name.

One of the most important psychological developments of 1941 was the elaboration of the Atlantic Charter at a dramatic and highly secret meeting of Roosevelt and Churchill at Argentia Bay off Newfoundland (August 10–12).[6] Roosevelt departed from Washington

---

[6] The meeting took place shortly after the German attack on Russia (June 22) which elicited Roosevelt's promise of lend-lease aid to the Soviets; on the last day of the meeting, too, Congress complied with his earlier request to extend the term of those inducted into service under the Act of 1940. On the meeting, see C. A. Beard, *President Roosevelt and the Coming of the War, 1941: A Study in Appearances and Realities,* Yale University Press, 1948, pp. 118–132; Winston S. Churchill, *The Grand Alliance,* Houghton Mifflin, 1950, pp. 433–450; Davis and Lindley, *op. cit.,* pp. 250–284; J. T. Flynn, *The Roosevelt Myth,* Devin-Adair, 1948, pp. 299–303; Hull, *op. cit.,* pp. 974–976, 1017–1020; Elliott Roosevelt, *As He Saw It,* Duell, Sloan, and Pierce, 1946, pp. 19–46; R. E. Sherwood, *Roosevelt and Hopkins,* Harper, 1948, pp. 349–365; Welles, *Time for Decision,* pp. 173–177.

on August 3, ostensibly on one of the fishing trips by which he periodically recouped his energies. Transferring to a warship, he proceeded to the rendezvous, to be joined by Churchill for a number of sessions devoted to discussion and drafting. The resultant document furnished the ideological counterpart of the concrete aid being offered by lend-lease and a logical, if partial, extension of the principles which Roosevelt had enunciated in his address of January 6 claiming for the peoples of the world Four Freedoms—freedom of speech and worship, and freedom from want and fear.[7]

The chiefs of state, aided in drafting by Sumner Welles and Sir Alexander Cadogan, optimistically set forth their common desires for the postwar world which seemed then a long way in the future. The document performed the useful and necessary wartime function of furnishing a nucleus around which the ultimate purposes of belligerents might be clustered and to which their peoples, and those subjected for the moment to enemy tyranny, might look for hope and inspiration. It was not a binding legal commitment, nor, as has sometimes been said, an alliance in realms other than those of hopes and desires. Severely condensed, the Charter expressed the two powers' position:

1. renouncing for themselves territorial or other aggrandizement;
2. opposing territorial changes contrary to the wishes of those immediately concerned;
3. supporting the right of peoples to choose their own form of government;
4. upholding, *with due respect for existing obligations,* the easing of existing restrictions on trade and access to raw materials;[8]
5. supporting coöperative efforts to improve the economic position and social security of the world's workers;

---

[7] The Charter said nothing about freedom of speech and worship, perhaps because Russia, not exactly distinguished in these directions, was now in the war; not all the evidence on this matter is yet in.

[8] The italicized qualification was inserted in deference to the so-called Ottawa Agreements establishing preferential tariff relations within the British Empire; Churchill insisted that, though personally disposed toward easing trade restrictions, he could make no promises without the consent of the Dominions. The possible implications for the United States, even with the qualification, would hardly be lost on high-tariff Americans.

6. looking forward to a postwar world from which want and fear would be banished;

7. and where the seas should be free to all;

8. and in which, to secure the future peace, nations given to aggression should be disarmed, pending the establishment of permanent peace-keeping machinery.

The inevitable comparison between the Charter and Wilson's Fourteen Points brings out both similarities and differences. Both were born of the psychological need for an ideological staff on which to lean in time of trouble. Each stated general principles rather than posing firm commitments, and though neither bound anyone without further implementation, both registered the profound desires of their formulators. The Charter, due to its multilateral support, carried more weight than Wilson's unilateral pronouncement; this perhaps because of, rather than in spite of, the fact that one party, the United States, was not even in the war. This, indeed, lent a touch of drama to Roosevelt's action, as well as creating at least a promise of future fulfillment. Building on Wilson's unwisdom in proposing specific territorial settlements which rose to plague him at Versailles, Roosevelt and Churchill stuck to generalities, though even these evoked disturbing questions of self-determination. Finally, Wilson's emphasis was almost entirely political; the Charter's additional emphasis on the social and the economic gave promise that even in the midst of war's alarms statesmen's thoughts in 1941 were following directions different from those of 1918.

War-Winds Blow from the East

The climax of the prewar drama was played in Washington, but faced toward the East.[9] The blitzkrieg year (1940) saw Japan inching southward to the accompaniment of tentative and ineffective opposition by the United States, where European developments commanded major attention. The expiration of the commercial

---

[9] For Japanese-American relations, 1940–1941, see Beard, *Roosevelt and the Coming of the War;* Bisson, *op. cit.,* pp. 125–135; Davis and Lindley, *op. cit.,* pp. 319–332; Grew, *op. cit.,* pp. 285–538; Hull, *op. cit.,* pp. 982–1037, 1054–1105; Frederick Moore, *With Japan's Leaders,* Scribner, 1942; *Peace and War,* pp. 92–98, 118–150; Quigley, *op. cit.,* pp. 194–227.

treaty according to notice on January 26 was the only important event until April, when obvious Japanese designs on the Netherlands East Indies drew a sharp protest. The summer and early autumn were more active; in July Congress authorized the establishment of a two-ocean Navy, with obvious Far Eastern implications. During the same month the National Defense Materials Act authorized the President to prescribe licensing regulations (which might extend to the point of complete prohibition) for the exportation of numerous commodities useful in war and therefore essential to domestic security. Roosevelt immediately applied this to the export of munitions and their components, machine tools, and non-ferrous metals. On the 26th he extended the regulation to cover petroleum products, tetraethyl lead, and high-grade scrap iron and steel. On August 2 the export of aviation gasoline outside the Western Hemisphere was banned. While these were not embargoes, they were capable of manipulation to Japan's disadvantage.

The shortages thus induced probably contributed to two developments during September, when Japan forced France to cede bases in northern Indo-China and, on the 27th, joined the Axis in a Tripartite Pact of full mutual assistance in case of attack by any power not presently involved in the European or Sino-Japanese conflicts. The obvious object of such an arrangement was to immobilize the United States by the threat of a two-front war. The day previously Roosevelt had embargoed exports of iron and scrap steel except to Western Hemisphere ports and to Great Britain, and within two weeks the Japanese Ambassador was chiding Secretary Hull about the curtailment of aviation gasoline and scrap iron. It should be noted that the licensing system for the time being permitted exportation of all petroleum products except the highest-quality aviation fuel. This seemingly pusillanimous policy was dictated by the existence of alternative sources of supply in the Netherlands East Indies, and the likelihood of forcible exploitation of these if California petroleum were embargoed. By playing a role something less than heroic the United States was able to hold a club, though a weak one, over Japan; complete embargo would probably have meant war, particularly Far Eastern War, in 1940.

Developments of 1941 counseled further pursuit of the American policy of not forcing Japan's hand while strengthening her own, applying, meanwhile, such economic pressures as could be employed without forcing matters to an issue. Japan, for her part, followed her appetite for empire ever deeper into Southeast Asia, increasing the hazards of American policy. American temporizing was further encouraged by the discovery as early as January of Hitler's plan to attack Russia, which would relieve a great potential pressure upon Japan. Japan discounted the possibility that Hitler might not move eastward by concluding (April 13) a nonaggression pact with the Soviets.

Japan's opening move came in February with the appointment to the Washington Embassy of Admiral Kichisaburo Nomura, Annapolis-trained and a former friend of President Roosevelt, whom Secretary Hull credited with being "honestly sincere" in desiring to avoid war. Between his arrival and Pearl Harbor, between forty and fifty evening conferences were held in the Hull apartment in which the aged statesman tested his endurance to the limit in an effort to gain time for his country. These were under way when, on June 22, Hitler moved on Russia. This of course caused a considerable stiffening of Japanese proposals, at a time when Europe demanded American attention. The Department of State knew as early as July 2 that Japan was preparing to attack southern Indo-China, a maneuver successful by the 21st of that month.[10] Two days later a reproof was handed to the Japanese Ambassador, and on the 24th Roosevelt hinted at forthcoming action by announcing that oil exports to Japan had been continued primarily in order to maintain peace in the Pacific. The American answer to Japanese violation of her part of the implied bargain was to freeze $138,000,000 of Japanese assets in the United States (July 26), virtually stopping Japanese-American trade.

This was the situation when Roosevelt met Churchill for the historic Atlantic Charter Conference in August. The leaders discussed

---

[10] Thanks to the interception and successful decoding of Japanese diplomatic messages, Hull was aware of exchanges between the Embassy and Tokyo during the crucial developments about to be recounted.

Far Eastern affairs and apparently agreed that Europe presented the most immediate emergency; they adopted a tactic of continuing the Hull-Nomura conversations in a double effort to gain time and to explore all possibilities, however slight (Hull said later that he had never felt his chances better than one in fifty), of discouraging further Japanese aggressions. As weeks passed the conversations grew less encouraging, Japanese actions more and more ominous, and the buying of time with words came to be of increasing and finally of paramount importance. Hull's account of these days, however, emphasizes that to the very end he sought a real solution: "We wanted peace with Japan; but if we could not have peace, then we needed time." After the furore of the Argentia Bay meeting Japan formally requested (August 28) a similar meeting between the President and Premier Fumimaro Konoye; the request probably combined a desire to gain "face" internationally by securing what the British had, and a desperate effort to bolster the declining fortunes of the Konoye Government. The meeting was never refused, but was deferred from time to time through September until Japan should properly approach the problem of agreement on basic principles. The Konoye Ministry presently fell, and was succeeded (October 17) by one headed by General Hideki Tojo, with Shigenori Togo as Foreign Minister.

Responding to Roosevelt's request for clarification of attitude on fundamentals, Japan submitted a set of proposals (September 6) whose demanding tone showed clearly the ineffectiveness of curtailed trade relations (which since July had filled Japanese warehouses with raw silk and emptied Japanese cotton mills of employees for want of raw materials) as a means of political coercion. This marked the beginning of a complicated set of exchanges which was dissolved only by the Pearl Harbor explosion. The lengthy United States reply (October 2) to the Japanese proposals of September 6 was followed by two weeks of futile effort to narrow the differences between Japan's insistence on domination over East Asia and American insistence upon Japanese surrender of the fruits of conquest and cessation from further aggression. In the course of these discussions a Japanese spokesman informed Joseph C. Grew, the American Ambassador to Tokyo, that since Nomura appeared to be "very fatigued" (the words are Hull's paraphrase) the Government was considering sending an experienced diplomat to assist him. The Tojo Government adopted this plan and on November 3 Saburo Kurusu, a career diplomat who as Ambassador to Germany had signed the Tripartite Pact, was ordered to the United States, in Hull's opinion for the purpose of stiffening Nomura's determination; Kurusu arrived on November 15.

The drama now mounted swiftly to its climax. In an intercepted message to Nomura (November 5) Togo indicated the pressing nature of affairs: "Because of various circumstances, it is absolutely necessary that all arrangements for the signing of this agreement [the proposals then under negotiation] be completed by the 25th of this month. I realize that this is a difficult order, but under the circumstances it is an unavoidable one. Please understand this thoroughly and tackle the problem of saving the Japanese-American relations from falling into a chaotic condition." Hull took this to mean that Japan's war machine was already in motion, to be stopped only if the United States capitulated to her demands by November 25. On November 7 he warned the Cabinet of the dangers ahead, and on Kurusu's arrival resumed the task of negotiation; both sides were now buying time with words—Japan to keep the United States quiet while she chose the hour to strike; the United States to try to complete general defense preparations and, in particular, to equip the badly undergarrisoned Philippines to make a real fight if invaded. On Thanksgiving Day (November 20) Nomura and Kurusu brought a set of proposals which intercepted information indicated to be Japan's last word.[11]

Japan demanded that the United States abandon China to her own tender mercies, withdrawing the moral and material aid hitherto vouchsafed; lift the freezing orders and resume full trade relations with Japan, particularly in oil; exert pressure to aid Japan in

---

[11] Two days earlier, likewise according to the intercepts, Nomura had received instructions regarding evacuation of Japanese nationals and a code whereby, through statements about wind directions, contained in Japanese short-wave broadcasts, he could determine whether diplomatic contacts were to be severed with the United States, Great Britain, or Russia.

securing needed supplies from the Dutch East Indies; and stop increasing her own armaments in the Western Pacific. In return Japan would agree not to push her military advance beyond Indo-China, would evacuate its southern area and withdraw completely upon restoration of peace between China and Japan. Though Hull felt that the demands were "preposterous" and the diplomatic situation "virtually hopeless," the urgent need of military and naval leaders for "more time" constrained him to keep talking. His first idea was to try to buy three months' time through a *modus vivendi,* but the intercepts presently stated that the Japanese deadline had been moved from November 25 to the 29th, and "After that things are automatically going to happen." The *modus vivendi* scheme was then dropped, partly because Japan was extremely unlikely to accept it, and partly because of its adverse effect on beleaguered China, and on November 26 Hull presented a series of counterproposals carefully called "Outline of a Proposed Basis for Agreement between the United States and Japan," a title indicative of American desire to prolong discussion.

Here Hull asked Japan to withdraw troops from China and Indo-China and sign a multilateral nonaggression pact. In return he would unfreeze Japanese assets, resume treaty-based trade relations, and assist in stabilizing the Japanese yen. To Japan this of course constituted a rejection; with the Pearl Harbor expedition already at sea, Tokyo asked for two weeks to study the proposals. Japanese mechanized equipment continued to pour into Indo-China, and on December 6 word arrived of a fleet movement from that area toward the Kra Peninsula. Since Washington believed that this was to be the long-expected overt act, last-minute measures were instituted accordingly. Since October American officials had been considering the utility of a direct presidential appeal to Emperor Hirohito to use his influence to preserve the peace. A message to this effect, on Roosevelt's desk since December 1, was despatched to Grew on the evening of the 6th, for transmission to the Emperor—too late, of course, for any effective results.

During the morning of Sunday, December 7, the Japanese reply to the November 26 proposals arrived, with instructions to Nomura and Kurusu to present it to Hull at 1:00 P.M., Washington time. The appointment was made accordingly, but postponed until 1:45 because of decoding delays; the envoys arrived late, appearing in Hull's office at 2:05 P.M., just as he received Roosevelt's telephoned report, as yet unconfirmed, of the sneak attack on Pearl Harbor at 1:20 P.M. After some discussion with his associates, Hull received the Japanese at 2:20 and accepted their statement, the contents of which he knew already through the intercepts. After glancing at it he dismissed the bearers without permitting them to comment upon it, after delivering this scathing statement: "In all my fifty years of public service I have never seen a document that was more crowded with infamous falsehoods and distortions—infamous falsehoods and distortions on a scale so huge that I never imagined until today that any Government on this planet was capable of uttering them."

With report of the Japanese attack disastrously confirmed, matters moved rapidly from the realm of diplomacy to that of war.[12] Military plans were placed in operation and on December 8 Roosevelt succinctly reported to Congress: "Yesterday, December 7, 1941—a date which will live in infamy—the United States of America was suddenly and deliberately attacked by naval and air forces of the Empire of Japan." On the same day Congress announced that "the state of war . . . which had thus been thrust upon the United States is hereby formally declared." On the 11th Germany and Italy fulfilled their obligations under the Tripartite Pact and declared war upon the United States. Churchill had already promised (November 10) that Japanese-American hostilities would bring Britain in "within the hour." Axis satellites played follow-my-leader (Hungary and Bulgaria declaring war on the United States December 13 and Thailand on January 25, 1942), and the war became a global one. The circumstances of its outbreak, though constituting the greatest military and naval disaster in American history, served one useful pur-

---

[12] No attempt is here made to cover the much-debated story of Pearl Harbor. The documents are contained in *Pearl Harbor Attack*, thirty-nine volumes of hearings before a joint congressional committee (Government Printing Office, 1946), resulting in majority and minority reports printed in *Senate Document 244*, 79th Cong., 2d Sess., Government Printing Office, 1946. Studies based on these are Beard's volume, cited earlier in this chapter, Walter Millis, *This Is Pearl! The United States and Japan-1941*, Morrow, 1947, and George Morgenstern, *Pearl Harbor: The Story of the Secret War*, Devin-Adair, 1947.

pose in silencing the still-vocal isolationists and uniting the nation for the task ahead.

Uphill Road to Victory

Previous pages have attempted to keep the main features of the war moving in step with the development of American pre-Pearl Harbor policy. The narrative has mentioned the German attack on Poland and the phony war of the winter of 1939–1940 which erupted into action in April with the attack on Norway and Denmark, followed by the blitz through the Low Countries and France, the Italian entry in June, and the air attack on England. The year 1940 also saw Japan join the Axis and begin her southward progress, continued more freely in 1941 as Hitler occupied Russian attention and the United States sparred for time. Pearl Harbor altered war psychology by moving the United States into belligerent ranks, but made little immediate difference in operations since the nation was already committed economically and its military and naval potential still awaited full development.[13] Reversing the procedure adopted while the United States was neutral, the present section will recapitulate briefly the chief military and naval occurrences as a background for the development of Allied policy.

A Roosevelt-Churchill meeting in late December, 1941, accepted a grand strategy forced upon the Allies by pressure of rushing events: To concentrate upon defeating the Axis in Europe, practicing containment in the Far East until European success, or mounting Allied potential, or both, permitted stepping up the Oriental war. The combination of Japanese momentum, already acquired in the southward push, the bloody handicap of Pearl Harbor, the great importance of European affairs, and the tremendously long supply-lines permitted Japan to expand almost at will in 1941–1942. From the running start at Pearl Harbor she proceeded, by the end of December, to complete the conquest of Guam, Wake, the northern Gilberts, and Thailand, together with the establishment of beach-

---

[13] The voluminous bibliography of military and naval operations lies outside the present story. A useful chronicle, written close to the events, is found in six volumes by Edgar McInnis, *The War: First Year*, *The War: Second Year*, etc., Oxford University Press, 1940–1946.

heads in the Philippines and Malaya, the last accompanied by the destruction of two of Britain's proudest naval units, the *Prince of Wales* and the *Repulse.* The year 1942 saw Japan's continuation of the Philippines-Malaya conquest with the fall of Corregidor (May 6) and Singapore (February 15); her continental moves included a drive on Burma resulting in the capture of Rangoon and a consequent threat to China's supply lines; the southward drive continued into Borneo, Java, and the Solomons. By mid-year Australia was in danger and few effective countermeasures had been possible. American troops reached the island continent, but naval action in the Straits of Macassar failed to halt the Japanese move into Borneo; the Battle of the Java Sea was likewise unsuccessful for Allied arms. Allied stock rose somewhat during the second half of 1942. Some inspiration was drawn from the token bombing of Tokyo (April 15) by a squadron under Brigadier General James H. Doolittle. A naval victory in the Battle of the Coral Sea (May 4–8) kept the Australian supply lines open. In June (3–6) the Navy won the Battle of Midway, and on August 7 occurred the first effective countermove in the establishment of a beachhead on Guadalcanal, in the Solomons.

Meantime Britain survived the 1940 blitz and defeated the Italian fleet in the Mediterranean. The German attack on Russia in June, 1941, somewhat eased the terrific pressure in the West; increasing American assistance during the summer made matters much less desperate than a year earlier. Sufficient confidence was engendered, in fact, to justify plans for a late-1942 invasion of North Africa as the first step on the uphill road. This was mounted on November 8, resulting in the early capture of most French troops in the area, which opened the way for further successful operations.[14] By May 9,

---

[14] After the capitulation of France (June 22, 1940) a fascist regime was set up at Vichy under the aged Marshal Henri-Philippe Pétain. The United States maintained a working arrangement with this regime despite its unsavory affiliations, in the hope of preventing surrender of the French fleet or of North Africa to the Germans and as a pipeline for information on continental and North African affairs. Admiral Jean Darlan, a Vichyite, was captured early in the 1942 invasion and was persuaded to issue the orders which resulted in surrender to the Allied invaders. On the Vichy policy of the United States see W. L. Langer, *Our Vichy Gamble,* Knopf, 1947, and W. D. Leahy (who was American Ambassador to the Pétain Government), *I Was There: The Personal Story of the Chief of Staff to Presidents Roosevelt and Truman, Based on His Notes and Diaries Made at the Time,* Whittlesey, 1950, pp. 6–94. A

1943, Axis forces in North Africa had surrendered, Mediterranean sea lanes continued intact, and the way to Italy lay open. Meantime, late in November, 1942, the Russians, in one of the war's epic engagements, began the envelopment and eventual destruction of a Nazi force which for months had besieged Stalingrad with fierce intensity. The optimistic could see a small turn of the tide by the end of the year.

The Pacific balance tilted still further in 1943. The Coral Sea–Midway victories of 1942 had weakened the Japanese offensive drive; Guadalcanal fell on February 9 and the combination of jungle-fighting experience and new bases gained in this campaign aided in future operations. General Douglas MacArthur embarked on the reconquest of New Guinea, closest Japanese approach to Australia, and the remaining Solomons, the Gilberts, and New Britain were either recaptured or invaded. Japan also evacuated footholds established on the Aleutian Islands. In Europe an invading campaign of thirty-nine days (opening July 9) recaptured Sicily. Vainly Mussolini appealed for German aid against the threatened mainland invasion; a domestic political upheaval ousted him from power (July 25). The invasion promise was fulfilled on September 3, the same day on which the new government under Marshal Pietro Badoglio surrendered unconditionally, leaving the Germans to counter the Allied invasion. This they did most effectively in the mountains of the southern peninsula; only on June 4, 1944, did the invaders enter Rome.

The year 1944 saw the invasion pattern developed at Guadalcanal and the Solomons applied to Marshall, Admiralty, Mariana, Guam, and other islands, pushing Japan increasingly back upon herself and neutralizing the great naval base at Truk by cutting off its supply

policy somewhat similar, but more expensive, was maintained toward the fascist dictatorship of Francisco Franco, in Spain, where a heavy program of buying tungsten ore kept that product from going to Germany and, along with other factors, helped to keep Franco first neutral and then "nonbelligerent" as German fortunes waxed. An academic practitioner of diplomacy, Professor Carlton J. H. Hayes of Columbia, aided in keeping Franco from slipping off the tightrope on the Nazi side until the shifting tides of war showed him that his bread would be more thickly buttered by the Allies. See C. J. H. Hayes, *Wartime Mission in Spain, 1942–1945*, Macmillan, 1945.

lines. From a landing at Leyte Gulf (October 19) MacArthur proceeded to the conquest of that Philippine Island by Christmas, before which time the Japanese fleet had been mauled in the Battle of the Philippine Sea (October 23–24). Occupied Burma was subjected to increasing pressure; mainland bases became available in mid-year for B-29 raids on the Japanese home islands, which were also attacked from the Marianas. At the Teheran Conference of December, 1943, agreement was finally reached for the invasion of Europe via Normandy in 1944, the way to which had been opened by increasingly heavy bombing of Germany itself, beginning in 1942 and intensifying in 1943, when the Americans took the day shift and the British worked at night. After months of defensive operations Germany tried an offensive against this combined onslaught, and within a week in February, 1944, lost the majority of her planes; by this time the Allies were shuttle-bombing Germany from British and Italian fields. The Normandy invasion opened on June 6, and after moving slowly for some time because of German resistance, unfavorable terrain, and bad weather, picked up momentum by the end of July, shortly after which (August 15) another front was opened up from around Marseilles in southern France. By the end of August the Germans were on the run through France and, later, Belgium and Luxembourg, only to turn upon their pursuers in the Battle of the Bulge in December. By the close of the year it was apparent that German collapse was but a matter of time.

The end came in 1945, with Germany falling first. A Rhine crossing was effected on March 7 and on April 27 American and Russian troops met at Torgau on the Elbe River. German forces in Italy surrendered on May 2, the day after Hitler's suicide was announced from Berlin; formal surrender terms were signed May 8, effective at 12:01 A.M. on May 9. In the Pacific, meanwhile, MacArthur pressed his Philippine invasion to Lingayen Gulf on Luzon (January 5), and captured Manila, Bataan, and Corregidor before the end of February; the reconquest was virtually completed early in July. Meantime, in another sector, the chain of islands running south from Japan was attacked; the conquest of the Bonins was accomplished by March 17, and on June 21, after some of the war's bitterest fighting, Okinawa fell. On July 26, from Berlin, the United States, Britain, and China threatened Japan with dire consequences if she did not surrender immediately; when this was ineffective, the atom bomb, World War II's gift to the art of destruction, was tried out at Hiroshima (August 6) and again at Nagasaki (August 9). Russia presently entered the Far Eastern War (August 9), in time to invade Korea and Manchuria and establish claim to a share of the Oriental loot. After complicated negotiations Japan signed preliminary surrender terms at Manila (August 19); the final act of Japanese humiliation took place on board the U.S.S. *Missouri* in Tokyo Bay on September 2. The long military road trod by the world since Hitler's invasion of Poland in 1939 was at an end.

War-by-Conference

There was more top-level planning by personal conference between chiefs of state during the War of 1939–1945 than in any previous conflict. The airplane, the fast battleship, the predilection of Roosevelt and Churchill for man-to-man discussion and, presently, Roosevelt's desire to sway Joseph Stalin, the Russian dictator, by immediate contact, account for this new development which profoundly influenced the diplomacy of the war years. Roosevelt and Churchill met repeatedly, often far from war's alarms, sometimes uncomfortably close to hostilities, on occasion roving far afield in deference to Stalin. These meetings were, moreover, more than merely political, as they frequently became the occasion for simultaneous conferences of the Joint Chiefs of Staff, who worked out their military plans and submitted them to the civilian leaders for modification or ratification. A not unimportant aspect of this war-by-conference, too, was its contribution to the emerging pattern of postwar organization.[15]

---

[15] The literature of war-by-conference is already considerable. For the reader's convenience a parenthesis following each title indicates the conferences covered. H. W. Baldwin, *Great Mistakes of the War,* Harper, 1949 (Casablanca, Teheran, Yalta); J. F. Byrnes, *Speaking Frankly,* Harper, 1947, pp. 21–45, 67–87 (Yalta, Potsdam); J. R. Deane, *The Strange Alliance,* Viking, 1947, pp. 13–26, 39–45, 240–254, 267–285 (Moscow, Cairo, Teheran, Yalta, Potsdam); Hull, *op. cit.,* pp. 1227–1318 (First Quebec, Moscow); Leahy, *op. cit.,* pp. 165–179, 259–266, 195–218, 291–323, 394–429 (First Quebec, Second Quebec, Cairo, Teheran, Yalta, Potsdam); Elliott

Roosevelt and Churchill had eight meetings, beginning with one at Washington in December, 1941, opening fifteen days after Pearl Harbor. Here in private conversations were confirmed the trends of the Argentia Bay discussions of the previous August when Roosevelt, the pseudo-neutral, promised all possible aid to Britain while seeking to keep Japan quiet. Now Roosevelt the full belligerent agreed with Churchill that victory in Europe must take precedence over the reconquest of the Far East. Other discussions produced a "Declaration by United Nations," publicly subscribed to on January 1, 1942, by the representatives of Britain, the United States, China, and Russia, and on the following day by the diplomatic representatives of twenty-two additional states, pledging each other to a full war effort against the Axis and vowing not to make peace separately. In June, 1942, at Washington and Hyde Park, the two leaders were forced to alter previous plans. With Germany on the warpath against Russia, Stalin clamored loudly for a second front to relieve the pressure: To him this meant only a second front in France, and Roosevelt had assured Vyacheslav M. Molotov in May that such would be established during the current year. German and Japanese victories, however, made a continental invasion impracticable, and in June it was decided to shift the scene to North Africa, which struck Stalin as a somewhat circuitous approach when Churchill explained the decision to him in August.

The successful landings in North Africa set the stage for the Casablanca Conference (January 14–26, 1943) where behind the lines the leaders arrived at a decision and made a compromise. The decision was one of the war's most fateful and was, in the judgment of most near-contemporary critics, an unfortunate one. At a press conference announcing the achievements of the meeting the President announced that the war would be prosecuted until the "unconditional surrender" of the enemy had been obtained. The evidence

Roosevelt, *op. cit., passim* (Casablanca, Cairo, Teheran); R. E. Sherwood, *Roosevelt and Hopkins,* Harper, 1948, pp. 667–697, 758–808, 850–870 (Casablanca, Cairo, Teheran, Yalta); J. T. Shotwell, *The Great Decision,* Macmillan, 1944, pp. 51–66 (Moscow); E. R. Stettinius, Jr. (ed. by Walter Johnson), *Roosevelt and the Russians: The Yalta Conference,* Doubleday, Doran, 1949.

seems fairly clear that this phrase (which was not included in the official communiqué) was first suggested by Roosevelt and that it was accepted by Churchill, who transmitted it, prior to the public announcement, to the British Cabinet, which did not object. In the words of Mr. Hanson W. Baldwin, military commentator for the New York *Times*, this "was perhaps the biggest political mistake of the war. . . . Unconditional surrender was an open invitation to unconditional resistance. . . ." There is of course no technique of measuring the significance of such a remark in nerving the Germans to resistance, but the Combined Chiefs of Staff, who were apparently not consulted in its formulation, were on later occasions embarrassed by being unable to accept conditional surrender in particular areas.

The compromise involved a second front, of great consequence to the Russians, now so hard-pressed by the German invasion. The leaders agreed that a second front should be created, but differed on its locale. American military men, whose ideas Roosevelt shared, favored an invasion via France as the quickest way to the military victory which seems to have been the chief objective of American thinking. Churchill thought in longer terms; after victory would come peace, with its own problems, which Britain had faced for generations. Among these was control of the Mediterranean approaches to the Suez Canal and the way to the Indies; moreover, although Russia was momentarily an ally, Britain had long been plagued by the specter of the Russian bear lumbering southward toward warm water through areas like Greece and Turkey where British interests had long been economic as well as political. Finally, the Balkans, which could be used as an avenue of approach to Germany could also, if filled with Russians and their ideology, pose as great a threat as Russia at the Dardanelles. Britain, then, supported at Casablanca and later the idea of using Sicily and Italy as stepping stones to an attack on the "soft underbelly" of Europe, both as a means of affirmatively protecting British imperial interests and of thwarting possible Russian expansion inimical to those interests. At Casablanca deadlock between both military and political leaders was followed by a compromise agreeing to the invasion of Sicily and Italy without prejudice to the ultimate invasion of Europe from the West.

This hardy perennial cropped up again at a meeting of Roosevelt, Churchill, and the Combined Chiefs at Washington (May 11–25, 1943). Here Churchill urged a knockout blow against Italy in 1943 and, while agreeing to an invasion of the Continent, argued that a cross-Channel invasion could not be mounted in the spring of 1944. Roosevelt objected to carrying Italian conquest beyond Sicily and Sardinia, and pressed for a drive across the Channel as soon as possible and not later than 1944.

The second front was also prominent at the First Quebec Conference (August 11–24, 1943), resulting from the necessity of new planning with Italy's approaching defeat. After a sharp conflict of wills, Churchill agreed on a cross-Channel invasion in the spring of 1944, and plans were concerted to this end; he continued, however, to press for the Balkan move. Plans for pressure on the Japanese in Burma were also initialled. The presence of Mr. T. V. Soong marked the first time that China had been invited to participate in discussions among the warring nations. Here, too, came a step in the planning of postwar international unity in conversations between Secretary Hull and Anthony Eden, British Foreign Minister, on a State Department plan for continuing the wartime unity of the Big Four nations into the postwar era. The way was opened for further consideration of this project when, on the last day of the meeting, Stalin accepted a suggestion that the Foreign Ministers of the Big Three confer among themselves.

Roosevelt had long been trying, unsuccessfully, to bring Churchill, Stalin, and himself together. The Soviet leader proved consistently coy, however, insisting that the conduct of military operations was so demanding as to preclude distant travel. During the Quebec Conference a section of the docile Russian press touted the idea of a meeting of Foreign Ministers; Churchill and Roosevelt took the bait and when Stalin replied favorably the meeting was arranged. The aging Secretary Hull undertook the assignment, although it involved his first trip by air, arriving safely in Moscow for sessions which continued from October 19–30, 1943.

The wide-ranging discussions, being below the top level, raised more questions than they answered, but bore importantly on many war and postwar problems. They disclosed a sharp difference over Poland between Russia and her two Allies, a clash which caused much trouble in succeeding months. The United States and Britain had recognized and supported an anti-Soviet Polish Government-in-exile resident in London; its members were fearful, correctly as events were to show, that a Russian victory would bring Soviet claims to Polish territory, particularly after Russia severed relations with the Polish Government in London on April 25, 1943. Despite Anglo-American efforts the Moscow discussion failed to secure Russian recognition of the London Poles. Although it had been clearly stipulated that Moscow was not a military conference, the Anglo-American delegates spent considerable time reassuring the Russians that the plans for the second front were actually under way and that the commitment would be honored on schedule. The postwar treatment of Germany came in for some comment. Hull presented a tentative plan calling for unconditional surrender and a fairly decentralized postwar political organization. Stalin's reaction, according to Hull's report, was "enthusiastic." The plan was turned over to the European Advisory Commission which was then in process of formation.

A Soviet request for a share of the recently surrendered Italian Navy and merchant fleet was a feature of the conversations. Hull raised Russian dudgeon by relaying Roosevelt's dictum that the ships must presently be employed where they were most useful, and that the ultimate decision would have to be deferred. Secretary Hull talked inconclusively with Stalin concerning a meeting of the Big Three. Roosevelt had asked Hull to explain to Stalin the difficulties inherent for him in a meeting at Teheran, then being proposed; the problem involved the difficulty of getting legislation from the Congress to Teheran and back to Washington within the ten-day period granted the President under the American Constitution for signing or vetoing domestic legislation. Still coy, Stalin suggested postponement until spring, when the conference might be held at Fairbanks, Alaska. A partial offset to this disappointment was Stalin's unsolicited and unconditional promise, made at the final banquet on October 30, that after Germany's defeat Russia would enter the war against Japan.[16]

Probably the most significant action of the Conference was the signature on the final day of the Four-Nation Declaration.[17] In this the signatories recognized "the necessity of establishing at the earliest practicable date a general international organization, based on the principle of the sovereign equality of all peace-loving states, and open to membership by all such states, large and small, for the maintenance of international peace and security." Thus Hull, who had quietly had a Departmental staff at work for over three years on postwar planning, sought to establish the principle of international organization while the struggle was still in progress; this technique would avoid at least one of Wilson's mistakes, that of postponing active consideration of his plan until postwar disillusionment had set in.

That a program as bold as this could be brought forward with even a faint hope of adoption in the United States pointed to a fundamental revolution in American thinking on world affairs. That the cautious Hull brought it forward was equal evidence that the revolution was well advanced. As early as September 21, 1943, the House of Representatives had adopted, 360 to 29, a resolution introduced by J. W. Fulbright of Arkansas: "That the Congress hereby expresses itself as favoring the creation of appropriate international machinery with power adequate to establish and to maintain a just

---

[16] This is usually given as Stalin's initial statement. Admiral Leahy points out, however, that Stalin had made a similar promise in an interview with Brigadier General Patrick Hurley in January, 1943. Leahy, *op. cit.*, pp. 147–148, 208.

[17] China was included in the ceremonies by courtesy and under some pressure by Hull on both Russia and the Chinese. Molotov, not involved in the Far Eastern war, had originally objected to including the Chinese, but finally agreed (October 26) if the necessary arrangements could be concluded. Hull secured Chinese assent to the document, operating through the Department in Washington and the Chinese Ambassador at Moscow, and the latter dignitary signed on behalf of his Government. Thus for the first time the Far Eastern member of the anti-Axis coalition signed an important document.

and lasting peace, among the nations of the world, and as favoring
the participation of the United States therein." A group of top-flight
Republican leaders meeting at Mackinac Island (in early September) had approved American participation in postwar international
organization.

There still remained, however, the United States Senate, former
stronghold of isolationism, which would be the final hurdle to be
topped by any such scheme, and until the Moscow Declaration no
open headway had been made in that quarter. Hull had, however,
been conferring during the spring with various leaders and as one
result of this groundwork Senator Tom Connally had introduced a
resolution (October 14); action was deferred until a majority was in
sight. The events just chronicled furnished this assurance and on
November 5 an amended resolution embodying the obligation of
the Moscow Agreement was adopted, 85 to 5, concluding, however,
on a characteristic note of Senatorial caution:

That the United States, acting through its constitutional processes, join
with free and sovereign nations in establishment and maintenance of
international authority with power to prevent aggression and to preserve
the peace of the world.

That the Senate recognizes the necessity of there being established at
the earliest practicable date a general international organization, based
on the principle of the sovereign equality of all peace-loving states, and
open to membership by all such states, large and small, for the maintenance of international peace and security.

That, pursuant to the Constitution of the United States, any treaty
made to effect the purposes of this resolution, on behalf of the Government of the United States with any other nation or any association of nations, shall be made only by and with the advice and consent of the
Senate of the United States, provided two-thirds of the Senators present
concur.

Two weeks later Hull, newly returned from Moscow, was invited
to describe his mission to a joint session of Congress, a tribute never
accorded one of his predecessors. Thus in the midst of war's alarms
(for it should be remembered that although Italy had surrendered
the sands of German might had not yet run out and the tide of the
Pacific war was just turning) a beginning attempt was made to point

the nations to a future unity of endeavor. Russian participation in the commitment gave added reason for optimism.

Matters moved rapidly after Hull had reassured Stalin of Allied determination on the cross-Channel invasion, code-named "Overlord." Stalin, however, persistently refused to travel beyond Teheran, and Roosevelt pocketed his constitutional scruples and agreed to go to the Iranian capital. As part of the wartime technique of promoting China to the top brackets, Generalissimo and Madame Chiang Kai-shek were invited to confer with Roosevelt and Churchill; since Russia was not a party to the Far Eastern war, these conferences were held prior to and succeeding the Teheran meeting, at a convenient way-point in Cairo (the first on November 22–26, 1943). The most important political result was the Declaration of Cairo, elaborated after the military men had made plans for the defeat of Japan. The three powers agreed that the Island Empire should be deprived of all Pacific Islands acquired since 1914, whether by capture or League of Nations mandate; moreover, all gains at the expense of China must be disgorged—Formosa, the Pescadores, and Manchuria. Politico-military discussions, less publicized than the Declaration, ranged widely. Here British influence, political and military, counseled delaying the Overlord invasion in favor of a move on the Island of Rhodes and the Aegean Sea. Here, too, was discussed the problem of a diversionary offensive against Burma to relieve the pressure upon South China and to permit increase in the flow of supplies; no decision was reached, though Chiang had been promised aid months before. The meetings then moved from the shadow of the Sphinx to that of that other Great Inscrutable whose riddle Roosevelt blithely undertook to solve.

The meeting at Teheran (November 27–December 2, 1943) was important in the realm of the intangibles in that it marked the initial success of Roosevelt's long quest for a meeting of the Big Three. Here the facile, confident, and egocentric President focused his charm upon the Russian in a series of contacts which found the two now agreeing, now differing, with, probably, more of the former than the latter since, in at least one important respect (the second front) their ideas coincided. Operation Overlord was still the subject of prolonged discussion, though the principle was now well established. British opinion, unitedly opposed by Stalin and Roosevelt, urged postponement of the prearranged spring jumpoff until the summer. Ultimately the British capitulated and agreed to move in May, on an exact date to be determined, and to support a flanking invasion through Southern France, favored by Russian and American opinion, as against Churchill's project of capturing Rhodes. In return for Anglo-American promises Stalin again promised to enter the Far Eastern war upon defeat of Germany.

Roosevelt spent considerable time expounding the nature of the proposed postwar organization, promise of which was embodied in the Declaration of Teheran (December 1, 1943), holding out hope of membership to all the well-intentioned: "We shall seek the coöperation and active participation of all nations, large and small, whose peoples in heart and mind are dedicated, as are our own peoples, to the elimination of tyranny and slavery, oppression and intolerance. We will welcome them, as they may choose to come, into a world family of Democratic Nations." Again, as at Moscow, Stalin claimed a share of Italian shipping. Whereas Roosevelt had originally replied unfavorably via Hull, face to face with the Russian he compromised and promised partial delivery in late January, 1944. Potentially embarrassing questions of Germany's postwar fate, and of Polish boundaries, were canvassed without decision; in the latter case the Curzon Line was again suggested as the eastern limit, without specific commitment on Roosevelt's part, and it seemed tacitly agreed, though not detailed precisely, that Poland should be compensated for this loss of territory by moving her own boundary westward at Germany's expense. The President departed in high spirits at this, his initial contact with his great contemporary.

The Cairo Conference was repeated in reverse (December 4–6, 1943), minus the presence of Chiang Kai-shek. Much time was spent in vigorous argument over the respective merits of the Rhodes project, still dear to Churchill's heart, and the Burma campaign that Roosevelt had promised the Chinese leader, the way to which was to be cleared by amphibious landings on the Andaman Islands in the Bay of Bengal. Both military and civilian Britishers opposed the

Andaman Islands scheme so stoutly that Roosevelt finally gave it up; apparently the price of securing British abandonment of Rhodes was violation of an American pledge to Chiang. While at Cairo Roosevelt ended a period of some hesitancy and conferred command of the Overlord expedition upon Dwight D. Eisenhower. This was the last meeting between Roosevelt and Churchill prior to the launching of the Overlord expedition the following year.

With the invasion a going concern in the summer of 1944 Churchill and Roosevelt foregathered again at Quebec (August 11–24). During the Conference the flanking movement in southern France was inaugurated (August 15); the summer, however, saw Churchill still trying for a thrust at the underbelly. The Quebec Conference planned completion of the war in Europe and in Asia, and witnessed the composition of sharp Anglo-American differences over delimiting zones of occupation following the conquest of Germany, a problem which had to be resolved in order to present a united front against expected Russian demands. Roosevelt wished to occupy northwestern Germany, with access to the sea. Churchill, too, wanted this area, with its industrial raw materials, its maritime advantages, and its proximity to Britain, for his own. Roosevelt finally capitulated and accepted a zone in southern Germany, well in the interior of Europe, and between the Soviet and French zones. Seaborne access was possible only via Bremen, surrounded by British territory, followed by a long overland passage through the British-held northwest. At this session, too, Churchill and Roosevelt initialled an utterly fantastic plan sponsored by Henry Morgenthau, Secretary of the Treasury, for reducing Germany to an agrarian economy to prevent the rise of another German war potential. Each apparently signed in an absent-minded moment, for neither had his heart in the scheme, and it was soon side-tracked.

With the end of 1944 approaching and the tide of victory nearing the flood, political questions moved to the front of the stage. These raised such complicated problems that Churchill sought a Big Three meeting in the autumn, hoping to adjust European affairs so as to preserve the continental power-balance. American practice, however, required Roosevelt to go before the voters in November;

though he had topped his highest hurdle in breaking the third-term tradition in 1940, nevertheless he refused to leave the country until after the election. Churchill's exigencies compelled a pilgrimage to Moscow in the hope of securing an Anglo-Russian division of Eastern Europe, likely to become a political vacuum in the near future. At a Moscow Conference (October 9–18, 1944) Churchill and Stalin seem to have agreed generally that the Curzon Line should bound Poland on the east and the Oder River on the west; they divided the Balkans into spheres, Russia to predominate in Rumania, Bulgaria, and Hungary, Britain in Greece, with Yugoslavia to be shared. Roosevelt, not a party to these arrangements, let it be known that he would not be bound by them.

With the election won, Roosevelt postponed until after inauguration his departure for the Big Three Conference at Yalta, in the Russian Crimea. Here, in one of the world's fateful weeks (February 4–11, 1945), the leaders wrestled with questions increasingly political in character, a natural result of the growing military success. Here Roosevelt, finally showing the strain of the long war years, acted as arbiter of sharpening Anglo-Russian differences. Here, in a give-and-take over which scholars are already divided and over which controversy will range for years as the record is amplified and clarified, compromises were made on both sides. Those close to the President during the negotiations (Admiral William D. Leahy and the new Secretary of State, Edward R. Stettinius, Jr.—Hull had resigned for reasons of health on November 30, 1944) have defended his conduct of affairs, particularly in the crucial Far Eastern phase. A mild critic (such as Robert E. Sherwood) suggests that fatigue led him to make commitments which were out of character; finally, a severe critic (Hanson W. Baldwin) asserts that "Perhaps the saddest chapter in the long history of political futility which the war recorded was the Yalta conference. . . ." The historian of the future, striking a balance among these views, should keep in mind that those who attended the Conference came away in a mood of jubilation, convinced that a world containing Russia and other powers of different domestic ideologies could live at peace and in harmony.

With European victory in sight, it was inevitable that the fate of

Germany should be high on the agenda. Military measures were concerted to complete the defeat now clearly predictable; the unconditional surrender formula was repeated, with the added penalty of being "dismembered" and administered in zones divided among the Big Three and France, now back in the international fold under a regime headed by General Charles de Gaulle. A Joint Allied Control Commission composed of the four national commanders would exercise overall supervision. Including France in this arrangement, be it noted, involved some concession on Stalin's part. Reparations problems followed logically upon the German defeat; much discussion at Yalta led to no conclusions. The Russians demanded twenty billion dollars from Germany, payable in kind, and half payable to themselves; Churchill refused this high figure and the matter was eventually referred to a Reparations Commission, with the understanding that this body would base its discussions on the Russian figure. Again, Russia agreed to less than her full desires.

The issue of Polish government and boundaries, boiling more vigorously than ever, became Yalta's most time-consuming problem. The Anglo-American desire for a free Poland with moderately expanded boundaries was written into the record, again at some expense to Russia's extreme demands; this time, however, the language was elastic enough to leave room for variant interpretations which later bred bad feeling. Politically, Roosevelt and Churchill desired a free government which would include all political parties, implying that such might grow out of the London Government with which they had retained relations. Territorially, they desired the Curzon Line (the eastern boundary) modified at its southern end to give Poland the city of Lvov and a share of the nearby oilfields. Stalin exploded at these proposals, showered contempt on the London Government, and presently insisted that a free, independent, and powerful Poland could only develop from the Soviet-sponsored Lublin regime. He agreed to the Curzon Line to the east, but demanded a western boundary at the Neisse River, giving Poland a much larger slice of Germany than the Oder River line favored by the others. Long argument produced an equivocal statement which on its face made possible the establishment of the type of govern-

ment desired by the Western leaders but which under proper manipulation could (and eventually did) result in a pro-Soviet regime.
As a corollary to the Polish settlement the Conference issued a Declaration of Liberated Europe pledging the Big Three to support
postwar governments in the liberated states which would be representative of the popular will expressed through free elections. The
Curzon-Line-with-modifications was accepted as one boundary, but
the Neisse-Oder controversy was not resolved, and a compromise
passed the western boundary question to the Peace Conference,
with the statement that Poland "must receive substantial accessions
of territory in the North and West."

Roosevelt's most cherished object at Yalta was the furtherance of
postwar international organization. This had already been carried
well into the planning stage by the Dumbarton Oaks Conference to
be noted below (pp. 505–506), and his principal task was to iron
out, if possible, one problem upon which the Dumbarton Oaks conferees had been unable to agree and then to secure Russian acceptance of the fundamental notion involved in the proposed United
Nations. The point of difference concerned the so-called veto upon
actions to be taken by the proposed Security Council, composed of
the five major powers as permanent members, plus six rotating representatives of the remaining member-states. At Dumbarton Oaks
the Russians had insisted that any Council action affecting world
peace (except matters of a procedural character) must receive seven
affirmative votes, including those of all five permanent members,
thus enabling each major power to block Council action. American
planners were almost as devoted to the veto as the Russians, since
the Senate could not be expected to submit itself to an international
power with control over American armed forces; they believed, however, that its exercise might be mildly limited, and worked out a
formula which Roosevelt proposed at Yalta.

This formula started by distinguishing between "procedural" and
"substantive" questions, the former dealing with matters involving
the organization and operation of the Council itself. On procedural
matters it was proposed that the affirmative vote of seven members
of the Council should be decisive, even if one or more permanent

members dissented. On other decisions, including those involving the use of force, the seven affirmative votes must include those of *all* the permanent members; here a great power could veto the use of force against itself or in any other contingency. However, in case a question arose which could be settled by *peaceful* means, presumably of a quasi-judicial nature, a great power which was party to the dispute would not vote in determining the issue. Thus each great power could prevent the use of force against itself while remaining amenable to unfavorable decisions of a peaceful nature. This formula had been presented to Stalin early in December, 1944, but when the matter first came up at Yalta he had evidently given it no consideration. Overnight, however, he accepted the plan, which became the basis of the final United Nations Charter provisions. He demanded his pound of flesh, however, by insisting that White Russia and the Ukraine, constituent members of the U.S.S.R., become charter members of the United Nations. This was agreed to privately, though Roosevelt informed Stalin that he might be forced to seek additional votes to place the United States on equal terms; Stalin assented to this, also privately, but Roosevelt's threat was never implemented. Publicly the Yalta conferees simply announced that they had worked out a formula for voting in the Security Council (publication of which followed French and Chinese acceptance), and that a conference to elaborate the United Nations Charter would convene at San Francisco on April 25, 1945.

Yalta's most controverted action was a secret written agreement of February 11, reiterating Stalin's promise freely proffered to Hull on October 30, 1943—this time, however, for a price. Now Russia agreed to enter the Far Eastern War "in two or three months after Germany has surrendered," in return for the following concessions: (1) recognition of the autonomy of Outer Mongolia, which had severed its connections with China and entered the Russian orbit; (2) return to Russia of the Manchurian rights lost by the Russo-Japanese War (it will be remembered that at Cairo Chiang Kai-shek had been promised return of Manchuria to China), including in particular restoration of the share in control of the Chinese railroads in that province which Russia had enjoyed prior to the current hostilities; moreover, Dairen was to become an international free port in which Russian "preëminent interests" would be recognized, and the Soviets would obtain a long-term lease of Port Arthur; (3) the Kurile Islands and the southern half of Sakhalin would go to Russia. Roosevelt agreed to secure Chinese acceptance of this severe blow to China's natural aspirations, and the Sino-Soviet Treaty of Moscow (August 14, 1945) formalized Chiang's consent.

The evidence available seems to indicate that Roosevelt's concessions rested on the conviction that only Russian entry into the Far Eastern War could prevent a tremendous waste of American lives in a headlong assault on Japanese island and continental strongholds which would be defended with fanatical intensity and considerable effectiveness; in other words, it was largely a military decision. There is some evidence to indicate that this conclusion was erroneous, and that naval and air activities in the Pacific had vitiated Japan's powers of resistance to a point where neither the Russian entry nor the atom bomb was necessary to insure her surrender.[18] The advisers to whom Roosevelt turned, however, were influenced by pessimistic intelligence reports of the prospective vigor of Japanese resistance and the resulting bargain violated promises to China and permitted Russian influence to unsettle the Far Eastern balance of power. In justice to Roosevelt, however, it should be pointed out that Far Eastern arrangements occupied little of Yalta's time, that no objections were made to Russian requests, and that there is no way of proving that, had the Yalta Agreement not been signed, the situation in the Far East would have differed greatly from the one which developed under its aegis. Again, it should be remembered, Roosevelt secured at Yalta, in return for the concessions just described, counterconcessions which on paper appeared to be not inconsiderable; the fact that subsequent history has proven Russian

---

[18] Rear Admiral Ellis M. Zacharias, "The Inside Story of Yalta," *United Nations World*, vol. 3 (1949), pp. 12–16. Baldwin, *op. cit.*, strongly supports this view; he shows that Japan had approached Russia regarding the possibility of mediating a surrender during the very month of the Yalta meeting, and that other peace moves were under way nearly a month before the first bomb fell on Hiroshima on August 6.

promises something less than valid should not obscure the fact that Russian promises had hitherto been kept with reasonable honesty. The conference closed with Russian-American relations at a peak of good will which began to disintegrate before Roosevelt's sudden death a few weeks later.

The Berlin (Potsdam) Conference (July 17–August 2, 1945), code-named "Terminal," could more aptly have been called "Transitional," for it was here that war-born unity among the great powers began that open deterioration which contributed to the substitution of two worlds for that One World which had been so bravely dreamed in the flush of wartime coöperation; this in spite of the largely successful San Francisco Conference but recently concluded (see pp. 506–509). New hands were at the helm; Roosevelt's death (April 12) had brought into the White House Harry S. Truman, product of none too savory Midwestern politics and a capable if not overly distinguished Senatorial career prior to his election as Vice-President in 1944. He brought with him to Berlin a team headed by a new Secretary of State, James F. Byrnes, whose principal international experience had been attendance at Yalta in an advisory capacity. During the Conference the British ship of state changed pilots also, Churchill being displaced by a Labor Government headed by Clement R. Attlee, with Ernest Bevin as Foreign Minister. Stalin and Molotov, therefore, remained the only veterans at the close of the negotiation.

The power-balance, as well as personalities, had changed drastically since Yalta. Germany's surrender (May 8) achieved Russia's chief war objective, permitting her tremendous energies to be channeled into postwar activities. Prior to Potsdam a Polish situation contrary to the Yalta agreements and subservient to Russia had become a fact; Soviet influence had flowed into the wake of declining military activity and organized puppet regimes in Rumania, Bulgaria, and Hungary. As Russian influence increased, the British power position correspondingly worsened, though this was hardly as evident at Potsdam as it became in succeeding months. By the same token, military victory and political success stiffened the Russian attitude to a point where Secretary Byrnes and Admiral Leahy, who attended both Yalta and Potsdam conferences, left the latter in a distinctly less optimistic frame of mind.[19]

European decisions dealt largely with peacemaking and occupation policy. The Council of Foreign Ministers, a new piece of machinery, was immediately charged with preparing draft treaties with Italy, Austria, Hungary, Rumania, Bulgaria, and Finland; whenever a German Government capable of negotiating should materialize, the Council would draft a German agreement as well. Meantime Germany was to be managed largely as proposed at Yalta, divided into four zones each under military control with an overall Control Council to deal with general problems. The occupation authorities were to conduct programs designed to de-Nazify and disarm Germany, which was to be treated during the occupation period as a single economic unit. War criminals were to be tried under regulations even then being negotiated in London. Frontiers and reparations remained undetermined. Final delimitation of the Polish-German frontier was left to the peace treaty, but meantime Russia, contrary to the Yalta agreement, had established Polish administrative control over the territory Stalin had demanded at Yalta; he refused to budge from this position. Yalta had postponed reparations to subsequent settlement, with the twenty-billion-dollar Russian demand as a basis of discussion; meantime Russia had been systematically stripping Germany, Austria, and Hungary of available equipment. After acrimonious argument Russia abandoned her Yalta demand for a specific dollar-total and agreed to take her reparations from the Eastern zone plus 10 percent of the useful capital equipment of the Western zone, plus a further 15 percent of the same in exchange for equivalent materials more plentiful in the Eastern zone. The Americans took this to mean that Russia had abandoned her demand for reparations out of current production, which had been a bone of contention at Yalta. But within a few months she had reverted to both specific dollar-total and reparation-from-current-production positions. At Potsdam she promised, in addition, to pay

---

[19] Since the developing antagonism which culminates in the cold war of the later 'forties will be the principal subject of the next chapter, the present account of Potsdam will deal mainly with immediate war and postwar problems.

Polish reparations from her own takings, and not to demand reparations of Austria.

Finally, Britain and the United States, with Chiang's approval, presented to Japan (July 26) a carefully worded ultimatum designed to facilitate acceptance of surrender terms, and couched in language making it clear that "unconditional surrender" did not mean, in Admiral Leahy's words, "the complete destruction of the Japanese Government." It was likewise an indirect appeal to the Emperor, whose word was thought to be important in stopping hostilities. This point may only be guessed at, but it is not impossible that the relative leniency of the suggested terms may have been dictated by a desire to remove Japan from the war prior to Russia's entry. This was not to be, however, as Japan delayed, despite peace feelers already under way, and the first atomic bomb was dropped on Hiroshima on August 6, to be followed three days later by a Russian declaration of war. Matters then proceeded to their denouément aboard the U.S.S. *Missouri* on September 2, while Russia speedily implemented Yalta's promises by overrunning Manchuria.

The New Order Emerges

Postwar planning, inaugurated long before the United States entered the conflict, led through a series of carefully developed steps within the Department of State into domestic and international contacts culminating in the Dumbarton Oaks Conversations and the San Francisco Conference which formally launched the United Nations. Things moved much more systematically than in 1917–1918, and with greater attention to cultivating the public, Congressional, and inter-Allied consultations so important in building a proper climate of opinion for the launching of a new and somewhat risky enterprise. The success achieved remains a tribute to the foresightedness and industry of Cordell Hull and his departmental associates on both the working and policy-forming levels.[20]

---

[20] Vera M. Dean, "The San Francisco Conference: With Text of Charter," *Foreign Policy Reports*, July 15, 1945; L. M. Goodrich and E. Hambro, *Charter of the United Nations: Commentary and Documents*, World Peace Foundation, 1946; Hull, *op. cit.*, pp. 1109–1126, 1625–1713; G. L. Kirk and L. H. Chamberlain, "Organization of the San Francisco Conference," *Political Science Quarterly*, vol. 60 (1945), pp. 321–342;

Some public results of the behind-the-scenes preparation about to be described have already been placed in the record. First came the statement of the Atlantic Charter (August, 1941), almost an aside and subordinate to a plea for the future disarmament of the ill-intentioned, "pending the establishment of a wider and permanent system of general security. . . ." Next came the Declaration of United Nations of early January, 1942, resulting from the first Roosevelt-Churchill conference, and the first to bear the name supposedly suggested by the President while the Prime Minister was in the bath and accepted from the midst of the Churchillian ablutions. While principally devoted to winning the war, it was designed to commit the belligerent nations, as well as later signatories, to certain basic principles of right and justice. By the First Quebec Conference (August, 1943) planning had reached a stage where postwar organization could be discussed with the British and broached to the Russians. Hull's pilgrimage to Moscow followed shortly (October, 1943); from it emerged the Four-Nation Declaration accepting the idea of a postwar security organization open to all peace-loving nations, to be reënforced by further discussion at Teheran.

These public statements resulted from much careful backstage planning. The war was barely a fortnight old when Hull appointed (September 16, 1939) a Special Assistant (Mr. Leo Pasvolsky) to deal with problems connected with peace. The next step, tentative and temporary, was the establishment of an Advisory Committee on Problems of Foreign Relations (January 8, 1940), headed by Sumner Welles and composed with two exceptions of high-level departmental personnel already heavily burdened with regular assignments. Under the circumstances it was inevitable that such a group

---

Harley Notter, *Postwar Foreign Policy Preparation, 1939–1945*, Government Printing Office, 1949. Hull's memoirs and the Notter account, the latter the official departmental report on postwar planning activities down to the San Francisco Conference, are the chief "inside" stories published to date. To the student interested in the actual mechanical evolution of foreign policy the Notter volume affords one of the best case studies in the literature of American foreign relations. The Department has not yet published a companion volume on the San Francisco Conference, but two source collections are available: *Documents of the United Nations Conference on International Organization, San Francisco, 1945*, The United Nations, 1945, 16 vols., and *The United Nations Conference on International Organization, San Francisco, California, April 25 to June 26, 1945: Selected Documents*, Government Printing Office, 1946.

had to spend most of its energies on current problems at the expense of long-range planning. A Division of Special Research was created early in 1941 (February 3) and "charged with appraisal of developments and conditions arising out of present-day disturbed international relations and requiring special study as an aid to formulation of foreign policy." Its function was to conduct the preliminary research necessary to the intelligent determination of policy; it worked slowly because of lack of personnel, and secretly since the United States was not in the war, through the remainder of 1941, concerning itself primarily with political problems.

With the United States in the war and with the Division's work program established in skeleton form, Roosevelt approved (on or about December 28, 1941) the appointment of an Advisory Committee on Postwar Foreign Policy as an overall body to make use of the work of the Division of Special Research in the formulation of policy recommendations for submission to the President. This group, with Hull as chairman and with an expanding membership eventually totaling forty-five, furnished a highly useful nonpartisan liaison with the public, with capital and labor, and with the Congress. It operated mainly through nine subcommittees which kept in close working contact with the Division of Special Research which by this time was equipped to furnish expert studies of postwar problems. On January 1, 1943, as problems grew in number and complexity, and as funds became more easily available, the Division was subdivided into the Division of Political Studies and the Division of Economic Studies, and the technical preparations were speeded accordingly.

By the summer of 1943, after a year of preliminary drafting, it was judged time to formulate specific proposals for an international organization, and by August the experts had evolved a tentative draft and charter for a United Nations organization, sufficiently detailed to become the basis of Hull's negotiations at Quebec and at Moscow and sufficiently advanced in content to contribute largely to American proposals at Dumbarton Oaks a year later. A memorandum presented to Roosevelt on December 29, 1943, embodied the results of still further study and contained a distillation of eighteen months of intensive thinking on postwar organization. On February 3, 1944, the President issued orders to use the memorandum as a basis of formal recommendations. Already (January 15) a departmental Postwar Programs Committee had been set up to facilitate the enlarged activities made necessary by the increasingly international aspects of the negotiations. At the same time a two-way channel for information and advice was proposed in the creation of an Advisory Council on Postwar Foreign Policy, to succeed the Advisory Committee on Postwar Foreign Policy, virtually inactive since midsummer, 1943. Like its predecessor, the Council was to be nonpartisan, enlisting members of Congress and influential private citizens, as well as departmental officials, and was designed to give overall advice on the formulation of broad policy. Although the Council was never activated, the planning which went into its preliminaries was put to effective use through other agencies. It was with this equipment that the Department entered the international stage of planning in 1944. Attention to the foregoing somewhat complicated details should not obscure the essential character of developments to date—the careful combination of expert study with repeated attempts to keep in touch with Congress and public through the larger committees.

Matters moved into the international stage early in 1944 when the Russian and British Embassies received word (February 8) of American desire to exchange views on postwar international organization. By April American plans were fairly well advanced, at which time they were submitted to a bipartisan group of elder statesmen —Charles Evans Hughes, Nathan L. Miller, and John W. Davis— for consideration and criticism. Meantime Hull had been actively promoting Congressional support by personal conference and repeated appearances at committee hearings. By the end of May these discussions, though productive of searching questions, had proceeded far enough to justify approaching London and Moscow; on May 30 Hull requested the respective Ambassadors to proceed with the formalities of arranging discussions. Favorable replies eventually arrived though Russia delayed for some time and insisted that because of her own noninvolvement in the Pacific war the negotiations must proceed in two phases, from the first of which the Chinese must be excluded, and from the last of which she must absent herself.

All this was preliminary to the Dumbarton Oaks Conversations at which the Big Three conferred from August 21 to September 28, following which Russia withdrew and Anglo-American conferences with China followed from September 29 to October 7. Documentary studies of these conversations are not yet available. Hull's *Memoirs,* however, indicate the main points of difference, among which were the position to be occupied by the proposed Assembly of the United Nations, whose functions were minimized in the Anglo-Russian proposals, but which acquired added importance under American urging; the question of whether the proposed Security Council should decide questions by two-thirds or by a bare majority (left open because of inability to agree); the problem of whether economic and social matters came within the scope of a security organization, at first opposed by Russia, which later agreed that the Assembly might handle them. The veto question could not be solved at Dumbarton Oaks. In his conversations with Senators Hull had made it clear that the veto had been provided "primarily on account of the United States." It was, therefore, a cardinal principle of action on questions involving American security; the American delegation was willing, however, to modify this position to the extent that a member of the Security Council should be barred from voting on a question to which it was itself a party. Russia refused to yield this right, despite a 7:30 A.M. conference between Roosevelt and the Russian Ambassador, Andrei A. Gromyko, and a direct appeal to Stalin, and the Conference was recessed with the matter still unresolved.[21] Other questions remaining unsolved upon adjournment were those of initial membership in the new organization, the problem of trusteeships over dependent areas, the statute of a proposed Court of International Justice, and the procedure of liquidating the League of Nations.

Discussions at Yalta underwrote the proposals made at Dum-

---

[21] See above, pp. 495–499 for the discussion of this question at the Yalta Conference.

barton Oaks and set the date for the assembling of the United Nations Conference on International Organization at San Francisco
for the period from April 25 until June 26, 1945. Meantime there had
occurred Roosevelt's death, the approaching end of the European
war (Germany surrendered May 8), and, backstage, the beginnings
of Russo-American antagonism. It was in the light of these, and of
the rapid approach of victory in the East, that the delegates of forty-
six nations (increased to fifty by admission of White Russia, the
Ukraine, Argentina, and Denmark prior to adjournment) heard
President Truman's voice call the assembly to order. Wilson's experience had demonstrated the error of combining peace negotiations
with the establishment of international organization; this mistake
was not repeated. Another source of Wilsonian discomfiture, his
disregard of Congress and, largely, of the opposing political party,
was likewise avoided. The American delegation, chosen with nice
regard for the political proprieties, was actively headed by Secretary
of State Edward R. Stettinius, Jr. (Hull's health precluded his attendance, but in deference to his earlier efforts he was designated
Senior Adviser) and included prominent Republicans Harold E.
Stassen, Senator Arthur H. Vandenberg, and Representative Charles
A. Eaton, with Tom Connally and Sol Bloom as their Democratic
opposite numbers. A delicate touch was the choice of Dean Virginia
C. Gildersleeve of Barnard College to represent both her sex and
her profession.

Charged with completing the work inaugurated in the Department of State, accepted by the Moscow and Teheran conversations
and carried forward at Dumbarton Oaks, the conference wrestled
manfully with the remaining questions. With the war's end approaching, many were apprehensive as to where Russian policy
might turn; the Russian delegation promptly justified such suspicion.
The powers had been unable to resolve the dispute as to Poland's
government; Britain and the United States continued to recognize
the London Poles, while Russia demanded seats for her hand-picked
Lublin group. The ensuing controversy left Poland unrepresented at
San Francisco. Russia was more successful in demanding conference
and United Nations Assembly seats for White Russia and the

Ukraine, as Roosevelt had committed himself to this action at Yalta. Finally, and with more brusqueness than good manners, she violated the custom that the host nation provides the presiding officer by successfully insisting upon a rotating chairmanship for the conference. Russia was not the only disturbing influence, however, as representatives of the small nations, jealous of the pretensions of the great powers, sought to wield influence more in accord with their numbers than their power potential.

Several specific topics caused particular discussion, important among which was the question of trusteeships. The problem of managing backward and dependent areas, many of them mainly of strategic significance, was of basic importance and had received lengthy study in the Department of State. It was, however, passed over at Dumbarton Oaks because of inability to reach agreement. American desire to maintain control over certain strategically important Pacific islands led the United States delegation to emphasize the strategic aspects of the problem at San Francisco and the Charter eventually contained provisions sufficiently elastic to permit the United States to secure the desired bases while in general promising to promote "progressive development towards self-government or independence. . . ." The broad program, it should be noted, constituted an enlightened approach to the problem of backward areas.

One triumph of the conference, which was to have considerable importance in coming years, was the reconciliation of general and regional security. At Chapultepec, in March, 1945, the American republics had concluded a regional security agreement applicable to themselves; other nations, notably Russia, felt that bilateral security arrangements were essential insurance-policies against recurrent German aggression until such time as the United Nations might function effectively; they feared that such agreements as that of Chapultepec would dangerously weaken the united front of the United Nations. By compromise it was finally agreed in Article 51 (Chapter 7) that nothing in the Charter should "impair the inherent right of individual or collective self-defense," pending action by the Security Council, in case of an armed attack. Chapter 8 authorized the formation of security organizations to deal with matters of regional concern. Such agencies were to act only in agreement with the principles of the U.N., and were to keep the Security Council informed of actions taken or contemplated. The Pact of Rio, already noted in other connections, is an example of such a regional agreement.

Probably the most arrant example of Russian obstreperousness occurred in connection with the veto question, deadlocked at Dumbarton Oaks and supposedly clarified at Yalta. The Russians at San Francisco interpreted the Yalta formula to mean that a nation could use the veto to forbid the Council even to discuss questions which might need forcible measures in their settlement. Stettinius finally threatened to remain aloof from the organization if this Russian view persisted, at which point of deadlock Truman enlisted the services of Harry Hopkins, then on his last public mission in Moscow, to take the matter direct to Stalin. Stalin broke the impasse by reversing the Russian position and agreeing that the veto should not be used to prevent discussion. Substantive matters were still subject to great-power veto, but no important issue could be barred from the forum of debate.

Space is inadequate to make a lengthy analysis of the Charter. The obvious intention of its framers was to make the Big Five (the United States, Britain, Russia, France, and China) responsible through the Council, over whose actions each retained a veto on questions involving enforcement action, for securing the world against aggression—this on the principle of authority commensurate with responsibility. By the same token the small nations were given a forum in the General Assembly for the discussion of "any questions relating to the maintenance of international peace and security brought before it by any member of the United Nations, or by the Security Council, or by a state which is not a member of the United Nations. . . ." As long as small nations remained alert no untoward action need ever go unchallenged. Outstanding features of the Charter, moreover, were those which, operating technically under the General Assembly through the Economic and Social Council, envisioned objectives whose scope might in time become of vast importance for human welfare.

The Charter came before the Senate under much more favorable auspices than did the League of Nations of an earlier day. Truman presented it on July 2, just prior to his departure for the Potsdam meeting. The hearings of 1945 were more favorable and less lengthy (five days as against six weeks) than those of 1919, and the Foreign Relations Committee made a favorable report, minus the crippling provisions which had burdened Wilson's League. A surge of public approbation helped to shorten debate to six days and, on July 28, 1945, the Senate gave a resounding affirmative vote of 89 to 2. Woodrow Wilson, watching from some Elysian field, could well rejoice that his country had at last assumed the international obligations to which he had tried to commit it; unless still inhibited by his stern Calvinistic repressions, he might well have shed a tear, too, at the travail which had been necessary to bring about the return to grace.

20 One World Becomes Two Worlds

As the war of 1939–1945 passed from the realm of memory into that of history, and as wartime unity descended into postwar antagonisms, world hopes and world fears increasingly centered about the United States and the Union of Soviet Socialist Republics. Before entering this chapter's task of chronicling the later 1940's, a brief glance at the protagonists is in order.[1]

After the War of 1914–1918 Soviet Russia, increasingly strong and continuingly revolutionary, long remained aloof from the international community and, although grudgingly recognized by all but the United States, remained more or less of a pariah. In the 1930's the rise of fascist power in Japan, Italy, and Germany posed urgent problems for the Soviet planners. Twice terribly invaded from the West within a century, Russia sought security in the fold of the League of Nations (1934) against a third onslaught. Successive League failures to stop aggression by Japan (1931 and 1937) and by Italy (1935) were followed by the swaggering Nazi *diktat* at Mu-

---

[1] Able attempts at the difficult task of writing contemporary history are found in the successive volumes prepared by John C. Campbell for the Council on Foreign Relations under the title *The United States in World Affairs, 1945–1947, 1947–1948, 1948–1949, and 1949,* Harper, 1947, 1948, 1949, and 1950, respectively, and by the International Studies Group of the Brookings Institution, *Major Problems of United States Foreign Policy, 1947: A Study Guide; Major Problems of United States Foreign Policy, 1948–1949: A Study Guide;* and *Major Problems of United States Foreign Policy, 1949–1950,* Brookings Institution, 1947, 1948, 1949. Documents covering the war and postwar years are conveniently collected under changing editorship in a series of *Documents on American Foreign Relations,* numbering, as this is written, ten volumes (Princeton University Press, 1939 ff.).

511

nich (1938), and the Russians negotiated the insurance policies of the Nazi-Soviet Pact (1939) and the Russo-Japanese Neutrality Agreement (1941). Hitler's attack canceled one of these in 1941 and drove Russia to fight a war on the side of Hitler's enemies. Putting on the sheep's clothing of democracy for, as it appeared later, an ulterior purpose, the Russians masqueraded successfully enough to persuade more hopeful Westerners of a change of heart. The disguise was wearing thin even before the end of the Pacific War, however, and within a matter of months the Soviets changed from willful but well-intentioned partners to their more familiar character of apostles of revolution, a role made infinitely more threatening by greatly expanded territorial influence and vastly increased power potential.

This reversion to type jarred most rudely the nation whose leader had apparently been most convinced that he, and the world, could "get along" with the Russians. The war's end found the United States, after decades of isolationism, newly committed to the doctrine of internationalism embodied in the United Nations, founded on the premise that the war-born compulsions which had produced unity among the great powers could be transformed into a will to work together in the no less difficult tasks of peace and reconstruction. Since the United Nations was a great-power organization (made so largely by the veto, upon which the United States was as insistent as the Russians), its success depended upon the possibility of establishing and maintaining a basis of agreement, both within and outside the organization, among those major nations. The increasing Russian intransigence just noted soon destroyed this possibility.

As a result the United States, the only remaining first-rate power, was increasingly forced to pursue (and become the focal point around which others might rally) a dual policy. Its first element was an honest, almost a stubborn, adherence to the coöperative program marked out in the United Nations Charter. Frustrated in the United Nations by Russian obstructionism in the Security Council, and prevented from achieving peace by Russian tactics outside the organization, the United States turned, first gradually and reluctantly and then with increasing vigor, to a second tactic designed to provide security outside the United Nations. Here refuge was taken in national rearmament, the fostering of regional agreements separate from but not incompatible with the United Nations, and the extension of economic and military aid to those nations whose opposition to the tide of Soviet aggression might be counted upon. An increasing crescendo of Russian talk and action accompanied these twin developments until the end of the war decade saw the world divided into two camps, waging a "cold" war which observers watched fearfully lest some untoward incident turned it suddenly into a "hot" one.

Antagonism Emerges

Yalta's sharp and unresolved differences afford a convenient starting point for observing the developing antagonism between Russia and her allies. Here, it will be recalled, had appeared differences over the amount of German reparations and over the boundaries and government of Poland. The Yalta Declaration on Liberated Europe had promised that the Allies would "jointly assist the people in any European liberated state or former Axis satellite state in Europe . . . to form interim governmental authorities *broadly representative* of all *democratic elements* in the population and pledged to the earliest possible establishment through *free elections* of governments responsive to the will of the people. . . ." There was, however, no attempt to define such fine phrases as those to which emphasis has been added. Secretary of State Stettinius records that less than a month after Yalta the Russians had become noncoöperative on the occupation of Germany and Rumania and the government of Poland.[2]

Russia showed a new face, too, in a dispute which developed in March, 1945, over surrender negotiations. Learning of German feelers for preliminary discussions in Switzerland, Russia requested

---

[2] Stettinius, *Roosevelt and the Russians*, pp. 312–314. Russia initially promised, then refused, to send delegates to London to establish the Allied Control Commission for Germany; in disregard of the local Allied Control Commission, Andrei Vishinsky late in February personally interfered with the government of Rumania; and Molotov disregarded the Yalta pledge to broaden the base of the Polish government.

representation. Due partly to the extremely tentative nature of the proceedings and partly to a desire to prevent Russia from playing an arrogant role when they should become more formal, the request was refused. On March 16 Molotov bluntly insisted that the conversations be terminated and a week later informed Ambassador Averell Harriman that the negotiations were "absolutely inadmissible." Such bad manners drew a direct cable from Roosevelt to Stalin (March 24) denying that formal negotiations had occurred and refusing to suspend the investigations "because of objection on the part of Mr. Molotov for some reason that is completely beyond my understanding." Stalin's insulting reply questioned Roosevelt's veracity, and it was not until Admiral William D. Leahy and General George C. Marshall drafted the following sharp retort for Roosevelt's approval (April 4) that the atmosphere was somewhat cleared: "Frankly, I cannot avoid a feeling of bitter resentment toward your informers, whoever they are, for such vile misrepresentations of my actions or those of my trusted subordinates." The tension caused by this episode was lightened somewhat by Russian denunciation (April 8) of the Japanese neutrality pact and a more conciliatory message from Stalin; Roosevelt's cable of April 11 expressed his pleasure that the incident was closed.[3]

Meantime, however, Yalta rose to plague relations once more. By the end of March Churchill was expressing to Roosevelt his fear for the permanence of the Yalta agreements, and on April 1 a Presidential cable chided Stalin for not honoring the Yalta commitments on Poland and Rumania. Stalin's reply of April 7 admitted a stalemate and threw the blame on Anglo-American deviations. A reply to this sally was under consideration when Roosevelt died. One of his last statements, an hour before his death (April 12), was a message to Churchill, who had asked for advice concerning a forthcoming address: "I would minimize the general Soviet problem as much as possible because these problems, in one form or another, seem to arise every day and most of them straighten out as in the case of the Bern meeting.

---

[3] Byrnes, *op. cit.*, pp. 57–58; Leahy, *op. cit.*, pp. 329–335.

"We must be firm, however, and our course thus far is correct."
These episodes illustrate a Russian attitude which was changing before Roosevelt's death, the collapse of Germany, and the convening
of the San Francisco Conference had opened a new chapter.[4]

The first round of the new game (really a continued one) was
played at Potsdam by the new team of Truman and Byrnes, which
started using the old signals that had previously worked well
enough, but soon fell back on a defensive alignment against an
overtly aggressive Russian adversary. Reparations, Polish territorial
settlements, and implementation of the Declaration on Liberated
Europe caused heated discussions in the alternate meetings of Foreign Ministers and of Chiefs of State.[5] The Americans tried to moderate renewed Russian demands for twenty billion dollars in reparations, half payable to the Soviets; they succeeded in providing that
payments should be in kind rather than in currency, and shifted the
Russian emphasis away from a specific dollar amount. It seemed
agreed, also, that reparations from current production should begin
only when essential imports had been provided for, though the final
protocol contained no mention of this. The price of these gains,
however, was an agreement that each nation should draw reparations from its own occupation zone, with Russia receiving some
payments from the Anglo-American zones; meantime the Russians
had been industriously relieving occupied areas of useful movable
equipment.

The Potsdam negotiators faced a *fait accompli* in Poland, where
the Russians, without consultation, had given Poland administrative
control of German territory east of the Neisse River, including some
of Germany's best agricultural areas. Long and bitter discussions
produced a statement in the final protocol postponing final decision
of the Polish boundary until the peace negotiations, but in view of

---

[4] Byrnes, *op. cit.*, pp. 49–59. Truman sent Harry Hopkins on his last European
journey to assure Stalin of continued American coöperation despite the change of
leaders. In his last interview with Hopkins, May 27, 1945, Stalin listed five factors
which, he claimed, indicated that the American attitude toward Germany had
changed since that nation's defeat, justifying, of course, a stiffer Russian attitude
toward the West. Sherwood, *op. cit.*, pp. 893–895.

[5] Byrnes, *op. cit.*, pp. 67–87, and Leahy, *op. cit.*, pp. 397–428, are participants'
accounts of the meeting.

Stalin's determined attitude and the fact of Polish occupation of German territory, the prospects of agreement were hardly bright.

The American delegation vigorously criticized Russian policy in the Balkans, asserting flatly that the Yalta Declaration on Liberated Europe had not been fulfilled in Hungary, Bulgaria, or Rumania. When Truman proposed to draft an Italian peace treaty, Stalin adroitly attempted to link recognition of the satellite governments, established under Russian auspices, to the Italian question. The net result was a weak statement, piously hoping that peace treaties for Italy, Bulgaria, Hungary, Rumania, and Finland would soon be made, and that these nations would soon develop governments sufficiently democratic to entitle them to membership in the United Nations. Both sides won and lost: Truman failed to secure the democratization called for in the Yalta Declaration, and Stalin missed his important objective of securing Western recognition for the satellite governments. In Admiral Leahy's judgment the impasse over this question provided an appropriate starting point for the cold war of the later decade. His conclusion on the meeting, less optimistic than Byrnes', though more realistic in the light of later developments, may well conclude the Potsdam discussion:

My general feeling about the Potsdam Conference was one of frustration. Both Stalin and Truman suffered defeats. Several important proposals advanced by our Chief Executive—proposals that would have measurably aided the cause of lasting peace in Europe—were either turned down, watered down, or passed down to subordinate councils or commissions.

The Soviet Union emerged at this time as the unquestioned all-powerful influence in Europe. Britain and the United States had to accept at Potsdam many unilateral actions taken by Moscow since Yalta, although this acceptance was concealed in the diplomatic verbiage of the final report. . . . At Potsdam the only possibility of agreement would have been to accept the Russian point of view on every issue.

A word should be said at this point concerning the establishment of the satellite states which have become Russia's chief bulwark on the west and a major source of fear and suspicion between Russia and her erstwhile allies. Subsequent developments appear to bear out the political wisdom of Churchill's obstinate efforts to secure a military thrust at Europe's underbelly, for wherever Russian troops have gone a pro-Soviet government has eventually emerged. Prior to the Yalta meeting, advancing Russian legions had ousted pro-Nazi regimes in Hungary, Rumania, and Bulgaria; Marshal Tito's pro-Soviet forces controlled most of Yugoslavia; Greece alone fell under British military control and so escaped Russian domination. Inevitably, the succession governments leaned toward Moscow, which had already prepared a group for the administration of Poland. As agreed, Allied Control Commissions were established to manage the occupied areas, but admission of Western members was a mere formality.

The purpose of the Yalta Declaration on Liberated Europe was to liberalize these succession governments. Under its pressure and the fierce urges of the long-repressed peoples to practice self-government, the succession regimes were, for a time, liberalized. However, establishment of Communist control over key ministries such as interior, justice, and war, and frequently over domestic police, facilitated the acquisition of complete authority after longer or shorter intervals. Bulgaria, Rumania, Yugoslavia, and Albania successively paraded under the Communist banner. Complete downing of opposition in Poland was slower; Hungary did not succumb until June, 1947, and the coup which reduced Czechoslovakia to submission was delayed until February, 1948. Finland, last unit in a barrier between Russia and the West extending from the Adriatic to the Arctic Ocean, was not Communized, but has been kept more or less in the Russian orbit by the facts of geography and judiciously exacted treaties. The first sign of weakness in this dike was the flaring of Yugoslav hostility against Moscow in June, 1948. Thus it was that when Russia chose to drop an "iron curtain" between herself and the West, she had willing stage-hands in the wings to ring it down.

Peace and Trouble—Treaties with Minor Enemies

Russo-American antagonism next developed in the negotiation of peace treaties with the minor enemy powers, Italy, Bulgaria, Rumania, Hungary, and Finland (the United States was not a party to this last, not having declared war on the northern republic). Here the Council of Foreign Ministers worked out (between September, 1945, and December, 1946) the best possible solution in view of conflicting desires. In the process Secretary of State James F. Byrnes, willing heir of Roosevelt's policy of trying to get along with Russia, found himself driven to stronger and stronger tactics as the only feasible alternative to complete capitulation. During this period emerges the policy of "patience and firmness" which shortly strengthened into one of "getting tough" and, in turn, hardened into one of containment.[6]

A three-week session of the Council of Foreign Ministers opening at London (September 11, 1945) followed a flurry of end-of-the-fighting activities (Japan had signed surrender terms on September 2). Molotov aggressively renewed demands first made at Potsdam for Russian trusteeship over Tripolitania, insisted upon friendly Yugoslav control over Trieste, and refused to return the Dodecanese Islands to Greece. Byrnes did not cater to Russian demands—in his own words, Christmas was over, the first-of-January bills were coming due, and he resolved to collect some of these instead of being a perpetual payor. This sharp difference prevented positive accomplishment. Compromises made at a further meeting of the Council at Moscow (December 16–27, 1945) brought the likelihood of treaties somewhat closer. Byrnes accepted the pro-Soviet *status quo* in Bulgaria and Rumania in return for promises of token representation for non-Communist groups in those two governments, Russian concessions enabled the new United Nations organization to establish an Atomic Energy Commission, and some progress was made on Far Eastern matters hitherto in dispute; the tense situation in Iran was not resolved. Matters were then turned over to the Council of Deputies which, meeting in London from mid-January into March, 1946, at the same time as the first session of the United Nations General Assembly, accomplished nothing.

---

[6] All current accounts rely heavily on Byrnes, *op. cit.*, pp. 91–115, for the negotiation of the minor peace treaties. His participation in abortive efforts to make peace with Germany and Austria are recounted in *ibid.*, pp. 159–178. The official story may be found in *Making the Peace Treaties, 1941–1947*, Government Printing Office, 1947. The minor treaties were completed, except for drafting, on December 12, 1946, and signed at Paris, February 10, 1947; the United States Senate consented to their ratification on June 5, 1947.

Meantime United Nations matters had likewise developed Russo-American antagonisms, and in February and March, 1946, several pronouncements underlined the stronger approach to Russia foreshadowed at the London meeting the preceding autumn. On February 28 Byrnes administered a public reproof by asserting that the United States could not "overlook a unilateral gnawing away at the *status quo* . . . we cannot allow aggression to be accomplished by coercion or pressure or by subterfuges such as political infiltration . . . the United States intends to defend the Charter." Senators Tom Connally and Arthur H. Vandenberg and Republican foreign policy counselor John Foster Dulles also chided Russia publicly. And on March 16 Byrnes told Russia, via an address to the Friendly Sons of St. Patrick on the eve of their patron's day, that "It takes time to pass from the psychology of war to the psychology of peace. We must have patience, as well as firmness. . . ." Without abandoning patience, firmness came to bulk larger in American policy, and in a radio address on May 20 the Secretary announced that his country would not relapse into isolationism.

Byrnes' eleventh trans-Atlantic trip within a year took him to Paris for a new meeting of the Foreign Ministers (June 15–July 12, 1946), the chief accomplishment of which was the decision to invite representatives of twenty-one nations to the French capital for a Peace Conference which lasted from July 29 to October 15. Byrnes interrupted its endless wrangles to make a landmark speech at Stuttgart, Germany, on September 6 in which he announced that the United States was in Europe to stay. The Conference, hampered by Russian delaying tactics but acting without a veto provision, handed up recommendations to the Foreign Ministers' Council characterized generally by sacrificing principle in the interest of peace. Final agreement was reached at the Council meeting in New York (November 4–December 12) by applying the Byrnes patience/firmness formula with a preponderance of the latter. At a private session in Byrnes's hotel room the Secretary apparently told Molotov to agree or go home, and a rapid accommodation followed, with both sides participating in the concessions. The result was agreement on the basic form of the treaties, leaving only the tech-

nical drafting as an obstacle to completion. On the Russian side of
the balance the United States recognized the pro-Soviet government
of Bulgaria and virtually accepted Russian control of eastern Europe, at long last admitting that the Yalta formula was unworkable
in the face of Soviet aggression. A prime objective of Anglo-American diplomacy, the ousting of Russia from the Danube Valley, was
not achieved. On the other hand, Yugoslavia failed to secure the important port of Trieste, which Molotov had sought avidly, nor did
the Soviets realize their cherished dream of a foothold on the Mediterranean by gaining a share in administering the Italian colonies.
Most of all, the way to peace had been opened, though it was to be
months before the treaties became operative; and finally, the way
was cleared for consideration of the major peace settlements with
Germany and Austria.

This last hope was long deferred, since prospects for major peace
settlements, never bright, rapidly merged into and were lost in the
struggle for control of Europe. The increasingly apparent fact was
that Russia did not want an early German peace; continued occupation afforded golden opportunity for consolidation, indoctrina-
tion, and siphoning eastward of German resources. The Western
powers, moreover, had reached the limit of concessions in the minor
treaties and, when faced with demands for further surrender, sought
other protective measures. The result was a total lack of progress
which has persisted to the present time. At the Paris Foreign Ministers' meeting in April, 1946, Byrnes unsuccessfully sought the appointment of deputies for consideration of a German peace treaty;
Molotov announced that the establishment of a single German government, able to wipe out all vestiges of fascism and to sustain
reparations payments, must precede a peace settlement. By the
Moscow meeting of March, 1947, Anglo-American consolidation of
western Germany had already begun; it was apparent that surrender
on Germany might mean the loss of Europe and a deadlock ensued.
Two days after the Ministers convened, announcement of the Truman Doctrine sounded the knell of full coöperation for European
peace. Though preparation of a German peace treaty was on the
agenda of the London Council of Foreign Ministers' meeting of

December, 1947, disagreement on more fundamental matters prevailed and peace passed into limbo.

The Not So United Nations

The United Nations, established as the vehicle of international order through coöperation of the great powers, could not fulfill the founders' high hopes because the essential great-power coöperation failed to materialize. Russian intransigence and an insistent American urge to counter Russian aggressiveness, within and without the United Nations, furnish the theme of the postwar years and go far to explain the rough road which the organization has had to travel, its no more than modest success in many of its undertakings, and the development, late in the decade, of other devices of security to compensate for its shortcomings. Mankind, fortunately or unfortunately, has not made his social and political institutions operate as automatically as his complicated mechanical devices. These institutions, therefore, seldom reach a potential higher than the collective will of their members, a potential which the indifference or ill-will of a single component can reduce to a point approaching impotence. Thus it has resulted that the United Nations, while accomplishing much good in social and economic spheres, has fallen short of its founders' hopes in the political area which draws most public attention.

Among the factors accounting for this failure to reach the expected efficiency have been Russia's in-season and out-of-season use of the veto and her consistent disinclination to grant the U.N. that physical force which alone could make it effective. Even before it was well organized the Security Council faced (early in 1946) a test which brought out the barely latent antagonism between Russia and the West. Iran, enormously rich in oil, had been partially occupied by Russian troops. These remained in the northern province of Azerbaijan, despite a treaty promise of withdrawal by March 2, 1946, when the Security Council convened in New York on March 25. Iran asked the Security Council to consider this thorny problem and when the Council voted, over Russia's objections, to do so, Andrei Gromyko, the Russian delegate, took the first of many Russian departures from the Council chamber. Eventually a solution was found, but the Council had hardly made an auspicious beginning; between February and September, 1946, moreover, Russia vetoed no less than eight proposals, many of them unimportant in themselves, but cumulatively indicative of Russian intention to expand the veto far beyond the point intended by the San Francisco framers of the Charter. The Assembly, on the other hand, soon promised to become a working organization, despite the Russian tendency to view the most inconsequential matters as crises in the struggle between true democracy (Soviet pattern) on the one side and fascists and warmongers on the other.

During 1947, with American resistance to Russian expansionism emerging through the Truman Doctrine and the incipient Marshall Plan, the United Nations again became a sounding board for Russian-American rivalry. The Security Council made but little headway in solving several disputes referred to it, while Andrei Vishinsky again castigated a long and specific list of American warmongers, including John Foster Dulles. Russian obstructionism in the Council was signalized by Secretary Marshall's proposal for creation of an Interim Committee of the Assembly, representative of each member state, to sit between sessions and exercise broad powers of discussion and recommendation. The "Little Assembly" was established despite the united opposition of the Soviet bloc of six votes.

By 1948 continued Russian obstructionism (four vetoes occurred between the Assembly sessions of 1947 and 1948) had raised the question of modifying the organization in an effort to by-pass the veto; serious and clamorous groups were advocating one or another form of world government designed to obviate its evils. Responsible government officials, decrying such schemes, preferred to retain the U.N. with its increasingly obvious shortcomings, as a means of keeping Russia within the international community and maintaining an organization which time might strengthen, rather than risking the inevitable final Russian walkout which would follow any attempt to tamper with the veto. Frankly recognizing, however, the existing shortcomings of the U.N., American policy in 1948 found its two most important avenues, the Marshall Plan and the Atlantic Pact (which supplemented the Rio Pact of 1947, an all-American regional agreement), outside the framework of the Charter. The U.N. remained, nevertheless, a going concern. It is impossible to chronicle here the constructive work being done by many of its specialized agencies; space must be spared, however, for bare mention of one major accomplishment at the autumn session of the Assembly in the adoption of a Universal Declaration of Human Rights, largely a monument to the perseverance of Mrs. Eleanor Roosevelt.

Extra-U.N. agencies of security received continued emphasis in 1949 in the further implementation of the Atlantic Pact. It now became reasonably apparent that the U.N. was a holding operation on the political front, maintained as a forum of discussion and a means of preserving contact with Russia, however precarious, in the hope of long-run improvement in the temper of international affairs. Meantime the U.N., like the League of Nations before it, continued its usefulness in nonpolitical fields.

One item repeatedly on the U.N. agenda, productive there of bitter disagreement and ending in stalemate, was of terrifying importance not only to the investigators and debaters of the world organization but also, in its implications for the peace of the world, to all thinking men everywhere. This, the control of atomic weapons and energy, was perhaps of more pressing importance than any single problem facing the U.N. Brought to world attention by the detonation at Hiroshima on August 6, 1945, the bomb's lethal character evoked more early comment than did its political potentialities; when Truman spoke of it to Stalin at Potsdam, the Generalissimo is said to have shown little interest. This engine of mass destruction promptly developed political overtones, and the urgent problem of control in the interests of human existence soon pressed itself upon the attention of the U.N. The fact that the United States alone possessed the bomb became the key to Russian policy. This policy combined efforts to postpone effective controls over its manufacture and use until Russia herself could master its secret with bitter attacks upon the United States for allegedly planning to use the bomb to establish world domination. Indeed, it would not be a great exaggeration to suggest that American possession of the bomb became one of Russia's strongest propaganda weapons—knowing well that it would only be used defensively, the Soviets could afford to damn the United States as a potential aggressor through its agency.

Alert to the implications of atomic power, its chief producers took early steps toward international control. At a meeting on November 15, 1945, President Truman, with Prime Ministers Attlee and W. L. Mackenzie King of Canada, decided to propose the creation of a U.N. commission to establish the necessary safeguards. At the December, 1945, session of the Council of Foreign Ministers Russia agreed to enter a six-power sponsoring group, composed of Canada and the five permanent members of the Security Council, to underwrite a resolution establishing a United Nations Atomic Energy Commission. The U.N. Assembly passed such a resolution, January 24, 1946. American thinking produced the Acheson-Lilienthal Report (March 16, 1946), which was presently adopted as government policy and became the basis of American action in the Atomic Energy Commission.[7] Briefly, this Report proposed to subject all atomic energy activity likely to threaten world security to international control and to place under similar inspection and licensing all other phases of atomic activity. Military use of the bomb would be forbidden and the international agency would be authorized to use force against violators. In return for such safeguards the United States would manufacture no more bombs and would, after the new authority became fully operative, get rid of its existing supplies. Bernard M. Baruch, elder statesman, was chosen as the American representative on the Atomic Energy Commission.

Early sessions of the Commission (which first met on June 14, 1946) disclosed a fundamental difference between Russian and American policy. Baruch presented the American scheme, based on the Acheson-Lilienthal Report, and proposing that those who violated a promise not to use atomic energy as a weapon of offense be

---

[7] The main outlines of the struggle for control of atomic energy may be traced through the following: *A Report of the International Control of Atomic Energy,* Government Printing Office, 1946; *The International Control of Atomic Energy: Growth of a Policy,* Government Printing Office, 1946; and *International Control of Atomic Energy: Policy at the Crossroads,* Government Printing Office, 1948.

subjected to automatic penalties without benefit of veto. Russian counterproposals called for prompt international agreement to outlaw atomic weapons, on such terms as would nullify the American advantage before establishment of safeguards against future misuse of the bomb. Instead of the automatic sanctions advocated by the United States, Russia suggested that the Security Council punish violators, thus maintaining great-power veto over such action. Late in 1946 (December 31) the Commission's first report to the Security Council adopted the United States plan with Russia and Poland abstaining. On February 10, 1947, Russia offered various amendments embodying its ideas and on March 10, 1947, the Council returned the report to the Commission for further study. During the long discussions the United States had consistently refused to bow to Russian insistence upon disarmament without adequate guarantees.

After considerable further discussion which failed to narrow the gap between the two positions, the Commission rendered a third report in May, 1948, concluding that coöperative control of atomic energy could only follow the establishment of a clearer atmosphere in general international relations, and recommending suspension of its work pending such clarification. An American resolution in the Security Council the following month putting the Council on record as approving the controls suggested by the Commission's majority was vetoed by the U.S.S.R. and the Commission's three reports turned over to the Assembly. That body accepted (November 4, 1948), over Russian opposition, the findings of the Commission, which thus became United Nations policy, even though Russian opposition prevented its implementation. Acting under instructions of the Assembly, the Commission worked further but was unable to resolve the three fundamental problems dividing Russian and western thinking: (1) the Russian demand for immediate conventional prohibition of the bomb as against gradual abolition paralleling development of international controls; (2) insistence upon national management and international inspection instead of international machinery in both fields; and (3) Security Council control of action against violators instead of inexorable vetoless sanctions. Matters

remained in this state of suspended animation until the announcement (September 24, 1949) that Russia had achieved an atomic
explosion made the controversy over controls somewhat academic
if even more urgent than ever.

Far Eastern Troubles

American postwar policy in Eastern Asia, as in Europe, has generally involved building dikes at various levels against insurgent
Communism. As in Eastern Europe, Russian forces, after the Soviet's
tardy commitment to the Pacific war, moved rapidly to fill the voids
created by the collapse of Japanese power on the mainland. Manchuria and North Korea were speedily occupied; American forces
took over Japan and South Korea, and an arbitrary line fixed at 38°
divided the former Hermit Kingdom, long held by Japan, into two
zones. These points of vantage formed the bases upon which subsequent policy has developed.

American China policy went back to the Yalta decisions, later
written into the Sino-Soviet agreement of August 14, 1945, granting
the U.S.S.R. essentially the same rights as Czarist Russia had enjoyed in Manchuria prior to 1904 and certain rights in the coastal
towns of Port Arthur and Dairen; in return, Stalin agreed to support
no other Chinese government than that of the Kuomintang. Soviet
troops presently evacuated Manchuria except for the Port Arthur-
Dairen areas, leaving large amounts of abandoned Japanese matériel
to the local Communists. Under these circumstances American policy during 1946 was directed mainly to efforts to persuade Chiang
Kai-shek to modify the Kuomintang's reactionary leadership.

Both President Truman and Secretary of State Byrnes made public statements toward the end of 1945 intimating that the "strong,
united, and democratic" China which all desired could be best obtained by broadening the political base "to include other political
elements in the country." The agent of this mediation was General
George C. Marshall, just retired as Chief of Staff of the victorious
armies and now called to a political mission of the utmost delicacy.
By mid-January, 1946, his great personal prestige secured a truce
between Chiang and the native Communists which, it was hoped,

would provide time for the negotiations which could implement American desires for liberalization of the government. However, when the General came home to report on his mission in March, fighting promptly broke out and, although he returned and spent weary months in negotiation, his position became intolerable by the end of the year. Both Chinese and Soviet Communists were attacking him, and the local disciples of Lenin had contemptuously rejected all government overtures.[8]

Under these circumstances Marshall felt he would best serve China's interests by going home and, departing, issuing a blunt statement on China's needs and shortcomings. These developments occurred early in January, 1947, shortly after Chiang proclaimed a new constitution, to become effective on the following December 25. Marshall's parting shot, repeating earlier advice to Chiang to broaden the governmental base, missed the mark, and little change in the Chinese political picture resulted. The General's mission, by and large a failure, had fallen between the two stools of dominant reaction in the Kuomintang and intransigent Communism which refused all compromise save on its own grounds. In China, negotiation soon gave way to out-and-out civil war, with the Communists making considerable headway in 1947.

In this year the United States, with General Marshall succeeding Byrnes as Secretary of State, pursued a tentative policy which offended Chiang, now more than ever opposed to the Communists, without appreciably improving the general situation. American military aid was much reduced, and General Albert C. Wedemeyer went to China as the Administration's observer. On leaving (August 24), he stated that in his opinion China should initiate "drastic and far-reaching political and economic reforms. Promises," he said, "will no longer suffice. Performance is absolutely necessary. . . ." This was hardly calculated to add to Chiang's peace of mind. By the end of the year it seemed apparent that the Administration's principal effort in the immediate future was to be devoted to containing

---

[8] *United States Relations with China: With Special Reference to the Period 1944– 1949*, Government Printing Office, 1949, carries the official explanation and analysis of government policy on China.

Communism in Europe through the Truman Doctrine and the Marshall Plan, implementation of which was already afoot. The calculated risk which had been discounted and assumed in Europe was not to be undertaken in China.

Rapid advance of the Chinese Communists, corresponding deterioration of Nationalist resistance, and renewal of American aid on a limited basis characterized 1948. In September the Chinese Reds took Tsinan, the capital of Shantung, and the following month completed the conquest of Manchuria and moved on Nanking, the Nationalist capital. The Communist threat had contributed to Congressional authorization of $463,000,000 in economic aid and $125,-000,000 in military assistance (April 3, 1948), but when military desperation caused Mme. Chiang to fly to Washington in December seeking more and more immediate assistance, she met with a chilly reception. By this time American eggs were in the European basket and the Administration was unwilling to make further commitments, desiring to remain free to act as events might dictate.

This freedom of action was maintained only at the cost of considerable embarrassment, however, since sooner or later a choice would have to be made between the enormous cost of full-scale aid to China and the loss of face involved in withdrawal after assuming the role of chief foe of Communism—particularly when European policy was still being conducted on just this basis. Events hastened the decision; on April 20, 1949, the Reds crossed the Yangtze River and four days later entered Nanking. Secretary of State Dean Acheson had already (March 15) informed Senator Connally that the Department did not favor extensive aid to China, and the White Paper of August 5 indicated that for the time being at least the United States, after spending $2,254,000,000 in China since the Japanese surrender without appreciable results, would now pursue a wait-and-see policy, permitting Chinese events to seek their own solution. By the end of this year the Nationalist Government had retreated to the Island of Formosa, Mao Tse-tung's Communists were in the saddle, that leader himself was on the usual pilgrimage to Moscow in search of Stalin's blessing and favorable treaties, and questions were being raised as to whether Nationalist China was

longer entitled to sit in the United Nations, where a Communist vote (and veto) would prove a useful adjunct to Soviet obstructionism. Here the American dike against Communism had not been built sufficiently high. By the end of the year, indeed, it was increasingly apparent that Soviet policy, balked in a measure by Western firmness over Berlin, was successfully pursuing, with the willing aid of Mao Tse-tung and the Chinese Communists, a familiar tactic of pushing out in another direction—a tactic which, as 1949 ended, had swung the pendulum against the West in China.

In Japan American policy was more successful. Here circumstances enabled that nation, like Germany, whose story will be treated below, to advance fairly rapidly from the status of a hated and conquered foe to that of a sort of below-the-salt retainer in the anti-Communist campaign. Among the factors involved were: The preponderant part played by American arms in the Pacific conquest, the mechanics of the occupation, the personality of the American administrator, the development of world and Far Eastern politics, and the increasing burden on the American taxpayer.[9]

Punishment and reform, the original purposes of the Japanese occupation, were carried out promptly and efficiently by General Douglas MacArthur, who became Supreme Commander for the Allied Powers (SCAP). Policy was designed to make Japan pay reparations for damages done, place her on an economic level where her power potential could never endanger world peace and security, and, withal, give her people a deeper knowledge of the democratic way of life than had ever been opened to them before. The occupation machinery was well adapted to these ends. Having achieved Japan's defeat alone, the United States assumed the chief role in affairs, not without some mutterings on the part of China and the Soviets. As a result machinery was set up ostensibly to direct SCAP's activities but, thanks in part to MacArthur's impatience at supervision, whether by his own or other Foreign Offices, it soon became advisory rather than supervisory.

---

[9] *Occupation of Japan: Policy and Progress,* Government Printing Office, 1946, and a series of articles by Ardath W. Burks on "Occupied Japan" in *The American Year Book, 1947, 1948* and *1949,* Nelson, 1948, 1949, 1950, pp. 105–115, 81–87, 84–91, round out the story told in authorities already cited.

Two boards were established. The Far Eastern Commission (FEC), composed of representatives of eleven immediately interested nations, sat in Washington. Its duties were to "formulate and review" policies relative to Japan's fulfillment of her surrender obligations. Presumably, the veto operated in its deliberations. In Tokyo the Big Four were represented on the Allied Council, whose advisory powers SCAP might disregard except that important matters were supposed to be reviewed by the Far Eastern Commission before becoming effective. Inasmuch as the United States might instruct SCAP in emergencies, and inasmuch as many FEC directives merely registered policies already effected by MacArthur, it will be seen that SCAP was driven with a very light rein. Under MacArthur's leadership vast changes in Japan's outward way of life occurred in a year and a half. Shinto, the state cult of emperor worship, was abolished; prompted by MacArthur Emperor Hirohito personally divested himself of the divinity which had hedged previous Japanese monarchs even when, as in the case of his own father, their mental equipment was less than normal. Japan became a limited monarchy under a westernized constitution patterned in considerable measure upon that of the United States; free elections, in which women voted for the first time, chose a Diet; and the institutions of local government were reformed.

In January, 1947, just as Marshall was completing his frustrating mission in China, and before the United States had committed itself fully to European containment, the Far Eastern Commission found it advisable to allow Japan a higher level of industrial production than that originally set. On March 17 MacArthur told a press conference that it was time to make peace, terminate the occupation, and surrender management of Japan to the United Nations. On July 11 the United States proposed that delegates of the FEC states meet in August to take preliminary action on peace terms, decisions to be taken by two-thirds vote, the veto not to apply, and the final draft to be submitted to the Foreign Ministers of the FEC powers. Russia countered with a suggestion that the veto-ridden Council of Foreign Ministers should take primary responsibility for negotiations;

previous experience caused the United States to shy away from this profitless exercise.

With peace a dream vanishing into a prospectively endless "armistice," with the Communist menace strong in Europe and waxing in East Asia, and with the American taxpayer facing increasing burdens resulting from European commitments, American practice sought to provide an anchor to windward by strengthening the Japanese economy. This was first done informally, but in the spring of 1948 an official mission composed of George Kennan and W. H. Draper visited the islands and recommended emphasizing economic recovery as opposed to reform. By December MacArthur was warning Washington that more force was needed in Japan to offset the flanking Communist positions being established in the Kuriles, Kamchatka, and China.

The year 1949 witnessed a curious series of developments. Japan passed more and more out of the status of conquered enemy into that of informal ally, despite the absence of formal peace arrangements. American policy tended to permit Japan, still under occupation, to assume considerable control over external as well as internal affairs. The economy was relieved of a heavy burden by suspension (May 12, 1949) of reparations payments. With China well on the way to Communism, it was Russia's turn to seek a peace treaty and the West's turn to ignore the request. Communism, strong on the mainland across from Japan, found MacArthur a stern and unrelenting foe. Chinese and Russian Communism could only look askance at this development and hope for better things in the future; in Japan the dike was high enough, for the time being at least, to keep out the flood.

Japan's defeat failed to unify troubled Korea. The end of hostilities found the country arbitrarily divided at the thirty-eighth parallel between Russian occupation troops on the north and Americans on the south. This division was economic as well as military, since Russia controlled the principal natural resources and the agricultural South was hardly self-sustaining. The result was a continuing tug of war between sharply divergent political ideologies, each seeking to claim all of Korea. North Korea was thoroughly Communized and regimented on the Soviet pattern, while the South remained under American control with the United Nations assuming increasing responsibilities. Toward the end of 1947 the United Nations sought to sponsor a free election for the whole country which would precede withdrawal of all occupation forces and the establishment of an autonomous Korea. This move failed to find favor with the northern Communists, and when the election was held in the spring of 1948 it was confined to South Korea and even there was boycotted by the local Communists and some rightist elements. The new National Assembly adopted a conservative constitution and chose as President Mr. Syngman Rhee; the American military government was ended, though troops remained on Korean soil. To the North a sovietized election was held (August 25, 1948) and the resulting "National Assembly" claimed jurisdiction over all Korea.

This pointed up another Russia-vs.-the-West struggle, for at the General Assembly session of September, 1948, the Russians announced withdrawal of their occupation forces by the end of the year; this was a move to force the United States to follow suit in South Korea, where local military and political instability afforded opportunities for aggressive penetration from the Communist North. After a bitter debate the Assembly established a Commission to try to bring unity out of Korean chaos, but neither of the rival governments would coöperate with it, each hoping to unify the country on its own pattern.

Russian troops allegedly withdrew on schedule and on January 1, 1949, the United States accorded South Korea diplomatic recognition, but a Russian veto defeated an American move to seat a Korean delegation in the United Nations. In mid-April President Rhee announced that his army was about ready to take over, provided the Republic was "not called upon to face attack from foreign sources." American troops were then on the way out of Korea (evacuation was completed in June, save for advisory groups), and matters remained in an indeterminate status for some months, with the artificial boundary still in effect, with Korea still divided economically, and with the Rhee Government unable either to consolidate its power effectively at home or to extend its influence northward. The weak dike erected at 38° held, however, until late June, 1950, when the Communist North launched a sudden military attack which broke the dike and threatened to turn the Far Eastern cold war into one of higher temperature.

Cold War in Europe

The preceding pages have described various phases of the growing friction between Russia and the West. One of the most crucial aspects of this conflict developed simultaneously over the control of Germany, where Russian influence met sterner opposition than in its rapid expansion into the Balkan satrapies. There ensued a power-conflict which, starting as a struggle for the domination of Germany, entered into a phase where the stakes were Europe-wide and thence, by rapidly shifting gradations, into a contest for world domination. It was a contest fought across peace tables, in the United Nations, in the economic organization of Germany, in the airlift, and in regional political pacts; fought with all the fanfare of ideological propaganda and, as the lines became more and more sharply drawn, fought with the weapons of food and dollars, in the decreasingly optimistic hope that these weapons might forestall the use of others too recently set aside. Again, as in contests already described, the chief protagonists were Russia and the United States, the latter aided, as the urgency of the situation became increasingly apparent, by most of the western European nations, fearful of their future.

Germany furnished the initial field of conflict. The sources of that conflict lay in wartime agreements (at Potsdam) which decreed that Germany should be disarmed, dismembered, denazified, "democratized," and reduced to an economic level where she could never again become a threat to world security and peace. The European Advisory Commission provided at Teheran wrestled manfully with the establishment of occupation zones, finally (June 5, 1945) assigning eastern Germany to Russia, dividing the south between France and the United States, placing Britain in charge of the west, and laying up trouble for all concerned by sharing Berlin, in the

(*From Brookings Institution,* Major Problems of the United States Foreign Policy, 1949–1950,
p. 108.)

heart of the Russian zone, among the occupying powers, leaving all ground approaches dominated by the Soviets.[10] According to the Potsdam agreement Germany was to be managed, pending the peace settlement, by an Allied Control Council composed of the four zonal military commanders. These wielded supreme local power

---

[10] Philip F. Mosely, "The Occupation of Germany: New Light on How the Zones Were Drawn," *Foreign Affairs,* vol. 28 (1950), pp. 580–604.

which was supposed to be tempered into overall agreement on the principle of unanimity; failing agreement, each continued to pursue his own devices in his own zone. A military Kommandatura was to manage Berlin's precarious destinies. Economically, occupied Germany was to be considered as a unit, managed under agreed Allied policies designed to assure minimum living standards, with primary emphasis on agriculture and nonmilitary industry. The leaders failed to draw finally the German-Polish boundary, leaving Poland in temporary control of Russia's maximum demands, but paying lip service to the idea that the peace settlement would make final (and possibly different) arrangements.

During the winter of 1945–1946, while the Conference of Foreign Ministers (Moscow, December, 1945) and their Deputies (London, January-March, 1946) made slow headway with the minor peace treaties, and while the infant United Nations wrestled with Iran and the Russian veto, friction developed over German affairs. Russia began to hint darkly, during the winter, that the slow pace of disarmament in the western zone was deliberately calculated to contribute to a strong German bulwark against Russian influence, and to justify her own interference to the east and south as a countermeasure for purposes of security. Serious problems in the economic and political management of Germany appeared during the year, and the outline of conflicting policies emerged. The United States favored the economic unification of Germany postulated in the Potsdam agreements; this in order to provide Germany with a viable economy which, in turn, would lighten the $200,000,000 annual burden which Germany was imposing on the American taxpayer. Since the Russian zone was more nearly self-supporting than the western zones, and since economic unity might demand that their zone contribute to western deficiencies, the Russians, though paying occasional lip service, showed little interest in economic unification. Differences developed, too, over the level of industry to be permitted the German economy. An agreement of March, 1946, set this at a low figure. Preliminary discussions showed that the Russians desired a still lower one, in order to make possible higher reparations payments, while the British desired a higher level in order to speed European recovery and to relieve the British taxpayer of occupation costs. American official opinion at first supported the Russian point of view for security reasons, but later in the year began to approach the British position that Germany ought to be made a going concern.

In the face of continued Russian unwillingness to unify, Secretary Byrnes, still in his "patience and firmness" phase, offered (July 11) to integrate the United States zone economically with that of any other nation. Russia refused this proposal as divisive of Germany, and France seconded the motion. Byrnes returned to the charge in his Stuttgart speech (September 6), admitting that the Allied Control Council was not carrying out the Potsdam agreements which, he argued, made economic unification more urgent than ever. The British accepted this overture and negotiations produced an agreement (signed December 2, to take effect January 1, 1947) for the economic fusion of the Anglo-American zones.

On the political side a fundamental difference also emerged. As the year passed it became apparent that the United States favored increasing German participation in governmental affairs, in the interest of the democratization posited at Potsdam, and as a means of lifting the German burden from the American fiscal system. The United States looked to a Germany organized upon a decentralized and democratic model which would minimize the likelihood of a "strong" government that might move toward dictatorship, either of the right or of the left. Russia, on the other hand, favored more centralized political institutions. Russia interpreted the developing American policy of 1946 in both economic and political spheres as opposing her own interests and as an American plea for German support against Russian efforts to dominate the German scene. This aspect of affairs became more apparent during 1947, when, too, the German situation began to merge into a larger European picture of great-power rivalry.

This year opened an era reminiscent of the mid-1930's, save that the threat came from a new quarter. Although the second half of the Byrnes patience-firmness formula had received major emphasis during the latter part of 1946, American policy-makers still clung to the increasingly forlorn hope that Russia would honor her pledges of coöperation. Before the year was half gone, however, the United States had become convinced that a new aggressor must be dealt with; because of this conviction, American policy hardened into one of containment, as expressed in the Truman Doctrine and the Marshall Plan.[11] Continued disagreement on Germany, developing during successive meetings of the Council of Foreign Ministers at Moscow (March-April) and London (November-December), reenforced this conviction and produced increasing harmony in Anglo-American policy.

Mention has already been made of the economic unification of British and American zones, formally effective on January 1, 1947, but continuing in the organizational stage until after the Moscow Conference. This was designed to increase west-German self-sufficiency and, as a result, to contribute to west-European recovery. The Moscow discussions, involving both the peace and the current management of Germany, renewed earlier disagreements over economic unification and centralized vs. federalized governmental institutions; they served no purpose other than to point up the irreconcilable differences between Russia on the one hand and Britain and the United States on the other, and to make crystal clear that any four-power agreement on Germany was a matter of the indeterminate future. The new orientation of American policy contained in the Truman Doctrine (announced March 12, 1947, two days after the Moscow conversations opened) and the Marshall Plan (foreshadowed in Marshall's pronouncement of June 5) broadened the area of Russian-American differences to include all of Europe, and tended to obscure the German question save as the latter was part of the larger whole.

With American efforts directed, after Moscow, to hastening the economic recovery of Europe, the tendency was to integrate German policy into this objective. On July 11 a new directive instructed General Lucius D. Clay, American military commander, that the

---

[11] An article by "X," usually attributed to George Kennan of the Department of State, "The Sources of Soviet Conduct," *Foreign Affairs*, vol. 25 (1947), pp. 566–582, analyzes the factors in Russian policy which pushed the United States toward an effort at containment.

basic purpose was now to be the "creation of those political, economic and moral conditions in Germany which will contribute to a
stable and prosperous Europe." Authorization in August of a higher
level of industry in the three west-German zones was further earnest
of this intention and further notice to Russia of democratic determination. Under the circumstances the deliberations of the Foreign
Ministers at London tended to assume an academic character. As on
earlier occasions, economic unification posed a stumbling block. The
United States insisted that economic unification must precede any
political steps, while Russia now refused economic unity until after
the establishment of a political structure agreeable to its interests.
There was no meeting of the minds, and the discussions convinced
the West that compromise was impossible. Germany was now important mainly as a factor in the general European situation.

Though events had for months pointed toward larger American
participation in general European events, the final plunge came
with startling suddenness. Developments began on a plane of simple
containment of Soviet expansionism in the Greco-Turkish aid program implementing the Truman Doctrine, but soon entered a
broader and more positive phase of attempting to unify Europe
economically as envisioned in the Marshall Plan. General Marshall
became Secretary of State on January 21, 1947, and was busily planning for the Moscow Conference, which he hoped would begin the
stabilization of Germany; President Truman was preparing to re-
build some inter-American fences by a trip to Mexico. On February
24 Marshall learned that the British, having poured a half-billion
dollars into the neighborhood of the Dardanelles since the end of
hostilities, felt compelled to withdraw further aid to Greece and
Turkey as of March 31. The obvious reason for this retrenchment
was Britain's straitened postwar circumstances; it has been suggested also that, with India's ties loosening, the eastern lifeline was
becoming less important and that British strategists preferred to
build their defenses on holdings in Kenya, Nigeria, and South Africa.

Whatever Britain's motivation, the impact of her decision was
tremendous. Greece and Turkey had become focal points of Russian
pressure on non-Sovietized Europe, outside aid was being furnished

to Communist revolutionaries against Greek authority, and Turkey was vulnerable as custodian of the Straits. Removal of British assistance would turn an outpost of resistance into a political vacuum—and Russian affinity for such was by now well established. A vigorous American stand would therefore constitute a definite threat to Soviet expansionism; it would transcend the repeated "Nay, Nay," of Secretary Byrnes across the conference table; it would entail assumption of international responsibilities, on a unilateral basis, such as those who took the United States into the United Nations had thought would only be the function of international organization.

The decision was taken promptly, so promptly, indeed, that the Administration earned itself sharp criticism for its method of procedure. In a dramatic message to Congress (March 12) Truman asserted that American policy would be "to support free peoples who are resisting attempted subjugation by armed minorities or by outside pressures." He asked for $300,000,000 (half of which was for military expenditures) for Greece and $100,000,000 (all military) for Turkey. Previous American policy-makers had received bitter condemnation for extending the frontier of American security to the British Isles and the Rhine; at one fell swoop Truman's announced policy of containment moved it eastward to the Dardanelles. The "Truman Doctrine" had been elaborated so speedily that its ramifications in other areas of American policy had not been fully explored. Critics soon made sharp outcry at this by-passing of the United Nations through a proposal which would undertake single-handed remedies with hardly a bow toward existing machinery. The American representative, Warren R. Austin, hastened to assure the Security Council that no slight had been intended, and Senator Arthur H. Vandenberg gave the critics *ex post facto* assurance by obtaining insertion of an amendment to the enabling legislation providing that the American program would be discontinued whenever either the Assembly or the Security Council should determine that United Nations action made further United States steps unnecessary or undesirable. The legislation was then passed and the die was cast.

The Truman Doctrine was essentially a negative approach, and Administration planners soon concluded that containment pure and simple, no matter how important, was not a whole solution to exist-ing problems. American funds could not be poured out indefinitely to dam the Communist flood; huge sums had already been expended since the conclusion of hostilities, and there appeared to be no end to the need. Some positive program must be developed whereby Europe's economy could be made self-supporting before the Amer-ican taxpayer's cash—and patience—gave out.[12] The suggested rem-edy was contained in an address delivered by General Marshall at Harvard University on June 5, 1947, which set in motion machinery which resulted in the Marshall Plan. This reoriented governmental policy from the negative Truman Doctrine and laid the foundation for an affirmative program designed to restore to full economic vigor a group of nations which together could, it was hoped, create a bar-rier to Russian Communism. No one nation, even one as willing to incur apparently unlimited deficits as the United States, could in-definitely maintain such a barrier.[13]

Since the proposal was essentially simple, asking for no money and carrying no commitments, it created much less of an initial stir than had the Truman Doctrine. Adopting an essentially economic ap-proach, Marshall proposed a campaign against "hunger, poverty, desperation and chaos," without mention of political ideology. He suggested that any nations interested (which of course might in-clude Russia and her satellites) should plan a coöperative recon-struction program; having done so, they were invited to submit it

---

[12] European aid had undergone considerable shifts since V-E day. Truman had turned off the spigot in the lend-lease pipeline on August 30, 1945, only to be beset by British urgency for continuation of assistance during the demobilization period. Political considerations counseled a new name, and for some months outright relief assistance was extended through the United Nations Relief and Rehabilitation Ad-ministration, an internationally supported scheme based largely on American funds. On December 23, 1946, the President announced that the program would be con-cluded during the first half of 1947, and the last payments under UNRRA were made about the time that Congress passed the Greco-Turkish aid legislation. Thereafter, it was announced, individual nations must make individual arrangements for funds. In line with this policy Congress subsequently appropriated $350,000,000 for aid to Italy, Austria, Poland, China, Trieste, and Greece, and on December 17, 1947, before the Marshall Plan went into effect, added $597,000,000 of interim aid.

[13] A speech of Undersecretary Dean Acheson at Cleveland, Mississippi, on May 8, "The Requirements of Reconstruction," deserved greater publicity than it received in impressing upon the public the wider implications of American foreign-aid pro-grams.

to the United States for scrutiny. The United States would then examine the plan and decide whether it was worth a trial. This forced the initiative upon Europe which, of late, had done little but seek largesse.

European action was prompt, but not unanimous. The three principal Foreign Ministers, Bevin, Molotov, and Georges Bidault, met at Paris late in June, raising short-lived hopes that Russia was at last entering a coöperative phase. These hopes proved false when Molotov proposed that instead of the concerted plan requested by Marshall, the nations should petition aid individually and independently. Since the combined operation was the heart of Marshall's scheme, it was apparent that the Molotov move was obstructionist. Molotov left Paris on July 3, taking with him not only Russian coöperation but the hopes of many East Europeans, for several Soviet-orbit nations, including Finland, Czechoslovakia, and Hungary, were eager to push goods trains through the iron curtain and restore former lucrative contacts with Western Europe. Most satellites came quickly to heel, but Czechoslovakia had the temerity to accept an invitation to the Paris parleys "in principle." It was necessary to summon Klement Gottwald and Jan Masaryk to Moscow before they saw the light and agreed to avoid the capitalist snare. Soviet and iron-curtain nations' abstention drew the lines more sharply than ever, and the Marshall Plan evolved (though not originally couched in such terms) into a defensive organization of the West against Communism.

Representatives of sixteen nations convened at Paris on July 12 and, working under forced draft, were able to lay a two-volume report and plan of campaign on Secretary Marshall's desk on September 22. Western Germany was included in their calculations at a late stage in the deliberations, further earnest of growing feeling that German and European prosperity were integrally connected. The move, moreover, placed the German problem on a broader than Big-Four basis, and made it part of the world equation again. After receiving expert reports that the American economy could stand the prospective strain, Truman presented the European Recovery Program (ERP) to Congress on December 19, 1947, and it was soon clothed in legislative language in the Economic Coöperation Act

(ECA), which asked the American taxpayer to underwrite a sum of seventeen billion dollars over the four and one-half years estimated as necessary to put Europe back on its feet.

Congress assumed the obligation, though with sufficient grumbling and delay to cause European misgivings as to the sincerity of American intentions. The decision entailed immense political consequences. The emergent Western European economic bloc forced Russia to plan counterstrokes. A series of politico-economic agreements was designed to offset the effects of Marshall Plan aid, and in October, 1947, Communist delegates from eight nations met in Poland to be indoctrinated in methods of offsetting this latest threat. Threat it was, indeed, as its implications were not alone economic; the political attractions that a prosperous and democratic West might exert on the satellites were too horrible to contemplate with equanimity; they might even go so far as to consider exchanging their existing orbit for one oriented westward.

German affairs developed on a divided base in 1948–1949, with the Western powers submerging their differences in the face of a rapidly developing Russian threat. Western policy toward Germany now became a two-phase operation, based upon the conviction that a revived Germany was essential to the recovery of Europe and less politically dangerous than the Communist menace, and upon the expansion of economic coöperation into the political sphere. Frankly abandoning hope of four-power coöperation in Germany, plans were initiated in January, 1948, for the economic integration of the Anglo-American zones. Between February and mid-June complicated negotiations among the United States, France, Britain, and the Benelux nations (Belgium, the Netherlands, and Luxembourg) resulted in an overall economic and political plan for Western Germany.

The Anglo-American bizonia became a tri-zone with the integration of the French holdings; agreement was reached (December 12, 1948) for establishment of a six-power International Authority to manage Ruhr industries, with German representation to be added when a political organization was established; it was decided to establish a federal republic in Western Germany, which went into operation in the spring of 1949 under a constitution drafted at Bonn, which became the new capital. Meantime an Occupation Statute had been agreed upon (proclaimed April 10, 1949) under which Germany resumed control of her own affairs except in the realms of foreign relations, security, and trade and foreign exchange. Military Government gave way to a High Commission composed of delegates from each of the occupying powers, and the new federal Parliament assembled at Bonn on September 7, 1949. Not to be outdone, the Soviets countered the Ruhr agreement of December, 1948, by establishment (January 25, 1949) of a Council of Mutual Assistance, linking all the satellites save Yugoslavia, now impatient of Russian dictation and very much in the Kremlin's bad books. An East German state was organized in October, 1949, and the division of Germany was more complete than ever. Thus after four years the Potsdam proposals for four-power control of Germany had been swallowed up in the cold war.

These steps integrating German recovery with the operation of the ERP (the enabling legislation for the Marshall Plan was signed April 3, 1948, and its pump-priming activities became operative during the year) were punctuated by one of the most dramatic episodes of the long struggle between Communism and the democracies. Anglo-American bizonal arrangements of the winter of 1948 were, of course, a threat to the Russian position in Germany; equally dangerous were plans for the establishment of West German political autonomy. The Soviets accordingly adopted an aggressive policy at first designed to challenge the West's right to continue a share in the occupation of Berlin, later shifting to an effort to reopen four-power negotiations on Germany as a whole.[14]

Attention has already been called to the curious zonal arrangements which created French, British, and American sectors in Berlin, containing roughly two millions of people, whose ground connections with western Germany were completely at the mercy of Soviet power. As it became apparent that the western zones would evolve some form of economic unification, Russia tightened controls on

---

[14] On the Berlin blockade and the resulting airlift see Walter Bedell Smith, *My Three Years in Moscow*, Lippincott, 1950, pp. 230–260; *The Berlin Crisis: A Report on the Moscow Discussions, 1948*, Government Printing Office, 1948.

access to Berlin; by April, 1948, it was very difficult for travelers to surmount the alleged "technical difficulties" connected with passing in and out of the city. Multiplying frictions made it fairly evident that Russia was intent on challenging the continued validity of the occupation agreements and the relative positions of the parties in Berlin and Germany as a whole, inevitably jeopardizing the lives of the west-zone Berliners. The Western powers obligingly furnished an excuse for further Russian restrictions by announcing (June 18) the inauguration of a new currency in their zones; they delayed introducing it into Berlin, however, in the hope of securing a four-power agreement for the city. Russia promptly refused this proposal, and announced that Russian currency would be used in the entire city, whereupon (June 23) the West put the new Deutsche Mark into circulation in West Berlin. On June 24 Russian orders halted all traffic between Berlin and Western Germany, and the West retaliated by stopping the flow of goods in the reverse direction.

This stalemate forced the West to take to the air in order to keep West Berliners alive, and for 321 days an operation aptly dubbed the airlift moved a gradually increasing volume of goods into the beleaguered city. The Western powers promptly took their case to headquarters and in July and August conferred with Molotov and Stalin in an effort to lift the blockade. General Walter Bedell Smith, the American Ambassador, stated bluntly in opening the discussions that "The three governments must reemphasize their rights to be in Berlin to be unquestionable and absolute. They do not intend to be coerced by any means whatsoever into abandoning this right." This refusal to negotiate under duress contributed to the length and fruitlessness of the meeting, during which it became apparent that the Russians wished to use Berlin, where they were strong, to force the Allies to forego their plans, now well advanced (the drafting body to draw up the West German constitution was to meet in September), for the creation of a West German government. Neither side would make concessions and the talks ended inconclusively.

The West, risking the stability of the United Nations, took the blockade to the Security Council under Section 7 of the Charter, dealing with threats to the peace. Russia boycotted the discussions, but remained active in other phases of the Council's activity. The small powers proposed a solution which the Soviet delegate vetoed and the airlift continued throughout the winter, ferrying goods enough to keep the populace alive, if neither warm nor happy. Its surprising success brought a shift in the Russian attitude and Soviet-initiated negotiations produced an order reopening channels of communication as of midnight, May 11, 1949. The price was a mere token, recognition of the blockade's ineffectiveness: The Council of Foreign Ministers must renew discussion of Berlin, of the entire German question, and of an Austrian peace treaty. The Foreign Ministers met in Paris in May and June, 1949, without positive results. Western economic and political plans for West Germany had proceeded so far, and so successfully, as to link the area prospectively into the European complex. Therefore, Vishinsky's proposed renewal of four-power controls seemed likely to undo the progress of previous months. On the other hand, Western proposals to include East Germany in the new Republic were equally unpalatable to Russia; there was no meeting of the minds, and the best that could be secured was an arrangement designed to minimize the likelihood of another Berlin crisis. On the credit side was a renewal of contact over the German question and a momentary lessening of the terrific tensions which it had generated.

Paralleling much of the foregoing story was a growing conviction that the politico-economic consolidation being achieved under Soviet auspices must be matched by a corresponding grouping of those in disagreement, a tragic recourse to the theory of balanced powers which idealists had sought to bury in the great-power coöperation of the United Nations. As early as September 19, 1946, Winston Churchill voiced the unspoken thought of many by openly proposing a United States of Europe. The same year saw integration of the economic policies of Belgium, the Netherlands, and Luxembourg (the so-called Benelux nations). On March 4, 1947, France and Belgium signed the Treaty of Dunkirk, a 50-year promise of full military assistance in case either became a target of German aggression. Although this was carefully phrased so as to come within the provisions of the previous Anglo-Soviet and Franco-Soviet treaties (of 1942 and 1944), Moscow organs were permitted to hint, particularly in the light of the Truman Doctrine announced on March 12, that an anti-Soviet bloc seemed to be emerging.

More important was the Brussels Treaty of March 17, 1948, uniting France, Britain, and the Benelux nations in an old-line fifty-year military alliance, combined with peripheral economic arrangements. The treaty bound the signatories to immediate military assistance of any member subjected to military attack on European soil; though modeled on the Rio Pact of Inter-American Defense, its obligation was more binding, since the Rio agreement left to each party the ultimate decision as to whether to resort to war. Adopted during a year of Soviet aggression, it reflected increasing uncertainty as to the efficacy of United Nations machinery and caused many leaders, including some in the United States, to consider the regional approach to security.

With the Marshall Plan about to afford Europe a measure of economic assistance, and with a Presidential campaign in the offing in the United States, it became desirable to establish a pattern which would at once reassure Europe politically and remove foreign policy from the domestic political arena. Here the regional approach proved a fruitful one. On May 19, 1948, Senator Vandenberg introduced a resolution favoring regional arrangements as agencies of self-defense. This steered a middle course between two politically dangerous alternatives: The Senate would not view favorably such an agreement as the Brussels Treaty, which infringed upon the constitutional right of Congress to declare war; on the other hand, the Administration desired to continue operations within the framework of the United Nations in order to maintain a forum of discussion and a vehicle of possible later agreement with Russia, although many honest and earnest Americans were by this time seriously questioning the usefulness of the U.N. and demanding drastic reforms in its organization. Vandenberg's proposal urged American support of "Progressive development of regional and other collective arrangements for individual and collective self-defense in accordance with the purposes, principles, and provisions of the Charter." It affirmed the American intention to exercise the individual and collective rights of self-defense against armed attack posited under Article 51

NORTH ATLANTIC AREA

—— AREA DEFINED IN ARTICLE 6 OF THE
NORTH ATLANTIC TREATY

SOURCE. SENATE DOCUMENT 48, 81ST CONG., 1ST SESS.

(*From Brookings Institution, Major Problems of the United States Foreign Policy, 1949–1950, p. 270.*)

of the Charter, and proposed to underwrite "association of the United States, by constitutional process, with such regional and other collective arrangements as are based on continuous and effective self-help and mutual aid, and as affect its national security." This tacit admission that the U.N. was not performing its expected functions as an agency of security caused very little debate on its passage through the Senate on June 11.

This, along with the Marshall Plan, was reassuring to Europe, but not too reassuring, for there was no way of knowing just how far it would carry the United States toward the military assistance of which Europe by this time stood desperately in need. With this situation in mind, conversations were opened in Washington in July, 1948, among the Brussels treaty powers, Canada, and the United States; after recessing in September, they were resumed on December 10, this time to discuss a draft treaty. Matters were sufficiently advanced that President Truman could speak in his Inaugural Address on January 20, 1949, of the American purpose to "strengthen freedom-loving nations against the dangers of aggression" by "a joint agreement designed to strengthen the security of the North Atlantic area," and by furnishing "military advice and equipment to free nations which will cooperate with us in the maintenance of peace and security."

Further negotiations preceded the signature (April 4, 1949) of the North Atlantic Pact by representatives of the United States, the United Kingdom, France, Belgium, the Netherlands, Luxembourg, Denmark, Norway, Iceland, Portugal, and Italy.[15] Its drafting represented a triumph in harmonizing dangerous alternatives: It was strong enough to reassure Europe, safe enough to find favor in the United States Senate (which consented to ratification on July 21, 1949), and withal, consistent with the provisions of the United Nations Charter. Its heart was Article 5 in which

The Parties agree that an armed attack against one or more of them in Europe or North America shall be considered an attack against them all; and consequently they agree that, if such an armed attack occurs, each of them, in exercise of the right of individual or collective self-defense recognized by Article 51 of the Charter of the United Nations,

---

[15] Halford L. Hoskins, *The Atlantic Pact,* Public Affairs Press, 1949.

will assist the Party or Parties so attacked by taking forthwith, individually and in concert with the other Parties, such action as it deems necessary, including the use of armed force, [this to safeguard Congressional exercise of the war-making power] to restore and maintain the security of the North Atlantic area.

Any such armed attack and all measures taken as a result thereof shall immediately be reported to the Security Council. Such measures shall be terminated when the Security Council has taken the measures necessary to restore and maintain international peace and security.

In September Congress passed the Mutual Defense Assistance Act allocating a billion dollars for military assistance to Pact nations.

Senatorial approval of the Pact in July probably marked the highest point of the Western position in the cold war. Russia, it might seem, was fairly well in check. Marshall Plan aid was reviving German and European economy; the airlift had demonstrated the West's determination to contain Russian aggressiveness in Berlin; a chink, albeit a small one, had been made in the Soviet front by Tito's insistence upon an unsatellite-like control of his own affairs (June, 1948); the Atlantic Pact had geared American money and military supplies, if not armed assistance, into the defense of Western Europe. All this had been achieved, however, at the cost of principles of coöperation written into the Charter of the United Nations; it had made necessary the by-passing of the peace-keeping machinery established at San Francisco; and it had been marked by a return to the opposing alliances which the Charter had sought once and for all to end.

Whatever feeling of security the above developments may have generated was short-lived. President Truman's announcement (September 23, 1949) of an atomic explosion in the Soviet Union shattered at once any feeling of confidence based on a monopoly of atomic-energy weapons and made the difference in Russian and American power potentials no longer a matter of kind, but merely one of degree. Now all considerations, economic, political, military, and diplomatic, had to be reassessed in the light of this development. The prospect was not bright, for the bright new One World of the mid-'forties had split into the Two Worlds of the mid-century, with none to tell how soon a new crisis might destroy even this precarious balance.

Selected Bibliography

The following bibliography, which includes only the sources and authorities cited in the footnotes, is highly selective but sufficiently inclusive to serve as a working tool. It is made up principally of secondary accounts, through which the inquiring student may find his way back into the sources. Much additional material, both primary and secondary, may be located by using Samuel Flagg Bemis and Grace Gardner Griffin, Guide to the Diplomatic History of the United States, 1775–1921, Washington, D.C., Government Printing Office, 1935.

CHAPTER 1

The Problem of Diplomacy

Nicolson, Harold, *Diplomacy*, New York, Harcourt, Brace, 1939.
Satow, Sir E. M., *A Guide to Diplomatic Practice*, 3d ed., London, Longmans, Green, 1932.

CHAPTER 2

Europe and America Before the Revolution

Alvord, C. W., *The Mississippi Valley in British Politics*, 2 vols., Cleveland, Arthur H. Clark, 1917.
Lybyer, A. H., "The Influence of the Ottoman Turks upon the Routes of Oriental Trade," *Report of the American Historical Association, 1914*, 2 vols., Washington, D.C., Government Printing Office, 1916, 1, pp. 125–133.
Lybyer, A. H., "The Ottoman Turks and the Routes of Oriental Trade," *English Historical Review*, 30 (1915), pp. 577–585.

Osgood, H. L., *The American Colonies in the Eighteenth Century*, 4 vols., New York, Columbia University Press, 1924.

Osgood, H. L., *The American Colonies in the Seventeenth Century*, 3 vols., New York, Macmillan, 1904–1907.

CHAPTER 3

Revolution and Peace

Bemis, Samuel Flagg (ed.), *The American Secretaries of State and Their Diplomacy*, 10 vols., New York, Knopf, 1927–1929.

Bemis, Samuel Flagg, *The Diplomacy of the American Revolution*, New York, Appleton-Century, 1935.

Corwin, E. S., *French Policy and the American Alliance*, Princeton, Princeton University Press, 1916.

Journals of the Continental Congress, 34 vols., Washington, D.C., Government Printing Office, 1904–1937.

Miller, Hunter (ed.), *Treaties and Other International Acts of the United States of America*, 7 vols., Washington, D.C., Government Printing Office, 1931 ff.

Sparks, Jared (ed.), *The Works of Benjamin Franklin*, 10 vols., Boston, Hilliard, Gray, 1840.

Wharton, Francis (ed.), *The Revolutionary Diplomatic Correspondence of the United States*, 6 vols., Washington, D.C., Government Printing Office, 1889.

CHAPTER 4

The Machinery of Diplomacy Under the Constitution

Beard, Charles A. (ed.), *The Journal of William Maclay*, New York, Boni, 1927.

Bolles, Blair, "Reorganization of the State Department," *Foreign Policy Reports*, August 15, 1947.

Corwin, E. S., *The President's Control of Foreign Relations*, Princeton, Princeton University Press, 1917.

Dangerfield, Royden J., *In Defense of the Senate*, Norman, University of Oklahoma Press, 1933.

Dickey, John Sloan, "Our Treaty Procedure Versus Our Foreign Policies," *Foreign Affairs*, 25 (1947), pp. 357–377.

Fleming, Denna Frank, *The Treaty Veto of the American Senate*, New York, Putnam, 1930.

Haynes, George H., *The Senate of the United States: Its History and Practice*, 2 vols., Boston, Houghton Mifflin, 1938.

Holt, W. Stull, *Treaties Defeated by the Senate*, Baltimore, Johns Hopkins Press, 1933.

Hulen, Bertram D., *Inside the Department of State*, New York, McGraw-Hill, 1939.

Hunt, Gaillard, *The Department of State of the United States: Its History and Functions*, Washington, D.C., Department of State, 1893.

Lauterpacht, H., *Recognition in International Law*, Cambridge, Cambridge University Press, 1947.

Lay, T. C., *The Foreign Service of the United States*, New York, Prentice-Hall, 1928.

McCamy, James L., *The Administration of American Foreign Affairs*, New York, Knopf, 1950.

McClure, Wallace, *International Executive Agreements: Democratic Procedure under the Constitution of the United States*, New York, Columbia University Press, 1941.

Mathews, J. M., *American Foreign Relations: Conduct and Policies*, New York, Century, 1928.

Stuart, Graham H., *American Diplomatic and Consular Practice*, New York, Appleton-Century, 1936.

Stuart, Graham H., *The Department of State: A History of Its Organization, Procedure, and Personnel*, New York, Macmillan, 1949.

Thayer, William Roscoe, *The Life and Letters of John Hay*, 2 vols., Boston, Houghton Mifflin, 1915.

CHAPTER 5

America in the World

Albion, Robert G., and Pope, Jennie B., *Sea Lanes in Wartime: The American Experience, 1775–1942*, New York, Norton, 1942.

Allen, Gardner W., *Our Naval War with France*, Boston, Houghton Mifflin, 1909.

Ames, Herman V. (ed.), *The X.Y.Z. Letters: University of Pennsylvania Translations and Reprints* . . . , vol. 6, No. 2, Philadelphia, University of Pennsylvania Press, 1899.

Bemis, Samuel Flagg, *Jay's Treaty*, New York, Macmillan, 1923.

Bemis, Samuel Flagg, "Jay's Treaty and the Northwest Boundary Gap," *American Historical Review*, 27 (1922), pp. 465–486.

Beveridge, Albert J., *The Life of John Marshall*, 4 vols., Boston, Houghton Mifflin, 1916–1919.

Bond, Beverly W., Jr., *The Monroe Mission to France, 1794–1796*, Baltimore, Johns Hopkins Press, 1907.

Borchard, Edwin M., and Lage, William P., *Neutrality for the United States,* New Haven, Yale University Press, 1937.

Burt, A. L., *The United States, Great Britain and British North America,* New Haven, Yale University Press, 1940.

Graham, G. S., *Sea Power and British North America, 1783–1820: A Study in British Colonial Policy,* Cambridge, Harvard University Press, 1921.

Henderson, Archibald, "Isaac Shelby and the Genêt Mission," *Mississippi Valley Historical Review,* 6 (1920), pp. 451–469.

Jessup, Philip C., and Deak, Francis, *Neutrality, Its History, Economics and Law,* 4 vols., New York, Columbia University Press, 1935–1936.

King, G. A., *The French Spoliation Claims, Senate Document 451,* 64th Congress, 1st Session.

Manning, William R., "The Nootka Sound Affair," *Report of the American Historical Association, 1904,* Washington, D.C., Government Printing Office, 1905, pp. 279–478.

Monaghan, Frank, *John Jay,* Indianapolis, Bobbs-Merrill, 1935.

Thomas, C. M., *American Neutrality in 1793,* New York, Columbia University Press, 1931.

Woolery, W. K., *The Relation of Thomas Jefferson to American Foreign Policy, 1783–1793,* Baltimore, Johns Hopkins Press, 1927.

CHAPTER 6

Neutrality Loses

Albion, Robert G., and Pope, Jennie B., *Sea Lanes in Wartime: The American Experience, 1775–1942,* New York, Norton, 1942.

Bemis, Samuel Flagg (ed.), *The American Secretaries of State and Their Diplomacy,* 10 vols., New York, Knopf, 1927–1929.

Burt, A. L., *The United States, Great Britain and British North America,* New Haven, Yale University Press, 1940.

Clauder, A. C., *American Commerce as Affected by the Wars of the French Revolution and Napoleon, 1793–1812,* Philadelphia, University of Pennsylvania Press, 1932.

Coleman, C. B., "The Ohio Valley in the Preliminaries of the War of 1812," *Mississippi Valley Historical Review,* 7 (1920), pp. 39–50.

Elliott, C. B., "The Doctrine of Continuous Voyages," *American Journal of International Law,* 1 (1907), pp. 65–95.

Golder, F. A., "The Russian Offer of Mediation in the War of 1812," *Political Science Quarterly,* 3 (1916), pp. 380–391.

Goodman, W. H., "The Origins of the War of 1812: A Survey of Changing Interpretations," *Mississippi Valley Historical Review,* 28 (1941), pp. 171–186.

Heckscher, R. F., *The Continental System: An Economic Interpretation,* Oxford, Clarendon, 1922.

Hill, C. E., *Leading American Treaties,* New York, Macmillan, 1924.

Mayo, Bernard, *Henry Clay: Spokesman of the New West,* Boston, Houghton Mifflin, 1937.

Philips, W. Alison, and Reede, Arthur H., *Neutrality, Its History, Economics and Law, Volume II, The Napoleonic Period,* New York, Columbia University Press, 1936.

Pratt, Julius W., *Expansionists of 1812,* Baltimore, Johns Hopkins Press, 1925.

Sears, Louis M., *Jefferson and the Embargo,* Durham, Duke University Press, 1927.

Smith, Abbot, "Mr. Madison's War: An Unsuccessful Experiment in the Conduct of National Policy," *Political Science Quarterly,* 57 (1942), pp. 229–246.

Updyke, F. A., *The Diplomacy of the War of 1812,* Baltimore, Johns Hopkins Press, 1915.

Zimmerman, J. F., *Impressment of American Seamen,* New York, Columbia University Press, 1925.

CHAPTER 7

The Infant Nation Starts to Grow

Adams, E. D., *British Interests and Activities in Texas, 1838–1846,* Baltimore, Johns Hopkins Press, 1910.

Adams, Henry, *History of the United States of America,* 9 vols., New York, Scribner, 1889–1891.

Barker, E. C., "The Influence of Slavery in the Colonization of Texas," *Mississippi Valley Historical Review,* 11 (1924), pp. 3–36.

Barker, E. C., *The Life of Stephen F. Austin, Founder of Texas, 1793–1836,* Nashville, Dallas, Cokesbury, 1926.

Barker, E. C., *Mexico and Texas, 1821–1835,* Dallas, P. L. Turner, 1928.

Barker, E. C., "The United States and Mexico, 1835–1837," *Mississippi Valley Historical Review,* 1 (1914), pp. 3–30.

Bassett, J. S., *The Life of Andrew Jackson,* 2 vols., Garden City, Doubleday, 1911.

Bemis, Samuel Flagg, *The Latin American Policy of the United States, An Historical Interpretation,* New York, Harcourt, Brace, 1943.

Bemis, Samuel Flagg, *Pinckney's Treaty: A Study of America's Advantage from Europe's Distress,* Baltimore, Johns Hopkins Press, 1926.

Boucher, C. S., "In Re That Aggressive Slaveocracy," *Mississippi Valley Historical Review,* 8 (1921), pp. 13–77.

Brooks, P. C., *Diplomacy and the Borderlands: The Adams-Onís Treaty of 1819*, Berkeley, University of California Press, 1939.

Chambers, H. E., *West Florida and Its Relation to the Historical Cartography of the United States*, Baltimore, Johns Hopkins Press, 1898.

Cox, I. J., *The West Florida Controversy, 1798–1813*, Baltimore, Johns Hopkins Press, 1918.

Fish, C. R., *American Diplomacy*, New York, Holt, 1915.

Fuller, H. B., *The Purchase of Florida*, Cleveland, Burrows, 1906.

Garner, James W., *American Foreign Policies*, New York, New York University Press, 1928.

Griffin, C. C., *The United States and the Disruption of the Spanish Empire, 1810–1822*, New York, Columbia University Press, 1937.

James, Marquis, *Andrew Jackson: The Border Captain*, Indianapolis, Bobbs-Merrill, 1933.

James, Marquis, *The Raven: A Biography of Sam Houston*, Indianapolis, Bobbs-Merrill, 1929.

Lyon, E. W., "The Closing of the Port of New Orleans," *American Historical Review*, 37 (1932), pp. 280–296.

Lyon, E. W., *Louisiana in French Diplomacy*, Norman, University of Oklahoma Press, 1934.

Reeves, J. S., *American Diplomacy under Tyler and Polk*, Baltimore, Johns Hopkins Press, 1907.

Rippy, J. F., *America and the Strife of Europe*, Chicago, University of Chicago Press, 1938.

Rives, G. L., *The United States and Mexico, 1821–1848*, 2 vols., New York, Scribner, 1913.

Smith, Justin H., *The Annexation of Texas*, New York, Baker and Taylor, 1911.

Washington, H. A. (ed.), *The Writings of Thomas Jefferson*, 9 vols., Washington, D.C., Taylor and Maury, 1853–1854.

Whitaker, A. P., *The Mississippi Question, 1795–1803: A Study in Trade, Politics, and Diplomacy*, New York, Appleton-Century, 1934.

Whitaker, A. P., "New Light on the Treaty of San Lorenzo," *Mississippi Valley Historical Review*, 15 (1929), pp. 435–454.

Whitaker, A. P., "The Retrocession of Louisiana in Spanish Policy," *American Historical Review*, 39 (1934), pp. 454–476.

Whitaker, A. P., *The Spanish-American Frontier, 1783–1795*, Boston, Houghton Mifflin, 1927.

CHAPTER 8
Retreat to the West

Bailey, T. A., *A Diplomatic History of the American People*, 3d ed., New York, Crofts, 1946.

Bailey, T. A., "The Lodge Corollary to the Monroe Doctrine," *Political Science Quarterly*, 48 (1933), pp. 220–239.

Bemis, Samuel Flagg (ed.), *The American Secretaries of State and Their Diplomacy*, 10 vols., New York, Knopf, 1927–1929.

Bemis, Samuel Flagg, *The Latin American Policy of the United States, An Historical Interpretation*, New York, Harcourt, Brace, 1943.

Bemis, Samuel Flagg, "Washington's Farewell Address: A Foreign Policy of Independence," *American Historical Review*, 39 (1934), pp. 250–268.

Blake, N. M., "Background of Cleveland's Venezuela Policy," *American Historical Review*, 47 (1942), pp. 259–297.

Bornholdt, Laura, "The Abbe de Pradt and the Monroe Doctrine," *Hispanic American Historical Review*, 24 (1944), pp. 201–221.

Clark, J. Reuben, *Memorandum on the Monroe Doctrine*, Washington, D.C., Government Printing Office, 1930.

Cleveland, Grover, *Presidential Problems*, New York, Century, 1904.

The Congressional Record, 58th Congress, 3d Session; 64th Congress, 2d Session, Washington, D.C., Government Printing Office, 1904, 1917.

Cresson, W. P., *The Holy Alliance: The European Background of the Monroe Doctrine*, New York, Oxford University Press, 1922.

Dennis, A. L. P., *Adventures in American Diplomacy, 1896–1906*, New York, Dutton, 1928.

Ford, W. C., "John Quincy Adams and the Monroe Doctrine," *American Historical Review*, 7 (1902), pp. 676–696; 8 (1902), pp. 28–52.

Fossum, P. R., "The Anglo-Venezuelan Boundary Controversy," *Hispanic American Historical Review*, 8 (1928), pp. 299–329.

Garner, James W., *American Foreign Policies*, New York, New York University Press, 1928.

Goebel, J. L., *The Struggle for the Falkland Islands: A Study in Legal and Diplomatic History*, New Haven, Yale University Press, 1927.

Hill, H. C., *Roosevelt and the Caribbean*, Chicago, University of Chicago Press, 1927.

Kunz, J. L., "The Inter-American Treaty of Reciprocal Assistance," *American Journal of International Law*, 42 (1948), pp. 111–120.

Langer, W. L., *The Diplomacy of Imperialism*, 2 vols., New York, Knopf, 1935.

Livermore, S. A., "Theodore Roosevelt, the American Navy, and the Venezuelan Crisis of 1902–1903," *American Historical Review*, 51 (1946), pp. 452–471.

Lodge, H. C., "England, Venezuela, and the Monroe Doctrine," *North American Review*, 160 (1895), pp. 651–658.

MacCorkle, W. A., *The Personal Genesis of the Monroe Doctrine*, New York, Putnam, 1923.

Nevins, Allan, *Grover Cleveland: A Study in Courage,* New York, Dodd, Mead, 1932.

Papers Relating to the Foreign Relations of the United States, 1895, Washington, D.C., Government Printing Office, 1896.

Perkins, Dexter, *The Monroe Doctrine, 1823–1826,* Cambridge, Harvard University Press, 1927.

Perkins, Dexter, *The Monroe Doctrine, 1826–1867,* Baltimore, Johns Hopkins Press, 1933.

Perkins, Dexter, *The Monroe Doctrine, 1867–1907,* Baltimore, Johns Hopkins Press, 1937.

Perkins, Dexter, *Hands Off: A History of the Monroe Doctrine,* Boston, Little, Brown, 1941.

Perkins, Dexter, "The Monroe Doctrine To-Day," *Yale Review,* 30 (1941), pp. 686–702.

Perkins, Dexter, "The Monroe Doctrine Up to Date," *Foreign Affairs,* 20 (1942), pp. 253–265.

Powell, J. H., *Richard Rush, Republican Diplomat, 1780–1859,* Philadelphia, University of Pennsylvania Press, 1942.

Pringle, H. F., *Theodore Roosevelt, A Biography,* New York, Harcourt, Brace, 1931.

Richardson, J. D. (comp.), *A Compilation of the Messages and Papers of the Presidents, 1789–1897,* 10 vols., Washington, D.C., Government Printing Office, 1896–1899.

Rippy, J. F., *The Caribbean Danger Zone,* New York, Putnam, 1940.

Rippy, J. F., "The Initiation of the Customs Receivership in the Dominican Republic," *Hispanic American Historical Review,* 17 (1937), pp. 419–457.

Rippy, J. F., and Debo, Angie, *The Historical Background of the American Policy of Isolation,* Northampton, Department of History, Smith College, 1924.

Schellenberg, T. R., "Jeffersonian Origins of the Monroe Doctrine," *Hispanic American Historical Review,* 14 (1934), pp. 1–31.

Smith, T. C., "Secretary Olney's Real Credit in the Venezuelan Affair," *Proceedings of the Massachusetts Historical Society,* 65 (1933), pp. 112–147.

Tansill, C. C., *The Foreign Policy of Thomas F. Bayard, 1885–1897,* New York, Fordham University Press, 1940.

Tansill, C. C., *The United States and Santo Domingo, 1798–1873,* Baltimore, Johns Hopkins Press, 1938.

Tatum, E. H., Jr., *The United States and Europe, 1815–1823,* Berkeley, University of California Press, 1936.

Vagts, A., *Deutschland und die Vereinigten Staaten in der Weltpolitik*, 2 vols., New York, Macmillan, 1935.

Weinberg, A. K., "The Historical Meaning of the American Doctrine of Isolation," *American Political Science Review*, 34 (1940), pp. 539–547.

Weinberg, A. K., "Washington's 'Great Rule' In Its Historical Evolution," in Goldman, E. F. (ed.), *Historiography and Urbanization: Essays in American History in Honor of W. Stull Holt*, Baltimore, Johns Hopkins Press, 1941.

Whitaker, A. P., *The United States and the Independence of Latin America, 1800–1823*, Baltimore, Johns Hopkins Press, 1941.

Wilcox, F. O., "The Monroe Doctrine and World War II," *American Political Science Review*, 36 (1942), pp. 433–453.

CHAPTER 9

Mexico and Her Northern Neighbor

Atwater, Elton, *American Regulation of Arms Exports*, Washington, Carnegie Endowment, 1941.

Baker, Ray Stannard, *Woodrow Wilson: Life and Letters*, 8 vols., Garden City, Doubleday, Page, 1927–1939.

Briggs, H. W., "The Settlement of Mexican Claims Act of 1942," *American Journal of International Law*, 37 (1943), pp. 222–232.

Bryn-Jones, D., *Frank B. Kellogg: A Biography*, New York, Putnam, 1937.

Callahan, James Morton, *American Foreign Policy in Mexican Relations*, New York, Macmillan, 1932.

Cumberland, Charles C., *Francisco I. Madero, Revolutionary*, Unpublished dissertation, University of Texas, 1949.

Daniels, J., *The Wilson Era: Years of Peace, 1910–1917*, Chapel Hill, University of North Carolina Press, 1944.

Foreign Policy Reports, August 1, 1937, August 15, 1937, August 15, 1938.

Fuller, J. D. P., *The Movement for the Acquisition of All Mexico, 1846–1848*, Baltimore, Johns Hopkins Press, 1936.

Gaither, R. B., *Expropriation in Mexico: The Facts and the Law*, New York, Morrow, 1940.

Garber, P. N., *The Gadsden Treaty*, Philadelphia, University of Pennsylvania Press, 1923.

Gordon, W. C., *The Expropriation of Foreign-Owned Property in Mexico*, Washington, D.C., American Council on Public Affairs, 1941.

Gruening, Ernest, *Mexico and Its Heritage*, New York, Century, 1928.

Jones, C. L., "Roots of the Mexican Church Conflict," *Foreign Affairs*, 14 (1935), pp. 135–146.

Kirk, Betty, *Covering the Mexican Front: The Battle of Europe Versus America*, Norman, University of Oklahoma Press, 1943.

Lippmann, Walter, "Church and State in Mexico: The American Mediation," *Foreign Affairs*, 8 (1930), pp. 186–208.

MacCorkle, S. A., *The American Policy of Recognition towards Mexico*, Baltimore, Johns Hopkins Press, 1933.

MacMahon, A. W., and Dittmar, W. R., "The Mexican Oil Industry since Expropriation," *Political Science Quarterly*, 57 (1942), pp. 28–50, 161–189.

Nicolson, Harold, *Dwight Morrow*, New York, Harcourt, Brace, 1935.

Notter, Harley, *The Origins of the Foreign Policy of Woodrow Wilson*, Baltimore, Johns Hopkins Press, 1937.

Papers Relating to the Foreign Relations of the United States, 1913, Washington, D.C., Government Printing Office, 1920.

Person, H. S., *Mexican Oil: Symbol of Recent Trends in International Relations*, New York, Harper, 1942.

Proceedings of the United States-Mexican Commission Convened at Mexico City, May 14, 1923, Washington, D.C., Government Printing Office, 1925.

Relyea, P. S., *Relations between the United States and Mexico under Porfirio Diaz, 1876–1910*, Northampton, Department of History, Smith College, 1924.

Rippy, J. F., *The United States and Mexico*, rev. ed., New York, Knopf, 1931.

Scroggs, W. O., "Mexican Anxieties," *Foreign Affairs*, 18 (1940), pp. 266–279.

Sears, L. M., *John Slidell*, Durham, Duke University Press, 1925.

Sears, L. M., "Nicholas P. Trist, A Diplomat with Ideals," *Mississippi Valley Historical Review*, 11 (1924), pp. 85–99.

Shepardson, W. H., and Scroggs, W. O., *The United States in World Affairs: An Account of American Foreign Relations, 1937*, New York, Harper, 1938.

Smith, Justin H., *The War with Mexico*, 2 vols., New York, Macmillan, 1919.

Stephenson, G. M., *John Lind of Minnesota*, Minneapolis, University of Minnesota Press, 1935.

Strode, Hudson, *Timeless Mexico*, New York, Harcourt, Brace, 1944.

Whetten, N. L., *Rural Mexico*, Chicago, University of Chicago Press, 1948.

Wriston, H. M., *Executive Agents in American Foreign Relations*, Baltimore, Johns Hopkins Press, 1929.

CHAPTER 10
The United States and Britain, 1815–1903

Adamov, E. A., "Russia and the United States at the Time of the Civil War," *Journal of Modern History*, 2 (1930), pp. 586–603.

Adams, R. G., *A History of the Foreign Relations of the United States*, New York, Macmillan, 1925.

Bailey, T. A., "The North Pacific Sealing Convention of 1911," *Pacific Historical Review*, 4 (1935), pp. 1–14.

Bailey, T. A., "Theodore Roosevelt and the Alaska Boundary Settlement," *Canadian Historical Review*, 18 (1937), pp. 123–131.

Bailey, T. A., "Why the United States Purchased Alaska," *Pacific Historical Review*, 3 (1934), pp. 37–49.

Bonham, M. L., "Alexander McLeod, Bone of Contention," *New York History*, 18 (1937), pp. 189–217.

Burt, A. L., *The United States, Great Britain and British North America*, New Haven, Yale University Press, 1940.

Callahan, James Morton, *American Foreign Policy in Canadian Relations*, New York, Macmillan, 1937.

Corey, A. B., *The Crisis of 1830–1842 in Canadian-American Relations*, New Haven, Yale University Press, 1941.

Current, R. N., "Webster's Propaganda and the Ashburton Treaty," *Mississippi Valley Historical Review*, 34 (1947), pp. 187–200.

Dennett, Tyler, *John Hay: From Poetry to Politics*, New York, Dodd, Mead, 1934.

Dennis, A. L. P., *Adventures in American Diplomacy, 1896–1906*, New York, Dutton, 1928.

Dulles, F. R., *America in the Pacific: A Century of Expansion*, Boston, Houghton Mifflin, 1932.

Dunning, W. A., "Paying for Alaska," *Political Science Quarterly*, 27 (1912), pp. 385–399.

Falk, E. A., *From Perry to Pearl Harbor: The Struggle for Supremacy in the Pacific*, Garden City, Doubleday, Doran, 1943.

Farrar, V. J., *The Annexation of Russian America to the United States*, Washington, D.C., W. F. Roberts, 1937.

Fuess, C. M., *Daniel Webster*, 2 vols., Boston, Little, Brown, 1930.

Golder, F. A., "The Purchase of Alaska," *American Historical Review*, 25 (1920), pp. 411–425.

Golder, F. A., "The Russian Fleet and the Civil War," *American Historical Review*, 20 (1915), pp. 801–813.

Hill, C. E., *Leading American Treaties*, New York, Macmillan, 1924.

Johnson, C. O., "George Turner," *Pacific Northwest Quarterly*, 34 (1943), pp. 367–392.

Keenleyside, Hugh, *Canada and the United States*, New York, Knopf, 1929.

Lansing, Robert, "The North Atlantic Coast Fisheries Arbitration," *American Journal of International Law*, 5 (1911), pp. 1–31.

LeDuc, T., "The Maine Frontier and the Northeast Boundary Controversy," *American Historical Review*, 53 (1947), pp. 30–41.

Luthin, R. H., "The Sale of Alaska," *Slavonic Review*, 16 (1937), pp. 168–182.

McInnis, E. W., *The Unguarded Frontier: A History of American-Canadian Relations*, Garden City, Doubleday, Doran, 1942.

Martin, L. F., and Bemis, Samuel Flagg, "Franklin's Red-Line Map Was a Mitchell," *New England Quarterly*, 10 (1937), pp. 105–111.

Martin, T. P., "Free Trade and the Oregon Question," in *Facts and Factors in Economic History: Articles by Former Students of Edwin Francis Gay*, Cambridge, Harvard University Press, 1932.

Masters, D. C., *The Reciprocity Treaty of 1854*, New York, Longmans, Green, 1937.

Merk, Frederick, "The British Corn Crisis of 1846," *Agricultural History*, 8 (1934), pp. 95–123.

Merk, Frederick, "British Government Propaganda and the Oregon Treaty," *American Historical Review*, 40 (1934), pp. 38–63.

Merk, Frederick, "British Party Politics and the Oregon Treaty," *American Historical Review*, 37 (1932), pp. 653–678.

Merk, Frederick, "The Oregon Pioneers and the Boundary," *American Historical Review*, 29 (1924), pp. 681–699.

Miller, Hunter (ed.), *Treaties and Other International Acts of the United States of America*, 7 vols., Washington, D.C., Government Printing Office, 1931 ff.

Nagengast, William E., "The Visit of the Russian Fleet to the United States: Were Americans Deceived?", *The Russian Review*, 8 (1949), pp. 46–55.

Nevins, Allan, *Hamilton Fish: The Inner History of the Grant Administration*, New York, Dodd, Mead, 1936.

Nevins, Allan, *Henry White: Thirty Years of American Diplomacy*, New York, Harper, 1930.

Powell, J. H., *Richard Rush, Republican Diplomat, 1780–1859*, Philadelphia, University of Pennsylvania Press, 1942.

Pratt, Julius W., "James K. Polk and John Bull," *Canadian Historical Review*, 24 (1943), pp. 341–349.

Reeves, J. S., *American Diplomacy under Tyler and Polk,* Baltimore, Johns Hopkins Press, 1907.

Sage, Walter, "The Oregon Treaty of 1846," *Canadian Historical Review,* 27 (1946), pp. 349–367.

Shippee, L. B., *Canadian-American Relations, 1849–1874,* New Haven, Yale University Press, 1941.

Smith, Goldwin, *The Treaty of Washington,* Ithaca, Cornell University Press, 1941.

Stanley-Brown, J., "The Bering Sea Controversy from an Economic Standpoint," *Yale Review,* 2 (1893), pp. 194–210.

Tansill, C. C., *Canadian-American Relations, 1875–1911,* New Haven, Yale University Press, 1944.

Tansill, C. C., *The Foreign Policy of Thomas F. Bayard, 1885–1897,* New York, Fordham University Press, 1940.

Thayer, William Roscoe, *The Life and Letters of John Hay,* 2 vols., Boston, Houghton Mifflin, 1915.

Thomas, B. P., *Russo-American Relations, 1815–1867,* Baltimore, Johns Hopkins Press, 1930.

Tompkins, S. R., "Drawing the Alaska Boundary," *Canadian Historical Review,* 26 (1945), pp. 1–24.

Watt, Alastair, "The Case of Alexander McLeod," *Canadian Historical Review,* 12 (1931), pp. 145–167.

The Works of Daniel Webster, 6 vols., Boston, Little, Brown, 1851.

CHAPTER 11

The United States and Britain, 1815–1903

Adams, C. F., *Charles Francis Adams,* Boston, Houghton Mifflin, 1900.

Adams, E. D., *Great Britain and the American Civil War,* 2 vols., London, Longmans, Green, 1925.

Albion, Robert G., and Pope, Jennie B., *Sea Lanes in Wartime: The American Experience, 1775–1942,* New York, Norton, 1942.

Baker, Ray Stannard, *Woodrow Wilson: Life and Letters,* 8 vols., Garden City, Doubleday, Page, 1927–1939.

Bancroft, F., *The Life of William H. Seward,* 2 vols., New York, Harper, 1900.

Baxter, J. P., 3rd, "The British Government and Neutral Rights, 1861–1865," *American Historical Review,* 34 (1928), pp. 9–29, 77–91.

Baxter, J. P., 3rd, "Some British Opinions as to Neutral Rights, 1861 to 1865," *American Journal of International Law,* 23 (1929), pp. 517–537.

Bemis, Samuel Flagg (ed.), *The American Secretaries of State and Their Diplomacy,* 10 vols., New York, Knopf, 1927–1929.

Bunau-Varilla, P., *Panama, the Creation, Destruction, and Resurrection,* New York, McBride, Nast, 1914.

Callcott, W. H., *The Caribbean Policy of the United States, 1890–1920,* Baltimore, Johns Hopkins Press, 1942.

Claussen, M. P., "Peace Factors in Anglo-American Relations, 1861–1865," *Mississippi Valley Historical Review,* 26 (1940), pp. 511–522.

Dennett, Tyler, *John Hay: From Poetry to Politics,* New York, Dodd, Mead, 1934.

Dennis, A. L. P., *Adventures in American Diplomacy, 1896–1906,* New York, Dutton, 1928.

Dennison, Eleanor, *The Senate Foreign Relations Committee,* Stanford University, Stanford University Press, 1942.

Elliott, C. B., "The Doctrine of Continuous Voyages," *American Journal of International Law,* 1 (1907), pp. 65–95.

Hill, C. E., *Leading American Treaties,* New York, Macmillan, 1924.

Hyde, C. C., "The Isthmian Canal Treaty," *Harvard Law Review,* 14 (1900), pp. 52–58.

Jones, C. L., *The Caribbean Since 1900,* New York, Prentice-Hall, 1936.

Jordan, H. D., and Pratt, E. J., *Europe and the American Civil War,* Boston, Houghton Mifflin, 1931.

Lockey, J. B., "A Neglected Aspect of Isthmian Diplomacy," *American Historical Review,* 41 (1936), pp. 295–306.

McDiarmid, A. M., "American Civil War Precedents: Their Nature, Application, and Extension," *American Journal of International Law,* 34 (1940), pp. 220–237.

Mack, Gerstle, *The Land Divided,* New York, Knopf, 1944.

Miner, D. C., *The Fight for the Panama Route: The Story of the Spooner Act and the Hay-Herran Treaty,* New York, Columbia University Press, 1940.

Monaghan, Jay, *Diplomat in Carpet Slippers: Abraham Lincoln Deals with Foreign Affairs,* Indianapolis, Bobbs-Merrill, 1945.

Nevins, Allan, *Hamilton Fish: The Inner History of the Grant Administration,* New York, Dodd, Mead, 1936.

The New York Times, May 29, 1902.

Owsley, F. L., *King Cotton Diplomacy,* Chicago, University of Chicago Press, 1931.

Parks, E. T., *Colombia and the United States,* Durham, Duke University Press, 1935.

Perkins, Dexter, *The Monroe Doctrine, 1826–1867,* Baltimore, Johns Hopkins Press, 1933.

Randall, J. G., *Lincoln the President: Springfield to Gettysburg,* 2 vols., New York, Dodd, Mead, 1945.

Rippy, J. F., *The Capitalists and Colombia*, New York, Vanguard, 1931.

Sears, L. M., *John Slidell*, Durham, Duke University Press, 1925.

Stowell, E. C., and Munro, H. F., *International Cases: Arbitrations and Incidents Illustrative of International Law as Practised by Independent States*, 2 vols., Boston, Houghton Mifflin, 1916.

Tansill, C. C., *The United States and Santo Domingo, 1798–1873*, Baltimore, Johns Hopkins Press, 1938.

Van Alstyne, R. W., "British Diplomacy and the Clayton-Bulwer Treaty, 1850–1860," *Journal of Modern History*, 11 (1939), pp. 149–183.

Van Alstyne, R. W., "The Central American Policy of Lord Palmerston, 1846–1848," *Hispanic American Historical Review*, 16 (1936), pp. 352–357.

Williams, M. W., *Anglo-American Isthmian Diplomacy, 1815–1915*, Baltimore, Lord Baltimore Press, 1916.

CHAPTER 12

Expansionism: World Phase

Bailey, T. A., "Dewey and the Germans at Manila Bay," *American Historical Review*, 45 (1939), pp. 59–81.

Bailey, T. A., "Hawaii and the United States during the Spanish-American War," *American Historical Review*, 36 (1931), pp. 552–560.

Brookes, Jean I., *International Rivalry in the Pacific Islands, 1800–1875*, Berkeley, University of California Press, 1941.

Butt, Archie W., *Taft and Roosevelt: The Intimate Letters of Archie Butt*, 2 vols., Garden City, Doubleday, Doran, 1930.

Chadwick, F. E., *The Relations of the United States and Spain: Diplomacy*, New York, Scribner, 1909.

Dennis, A. L. P., *Adventures in American Diplomacy, 1896–1906*, New York, Dutton, 1928.

Dozer, D. M., "The Opposition to Hawaiian Reciprocity, 1876–1888," *Pacific Historical Review*, 14 (1945), pp. 157–183.

Dulles, F. R., *America in the Pacific: A Century of Expansion*, Boston, Houghton Mifflin, 1932.

Ellison, J. W., *Opening and Penetration of Foreign Influence in Samoa to 1880*, Corvallis, Oregon State College Press, 1938.

Ellison, J. W., "The Partition of Samoa: A Study in Imperialism and Diplomacy," *Pacific Historical Review*, 8 (1939), pp. 259–288.

Flack, H. E., *Spanish-American Diplomatic Relations Preceding the War of 1898*, Baltimore, Johns Hopkins Press, 1906.

Foster, John W., *American Diplomacy in the Orient*, Boston, Houghton Mifflin, 1903.

Harrington, F. H., "The Anti-Imperialist Movement in the United States, 1898–1900," *Mississippi Valley Historical Review*, 22 (1935), pp. 211–230.

Hill, C. E., *Leading American Treaties*, New York, Macmillan, 1924.

Holt, W. Stull, *Treaties Defeated by the Senate*, Baltimore, Johns Hopkins Press, 1933.

Masterman, Sylvia, *The Origins of International Rivalry in Samoa, 1845 to 1884*, Stanford University, Stanford University Press, 1934.

Millis, Walter, *The Martial Spirit: A Study of Our War with Spain*, Boston, Houghton Mifflin, 1931.

Nevins, Allan, *Grover Cleveland: A Study in Courage*, New York, Dodd, Mead, 1932.

Pratt, Julius W., "American Business and the Spanish-American War," *Hispanic American Historical Review*, 14 (1934), pp. 163–201.

Pratt, Julius W., *Expansionists of 1898*, Baltimore, Johns Hopkins Press, 1936.

Pratt, Julius W., "The Hawaiian Revolution, A New Interpretation," *Pacific Historical Review*, 1 (1932), pp. 273–294.

Pratt, Julius W., "The 'Large Policy' of 1898," *Mississippi Valley Historical Review*, 19 (1932), pp. 219–242.

Russ, W. A., "The Role of Sugar in Hawaiian Annexation," *Pacific Historical Review*, 12 (1943), pp. 339–350.

Ryden, G. H., *The Foreign Policy of the United States in Relation to Samoa*, New Haven, Yale University Press, 1933.

Shippee, L. B., "Germany and the Spanish-American War," *American Historical Review*, 30 (1925), pp. 754–777.

Tansill, C. C., *The Foreign Policy of Thomas F. Bayard, 1885–1897*, New York, Fordham University Press, 1940.

Tyler, A. F., *The Foreign Policy of James G. Blaine*, Minneapolis, University of Minnesota Press, 1927.

Wilkerson, M. M., *Public Opinion and the Spanish-American War*, Baton Rouge, Louisiana State University Press, 1932.

Wisan, J. E., *The Cuban Crisis as Reflected in the New York Press*, New York, Columbia University Press, 1934.

CHAPTER 13

Advance and Retreat in the Caribbean

Adler, Selig, "Bryan and Wilsonian Caribbean Penetration," *Hispanic American Historical Review*, 20 (1940), pp. 198–226.

Beals, Carleton, *The Crime of Cuba*, Philadelphia, Lippincott, 1934.

Bemis, Samuel Flagg, *The Latin American Policy of the United States, An Historical Interpretation*, New York, Harcourt, Brace, 1943.

A Brief History of the Relations between the United States and Nicaragua, 1909 to 1928, Washington, D.C., Government Printing Office, 1928.

Bryn-Jones, D., *Frank B. Kellogg, A Biography*, New York, Putnam, 1937.

Buell, R. L., "The American Occupation of Haiti," *Foreign Policy Information Service*, November-December, 1929.

Buell, R. L., "Union or Disunion in Central America," *Foreign Affairs*, 11 (1933), pp. 478–490.

Buell, R. L., et al., *Problems of the New Cuba*, New York, Foreign Policy Association, 1935.

Callcott, W. H., *The Caribbean Policy of the United States, 1890–1920*, Baltimore, Johns Hopkins Press, 1942.

Chapman, C. E., *A History of the Cuban Republic: A Study in Hispanic American Politics*, New York, Macmillan, 1927.

Cox, I. J., *Nicaragua and the United States, 1909–1927*, Boston, World Peace Foundation, 1929.

Dennis, Lawrence, "Nicaragua: In Again, Out Again," *Foreign Affairs*, 9 (1931), pp. 496–500.

Dennis, Lawrence, "Revolution, Recognition, and Intervention," *Foreign Affairs*, 9 (1931), pp. 204–221.

Denny, Harold, *Dollars for Bullets*, New York, Dial, 1929.

Douglas, P. H., "The American Occupation of Haiti," *Political Science Quarterly*, 42 (1927), pp. 228–259, 368–397.

Fitzgibbon, R. H., *Cuba and the United States*, Menasha, Banta, 1935.

Green, Laurence, *The Filibuster: The Career of William Walker*, Indianapolis, Bobbs-Merrill, 1937.

Guggenheim, H. F., *The United States and Cuba*, New York, Macmillan, 1934.

Hill, H. C., *Roosevelt and the Caribbean*, Chicago, University of Chicago Press, 1927.

Hollander, Jacob, "The Convention of 1907 between the United States and the Dominican Republic," *American Journal of International Law*, 1 (1907), pp. 287–296.

Hollander, Jacob, "The Financial Difficulties of Santo Domingo," *Annals of the American Academy of Political and Social Science*, 30 (1907), pp. 93–103.

Hollander, Jacob, "The Readjustment of Santo Domingo's Finances," *Quarterly Journal of Economics*, 21 (1907), pp. 405–426.

Jenks, L. H., *Our Cuban Colony*, New York, Vanguard, 1928.

Jessup, P. C., *Elihu Root*, 2 vols., New York, Dodd, Mead, 1938.

Jones, C. L., *The Caribbean Since 1900*, New York, Prentice-Hall, 1936.

Kelsey, C., "The American Intervention in Haiti and Santo Domingo," *Annals of the American Academy of Political and Social Science*, 100 (1922), pp. 113–165.

Knight, M. M., *The Americans in Santo Domingo*, New York, Vanguard, 1928.

Lockmiller, D. A., *Magoon in Cuba*, Chapel Hill, University of North Carolina Press, 1938.

Millspaugh, A. C., *Haiti under American Control*, Boston, World Peace Foundation, 1931.

Montague, L. L., *Haiti and the United States, 1714–1938*, Durham, Duke University Press, 1940.

Munro, D. G., *The United States and the Caribbean Area*, Boston, World Peace Foundation, 1934.

Nevins, Allan, *Hamilton Fish: The Inner History of the Grant Administration*, New York, Dodd, Mead, 1936.

Perkins, Dexter, *The United States and the Caribbean*, Cambridge, Harvard University Press, 1947.

Powell, Anna A., "Relations between the United States and Nicaragua, 1898–1916," *Hispanic American Historical Review*, 8 (1928), pp. 43–64.

Rippy, J. F., *The Caribbean Danger Zone*, New York, Putnam, 1940.

Scroggs, W. O., *Filibusters and Financiers*, New York, Macmillan, 1916.

Scroggs, W. O., "William Walker and the Steamship Corporation in Nicaragua," *American Historical Review*, 10 (1905), pp. 792–811.

Smith, Arthur D. H., *Commodore Vanderbilt*, New York, McBride, 1927.

Stimson, H. L., *American Policy in Nicaragua*, New York, Scribner, 1927.

Tansill, C. C., *The United States and Santo Domingo, 1798–1873*, Baltimore, Johns Hopkins Press, 1938.

Thomson, C. A., "The Cuban Revolution: Fall of Machado," *Foreign Policy Reports*, December 18, 1935.

Thomson, C. A., "The Cuban Revolution: Reform and Reaction," *Foreign Policy Reports*, January 1, 1936.

Torriente, C. de la, "The Platt Amendment," *Foreign Affairs*, 8 (1930), pp. 364–379.

Welles, Sumner, *Naboth's Vineyard: The Dominican Republic, 1844–1924*, 2 vols., New York, Payson and Clarke, 1928.

Welles, Sumner, *The Time for Decision*, New York, Harper, 1944.

Wright, P. G., *The Cuban Situation and Our Treaty Relations*, Washington, D.C., Brookings Institution, 1931.

CHAPTER 14

The Far East: China

Abend, H., *Treaty Ports*, Garden City, Doubleday, Doran, 1944.

Backhouse, E. T., and Bland, J. O. P., *Annals and Memoirs of the Court of Peking*, London, Heineman, 1914.

Bailey, T. A., "The Root-Takahira Agreement of 1908," *Pacific Historical Review*, 9 (1940), pp. 19–35.

Biggerstaff, K., "The Official Chinese Attitude toward the Burlingame Mission," *American Historical Review*, 41 (1936), pp. 682–701.

Borg, Dorothy, *American Policy and the Chinese Revolution*, New York, Macmillan, 1947.

Clyde, Paul H., *The Far East: A History of the Impact of the West on Eastern Asia*, New York, Prentice-Hall, 1948.

Coolidge, M. R., *Chinese Immigration*, New York, Holt, 1909.

Croly, Herbert, *Willard Straight*, New York, Macmillan, 1924.

Dennett, Tyler, *Americans in Eastern Asia*, New York, Macmillan, 1922.

Dennett, Tyler, *John Hay: From Poetry to Politics*, New York, Dodd, Mead, 1934.

Dennett, Tyler, "Seward's Far Eastern Policy," *American Historical Review*, 28 (1922), pp. 45–62.

Dennis, A. L. P., *Adventures in American Diplomacy, 1896–1906*, New York, Dutton, 1928.

Dulles, F. R., *China and America: The Story of Their Relations Since 1784*, Princeton, Princeton University Press, 1946.

Dulles, F. R., *The Old China Trade*, Boston, Houghton Mifflin, 1930.

Elliston, H. B., "China in the World Family," *Foreign Affairs*, 7 (1929), pp. 616–627.

Fairbank, J. K., *The United States and China*, Cambridge, Harvard University Press, 1948.

Griswold, A. W., *The Far Eastern Policy of the United States*, New York, Harcourt, Brace, 1938.

Holcombe, A. N., *The Chinese Revolution: A Phase in the Regeneration of a World Power*, Cambridge, Harvard University Press, 1930.

House Executive Document 1, 38th Congress, 1st Session, Washington, D.C., Government Printing Office, 1864.

Huntington-Wilson, F. M., *Memoirs of an Ex-Diplomat*, Boston, Humphries, 1945.

Kuo, P. C., "Caleb Cushing and the Treaty of Wanghia," *Journal of Modern History*, 5 (1933), pp. 34–54.

LaFargue, T. E., *China and the World War*, Stanford University, Stanford University Press, 1937.

Langer, W. L., *The Diplomacy of Imperialism*, 2 vols., New York, Knopf, 1935.

McKenzie, R. D., *Oriental Exclusion*, Chicago, University of Chicago Press, 1928.

Mallory, W. H., "The Passing of Extraterritoriality in China," *Foreign Affairs*, 9 (1931), pp. 346–349.

Martin, W. A. P., *A Cycle of Cathay; or, China, South and North*, New York, Revell, 1896.

Morse, H. B., and MacNair, H. F., *Far Eastern International Relations*, Boston, Houghton Mifflin, 1931.

Nevins, Allan, *Henry White: Thirty Years of American Diplomacy*, New York, Harper, 1930.

Oberholtzer, E. P., *A History of the United States Since the Civil War*, 5 vols., New York, Macmillan, 1917–1937.

Paul, R. W., "The Origin of the Chinese Issue in California," *Mississippi Valley Historical Review*, 25 (1938), pp. 181–196.

Pollard, R. T., *China's Foreign Relations, 1917–1931*, New York, Macmillan, 1933.

Remer, C. F., *Foreign Investments in China*, New York, Macmillan, 1933.

Sprout, Harold and Margaret, *Toward a New Order of Sea Power*, Princeton, Princeton University Press, 1940.

Tsiang, T. F., "The Extension of Equal Commercial Privileges to Other Nations than the British after the Treaty of Nanking," *Chinese Social and Political Science Review*, 15 (1931), pp. 422–444; 16 (1932), pp. 105–109.

Vinacke, Harold M., *A History of the Far East in Modern Times*, 5th ed., New York, Appleton-Century-Crofts, 1950.

Walsh, Warren B., "The Beginnings of the Burlingame Mission," *Far Eastern Quarterly*, 4 (1945), pp. 274–277.

Williams, F. W., *Anson Burlingame and the First Chinese Mission to Foreign Powers*, New York, Scribner, 1912.

Willoughby, W. W., *Foreign Rights and Interests in China*, Baltimore, Johns Hopkins Press, 1927.

Zabriskie, E. H., *American-Russian Rivalry in the Far East*, Philadelphia, University of Pennsylvania Press, 1946.

CHAPTER 15

The Far East: Japan

Bailey, T. A., *A Diplomatic History of the American People*, 3d ed., New York, Crofts, 1946.

Bailey, T. A., "Japan's Protest Against the Annexation of Hawaii," *Journal of Modern History*, 3 (1931), pp. 46–61.

Bailey, T. A., *Theodore Roosevelt and the Japanese-American Crises*, Stanford University, Stanford University Press, 1934.

Barrows, E. M., *The Great Commodore: The Exploits of Matthew Calbraith Perry*, Indianapolis, Bobbs-Merrill, 1936.

Bisson, T. A., *America's Far Eastern Policy*, New York, Macmillan, 1945.

Brebner, J. B., "Canada, the Anglo-Japanese Alliance, and the Washington Conference," *Political Science Quarterly*, 50 (1935), pp. 45–58.

Buell, R. L., "The Development of the Anti-Japanese Agitation in the United States," *Political Science Quarterly*, 37 (1922), pp. 605–638; 38 (1923), pp. 57–81.

Buell, R. L., *Isolated America*, New York, Knopf, 1940.

Buell, R. L., *Japanese Immigration*, World Peace Foundation Pamphlets, vol. 7, Nos. 5 and 6, Boston, World Peace Foundation, 1924.

Buell, R. L., *The Washington Conference*, New York, D. Appleton, 1922.

Clyde, Paul H., "The American Policy of 'Playing No Favorites': Secretary Stimson and Manchuria, 1931," *Mississippi Valley Historical Review*, 35 (1948), pp. 187–202.

Clyde, Paul H., *International Rivalries in Manchuria*, Columbus, Ohio State University Press, 1928.

Cole, Allen B. (ed.), *With Perry in Japan: The Diary of Edward Yorke McCauley*, Princeton, Princeton University Press, 1943.

Conference on the Limitation of Armaments, November 12, 1921–February 6, 1922, Washington, D.C., Government Printing Office, 1922.

Cosenza, M. E. (ed.), *The Complete Journal of Townsend Harris*, Garden City, Doubleday, Doran, 1930.

Crow, Carl, *He Opened the Door of Japan*, New York, Harper, 1939.

Dennett, Tyler, *Roosevelt and the Russo-Japanese War*, Garden City, Doubleday, Page, 1925.

Dennis, A. L. P., *Adventures in American Diplomacy, 1896–1906*, New York, Dutton, 1928.

Dulles, F. R., *America in the Pacific: Forty Years of American-Japanese Relations*, New York, Appleton-Century, 1937.

Falk, E. A., *From Perry to Pearl Harbor: The Struggle for Supremacy in the Pacific*, Garden City, Doubleday, Doran, 1943.

Galbraith, John S., "The Imperial Conference of 1921 and the Washington Conference," *Canadian Historical Review*, 29 (1948), pp. 143–152.

Gowen, H. H., *Five Foreigners in Japan*, New York, Revell, 1936.

Graves, W. S., *America's Siberian Adventure, 1918–1920*, New York, P. Smith, 1931.

Griswold, A. W., *The Far Eastern Policy of the United States*, New York, Harcourt, Brace, 1938.

Hawks, F. L., *Narrative of the Expedition of an American Squadron to the China Seas and Japan*, New York, D. Appleton, 1856.

Hoag, D. L., *Preface to Preparedness: The Washington Disarmament Conference and Public Opinion*, Washington, D.C., American Council on Public Affairs, 1941.

Howard, H. P., and Dennett, Tyler, "America's Role in Asia," *Pacific Affairs*, 16 (1943), pp. 485–492.

Ichihashi, Yamato, *The Washington Conference and After: A Historical Survey*, Stanford University, Stanford University Press, 1928.

Jessup, P. C., *Elihu Root*, 2 vols., New York, Dodd, Mead, 1938.

Jones, F. C., *Extraterritoriality in Japan and the Diplomatic Relations Resulting from Its Abolition, 1853–1889*, New Haven, Yale University Press, 1931.

Kawakami, K. K., *American-Japanese Relations: An Inside View of Japan's Policies and Purposes*, New York, Revell, 1912.

Langdon, W. R. (tr.), *Diplomatic Commentaries, by Viscount Kikujiro Ishii*, Baltimore, Johns Hopkins Press, 1936.

Lansing, Robert, *The War Memoirs of Robert Lansing*, Indianapolis, Bobbs-Merrill, 1935.

Lippmann, Walter, and Scroggs, W. O., *The United States in World Affairs: An Account of American Foreign Relations, 1931*, New York, Harper, 1932.

Lippmann, Walter, and Scroggs, W. O., *The United States in World Affairs: An Account of American Foreign Relations, 1932*, New York, Harper, 1933.

Morris, R. S., *Townsend Harris: A Chapter in American Diplomacy*, New York, Japan Society, 1921.

Myers, W. S., *The Foreign Policies of Herbert Hoover, 1929–1933*, New York, Scribner, 1940.

Papers Relating to the Foreign Relations of the United States, 1924, Washington, D.C., Government Printing Office, 1939.

Papers Relating to the Foreign Relations of the United States: Japan, 1931–1941, 2 vols., Washington, D.C., Government Printing Office, 1943.

Paul, R. W., *The Abrogation of the Gentlemen's Agreement*, Cambridge, The Phi Beta Kappa Society, 1936.

Paullin, C. O., *Diplomatic Negotiations of American Naval Officers*, Baltimore, Johns Hopkins Press, 1912.

Paxson, F. L., *American Democracy and the World War: Postwar Years: Normalcy, 1918–1923*, Berkeley, University of California Press, 1948.

Pratt, Sir John T., and Dennett, Tyler, "Correspondence," *Pacific Affairs*, 18 (1945), pp. 369–374.

Sansom, Sir George B., *The Western World and Japan*, New York, Knopf, 1950.

Simonds, F. H., *American Foreign Policy in the Post-War Years*, Baltimore, Johns Hopkins Press, 1935.

Smith, Sara R., *The Manchurian Crisis, 1931–32: A Tragedy in International Relations*, New York, Columbia University Press, 1948.

Sprout, Harold and Margaret, *Toward a New Order of Sea Power*, Princeton, Princeton University Press, 1940.

Stimson, H. L., *The Far Eastern Crisis*, New York, Harper, 1936.

Stimson, H. L., and Bundy, McGeorge, *On Active Service in Peace and War*, New York, Harper, 1947.

Sullivan, Mark, *The Great Adventure in Washington: The Story of the Conference*, Garden City, Doubleday, Page, 1922.

Tompkins, Pauline, *American-Russian Relations in the Far East*, New York, Macmillan, 1949.

Treat, Payson J., *Diplomatic Relations between the United States and Japan, 1853–1895*, 2 vols., Stanford University, Stanford University Press, 1932.

Treat, Payson J., *Diplomatic Relations between the United States and Japan, 1895–1905*, Stanford University, Stanford University Press, 1938.

Treat, Payson J., *The Early Diplomatic Relations between the United States and Japan, 1853–1865*, Baltimore, Johns Hopkins Press, 1917.

Treat, Payson J., *The Far East: A Political and Diplomatic History*, New York, Harper, 1928.

Treat, Payson J., *Japan and the United States, 1853–1921*, Boston, Houghton Mifflin, 1921.

Tupper, E., and McReynolds, G. E., *Japan in American Public Opinion*, New York, Macmillan, 1937.

Vagts, A., *Deutschland und die Vereinigten Staaten in der Weltpolitik*, 2 vols., New York, Macmillan, 1935.

Wallace, B. J., "How the United States 'Led the League' in 1931," *American Political Science Review*, 39 (1945), pp. 101–116.

Walworth, Arthur, *Black Ships off Japan*, New York, Knopf, 1946.

Wilbur, R. L., and Hyde, A. M., *The Hoover Policies*, New York, Scribner, 1937.

Wildes, H. E., *Aliens in the East: A New History of Japan's Foreign Intercourse*, Philadelphia, University of Pennsylvania Press, 1937.

Williams, F. W., *The Life and Letters of Samuel Wells Williams, Missionary, Diplomatist, Sinologue*, New York, Putnam, 1889.

Young, Eugene J., *Powerful America*, New York, Stokes, 1936.

CHAPTER 16

Neutrality Fails Again

Adler, Selig, "The Congressional Election of 1918," *South Atlantic Quarterly*, 36 (1937), pp. 447–465.

Albion, Robert G., and Pope, Jennie B., *Sea Lanes in Wartime: The American Experience, 1775–1942*, New York, Norton, 1942.

Bailey, T. A., "The Sinking of the *Lusitania*," *American Historical Review,* 41 (1935), pp. 54–74.

Bailey, T. A., "The United States and the Blacklist during the Great War," *Journal of Modern History,* 6 (1934), pp. 14–35.

Bailey, T. A., *Woodrow Wilson and the Great Betrayal,* New York, Macmillan, 1945.

Bailey, T. A., *Woodrow Wilson and the Lost Peace,* New York, Macmillan, 1944.

Baker, Ray Stannard, *Woodrow Wilson: Life and Letters,* 8 vols., Garden City, Doubleday, Page, 1927–1939.

Baker, Ray Stannard, *Woodrow Wilson and World Settlement,* 3 vols., Garden City, Doubleday, Page, 1922.

Berdahl, C. A., *The Policy of the United States with Respect to the League of Nations,* Geneva, Librairie Kundig, 1932.

Binkley, R. C., "New Light on the Paris Peace Conference," *Political Science Quarterly,* 46 (1931), pp. 335–361, 509–547.

Binkley, R. C., "Ten Years of Peace Conference History," *Journal of Modern History,* 1 (1929), pp. 607–629.

Birdsall, Paul, "The Second Decade of Peace Conference History," *Journal of Modern History,* 11 (1939), pp. 362–378.

Birdsall, Paul, *Versailles Twenty Years After,* New York, Reynal and Hitchcock, 1941.

Borchard, Edwin M., and Lage, William P., *Neutrality for the United States,* New Haven, Yale University Press, 1937.

Curti, M. E., *Bryan and World Peace,* Smith College Studies in History, vol. 16, Nos. 3 and 4, Northampton, Smith College, 1931.

Darling, H. M., "Who Kept the United States Out of the League of Nations?", *Canadian Historical Review,* 10 (1929), pp. 196–211.

Finch, G. A., "The Treaty of Peace with Germany in the United States Senate," *American Journal of International Law,* 14 (1920), pp. 155–206.

Fleming, Denna Frank, *The Treaty Veto of the American Senate,* New York, Putnam, 1930.

Fleming, Denna Frank, *The United States and the League of Nations, 1918–1920,* New York, Putnam, 1932.

Forster, K., *The Failures of Peace,* Washington, American Council on Public Affairs, 1941.

Grattan, C. Hartley, *Why We Fought,* New York, Vanguard, 1929.

Haskins, C. H., and Lord, R. H., *Some Problems of the Peace Conference,* Cambridge, Harvard University Press, 1920.

Hendrick, B. J., *The Life and Letters of Walter Hines Page,* 2 vols., Garden City, Doubleday, Page, 1923.

Holt, W. Stull, *Treaties Defeated by the Senate*, Baltimore, Johns Hopkins Press, 1933.

House, E. M., and Seymour, Charles, *What Really Happened at Paris: The Story of the Peace Conference, 1918–1919*, New York, Scribner, 1921.

Howland, C. P., *Survey of American Foreign Relations, 1928*, New Haven, Yale University Press, 1928.

Lansing, Robert, *The Peace Negotiations: A Personal Narrative*, Boston, Houghton Mifflin, 1921.

Lansing, Robert, *The War Memoirs of Robert Lansing*, Indianapolis, Bobbs-Merrill, 1935.

Leopold, R. W., "The Problem of American Intervention, 1917: An Historical Retrospect," *World Politics*, 2 (1950), pp. 405–425.

Lloyd George, David, *Memoirs of the Peace Conference*, 2 vols., New Haven, Yale University Press, 1939.

Marston, F. S., *The Peace Conference of 1919: Organization and Procedure*, London, Oxford, 1944.

Miller, David Hunter, *The Drafting of the Covenant*, New York, Putnam, 1928.

Millis, Walter, *The Road to War*, Boston, Houghton Mifflin, 1935.

Morrissey, Alice M., *The American Defense of Neutral Rights, 1914–1917*, Cambridge, Harvard University Press, 1939.

Nevins, Allan, *Henry White: Thirty Years of American Diplomacy*, New York, Harper, 1930.

The New York Times, February 4, 1924.

Nicolson, Harold, *Peacemaking, 1919*, Boston, Houghton Mifflin, 1933.

Notter, Harley, *The Origins of the Foreign Policy of Woodrow Wilson*, Baltimore, Johns Hopkins Press, 1937.

Papers Relating to the Foreign Relations of the United States: The Lansing Papers, 2 vols., Washington, D.C., Government Printing Office, 1939–1940.

Perkins, Dexter, *America and the Two Wars*, Boston, Little, Brown, 1944.

Paxson, F. L., *American Democracy and the World War: Postwar Years: Normalcy, 1918–1923*, Berkeley, University of California Press, 1948.

Paxson, F. L., *American Democracy and the World War: Pre-War Years, 1913–1917*, Boston, Houghton Mifflin, 1936.

Peterson, H. C., *Propaganda for War*, Norman, University of Oklahoma Press, 1939.

Savage, C. (comp.), *The Policy of the United States toward Maritime Commerce in War*, 2 vols., Washington, D.C., Government Printing Office, 1936.

Schmitt, Bernadotte E., "The Peace Conference of 1919," *Journal of Modern History*, 16 (1944), pp. 49–59.

Schriftgiesser, K., *The Gentleman from Massachusetts: Henry Cabot Lodge*, Boston, Little, Brown, 1944.

Seymour, Charles, *American Diplomacy during the World War*, Baltimore, Johns Hopkins Press, 1934.

Seymour, Charles, *American Neutrality, 1914–1917: Essays on the Causes of American Intervention in the World War*, New Haven, Yale University Press, 1935.

Seymour, Charles (ed.), *The Intimate Papers of Colonel House*, 4 vols., Boston, Houghton Mifflin, 1926–1928.

Shotwell, James T., *At the Paris Peace Conference*, New York, Macmillan, 1937.

Squires, J. D., *British Propaganda at Home and in the United States from 1914 to 1917*, Cambridge, Harvard University Press, 1935.

Tansill, C. C., *America Goes to War*, Boston, Little, Brown, 1938.

Van Alstyne, R. W., "The Policy of the United States Regarding the Declaration of London, at the Outbreak of the Great War," *Journal of Modern History*, 7 (1935), pp. 434–447.

Wilson, Edith Bolling, *My Memoir*, Indianapolis, Bobbs-Merrill, 1939.

CHAPTER 17

A Decade of Contradictions, 1922–1933

American Coöperation with the League, Geneva Special Studies, vol. 11, No. 7, July, 1931, Geneva, Geneva Research Information Committee.

Barck, O. T., and Blake, N. M., *Since 1900*, New York, Macmillan, 1947.

Berdahl, C. A., "Relations of the United States to the Council of the League of Nations," *American Political Science Review*, 26 (1932), pp. 497–526.

Bryn-Jones, D., *Frank B. Kellogg: A Biography*, New York, Putnam, 1937.

Fleming, Denna Frank, *The United States and the World Court*, Garden City, Doubleday, Doran, 1945.

Fleming, Denna Frank, *The United States and World Organization, 1920–1933*, New York, Columbia University Press, 1938.

Fosdick, R., "Secretary Hughes and the League of Nations," *The New York Times*, October 19, 1924.

Hudson, Manley O., *The World Court, 1921–1938*, Boston, World Peace Foundation, 1938.

Johnson, Claudius O., *Borah of Idaho*, New York, Longmans, Green, 1936.

Langsam, W. C., *The World Since 1914,* 6th ed., New York, Macmillan, 1948.

Lippmann, Walter, and Scroggs, W. O., *The United States in World Affairs: An Account of American Foreign Relations, 1931,* New York, Harper, 1932.

Lippmann, Walter, and Scroggs, W. O., *The United States in World Affairs: An Account of American Foreign Relations, 1932,* New York, Harper, 1933.

Lippmann, Walter, and Scroggs, W. O., *The United States in World Affairs: An Account of American Foreign Relations, 1933,* New York, Harper, 1934.

Miller, David Hunter, *The Peace Pact of Paris: A Study of the Briand-Kellogg Treaty,* New York, Putnam, 1928.

Moulton, H. G., and Pasvolsky, Leo, *War Debts and World Prosperity,* New York, Scribner, 1932.

Moulton, H. G., and Pasvolsky, Leo, *World War Debt Settlement,* New York, Macmillan, 1926.

Myers, Denys P., *Origin and Conclusion of the Paris Pact: The Renunciation of War as an Instrument of National Policy,* World Peace Foundation Pamphlets, vol. 12, No. 2, Boston, World Peace Foundation, 1929.

Noel-Baker, P. J., *Disarmament and the Coolidge Conference,* London, Woolf, 1927.

Pearson, Drew, and Brown, Constantine, *The American Diplomatic Game,* Garden City, Doubleday, Doran, 1935.

Perkins, Dexter, *The Evolution of American Foreign Policy,* New York, Oxford, 1948.

Shotwell, James T., *On the Rim of the Abyss,* New York, Macmillan, 1936.

Shotwell, James T., *War as an Instrument of National Policy and Its Renunciation in the Pact of Paris,* New York, Harcourt, Brace, 1929.

Stimson, H. L., and Bundy, McGeorge, *On Active Service in Peace and War,* New York, Harper, 1947.

Stoner, J. E., *S. O. Levinson and the Pact of Paris: A Study in the Techniques of Influence,* Chicago, University of Chicago Press, 1942.

Tate, Merze, *The United States and Armaments,* Cambridge, Harvard University Press, 1948.

Williams, B. H., *Economic Foreign Policy of the United States,* New York, McGraw-Hill, 1929.

Williams, B. H., *The United States and Disarmament,* New York, Whittlesey House, 1931.

CHAPTER 18

Descent into Isolationism

Barnes, H. E., *The Genesis of the World War: An Introduction to the Problem of War Guilt,* New York, Knopf, 1926.

Bausman, Frederick, *Facing Europe,* New York, Century, 1926.

Beard, Charles A. and Mary, *America in Midpassage,* 2 vols., New York, Macmillan, 1939.

Beckett, Grace, *The Reciprocal Trade Agreements Program,* New York, Columbia University Press, 1941.

Bisson, T. A., *America's Far Eastern Policy,* New York, Macmillan, 1945.

Borchard, Edwin M., and Lage, William P., *Neutrality for the United States,* New Haven, Yale University Press, 1937.

Chambers, F. P., Grant, C. P., and Bayley, C. C., *This Age of Conflict,* New York, Harcourt, Brace, 1943.

Culbertson, W. S., *Reciprocity: A National Policy for Foreign Trade,* New York, Whittlesey House, 1931.

Dulles, A. W., and Armstrong, H. F., *Can America Stay Neutral?,* New York, Harper, 1939.

Dulles, F. R., *The Road to Teheran: The Story of Russia and America, 1781–1943,* Princeton, Princeton University Press, 1944.

Engelbrecht, H. C., and Hanighen, F. C., *Merchants of Death: A Study of the International Arms Industry,* New York, Dodd, Mead, 1934.

Fairlie, J. A. (ed.), *Studies in Government and International Law, by James Wilford Garner,* Urbana, University of Illinois Press, 1943, as follows:
　　"Recent Neutrality Legislation of the United States," pp. 515–523; "The United States 'Neutrality' Legislation of 1937," pp. 524–544.

Fenwick, C. G., *American Neutrality: Trial and Failure,* New York, New York University Press, 1940.

Fenwick, C. G., *The Inter-American Regional System,* New York, McMullen, 1949.

Grattan, C. Hartley, *Why We Fought,* New York, Vanguard, 1929.

Grew, Joseph C., *Ten Years in Japan,* New York, Simon and Schuster, 1944.

Guerrant, E. O., *Roosevelt's Good Neighbor Policy,* Albuquerque, University of New Mexico Press, 1950.

Hull, Cordell, *The Memoirs of Cordell Hull,* 2 vols., New York, Macmillan, 1948.

Johnson, Walter, *The Battle Against Isolation,* Chicago, University of Chicago Press, 1944.

Langsam, W. C., *The World Since 1914*, 6th ed., New York, Macmillan, 1948.

Larkin, J. D., *Trade Agreements: A Study in Democratic Methods*, New York, Columbia University Press, 1940.

Leopold, R. W., "The Problem of American Intervention, 1917: An Historical Retrospect," *World Politics*, 2 (1950), pp. 405–425.

Lippmann, Walter, and Scroggs, W. O., *The United States in World Affairs: An Account of American Foreign Relations*, 1933, New York, Harper, 1934.

MacMahon, John L., *Recent Changes in the Recognition Policy of the United States*, Washington, D.C., The Catholic University of America, 1933.

Moley, Raymond, *After Seven Years*, New York, Harper, 1939.

Peace and War: United States Foreign Policy, 1931–1941, Washington, D.C., Government Printing Office, 1943.

Perkins, Dexter, *The Evolution of American Foreign Policy*, New York, Oxford, 1948.

Quigley, H. S., *Far Eastern War, 1937–1941*, Boston, World Peace Foundation, 1942.

Shepardson, W. H., and Scroggs, W. O., *The United States in World Affairs: An Account of American Foreign Relations, 1934–1935*, New York, Harper, 1935.

Shepardson, W. H., and Scroggs, W. O., *The United States in World Affairs: An Account of American Foreign Relations, 1936*, New York, Harper, 1937.

Shepardson, W. H., and Scroggs, W. O., *The United States in World Affairs: An Account of American Foreign Relations, 1937*, New York, Harper, 1938.

Shepardson, W. H., and Scroggs, W. O., *The United States in World Affairs: An Account of American Foreign Relations, 1938*, New York, Harper, 1939.

Shepardson, W. H., and Scroggs, W. O., *The United States in World Affairs: An Account of American Foreign Relations, 1940*, New York, Harper, 1941.

Tasca, H. J., *The Reciprocal Trade Policy of the United States*, Philadelphia, University of Pennsylvania Press, 1938.

Tompkins, Pauline, *American-Russian Relations in the Far East*, New York, Macmillan, 1949.

Turner, J. K., *Shall It Be Again?*, New York, Huebsch, 1922.

CHAPTER 19

Through War to Coöperation

Baldwin, Hanson W., *Great Mistakes of the War*, New York, Harper, 1949.

Beard, C. A., *President Roosevelt and the Coming of the War: A Study in Appearances and Realities*, New Haven, Yale University Press, 1948.

Bisson, T. A., *America's Far Eastern Policy*, New York, Macmillan, 1945.

Byrnes, J. F., *Speaking Frankly*, New York, Harper, 1947.

Churchill, Winston S., *The Grand Alliance*, Boston, Houghton Mifflin, 1950.

Davis, Forrest, and Lindley, E. K., *How War Came: An American White Paper; from the Fall of France to Pearl Harbor*, New York, Simon and Schuster, 1942.

Dean, Vera M., "The San Francisco Conference: With Text of Charter," *Foreign Policy Reports*, July 15, 1945.

Deane, John R., *The Strange Alliance*, New York, Viking, 1947.

Documents of the United Nations: Conference on International Organization, San Francisco, 1945, 16 vols., London and New York, United Nations, 1945.

Flynn, John T., *The Roosevelt Myth*, New York, Devin-Adair, 1948.

Goodrich, L. M., and Hambro, E., *Charter of the United Nations: Commentary and Documents*, Boston, World Peace Foundation, 1946.

Grew, Joseph C., *Ten Years in Japan*, New York, Simon and Schuster, 1944.

Guerrant, E. O., *Roosevelt's Good Neighbor Policy*, Albuquerque, University of New Mexico Press, 1950.

Hayes, C. J. H., *Wartime Mission in Spain, 1942–1945*, New York, Macmillan, 1947.

Hull, Cordell, *The Memoirs of Cordell Hull*, 2 vols., New York, Macmillan, 1948.

Kirk, G. L., and Chamberlain, L. H., "Organization of the San Francisco Conference," *Political Science Quarterly*, 60 (1945), pp. 321–342.

Langer, W. L., *Our Vichy Gamble*, New York, Knopf, 1947.

Leahy, W. D., *I Was There: The Personal Story of the Chief of Staff to Presidents Roosevelt and Truman, Based on His Notes and Diaries Made at the Time*, New York, Whittlesey House, 1950.

McInnis, Edgar, *The War: First Year*, London, Oxford, 1940. Companion volumes carry the story through the six war years.

Millis, Walter, *This is Pearl! The United States and Japan—1941*, New York, Morrow, 1947.

Moore, Frederick, *With Japan's Leaders*, New York, Scribner, 1942.

Morgenstern, George, *Pearl Harbor: The Story of the Secret War,* New York, Devin-Adair, 1947.

Notter, Harley, *Postwar Foreign Policy Preparation, 1939–1945,* Washington, D.C., Government Printing Office, 1949.

Peace and War: United States Foreign Policy, 1931–1941, Washington, D.C., Government Printing Office, 1943.

Pearl Harbor Attack, 39 vols., Washington, D.C., Government Printing Office, 1946.

Quigley, H. S., *Far Eastern War, 1937–1941,* Boston, World Peace Foundation, 1942.

Roosevelt, Elliott, *As He Saw It,* New York, Duell, Sloan, and Pierce, 1946.

Senate Document 244, 79th Congress, 2d Session, Washington, D.C., Government Printing Office, 1947.

Shepardson, W. H., and Scroggs, W. O. *The United States in World Affairs: An Account of American Foreign Relations, 1940,* New York, Harper, 1941.

Sherwood, R. E., *Roosevelt and Hopkins: An Intimate History,* New York, Harper, 1948.

Shotwell, James T., *The Great Decision,* New York, Macmillan, 1944.

Stettinius, E. R., Jr., *Lend-Lease, Weapon for Victory,* New York, Macmillan, 1944.

Stettinius, E. R., Jr., *Roosevelt and the Russians: The Yalta Conference,* Garden City, Doubleday, Doran, 1949.

The United Nations Conference on International Organization, San Francisco, California, April 25 to June 26, 1945: Selected Documents, Washington, D.C., Government Printing Office, 1946.

Welles, Sumner, *The Time for Decision,* New York, Harper, 1944.

Zacharias, Rear Admiral Ellis M., "The Inside Story of Yalta," *United Nations World,* 3 (1949), pp. 12–16.

CHAPTER 20

One World Becomes Two Worlds

The Berlin Crisis: A Report on the Moscow Discussions, 1948, Washington, D.C., Government Printing Office, 1948.

Burks, Ardath W., "Occupied Japan," in *The American Year Book, 1948,* pp. 105–115; *1949,* pp. 81–87; *1950,* pp. 84–91, New York, Nelson, 1948, 1949, 1950.

Byrnes, J. F., *Speaking Frankly,* New York, Harper, 1947.

Campbell, John C., *The United States in World Affairs, 1945–1947,* New York, Harper, 1947.

Campbell, John C., *The United States in World Affairs, 1947–1948*, New York, Harper, 1948.

Campbell, John C., *The United States in World Affairs, 1948–1949*, New York, Harper, 1949.

Dennett, Raymond, and Turner, Robert K. (eds.), *Documents on American Foreign Relations*, 10 vols. (in progress), Princeton, Princeton University Press, 1939 ff.

Hoskins, Halford L., *The Atlantic Pact*, Washington, D.C., Public Affairs Press, 1949.

The International Control of Atomic Energy: Growth of a Policy, Washington, D.C., Government Printing Office, 1946.

International Control of Atomic Energy: Policy at the Crossroads, Washington, D.C., Government Printing Office, 1948.

International Studies Group of the Brookings Institution, *Major Problems of United States Foreign Policy, 1947: A Study Guide; 1948–49; 1950*, Washington, D.C., Brookings Institution, 1947, 1948, 1950.

Leahy, W. D., *I Was There: The Personal Story of the Chief of Staff to Presidents Roosevelt and Truman, Based on His Notes and Diaries Made at the Time*, New York, Whittlesey House, 1950.

Making the Peace Treaties, 1941–1947, Washington, D.C., Government Printing Office, 1947.

Moseley, Philip E., "The Occupation of Germany: New Light on How the Zones Were Drawn," *Foreign Affairs*, 28 (1950), pp. 580–604.

Occupation of Japan: Policy and Progress, Washington, D.C., Government Printing Office, n.d.

A Report of the International Control of Atomic Energy, Washington, D.C., Government Printing Office, 1946.

Sherwood, R. E., *Roosevelt and Hopkins: An Intimate History*, New York, Harper, 1948.

Smith, Walter Bedell, *My Three Years in Moscow*, Philadelphia, Lippincott, 1950.

Stebbins, Richard P., *The United States in World Affairs, 1949*, New York, Harper, 1950.

Stettinius, E. R., Jr., *Roosevelt and the Russians: The Yalta Conference*, Garden City, Doubleday, Doran, 1949.

United States Relations with China: With Special Reference to the Period 1944–1949, Washington, D.C., Government Printing Office, 1949.

X, "The Sources of Soviet Conduct," *Foreign Affairs*, 25 (1947), pp. 566–582.

Index

583